Building Codes ILLUSTRATED

Building Codes ILLUSTRATED

Fifth Edition

*A Guide to Understanding the
2015 International Building Code®*

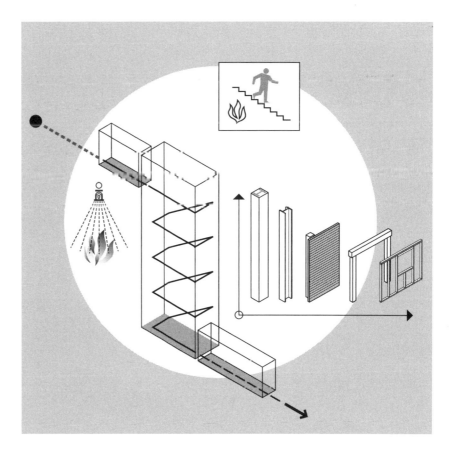

FRANCIS D. K. CHING / STEVEN R. WINKEL, FAIA

WILEY

Cover Design: Wiley
Cover Illustration: Francis D.K. Ching

This book is printed on acid-free paper. ∞

Library of Congress Cataloging-in-Publication Data

Ching, Frank, 1943-

Building codes illustrated : a guide to understanding the 2015 international building code /
Francis Ching, Steven Winkel. -- Fifth edition.
 Includes index.
  ISBN 978-1-119-15092-3; ISBN 978-1-119-15094-7 (ebk); ISBN 978-1-119-15095-4 (ebk)

Printed in the United States of America.

10 9 8 7 6 5 4 3 2 1

Disclaimer

The book contains the authors' analyses and illustrations of the intent and potential interpretations of the *2015 International Building Code®* (IBC). The illustrations and examples are general in nature and not intended to apply to any specific project without a detailed analysis of the unique nature of the project. As with any code document, the IBC is subject to interpretation by the Authorities Having Jurisdiction (AHJ) for their application to a specific project. Designers should consult the local Building Official early in project design if there are questions or concerns about the meaning or application of code sections in relation to specific design projects.

The interpretations and illustrations in the book are those of the authors. The authors do not represent that the illustrations, analyses, or interpretations in this book are definitive. They are not intended to take the place of detailed code analyses of a project, the exercise of professional judgment by the reader, or interpretive application of the code to any project by permitting authorities. While this publication is designed to provide accurate and authoritative information regarding the subject matter covered, it is sold with the understanding that neither the publisher nor the authors are engaged in rendering professional services. If professional advice or other expert assistance is required, the services of a competent professional person should be sought.

The authors and John Wiley & Sons would like to thank Doug Thornburg and Jay Woodward of the International Code Council for their thorough review of the manuscript. Their review does not reflect in any way the official position of the International Code Council. Any errors in the interpretations or illustrations in the book are solely those of the authors and are in no way the responsibility of the International Code Council.

We would also like to thank David Collins, FAIA, of The Preview Group, Inc., for his insightful review. The book was made clearer and our interpretations were improved by his comments and suggestions.

About the International Code Council®

The International Code Council (ICC®), a membership association dedicated to building safety, fire prevention and energy efficiency, develops the codes and standards used to construct residential and commercial buildings, including homes and schools. The mission of ICC is to provide the highest quality codes, standards, products and services for all concerned with the safety and performance of the built environment. Most United States cities, counties and states choose the International Codes, building safety codes developed by the International Code Council. The International Codes also serve as the basis for construction of federal properties around the world, and as a reference for many nations outside the United States. The Code Council is also dedicated to innovation and sustainability and Code Council subsidiary, ICC Evaluation Service, issues Evaluation Reports for innovative products and reports of Sustainable Attributes Verification and Evaluation (SAVE).

Headquarters: 500 New Jersey Avenue, NW, 6th Floor, Washington, DC 20001-2070
District Offices: Birmingham, AL; Chicago. IL; Los Angeles, CA
1-888-422-7233
www.iccsafe.org

Contents

Preface

The primary purpose of this book is to familiarize code users with the *2015 International Building Code®* (IBC). It is intended as an instructional text on how the Code was developed and how it is organized, as well as a primer on how to use the Code. It is intended to be a companion to the IBC, not a substitute for it. This book must be read in concert with the IBC.

Many designers feel intimidated by building codes. They can seem daunting and complex at first glance. It is important to know that they are a product of years of accretion and evolution. Sections start simply and are modified, and new material is added to address additional concerns or to address interpretation issues from previous code editions. The complexity of a building code often comes from this layering of new information upon old without regard to overall continuity. It is important to keep in mind that there is no single author of the building code. Each section has a different author. Building codes are living documents, constantly under review and modification. It is vital to an understanding of codes to keep in mind that they are a human institution, written by ordinary people with specific issues in mind or specific agendas they wish to advance.

Over the past several editions of the IBC there has been an increase in the number of code revisions made to "clarify" the code. This trend has often resulted in the reorganization of code sections, often without any substantive changes. For those code users who are familiar with the previous code editions these changes can be upsetting and confusing. It may seem that familiar and well-understood code provisions have disappeared when in actuality they have just been relocated and renumbered. We strongly recommend that code users obtain electronic copies of the codes. These lend themselves to keyword searches that make it possible to find moved provisions based on the unchanged text content.

This book is designed to give an understanding of how the International Building Code is developed, how it is likely to be interpreted, and how it applies to design and construction. The intent of this book is to give a fundamental understanding of the relationship of codes to practice for design professionals, especially those licensed or desiring to become licensed as architects, engineers, or other registered design professionals. Code knowledge is among the fundamental reasons for licensing design professionals, for the protection of public health, safety, and welfare. It is our goal to make the acquisition and use of code knowledge easier and clearer for code users.

BUILDING CODE

Webster's Third New International Dictionary defines a building code as: "A set of rules of procedure and standards of materials designed to secure uniformity and protect the public interest in such matters as building construction and public health, established usually by a public agency and commonly having the force of law in a particular jurisdiction."

How This Book Is Organized

The first two chapters of this book give background and context regarding the development, organization, and use of the IBC. Chapters 3 through 18 are organized and numbered the same as the corresponding subject-matter chapters in the IBC. Chapter 19 summarizes the requirements in the remaining IBC chapters. Chapter 13 refers briefly to the energy provisions of the International Code family, which are contained in a separate code, the *International Energy Conservation Code* (IECC), and which are beyond the scope of this book. Chapter 20 touches on the code provisions for existing buildings, which are no longer included in the IBC, but occur in the *International Existing Building Code* (IEBC).

- *Text that is new or revised for the Fifth Edition is denoted by a vertical gray bar ▌ in the margins. This is similar to markings used in the IBC to indicate changes in code provisions.*
- *The IBC uses solid black vertical bars ▌ to denote changes and arrows ➡ to denote deletions. We strongly recommend that users study the Code very carefully for changes and compare old copies of the Code to the new copies as you become familiar with the new Code.*
- *Note that relocated items are marked with an arrow indicating a deletion from that section, with no cross-reference about where the section was moved. This can be very confusing, especially when requirements are merely relocated without any substantive technical changes.*

- *Page headings refer to major sections within each chapter of the Code.*
- *Text is arranged in columns, typically on the left side of a single page or of two facing pages.*

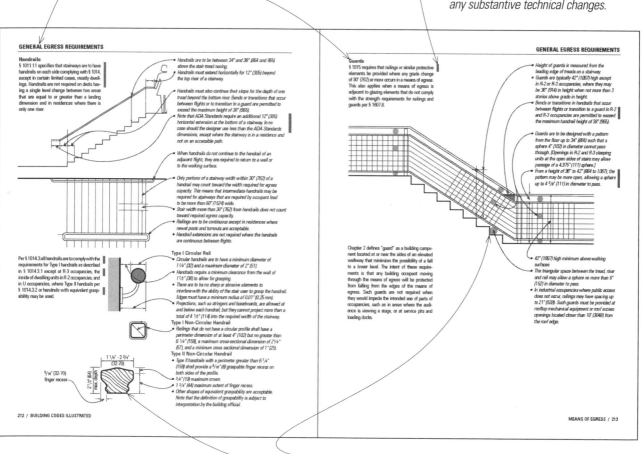

- *Drawings are typically to the right, accompanied by captions or explanatory notes. The illustrations are intended to help the reader visualize what is described in the text. They should therefore be considered to be diagrams that explain and clarify design relationships rather than represent specific design solutions.*

For the Student

The book is part of the introduction to building codes that are an integral part of professional studies in architecture, structural engineering, and civil engineering. It will serve as explanatory text to accompany analysis of the organization, intent, and use of codes in general and the *International Building Code* in particular. The introductory chapters will instill in undergraduate design students the reasons codes exist and how they form an integral part of the design process for every building project. Most design problems in school are at the schematic design level, so that detailed code analysis will not typically be undertaken in most undergraduate classes. In graduate classes the book can serve to organize and facilitate a deeper understanding of detailed requirements common to all building codes. The book also gives guidance on best practices for code analysis to lay a foundation for future practitioners to better meet the health, safety, and welfare criteria that are the basis for professional licensure.

For Emerging Professionals

Whether you are engaged in design, production, management, or construction administration, codes and standards are an integral and inescapable part of the practice of architecture and engineering. New practitioners need to refine their skills and knowledge of codes to make their projects safe and buildable with few costly changes. The more practitioners know about the code, the more it can become a tool for design rather than an impediment. The better the underlying criteria for code development and the reasons for code provisions are understood, the easier it is to create code-compliant designs. Early understanding and incorporation of code-compliant design provisions in a project reduces the necessity for costly and time-consuming rework or awkward rationalizations to justify dubious code decisions late in project documentation, or even during construction. Code use and understanding should be part of accepted knowledge for professionals, so that it becomes a part of the vocabulary of design.

For Experienced Practitioners

The greatest value of this book is that it is based on the widely adopted *International Building Code*. This is a code that is similar but by no means identical to the three model codes—the Uniform Building Code, the National Building Code, and the Standard Building Code—that most experienced practitioners have used in the past. Also, as noted above, items have been moving around in recent editions of the IBC and this book can serve as a guide in keeping track of reorganized code sections. This book will guide experienced practitioners out of the old grooves of code use they may have fallen into with the old codes. The code-analysis methods and outcomes will vary from prior codes to the new IBC. While there are seemingly familiar aspects from each code interspersed throughout the new code, the actual allowable criteria and how they are determined are often quite different. It is likely that the illustrations and the underlying reasons for the development of each code section will look familiar to experienced practitioners. The experienced practitioner must not rely on memory or old habits of picking construction types or assemblies based on prior practice. Each building must be looked at anew until the similarities and sometimes-critical differences between the new code and old habits are understood and acknowledged. This admonition also applies to the need to determine local modifications to codes and not assume new projects in new locations are identical to similar prior projects.

How to Use This Book

This book focuses on the use and interpretation of the nonstructural provisions of the *International Building Code*. There are references to basic structural requirements, but this book does not attempt to go into structural requirements in depth. That is the subject for another volume.

The organization of this book presumes that the reader has a copy of the latest version of the IBC itself as a companion document to this book. The book is intended to expand on, interpret, and illustrate various provisions of the Code. The IBC has been adopted in many jurisdictions. As it is now being extensively applied, there is an evolving body of precedent in application and interpretation. It is our hope that the analysis and illustrations in the book will aid the designer and the Authorities Having Jurisdiction (AHJ) in clarifying their own interpretations of the application of code sections to projects.

The book is not intended to take the place of the *2015 International Building Code®* (IBC) in any way. The many detailed tables and criteria contained in the IBC are partially restated in the book for illustrative purposes only. For example, we show how various tables are meant to be used and how we presume certain parts will be interpreted. When performing a code analysis for a specific project, we anticipate the reader will use our book to understand the intent of the applicable code section and then use the Code itself to find the detailed criteria to apply. One can, however, start with either the IBC or this book in researching a specific topic.

Beginning with the *2015 International Building Code®*:
- Search Contents or Index.
- Read relevant section(s).
- For further explanation and/or clarification, refer to this book.

Beginning with *Building Codes ILLUSTRATED*:
- Search Code Index for section number or Subject Index for topic.
- Refer back to specific text of *2015 International Building Code®*.

The text is based on the language of the Code and interprets it to enhance the understanding of the user. The interpretations are those of the authors and may not correspond to those rendered by the AHJ or by the International Code Council (ICC). This book, while based on a publication of the ICC, does not in any way represent official policies, interpretations, or positions of the ICC. We would encourage the users of the book to confer with the AHJ, using the illustrations from this book to validate interpretations. Reconciling text with construction drawings often benefits from additional illustrations. We trust that this will be the case with the explanations and graphics in this book.

Note that the text of the 2015 IBC contains terms in *italic type*. These italicized terms appear in the definitions in Chapter 2 of the IBC. Where defined terms are used in ways intended by their definitions, they are italicized in the body of the IBC. Italicized type is not used in this book in the same way. The IBC publisher's intent for this notification method is to highlight for the code user that the definitions should be read carefully to facilitate a better understanding of how they are used in the context where they appear in italics. It is critical that the code user go back to the IBC's definitions when attempting to understand the literal and figurative meaning of code requirements. All code definitions are now located in Chapter 2 of the IBC.

The primary purpose of the *International Building Code* (IBC) is to provide reasonable safeguards for the design, construction, use, occupancy, and maintenance of buildings. Participation by numerous volunteers representing all segments of the building community continue to log countless hours to ensure the code is updated every three years and reflects the current state of the art advances in building safety and performance. Developed through an open and transparent process, the IBC provides a balanced approach to safety, affordability, sustainability, and resiliency of buildings.

To the uninformed, building codes can appear limiting or even serve as a roadblock to building design and construction. Building codes have also been accused of being too rigid or static and unable to stay abreast of innovation or the latest advances in technology. While no one denies the need for a building regulatory system to address the safety and welfare of the public, everyone wants it to be effective, flexible, and allow for innovation. To the informed user of the IBC, the opportunity has always existed for designers, builders, manufacturers, and code officials to apply the performance-based provisions of the code in a manner that allows for creativity, flexibility, and affordability in building construction. The current *2015 International Building Code* states the following:

"The provisions of this code are not intended to prevent the installation of any material or to prohibit any design or method of construction not specifically prescribed by this code, provided that any such alternative has been approved. An alternative material, design or method of construction shall be approved where the building official finds that the proposed design is satisfactory and complies with the intent of the provisions of this code, and that the material and method of work offered is, for the purpose intended, at least the equivalent of that prescribed in this code in quality, strength, effectiveness, fire resistance, durability and safety."

With advances in technology, competition, and the globalization of our economy, it is critical that building codes be dynamic and provide a pathway for the approval of new and innovative materials, designs, and methods of construction. Often, Code officials utilize research reports, listings, and/or test reports from approved sources providing verification of code compliance. The independent source utilized frequently by code officials to verify that a product certified to a standard within the code, or an innovative or new product evaluated to a criteria meet the Building Code requirements in terms of, strength, effectiveness, fire resistance, durability, and safety is the ICC Evaluation Service, Inc.[R] (ICC-ES). Functioning as a subsidiary of the International Code Council, ICC-ES works hand in glove with manufacturers, code officials, and the design community in an effort to facilitate the acceptance of products in the marketplace without compromising public safety. Information on products that have been reviewed by ICC-ES for code compliance can be downloaded at no cost by visiting: http://www.icc-es.org/Evaluation_Reports/ orhttp://www.icc-es.org/listing/listing_directory.cfm.

The *Fifth Edition of Building Codes Illustrated* builds on the successful foundation laid by previous editions. Codes by their very nature tend to be tedious, dry documents that can also serve the late-night insomniac in search of relief. *Building Codes Illustrated* brings the code to life through its use of numerous illustrations accompanied with clear, concise, easy-to-understand text that spares the reader the normal legalese contained in regulatory documents. This updated guide continues its long tradition of serving as a key resource for those interested in not only understanding the code, but applying it as well.

Mark A. Johnson
Executive Vice President and Director of Business Development
International Code Council, Inc..

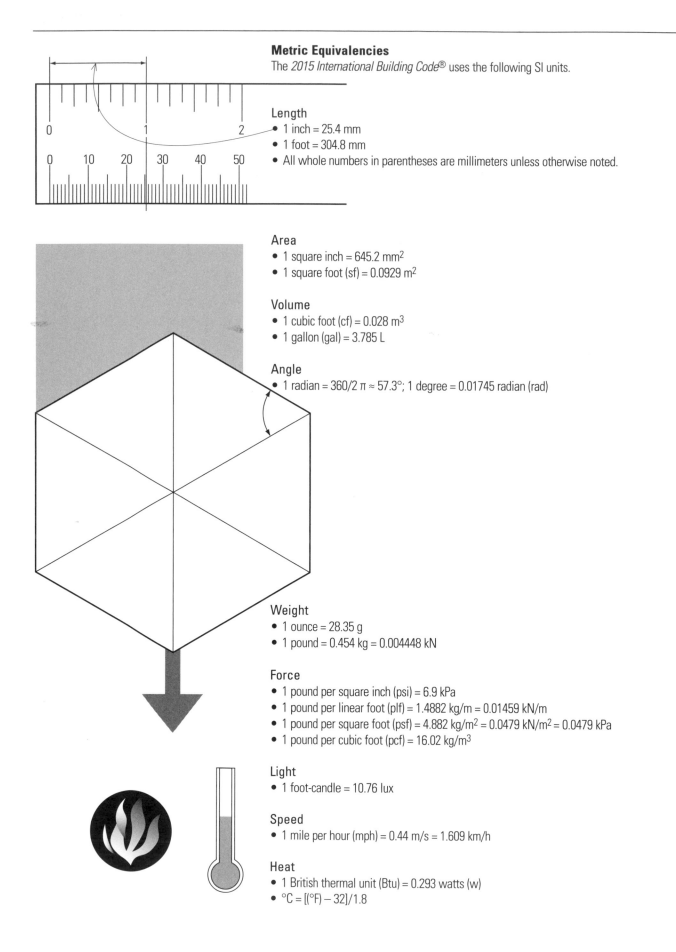

Metric Equivalencies

The *2015 International Building Code*® uses the following SI units.

Length
- 1 inch = 25.4 mm
- 1 foot = 304.8 mm
- All whole numbers in parentheses are millimeters unless otherwise noted.

Area
- 1 square inch = 645.2 mm^2
- 1 square foot (sf) = 0.0929 m^2

Volume
- 1 cubic foot (cf) = 0.028 m^3
- 1 gallon (gal) = 3.785 L

Angle
- 1 radian = 360/2 $\pi \approx$ 57.3°; 1 degree = 0.01745 radian (rad)

Weight
- 1 ounce = 28.35 g
- 1 pound = 0.454 kg = 0.004448 kN

Force
- 1 pound per square inch (psi) = 6.9 kPa
- 1 pound per linear foot (plf) = 1.4882 kg/m = 0.01459 kN/m
- 1 pound per square foot (psf) = 4.882 kg/m^2 = 0.0479 kN/m^2 = 0.0479 kPa
- 1 pound per cubic foot (pcf) = 16.02 kg/m^3

Light
- 1 foot-candle = 10.76 lux

Speed
- 1 mile per hour (mph) = 0.44 m/s = 1.609 km/h

Heat
- 1 British thermal unit (Btu) = 0.293 watts (w)
- °C = [(°F) − 32]/1.8

1
Building Codes

The existence of building regulations goes back almost 4,000 years. The Babylonian Code of Hammurabi decreed the death penalty for a builder if a house he constructed collapsed and killed the owner. If the collapse killed the owner's son, then the son of the builder would be put to death; if goods were damaged then the contractor would have to repay the owner, and so on. This precedent is worth keeping in mind as you contemplate the potential legal ramifications of your actions in designing and constructing a building in accordance with the code. The protection of the health, safety, and welfare of the public is the basis for licensure of design professionals and the reason that building regulations exist.

"If a builder build a house for some one, and does not construct it properly, and the house which he built fall in and kill its owner, then that builder shall be put to death.

If it kill the son of the owner, the son of that builder shall be put to death.

If it kill a slave of the owner, then he shall pay slave for slave to the owner of the house.

If it ruin goods, he shall make compensation for all that has been ruined, and inasmuch as he did not construct properly this house which he built and it fell, he shall re-erect the house from his own means.

If a builder build a house for some one, even though he has not yet completed it; if then the walls seem toppling, the builder must make the walls solid from his own means."

Laws 229–233
Hammurabi's Code of Laws
(ca. 1780 BC)

From a stone slab discovered in 1901 and preserved in the Louvre, Paris.

Various civilizations over the centuries have developed building codes. The origins of the codes we use today lie in the great fires that swept American cities regularly in the 1800s. Chicago developed a building code in 1875 to placate the National Board of Fire Underwriters, who threatened to cut off insurance for businesses after the fire of 1871. It is essential to keep the fire-based origins of the codes in mind when trying to understand the reasoning behind many code requirements.

The various city codes and often conflicting codes were refined over the years and began to be brought together by regional nongovernmental organizations to develop so-called model codes. The first model codes were written from the point of view of insurance companies to reduce fire risks. Model codes are developed by private code groups for subsequent adoption by local and state government agencies as legally enforceable regulations. The first major model-code group was the Building Officials and Code Administrators (BOCA), founded in 1915 and located in Country Club Hills, Illinois. Next was the International Conference of Building Officials (ICBO), formed in 1922, located in Whittier, California. The first edition of their *Uniform Building Code* was published in 1927. The Southern Building Code Congress, founded in 1940 and headquartered in Birmingham, Alabama, first published the *Southern Building Code* in 1946. The first BOCA *National Building Code* was published in 1950.

These three model-code groups published the three different building codes previously in widespread use in the United States. These codes were developed by regional organizations of building officials, building materials experts, design professionals and life safety experts to provide communities and governments with standard construction criteria for uniform application and enforcement. The ICBO *Uniform Building Code* was used primarily west of the Mississippi River and was the most widely applied of the model codes. The BOCA *National Building Code* was used primarily in the north-central and northeastern states. The SBCCI *Standard Building Code* was used primarily in the Southeast. The model-code groups merged in the late 1990s to form the International Code Council and BOCA, ICBO, and SBCCI ceased maintaining and publishing their legacy codes.

The International Building Code

The new ICC process was a real revolution in the development of model codes. There was recognition in the early 1990s that the nation would be best served by a comprehensive, coordinated national model building code developed through a general consensus of code writers. There was also recognition that it would take time to reconcile the differences between the existing codes. To begin the reconciliation process, the three model codes were reformatted into a common format. The International Code Council, made up of representatives from the three model-code groups, was formed in 1994 to develop a single model code using the information contained in the three current model codes. While detailed requirements still varied from code to code, the organization of each code became essentially the same during the mid-1990s. This allowed direct comparison of requirements in each code for similar design situations. Numerous drafts of the new International Building Code were reviewed by the model-code agencies along with code users. From that multiyear review grew the original edition of the *International Building Code* (IBC), first published in 2000. There is now a single national model code maintained by a group composed of representatives of the three prior model-code agencies, the International Code Council, headquartered in Washington, D.C. The three organizations have now accomplished a full merger of the three model-code groups into a single agency to update and maintain the IBC.

Note that in addition to the *International Building Code* (IBC), code users must be familiar with the *International Residential Code* (IRC). This code is meant to regulate construction of detached one- and two-family dwellings and townhouses that are not more than three stories in height. This code supplants residential requirements in the IBC in jurisdictions where it is adopted.

Note also that most local jurisdictions make other modifications to the codes in use in their communities. For example, many jurisdictions make amendments to require fire sprinkler systems where they may be optional in the model codes. In such cases mandatory sprinkler requirements may change the design trade-offs offered in the model code for inclusion of sprinklers where "not otherwise required" by the code. It is imperative that the designer determines what local adoptions and amendments have been made to be certain which codes apply to a specific project.

A major revision has taken place in the 2015 IBC. The provisions for existing buildings, contained in Chapter 34 of the previous code, have been removed. Therefore the IBC applies only to new buildings. The provisions for existing buildings are now contained exclusively in the *International Existing Building Code* (IEBC). The provisions in the IEBC for alterations and additions refer back to the IBC or adopt similar requirements, but the two codes are now intended to be used separately. For the purposes of this book, assume that the requirements discussed are to apply to new buildings or to additions to new buildings unless noted otherwise.

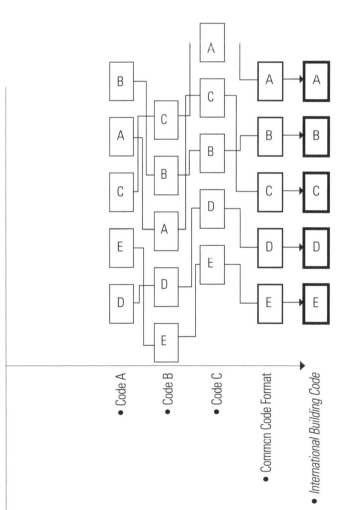

There are also specific federal requirements that must be considered in design and construction in addition to the locally adopted version of the model codes. Among these are the Americans with Disabilities Act of 1990 and the Federal Fair Housing Act of 1988.

Americans with Disabilities Act

The Americans with Disabilities Act (ADA) of 1990 is federal civil-rights legislation requiring that buildings be made accessible to persons with physical disabilities and certain defined mental disabilities. The *ADA Accessibility Guidelines* (ADAAG) are administered by the Architectural and Transportation Barriers Compliance Board (ATBCB), and the regulations are administered by the U.S. Department of Justice. Enforcement of the law is through legal actions brought by individuals or groups asserting violations of their rights of access, as civil rights. A new version of the ADA accessibility guidelines known as the *ADA/ABA Accessibility Guidelines* goes into effect on March 15, 2012. Designers can obtain copies of the new guidelines from the Access Board at www.access-board.gov/ada.

It is critical for designers to understand that the ADA is not subject to interpretation by local building officials; it is enforced by legal action, through the courts. Access is to be provided for all disabilities, not just for people with mobility impairments. These include hearing, vision, speech, and cognitive impairments, as well as persons of short stature and with limited mobility not necessarily requiring the use of a wheelchair. The ADA applies to all new construction. The ADA also requires that barriers to access be removed from existing buildings where such work is readily achievable. The definition of readily achievable is an economic one and should be addressed by the building owner, not by the building architect.

The ADA is one of the few building regulations—in this case a law, not a code—that requires retrofitting of projects apart from upgrading facilities during remodeling or renovation. Most codes apply to existing buildings only when renovation is undertaken. Under the ADA those access improvements that are readily achievable should be undertaken by the owner whether or not any other remodeling work is to be done. The **owner**, not the architect, must make this determination.

As the ADA is not enforced by local building officials we will concentrate here only on those accessibility codes that are enforced locally and subject to review and interpretation as part of the permit process. Designers must first concentrate on complying with codes and standards adopted locally but must also keep national statutory requirements such as the ADA in mind. It is prudent to review design work against ADAAG at the same time as the model-code review. It is often a judgment call as to which is the most stringent requirement where requirements between codes and legislation differ. In these situations, it is essential and prudent to make the client aware of these discrepancies and have them actively participate in any decisions as to which part of which requirements will govern the design of project components.

Space requirements for accessibility are related to ergonomics. Bigger is not automatically better. The 18" (457) dimension between a toilet and adjacent grab bars is based on reach ranges and leverage for movement using one's arms. A longer reach reduces leverage and thus may be worse than too little space.

Federal Fair Housing Act

The Federal Fair Housing Act (FFHA) of 1988 includes Department of Housing and Urban Development (HUD) regulations requiring all residential complexes of four or more dwelling units constructed after March 13, 1991, to be adaptable for use by persons with disabilities. For example, residential complexes must provide access to all units on the ground floor, and all units must be accessible from grade by a ramp or elevator. Many state housing codes also incorporate these requirements. A very good reference for the FFHA is the *Fair Housing Act Design Manual*, which can be obtained free of charge at http://www.huduser.org/portal/publications/destech/fairhousing.html.

State Building Codes

Each state has a separate and distinct code adoption process. In the past many states adopted one of the three previous model codes, and some states even had their own building codes. The geographic areas for state model-code adoptions corresponded roughly to the areas of influence of the three previous model codes as noted on page 3. The BOCA *National Building Code* predominated in the northeastern United States. The *Southern Building Code* was adopted throughout the southeastern United States. The *Uniform Building Code* was adopted in most states west of the Mississippi River. Many states allowed local adoption of codes so that in some states, such as Texas, adjacent jurisdictions in the same state had different building codes based on different model codes. Now, the advent of the International Codes has altered this landscape drastically. The "I Codes" are now the basic model codes in essentially every state. However, be aware that most state processes still allow amendments to the IBC, which means that there will likely be state-adopted amendments to the IBC. Make certain you know what code you are working with at the permitting level.

Local Building Codes

Many localities adopt the model-code documents with little modification except for the administrative chapters that relate to local operations of the building department. Larger cities, such as Los Angeles, New York City, Chicago, and San Francisco, typically adopt much more sweeping revisions to the model codes. The codes for such cities often bear little resemblance to the underlying model codes and in some cases have no basis in them at all. Interpretations, even of the unaltered model code made by big-city building departments, often tend to be very idiosyncratic and nonuniform when compared to smaller jurisdictions that use less modified versions of the model codes. The adoption of the IBC at the state level has generated a review of big-city building codes so that these city codes are moving toward greater conformity with the model codes. For example, San Francisco and Los Angeles previously used a UBC-based state code, which has now been converted to an IBC-based, locally modified state code. This will require a careful analysis of the city-code

amendments to ensure conformance with the new model code. This redevelopment of codes has also been occurring in other large cities, such as Dallas and New York, as their states adopt the IBC. Be aware of local modifications and be prepared for varying interpretations of the same code sections among various jurisdictions. Do not proceed too far in the design process based on review of similar designs in another jurisdiction without verification of the code interpretation in the jurisdiction where the project is located. Similarly, although this book offers opinions of what code sections mean, all such opinions are subject to interpretation by local authorities as codes are applied to specific projects.

Codes and standards are related, but serve different purposes. A building code (e.g., the International Building Code) establishes a jurisdictional "floor" relative to occupants' health, safety, and welfare. A building standard (e.g., NFPA 13) is a "standard practice" often referred to within the codes. In short, a code is what you must do; a standard is a guide on how you do it. There are thus a number of other codes and standards that the designer must be familiar with. They are mentioned here in brief to remind users of the *International Building Code* that other documents must also be consulted during project design.

While building code and accessibility regulations are usually the focus of interest for architectural and structural work, you need to be aware of the existence of other separate codes for such work as electrical, plumbing, mechanical, fire sprinklers, and fire alarms. Each of these may impact the work of design consultants and in turn the work of the architect. Detailed consideration of the requirements in these other codes is beyond the scope of this book.

Among other specialized codes is the *Life Safety Code* (NFPA-101) published by the National Fire Protection Association. This code serves as a basis for the egress provisions in the other model codes. Designers may encounter NFPA-101 when doing federal and hospital work. The NFPA also publishes various other standards that are adopted to accompany the model codes. Primary examples are NFPA-13: Standard for the Installation of Sprinkler Systems, and NFPA-70, which is the National Electrical Code.

The National Fire Protection Association has developed a new model building code, NFPA 5000, to rival the *International Building Code*. The development of this code is meant to offer an alternative to the "I" codes. The NFPA 5000 has, to date, been adopted in very few jurisdictions. Some jurisdictions may move to adopt either the International code family or the NFPA family of codes, or even portions of each. This is yet another reason for designers to verify in detail what model code documents are adopted by the Authorities Having Jurisdiction (AHJ)—a catch-all phrase for all planning, zoning, fire, and building officials having something to say about building—where a project is located.

Fire codes are typically considered maintenance codes. They are intended to provide for public health and safety in the day-to-day operation of a structure. They are also meant to assure that building life-safety systems remain operational in case of emergency. The various model-code agencies have developed model fire codes for these purposes. They are developed with primary input from the fire services and less input from design professionals. Note, however, that fire codes can have an impact on building design. They contain requirements for such elements as fire-truck access, locations and spacing of fire extinguishers, as well as requirements for sprinklers and wet or dry standpipes. The fire code also may contain requirements for added fire protection related to the ease or difficulty of fire equipment access to structures.

Plumbing codes often dictate the number of plumbing fixtures required in various occupancies. Some codes place this information in the building code, some in the plumbing code, and some in appendices that allow local determination of where these requirements may occur in the codes. The designer must determine which course of legal adoption the local authority has chosen. The determination of the required number of plumbing fixtures is an important design consideration. It is essential to use the adopted tables and not automatically assume those in the model building code apply.

Code Interactions

The AHJ may not always inform the designer of overlapping jurisdictions or duplication of regulations. Fire departments often do not thoroughly check plan drawings at the time building permit documents are reviewed by the building department. Fire-department plan review deficiencies are often discovered at the time of field inspections by fire officials, usually at a time when additional cost and time is required to fix these deficiencies. The costs of tearing out noncomplying work and replacing it may be considered a designer's error. Whenever starting a project, it is therefore incumbent upon the designer to determine exactly which codes and standards are to be enforced for the project and by which agency. It is also imperative to obtain copies of any revisions or modifications made to model codes by local or state agencies. This must be assured for all AHJs.

The model codes have no force of law unto themselves. Only after adoption by a governmental agency are they enforceable under the police powers of the state. Enforcement powers are delegated by statute to officials in various levels of government. Designers must verify local amendments to model codes to be certain which code provisions apply to specific projects.

There are many different codes that may apply to various aspects of construction projects. Typically the first question to be asked is whether the project requires a permit. Certain projects, such as interior work for movable furniture or finishes, are usually exempt. Carpeting may be replaced and walls painted without a permit, but moving walls, relocating doors, or doing plumbing and electrical work will require a permit in most jurisdictions.

Traditionally, codes have been written with new construction in mind. In recent years more and more provisions have been made applicable to alteration, repair, and renovation of existing facilities. One of the emerging trends in code development is the creation of an *International Existing Building Code* (IEBC). As the importance of preservation of historic structures and the sustainable design implications of reusing existing buildings become more important, the IEBC will take on greater impact. The reuse of existing buildings is also of concern for accessibility issues. One of the most crucial aspects of remodeling work is to determine to what extent and in what specific parts of your project do building codes and access regulations apply. Most codes are not retroactive. They do not require remedial work apart from remodeling or renovation of a building.

A notable exception to this is the Americans with Disabilities Act, which requires that renovation be undertaken to provide access for persons with disabilities if access can be readily provided. However, this is a civil-rights law and not a code. As such, it is not enforced by building officials. In existing buildings it is critical for the designer to determine with the AHJ what the boundaries of the project are to be and to make certain that the AHJ, the designer, and the client understand and agree upon the requirements for remedial work to be undertaken in the project area.

Rating Systems

There are also rating systems, the most well known and widespread of which is the *Leadership in Energy and Environmental Design*, or LEED program, developed by the U.S. Green Building Council (USGBC). LEED is not intended to be a code, although some jurisdictions have adopted LEED criteria as code language. Typically, a rating system is a voluntary program based on options selected by the owner and the design team rather than being a set of requirements. Rating systems serve as an ever-being-raised "ceiling" for practice.

Standard of Care

The designer should always remember that codes are legally and ethically considered to be minimum criteria that must be met by the design and construction community. The protection of health, safety, and welfare is the goal of these minimum standards. It is important to also understand that registered design professionals will be held by legal and ethical precedents to a much higher standard than the code minimum.

The so-called "standard of care" is a legal term defining the level of quality of service that a practitioner is expected to meet. This is higher than the minimum standard defined by the code. The code is the level that a practitioner must never go below. Because professional work involves judgment, perfection is not expected of a design professional. The standard of care is defined for an individual designer as being those actions that any other well-informed practitioner would have taken given the same level of knowledge in the same situation. It is a relative measure, not an absolute one.

Life Safety vs. Property Protection

The basis for building-code development is to safeguard the health, safety, and welfare of the public. The first and foremost goal of building codes is the protection of human life from the failure of life safety provisions in a building, or from structural collapse. But there is also a strong component of property protection contained in code requirements. Sprinkler provisions can serve both purposes. When buildings are occupied, sprinklers can contain or extinguish a fire, allowing the building occupants to escape. The same sprinkler system can protect an unoccupied structure from loss if a fire occurs when the structure is not occupied.

While many systems may perform both life safety and property protection functions, it is essential that code developers keep the issue of life safety versus property protection in mind. For example, security measures to prevent intrusion into a structure may become hazards to life safety. A prime example of this is burglar bars on the exterior of ground-floor windows that can trap inhabitants of the building in an emergency if there is not an interior release to allow occupants to escape while still maintaining the desired security. In no case should property-protection considerations have primacy over life safety.

The International Building Code is a living document. It is subject to regular review and comment cycles. A new code is published at regular intervals, usually every three years. This publication cycle gives some measure of certainty for building designers that the code will remain unchanged during the design-and-construction process. The code responds to new information, growing by accretion and adaptation. Now that the three model-code agencies have merged into one organization, detailed changes in the code-development process have evolved and have been refined. We will give only a general description of the code-development process. For a detailed description of the current code development process, see the ICC website.

Any person may propose a code revision. Any designer, material supplier, code official, or interested member of the public that feels they have a better way to describe code requirements or to accommodate new life-safety developments or new technology may prepare revised code language for consideration. Proposed code changes are published for review by all interested parties. They are then categorized based on what section of the code is being revised and assigned to a committee of people experienced in those matters for review and consideration. Committees are typically organized around specific issues such as means of egress, fire safety, structural, general and so forth. Anyone may testify at these committee hearings regarding the merits or demerits of the code change. The committee then votes to make its recommendation to the annual business meeting. At the annual business meeting, testimony will be heard from all interested parties, both from non-voting industry representatives and building officials who will be able to vote on the proposed changes. After testimony is heard only the government members of the organization, typically public employees serving as building and fire officials, are allowed to vote on the proposed changes. This is described as the "governmental consensus process" by the ICC.

Performance vs. Prescriptive Codes

There is now an ICC *International Performance Code*. It presents regulations based on desired outcomes rather than prescriptions. It encourages new design methods by allowing a broader parameter for meeting the intent of the International Codes. Where adopted locally it may be used in place of the regular IBC provisions. We will discuss briefly the distinctions between prescriptive and performance codes.

The *International Building Code*, as were the codes that preceded it, is predominately prescriptive in nature, but it does have some performance-based criteria as well. It is developed to mitigate concerns by creating mostly specific and prescribed responses to problems that have been identified. Designers identify the problem to be addressed, such as the height of guardrails, and then they look up the prescribed response in the applicable code section. For example, guardrail heights are prescribed to be 42" (1067) high and are required when adjacent changes in grade exceed 30" (762). The designer follows the prescribed requirements to avoid the problem the code has identified—that is, preventing falls over an edge higher than 30" (762). The code provides a defined solution to an identified problem.

Performance codes, such as the ICC International Performance Code, define the problem and allow the designer to devise the solution. The word "performance" in this context refers to the problem definition and to the setting of parameters for deciding if the proposed solution solves the problem adequately. These standards define the problem, but do not define, describe, or predetermine the solution.

The use of performance codes has been increasing in the past few years, due in large part to the development of new modeling techniques for predicting how a building will react under certain fire, earthquake, or other stimuli. Performance codes are used in many countries around the world. Their requirements may be as broad as "the building shall allow all of its prospective occupants to safely leave the building in the event of a fire." Most performance codes in reality have much more tightly defined requirements, but the exiting requirement stated above is a good example of the essence of what performance-code requirements can be.

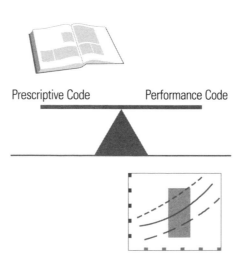

Prescriptive Code   Performance Code

The basic form of modern performance-code language can be described as objective-based. Each code requirement is broken into three sections. We will use fall prevention as our example. Note that provision of guardrails is only one example of many solutions to the performance objective, not the only solution.

- Objective: What is to be accomplished? In this case the prevention of falls from heights of more than 30" (762).

- Functional Statement: Why do we want to accomplish this? We wish to safeguard building occupants by preventing them from accidentally falling from a height great enough to result in an injury.

- Performance Requirement: How is this to be accomplished? Performance codes could become prescriptive at this juncture, mandating a guardrail. More likely such a performance standard would require that the barrier be high enough, strong enough and continuous enough to prevent falls under the objective circumstances. Note that a guardrail meeting current code standards would be deemed to satisfy those requirements, but alternate means and methods could also achieve the same ends. For example, landscaping could prevent access to the grade change, or innovative railing substitutes could be designed to function like automobile air bags to catch falling persons without having a visible rail present in most conditions. Let your imagination provide other alternatives.

Performance codes give designers more freedom to comply with the stated goals. They also require the designer to take on more responsibility for knowing the consequences of their design actions. We anticipate that performance codes will be used in limited ways for innovative projects, but that most typical, repetitive designs will continue to use prescriptive codes for speed, clarity, and assurance of compliance during design review. Also, given the legal climate, designers are often reluctant to take on the responsibility for long-term code compliance for innovative systems.

2
Navigating the Code

The key word to remember about how all building codes are developed and how they all work is intent. As we noted in the Preface, code sections have individual authors who had some problem in mind when they wrote a code-change proposal. The intent of the author of a building-code section is to solve a specific design problem with prescriptive language. Designers are usually trying to measure visual and spatial expressions against the language of the code. During this process, the designer should ask what problem or performance criteria the code section is addressing. The language will start to make more sense as one tries to go beyond the specific language to determine why the words say what they say.

Designers also have intent. They are trying to achieve certain functional or formal goals in the design of the building. Designers should measure their own intent for the design against their interpretations of the intent of the code. When examined together, the intent of the code and that of the design solution should be concurrent.

Do not try and ignore the code. Do not try and confuse or obfuscate code issues to achieve approvals. The responsibility for understanding, applying, and fulfilling the requirements of the code always rests with the design professional. Approvals by the AHJ do not relieve the designer of social and licensing responsibilities to maintain the health, safety, and welfare of society.

Each section of the code was developed to solve a certain problem. Code sections are typically written in relatively short paragraphs. Sections are organized into chapters based on common themes, but usually are developed in isolation from one another with little attention to continuity of the entire document. As you look at the code, try and visualize the intent of the writer of that section and try to understand the problem they were addressing. Code language usually arises from a specific issue the code writer wishes to address based on experience or on an actual construction or life safety issue. The writer then makes the requirements general so that they will apply to more typical conditions than the specific instance that generated the concern.

The intent of the code is a crucial idea to understand. *Why* is a much more important question than *what* when you are puzzled by the actual language of a code passage. The code is a general document that must then be interpreted for its specific application to a specific project. If you know the code in general and think about its intent, you will be in a better position to formulate your own interpretation of code sections as they apply to your specific project. You will thus be in a position to help building officials see the validity of your opinion when interpretation of the code is required for a specific design condition. Confidence will come with experience in use of the code. Learning the code is vital to your success as a well-rounded designer.

Note that in the 2015 IBC certain terms are in *italic type*. These italicized terms appear in the definitions in Chapter 2. Where terms are used in ways intended by their definitions they are italicized in the body of the code. Italicized type is **not** used in this book in the same way. The code publisher's intent for this notification method is to highlight for the code user that the code's definitions should be read carefully to facilitate better understanding of how they are used in the context where they appear in italics. It is critical that the code user go back to the code definitions when attempting to understand the literal and figurative meaning of code requirements. When attempting to interpret a code section be sure to examine the code definitions for the terms used in the code section. Do not assume that the meanings of terms are the same as in everyday speech, especially for italicized text.

While definitions occur in the IBC in Chapter 2, this book discusses definitions in context with where the defined items are used in the technical requirements in the code. We believe this makes the analysis in this book easier to follow. Defined terms from the IBC are noted in [*bracketed italic type*]. Thus defined terms will be found throughout the various chapters of this book.

Learn the table of contents and use the index. It is very useful to get the code in electronic form for use in your practice. This allows key word searches. Don't try and memorize passages of the code, because these may change or move around inside the code over time as the code is amended. Learn the organization of the code and learn where to find things that way. Use the index if the table of contents doesn't get you where you want to be. Think of synonyms for the topic you are researching to facilitate key word or index searches. You may have to scan large portions of the index to locate potential items. Try to remember associations of ideas, not specific language, to facilitate your use of the code.

In the code, solid vertical lines [▌] in the margins indicate a text change from the 2012 code edition. There will be an arrow in the margin [—>] indicating a deletion in the section. A single asterisk [*] placed in the margin indicates that text or a table has been relocated within the code. A double asterisk [**] placed in the margin indicates that the text or table immediately following it has been relocated there from elsewhere in the code.

You should probably own a personal printed copy of the model code, and an electronic copy as well. Remember that the model code is often amended during adoption by local agencies. Be certain to find out what local code amendments to the code apply to your specific project. Also determine if the local AHJ has published written opinions regarding their interpretation of the code in their jurisdiction.

intent
+
interpretation
=
- ## intent
- ## intent
- ## intent
- ## intent
- ## intent

Alternative Means and Methods

§ 104.11 states that the provisions of this code are not intended to prevent the installation of any material or to prohibit any design or method of construction not specifically prescribed by this code. While written around prescriptive descriptions of tested assemblies and rated construction, the code recognizes that there may be many different ways of solving the same design problems. It recognizes that there will be innovations in building types, such as covered malls, mixed-use buildings, and atrium buildings that do not fit neatly into prescribed occupancy classifications. The code also recognizes that there will be innovations in materials and construction technology that may happen faster than code revisions are made. Thus the code sets up a method for the building official to approve proposed alternative designs. Deviations from prescribed standards must be submitted for review and approval of the building official. The criteria they are to use are spelled out in the code. We have highlighted some of the key provisions of the approval in **bold italics**. The alternative is to be approved when "the proposed design is satisfactory and complies with the intent of the provisions of this code, and that the material, method, or work offered is, for the purpose intended, **not less than the equivalent of that prescribed in the code in quality, strength, effectiveness, fire resistance, durability, and safety**" (emphasis added). These words are also the fundamental criteria for why each and every code section is included in the basic code.

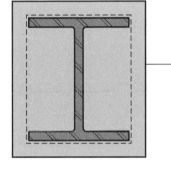

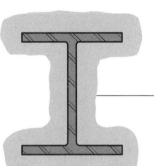

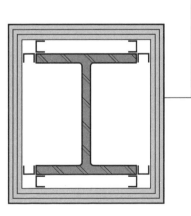

Evaluation of Innovative Products

Innovations in construction materials and methods need to be evaluated for code compliance. Testing agencies often perform standardized tests on new products. These tests and data about the product must then be evaluated for code compliance. One popular way of demonstrating compliance to the AHJ for products or construction methods is through the use of ICC Evaluation Service reports.

ICC-ES is a nonprofit, limited liability company that does technical evaluations of building products, components, methods, and materials. Reports are prepared at the request of companies wishing their products to be evaluated by ICC-ES. Supporting data, such as product information and test reports, is reviewed by the ICC-ES technical staff for code compliance. The evaluation process culminates with the issuance of a report on code compliance. The reports are public documents, readily available on the Internet. They may be used by designers in determining whether an innovative or unusual construction material or process is code-compliant. The designer may then use the ICC-ES report to demonstrate code compliance by submitting it for review by the AHJ.

Concrete, spray-on fireproofing, or gypsum board provide alternate means of fireproofing a structural steel member.

Code Interpretations

Designers and code officials approach interpretations from quite different perspectives. The designer is trying to make a functional or formal design code compliant while satisfying project requirements in an aesthetic, economical and practical way. The AHJ examines completed drawings for compliance with code requirements. While the AHJ is not unaware of the practical requirements contained in the building design, they are charged first and foremost with protecting the health, safety, and welfare of the public by verifying code compliance. It is the responsibility of the designer to demonstrate code compliance and to modify noncompliant areas identified during plan review by the AHJ while continuing to meet the project requirements.

Both the designer and the AHJ are working to apply generalized code provisions to a specific project. It is differences in opinion about the application of the general to the specific that most often give rise to differences in interpretation. Code officials also see many more similar examples of the relationship of code sections to various designs. Thus they may generalize interpretations from one project to another even though the projects may be different in significant ways. On the other hand, designers may find that similar designs receive quite different interpretations by the AHJ in different jurisdictions. When differences of opinion about interpretation occur, the designer must work with the AHJ to reconcile the intent of the design to the interpretations of the intent of the code. If reconciliation cannot be reached the designer must decide whether to revise the project to obtain approval or appeal the ruling of the AHJ to some civic body prescribed in the jurisdiction for hearing appeals. Often the AHJ can be requested to apply to the model-code agency that published the code for a ruling as to the publisher's opinion of the intent of the code section in question. Such appeals to the ICC are allowed to be made by any ICC member. It is thus prudent for design professionals to be ICC members to be able to access this service. In addition members receive discounts on ICC codes and have access to other interpretive and educational materials. Members may also participate in the code development process and gain deeper insights into code interpretations.

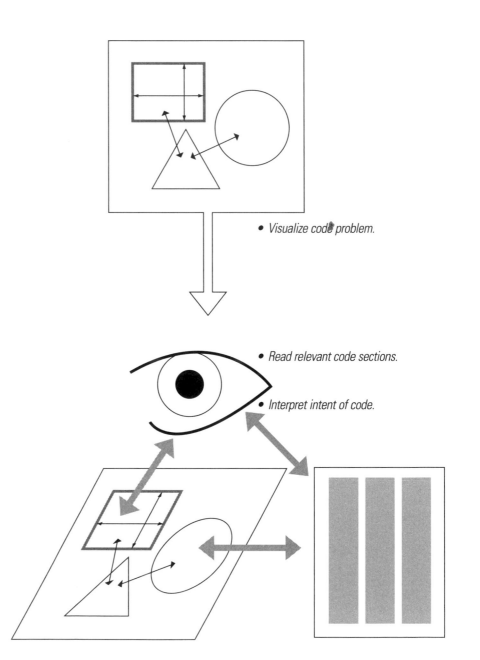

• Visualize code problem.

• Read relevant code sections.

• Interpret intent of code.

• Revisualize possible solution that satisfies both design intent and intent of the code.

Documenting Code Interpretations

Every project should receive a detailed code analysis that is recorded as a permanent part of the permit documents. All code interpretations and citations should have a reference to the code section in question to allow retracing steps in the code analysis. Without a code section citation it is very difficult to have a productive discussion about interpretations. Recording citations focuses code issues for the designer during the design process and facilitates plan reviews by the AHJ.

At minimum the analysis should contain the following items. We recommend the following format to unify code analysis for all projects. The code section citations used should be specific for the project and sections, not as limited as in our example.

Proposed Condition	Allowed per Code	Code Section or Table
Occupancy Classification	Select from Chapter 3	Chapter 3
Fire Protection (active)	Select per occupancy	Chapter 9
Building Height (feet/stories)	Allowed per proposed type	Tables 504.3 and 504.4
Building Area	Select per construction type	Table 506.2, as adjusted
Type of Construction	Determine from design	Chapters 5, 6, 7
Means of Egress	Select per occupancy	Chapter 10

A site plan and floor plan should be included that describes the location of the building on the property and any height area or construction-type credits or requirements related to location on the site and proximity to streets and other structures. The floor plan should also detail egress requirements, such as exit access widths, exit quantities and locations, and exit discharge paths to the public way. A recommended code room tag is shown below.

####	Room Number
Room Name	Assigned Room Use
Occupancy Group	Per IBC Chapter 3
Area - SF	"Gross" or "Net" per IBC Chapter 2
Occ. Load Factor	Per IBC Table 1004.1.2
# of Occupants	Area x OLF
Door Width	Width of required door(s) at least 32" (813) clear.

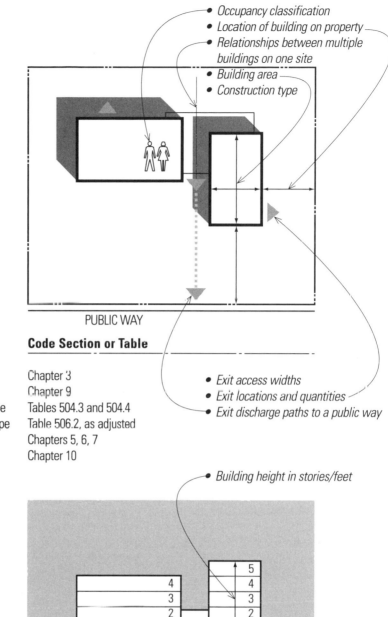

- Occupancy classification
- Location of building on property
- Relationships between multiple buildings on one site
- Building area
- Construction type

PUBLIC WAY

- Exit access widths
- Exit locations and quantities
- Exit discharge paths to a public way

- Building height in stories/feet

For the designer, many elements required to determine how the code should apply to a project are a given from the program and the site or zoning constraints:

- Occupancy classification—the client determines what functions they want;
- Location of building on property— determined by the building footprint, zoning, natural features, etc.;
- Building height and area—given the scope of the project, the designer will note how large the building needs to be and how many floors will be required.

With these pieces of information it is possible to determine how the code prescribes the minimum for:
- Construction type—determined by calculation;
- Exit locations and quantities;
- Exit access widths;
- Exit discharge to a public way.

The following procedure is recommended as being helpful in using the International Building Code. Note that most of the major issues are interactive and that iteration of relationships will be required to optimize design solutions. The procedure can be paraphrased as follows.

1. Classify the building according to occupancy, type of construction, location on property, floor area, height, and number of stories.

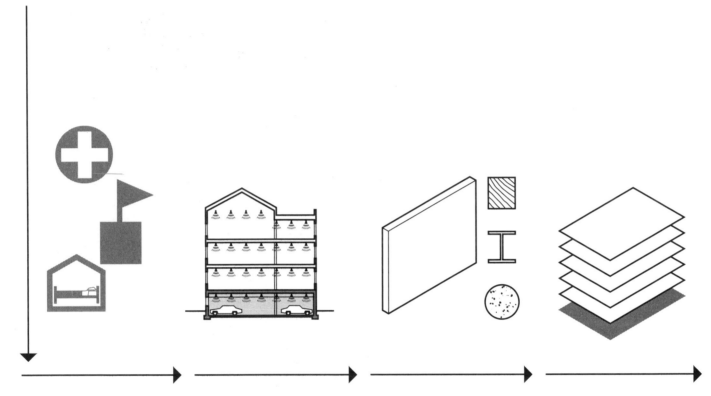

A. Occupancy Classification
Determine the occupancy group that the use of the building or portion thereof most nearly resembles. Compute the floor area and occupant load of the building or portion thereof. See the appropriate sections in Chapter 5 for requirements for buildings with mixed occupancies.

B. Sprinkler Systems
Determine if the occupancy is required to be protected by a sprinkler system and identify the threshold(s). Determine if the anticipated height of the building will require fire sprinklers. See the appropriate sections in Chapter 9 for thresholds based on the occupancy. Note also the sprinkler adjustments for heights and areas in Chapter 5 as described in Step "D."

C. Type of Construction
Determine the required minimum type of construction based on the occupancy, fire protection, and the designed height and area. This will dictate the materials used and the fire-resistance of the parts of the building as limited in Chapter 6.

D. Allowable Floor Area
Determine the allowable floor area of the building. Use the basic allowable floor area based on occupancy group and type of construction. Determine allowable floor area of multistory buildings. Determine allowable increases based on location on property and if there is installation of an approved automatic fire-sprinkler system.

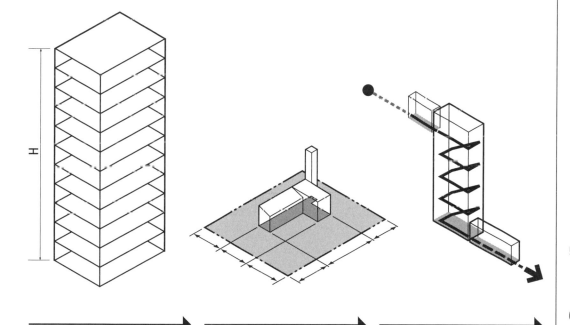

2. Review requirements for fire sprinkler protection.

3. Review the building for conformity with the type-of-construction requirements in relation to desired and allowable building heights and plan areas. Iteration may be required between heights, areas and construction types.

4. Review the effects on the building based on its location on the building site. Iteration may be required in reviewing location together with construction types and amount of openings in relation to property lines.

5. Review the building for conformity with egress requirements.

6. Review the building for other detailed code requirements.

7. Review the building for conformity with structural engineering regulations and requirements for materials of construction.

E. Height and Number of Stories
Compute the height of the building and determine the number of stories. Determine the maximum height and number of stories permitted based on occupancy group and type of construction. Determine allowable height and story increase based on the installation of an approved automatic fire-sprinkler system.

F. Location on Property
Determine the location of the building on the site and clearances to lot lines and other buildings from the plot plan. Determine the fire-resistance requirements for exterior walls and wall-opening requirements based on fire-separation distances to lot lines. The fire resistance requirements for exterior walls and the limitations on their openings are found in Chapter 7.

G. Means of Egress
Determine the requirements for means of egress from the building found in Chapter 10.

The following section is a review of the critical information required for a project code analysis, based on the analysis system noted above.

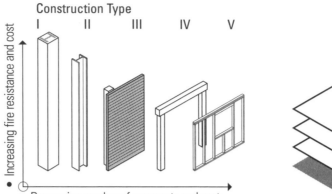

Construction Type

I   II   III   IV   V

Increasing fire resistance and cost

Decreasing number of occupants and cost

Occupancy Type

Projects are almost invariably defined for the designer based on occupancy type. A client almost always comes to a designer with a defined need for a facility. The use of that facility determines the occupancy classification to which it belongs. Each occupancy classification or type has specific requirements related to allowable area, height and exiting with potential construction types growing out of these requirements. The codes are fundamentally use (occupancy) based. Other criteria are derived from the first basic classification by occupancy. Occupancy classifications are defined in Chapter 3.

Fire Extinguishing Systems

Fire sprinklers, standpipes, fire detection, and fire-alarm systems are an integral part of most new buildings. Use of such systems, especially automatic fire sprinklers, often results in trade-offs for additional height or area. Trade-offs are listed in the code sections related to height and areas, but other requirements are listed in separate sections of the code. Fire-protection systems are covered in Chapter 9. Note also that sprinkler system requirements are another area where local amendments are often added to the model codes. These requirements should be verified for each project. It can be critical to a trade-off to know if a system is otherwise required in the jurisdiction where you are working, as it may remove the model-code option of using some items like a sprinkler trade-off in lieu of fire rating certain parts of the building structure. Trade-offs only apply when the systems are not otherwise required by the local code to be used for a project. The idea of a trade-off recognizes that this is a mitigation measure over and above basic code requirements to achieve the desired level of safety through other means than those spelled out in the basic code.

Construction Type

Construction types are typically categorized by materials based on their resistance to fire in structural applications. The construction type gives some indication of the amount of time available for evacuation of occupants, for fire fighting, and for emergency response under fire conditions. Buildings of fire-protected steel or concrete will provide more fire resistance than those of wood construction. More fire-resistant construction types are allowed to be of larger area and to have more stories as the fire-resistance increases. As a rough rule of thumb, allowable occupancy quantities and construction costs will both decrease with building type from Type I to Type V.

Types of construction are defined in Chapter 6. Table 601 gives a synopsis of the minimum fire-resistive requirements of each main element of building construction. As you go through a code analysis you will be referring to this table and to Table 506.2 to select the optimum balance of construction type, occupancy, and area requirements for a specific project. It is typically a budget goal to minimize construction costs by selecting the least costly construction type appropriate for the proposed use of the building.

Building or Floor Area

Once the occupancy classification and construction type are known it is important to establish the permissible area for each floor for each use and for the total building. Certain types of construction are limited in size based on occupancy and concentration of people. As noted above, selection of the allowable area and construction type may require iteration of selections of construction type and allowable area based on occupancy requirements.

Allowable areas are tabulated in Table 506.2. See § 506 for allowable area increases based on location on the property and allowance for installation of automatic fire-sprinkler systems.

Building Height

The allowable number of floors is usually tied closely to allowable area by construction type. Total height in feet and number of stories may also be limited by planning codes, not for technical reasons but as matters of public policy.

Building heights are tabulated in Tables 504.3 and 504.4. Study the definition of height and story as noted in the IBC. Also be aware that the definition of height and story is often subject to local amendment. Be certain to check these provisions with the local AHJ to be certain of the exact requirements for your project. This is especially true in older, hilly cities like San Francisco, where topography and historical development patterns may generate definitions of height or story different than in other jurisdictions. Do not confuse zoning height definitions and limits with those in the building code. They are usually different in almost all jurisdictions.

Exits/Egress

One of the most important functions of building codes is determining egress requirements and provision of safe means of egress for all of the anticipated occupants of a building. There are specific requirements for size, spacing, and travel distances for all components of the means of egress, such as floor plans, doors, corridors, and stairs. In simple terms a means of egress consists of three components: an exit access, an exit, and an exit discharge. Chapter 10 of the IBC relates to means of egress.

Building Separations and Shafts

Where buildings have mixed occupancies, codes often require fire-rated partitions separating the occupancies. Separations may also be used to allow more area for a particular occupancy on a single floor in certain types of construction where such sizes of use would not otherwise be permitted.

Openings between floors such as for stairs, elevators, and mechanical shafts can allow the passage of smoke, heat and flames in a fire. Therefore the codes have requirements based on occupancy, building type, and building height related to shaft protection. Basic shaft-protection requirements are contained in Chapter 7.

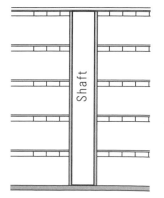

Fire Protection

Fire protection can be divided into two broad categories: passive or active protection. Passive protection is that built into the structure, either inherent in the material or added as part of protective membranes. Thus a steel building has more inherent passive protection capability than a wood one because steel is noncombustible whereas wood is not. Active systems are ones where a fire causes a reaction in a system that serves to combat the fire. Sprinklers are a prime example of active systems. A fire causes a sprinkler system to activate and extinguish the fire before exposing the passive systems to a fire. Code analysis and design often includes trade-offs between active and passive systems.

Fire-resistance standards include:

1. Structure Hour Rating: Requirements for the time it takes for a fire to weaken a structural element to the point of failure. These requirements are minimums based on providing enough time for fire-fighting and evacuation operations to take place for a specified time period without placing emergency responders and occupants in danger.
2. Area or Occupancy Separation Rating: Requirements of how long it will take for a fire to penetrate a wall partition, floor or roof assembly.
3. Flame Spread and Smoke Generation: Requirements of how long it takes for fire to move along the surface of a building material and how much smoke is generated under fire exposure. The density and toxicity of the smoke is also a factor to be considered in these criteria.

Fire-resistance requirements are found primarily in Chapters 7 and 8.

Engineering Requirements

A large portion of the code is devoted to engineering requirements. One of the bases of codes is structural adequacy of buildings for both static loading such as occupants and equipment and dynamic loading such as earthquakes, snow, and wind. Requirements for both structural systems and structural materials are contained in the code. Chapters 16–18 deal with forces, inspections, and foundations. Chapters 19–23 deal with structural materials: concrete, lightweight metals, masonry, steel, and wood.

Every project, no matter how small, should have a written code analysis included in the construction documents. We recommend organizing the code analysis in the same order as shown earlier in this chapter, so that the thought process you use in developing your code conclusions is revealed in the written code analysis. This should be done early in the design process so that any issues can be identified and discussed with the Authorities Having Jurisdiction.

As noted before, don't be shy about using the table of contents and index to locate sections of the code. DO NOT TRY AND MEMORIZE PARTS OF THE CODE! As sections change and interpretations alter meanings, memorization is a recipe for trouble in the future. Clients may expect you to be able to rattle off requirements at a moment's notice, but it is not in the best interest of the project or the client to be able to make snap code decisions. Remember where to look up information and check your decisions each time you apply them; do not proceed on memory or analogy from other jobs. Even seasoned code professionals use the index or an electronic code to locate familiar phrases when they cannot quite recall where the phrase is located in the code. It is worthwhile for designers to remember that as the new model code is adopted across the nation local code officials will often have little more hands-on experience with the IBC than design professionals.

Early Meetings

One advantage of larger projects is that they are often large enough to warrant pre-review and consultation with the building department prior to finalizing design. No matter what the size of your project, we recommend consulting with the applicable AHJ early in the process wherever it is possible, prior to commencing detailed design, even if a fee is charged. We also recommend that both the building and fire plan reviewers be at such meetings as they often do not always interpret the building and fire codes in the same way.

Do not expect the code official to do your work for you. Compliance is the responsibility of the designer. However, codes are subject to interpretation, and it is almost always in your best interest to determine what, if any, interpretations will be needed for any project. This should be done prior to expending a lot of time and energy designing a project that may be deemed not in compliance during plan review.

3

Use and Occupancy

The intended use or occupancy of a building is a fundamental consideration for the building code. Typically a client comes to an architect with a defined need for a facility. The desired use of that facility determines the occupancy group to which it is assigned under the code. Occupancy group classifications trigger specific requirements for the allowable area and height of a building, for means of egress, as well as for type of construction. The "I" codes are fundamentally occupancy based as were the three model codes from which it was born. Most other broad sets of code criteria are derived from the basic classification by occupancy.

The code separates uses into broad groups called Occupancies. Under these groups are subdivisions that further refine the detailed requirements. It is worth remembering that while the designer usually makes the first pass at categorizing uses in terms of occupancy according to the fire safety and relative hazard involved, the ultimate judge of occupancy classification is the Building Official per the provisions of Chapter 1 of the IBC. The intent regarding classification is best described by the language directing classification of atypical occupancies: "such structure shall be classified in the group which the occupancy most nearly resembles, *according to the fire safety and relative hazard involved.*" This reiterates the intent and purpose of the occupancy classifications that exist in the code. Each of the stated occupancy classifications was determined during the code development process by using fire-safety and relative hazard performance data to develop criteria.

Determination of the occupancy type flows in almost every case from the program given to the designer by the client. Other code requirements flow from the number of occupants and the hazards to their safety from external and internal factors. As we discussed previously, the code looks at property protection considerations along with life safety concerns. The occupancy's hazards are assessed relative to their impact on adjacent properties as well as on the building occupants. The code also analyzes the hazards posed by adjacent buildings; however, it places the responsibility for protection of the adjacent facilities on the building under consideration.

Among the considerations for occupancy classification are: how many people will be using a facility; whether there are assembly areas such as theaters and restaurants; whether people will be awake or asleep in the building; will they be drinking alcohol while using the building, or undergoing medical treatment, which makes them less capable of self-preservation in an emergency? The presence of hazardous materials or processes will also affect the requirements for allowable area, fire separations, and construction type.

Note that the criteria discussed in this book generally apply to non-hazardous occupancies. Hazardous occupancies are not addressed by most design professionals and are covered by a separate set of special requirements discussed in § 414 and 415. Because they are very specialized and encountered infrequently by most designers, the requirements for hazardous occupancies will only be lightly touched on in this book.

It is essential to read the detailed requirements for each type of occupancy in a project. There are often cross-references to various other code sections in the detailed occupancy criteria. Another factor that impacts occupancy classification is the mixture of various uses in a building and their sizes relative to the predominant use of the building. The sections regarding mixed occupancies and incidental uses were located in Chapter 3 in past editions of the code. They were moved to Chapter 5 in the 2006 edition of the IBC. In the 2012 edition, incidental uses were moved to their own section, § 509. This is one of the reasons why code analysis should not be done by memorization. Code users must be able to track changes by use of the index for new code

editions. Another good way to track changes is to use a PDF version of the code and use key word searches to find code items.

Several ideas common to most occupancy classifications, discussed in detail in Chapter 5, should be understood. First is the language: "structures or portions of structures." This distinction allows the use of mixed occupancies in a single building without having to consider the entire building as a single occupancy group. The concept of separated and nonseparated uses, discussed in Chapter 5, allows the designer two options for addressing mixed-use buildings. It also allows rooms within buildings to be considered as distinct occupancies that can then be addressed as either separated or non-separated uses at the designer's discretion.

The other concept to understand is that the laundry lists of examples in each occupancy group are not the sole definition of which uses are to be classified in which occupancy group. The code recognizes that not all occupancies are included in the lists and gives direction to the building official regarding classification of buildings not included in the examples.

The IBC establishes the following occupancy groups:
- Assembly (A)
- Business (B)
- Educational (E)
- Factory and Industrial (F)
- High Hazard (H)
- Institutional (I)
- Mercantile (M)
- Residential (R)
- Storage (S)
- Utility and Miscellaneous (U)

Group B: Less than 50 occupants

Group A: 50 or more occupants

Assembly Group A (303)

The examples noted in this group recognize that these uses bring large groups of people together in relatively small spaces. How the spaces are used in relationship to physical features and human behavior also enter into the distinction between assembly categories, which are meant to serve as cues for assigning buildings or parts of buildings to an occupancy class. The final determination of this classification, as for all classifications, is made by the building official. Note that the subcategories are examples, not a definitive or exhaustive list of possible assignments.

Be very careful in reading language where criteria are based on numbers. "Less than 50 persons" means that 49 or fewer people have one set of criteria and "50 or more" have another. The dividing line in this case is 50. Read such language very carefully when deciding if an issue belongs in one category or another. If in doubt be sure to verify the interpretation with your AHJ early in the design process to avoid costly errors.

Group A occupancies are typically defined as having 50 or more occupants, but the use of the space must be examined in relation to the code language stating that these are spaces "for purposes such as civic, social or religious functions, recreation, food or drink consumption…." For instance, retail stores in M Occupancies may have more than 49 occupants but are not considered as Group A. Per § 303.1.1, assembly areas with fewer than 50 occupants are to be classified as Group B Occupancies. Assembly areas of less than 750 sf (69.68 m^2) that are accessory to other uses are also not considered as Group A areas per § 303.1.2 Item 2.

Language in § 303.1.3 clarifies that assembly occupancies associated with Group E occupancies (educational facilities) need not be considered as separate "A" occupancies.

Accessory religious educational rooms and religious auditoriums with an occupant load of less than 100 are not considered separate occupancies and would be classified with the majority of the facility, likely as an A-3 occupancy.

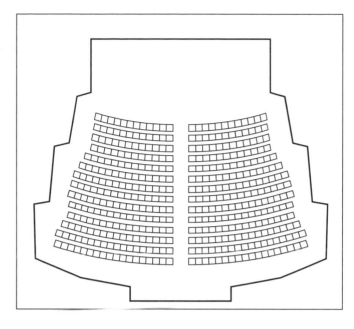

- Group A-1 per § 303.2 is for assembly areas, usually with fixed seats, intended for the viewing of performing arts or motion pictures. The presence or absence of a stage is not a distinguishing feature. Most uses classified in this occupancy will have fixed seats. The egress requirements in Group A-1 occupancies recognize that light levels may be low during performances and that people may panic in emergency situations under such circumstances.

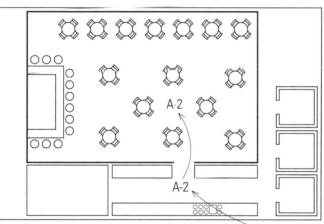

- Group A-2 per § 303.3 is for assembly areas where food and drink are consumed. The requirements for these occupancies presume that alcoholic beverages may be served, thus potentially impairing the occupants' responses to an emergency. It also presumes that chairs and tables will be loose and may obstruct or make unclear egress pathways for patrons. The requirements also recognize the poor fire history of such occupancies.

- Note that in the 2012 IBC, gaming areas in casinos were added to the list of examples.

- Also, note that the code addresses commercial kitchens. They are to be classified in the same A-2 occupancy as the dining areas they are associated with. See "B" and "F" occupancies for a discussion regarding food processing facilities and commercial kitchens not associated with assembly spaces.

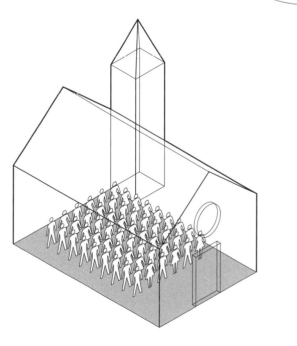

- Group A-3 occupancies per § 303.4 are assembly areas that do not fit into the other Group A categories. It also includes spaces used for worship, recreation, or amusement. The intent of this classification is that any use that seems to be an assembly occupancy and does not fit the criteria of the other four Group A categories should be classified as an A-3 occupancy.

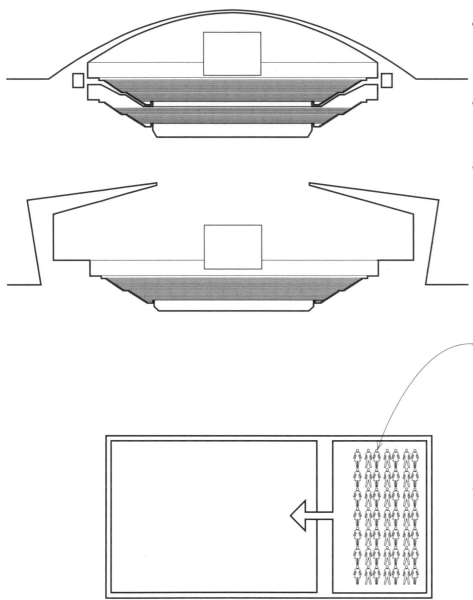

- Group A-4 occupancies per § 303.5 are assembly areas for the viewing of indoor sporting events.

- Group A-5 occupancies per § 303.6 are assembly areas for the participation or viewing of outdoor sporting events.

- The principal distinction between Group A-4 and A-5 occupancies is one of indoor versus outdoor facilities. Note also that Group A-4 occupancies are presumed to have spectator seating. Those assembly uses that are similar to these two classifications but do not meet all their criteria would most likely be considered Group A-3 occupancies.

- As noted in § 303.1.2 Item 1, "small" assembly spaces with less than 50 occupants are to be considered by exclusion as part of the overall occupancy. For example, having a conference room or a lunchroom with fewer than 50 occupants serving a larger use does not trigger classifying that space as an Assembly Group A occupancy.

- Per the same criteria, a large conference room in an office, where the room has more than 49 occupants, would be classified as an A-3 occupancy. This may trigger code provisions related to Group A occupancies that might not otherwise apply to the other office areas. It also may trigger occupancy separation requirements per § 508.4.

Business Group B

Office buildings are typically classified as Group B occupancies. Storage areas for offices, such as back-office file rooms, do not constitute a separate occupancy.

Outpatient clinics and ambulatory care facilities are also classified in this occupancy group. "Clinic-outpatient" defines a medical care facility where patients <u>are not</u> rendered incapable of self-preservation. Even where patients may be rendered incapable of unassisted self-preservation by anesthesia, the use could still be classified as a Group B occupancy. Such a facility, called an "Ambulatory Care Facility," is contained in the B occupancy list. It is defined in Chapter 2 as being a facility where patients stay for less than 24 hours but where such patients are rendered incapable of self-preservation.

The definition refers only to "care" facilities to broaden the applicability of this occupancy classification to more uses. While both uses are B occupancies, there are other distinctions, such as sprinkler requirements per § 903.2.2, which depend on whether patients are rendered incapable of self-preservation and how many of such patients there are at any time. There are also varying fire-alarm and detection requirements for B occupancies depending on their use, contained in § 907.2.2.

Testing and research laboratories that do not exceed the quantities of hazardous materials specified in the code are also classified as Group B occupancies. Those that exceed the minimums are classified as Group H occupancies.

Educational facilities for junior colleges, universities, and continuing education for classes above the 12th grade are considered Group B occupancies, not Group E. Assembly rooms in these facilities should be examined for conformance with the criteria for Group A occupancies. The code has also clarified that tutoring centers not associated with schools are to be classifed as Group B occupancies and not as Group E occunacies, regardless of the ages served. Prior to this change, tutoring or learning facilities for children in the ages for K-12 education had often been misclassified as Group E.

Note that procedures such as laser eye surgery or kidney dialysis should be considered as rendering patients incapable of unassisted self-preservaton. Note further that facilities accommodating people incapable of unassisted self-preservation may also be classified as I-2 occupancies, based on duration of stay; see page 27.

- *Small food-processing facilities, such as a take-out-only pizza shop or to-go Asian food restaurant where there are no dining or drinking areas and which are no more than 2,500 sf (232 m²) in area, are to be classified as Group B occupancies instead of an A-2 or an F-1. Stand-alone food processing facilities that are larger than 2,500 sf are to be classified as Group F-1.*

Educational Group E

Group E occupancies are used by six or more people for classes up to the 12th grade. Uses for the day care of six or more children over 2¹/₂ years of age make up another set of Group E occupancies. Day care uses with fewer than six children are to be classified with the larger occupancy they occur within. Those uses with fewer than six children in a dwelling unit are classified as Group R-3.

Assembly uses in school facilities are not excluded from this use group. However, most schools use their large rooms for assembly uses. Such facilities need not be considered as separate A occupancies per the provisions of § 303.1.3. Religious classrooms and auditoriums that are accessory to churches and have fewer than 100 occupants are to be considered as A-3 occupancies per § 303.1.4.

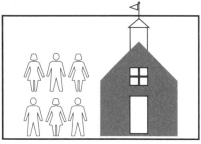

Factory and Industrial Group F

Factory occupancies are defined in part by what they are not. The two occupancy groups, Moderate-Hazard Occupancy F-1 and Low-Hazard Occupancy F-2, are based on an analysis of the relative hazards of the operations in these occupancies and a determination that they do not fall under the criteria set for Group H. Group F-1 is classified as those operations not falling within the definitions for Group F-2. The predominant difference between F-1 and F-2 is that in F-2 occupancies the materials of manufacture are considered to be noncombustible.

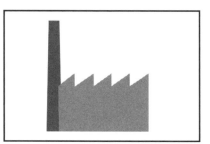

The classification of Group F occupancies assumes that these are not public areas. The users are presumed to be familiar with their surroundings and not occasional visitors. The processes themselves will determine which classification the use is to receive. Uses meeting the F-2 classification are limited. Occupancy classification determinations between Groups F-1 and H often are done by a process of elimination. When analyzing whether a use or occupancy should be classified as Group F-1 or Group H, the quantities of materials used in the process under consideration will determine to which group the use belongs. For example, an F occupancy manufacturing alcoholic beverages up to 16% alcohol content is considered to be an F-2 low-hazard occupancy, while those manufacturing beverages with an alcohol content above 16% are an F-1 occupancy. This is based on the idea that the presumed level of flammability of such beverages increases with alcohol content, with 16% being established as the threshold between conventionally fermented wines and wines "fortified" with added alcohol. Large commercial cooking operations not associated with restaurants are now called out to be F-1 occupancies.

The code now places a threshold of 2,500 sf (232 m²) for F-1 food-processing establishments and commerical kitchens. Facilites not exceeding the threshold, such as take-out restaurants with no seating or serving areas, are now called out to be classified as Group B occupancies.

High-Hazard Group H

Hazardous occupancies could easily be the subject of another book and will only be touched on in an introductory fashion in this text. The uses classified under this occupancy group are very specialized and require careful code and design analysis. Understanding the products, processes, hazard levels of materials used in the occupancy, and their quantities is essential. Variations in material quantities and hazards interact to set the design criteria for hazardous occupancies. The classification of uses in this category will almost undoubtedly require consultation with the client and with the building official at an early stage of design.

There are two sets of criteria for hazardous occupancies. The first set is related to the hazard of the materials in use and the quantities of those materials in use. High-Hazard Groups H-1 through H-4 fall in this category. The second set relates to the nature of the use as well as the quantity and nature of hazardous materials in use. This is High-Hazard Group H-5, which are semiconductor fabrication facilities and similar research and development facilities.

Areas that contain limited quantities of hazardous materials may occur in other occupancy groups when the amounts are less than the designated limits for exempt quantities. For example, small amounts of flammable cleaning fluids or paints might be stored in a room in a business occupancy. A mercantile occupancy can sell specified quantities of materials that may be considered hazardous without being designated a Group H occupancy as long as the amount of material is below the limit for exempt quantities. This exemption pertains only to occupancy classification related to quantities; it does not waive compliance with any other code provisions. Note also that the International Fire Code sets forth many additional construction and use requirements for Group H.

Control Areas

The other basic concept in the code provisions for High-Hazard Group H is that of control areas. The special detailed requirements for the separation of control areas are contained in Chapter 4 and outlined in Table 414.2.2. Chapter 4 must therefore be read in concert with Chapter 3 to determine all applicable code requirements. This applies both to subdivisions of buildings classified as hazardous occupancies and to areas where hazardous materials occur within other occupancies. The definition of this concept bears stating verbatim from § 202:

- Control areas are "spaces within a building where quantities of hazardous materials not exceeding the maximum allowable quantities per control area are stored, dispensed, used or handled."
- The control area concept allows multiple parts of a building to contain an array of hazardous materials when the areas are properly separated and the quantity of materials within each area meet the specified maximums for each type of material. These criteria reinforce the concept that hazard levels are mitigated by passive and/or active fire-protection measures. This concept is based on two primary considerations. The first is the nature of the hazard of the material in question. The second is that the level of hazard is primarily related to the quantity of materials within a given area.

- Control areas must be separated from one another by 1-hour fire-barrier walls and floors having a minimum fire-resistance rating of 2 hours. For the fourth and succeeding floors above grade, fire-barrier walls must have a 2-hour fire-resistance rating.

- Note that both the percentage of maximum allowable quantity of hazardous materials and the number of control areas decrease when proceeding up or down in the building to floors either above or below the first floor of a building.

- Higher than nine floors above grade, one control area with 5% of allowable quantity is permitted per floor.

- The seventh through ninth floors above grade may have two control areas per floor with 5% of allowable quantity per control area.

- The fourth through sixth floors above grade may have two control areas per floor with 12.5% of allowable quantity per control area.

- Third floor above grade may have two control areas with 50% of allowable quantity per control area.

- The second floor above grade and first floor below grade may have three control areas with 75% of allowable quantity per control area.

- The second floor below grade may have two control areas with 50% of the allowable quantity per control area.

- Control areas are not allowed more than two floors below grade.

Institutional Group I

Institutional occupancies are those where people have special restrictions placed on them. The occupancy groups in these groups are sub-divided by the abilities of the occupants to take care of themselves in an emergency. The different categories in this occupancy are determined by the number of occupants, their ages, health and personal liberty, and whether they are in the facility all day or part of the day or night. Whether or not the occupants are capable of unassisted self-prervation or are somehow incapacitated to the exent they will need help to escape danger also enters into the occupancy classification. Many of these occupancy groups have a residential character, and if they fall outside the designated thresholds for Group I occupancies, they will likely be classified as residential occupancies.

The different Group I occupancies have their distinguishing characteristics shown here in the same order to facilitate understanding the differences between them.

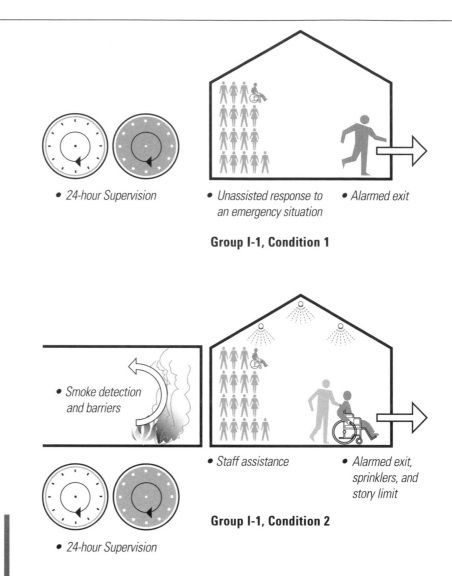

• 24-hour Supervision   • Unassisted response to an emergency situation   • Alarmed exit

Group I-1, Condition 1

• Smoke detection and barriers   • Staff assistance   • Alarmed exit, sprinklers, and story limit

• 24-hour Supervision

Group I-1, Condition 2

- Group I-1 has more than 16 people living under supervised conditions and receiving custodial care in a residential environment on a 24-hour basis. "Custodial Care" is defined in § 202 as "Assistance with day-to-day living tasks, such as assistance with cooking, taking medication, bathing, using toilet facilities, and other tasks of daily living." Custodial care includes persons receiving care who have the ability to respond to emergency situations and evacuate at a slower rate and/or who have mental and psychiatric complications. This classification includes halfway houses, assisted-living facilities, and group homes.

- Note that the term "convalescent facilities" has been deleted as it is not a contemporary term and is subject to a variety of confusing usages.

- I-1 occupancies have been broken down into two "Conditions" based on the abilities of the occupants to respond to emergencies and evacuate a building. The conditions are as follows:

* **Condition 1** occupants are presumed to be able to respond to an emergency independently and without assistance.
* **Condition 2** occupants are presumed to need "limited verbal or physical assistance" to respond to an emergency and evacuate the building.

- It is essential that the designer and the building client confer early in the design process to assess the capabilities of the prospective building occupants to determine the correct classification. This should also include consultation with the operator of the facility to determine what local licensing requirements may apply to the facility to assist in determining the proper classification.

Because the occupants under Condition 2 will likely take more time to evacuate the building during an emergency, the code places additional limitations for such things as the number of stories allowable for a given construction type, as well as requirements for smoke barriers, sprinkler protection, and smoke detection. If the understanding of the classification of the two conditions occurs late in the design process or in the course of construction, the change can have profound consequences on the building. Thus, it is important to make this determination early in the design process. If there is any doubt about how the building will be used it is prudent to assume it will have to meet Condition 2 criteria, which would allow the use of the building for Condition 1 occupants. The reverse would not be the case. Condition 2 occupants could not be housed in a Condition 1 facility.

- Similar occupancies with between 6 and 16 occupants are to be classified as an R-4 occupancy or an R-3 if there are 5 or fewer occupants.

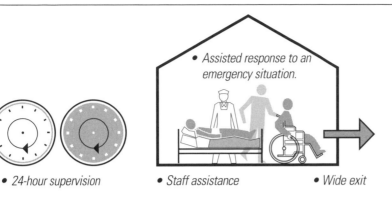

- *24-hour supervision*
- *Staff assistance*
- *Wide exit*

Group I-2, Condition 1

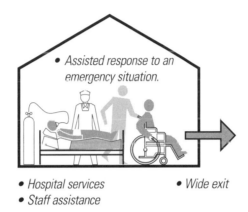
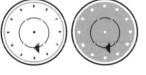

- *24-hour supervision*
- *Hospital services*
- *Staff assistance*
- *Wide exit*

Group I-1, Condition 2

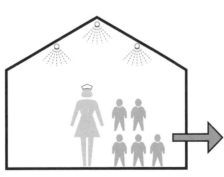

- *Less than 24-hour Care*
- *Supervisor*
- *Residents*

- *Group I-2 has more than five people living under supervised conditions and medical care on a 24-hour basis. The occupants are presumed under this classification to be incapable of unassisted self-preservation and thus cannot respond to emergencies without assistance from the staff. This classification includes hospitals, mental hospitals, detox facilities, and nursing homes.*

Group I-2 occupancies are now classified into two conditions. The conditions are as follows:

§ 308.4.1.1, Condition 1. This occupancy condition includes facilities that provide nursing and medical care but do not provide services typically associated with hospitals. This is considered to include nursing homes and foster care facilities.

§ 308.4.1.2, Condition 2. This occupancy condition is for hospitals, and includes facilities that provide nursing and medical care and could provide emergency care, surgery, obstetrics, or in-patient stabilization units for psychiatric or detoxification.

Similar occupancies with fewer than six occupants who stay for less than 24 hours may be allowed to be classified as R-3 occupancies. They may also comply with the IRC. This should be reviewed with the AHJ for their concurrence. Such facilities are to be fully sprinklered.

- Group I-3 has more than five people living under supervised conditions under restraint or security on a 24-hour basis. The occupants cannot respond to emergencies without assistance from the staff, not because of illness, infirmity, or age, but due to security measures outside their control. This group includes prisons, detention centers, and mental hospitals, and is further subdivided into five conditions based on the relative freedom of movement within areas inside the facility. These conditions also presume the areas are divided into smoke compartments with differing degrees of access controls between them.

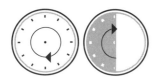

- 24-hour Supervision

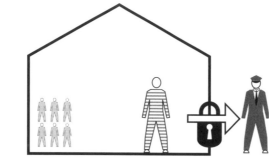

- Controlled Exit

- Group I-4 is for uses having more than five people under supervised conditions and under custodial care on a less than 24-hour basis. The occupants are presumed not to be able to respond to emergencies without assistance from the staff, although this is not stated in the code. This classification includes adult day care and child day care.

The group is further subdivided into care facilities for adults and for children under 2¹/₂ years of age. A child day-care facility for between 6 and 100 children under 2¹/₂ years of age, located on the exit discharge level with a direct exterior exit, is to be classified as an E occupancy.

Similar occupancies with five or fewer occupants may be classified as R-3 occupancies or shall comply with the International Residential Code.

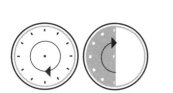

- Less than 24-hour Care

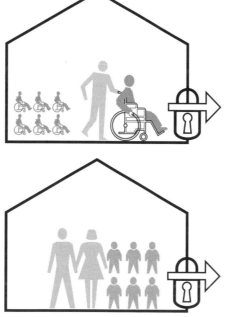

- Less than 24-hour Care

- Controlled Exit

Mercantile Group M

Uses in these groups are fairly self-explanatory. The occupancy group includes incidental storage, which will be regulated per the mixed use provisions in § 508. Accessory occupancies are regulated by § 508.2 and must still be individually classified. Larger storage areas would be classified as Group S. Typically for larger combinations of M and S occupancies, the nonseparated provisions of § 508.3 are used.

Most retail facilities, no matter what merchandise they sell, fall into this occupancy. There are limits to the quantities of hazardous materials that may be stored in mercantile occupancies without being classified as a Group H occupancy. These limits are shown in Table 414.2.5(1).

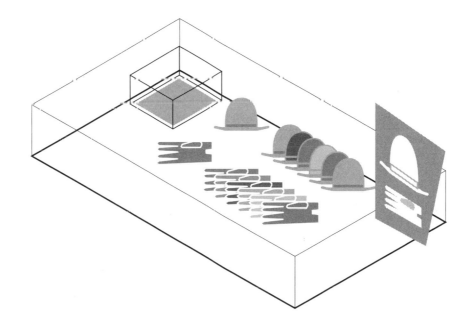

Residential Group R

Residential occupancies include typical housing units, distinguished mainly by the total number of occupants. A key criterion for this type of occupancy is that the occupants sleep in the building. This group also includes smaller-scale institutional occupancies that fall below certain thresholds for the number of occupants.

- Note that although defined terms related to residential occupancies are listed in the residential occupancy section, the definitions are in Chapter 2 and thus apply not only to this section but also throughout the code.

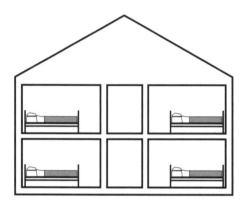

S	M	T	W	T	F	S
1	2	3	4	5	6	7
8	9	10	11	12	13	14
15	16	17	18	19	20	21
22	23	24	25	26	27	28
29						

- *Less than 30 Days Occupancy*

- *Group R-1 occupants are transient, sleeping in their rooms for 30 days or less, as in hotels and transient boarding houses. The requirements assume that the occupants are not familiar with the surroundings.*

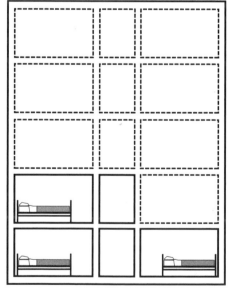

S	M	T	W	T	F	S
1	2	3	4	5	6	7
8	9	10	11	12	13	14
15	16	17	18	19	20	21
22	23	24	25	26	27	28
29	30					

S	M	T	W	T	F	S
		1	2	3	4	5
6	7	8	9	10	11	12
13	14	15	16	17	18	19
20	21	22	23	24	25	26
27	28	29	30			

- *Permanent Residency*

- *Group R-2 occupants are permanent, sleeping in buildings containing more than two dwelling units for more than 30 days. These include apartments, dormitories, and long-term residential boarding houses. Congregate living facilities with 16 or fewer occupants (note the cutoff is 16 or less) are permitted to comply with requirements for R-3 occupancies.*

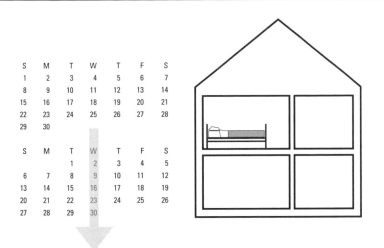

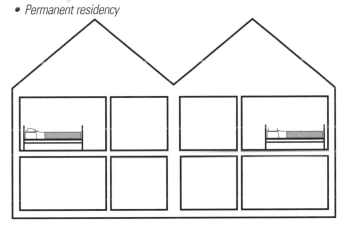

- *Permanent residency*

- Group R-3 occupants are permanent, and the group is defined as being those not meeting the criteria for R-1, R-2 or Group I occupancy groups. These are primarily single-family residences and duplexes. Day-care facilities for five or fewer people using the facility for less than 24 hours also fall into this occupancy group. In many jurisdictions these occupancies are regulated under the International Residential Code (IRC) when it is adopted by the local jurisdiction.

Boarding houses with 16 or fewer non-transient occupants or 10 or fewer transient occupants are also classified as R-3 occupancies. Lodging houses are now a defined term for facilities having one or more permanent occupants paying rent for guest rooms.

Care facilities for five or fewer persons are permitted to comply with the International Residential Code if an automatic sprinkler system is provided. Also, owner-occupied lodging houses with five or fewer guest rooms are allowed to be constructed in accordance with the IRC if they meet the IRC's height criteria of 3 stories or less. Taller R-3 occupancies are to use the IBC. Lodging houses with more than five guest rooms are to be classified as R-1 for transient lodging and R-2 if used for non-transient use, but only if they exceed the 10 or 16 occupant load threshold. Otherwise, they are R-3s.

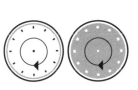

- *24-hour supervision*

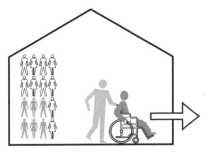

Group R-4, Condition 1

- Group R-4 occupancies are used for residential care or assisted-living uses with more than five but not more than 16 occupants receiving custodial care, excluding staff. Under these conditions, Group R-4 is used in lieu of Group I. This occupancy group is to meet the requirements for R-3 occupancies except as otherwise provided for in other sections of the IBC.

As for I-1 occupancies there are now two conditions related to the ability of residents to respond to instructions: **Condition 1 (§ 310.6.1)** occurs where persons receiving custodial care are capable of responding to an emergency situation to evacuate the building.

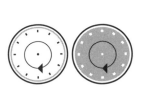

- *24-hour supervision*

Group R-4, Condition 2

Condition 2 (§ 310.6.2) includes buildings in which there are any persons receiving custodial care who require limited verbal or physical assistance while responding to an emergency situation to complete building evacuation. See the I-1 discussion for the impact of the conditions on building design. When in doubt uses should be classfied as Condition 2.

Storage Group S

Storage for materials with quantities or characteristics not considered hazardous enough to be considered a Group H occupancy is classified as Group S. The two subdivisions are similar to the distinctions made for F occupancies: Moderate-Hazard S-1 occupancies and Low-Hazard S-2 occupancies. The lists of examples for each category are quite lengthy and detailed. When occupancies contain mixed groups of various products it can be quite difficult to determine which occupancy group to use. Careful consideration of projected uses for the facility and potential changes in use over time must be considered. It is useful to confer with the building official early in the design process to get concurrence on the proposed classification. As in the distinction between F-1 and F-2 occupancies, the distinction between S-1 and S-2 is that S-2 is used for the storage of noncombustible materials.

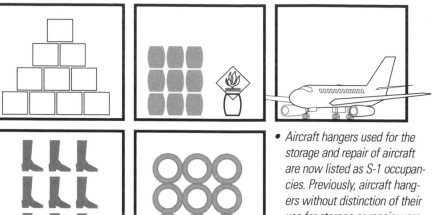

- Accessory storage spaces (§ 311.1.10) are described as rooms or spaces used for storage purposes, are less than 100 sf (9.3 m²) in area, are accessories to another occupancy, and are classified as part of that occupancy. The aggregate area of such rooms or spaces are not to exceed the allowable area limits of § 508.2, which are "accessory occupancies." Aggregate accessory occupancies are not to be more than 10 percent of the floor area of the story in which they are located and are not to exceed the tabular values for nonsprinklered buildings in Table 506.2 for each such accessory occupancy.

- Aircraft hangers used for the storage and repair of aircraft are now listed as S-1 occupancies. Previously, aircraft hangers without distinction of their use for storage or repair were classified as S-2 occupancies. Factories for aircraft manufacture are now included in the list for F-1 occupancies.

Utility and Miscellaneous Group U

This group is for incidental buildings of an accessory nature. These structures are typically unoccupied except for short times during a 24-hour period and are typically separate from and subservient to other uses. This occupancy group is used sparingly. It is not meant to be a catch-all for occupancy types that are not readily categorized. The AHJ has the ultimate responsibility for determination of occupancy classification using the criteria set forth in § 302.1. Note also that this group contains items that are not buildings, such as fences over 6' (1829) in height and retaining walls.

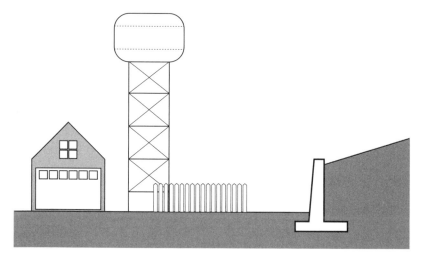

4

Special Uses and Occupancies

In addition to the requirements for typical occupancies, the code addresses detailed requirements for specific building types in Chapter 4. The occupancy of these buildings usually fits into one or more of the typical occupancy groups, but characteristics of these building types require additional code provisions. Examples of such building types are covered and open mall buildings, high-rise buildings, and atriums. A mall is basically a Group M occupancy, but with many stores, large occupant loads, and means of egress that also serve as pedestrian walkways. High-rise buildings are typically Group B or R occupancies with very large occupant loads and are defined as having occupied floors located above fire department ladder access. Atriums have large interior volumes open to pedestrian pathways and to occupied spaces. These buildings need added code consideration above and beyond more typical uses in the same occupancy group. The additional code requirements for these building types are determined by their configurations, not their uses.

The development of new types of buildings often happens in advance of code provisions specific to them. Code officials must respond to requests by owners to build such structures by addressing them on a case-by-case basis. As these new types of buildings or new uses become more prevalent, the code responds by collecting information about how different jurisdictions have addressed these new buildings. Then the code-development process generates new code provisions to address them. These provisions are meant to apply over and above the other provisions applicable to their occupancy group classification. After the designer has classified the building by occupancy, the building type must then be examined to see if it meets the definitions for these specialized use groups and thus must also meet the added criteria for them. The process of analysis of use and occupancy should commence with an analysis of how the proposed building fits into the uses and occupancies described in Chapter 3 of the code and then should be analyzed against the criteria in Chapter 4 to see which, if any, are applicable.

It is worth remembering that the detailed provisions of Chapter 4 of the code relate to and coordinate with the more basic requirements spelled out in Chapter 3 for use and occupancy requirements. The designer as code user should make a progression from the general to the specific in analyzing a building. Begin with the general categorization of uses and occupancies. Then proceed to review the detailed requirements of Chapter 4 for provisions applicable to the building in question. While one may begin the analysis of a specialized use by looking up the detailed requirements, the code is organized to proceed from determining the occupancy first and then applying detailed criteria. Just as one should not read up from footnotes to find table sections that may be misapplied, the user should not work backward in these analyses, as this may lead to erroneous code interpretations.

We will go through the specialized building types to describe their distinguishing criteria and touch on the major additional code provisions applicable to them. We will discuss those special uses most likely to be encountered by designers. Note that several very specialized uses have been omitted, as they are not seen frequently. Most are related to Group H Occupancies or to process-related special uses. Most designers do not frequently encounter these very specialized structures, or others such as underground buildings or amusement buildings. The criteria applicable to each of these other building types are used as noted above. The occupancy must first be determined before applying the specialized requirements contained in Chapter 4.

Many of the sections in Chapter 4 contain definitions of the uses or occupancies to which the special provisions apply. These definitions are listed in Chapter 2 of the code and cross-referenced for location and explanation in the section indicated. Note that although the definitions may seem familiar and similar to common construction terminology, they have very specific meanings in the code. Examine the building design conditions and definitions carefully to determine the applicability of the definition to the building design. This analysis of the definition may also point out necessary modifications to the design to make it code-compliant or reveal the need to reclassify it.

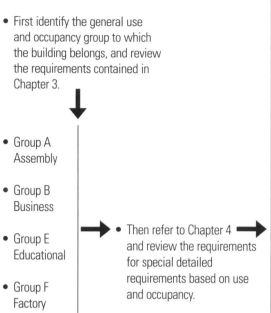

- First identify the general use and occupancy group to which the building belongs, and review the requirements contained in Chapter 3.

- Group A Assembly
- Group B Business
- Group E Educational
- Group F Factory
- Group H Hazardous
- Group I Institutional
- Group M Mercantile
- Group R Residential
- Group S Storage
- Group U Utility

- Then refer to Chapter 4 and review the requirements for special detailed requirements based on use and occupancy.

- Covered and Open Mall Buildings
- High-Rise Buildings
- Atriums
- Underground Buildings
- Motor-Vehicle Related Occupancies
- Institutional Groups I-2 and I-3
- Motion-Picture Projection Rooms
- Stages and Platforms
- Special Amusement Buildings
- Aircraft-Related Occupancies
- Hazardous Materials
- Application of Flammable Finishes
- Drying Rooms
- Organic Coatings
- Live/Work Units
- Special requirements for I-1, R-1, R-2, R-3, and R-4 Occupancies
- Hydrogen Fuel Gas Rooms
- Ambulatory Care Facilities
- Storm Shelters
- Children's Play Structures
- Hyperbaric Facilities
- Combustible Dusts, Grain Processing, and Storage

Institutional Groups I-2 and I-3
The code adds provisions related to Group I-2 occupancies in § 407 and Group I-3 occupancies in § 408 that must be read in concert with those in Chapter 3. Chapter 3 is intended to address the occupancy classification of a building and Chapter 4 is intended to address detailed requirements for certain uses and occupancies. Code analysis of these occupancy groups requires looking at both sets of provisions together. These are very specialized occupancies with many specific and detailed requirements. The discussion in this chapter of the special requirements for these occupancies is only an introduction. The code user must consult the detailed requirements in the IBC to determine the specific requirements for a specific project.

Other Specialized Uses
The remaining groups of uses in Chapter 4, beyond those discussed in this chapter, relate to specific uses of buildings or parts of buildings that are infrequently encountered in most occupancies. These include motion-picture projection rooms, stages and platforms, special amusement buildings, aircraft-related facilities, and high-piled combustible storage. These are specialized uses not often encountered in the normal course of work and will not be addressed in this book.

Covered and Open Mall Buildings

The code provisions in § 402 for covered mall buildings grew out of many years of application of special interpretations of existing codes in response to a then-new building type. It did not fit into the code criteria in use at the time this use type was first developing. Covered malls came into being based on design and retailing innovations. They combine the circulation paths used for means of egress with pedestrian routes. Spaces that might be considered exit discharge areas or safe egress terminations, such as a city street, became exit access areas with enclosures. Multiple tenants have access to the common pedestrian areas. There is a mixture of large department store type uses, termed "anchor" buildings, and smaller shops that open on the mall. It is also expected that there may be a mixture of other uses such as cinema and food court assembly areas as well as major anchor uses that are interconnected by the mall.

The 2009 IBC added language clarifying that the term *Covered Mall Building* is intended to also include open malls, which are defined as "unroofed common pedestrian ways serving two or more tenants and which do not have more than 3 levels open to each other." Thus an open mall is essentially the same as a covered mall, but without a cover over the mall circulation spaces. The open mall is flanked by "open mall buildings," which, as for covered malls, do not include anchor buildings.

New language was added in the 2012 IBC to clarify that open malls using the provisions of § 402 are to be treated in a similar manner to covered malls in how they relate to means of egress and major stores.

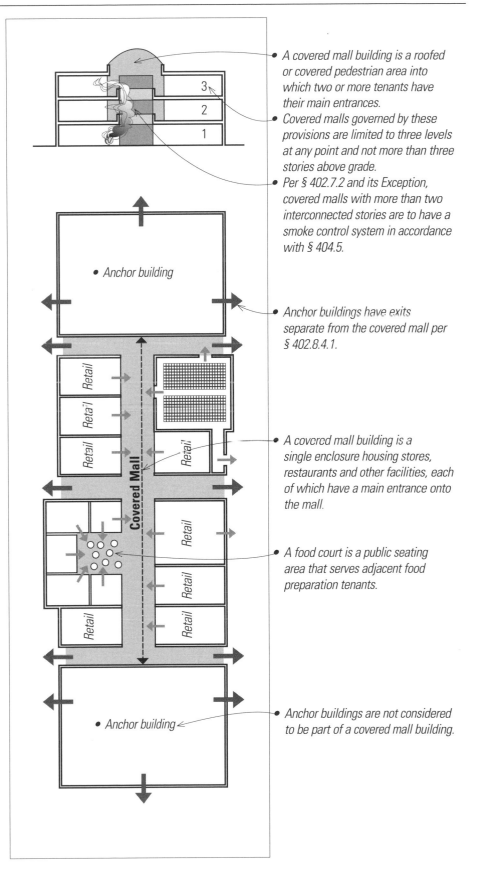

- A covered mall building is a roofed or covered pedestrian area into which two or more tenants have their main entrances.
- Covered malls governed by these provisions are limited to three levels at any point and not more than three stories above grade.
- Per § 402.7.2 and its Exception, covered malls with more than two interconnected stories are to have a smoke control system in accordance with § 404.5.

- Anchor buildings have exits separate from the covered mall per § 402.8.4.1.

- A covered mall building is a single enclosure housing stores, restaurants and other facilities, each of which have a main entrance onto the mall.

- A food court is a public seating area that serves adjacent food preparation tenants.

- Anchor buildings are not considered to be part of a covered mall building.

- An open mall is an unroofed common pedestrian way serving multiple tenants and not exceeding three levels.

- *Gross leasable area (GLA) is the total floor area available for tenant occupancy, measured from the centerlines of joint partitions to the outside of tenant walls. All tenant areas, including areas used for storage are to be included in the GLA.*

Example for Determining Occupant Load per § 402.8.2

Assume:
Retail Gross Leasable Area (GLA) = 200,000 sf (18 580 m²)
+ A food court having an area of 5000 sf (465 m²)
+ An assembly use with fixed seating for 500 (included in the 200,000 sf (18 580 m²) of the GLA)

To determine the Occupant Load Factor (OLF) for the mall, use Equation 4-1:

OLF = (0.00007) (GLA) + 25
OLF = (0.00007) (200,000) + 25
= 39 sf (3.62 m²) per occupant

To determine the occupancy of the food court, use Table 1004.1.2 and allow 15 sf (1.39 m²) net per occupant in the food court seating area (Assembly without fixed seats, unconcentrated, with tables and chairs):

5000 sf/15 sf (465 m²/1.39 m²) per occupant = 334 occupants

Total Occupant Load:
= (200,000/39) + 334
= 5129 + 334 = 5463 occupants

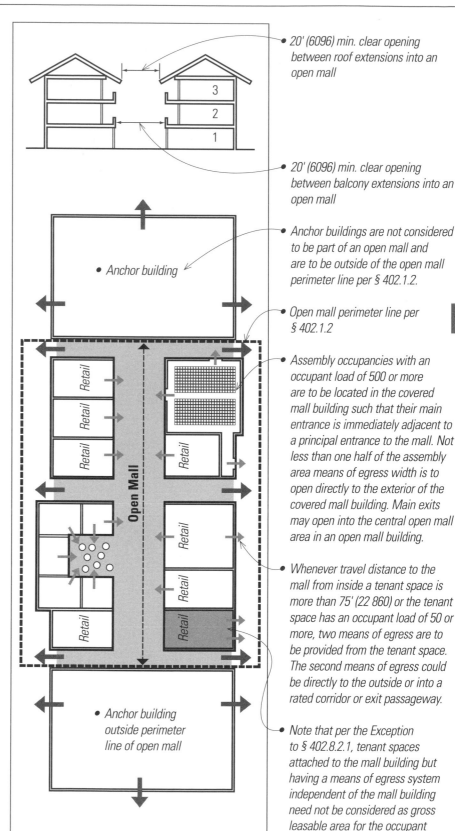

- *20' (6096) min. clear opening between roof extensions into an open mall*

- *20' (6096) min. clear opening between balcony extensions into an open mall*

- *Anchor buildings are not considered to be part of an open mall and are to be outside of the open mall perimeter line per § 402.1.2.*

- *Open mall perimeter line per § 402.1.2*

- *Assembly occupancies with an occupant load of 500 or more are to be located in the covered mall building such that their main entrance is immediately adjacent to a principal entrance to the mall. Not less than one half of the assembly area means of egress width is to open directly to the exterior of the covered mall building. Main exits may open into the central open mall area in an open mall building.*

- *Whenever travel distance to the mall from inside a tenant space is more than 75' (22 860) or the tenant space has an occupant load of 50 or more, two means of egress are to be provided from the tenant space. The second means of egress could be directly to the outside or into a rated corridor or exit passageway.*

- *Note that per the Exception to § 402.8.2.1, tenant spaces attached to the mall building but having a means of egress system independent of the mall building need not be considered as gross leasable area for the occupant load calculations since they do not contribute any occupant load to the mall means-of-egress system.*

The code provisions for covered and open malls rely on several basic ideas:

1. First is the provision of multiple clear paths of exit with widths sufficient to accommodate the occupant load, which is calculated according to criteria in this section.
2. Second is the requirement that the increased building area be offset by separation from other buildings by at least 60' (18 288) of permanent open space to allow safe egress areas for occupants. This permanent open space allows covered mall and anchor buildings to have unlimited area for all but Type V construction. Note that the open space may be reduced under certain conditions as illustrated below.
3. Third is the requirement that potentially hazardous uses such as parking structures be separated from the mall, either by a minimum distance or by construction type (fire barrier with a fire-resistance rating of 2 hours).
4. Fourth is a requirement for provision of active fire protection in the form of sprinklers, standby power, and a central fire department operations area.

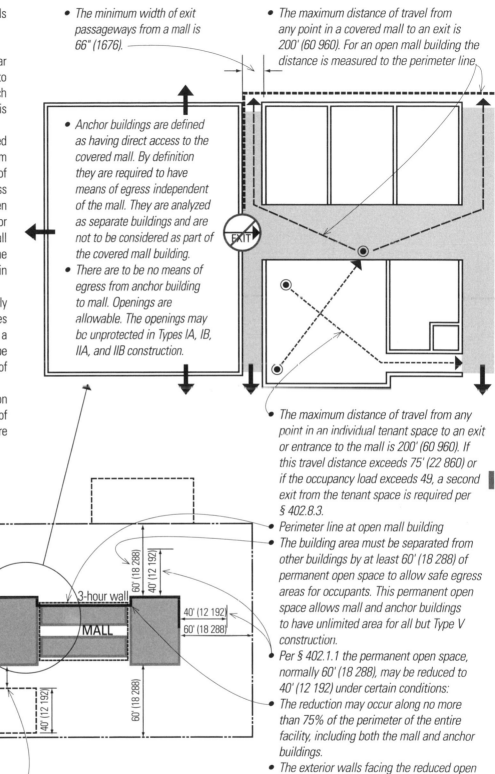

- The minimum width of exit passageways from a mall is 66" (1676).

- Anchor buildings are defined as having direct access to the covered mall. By definition they are required to have means of egress independent of the mall. They are analyzed as separate buildings and are not to be considered as part of the covered mall building.
- There are to be no means of egress from anchor building to mall. Openings are allowable. The openings may be unprotected in Types IA, IB, IIA, and IIB construction.

- The maximum distance of travel from any point in a covered mall to an exit is 200' (60 960). For an open mall building the distance is measured to the perimeter line.

- The maximum distance of travel from any point in an individual tenant space to an exit or entrance to the mall is 200' (60 960). If this travel distance exceeds 75' (22 860) or if the occupancy load exceeds 49, a second exit from the tenant space is required per § 402.8.3.
- Perimeter line at open mall building
- The building area must be separated from other buildings by at least 60' (18 288) of permanent open space to allow safe egress areas for occupants. This permanent open space allows mall and anchor buildings to have unlimited area for all but Type V construction.
- Per § 402.1.1 the permanent open space, normally 60' (18 288), may be reduced to 40' (12 192) under certain conditions:
- The reduction may occur along no more than 75% of the perimeter of the entire facility, including both the mall and anchor buildings.
- The exterior walls facing the reduced open space must have a fire-resistance rating of 3 hours and openings must have a fire protection rating of 3 hours.
- There can be no E, H, I, or R occupancies within the facility; thus, hotels and apartment buildings may not be in the facility if it utilizes the reduced distances.

3-hour wall

MALL

60' (18 288)
40' (12 192)
40' (12 192)
60' (18 288)
60' (18 288)
40' (12 192)
60' (18 288)
40' (12 192)

- Parking structures must be separated from the mall by construction type (fire barrier with a fire-resistance rating of 2 hours), or if separated by distance, the distance is to meet the requirements of Table 602.

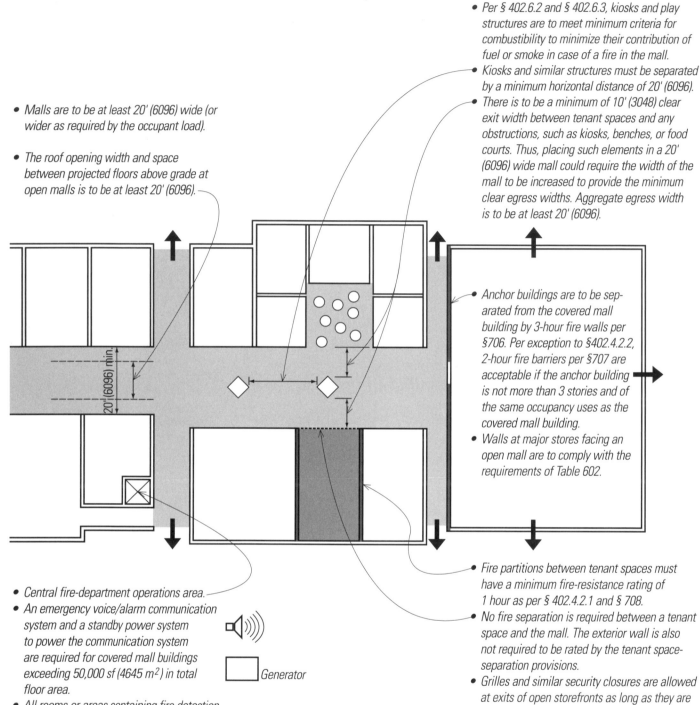

- Malls are to be at least 20' (6096) wide (or wider as required by the occupant load).

- The roof opening width and space between projected floors above grade at open malls is to be at least 20' (6096).

- Per § 402.6.2 and § 402.6.3, kiosks and play structures are to meet minimum criteria for combustibility to minimize their contribution of fuel or smoke in case of a fire in the mall.
- Kiosks and similar structures must be separated by a minimum horizontal distance of 20' (6096).
- There is to be a minimum of 10' (3048) clear exit width between tenant spaces and any obstructions, such as kiosks, benches, or food courts. Thus, placing such elements in a 20' (6096) wide mall could require the width of the mall to be increased to provide the minimum clear egress widths. Aggregate egress width is to be at least 20' (6096).

- Anchor buildings are to be separated from the covered mall building by 3-hour fire walls per §706. Per exception to §402.4.2.2, 2-hour fire barriers per §707 are acceptable if the anchor building is not more than 3 stories and of the same occupancy uses as the covered mall building.
- Walls at major stores facing an open mall are to comply with the requirements of Table 602.

20' (6096) min.

- Central fire-department operations area.
- An emergency voice/alarm communication system and a standby power system to power the communication system are required for covered mall buildings exceeding 50,000 sf (4645 m²) in total floor area.
- All rooms or areas containing fire detection and suppression systems must be identified for use by the fire department.

Generator

- Fire partitions between tenant spaces must have a minimum fire-resistance rating of 1 hour as per § 402.4.2.1 and § 708.
- No fire separation is required between a tenant space and the mall. The exterior wall is also not required to be rated by the tenant space-separation provisions.
- Grilles and similar security closures are allowed at exits of open storefronts as long as they are not closed during normal business hours.
- The mall itself is considered as a corridor, but is not required to be fire-rated if it is more than 20' (6096) wide, and all egress width provisions are met per § 402.8.1.

As building technology allowed advances in high-rise construction, the buildings often outstripped code provisions needed to address the new conditions impacting fire and life safety. High-rise buildings, made possible by innovative structural technology and elevators for transporting occupants, exceed the capabilities of fire-fighting procedures used for shorter buildings. They have occupied floors above the reach of even the longest ladders carried by fire department vehicles.

Note that high-rise egress systems are based on the occupant loads and egress requirements spelled out elsewhere in the code (see Chapter 10). Stairways are the primary means of egress, with elevators typically serving only firefighting functions as necessary. There are currently no refuge-area requirements in the code for harboring occupants not able to reach the stairway systems, other than requirements for areas of refuge for persons with disabilities where required by other sections of the code.

- The definition of a high-rise building In §403 is based on the height that typical fire-department extension ladders and hose streams can effectively fight a fire. Thus a building with an occupied floor more than 75' (22 860) above the lowest level of fire-department access is defined as a high-rise. Firefighting in a high-rise assumes that the firefighters must enter the building and go up inside the building to fight a fire.

With the advent of ever-taller buildings and in light of lessons learned from the September 11, 2001, World Trade Center disaster, a subset of requirements for "super high-rise" buildings, which are those taller than 420' (128 m) in height, has been added to the IBC. Most of these provisions are found in § 403 but many others are scattered throughout the code, most notably in Chapter 10, where additional means-of-egress provisions are required in such buildings. We will highlight these provisions with a notation where they apply to our discussion or illustrations.

Note that due to their limitations on heights and not being part of a mixed-use occupancy, buildings with Group H-1, H-2, and H-3 occupancies are excepted from the provisions in § 403, since in practical terms they will never be present in a high-rise structure.

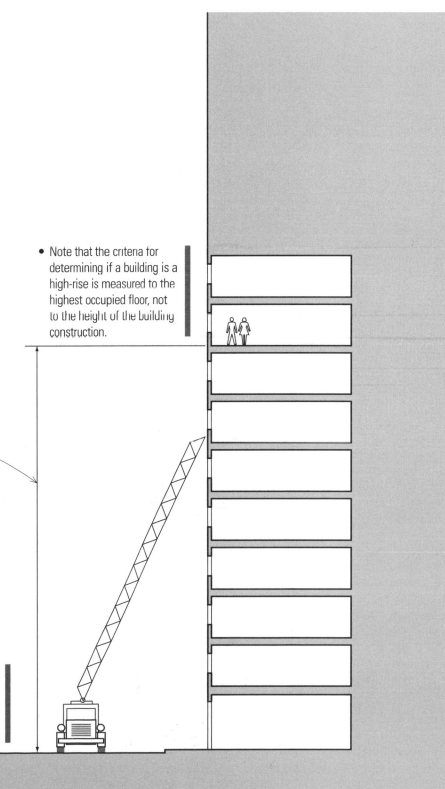

- Note that the criteria for determining if a building is a high-rise is measured to the highest occupied floor, not to the height of the building construction.

- Emergency phone every fifth floor in each required stairway where the doors to the stairway are locked.
- § 403.4.5 requires that emergency responder radio coverage is to be provided per § 510 of the IFC.

Code requirements for high-rises are a combination of passive and active fire-protection measures.

- The buildings must be constructed of noncombustible materials.
- Shafts and vertical penetrations must be enclosed to prevent the spread of smoke and fire.
- § 403.3 requires that automatic fire sprinklers be installed throughout high-rise buildings.
- In Seismic Design Categories C, D, E, or F, a secondary water supply capable of supplying the required hydraulic sprinkler demand, including the hose stream requirement, for up to 30 minutes is required.
- § 403.2.1 allows a reduction in fire-resistance rating if the automatic sprinkler system has control valves equipped with supervisory initiating devices and water-flow initiating devices for each floor. This reduction <u>does not apply</u> to high-rise buildings over 420' (128 m) in height.
- See table on facing page. ⟶

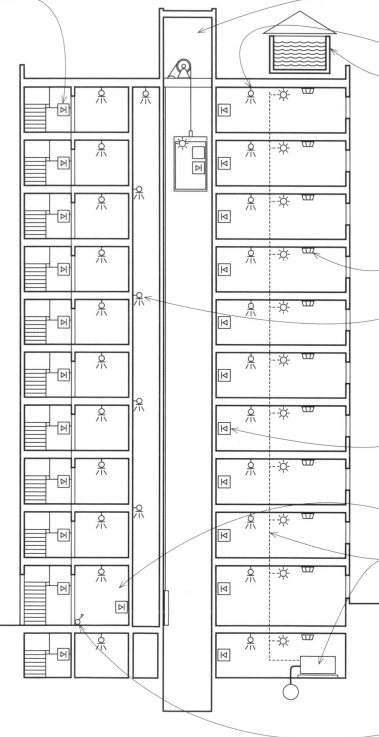

- § 403.4.1 requires smoke detectors connected to an automatic fire-alarm system per § 907.2.13.1.
- Where shafts have sprinklers installed in them at their tops and at alternate floor levels, the shaft fire-resistance rating may be reduced to one hour.
- This reduction <u>does not apply</u> to exit enclosure shafts or to elevator hoistway enclosures, or to any shafts in buildings over 420' (128 m) in height, whether sprinklered or not.
- § 403.4.4 requires an emergency voice/alarm communication system to be activated with the operation of any automatic fire detector, manual fire-alarm box or sprinkler device.
- § 403.4.6 requires a fire-fighting command center per § 911 in a location approved by the fire department.
- § 403.4.8 requires standby and emergency power systems to be located in a separate room enclosed with 2-hour fire-resistance-rated fire barriers and fueled by a 2-hour supply of on-site fuel. These power systems are required for the operation of systems necessary for evacuation or for firefighting, such as elevators, smoke control systems, emergency lights, and firefighting systems and operations. Confer with the AHJ to determine the Fire Code distinctions and requirements for standby and emergency power systems.
- § 403.5.3 requires stairway doors that are locked from the stairway side to be capable of being unlocked simultaneously from the fire command center.

Reduction in Fire-Resistance Rating per § 403.2.1

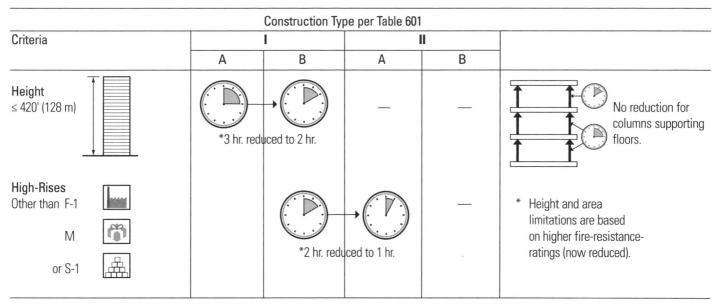

Criteria	Construction Type per Table 601				
	I		II		
	A	B	A	B	
Height ≤ 420' (128 m)	*3 hr. reduced to 2 hr.		—	—	No reduction for columns supporting floors.
High-Rises Other than F-1 M or S-1	*2 hr. reduced to 1 hr.		—		* Height and area limitations are based on higher fire-resistance-ratings (now reduced).

For <u>all</u> high-rises:

- Per § 403.5.1, stair enclosures are to be separated by at least 30' (9144) or not less than ¼ of the length of the maximum diagonal dimension, whichever is less. Where there are three stairs, at least two must meet this criteria.
- For high rises greater than 120' (36 576) in height, there is to be at least two fire-service access elevators complying with § 3007.

- Minimum bond strength of sprayed fire-resistant materials (SFRM) varies based on building height, with the major break occurring at a height of 420' (128 m).

- Buildings greater than 420' (128 m) in height or in Risk Categories III and IV per Table 1604.5 (i.e., hospitals, large assembly high-rises, and essential services) are to have hardened exit and elevator shafts per § 403.2.3. The hardening criteria are based on ASTM C1629/C1629M standards. Concrete or masonry walls are deemed to meet these requirements.

- Per § 403.5.2, a third egress stair is required for buildings other than R-2 occupancies greater that 420' (128 m) in height. (Note the requirement is dependent on building height, not just for Occupancy Categories III and IV.)

- Each sprinkler zone in buildings greater than 420' (128 m) in height is to have two fire sprinkler risers, with each riser supplying sprinklers on alternate floors.

- Note that per the Exception to § 403.5.2, a third egress stair is not required if occupant self-evacuation elevators complying with § 3008 are provided.

SFRM Minimum bond strength (psf)

1,000 psf

500 psf
430 psf

0

75' (22 m)   420' (128 m)   > 420' (128 m)

Building Height

Atriums were an innovative building type that required a specific building-code response as their use became more prevalent. The code requirements in § 404 for atriums combine aspects of malls and high-rise fire and life safety provisions.

As for covered malls and high-rise buildings, the code requires that a mixture of active and passive fire-protection measures be provided in atriums. Atrium buildings, however, rely more heavily on active systems for fire and life safety.

- The travel distance through the atrium cannot exceed 200' (60 960).
- Buildings containing atriums must be fully sprinklered throughout the building. There are limited exceptions to § 404.3 for certain areas, but the basic design assumption should be that such buildings are fully sprinklered.
- Openings into the atrium may be glazed if special fire-sprinkler protection is provided.

The greatest concern about atrium fire and life safety involves the control of smoke. Atriums that connect more than two stories are required to have smoke management systems conforming to § 909. These interconnect elaborate systems of detectors, fans, and controls to contain or move smoke to allow safe egress for occupants of atriums.

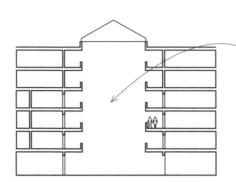

- *By definition, an atrium is an opening connecting two or more floor levels that is closed at the top. In other words, it is considered to be an interconnected series of floor openings inside of a building that create a physical connection and a common atmosphere between floor levels of the building. The code definition assumes that an atrium has an enclosed top.*

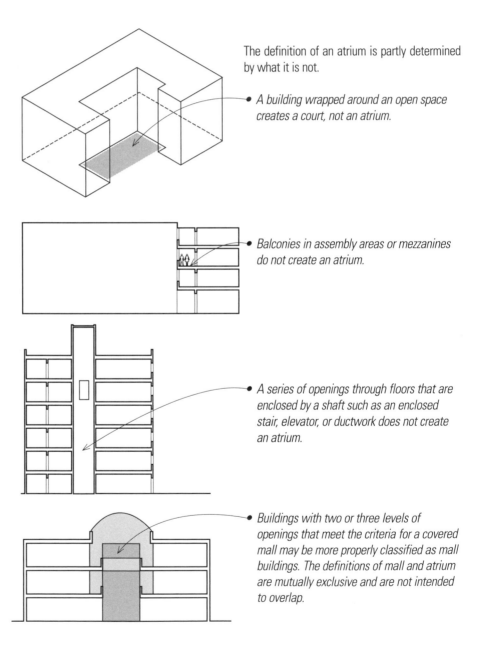

The definition of an atrium is partly determined by what it is not.

- *A building wrapped around an open space creates a court, not an atrium.*

- *Balconies in assembly areas or mezzanines do not create an atrium.*

- *A series of openings through floors that are enclosed by a shaft such as an enclosed stair, elevator, or ductwork does not create an atrium.*

- *Buildings with two or three levels of openings that meet the criteria for a covered mall may be more properly classified as mall buildings. The definitions of mall and atrium are mutually exclusive and are not intended to overlap.*

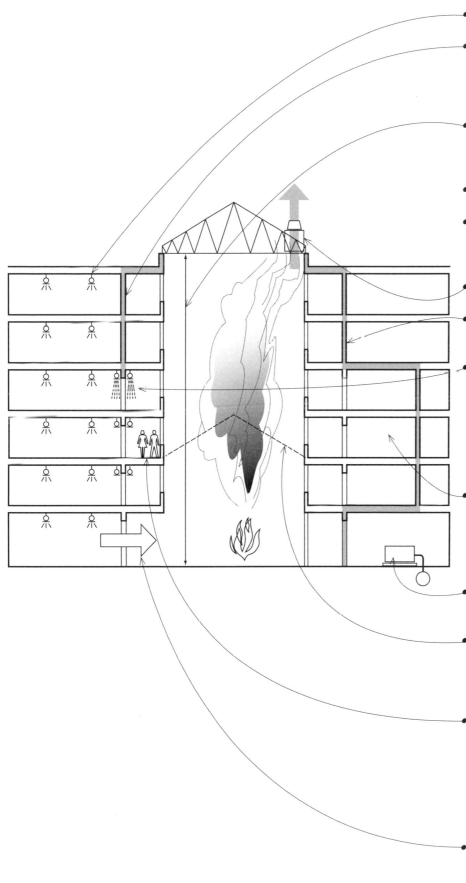

• *§ 404.3 requires an approved automatic fire-sprinkler system be installed throughout.*

• *The sprinkler requirement does not apply to the portion of a building adjacent to or above an atrium if that portion is separated from the atrium with 2-hour fire barrier walls or horizontal assemblies, or both.*

• *Automatic sprinkler protection for the ceiling of an atrium is not required if the ceiling is more than 55' (16 764) above the floor.*

• *§ 404.4 requires a fire alarm system complying with § 907.2.14.*

• *§ 404.5 requires a smoke-control system to be installed in accordance with § 909 so that the atrium space is kept clear of smoke and can be used as a safe means of egress.*

• *Means to exhaust air for smoke-control system.*

• *§ 404.6 requires atrium spaces to be separated from adjacent spaces with 1-hour fire-barrier walls.*

• *Glass walls separating an atrium space from adjacent spaces are permitted if they serve as smoke barriers and can be wetted upon activation of automatic sprinklers spaced along both sides at 6' (1829) on center and installed between 4" and 12" (102 and 305) away from the glass. Only one side need be protected if there is no walkway on the atrium side.*

• *The 1-hour protection may be omitted for the adjacent spaces of any three floors of the atrium if the spaces are included in computing the atrium volume for the design of the smoke-control system.*

• *§ 404.7 requires an emergency standby system per § 909.11 be available to power the smoke control system.*

• *2-story atrium does not require smoke control per Exception to § 404.5, unless the building houses I-1 Condition 1 or I-2 occupancies where a smoke-control system is required at two or more stories.*

• *§ 404.9 limits the exit-access travel distance to 200' (60 960), where the travel starts at a level other than the level of exit discharge. When the travel distance in the atrium occurs at the level of exit discharge, the distance is to comply with § 1017. This is also the case for means of egress that are open to the atrium but where the egress travel does not occur in the atrium.*

• *Means to allow air in for smoke-control system as make-up air for smoke exhaust.*

Building codes have traditionally had a great deal of difficulty classifying and addressing parking structures and garages. There is a long-standing perception among code writers that there are inherent dangers for vehicles carrying flammable fuels and emitting noxious gases. Yet buildings housing these types of uses have had a generally good safety record. Because of special concerns regarding these occupancies expressed in predecessor codes, § 406 has grouped these uses into a separate category that can be considered a distinct occupancy group.

Motor-vehicle-related uses break down into four general categories:
1. Private garages or carports
2. Public parking garages
    2a. Open parking garages
    2b. Enclosed parking garages
3. Motor-fuel dispensing stations
4. Repair garages

Private Garages and Carports

Private garages or carports are for private use and meet the common definition of what we all think of as parking for housing. These are typically considered Group U occupancies. Separation requirements are contained in Chapter 4, § 406.3.4. Note that one- and two-family dwellings and their accessory structures such as garages are intended to be regulated by the International Residential Code.

- An enclosed garage abutting a house is to have a minimum of one layer of 1/2" (12.7 mm) gypsum board on the garage side. Where rooms extend over the garage a minimum of 5/8" (15.9 mm) type-X gypsum board is to be used at the ceiling for separation.
- Doors between the garage and house are to be solid wood or solid-core doors at least 1 3/8" (35) thick or complying with § 716.5.3.
- Door is to be self-closing and self-latching.

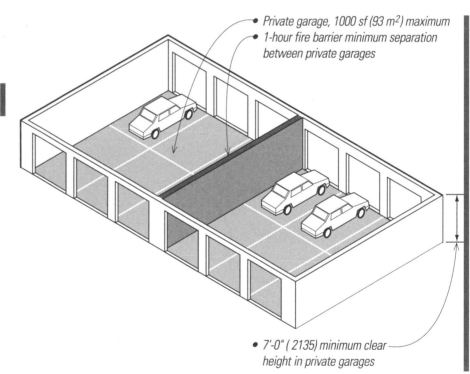

- Private garage, 1000 sf (93 m²) maximum
- 1-hour fire barrier minimum separation between private garages

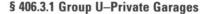

- 7'-0" (2135) minimum clear height in private garages

§ 406.3.1 Group U–Private Garages

Parking Garages

§ 406.4 classifies public parking garages into open parking garages and enclosed parking garages.

Open Parking Garages

Open parking garages are multiple-vehicle facilities used for parking or the storage of vehicles where no repairs take place. These are typically classified as Group S-2 occupancies. They are to be of Types I, II or IV construction per § 406.5.1. To meet this definition, the amount and distribution of openings are specified in § 406.5.2 of the code. Because these openings are distributed in a manner that provides cross-ventilation for the parking tiers, no mechanical ventilation is required.

• § 406.5.8 requires standpipes per § 905.3.

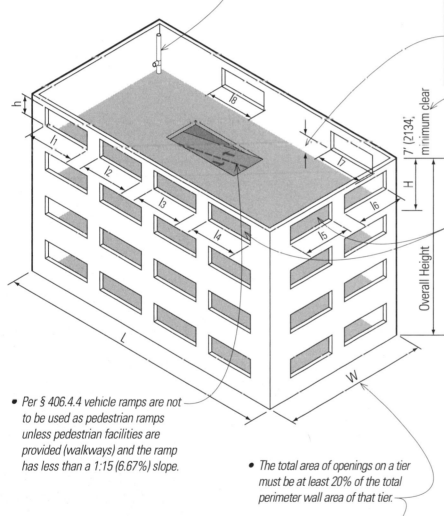

• Per § 406.4.4 vehicle ramps are not to be used as pedestrian ramps unless pedestrian facilities are provided (walkways) and the ramp has less than a 1:15 (6.67%) slope.

• § 406.4.2 requires guards in accordance with § 1015.
• Per § 406.4.3, vehicle barrier systems not less than 2'-9" (835) high are to be placed at the end of drive lanes and at the end of parking spaces that are more than 1' (305) above adjacent grade. Vehicle barriers are to be in accordance with § 1607.8.3.
• § 406.4.1 requires a minimum clear height of 7' (2135) at each floor level for vehicular and pedestrian travel in all parking garages. We construe this to mean that, in areas where vehicles or pedestrians are not moving through those areas, items such as ventilation ductwork or piping may be lower than 7' (2135). Areas to be used by vans for accessibility are to be higher per § 1106.5 and ICC A117.1
• § 406.5.2 requires uniformly distributed openings on two or more sides for the natural ventilation of open parking garages.
• The aggregate length of openings on a tier must be at least 40% of the total perimeter of the tier. Interior walls are to be at least 20% open, with uniformly distributed openings.
• Although openings on a third side are not required, openings on opposing sides are preferred for cross-ventilation.
• Table 406.5.4 determines the allowable floor areas and heights of open, single-use parking garages for private vehicles according to type of construction. The grade-level tier is permitted to contain an office, waiting, and toilet rooms having a combined area of not more than 1,000 sf (93 m^2). Such areas need not be separated from the open parking garage.
• § 406.5.5 permits area and height increases for open parking garages having a greater percentage of openings along a greater perimeter of the building and under specific conditions of use.

• The total area of openings on a tier must be at least 20% of the total perimeter wall area of that tier.

$$h \times [l_1 + l_2 + l_3 + l_4 + l_5 + l_6 + l_7 + l_8] \geq 20\% \text{ of } [H \times (2W + 2L)]$$

$$[l_1 + l_2 + l_3 + l_4 + l_5 + l_6 + l_7 + l_8] \geq 40\% \text{ of } [2W + 2L]$$

Enclosed Parking Garages

Enclosed parking garages are similar to open parking garages except that the amount of wall enclosure relative to the building area does not allow them to be considered as open garages. Because they do not meet the criteria for open parking garages and are considered enclosed, mechanical ventilation is required to compensate for the lack of cross-ventilation.

• Means to get exhaust air out for mechanical ventilation of the parking garage per § 406.6.2 and IMC

• Rooftop parking is permitted.

• Sprinklered per § 406.6.3

• 7' (2135) minimum clear height at each floor level.

• The allowable heights and areas for enclosed parking garages are limited to the allowable heights and areas specified in § 504 and 506 as modified by § 507.

• Means to get fresh air in for mechanical ventilation of the parking garage

Motor-Vehicle Service Stations

Motor-vehicle service stations are typically free-standing structures and are considered as Group M occupancies. Note the references to the Fire Code in which additional construction detail requirements are contained.

• Canopies are to have a clear height of not less than 13'-6" (4115) to the lowest projecting element of the canopy to allow vehicles to drive under the canopy.

Repair Garages

Repair garages are repair facilities not otherwise classified as service stations. The limitations on hazardous materials will dictate whether these facilities are considered as Group S or H occupancies. They are considered as Group S-1 occupancies when they do not use or store hazardous materials in quantities sufficient to require classification as a Group H occupancy. These facilities are required to be separated by fire barriers when in mixed-use conditions and treated as separated occupancies. S-1 occupancies may be treated as nonseparated occupancies per § 508.3, but H occupancies will always require separations.

Hazardous area

• Repair garage to be sprinklered per § 406.8.6.

Group I-2 occupancies include nursing homes and hospitals. Such occupancies serve populations that are not capable of self-preservation in an emergency and who will either require evacuation assistance or a "defend in place" egress strategy. Hospitals are very complex buildings that have extensive code requirements that need to be met by experienced designers. We will not touch on them in this book. However, Group I-2 Condition 1 occupancies include foster care homes and nursing homes, which many more design professionals may be engaged to design. We discuss here several examples of the specialized requirements for these uses to highlight how Chapter 4 must be consulted for information regarding the specific occupancies addressed in this chapter.

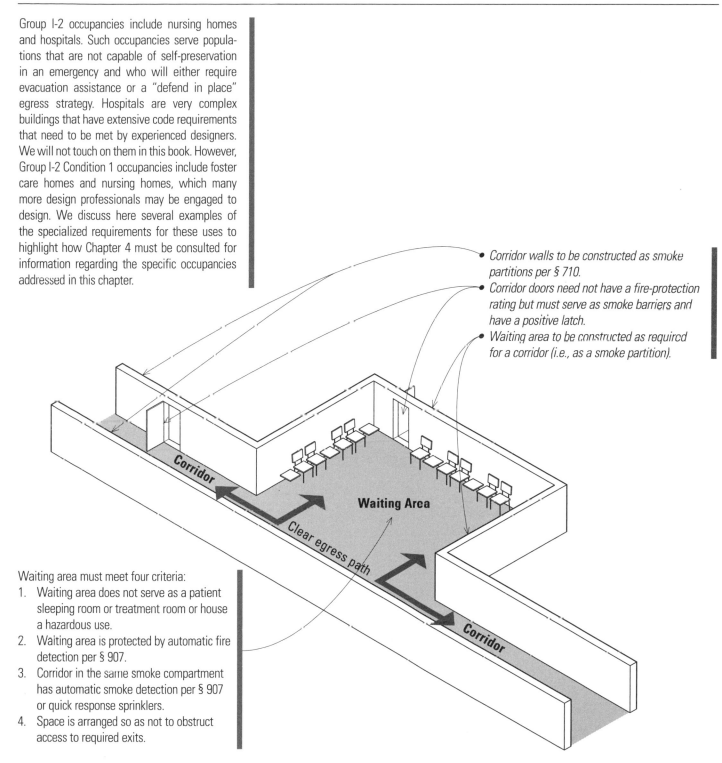

- *Corridor walls to be constructed as smoke partitions per § 710.*
- *Corridor doors need not have a fire-protection rating but must serve as smoke barriers and have a positive latch.*
- *Waiting area to be constructed as required for a corridor (i.e., as a smoke partition).*

Waiting area must meet four criteria:
1. Waiting area does not serve as a patient sleeping room or treatment room or house a hazardous use.
2. Waiting area is protected by automatic fire detection per § 907.
3. Corridor in the same smoke compartment has automatic smoke detection per § 907 or quick response sprinklers.
4. Space is arranged so as not to obstruct access to required exits.

§ 407.2.1 Corridors and Waiting Areas in Any Group I-2 Occupancy

Shared living or meeting spaces may be open to the corridor to facilitate interaction among residents if all of the following conditions are met:

1. Walls and ceilings are constructed as required for corridors.
2. Spaces do not serve as patient sleeping rooms or treatment rooms, or house incidental or hazardous uses.
3. Area is protected by automatic fire protection per § 907.
4. Corridor in the same smoke compartment is protected by automatic smoke detection per § 907 or has quick response sprinklers.
5. Space is arranged so as not to obstruct access to required exits.

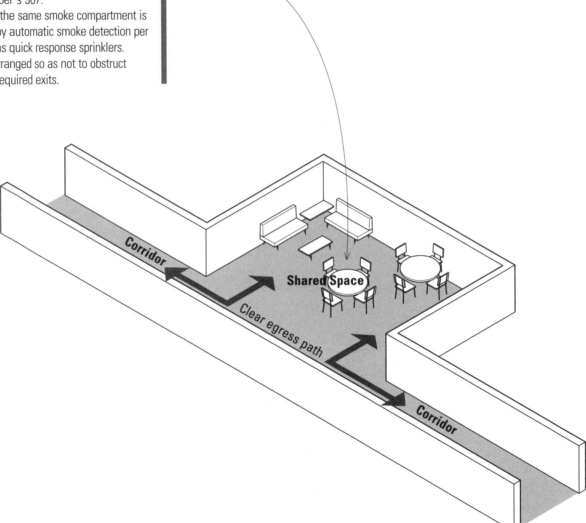

§ 407.2.5 Nursing Home Housing Units
[Group I-2, Condition 1 only: Nursing Homes and Foster Care Facilities]

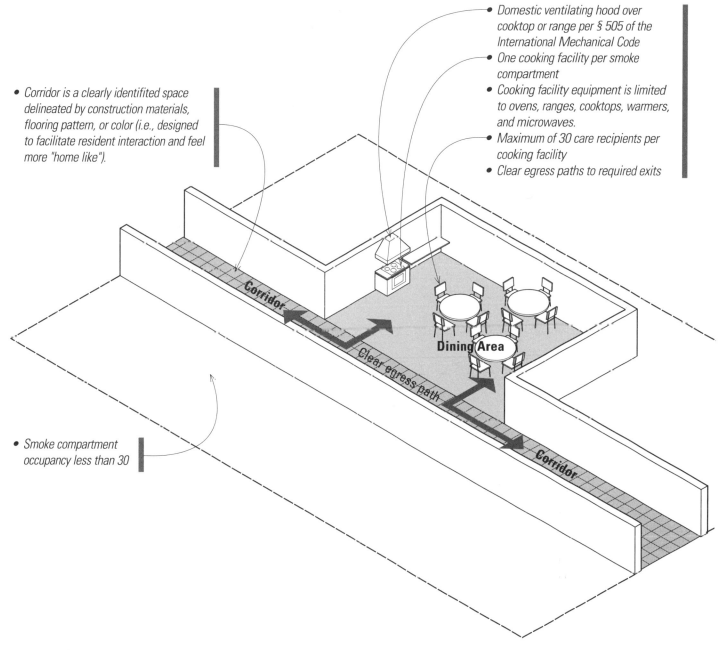

- Corridor is a clearly identifited space delineated by construction materials, flooring pattern, or color (i.e., designed to facilitate resident interaction and feel more "home like").

- Domestic ventilating hood over cooktop or range per § 505 of the International Mechanical Code
- One cooking facility per smoke compartment
- Cooking facility equipment is limited to ovens, ranges, cooktops, warmers, and microwaves.
- Maximum of 30 care recipients per cooking facility
- Clear egress paths to required exits

- Smoke compartment occupancy less than 30

§ 407.2.6 Cooking Facilities
[Group I-2, Condition 1 only: Nursing Homes and Foster Care Facilities]

Although not explicitly stated, assume corridor wall construction extends around the dining area as a space meeting the requirements of § 407.2.5.

Live-Work Units

§ 419 of the code addresses requirements for live-work units, which are classified as an R-2 occupancy.

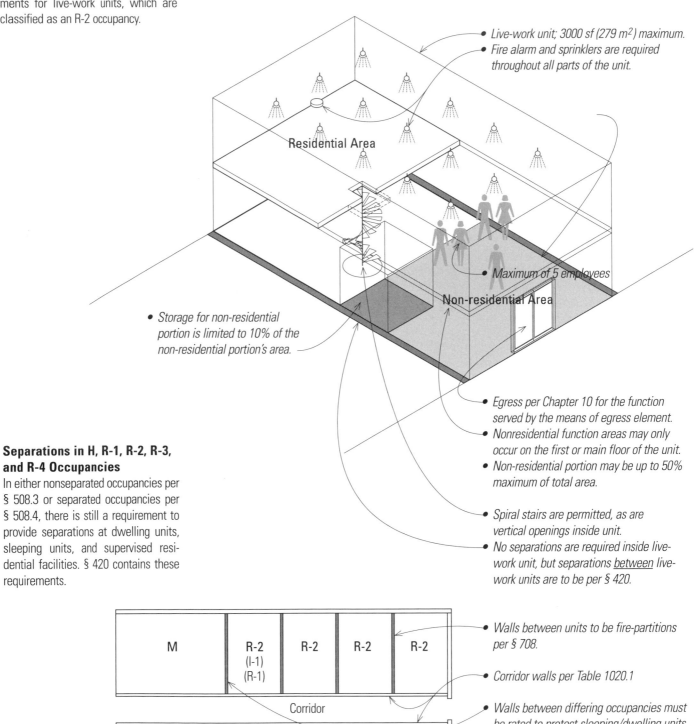

- Live-work unit; 3000 sf (279 m²) maximum.
- Fire alarm and sprinklers are required throughout all parts of the unit.

Residential Area

Maximum of 5 employees

Non-residential Area

- Storage for non-residential portion is limited to 10% of the non-residential portion's area.

- Egress per Chapter 10 for the function served by the means of egress element.
- Nonresidential function areas may only occur on the first or main floor of the unit.
- Non-residential portion may be up to 50% maximum of total area.

- Spiral stairs are permitted, as are vertical openings inside unit.
- No separations are required inside live-work unit, but separations *between* live-work units are to be per § 420.

Separations in H, R-1, R-2, R-3, and R-4 Occupancies

In either nonseparated occupancies per § 508.3 or separated occupancies per § 508.4, there is still a requirement to provide separations at dwelling units, sleeping units, and supervised residential facilities. § 420 contains these requirements.

M	R-2 (I-1) (R-1)	R-2	R-2	R-2

Corridor

R-2	R-2	R-2	R-2	R-2	R-2

- Walls between units to be fire-partitions per § 708.

- Corridor walls per Table 1020.1

- Walls between differing occupancies must be rated to protect sleeping/dwelling units in the same manner as the walls between the units themselves.
- Separation requirements also apply to horizontal assemblies between stacked units. These separations are to be per § 711.

Health Care Clinics

Health Care Clinics are B occupancies per the list in § 304. There are two categories of health care clinics: Ambulatory Care Facilities and Outpatient Clinics.

While health care clinics are a specialized use, the occupancy classification and application of code provisions to health clinics is often the subject of misunderstanding between project proponents and the AHJ. We have therefore included a discussion of the distinctions between the requirements for Ambulatory Care Facilities, discussed in the new § 422 of the IBC, and other types of clinics. Ambulatory Care Facilities, often called "outpatient surgical centers," often perform relatively complex surgical procedures, where patients are rendered unconsious during the procedure but go home in less than twenty-four hours; the facilities therefore do not function as hospitals. New code provisions have been written to address the increasing construction and operation of such facilities.

Outpatient Clinics

- § 304.1.1 defines Outpatient Clinics as buildings or portions thereof used to provide medical care on a _less than 24-hour basis_ to individuals who **are not** _rendered incapable of self-preservation_.

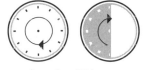

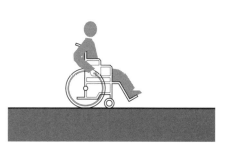

- _Less than 24-hour care_

- _Even if disabled, patients in outpatient clinics are presumed to be capable of self-preservation in an emergency and able to evacuate without assistance._

Ambulatory Care Facilities

- § 202 defines Ambulatory Care Facilities as buildings or portions thereof used to provide medical, surgical, psychiatric, nursing, or similar care on a _less than 24-hour basis_ to individuals who **are** _rendered incapable of self-preservation_ (i.e., anaesthetized or heavily sedated).

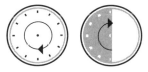

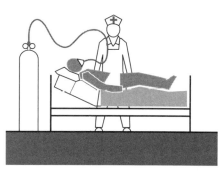

- _Less than 24-hour care_

- _Having patients rendered incapable of self-preservation (unconscious or semi-conscious) during some part of their stay in the facility is the distinguishing factor between ambulatory-care B occupancies and outpatient-clinic B occupancies._

Ambulatory Care Facilities

§ 422 contains special provisions for ambulatory care facilities based on the assumption that occupants may not be able to leave without assistance and thus need additional protection:

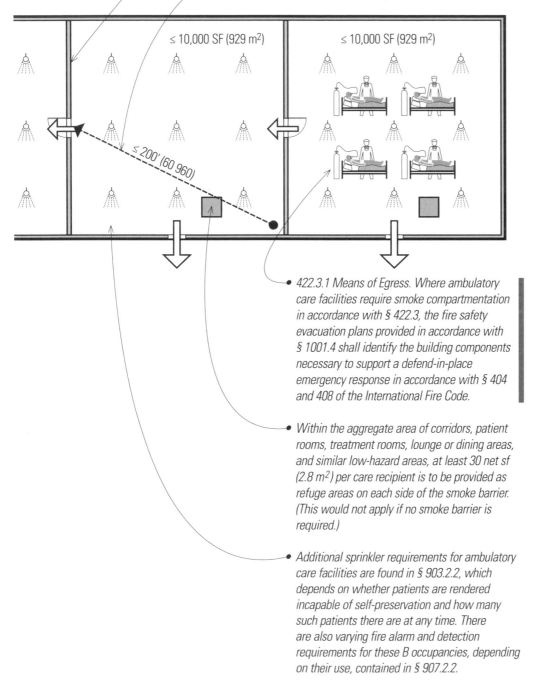

- Any ambulatory care facility greater than 10,000 sf (929 m²) is to be subdivided by a smoke barrier per § 709. Each smoke compartment to be less than or equal to 22,500 sf (2090 m²) in area.

- The travel distance from any point in a smoke compartment to a smoke-barrier door is not to exceed 200' (60 960).

≤ 10,000 SF (929 m²)

≤ 10,000 SF (929 m²)

≤ 200' (60 960)

- 422.3.1 Means of Egress. Where ambulatory care facilities require smoke compartmentation in accordance with § 422.3, the fire safety evacuation plans provided in accordance with § 1001.4 shall identify the building components necessary to support a defend-in-place emergency response in accordance with § 404 and 408 of the International Fire Code.

- Within the aggregate area of corridors, patient rooms, treatment rooms, lounge or dining areas, and similar low-hazard areas, at least 30 net sf (2.8 m²) per care recipient is to be provided as refuge areas on each side of the smoke barrier. (This would not apply if no smoke barrier is required.)

- Additional sprinkler requirements for ambulatory care facilities are found in § 903.2.2, which depends on whether patients are rendered incapable of self-preservation and how many such patients there are at any time. There are also varying fire alarm and detection requirements for these B occupancies, depending on their use, contained in § 907.2.2.

5

Building Heights and Areas

As noted in Chapter 3, building designers almost invariably start a project with a given occupancy. After a building's occupancy classification is determined, the code analysis task becomes one of determining what heights and areas are allowable for the occupancy classification, given various types of construction. Criteria for allowable building heights and areas are set forth in Chapter 5 of the IBC. Economics and utility generally dictate that buildings be built using the least costly and complicated type of construction that will meet the criteria set forth in the code.

There are two types of design choices that typically impact the use of Chapter 5 for determining allowable heights and areas. The first is when the design of a given occupancy must provide enough area to contain the known uses. The second choice comes into play in speculative buildings built for economic gain. The goal in these facilities, such as office buildings or retail uses, is to maximize the allowable height and area using the most economical construction type.

When addressing the question of maximizing the economically viable building size, the designer must use an iterative process to maximize the space for a given building. One must make assumptions regarding construction type and analyze the relative cost and return for various construction types before the owner can make a decision. This iterative process may also be used to maximize the economic efficiency of a building where the program size requirements are the primary consideration. In either case, the goal is to achieve the maximum area with the minimum investment in construction materials while still meeting or exceeding the code-mandated requirements to protect public health, safety and welfare.

The descriptions for the allowable heights and areas for buildings that are contained in Chapter 5 have been completely reorganized from the way they were presented in previous editions of the code. For those readers familiar with the old table and methods presented in prior code editions it is important to remember that this reorganization was NOT intended to make any substantive revisions to the heights or areas that would have been determined under prior codes. The reorganization was undertaken only to clarify and make more consistent how allowable heights and area are interpreted by code users and authorities having jurisdiction.

The organization of Chapter 5 in the code is based on a set of basic criteria that are then modified by mitigating factors to allow increases or trade-offs between heights, areas, construction types, fire protection, and life safety systems. Upon first reading, the tables in Chapter 5 may seem very restrictive, but there are modifications contained throughout the rest of the chapter that give the designer greater flexibility.

In summary:
1. The designer usually knows the occupancy classification of the building.
2. The program area is usually set either by program needs or by budget.
3. A construction type will usually be determined during schematic design.
4. Note that, as described previously in the text in Chapter 2 regarding fire extinguishing systems, code requirements for fire sprinkler systems from Chapter 9 must be determined at this time to fully understand how to use the provisions of Chapter 5.
5. Since almost any building has a mix of incidental and accessory occupancies, and perhaps a mixture of occupancy classifications as described in Chapter 3, the provisions of § 508 must be carefully examined.

The definitions listed in Chapter 5 of the code are cross-referenced back to the actual definitions detailed in Chapter 2. As with other similar definitions, they apply throughout the code, not just within Chapter 5. The definitions have very specific code-related criteria that may be different from the colloquial meanings of the terms. They should be studied carefully for applicability when determining allowable heights and areas.

Height limitations for buildings contained in planning and zoning regulations do not necessarily use the same definitions or criteria for determining heights. The definitions in the code are developed to facilitate uniform application of regulations. Read the documents that pertain to the regulations in question. Never apply building-code criteria to planning issues, or vice versa.

Building Area is usually considered to exclude the thickness of the exterior walls of a building. This is based on the language describing gross floor area as "the area included *within* surrounding exterior walls." The wording seems to imply the wall is not a part of the area to be considered. Therefore the building area is the area enclosed within the building and the area begins at the *inside* face of the exterior wall. Another real-estate term often used for building area is "gross building area," which is typically calculated to the exterior side of the exterior walls. The most conservative way to calculate building area is to measure from outside face of wall to outside face of wall. This generates the most building area when nearing the upper limit of allowable area, which should not ever be challenged by the authorities having jurisdiction.

The definitions of Basement, Grade Plane, and Building Height are correlated and based on the relationship of building parts below or above the grade plane as it is defined. Note that building height, as measured in feet, takes roof profiles into account. Building heights are measured to the average height of the highest roof, thus allowing for pitched roofs, varying parapet heights and rooftop equipment enclosures. The height is calculated using different criteria than those used to determine the height of a building in stories. "Story" is intended to mean occupiable or usable space located inside the building contained by a floor below and a plane (next story or roof) above. Thus, this would exclude such unoccupied spaces as depressed loading docks. This definition is found with other definitions in Chapter 2.

Building Area is "the area included within surrounding exterior walls." This is generally interpreted as meaning to the inside face of exterior walls. See the commentary at left for a description of a more conservative approach to calculating building areas.

Vent shafts and courts are excluded from Building Area, taking into account both the shaft's wall thickness and the area inside the shaft as part of the excluded area.

Areas included within the horizontal projection of a floor or roof above, even if not enclosed by surrounding walls, are included in Building Area at full value. Thus roof overhangs can matter in area calculations.

Basement is defined as what it is *not*. It is a story, but one that is "not a story above grade plane," which term is defined in § 202. (See facing page for an explanation of Grade Plane.)

If the finished surface of the floor above the lower level is more than 6' (1829) above the grade plane or if it is more than 12' (3658) above grade at any point, then that level is considered to be "a story above grade plane," as defined in Chapter 2 of the IBC.

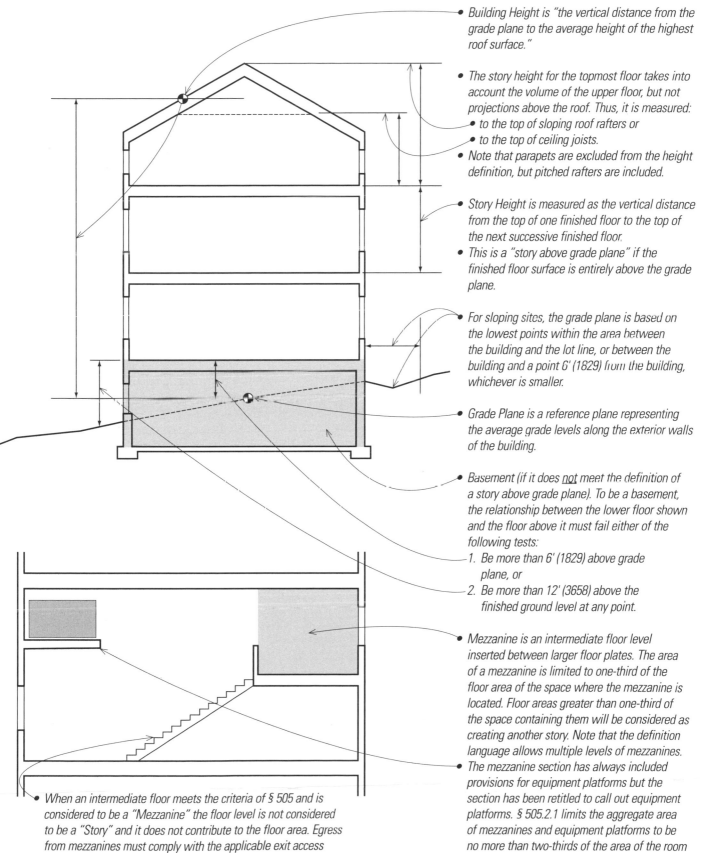

- Building Height is "the vertical distance from the grade plane to the average height of the highest roof surface."

- The story height for the topmost floor takes into account the volume of the upper floor, but not projections above the roof. Thus, it is measured:
  - to the top of sloping roof rafters or
  - to the top of ceiling joists.
- Note that parapets are excluded from the height definition, but pitched rafters are included.

- Story Height is measured as the vertical distance from the top of one finished floor to the top of the next successive finished floor.
- This is a "story above grade plane" if the finished floor surface is entirely above the grade plane.

- For sloping sites, the grade plane is based on the lowest points within the area between the building and the lot line, or between the building and a point 6' (1829) from the building, whichever is smaller.

- Grade Plane is a reference plane representing the average grade levels along the exterior walls of the building.

- Basement (if it does _not_ meet the definition of a story above grade plane). To be a basement, the relationship between the lower floor shown and the floor above it must fail either of the following tests:
  1. Be more than 6' (1829) above grade plane, or
  2. Be more than 12' (3658) above the finished ground level at any point.

- Mezzanine is an intermediate floor level inserted between larger floor plates. The area of a mezzanine is limited to one-third of the floor area of the space where the mezzanine is located. Floor areas greater than one-third of the space containing them will be considered as creating another story. Note that the definition language allows multiple levels of mezzanines.
- The mezzanine section has always included provisions for equipment platforms but the section has been retitled to call out equipment platforms. § 505.2.1 limits the aggregate area of mezzanines and equipment platforms to be no more than two-thirds of the area of the room or space where both of these elements are co-located.

- When an intermediate floor meets the criteria of § 505 and is considered to be a "Mezzanine" the floor level is not considered to be a "Story" and it does not contribute to the floor area. Egress from mezzanines must comply with the applicable exit access provisions of Chapter 10.

§ 503.1.1 exempts low-hazard, high-bay spaces, such as mills or foundries, from the height and building area limitations in § 504 and § 506. This recognizes the special-process requirements for such uses as well as their limited occupant loads with little or no public access.

§ 503.1.3 states that Type I buildings, permitted to be of unlimited height and area per § 504 and § 506, do not require the mitigations for unlimited-area building imposed on other construction types by other sections of this chapter. Note, however, that certain Group H occupancies have height and area restrictions even for Type I buildings.

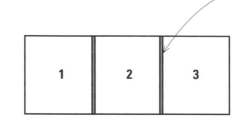

• *§ 503.1 allows one or more "fire walls" (defined and regulated by the provisions of Chapter 7) to divide a single structure into a number of "separate" buildings.*

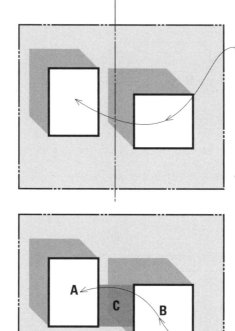

• *§ 503.1.2 states that multiple buildings on a single site may be considered as separate buildings (see also § 705.3 regarding assumption of an imaginary line between them), or as a single building for determining building areas.*

• *For a group of buildings to be considered as a single building, the group must meet the aggregate area limitations based on the most restrictive occupancy. Means of egress must also be carefully examined when multiple buildings are treated as one. When multiple buildings are treated as one, the walls between them (facing area C) do not have to conform to the requirements for exterior-wall fire separation in § 602 and opening protection per § 705.3.*

• *E.g., Areas of A + B must not exceed the single building area of the more restrictive occupancy. If Area C is open to the sky it does not contribute to the building area. If Area C were to be covered, it would be assigned an area and the building area would thus be A + B + C.*

The new provisions for determining allowable heights and areas are based on several factors. The first question to be determined is the type of occupancy (or multiple types in mixed-occupancy buildings) present in the proposed building. The second is whether the building is to be sprinklered or not. Next come determinations or assumptions about what construction type is desired or required for the proposed occupancies. The new organization of Chapter 5 uses the following abbreviations for conditions:

- NS: Buildings not equipped throughout with an automatic sprinkler system
- S = Buildings equipped throughout with an automatic sprinkler system installed in accordance with § 903.3.1.1 (NFPA 13)
- S1 = Buildings a maximum of one story above grade plane and equipped throughout with an automatic sprinkler system installed in accordance with § 903.3.1.1 (NFPA 13)
- SM = Buildings two or more stories above grade plane equipped throughout with an automatic sprinkler system installed in accordance with § 903.3.1.1 (NFPA 13)
- S13R = Buildings equipped throughout with an automatic sprinkler system installed in accordance with § 903.3.1.2 [NFPA 13R sprinkler systems in Group R occupancies up to and including four stories in height in buildings not exceeding 60 feet (18 288) in height above grade plane]

In prior editions of the IBC, Table 503 combined the basic information for heights of buildings in feet above grade plane, number of stories, and basic allowable areas per floor. These basic allowances were based on the intersection of occupancy groups and building construction types. There are new tables in the code which address heights in § 504 and areas in § 506. They are still organized around occupancies and construction types, but the tables are separated to address only one aspect of height and area allowances in each table. As in prior codes, the construction types are based on those described in Chapter 6, ranging from Type I fire-protected construction to Type V unrated construction. As in Table 601 "A" denotes construction that is "protected" with increased fire-resistance and "B" denotes construction not provided with fire-resistance protection.

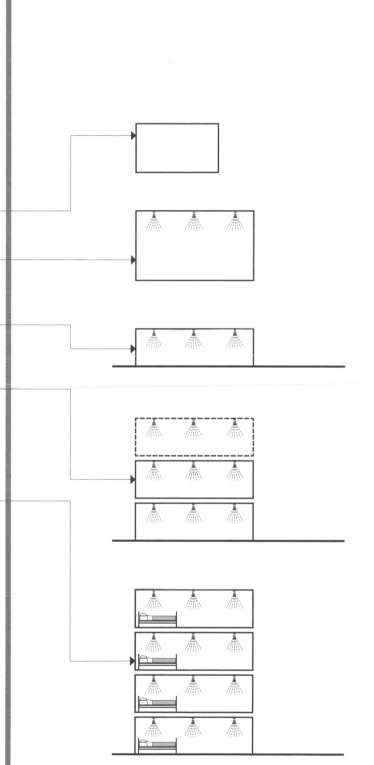

We will first discuss the standards in the new tables as general limitations. We will then examine in detail the allowable modifications contained in the new tables. For readers familiar with the presentation of these requirements in Table 503 in prior code editions it is important to remember that while the presentation of the information has changed, the technical requirements have not. A building designed under the 2015 IBC will be the same size and height as that same building would have been under the 2012 IBC.

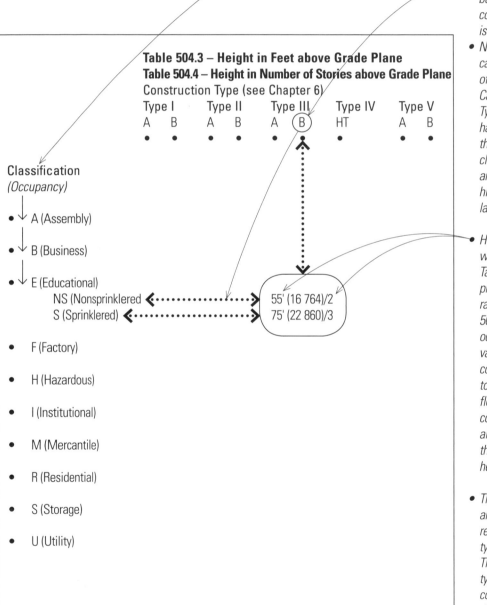

Table 504.3 – Height in Feet above Grade Plane
Table 504.4 – Height in Number of Stories above Grade Plane
Construction Type (see Chapter 6)

Type I		Type II		Type III		Type IV	Type V	
A	B	A	B	A	Ⓑ	HT	A	B

Classification
(Occupancy)

- ↓ A (Assembly)
- ↓ B (Business)
- ↓ E (Educational)
  - NS (Nonsprinklered) ◄┈┈┈┈┈► 55' (16 764)/2
  - S (Sprinklered) ◄┈┈┈┈┈► 75' (22 860)/3
- F (Factory)
- H (Hazardous)
- I (Institutional)
- M (Mercantile)
- R (Residential)
- S (Storage)
- U (Utility)

- *Allowable building height and building area, listed in § 502 but actually defined in Chapter 2, are determined by the intersection of occupancy group and construction type.*

- *As occupancy is usually determined before heights and areas, the table will typically be entered by reading down the list of occupancy groups to find the occupancy that fits the building design.*

- *Then reading across leads to the allowable building heights based on type of construction and whether or not the building is sprinklered.*

- *Note that the distinction between A and B categories of construction types is the level of fire resistance as described in Table 601. Category A is of higher fire resistance, thus Type A buildings of any construction type have higher allowable heights and areas than Type B buildings. Using the principle of classifying occupancies by degree of hazard and building types by fire-resistance, the higher the level of fire and life safety, the larger and taller a building can be.*

- *Heights are expressed in two ways, both of which refer to defined terms. The first, in Table 504.3, is height in feet above the grade plane and is generally tied to fire-resistance rather than occupancy. The second, in Table 504.4, is height in stories and is tied to occupancy. For discussion purposes, the values from Tables 504.3 and 504.4 are combined here. Both sets of criteria apply to any analysis. That is to avoid having high floor-to-floor heights between stories that could generate a building complying with the allowable number of stories but exceeding the height limit in feet above grade plane if heights were not also tabulated.*

- *The illustrations starting on the facing page are taken from Table 504.3 to show the relationship of occupancy and construction type to allowable building heights in feet. The examples are chosen from building types typically encountered by designers with the construction types chosen to highlight the differences as one proceeds from Type I fire-protected construction to Type V unrated construction. Entries in the table represent allowable heights in feet, as adjusted for inclusion of fire sprinklers or not.*

§ 504 has been reformatted to pertain only to the determination of allowable building heights in feet and stories above the grade plane. The values determined by the use of the tables in this section are the same as those that occured in Table 503 in prior editions of the IBC, but have been reformatted to make determination of allowable building heights clearer and less prone to error. As with building areas, building heights in feet and in stories are dependent on the occupancies to be included in the building and on the building's construction type. The inclusion of automatic sprinklers in the building also results in increases in allowable heights in feet and stories. Heights are described in two tables.

The first, Table 504.3, shows allowable building heights in feet only, based on occupancy type, construction type, and sprinkler conditions. The second, Table 504.4, shows allowable building heights in terms of the number of stories, also based on occupancy type, construction type, and sprinkler conditions. The new tables include all of the criteria necessary to determine allowable values for these variables. One looks in the tables under the chosen construction type, then reads down the chosen column to the occupancy in question and then makes a selection based on whether the building is sprinklered or not. The intersection of those variables in the tables give the code user the allowable values for height in feet (Table 504.3) or height in stories (504.4). There are no longer any adjustments necessary to the values in the tables for provision of sprinklers; those determinations are built into the two new tables.

Table 504.3

Allowable Building Heights in Feet Above Grade Plane (based on construction type, occupancy, and sprinklers)

Occupancy Classification	Sprinklers	Type I		Type II		Type III		Type IV	Type V	
		A	B	A	B	A	B	HT	A	B
A, B, E, F, M, S, U	NS	UL	160' (48.8 m)	65' (19.8 m)	55' (16.8 m)	65' (19.8 m)	55' (16.8 m)	65' (19.8 m)	50' (15.2 m)	40' (12.2 m)
	S	UL	180' (54.9 m)	85' (25.9 m)	75' (22.9 m)	85' (25.9 m)	75' (22.9 m)	85' (25.9 m)	70' (21.3 m)	60' (18.3 m)
H-1, H-2, H-3, H-5	NS[1,2]	UL	160' (48.8 m)	65' (19.8 m)	55' (16.8 m)	65' (19.8 m)	55' (16.8 m)	65' (19.8 m)	50' (15.2 m)	40' (12.2 m)
	S[1]	UL	160' (48.8 m)	65' (19.8 m)	55' (16.8 m)	65' (19.8 m)	55' (16.8 m)	65' (19.8 m)	50' (15.2 m)	40' (12.2 m)

Table 504.3 (cont'd)

Allowable Building Heights in Feet Above Grade Plane (based on construction type, occupancy, and sprinklers)

Occupancy Classification	Sprinklers	Type 1		Type II		Type III		Type IV	Type V	
		A	B	A	B	A	B	HT	A	B
H-4	NS[2]	UL	160' (48.8 m)	65' (19.8 m)	55' (16.8 m)	65' (19.8 m)	55' (16.8 m)	65' (19.8 m)	50' (15.2 m)	40' (12.2 m)
	S	UL	180' (54.9 m)	85' (25.9 m)	75' (22.9 m)	85' (25.9 m)	75' (22.9 m)	85' (25.9 m)	70' (21.3 m)	60' (18.3 m)
I-1 Condition 1 (Custodial care– evacuate without assistance) I-3 (Restrained occupants)	NS[2,3]	UL	160' (48.8 m)	65' (19.8 m)	55' (16.8 m)	65' (19.8 m)	55' (16.8 m)	65' (19.8 m)	50' (15.2 m)	40' (12.2 m)
	S	UL	180' (54.9 m)	85' (25.9 m)	75' (22.9 m)	85' (25.9 m)	75' (22.9 m)	85' (25.9 m)	70' (21.3 m)	60' (18.3 m)
I-1 Condition 2 (Custodial care– evacuate with limited assistance) I-2 (Nursing care, hospitals)	NS[2,3]	UL	160' (48.8 m)	65' (19.8 m)	55' (16.8 m)	65' (19.8 m)	55' (16.8 m)	65' (19.8 m)	50' (15.2 m)	40' (12.2 m)
	S	UL	180' (54.9 m)	85' (25.9 m)	55' (16.8 m)	65' (19.8 m)	55' (16.8 m)	65' (19.8 m)	50' (15.2 m)	40' (12.2 m)

Table 504.3 (cont'd)

Allowable Building Heights in Feet Above Grade Plane (based on construction type, occupancy, and sprinklers)

Occupancy Classification	Sprinklers	Type 1		Type II		Type III		Type IV	Type V	
		A	B	A	B	A	B	HT	A	B
I-4	NS[2, 5]	UL	160' (48.8 m)	65' (19.8 m)	55' (16.8 m)	65' (19.8 m)	55' (16.8 m)	65' (19.8 m)	50' (15.2 m)	40' (12.2 m)
	S	UL	180' (54.9 m)	85' (25.9 m)	75' (22.9 m)	85' (25.9 m)	75' (22.9m)	85' (25.9 m)	70' (21.3 m)	60' (18.3 m)
R	NS[2, 6]	UL	160' (48.8 m)	65' (19.8 m)	55' (16.8 m)	65' (19.8 m)	55' (16.8 m)	65' (19.8 m)	50' (15.2 m)	40' (12.2 m)
	S13R	60' (18.3 m)	60' (18.3 m)	60' (18.3 m)	60' (18.3 m)	60' (18.3 m)	60' (18.3 m)	60' (18.3 m)	60' (18.3 m)	60' (18.3 m)
	S	UL	180' (54.9 m)	85' (25.9 m)	75' (22.9 m)	85' (25.9 m)	75' (22.9m)	85' (25.9 m)	70' (21.3 m)	60' (18.3 m)

Footnotes:
1. New H occupancies must be sprinkered.
2. Non-sprinklered occupancies included only for evaluation of existing building height per the IEBC.
3. New I-1 and I-3 occupancies must be sprinklered.
4. New I-2 occupancies must be sprinklered.
5. For new I-4 occupancies, see Exceptions 2 and 3 to § 903.2.6 for day-care on the ground floor with direct egress or a sprinklered egress path if above the ground floor.
6. All R occupancies must be sprinklered.

Mezzanines

§ 505 considers mezzanines that meet the definition in Chapter 2 to be part of the story below them. If they meet the criteria limiting their area to one-third of the floor below, then they are not considered part of the overall building area, or as an additional story. However, the area must be counted toward the overall "Fire Area" as defined in Chapter 2.

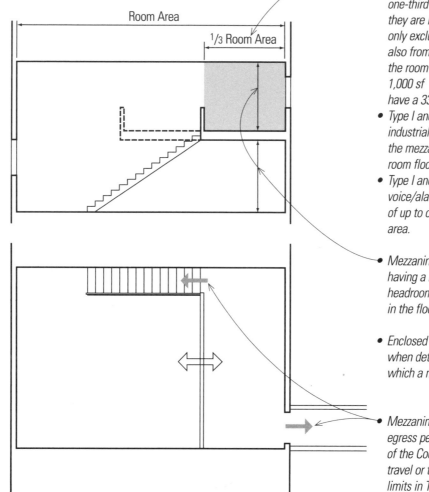

Room Area

¹/₃ Room Area

- Mezzanines are limited by the definition in Chapter 2, which in turn refers to § 505, to one-third of the area of the space in which they are located. Such a mezzanine is not only excluded from the overall area but also from the total floor-area calculation for the room containing the mezzanine. Thus a 1,000 sf (93 m²) floor space can typically have a 333 sf (31 m²) mezzanine.
- Type I and II buildings housing special industrial occupancies get a bonus allowing the mezzanine to be up to two-thirds of the room floor area.
- Type I and II buildings with sprinklers and voice/alarm systems may have mezzanines of up to one-half the area of the room floor area.

- Mezzanines must be of habitable height, having a minimum of 7' (2134) clear headroom at the mezzanine level as well as in the floor area under the mezzanine.

- Enclosed portions of a room are not included when determining the size of the room in which a mezzanine is located.

- Mezzanines are required to have means of egress per the requirements of Chapter 10 of the Code. Where the common path of travel or the occupant load exceeds the limits in Table 1006.2.1, then two means of egress will be required.

Mezzanines are conceived of by the code as open areas set above other spaces in a room. The code makes an absolute-sounding statement that all mezzanines shall be open and unobstructed to the room in which they are located, except for a railing-height wall at the edge. The statement is then followed by numerous exceptions. The basic idea is that if the mezzanine is small in area or occupant load, is furnished with a clearly defined separate exit path, or has two means of egress, it may be enclosed.

Allowable Building Areas per Table 506.2 As discussed previously, in prior code editions Table 503 combined allowable building heights in feet and stories with basic allowable areas. Each of the sets of tabular values for heights and areas were then adjusted for sprinkler conditions and location on property. The new code now breaks apart height in feet, height in number of stories, and allowable areas per level into three tables. It also includes modifications inside of each table based on whether the buildings are sprinklered or not.

The allowable areas are determined per Table 506.2. This table shows allowable building areas based on occupancy type and construction type. It also shows areas based on whether the building is nonsprinklered or is a sprinklered single-story or multiple-story building. It is very important to realize that under the increase formulas, the "NS" (nonspinklered) values in this table will be used in area-increase calculations, even for sprinklered buildings. When doing a code analysis for a proposed building, it is important to note the allowable area values for nonsprinklered buildings based on anticipated occupancies and proposed construction types so that you are able to insert them into the formulas from § 506.2 as described below.

Combined Table 504.4 and Table 506.2

The tables below and on the following pages show graphically the allowable areas taken from Table 506.2, based, as for heights, on the building's construction type, occupancy, and whether or not it is sprinklered. This table also graphically combines the number of allowable stories from Table 504.4 to represent the comparative heights and areas for the various combinations of the variables in the tables. This is a graphic tool to convey the use and implications of the choices for construction types for the various occupancies that may occur in a building. The intent of the code is that the determinations of the values from each table are made independently and then combined into a set of code criteria for design of the building.

Allowable Building Heights in Stories Above Grade Plane and Graphic Allowable Areas [based on construction type, occupancy, and sprinklers, and on values taken from Tables 504.4 and 506.2]

Occupancy Classification	Sprinklers	Type 1		Type II		Type III		Type IV	Type V	
	See footnotes	A	B	A	B	A	B	HT	A	B
A-1	NS	UL/UL	5/UL	3/15,500	2/8,500	3/14,000	2/8,500	3/15,000	2/11,500	1/5,500
	S1	1/UL	1/UL	1/62,000	1/34,000	1/56,000	1/34,000	1/60,000	1/46,000	1/22,000
	SM	UL/UL	6/UL	4/46,500	3/25,500	4/42,000	3/25,500	4/45,000	3/34,500	2/16,500

Allowable Building Heights in Stories Above Grade Plane (Table 504.4) and Graphic Allowable Areas (Table 506.2) [based on construction type, occupancy, and sprinklers]

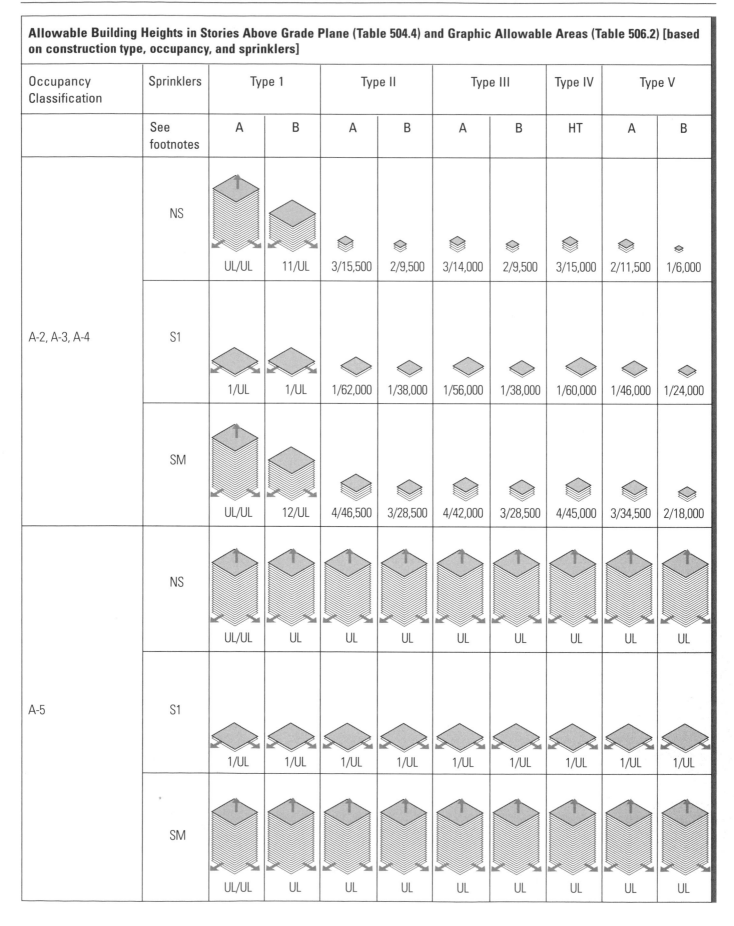

Occupancy Classification	Sprinklers	Type 1		Type II		Type III		Type IV	Type V	
	See footnotes	A	B	A	B	A	B	HT	A	B
A-2, A-3, A-4	NS	UL/UL	11/UL	3/15,500	2/9,500	3/14,000	2/9,500	3/15,000	2/11,500	1/6,000
	S1	1/UL	1/UL	1/62,000	1/38,000	1/56,000	1/38,000	1/60,000	1/46,000	1/24,000
	SM	UL/UL	12/UL	4/46,500	3/28,500	4/42,000	3/28,500	4/45,000	3/34,500	2/18,000
A-5	NS	UL/UL	UL	UL	UL	UL	UL	UL	UL	UL
	S1	1/UL	1/UL	1/UL	1/UL	1/UL	1/UL	1/UL	1/UL	1/UL
	SM	UL/UL	UL	UL	UL	UL	UL	UL	UL	UL

Allowable Building Heights in Stories Above Grade Plane (Table 504.4) and Graphic Allowable Areas (Table 506.2) [based on construction type, occupancy, and sprinklers]

Occupancy Classification	Sprinklers	Type 1		Type II		Type III		Type IV	Type V	
	See footnotes	A	B	A	B	A	B	HT	A	B
B	NS	UL/UL	11/UL	5/37,500	3/23,000	5/28,500	3/19,000	5/36,000	3/18,000	2/9,000
	S1	1/UL	1/UL	1/150,000	1/92,000	1/114,000	1/76,000	1/144,000	1/72,000	1/36,000
	SM	UL/UL	12/UL	6/112,500	4/69,000	6/85,500	4/57,000	6/108,000	4/54,000	3/27,000
E	NS	UL/UL	5/UL	3/26,500	2/14,500	3/23,500	2/14,500	3/25,500	1/18,500	1/9,500
	S1	1/UL	1/UL	1/106,000	1/58,000	1/94,000	1/58,000	1/102,000	1/74,000	1/38,000
	SM	UL/UL	6/UL	4/79,500	3/43,500	4/70,500	3/43,500	4/76,500	2/55,500	2/28,500

Allowable Building Heights in Stories Above Grade Plane (Table 504.4) and Graphic Allowable Areas (Table 506.2) [based on construction type, occupancy, and sprinklers]

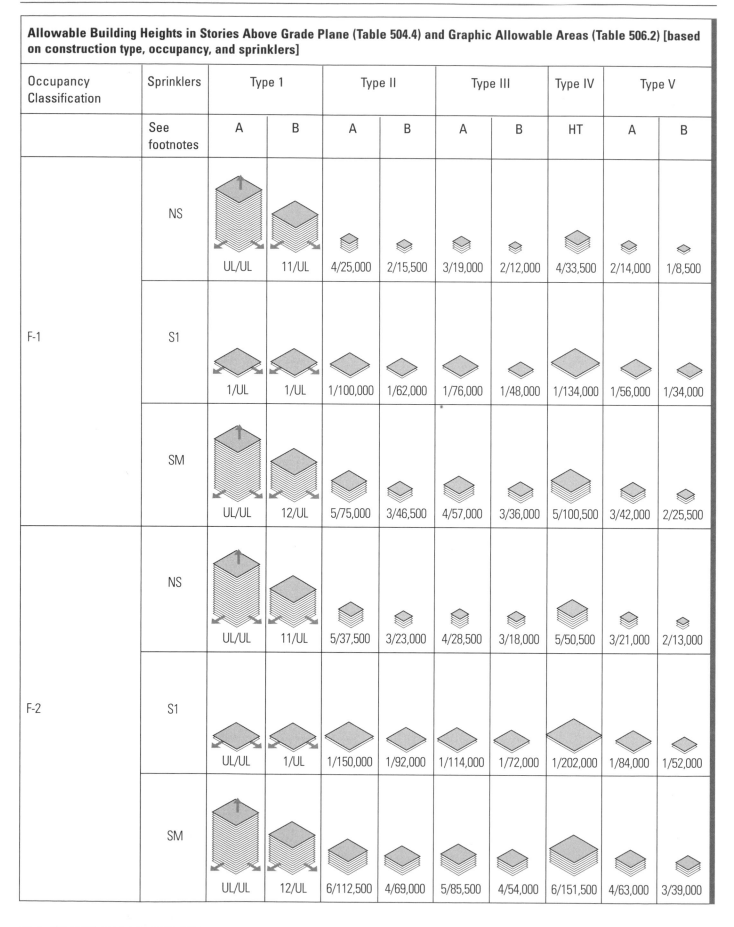

Occupancy Classification	Sprinklers	Type 1		Type II		Type III		Type IV	Type V	
	See footnotes	A	B	A	B	A	B	HT	A	B
F-1	NS	UL/UL	11/UL	4/25,000	2/15,500	3/19,000	2/12,000	4/33,500	2/14,000	1/8,500
	S1	1/UL	1/UL	1/100,000	1/62,000	1/76,000	1/48,000	1/134,000	1/56,000	1/34,000
	SM	UL/UL	12/UL	5/75,000	3/46,500	4/57,000	3/36,000	5/100,500	3/42,000	2/25,500
F-2	NS	UL/UL	11/UL	5/37,500	3/23,000	4/28,500	3/18,000	5/50,500	3/21,000	2/13,000
	S1	UL/UL	1/UL	1/150,000	1/92,000	1/114,000	1/72,000	1/202,000	1/84,000	1/52,000
	SM	UL/UL	12/UL	6/112,500	4/69,000	5/85,500	4/54,000	6/151,500	4/63,000	3/39,000

Allowable Building Heights in Stories Above Grade Plane (Table 504.4) and Graphic Allowable Areas (Table 506.2) [based on construction type, occupancy, and sprinklers]

Occupancy Classification	Sprinklers	Type 1		Type II		Type III		Type IV	Type V	
	See footnotes	A	B	A	B	A	B	HT	A	B
H-1	NS[1,2]	1/21,000	1/16,500	1/11,000	1/7,000	1/9,500	1/7,000	1/10,500	1/7,500	NP
	S1	1/21,000	1/16,500	1/11,000	1/7,000	1/9,500	1/7,000	1/10,500	1/7,500	NP
	SM	No SM @ H-1								
H-2	NS[1,2]	UL/21,000	3/16,500	2/11,000	1/7,000	2/9,500	1/7,000	2/10,500	1/7,500	1/3,000
	S1	1/21,000	1/16,500	2/11,000	1/7,000	2/9,500	1/7,000	2/10,500	1/7,500	1/3,000
	SM	UL/21,000	3/16,500	2/11,000	1/7,000	2/9,500	1/7,000	2/10,500	1/7,500	1/3,000

Allowable Building Heights in Stories Above Grade Plane (Table 504.4) and Graphic Allowable Areas (Table 506.2) [based on construction type, occupancy, and sprinklers]

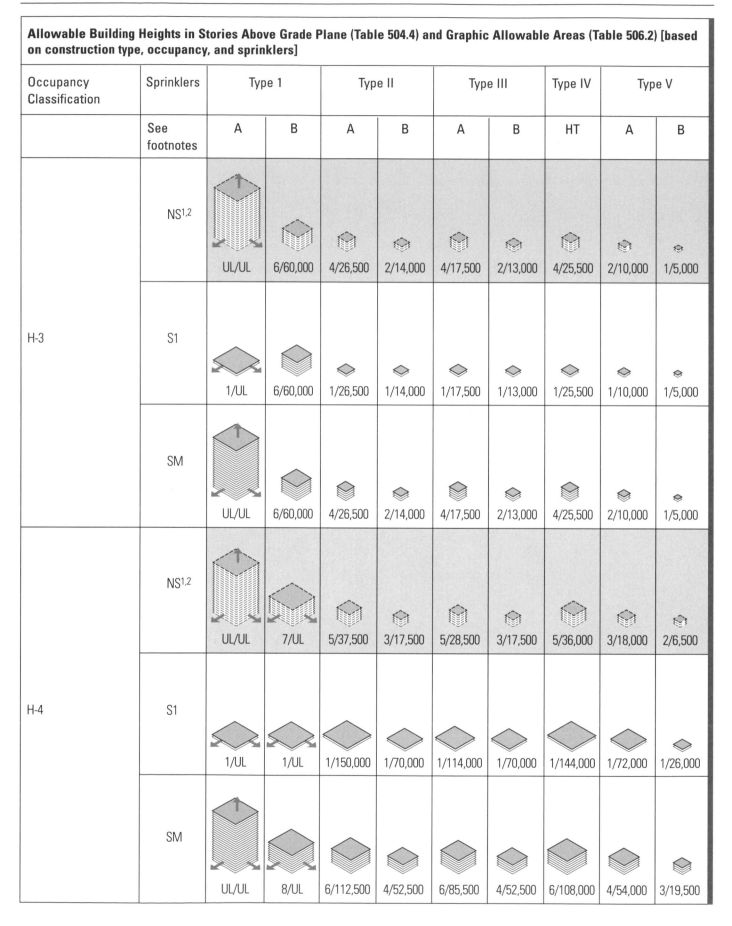

Occupancy Classification	Sprinklers	Type 1		Type II		Type III		Type IV	Type V	
	See footnotes	A	B	A	B	A	B	HT	A	B
H-3	NS[1,2]	UL/UL	6/60,000	4/26,500	2/14,000	4/17,500	2/13,000	4/25,500	2/10,000	1/5,000
	S1	1/UL	6/60,000	1/26,500	1/14,000	1/17,500	1/13,000	1/25,500	1/10,000	1/5,000
	SM	UL/UL	6/60,000	4/26,500	2/14,000	4/17,500	2/13,000	4/25,500	2/10,000	1/5,000
H-4	NS[1,2]	UL/UL	7/UL	5/37,500	3/17,500	5/28,500	3/17,500	5/36,000	3/18,000	2/6,500
	S1	1/UL	1/UL	1/150,000	1/70,000	1/114,000	1/70,000	1/144,000	1/72,000	1/26,000
	SM	UL/UL	8/UL	6/112,500	4/52,500	6/85,500	4/52,500	6/108,000	4/54,000	3/19,500

Allowable Building Heights in Stories Above Grade Plane (Table 504.4) and Graphic Allowable Areas (Table 506.2) [based on construction type, occupancy, and sprinklers]

Occupancy Classification	Sprinklers	Type 1		Type II		Type III		Type IV	Type V	
	See footnotes	A	B	A	B	A	B	HT	A	B
H-5	NS[1,2]	4/UL	4/UL	4/37,500	3/23,000	3/28,500	3/19,000	3/36,000	3/18,000	2/9,000
	S1	1/UL	1/UL	1/150,000	1/92,000	1/114,000	1/76,000	1/144,000	1/72,000	1/36,000
	SM	4/UL	4/UL	3/112,500	3/69,000	3/85,500	3/57,000	3/108,000	3/54,000	2/27,000
I-1 Condition 1 (Custodial care— evacuate without assistance)	NS[2,3]	UL/UL	9/55,000	4/19,000	3/10,000	4/16,500	3/10,000	4/18,000	3/10,500	2/4,500
	S1	1/UL	1/220,000	1/76,000	1/40,000	1/66,000	1/40,000	1/72,000	1/42,000	1/18,000
	SM	UL/UL	10/165,000	5/57,000	4/30,000	5/49,500	4/30,000	5/54,000	4/31,500	3/13,500

Allowable Building Heights in Stories Above Grade Plane (Table 504.4) and Graphic Allowable Areas (Table 506.2) [based on construction type, occupancy, and sprinklers]

Occupancy Classification	Sprinklers	Type 1		Type II		Type III		Type IV	Type V	
	See footnotes	A	B	A	B	A	B	HT	A	B
I-1 Condition 2 (Custodial care– evacuate with limited assistance)	NS[2,3]	UL/UL	9/55,000	4/19,000	3/10,000	4/16,500	3/10,000	4/18,000	3/10,500	2/4,500
	S1	1/UL	1/220,000	1/76,000	1/40,000	1/66,000	1/40,000	1/72,000	1/42,000	1/18,000
	SM	UL/UL	10/165,000	5/57,000	3/30,000	4/49,500	3/30,000	4/54,000	3/31,500	2/13,500
I-2	NS[2,4]	UL/UL	4/UL	2/15,000	1/11,000	1/12,000	NP	1/12,000	1/9,500	NP
	S1	1/UL	1/UL	1/60,000	1/44,000	1/48,000	NP	1/48,000	1/38,000	NP
	SM	UL/UL	8/UL	6/45,000	4/33,000	6/36,000	NP	1/36,000	1/28,500	NP

Allowable Building Heights in Stories Above Grade Plane (Table 504.4) and Graphic Allowable Areas (Table 506.2) [based on construction type, occupancy, and sprinklers]

Occupancy Classification	Sprinklers	Type 1		Type II		Type III		Type IV	Type V	
	See footnotes	A	B	A	B	A	B	HT	A	B
I-3	NS[2,3]	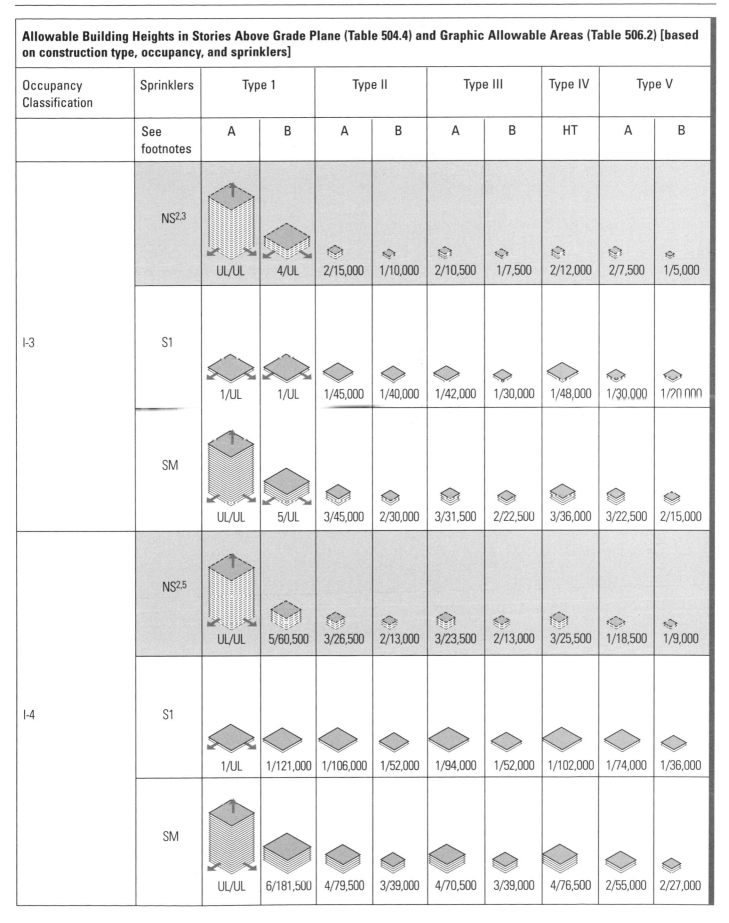 UL/UL	4/UL	2/15,000	1/10,000	2/10,500	1/7,500	2/12,000	2/7,500	1/5,000
	S1	1/UL	1/UL	1/45,000	1/40,000	1/42,000	1/30,000	1/48,000	1/30,000	1/20,000
	SM	UL/UL	5/UL	3/45,000	2/30,000	3/31,500	2/22,500	3/36,000	3/22,500	2/15,000
I-4	NS[2,5]	UL/UL	5/60,500	3/26,500	2/13,000	3/23,500	2/13,000	3/25,500	1/18,500	1/9,000
	S1	1/UL	1/121,000	1/106,000	1/52,000	1/94,000	1/52,000	1/102,000	1/74,000	1/36,000
	SM	UL/UL	6/181,500	4/79,500	3/39,000	4/70,500	3/39,000	4/76,500	2/55,000	2/27,000

Allowable Building Heights in Stories Above Grade Plane (Table 504.4) and Graphic Allowable Areas (Table 506.2) [based on construction type, occupancy, and sprinklers]

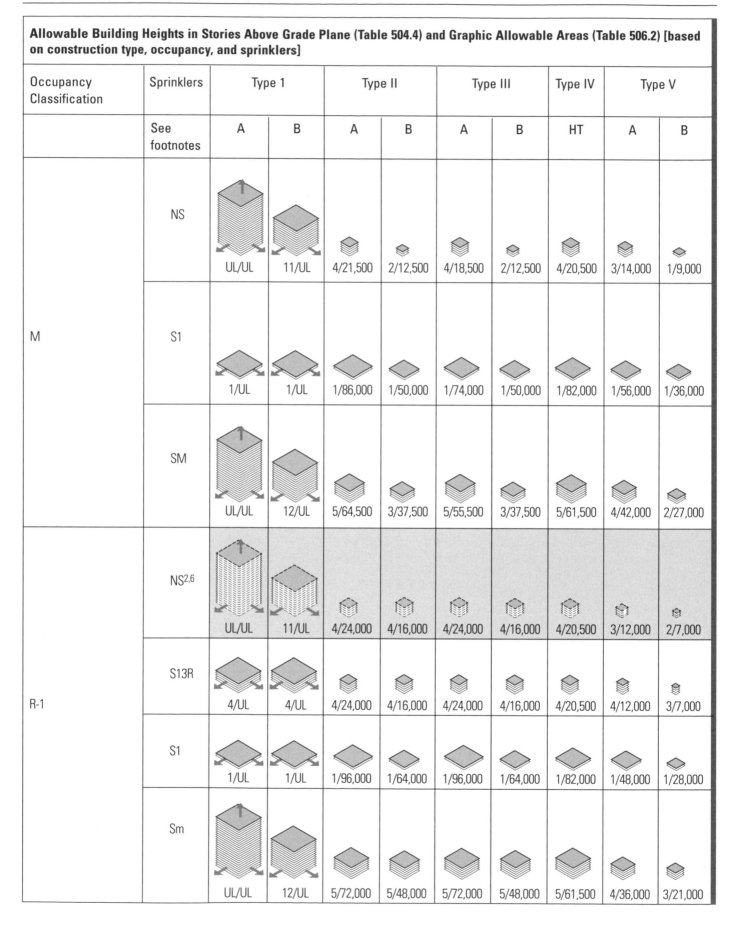

Occupancy Classification	Sprinklers	Type 1		Type II		Type III		Type IV	Type V	
	See footnotes	A	B	A	B	A	B	HT	A	B
M	NS	UL/UL	11/UL	4/21,500	2/12,500	4/18,500	2/12,500	4/20,500	3/14,000	1/9,000
	S1	1/UL	1/UL	1/86,000	1/50,000	1/74,000	1/50,000	1/82,000	1/56,000	1/36,000
	SM	UL/UL	12/UL	5/64,500	3/37,500	5/55,500	3/37,500	5/61,500	4/42,000	2/27,000
R-1	NS[2,6]	UL/UL	11/UL	4/24,000	4/16,000	4/24,000	4/16,000	4/20,500	3/12,000	2/7,000
	S13R	4/UL	4/UL	4/24,000	4/16,000	4/24,000	4/16,000	4/20,500	4/12,000	3/7,000
	S1	1/UL	1/UL	1/96,000	1/64,000	1/96,000	1/64,000	1/82,000	1/48,000	1/28,000
	Sm	UL/UL	12/UL	5/72,000	5/48,000	5/72,000	5/48,000	5/61,500	4/36,000	3/21,000

Allowable Building Heights in Stories Above Grade Plane (Table 504.4) and Graphic Allowable Areas (Table 506.2) [based on construction type, occupancy, and sprinklers]

Occupancy Classification	Sprinklers	Type 1		Type II		Type III		Type IV	Type V	
	See footnotes	A	B	A	B	A	B	HT	A	B
R-2	NS[2,6]	UL/UL	11/UL	4/24,000	4/16,000	4/24,000	4/16,000	4/20,500	3/12,000	2/7,000
	S13R	4/UL	4/UL	4/24,000	4/16,000	4/24,000	4/16,000	4/20,500	4/12,000	3/7,000
	S1	1/UL	1/UL	1/96,000	1/64,000	1/96,000	1/64,000	1/82,000	1/48,000	1/28,000
	SM	UL/UL	12/UL	5/72,000	5/48,000	5/72,000	5/48,000	5/61,500	4/36,000	3/21,000
R-3	NS[2,6]	UL/UL	11/UL	4/UL	4/UL	4/UL	4/UL	4/UL	3/UL	3/UL
	S13R	4/UL	4/UL	4/UL	4/UL	4/UL	4/UL	4/UL	4/UL	4/UL
	S1	1/UL	1/UL	1/UL	1/UL	1/UL	1/UL	1/UL	1/UL	1/UL
	SM	UL/UL	12/UL	5/UL	5/UL	5/UL	5/UL	5/UL	4/UL	4/UL

Allowable Building Heights in Stories Above Grade Plane (Table 504.4) and Graphic Allowable Areas (Table 506.2) [based on construction type, occupancy, and sprinklers]

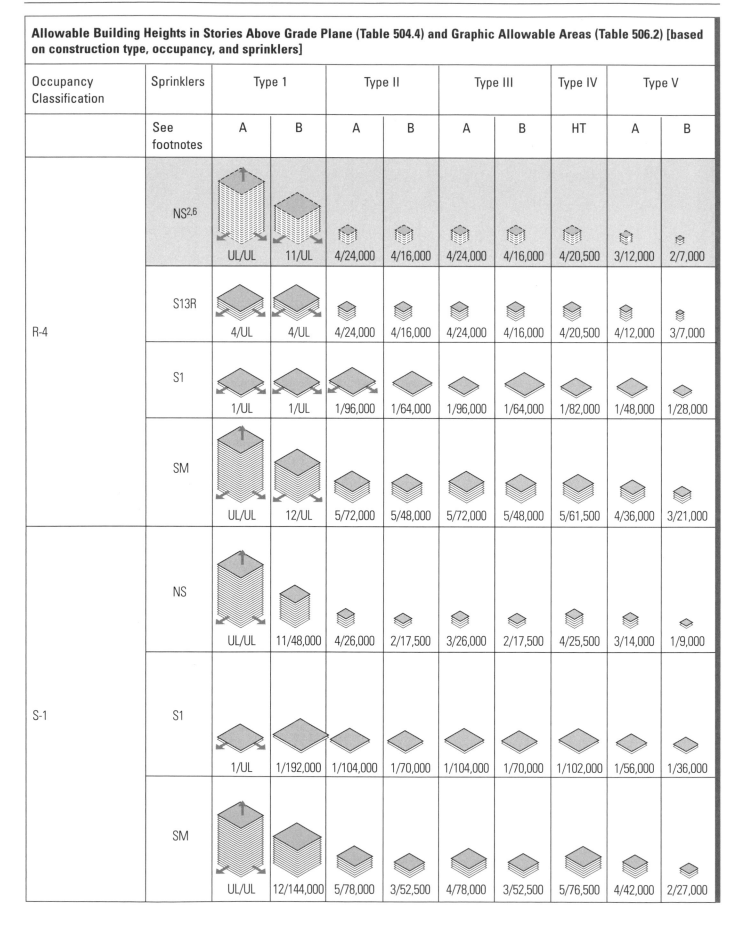

Occupancy Classification	Sprinklers	Type 1		Type II		Type III		Type IV	Type V	
	See footnotes	A	B	A	B	A	B	HT	A	B
R-4	NS[2,6]	UL/UL	11/UL	4/24,000	4/16,000	4/24,000	4/16,000	4/20,500	3/12,000	2/7,000
	S13R	4/UL	4/UL	4/24,000	4/16,000	4/24,000	4/16,000	4/20,500	4/12,000	3/7,000
	S1	1/UL	1/UL	1/96,000	1/64,000	1/96,000	1/64,000	1/82,000	1/48,000	1/28,000
	SM	UL/UL	12/UL	5/72,000	5/48,000	5/72,000	5/48,000	5/61,500	4/36,000	3/21,000
S-1	NS	UL/UL	11/48,000	4/26,000	2/17,500	3/26,000	2/17,500	4/25,500	3/14,000	1/9,000
	S1	1/UL	1/192,000	1/104,000	1/70,000	1/104,000	1/70,000	1/102,000	1/56,000	1/36,000
	SM	UL/UL	12/144,000	5/78,000	3/52,500	4/78,000	3/52,500	5/76,500	4/42,000	2/27,000

Allowable Building Heights in Stories Above Grade Plane (Table 504.4) and Graphic Allowable Areas (Table 506.2) [based on construction type, occupancy, and sprinklers]

Occupancy Classification	Sprinklers	Type 1		Type II		Type III		Type IV	Type V	
	See footnotes	A	B	A	B	A	B	HT	A	B
S-2	NS	UL/UL	11/79,000	5/39,000	3/26,000	4/39,000	3/26,000	4/38,500	4/21,000	2/13,500
	S1	I/UL	1/316,000	1/156,000	1/104,000	1/156,000	1/104,000	1/154,000	1/84,000	1/54,000
	SM	UL/UL	12/237,000	6/117,000	4/78,000	5/117,000	4/78,000	5/115,500	5/63,000	3/40,500
U	NS	UL/UL	5/35,500	4/19,500	2/8,500	3/14,000	2/8,500	4/18,000	2/9,000	1/5,500
	S1	1/UL	1/142,000	1/76,000	1/34,000	1/56,000	1/34,000	1/72,000	1/36,000	1/22,000
	SM	UL/UL	6/106,500	5/57,000	3/25,500	4/42,000	3/25,500	5/54,000	3/27,000	2/16,500

Footnotes:
1 New H occupancies must be sprinklered.
2 Non-sprinklered occupancies are included only for evaluation of existing building height per the IEBC.
3 New I-1 and I-3 occupancies must be sprinklered.
4 New I-2 occupancies must be sprinklered.
5 For new I-4 occupancies see Exceptions 2 and 3 to § 903.2.6 for daycares on the ground floor with direct egress or a sprinklered egress path if above the ground floor.
6 All R occupancies must be sprinklered.

Allowable Building Area Determination

The allowable area of a building is to be determined in accordance with the applicable provisions of § 506.2.1 through 506.2.4 and § 506.3 using the values from Table 506.2. The calculations for area increase have been changed dramatically from the way area increases were done under prior editions of the IBC. As noted above, the increases for heights in feet and stories based on sprinklers and construction type are now built into the tables in § 504. For those code users familiar with the old calculation methods it is very important to remember that the new methods are intended to yield the same results in terms of allowable building areas, and heights as well, as were allowed under previous editions of the IBC. Experienced code users may want to verify their calculations for allowable heights and areas using the new formulas against determinations for the allowances using formulas from the prior version of the IBC. This will help familiarize experienced users with the new methods while minimizing calculation errors. We have presented here in the new edition only the new formulas to avoid confusing new code users for whom such comparisons would not be helpful. This will also familiarize experienced code users with the procedures found in the new edition of the code.

Frontage Increases

§ 506 specifies that the areas set by Table 506.2 may be modified based on how much open space adjoins the building, including streets and open space. This is known as "frontage." As in prior editions of the code the equation numbering in Chapter 5 is somewhat misleading. The values for frontage increase (If) are determined per Equations 5-4 and 5-5 and then used in Equations 5-1, 5-2, and 5-3.

We will address the use of Equations 5-5 and 5-4 in reverse order and then go on to describe how to use them in calculating area modifications.

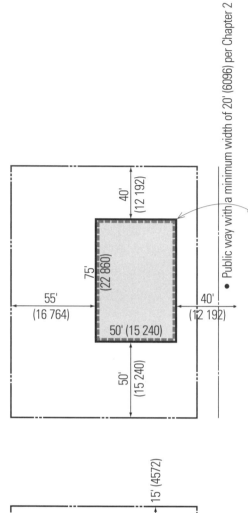

- Every building must adjoin or have access to a public way in order to receive area increases. When a building has more than 25 percent of its perimeter opening onto a public way or open space at least 20' (6096) wide, the building's area may be increased based on the added width of the public way(s) and/or open space(s) and the extent of the building perimeter surrounded by them.

- **Equation 5-5:**

$$
\begin{aligned}
I_f &= [F/P - 0.25)\, W/30 \\
&= [250/250 - 0.25]\, 40/30* \\
&= [1.0 - 0.25]1* \\
&= [0.75] = 75\%
\end{aligned}
$$

where

I_f = area increase due to frontage

F = building perimeter fronting on a public way or open space of 20' (6096) minimum width

P = total perimeter of the entire building

W = width of public way or open space (feet) per § 506.3.2

*W/30 cannot exceed 1.0 per § 506.3.2 with one exception: W/30 may be up to 2 when the building meets all criteria of § 507 except for compliance with the 60' (18 288) public way or yard requirement.

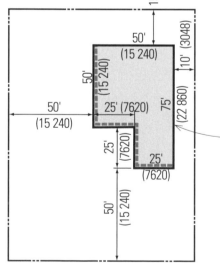

$$
\begin{aligned}
I_f &= [F/P - 0.25]\, W/30 \\
&= [125/250 - 0.25]\, 50/30* \\
&= [0.5 - 0.25]1* \\
&= [0.25] = 25\%
\end{aligned}
$$

------ Perimeter meeting criteria for frontage increase as per Equation 5-5.

- **Equation 5-4:**

Weighted Average (W) = $\dfrac{(L_1 \times W_1 + L_2 \times W_2 + L_xW_x...)}{F}$

where:

L_n = Length of exterior perimeter wall
W_n = Width of open space @ wall L_n
F = Building perimeter with $W_n \geq 20'$ (6096)

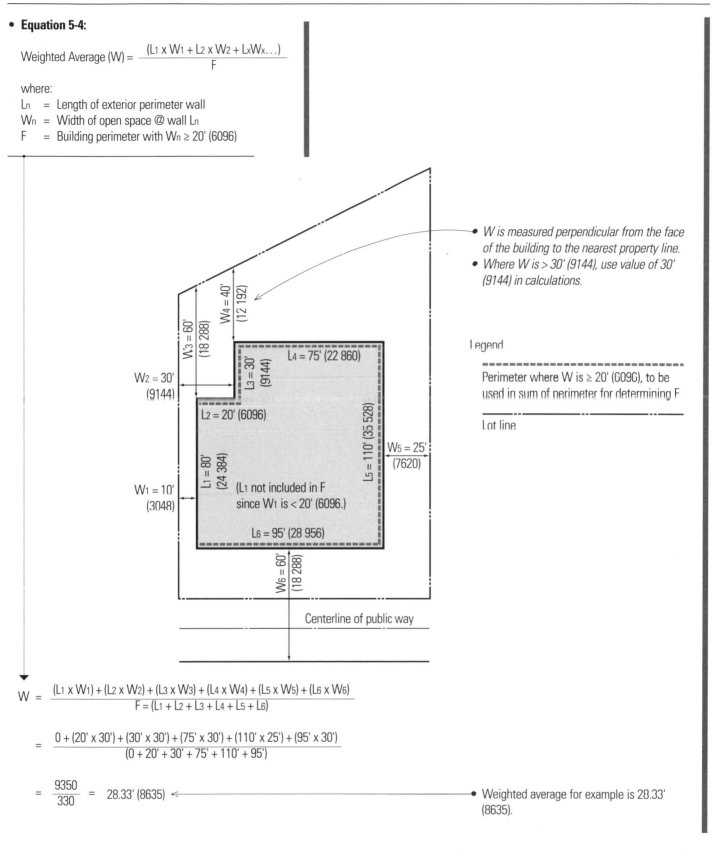

- W is measured perpendicular from the face of the building to the nearest property line.
- Where W is > 30' (9144), use value of 30' (9144) in calculations.

Legend

`-------------------------------------`

Perimeter where W is ≥ 20' (6096), to be used in sum of perimeter for determining F

Lot line

$W_4 = 40'$ (12 192)

$W'_3 = 60'$ (18 288)

$L_4 = 75'$ (22 860)

$L_3 = 30'$ (9144)

$W_2 = 30'$ (9144)

$L_2 = 20'$ (6096)

$L_5 = 110'$ (35 528)

$W_5 = 25'$ (7620)

$L_1 = 80'$ (24 384)

(L1 not included in F since W1 is < 20' (6096.)

$W_1 = 10'$ (3048)

$L_6 = 95'$ (28 956)

$W_6 = 60'$ (18 288)

Centerline of public way

$W = \dfrac{(L_1 \times W_1) + (L_2 \times W_2) + (L_3 \times W_3) + (L_4 \times W_4) + (L_5 \times W_5) + (L_6 \times W_6)}{F = (L_1 + L_2 + L_3 + L_4 + L_5 + L_6)}$

$= \dfrac{0 + (20' \times 30') + (30' \times 30') + (75' \times 30') + (110' \times 25') + (95' \times 30')}{(0 + 20' + 30' + 75' + 110' + 95')}$

$= \dfrac{9350}{330} = 28.33'$ (8635)

- Weighted average for example is 28.33' (8635).

§ 506.2 contains three formulas for calculating area modifications. The formulas make use of the frontage increase allowable per Equations 5-4 or 5-5. It is very important to keep in mind that while part of the area determination is based on whether the building is to have sprinklers, the "NS" value is to be used as well, regardless of whether the building is sprinklered. Be sure that for sprinklered buildings you do not duplicate the tabular values for sprinklered buildings, but use the NS values in the appropriate location in the equations.

The first formula is Equation 5-1 from § 506.2.1, which is for single occupancy, one-story buildings. The building is to have no more than a single story above the grade plane. The basic tabular area is taken from Table 506.2 and is based on the construction type and sprinkler status of the building in question.

For our example we have assumed a sprinklered B occupancy building of Type IIIA construction. The tabular area is thus for a sprinklered, single-occupancy, single-story building with added increase for frontage based on location on property.

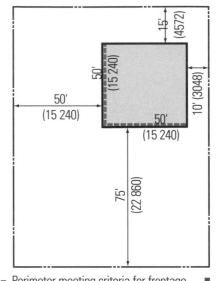

– – – – – – – Perimeter meeting criteria for frontage increase per Equation 5-5.

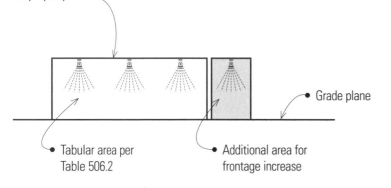

Grade plane

Tabular area per Table 506.2

Additional area for frontage increase

- **Equation 5-1:**

$$A_a = A_t + (NS \times I_f)$$

where:
A_a = Allowable area (square feet).
A_t = Tabular allowable area factor (NS, S1, or S13R value, as applicable) in accordance with Table 506.2.
NS = Tabular allowable area factor in accordance with Table 506.2 for nonsprinklered buildings (*regardless of whether the building is sprinklered*).
I_f = Area factor increase due to frontage (percent) as calculated in accordance with § 506.3. [Equations 5-4 and 5-5]

- Frontage Increase per § 506.3 (with Equation 5-5)

$$
\begin{aligned}
I_f &= [F/P - 0.25]\, W/30 \\
&= [(50' + 50')/(50' \text{ @ all 4 sides}) - 0.25]\, 50/30* \\
&= [100/200 - 0.25]\, 1* \\
&= [0.5 - 0.25]\, 1* \\
&= [0.25] = 25\%
\end{aligned}
$$

*W/30 cannot exceed 1.0 per § 506.3.2 with one exception: W/30 may be up to 2 when the building meets all criteria of § 507 except for compliance with the 60' (18 288) public way or yard requirement.

- Per Equation 5-1:

$$
\begin{aligned}
A_a &= A_t + (NS \times I_f) \\
A_a &= 114,000 \text{ sf } [10,591 \text{ m}^2] + (\,28,500 \text{sf } [2648 \text{ m}^2] \times 0.25) \\
&= 121,125 \text{ sf } [11,253 \text{ m}^2]
\end{aligned}
$$

The second formula is Equation 5-2, which is used for multistory buildings with a single occupancy group. This takes the allowable areas for single-story buildings and adds a factor for stories greater than one.

For this example, we assume a 3-story, B occupancy, Type IIIA building with sprinklers and the same frontage increase of 25% from the previous example.

- **Equation 5-2:**

$$A_a = A_t + (NS \times I_f) \times S_a$$

where:
A_a = Allowable area (square feet).
A_t = Tabular allowable area factor (NS, S1, or S13R value, as applicable) in accordance with Table 506.2.
NS = Tabular allowable area factor in accordance with Table 506.2 for nonsprinklered buildings (*regardless of whether the building is sprinklered*).
I_f = Area factor increase due to frontage (percent) as calculated in accordance with § 506.3. [Equations 5-4 and 5-5]
S_a = Actual number of stories above grade plane, not to exceed 3 for nonsprinklered buildings and not to exceed 4 for sprinklered Group R buildings with a 13R sprinkler system.

- Frontage Increase per § 506.3 (with Equation 5-5)

$$
\begin{aligned}
I_f &= [F/P - 0.25] \, W/30 \\
&= [(50' + 50')/(50' @ \text{ all 4 sides}) \quad 0.25] \, 50/30* \\
&= [100/200 - 0.25] \, 1* \\
&= [0.5 - 0.25] \, 1* \\
&= [0.25] = 25\%
\end{aligned}
$$

- Per Equation 5-2:

$$
\begin{aligned}
A_a &= A_t + (NS \times I_f) \times S_a \\
A_a &= 85{,}500 \text{ sf } [7943 \text{ m}^2] + (28{,}500\text{sf } [2648 \text{ m}^2] \times 0.25) \\
&= 92{,}625 \text{ sf } [8605 \text{ m}^2] \times 3 \\
&= 277{,}875 \text{ sf } [25\,814 \text{ m}^2]
\end{aligned}
$$

- Tabular area per Table 506.2

- Additional area for frontage increase

- Included sprinkler increase in Table 506.2

- Grade plane

- Single basement, no larger than the allowable area (A_a) for a building with no more than one story above the grade plane. This could result in a code-compliant basement that is larger than the floors above.

The 2015 IBC height and area calculation procedure as described in the supporting statement for the code change proposal is:

- **Step 1**: Read charging language at § 503.1.

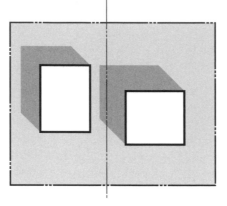

- *Determine the height and area of the proposed building and whether multiple buildings on a single lot are to be treated as a single building or as multiple buildings with assumed lines between them.*

- **Step 2**: Read charging language at § 504.1.

- *The height, in feet, and the number of stories of a building shall be determined based on the type of construction, occupancy classification, and whether there is an automatic sprinkler system installed throughout the building.*

- **Step 3**: Read § 504.1 through 504.3 and determine allowable building height in feet.

From Table 504.3			
Occupancy Classification	Sprinklers	Type III	
		A	B
A, B, E, F, M, S, U	NS	65' (19.8 m)	55' (16.8 m)
	S	85' (25.9 m)	75' (22.9 m)

- *Determine the height in feet of the proposed building using Table 504.3.*

- **Step 4**: Read § 504.4 and determine allowable building height in stories.

From Table 504.4			
Occupancy Classification	Sprinklers See footnotes	Type III	
		A	B
B	NS	5/28,500	3/19,000
	S1	1/114,000	1/76,000
	SM	6/85,500	4/57,000

- *Determine the height in stories of the proposed building using Table 504.4.*

- **Step 5**: Read § 506.1 through 506.2.3 and determine the values required for determining maximum building floor area in Equation 5-2. If need be, go to § 506.3. (See Step 6).

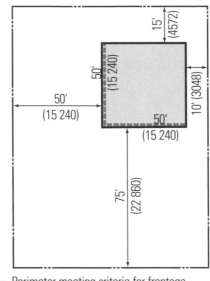

-------- Perimeter meeting criteria for frontage increase per Equation 5-5.

- Determine what frontage increases are available for the proposed building based on its location on property.

- **Step 6**: Read § 506.3 through 506.3.3 and determine applicable allowable area frontage increase from Equations 5-2 and 5-3.

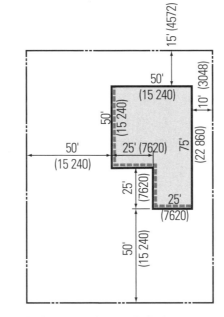

-------- Perimeter meeting criteria for frontage increase as per Equation 5-2.

- Determine if weighted averages are necessary for frontages per Equation 5-4 or whether basic frontage increase formulas can be used per Equation 5-5.

- **Step 7**: Using values obtained in Steps 5 and 6 determine the maximum building floor area using Equation 5-2, 5-3, or 5-4.

- *Insert values from Equations 5-4 and 5-5 into Equations 5-1, 5-2, or 5-3, depending on configuration of the building.*

- **Step 8**: Determine maximum allowable area per story for the building using Equation 5-2, 5-3, or 5-4.

- *Multiply allowable area by number of stories based on allowable increases for unsprinklered or sprinklered buildings.*

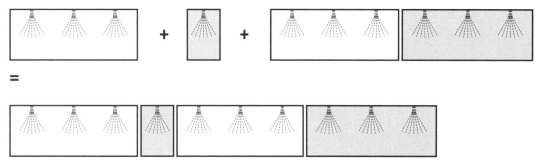

- Finished.

UNLIMITED-AREA BUILDINGS

§ 507 allows buildings of other than Type I construction to be of unlimited area when certain conditions are met. These exceptions overlay the height, story, and area tables in Chapter 5 and are summarized in the table below.

Unlimited-Area Buildings

Section	507.2	507.3	507.4	
	Nonsprinklered 60' yards (18 288)	Sprinklered 60' yards (18 288)	Sprinklered 60' yards (18 288)	Notes Yard = permanent open space around the sides of a building
Maximum Height	1 story	1 story	2 story	
Occupancy				
A-4	—	UL (other than Type V contruction)	—	§ 507.1 has been clarified regarding basements. Basements not more than one story below grade plane are permitted in unlimited area buildings.
B	—	UL	UL	
F-1	—	UL	UL	
F-2	UL	UL	UL	
M	—	UL	UL	
S-1	—	UL	UL	
S-2	UL	UL	UL	
Special Provisions	See section number at left column.			
A-3, Type II (§ 507.6)	—	UL	—	No stage other than a platform
A-3, Types III and IV (§ 507.7)	—	UL	—	No stage other than a platform, within 21" (533) of grade, with egress ramps.
E (§ 507.10)	—	UL	—	Construction Types II, III-A, IV only; 2 exits per classroom with 1 direct to exterior.
H-5 in Mixed Occupancies (§ 507.9)	—	UL	—	Buildings containing an H-5 occupancy are to meet these conditions: 1. Be of Type I or Type II construction. 2. H-5 occupancy is separated from other occupancies per § 415.11 and 508.4. 3. H-5 area may not exceed maximum allowable area per § 503.1 as modified by § 506 unless, per the exception, the H-5 area is subdivided into appropriate areas by 2-hour barriers.
Motion Picture Theaters (§ 507.11)	—	UL	—	Construction Type I or II only; yard reduction allowed if also compliant with § 507.5.

See illustration on facing page

- It is permissible to have other occupancies than those listed in the allowances for unlimted area buildings, such as having an A-2 restaurant in a retail space, if the occupancy meets the criteria for "Accessory" occupancies per § 508.2.

- For certain buildings, the required 60' (18 288) yard may be reduced to 40' (12 192) for not more than 75% of building perimeter if the exterior wall facing the reduced open space and openings in the exterior wall have a minimum fire resistance rating of 3 hours.

- Open space may be measured using the entire width of a public way to meet the 60' (18 288) criteria.

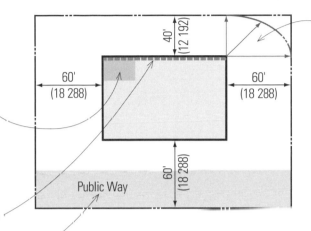

- As opposed to measurements for fire separation distance, this open space is primarily for fire department access and is to be measured "in all directions" when determining compliance with this code section.

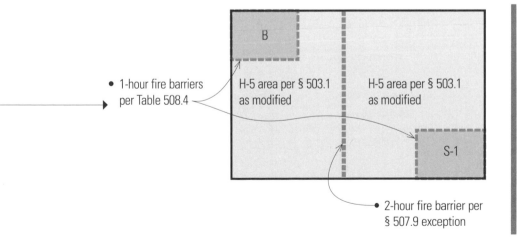

- 1-hour fire barriers per Table 508.4

- 2-hour fire barrier per § 507.9 exception

§ 508 Mixed Use and Occupancy

This section addresses three concepts that involve having more than one occupancy in a single building. They are:

- Accessory Occupancies (§. 508.2)
- Nonseparated Occupancies (§ 508.3)
- Separated Occupancies (§ 508.4)

Per exceptions to § 508.1, the following are not considered mixed occupancies for the purposes of applying § 508: occupancies separated per § 510; hazardous materials in separate buildings when required by Table 415.6.2; and the areas within live-work spaces complying with § 419.

Accessory Occupancies

When the occupancy contains a distinctly different ancillary use to the main occupancy of a building and aggregate accessory occupancies do not occupy more than 10 percent of the floor area of the story in which they are located based on the tabular area allowed for various nonsprinklered occupancies by Table 506.2, the accessory use need not be separated from the primary occupancy. Exceptions exist for hazardous uses or when required as an "incidental use."

- *Accessory occupancies are still to be classified by their uses in accordance with Chapter 3 of the code.*
- *Accessory occupancy areas need not be separated from the primary occupancy if they meet the criteria of § 508.2.3 as described at left on this page.*

- *The allowable building area and height is to be based on the main occupancy.*

- *Separations are required for the following accessory occupancies:*

- *Uses incidental to the basic or main occupancy per § 509.*

- *Group H-2, H-3, H-4 and H-5 accessory occupancies are to be separated per § 508.4.*

- *Dwelling units and sleeping units in I-1, R-1, R-2, and R-3 occupancies are to be separated from each other and from contiguous occupancies per § 420.*

Mixed Occupancies

When a building has a mix of occupancies that are each distinct or extensive enough to be considered as separate uses, each use is considered a separate and distinct occupancy. The mix of occupancies is addressed in several ways in addition to being treated as accessory occupancies:

1. **Nonseparated Occupancies**
   For nonseparated occupancies, the entire building is regulated according to the most restrictive of the height, area, and fire-protection requirements for each of the multiple occupancies under consideration.

2. **Separated Occupancies**
   Separated occupancies may require that an occupancy separation with a fire-resistance rating as defined by Table 508.4 be provided between the occupancies.

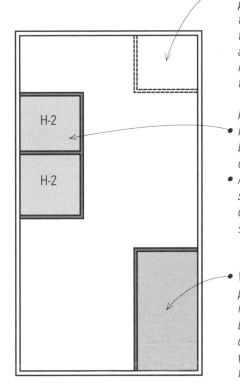

• When using nonseparated occupancy criteria per § 508.3, uses need not be separated from one another or from the remainder of the building, but the allowable height, area, and construction type for the entire building is governed by the most restrictive criteria for each of the unseparated uses.

Per exceptions to § 508.3.3:
• H-2, H-3, H-4 and H-5 occupancies must be separated, even in nonseparated occupancies.
• Also, I-1, R-1, R-2, and R-3 dwelling and sleeping units must be separated from each other and from contiguous occupancies per § 420.

• When using separated occupancy criteria per § 508.4, different uses may need to be separated from each other with a fire barrier, but the allowable height area and construction types for the building as a whole are determined by the requirements for each separate area.

Allowable Building Height and Building Area for Nonseparated Occupancies with M and A-2 Occupancies

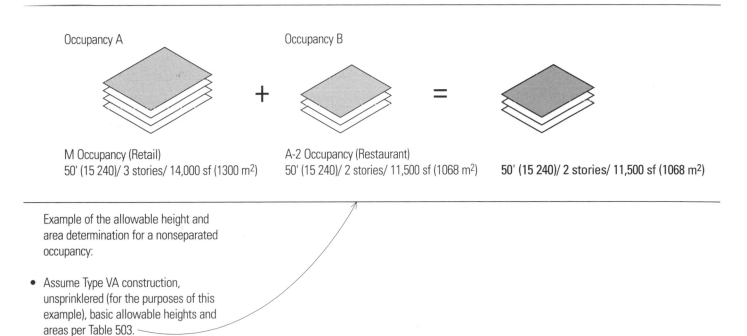

Occupancy A

M Occupancy (Retail)
50' (15 240)/ 3 stories/ 14,000 sf (1300 m²)

Occupancy B

A-2 Occupancy (Restaurant)
50' (15 240)/ 2 stories/ 11,500 sf (1068 m²)

50' (15 240)/ 2 stories/ 11,500 sf (1068 m²)

Example of the allowable height and area determination for a nonseparated occupancy:

• Assume Type VA construction, unsprinklered (for the purposes of this example), basic allowable heights and areas per Table 503.

MIXED USE AND OCCUPANCY

Example for a separated-occupancy height and area determination. Assume the same construction type and occupancies as on preceding page: Type V-A construction, unsprinklered, M-Occupancy (Retail/ 10,000 sf/929 m2), and A-2 Occupancy (Restaurant/ 3000 sf/279 m2), located on second floor.

Criteria	A-2 Occupancy		M Occupancy	
	Allowable (Chapter 5)	Proposed	Allowable (Chapter 5)	Proposed
Area Height (feet)	50' (15 240)	<50' (15 240)	50' (15 240)	<50' (15 240)
Area Height (stories)	2 stories	On first floor	3 stories	3 stories
Floor Area/Story (sf/m2)	11,500/1068 m2	3000/279 m2	14,000/1300 m2	10,000/929 m2

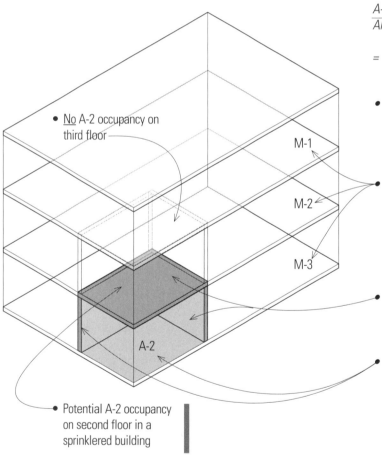

- No A-2 occupancy on third floor

M-1

M-2

M-3

A-2

- Potential A-2 occupancy on second floor in a sprinklered building

Calculation for the second floor per the example and §. 508.4.2 :

$$\frac{A\text{-}2 \ Actual \ Area}{Allowable \ Area} + \frac{M \ Actual \ Area}{Allowable \ Area} < 1.00$$

$$= \frac{3,000 \ sf}{11,500 \ sf} + \frac{10,000 \ sf}{14,000 \ sf} = 0.26 + 0.71 = 0.98 < 1.00\ldots OK$$

- *Each occupancy area is to comply with the height and area restrictions contained in § 503.*

- *The M occupancy area may be three stories in height and M uses may be located on any of the three floor levels since Table 503 allows the M occupancy to be three stories in height.*

- *The A-2 occupancy cannot be located above the second floor since an A-2 occupancy can only be 2 stories in height per Table 503.*

- *A-2 occupancy is to be completely separated from M occupancy by 2-hour fire barriers per § 707 and horizontal assemblies per § 712.*

Incidental Uses

Uses or occupancies that are incidental to the main occupancy are not considered to have enough impact to warrant their classification as an occupancy. The structure or portion thereof must be one of the uses listed in Table 509. These uses are typically considered to have a higher level of fire or safety risk than the occupancies within which they occur and Table 509 requires addtional protection or isolation from the areas within which they occur.

When the occupancy of a building contains one or more incidental uses as defined in Table 509, the areas are considered part of the main occupancy but require fire-resistance rated separations from the rest of the occupancy according to the requirements listed in the table. Note that separation requirements for incidental accessory occupancies are not applicable to dwelling units.

Designation of incidental use areas is limited to those uses listed in Table 509. Note that incidental uses do <u>not</u> change the occupancy group of the area where they occur. That is why they are called "incidental."

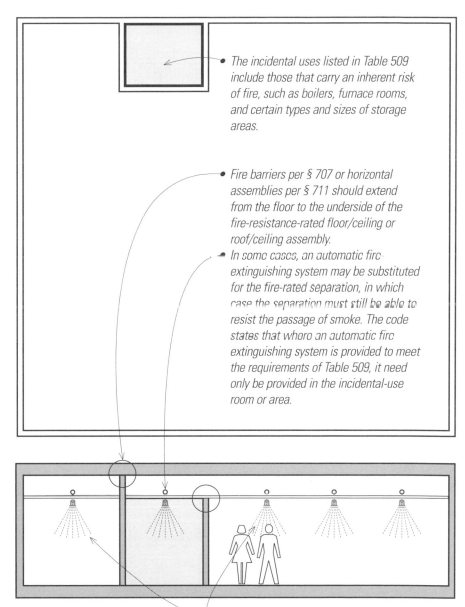

- *The incidental uses listed in Table 509 include those that carry an inherent risk of fire, such as boilers, furnace rooms, and certain types and sizes of storage areas.*

- *Fire barriers per § 707 or horizontal assemblies per § 711 should extend from the floor to the underside of the fire-resistance-rated floor/ceiling or roof/ceiling assembly.*

- *In some cases, an automatic fire extinguishing system may be substituted for the fire-rated separation, in which case the separation must still be able to resist the passage of smoke. The code states that where an automatic fire extinguishing system is provided to meet the requirements of Table 509, it need only be provided in the incidental-use room or area.*

- *The code notes in § 509.4.2 that even where Table 509 allows just the use of a sprinkler system to protect an incidental use, barriers around the use must be smoke-resistant.*
- *The code states in § 509.4.2.1 that "only the space occupied by the incidental use need be equipped with such a system." This is less than the full sprinkler provisions of NFPA 13, but based on the code conflict resolution provisions in § 102.4.1, the code allows for a very limited system instead of requiring the sprinklers throughout the building or in surrounding spaces.*

- *Because § 509.4.2.1 only requires the sprinkler system within the incidental use area, such a limited sprinkler system will not qualify a building for such things as area increases that are granted for provision of sprinkler systems throughout the building.*

The layout of the code places Table 509 after the text for that section. Do not confuse Table 508.4 regarding occupancy separations with the incidental use Table 509.

As examples we have highlighted the incidental uses most likely to be encountered in building design:

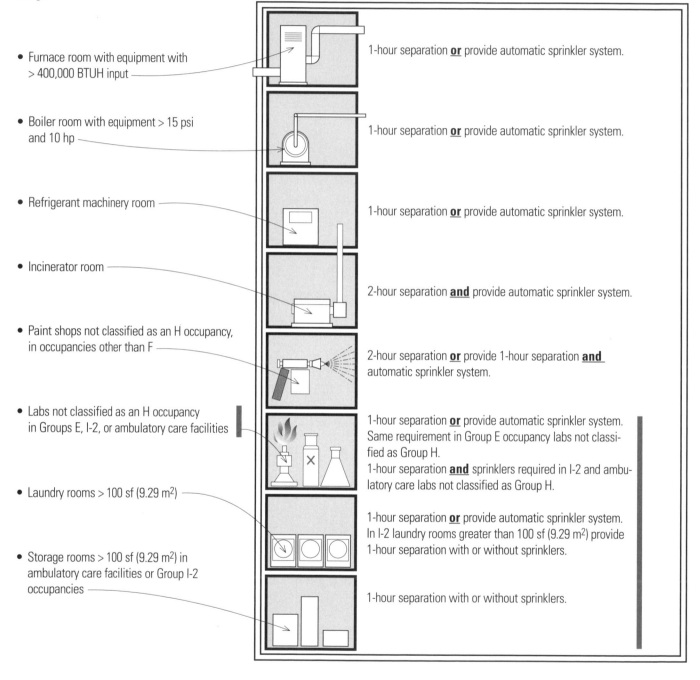

- Furnace room with equipment with > 400,000 BTUH input

  1-hour separation **or** provide automatic sprinkler system.

- Boiler room with equipment > 15 psi and 10 hp

  1-hour separation **or** provide automatic sprinkler system.

- Refrigerant machinery room

  1-hour separation **or** provide automatic sprinkler system.

- Incinerator room

  2-hour separation **and** provide automatic sprinkler system.

- Paint shops not classified as an H occupancy, in occupancies other than F

  2-hour separation **or** provide 1-hour separation **and** automatic sprinkler system.

- Labs not classified as an H occupancy in Groups E, I-2, or ambulatory care facilities

  1-hour separation **or** provide automatic sprinkler system. Same requirement in Group E occupancy labs not classified as Group H.
  1-hour separation **and** sprinklers required in I-2 and ambulatory care labs not classified as Group H.

- Laundry rooms > 100 sf (9.29 m²)

  1-hour separation **or** provide automatic sprinkler system. In I-2 laundry rooms greater than 100 sf (9.29 m²) provide 1-hour separation with or without sprinklers.

- Storage rooms > 100 sf (9.29 m²) in ambulatory care facilities or Group I-2 occupancies

  1-hour separation with or without sprinklers.

§ 510 is devoted to exceptions to the provisions of Tables 504.3, 504.4, and 506.2, and the other sections in Chapter 5. These exceptions apply only when all of the conditions in the subsections are met. These conditions are based on specific combinations of occupancy groups and construction types. These special provisions were code responses developed over time to meet construction conditions found in the jurisdictions of the model codes that preceded the IBC. These special provisions will usually give the designer greater flexibility in meeting the requirements of the building program than will § 503.1 alone. These conditions should be annotated in that table for reference by the designer to be certain that they are not overlooked when commencing design and code analysis.

Per § 510.2, parts of buildings shall be considered as separate and distinct buildings for the purpose of determining area limitations, continuity of fire walls, limitations on the number of stories, and type of construction <u>when all of the following conditions are met</u>:

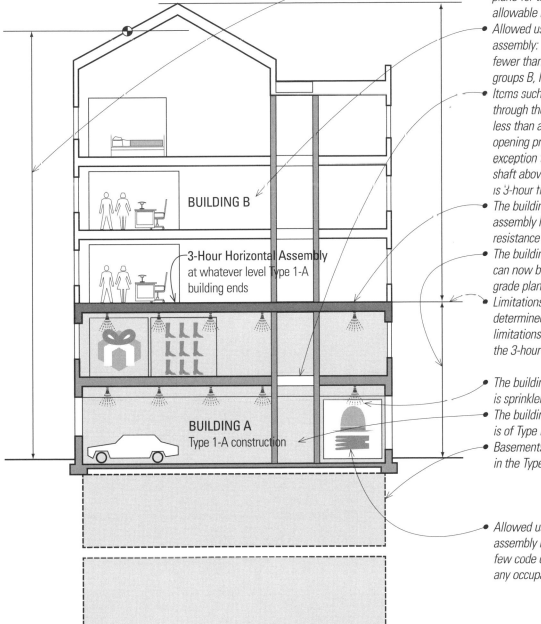

BUILDING B

3-Hour Horizontal Assembly
at whatever level Type 1-A
building ends

BUILDING A
Type 1-A construction

- *The maximum building height in feet is per § 504.3 and measured from the grade plane for the building having the smaller allowable height;*
- *Allowed uses above the horizontal assembly: assembly occupancies with fewer than 300 occupants and occupancy groups B, M, R, or S;*
- *Items such as shafts and stair enclosures through the horizontal assembly have not less than a 2-hour fire-resistance rating with opening protectives per § 716.5. (There is an exception to § 510.2, which allows a 1-hour shaft above if the lower portion of the shaft is 3-hour fire-resistance rated.);*
- *The buildings are separated by a horizontal assembly having a minimum 3-hour fire-resistance rating;*
- *The building below the horizontal assembly can now be more than one story above grade plane;*
- *Limitations for the number of stories is determined for each building; thus, the story limitations for Building B start at the top of the 3-hour horizontal assembly.*

- *The building below the horizontal assembly is sprinklered per § 903.3.1.1.*
- *The building below the horizontal assembly is of Type I-A construction.*
- *Basements below grade plane are allowed in the Type I portion of the building.*

- *Allowed uses below the horizontal assembly have been expanded over the last few code cycles and now basically include any occupancy other than Group H.*

Group S-2 Enclosed Parking Garage with S-2 Open Parking Garage Above

All parking garages for the storage of private motor vehicles are classified as S-2 occupancies; thus, they need not be separated. § 510.3 uses the same principle as that for mixed-use buildings in § 510.2. The criteria are different but § 510.3 basically allows an open garage to be built over an enclosed garage while treating the transition between them as a new ground plane when fire-resistance requirements are met.

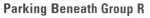

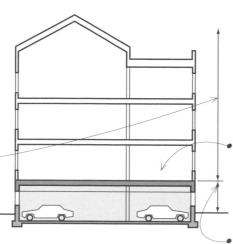

- *The sum of the ratios of actual areas divided by allowable areas shall be less than 1. The allowable areas for open and enclosed parking garages differ, per § 406.5, § 406.6, and Table 506.2.*

- *The height and the number of tiers at the open parking garage shall be per Table 406.5.4.*

- *Openings between the open and enclosed parking garages need not be protected except for exit openings.*

- *The floor assembly separating the open parking garage from the enclosed parking garage shall be protected per the requirements for an enclosed parking garage.*

- *The enclosed parking garage may be only one story above grade plane and must be of Type I or Type II construction and be at least equal to the fire-resistance requirements for the Group S-2 open parking garage.*

- *The enclosed parking garage is to be used only for parking of private motor vehicles (i.e., no auto repairs) but may have an office, waiting rooms, and toilet rooms of not more than 1,000 sf (93 m²) [assumed to be an aggregate area, not for each function] and mechanical equipment rooms incidental to the operation of the building.*

Parking Beneath Group R

Where an S-2 parking garage (either open or enclosed) is one story above the grade plane, has an entrance at grade, is of Type I construction, and is located beneath a Group R occupancy, the number of stories used to determine the minimum construction type is to be measured from the floor above the parking area.

- *The floor assembly between the parking garage and the Group R occupancy above is determined by the construction type requirements for the parking garage. It shall also have a fire-resistance rating as an occupancy separation per Table 508.4.*

- *One story maximum above grade plane*

Special Provisions for Groups R-1 and R-2

§ 510.5 and § 510.6 were written to address hotel and apartment construction issues. Where fire-resistance ratings are met, fire separations are provided, and/or buildings are separated by required distances, these sections allow greater design flexibility than noted in Table 504.3 and 504.4.

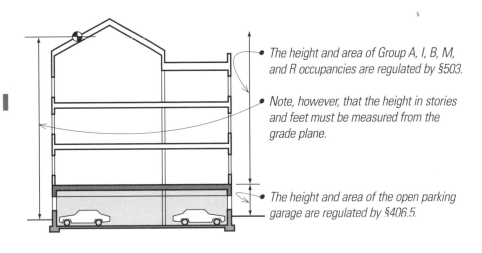

- Groups R-1 and R-2 buildings of Type III-A construction may be increased in height to 75' (22 860) and six stories when the first floor construction above the basement has a fire-resistance rating of at least 3 hours and the floor area is subdivided by 2-hour fire walls into areas of not more than 3,000 sf (279 m²).

- Groups R-1 and R-2 buildings of Type II-A construction may be increased in height to 100' (30 480) and nine stories when:

- the first-floor construction has a fire-resistance rating of at least 1-½ hours;
- the building is separated from any other building on the same lot and from property lines by no less than 50' (15 240); and
- exits are enclosed by 2-hour fire walls.

Open Parking Garage Beneath Groups A, I, B, M, and R

§ 510.7 allows constructing the use groups as indicated above an open parking garage and treating them as separate buildings for allowable height and area purposes. The height and area of the open garage are regulated by § 406.5, and the heights and areas of the groups above the garage are regulated by § 503.1. There is a restriction that heights in feet and stories for the part of the building above the garage be measured from the grade plane for the entire group of stacked uses. This section also requires fire resistance to be provided for the most restrictive of the uses. It also requires egress from the uses above the garage be separated by fire-resistance-rated assemblies of at least two hours.

- The height and area of Group A, I, B, M, and R occupancies are regulated by §503.

- Note, however, that the height in stories and feet must be measured from the grade plane.

- The height and area of the open parking garage are regulated by §406.5.

Group S-2 Open Parking Garage Above Group B or M

Per § 510.8, where Group B or M occupancies are located on the first story above grade plane, they may be considered as separate and distinct buildings for the purpose of determining the allowable construction types when there is an open parking garage above these occupancies and all of the noted conditions are met.

Note that while Building A and Building B may be considered as separate buildings, Item 4 of § 510.8 says the building below the horizontal assembly is to be of Type I or Type II construction, "but not less than the type of construction required for the Group S-2 parking garage above." How this is to be applied should be confirmed with the AHJ.

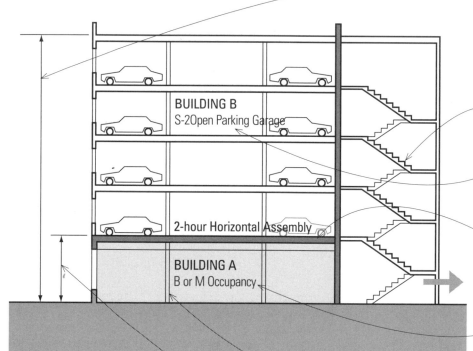

The height of the S-2 open parking garage does not exceed the limits of § 406.5. The height, in both feet and stories, of the open parking garage is to be measured from the grade plane, including the building below the horizontal assembly.

Exits serving the parking garage must be separated by 2-hour fire barriers and discharge directly to a street or public way.

The occupancy above the horizontal assembly is limited to a Group S-2 open parking garage.

The buildings must be separated with a horizontal assembly having a minimum 2-hour fire-resistance rating.

The occupancies in the building below the horizontal separation are limited to Groups B and M.

The building below the horizontal assembly is of Type I or Type II construction, but not less than the type of construction required for the Group S-2 open parking garage above.

The height of the area below the horizontal separation does not exceed the limits set forth in § 503.

6

Types of Construction

The classification of buildings by types of construction has been a part of most model codes from their inception. The Uniform Building Code contained these classifications in the first 1927 edition. The IBC also recognizes the relationships of occupancy and construction type contained in the predecessor codes, but the provisions of the IBC are organized in a much different manner and with less direct definitions than the older model codes. Many code sections became footnotes, and some provisions now appear in definitions in other chapters. Fire-resistance ratings that had more extensive written descriptions in the legacy codes that aided understanding in relation to known building materials have, in the IBC, briefer descriptions in § 602, with many distinctions made in relation to test criteria alone. However, those familiar with construction will understand the basic distinctions between construction-type classifications.

The simplification of the definitions and reduced description of the respective responsibilities of designers and building officials may make determinations easier. On the other hand, there may be more confusion in the application of these provisions as new users of the code apply the abstract provisions to real projects. The development of precedents for interpretations require the use of the code to generate a body of applied knowledge to set the tone for future interpretations.

Definitions of building construction in the older model codes went into greater detail about construction materials for such elements as structural framework and stair treads. The new criteria define the subdivision of materials between "combustible" and "noncombustible" by their test performance under given conditions. This is a more precise definition, but more obscure for the casual code user who understands intuitively that steel or concrete are noncombustible materials versus how they perform in testing per ASTM E 119, *Standard Test Methods for Fire Tests of Building Construction and Materials*. This change takes some adaptation by those code users steeped in the old model codes to adjust to the new IBC way of doing things.

The IBC classifies all buildings into five broad categories based on the fire-resistance capabilities of the predominant materials used for their construction. The five types of construction are given Roman-numeral designations, and progress downward in fire-resistance from Type I, the most fire-resistive construction, to Type V, the least fire-resistive.

The five types of construction classes are subdivided into two broad categories, A and B, based on the inherent fire-resistance or combustibility of the materials and the degree of fire protection applied over the structural members. "A" denotes "protected" construction and "B" denotes less protected construction. These are further subdivided according to the fire-resistance gained by the application of protection to major elements of the construction systems. This fire-resistance rating is predicated on the protection of the elements from exposure to fires both from within the building and from adjacent structures.

The tables in § 504 and § 506 correlate the five types of construction with the allowable heights and areas for buildings, based on their occupancy. The designer must work with three sets of dependent variables when making the initial code analysis. The desired occupancy and the desired building height and area will determine the type of construction allowable under the code.

Table 601 defines the required fire-resistance of major building elements for each type of construction. See pages 100–102 for a more detailed discussion. Note that Chapter 7 governs the actual materials and assemblies used in fire-resistance-rated construction. § 602.1 refers code users to § 703.2, which contains the criteria for fire-resistance ratings and fire tests. There is a direct relationship between occupancy type and number of occupants to the construction classification. Higher occupant quantities, more hazardous occupancies and occupants with special needs, such as children and the infirm, all require more fire resistance or additional levels of active fire-suppression systems.

Height and Area Tables from § 504 and § 506

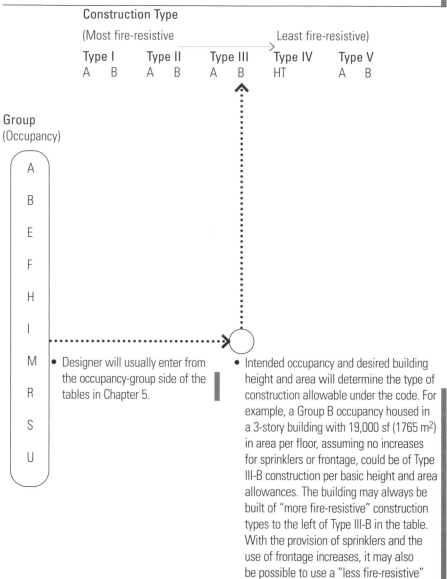

Construction Type

(Most fire-resistive   Least fire-resistive)

Type I	Type II	Type III	Type IV	Type V
A B	A B	A B	HT	A B

Group
(Occupancy)

A
B
E
F
H
I
M
R
S
U

- Designer will usually enter from the occupancy-group side of the tables in Chapter 5.

- Intended occupancy and desired building height and area will determine the type of construction allowable under the code. For example, a Group B occupancy housed in a 3-story building with 19,000 sf (1765 m²) in area per floor, assuming no increases for sprinklers or frontage, could be of Type III-B construction per basic height and area allowances. The building may always be built of "more fire-resistive" construction types to the left of Type III-B in the table. With the provision of sprinklers and the use of frontage increases, it may also be possible to use a "less fire-resistive" construction type to the right of Type III-B in the table. This is an iterative process.

The broadest distinction between the various types of construction can be summarized in the table below.

Materials	Protected Elements	Less Protected Elements	Unprotected Elements
Noncombustible	Type I-A, II-A	Type I-B (vis-à-vis Type 1-A; still > Type II-A)	Type II-B
Combustible	—	—	—
Mixed Systems	Type III-A	Type III-B	—
Heavy Timber	—	Type IV	—
Any Materials	Type V-A	—	Type V-B

• Note that levels of fire resistance decrease from left to right and top to bottom of this table.

Noncombustible Materials

The principal elements of construction Types I and II are made of noncombustible materials. The Uniform Building Code defined "noncombustible" as "material of which no part will ignite and burn when subjected to fire" (1997 UBC § 215). The IBC definition of noncombustibility is contained in § 703.5, and states that materials required to be noncombustible must meet the test criteria prescribed in the American Society for Testing and Materials (ASTM) Standard E 136.

Combustible Materials

The elements of Types III, IV, and V construction allow the use of combustible materials in varying degrees. Additional levels of fire protection can increase the fire-resistance rating of these three types of construction. Note that construction types with mixed elements of noncombustible and combustible construction are considered combustible and are of Types III, IV, or V.

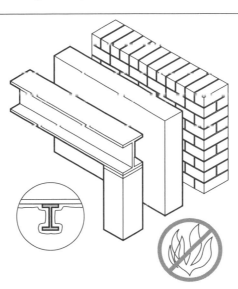

• Noncombustible materials include masonry, concrete and steel.

• Note that application of additional fire protection materials to the noncombustible elements of Types I and II construction yields higher Type I-A, I-B, and II-A ratings, above the basic II-B classification for unprotected noncombustible construction.

• There is no definition of "combustible construction" contained in the IBC. Technical dictionaries of construction or mining terms define it as "capable of undergoing combustion or of burning. Used esp. for materials that catch fire and burn when subjected to fire." By inference these materials, such as wood and plastics, would be those that do not comply with the requirements for noncombustibility contained in ASTM E 136.

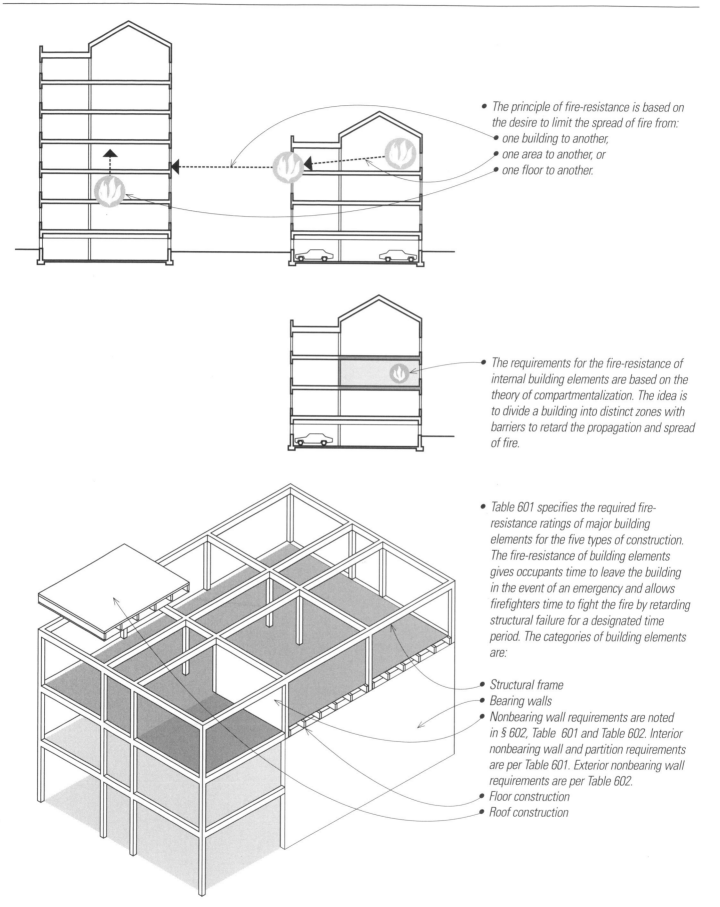

- The principle of fire-resistance is based on the desire to limit the spread of fire from:
  - one building to another,
  - one area to another, or
  - one floor to another.

- The requirements for the fire-resistance of internal building elements are based on the theory of compartmentalization. The idea is to divide a building into distinct zones with barriers to retard the propagation and spread of fire.

- Table 601 specifies the required fire-resistance ratings of major building elements for the five types of construction. The fire-resistance of building elements gives occupants time to leave the building in the event of an emergency and allows firefighters time to fight the fire by retarding structural failure for a designated time period. The categories of building elements are:

- Structural frame
- Bearing walls
- Nonbearing wall requirements are noted in § 602, Table 601 and Table 602. Interior nonbearing wall and partition requirements are per Table 601. Exterior nonbearing wall requirements are per Table 602.
- Floor construction
- Roof construction

The classification by types of construction determines the level of passive fire-resistance that is inherent in the building's structure and envelope. This is distinct from active fire-suppression systems such as sprinklers. As we will discuss in Chapters 7 and 9, there can be trade-offs under the code between passive and active systems. The idea is to look at the building as a whole and provide a balance of fire protection to achieve a predetermined level of structural protection and occupant safety.

It is important to remember that most building owners will opt for the lowest fire-resistance rating possible, as there is a direct relationship between providing fire resistance and cost of construction. The determination of construction type usually entails an analysis of both the desired occupancy and the requirements for fire-separation distance between buildings or parts of buildings. This helps determine the necessary minimum fire resistance of the building elements. Conversely, using higher fire-rated building systems for a portion of a building for reasons such as utility or aesthetics does not require the entire building to be of a higher fire rating than is required by the occupancy or location on the property. The standards applied to classification are minimum standards, but the minima and maxima apply to the whole building, not isolated components.

The building official will examine the classification assigned by the designer and make the final determination of classification. The building is to be looked at as a whole system and considered in the aggregate. § 602.1.1 notes that although portions of the building may exceed the requirements for the type and for the building occupancy, the whole building need not meet requirements higher than those necessary for the intended occupancy.

- Passive fire resistance results from the use of construction materials and assemblies that can be expected to withstand exposure to fire without collapsing or exceeding a certain temperature on the side facing away from a fire. Examining the Chapter 5 height and area tables discloses that the application of fire-resistive materials to construction materials can allow increases in the allowable heights and areas. This recognizes that combustible materials may be made more fire-resistive by the application of fire-retardant coverings to accomplish the goal of retarding the spread of fire and to extend the durability of the building structure in a fire. The application of passive fire-resistive materials can increase the durability of even noncombustible materials in a fire. Even steel or concrete, if unprotected, can lose strength under fire exposure.

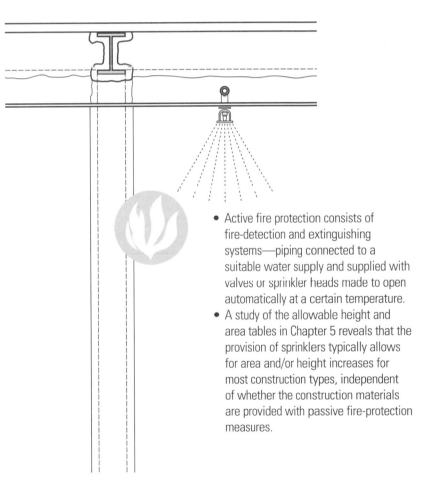

- Active fire protection consists of fire-detection and extinguishing systems—piping connected to a suitable water supply and supplied with valves or sprinkler heads made to open automatically at a certain temperature.
- A study of the allowable height and area tables in Chapter 5 reveals that the provision of sprinklers typically allows for area and/or height increases for most construction types, independent of whether the construction materials are provided with passive fire-protection measures.

TABLE 601

Table 601 specifies the fire-resistance rating requirements for the major building elements, based on a specified type of construction or construction classification. A building may only be classified as a single type of construction unless a fire wall divides it into separate structures, or it falls into the special provisions for mixed construction permitted under § 510. Even if some building elements satisfy the fire-resistance rating requirements for a higher type of construction, the building as a whole need only conform to the lowest type of construction that meets the minimum requirements of the code based on occupancy. Below is an abbreviated version of Table 601.

Required Fire-Resistance Ratings in Hours

Construction Type	Type I		Type II		Type III		Type IV	Type V	
	A	B	A	B	A	B	HT	A	B
Building Element*									
Primary Structural Frame** (See Table 601, Footnote f)	3[a]	2[a]	1	0	1	0	HT	1	0
Bearing Walls** (See Table 601, Footnotes e and f)									
Exterior (see Table 602 & § 704.10)	3	2	1	0	2	2	2	1	0
Interior	3[a]	2[a]	1	0	1	0	1/HT	1	0
Nonbearing Walls	Requirements for nonbearing exterior walls and interior partitions are noted in § 602 and Table 602.								
Floor Construction & Secondary Members (see § 202)	2	2	1	0	1	0	HT	1	0
Roof Construction & Secondary Members (see § 202)	1$1/2$[b]	1[b,c]	1[b,c]	0[c]	1[b,c]	0	HT	1[b,c]	0

* Under the previous model codes, elements such as stairways were also defined in terms of construction materials under the sections addressing types of construction. The new test-based criteria called out in § 1011.7 states that stairways be "built of materials consistent with the types permitted for the type of construction of the building." This new definition may lead to confusion when applied in conjunction with § 603, which allows the use of combustible materials in Type I and Type II construction.

** The footnotes to Table 601 contain essential information for the designer to consider when making design decisions and when reviewing Table 601 in conjunction with the height and area tables in Chapter 5, which correlates allowable height and building areas with types of construction and occupancies. The designer should read the footnotes carefully as they contain notable exceptions and trade-offs.

While it is important to understand the footnotes to Table 601, the code user must use great caution when "reading up" from the footnotes to be certain that the provisions of the footnote apply to the specific building in question. The table should typically be read from top to bottom in the column that applies to the construction being analyzed.

TABLE 601

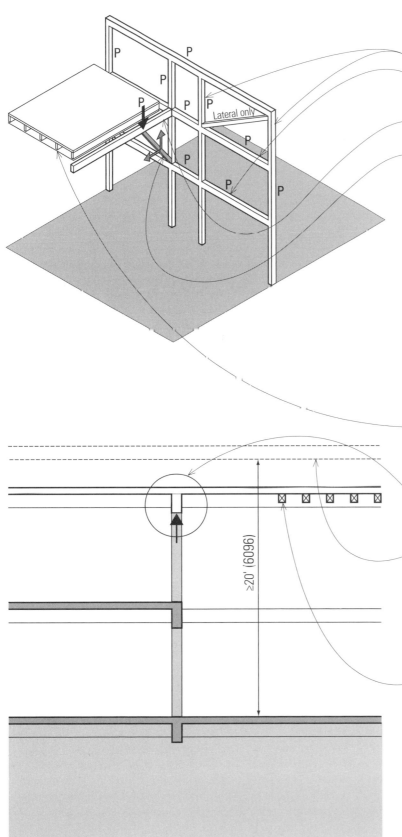

- The "primary structural frame" [P] is defined in § 202 as including all of the following structural members:

1. The columns;
2. Structural members having direct connection to the columns, including girders, beams, trusses, and spandrels;
3. Members of the floor construction and roof construction having direct connections to the columns; and
4. Bracing members that are essential to the <u>vertical stability</u> of the primary structural frame <u>under gravity loading</u> shall be considered part of the primary structural frame, whether or not the bracing members carry gravity loads. (emphasis added)

We construe the Definition 4 to mean that diagonal bracing that does not contribute to the vertical stability of the rest of the primary frame under gravity loading is not to be considered part of the primary framing system. Thus, such items as diagonal braces designed to carry lateral loads only would likely not require the same fire-resistance rating as the primary structural frame. This is a subject to discuss in detail with the project structural engineer and with the AHJ early in the code-analysis process.

- The other elements not making up the structural frame are covered by the requirements for floor and roof construction.

- Footnote a: This footnote recognizes that roof framing at interior bearing walls in Type I construction has a lighter fire load than does the primary structure for floors.

- Footnote b: The conditions in this footnote refer to special provisions related to fire protection and building element protection in roof construction. The footnote permits unprotected roof construction for roofs 20' (6096) or more above the floor below, except in Group F-1, H, M, and S-1 occupancies, and it allows the use of fire-retardant-treated wood for such unprotected members.

- Footnote c: Allows the use of heavy timbers where a 1-hour or less fire-resistance rating is required. This can even apply in buildings of "noncombustible" Type I or II construction.

TABLE 601

• Footnote d, which allowed providing an automatic sprinkler system as a substitute for 1-hour fire-resistance-rated construction, has been deleted. This provision, left over from much older predecessor codes, allowed the substitution when "sprinklers are not otherwise required by other provisions of the code..." When versions of the IBC increased the number of circumstances where sprinklers are required, the use of this provision became less and less frequent. The provision has often been misapplied by designers early in code analysis. This can lead to development of incorrect construction documents, which are found to be wrong during plan review. Having to change construction types late in the design process can be a costly and time-consuming effort. Because of its very limited use and potential for misapplication, the footnote has been deleted to remove this substitution method completely.

• Footnote d (old footnote "e"): This footnote is meant to remind the code user that other issues, such as corridor-rating requirements, may affect rating requirements for nonbearing walls.

• Footnote e (old footnote "f"): This footnote advises the designer to compare the requirements of both Tables 601 and 602 to determine the fire-resistive requirements for exterior bearing walls. It is possible that the requirements of Table 602 will require a higher fire-resistance rating for an exterior wall than Table 601; in the event of overlapping requirements, the most restrictive is to govern per § 102.1. For example, a Group M occupancy in a Type V-A building located within 5' (1524) of a property line would require a 2-hour wall rating per Table 602 and only a 1-hour rating per Table 601. In this case the 2-hour requirement would govern, as the code requires the most restrictive provision to govern per § 102.1. We also recommend examining § 705 for additional provisions that apply to exterior walls.

• Footnote f (old footnote "g"): This footnote refers the user to § 704.10 for the fire-resistance of the primary structural frame.

Footnote g to Table 602 correlates the requirements for fire-resistance ratings in nonbearing walls with the allowances for the amount of wall openings as described in Table 705.8. Where unlimited openings are allowed per Table 705.8 the wall rating may be 0 hours. This typically occurs at a fire-separation distance of 20 feet (6096) in sprinklered buildings.

TABLE 602

Table 602 specifies the fire-resistance rating requirements of exterior walls based on fire-separation distance as well as type of construction and occupancy groups. Use of the table requires that the occupancy group be known in order to determine the fire-resistance requirements for exterior walls. Note also that the exterior bearing wall requirements contained in Table 601 need to be compared to the requirements in Table 602. Where such comparisons result in a potential conflict, the most restrictive requirement will govern.

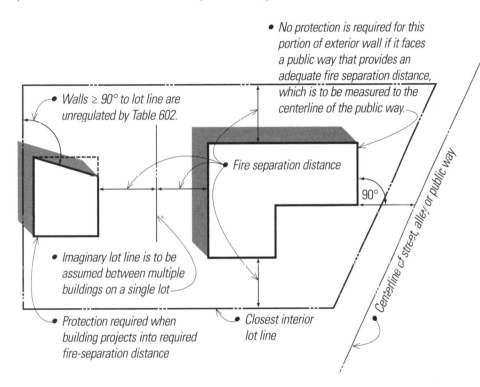

- No protection is required for this portion of exterior wall if it faces a public way that provides an adequate fire separation distance, which is to be measured to the centerline of the public way.

- Walls ≥ 90° to lot line are unregulated by Table 602.

- Imaginary lot line is to be assumed between multiple buildings on a single lot

- Protection required when building projects into required fire-separation distance

- Closest interior lot line

- The term "fire separation distance" is defined in Chapter 2. This is new terminology for some users of prior model codes. This definition replaces terminology related to "location on property" with a more general idea that encompasses not just the spatial relationship of buildings to their site boundaries but to adjacent buildings on the same site as well. There is an interrelationship between building occupancy, construction type, and location on the site. These are dependent variables with each impacting the other as a building design develops. Fire separation distance is to be measured perpendicular to the face of the building as illustrated.

- The fire-resistance requirements decrease with increasing distance between buildings. They also decrease in relation to decreasing construction-type requirements. Table 602 also builds in assumptions about the hazards of occupancies relative to fire-separation distances. The guiding principle is that increased distances offset the hazards presented by various occupancies. Distance also mitigates the reduction in resistance to external fires presented by less resistive construction types.

- The amount of opening area in exterior walls is governed by the area limitations set forth in Table 705.8. The opening protection levels are correlated between the wall protection requirements of Table 602 and the opening protection requirements of Tables 716.5 and 716.6. The designer must first ascertain the required fire-resistance rating of exterior walls to determine the required level of opening protection in the exterior walls. The designer can then determine the allowable amount of protected and unprotected openings in the exterior wall by using these two sections together.

Table 602
Required Fire-Resistance Rating of Exterior Walls Based on Fire-Separation Distance

Fire-Separation Distance (feet)	Type of Construction	Group H	Groups F-1, M, S-1	Groups A, B, E, F-2, I, R, S-2, U
		• Decreasing hazard →		
< 5	All	3	2	1
	I-A			
		Decreasing fire-resistance requirements →		
	V-B			
≥ 30	All	0	0	0

The building elements of Type I and Type II construction are of noncombustible materials. As noted on page 97, the definition of noncombustible is contained in § 703.5 and requires meeting the criteria of ASTM E 136.

- Type I-A construction, providing the highest level of fire-resistance-rated construction, requires passive protection for all elements of the structure.
- Type I-B construction is similar to Type I-A construction but permits a 1-hour reduction in fire-resistance rating for the structural frame, bearing walls, and floor construction, and a 1/2-hour reduction for roof construction.
- Type II-A construction allows active or passive protection of all elements of the structure.
- Type II-B construction allows unprotected noncombustible building elements. This type of construction was described as "Type II-nonrated" in some previous model codes.

Combustible Materials
in Types I and II Construction

The key to the use of combustible materials in a noncombustible construction type is understanding that these uses are ancillary to the primary structure of the building. The premise for allowing the use of these combustible materials is that they will be of limited quantity and used under defined conditions where they will not contribute in any large measure to compromising the desired level of fire-resistance in the structure. As one can see, the rules for Construction Types I and II, while calling for noncombustible materials, allow for a number of exceptions when all the requirements are taken together.

§ 603 contains a list of notes specifying which combustible materials can be used in buildings of Types I and II construction.

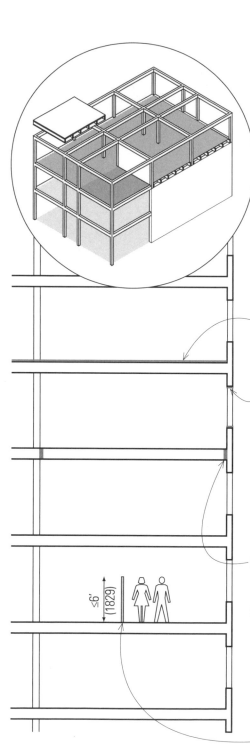

1. *Note 1 calls out allowances for the use of fire-retardant-treated wood for nonbearing walls and partitions, and for roof construction.*
2. *Thermal and acoustical insulation materials with a flame spread of less than 25 have ratings corresponding to Class A interior finishes per ASTM E 84. These indices may be higher, as noted in the exception, where insulation is encapsulated between layers of noncombustible materials without an air space.*
3. *Foam plastics are allowable if compliant with the provisions of Chapter 26 of the code. Note especially the provisions of § 2603.5 regarding the use of foam plastics on the exterior of Type I, II, III and IV buildings.*
4. *Most roof coverings have a classification of A, B, or C, so this should almost always be usable.*
5. *The code recognizes that combustible decorative and utilitarian interior finishes, such as wood floors, will be applied over the noncombustible structural elements if installed per § 804.*
6. *Millwork such as doors, door frames, window sashes, and window frames are acceptable.*
7. *Interior wall and ceiling finishes are acceptable if installed per § 801 and 803.*
8. *Trim installed per § 806.*
9. *Wood trim at or near grade level is acceptable where not beyond ready fire-fighting access up to a level of 15' (4572) above grade.*
10. *This note requires fire-stopping in wood floors in Type I and II construction per § 805. This is similar to Note 5.*
11. *The key item in this section is that the area in question be occupied and controlled by a single tenant. These provisions do not apply for multi-tenant spaces. Also, these partitions must not define exit access passages that could be construed as corridors for the use of more than 30 occupants. This note also recognizes that single-tenant floors can have partitions of wood or similar light construction if they are lower than 6' (1829) and allow standing occupants to generally survey the occupied space in the event of an emergency.*

≤6' (1829)

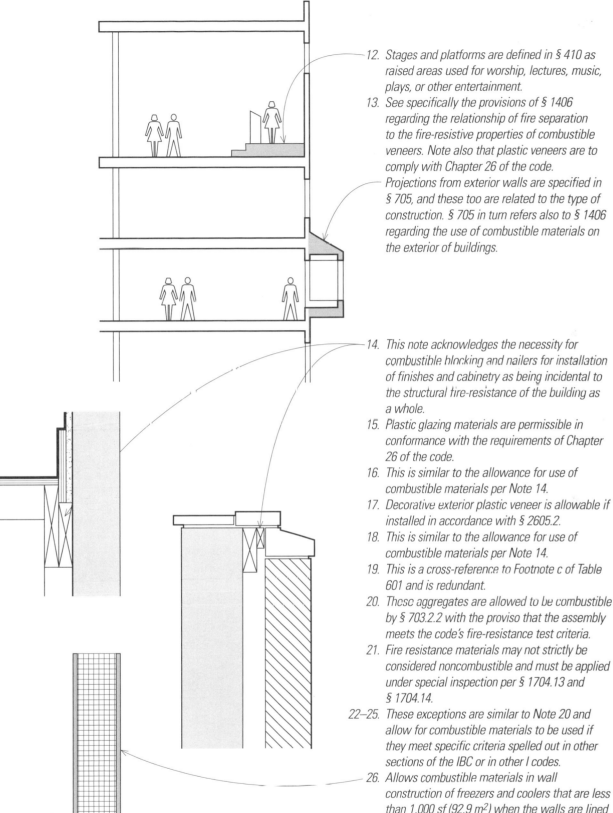

12. Stages and platforms are defined in § 410 as raised areas used for worship, lectures, music, plays, or other entertainment.

13. See specifically the provisions of § 1406 regarding the relationship of fire separation to the fire-resistive properties of combustible veneers. Note also that plastic veneers are to comply with Chapter 26 of the code. Projections from exterior walls are specified in § 705, and these too are related to the type of construction. § 705 in turn refers also to § 1406 regarding the use of combustible materials on the exterior of buildings.

14. This note acknowledges the necessity for combustible blocking and nailers for installation of finishes and cabinetry as being incidental to the structural fire-resistance of the building as a whole.

15. Plastic glazing materials are permissible in conformance with the requirements of Chapter 26 of the code.

16. This is similar to the allowance for use of combustible materials per Note 14.

17. Decorative exterior plastic veneer is allowable if installed in accordance with § 2605.2.

18. This is similar to the allowance for use of combustible materials per Note 14.

19. This is a cross-reference to Footnote c of Table 601 and is redundant.

20. These aggregates are allowed to be combustible by § 703.2.2 with the proviso that the assembly meets the code's fire-resistance test criteria.

21. Fire resistance materials may not strictly be considered noncombustible and must be applied under special inspection per § 1704.13 and § 1704.14.

22–25. These exceptions are similar to Note 20 and allow for combustible materials to be used if they meet specific criteria spelled out in other sections of the IBC or in other I codes.

26. Allows combustible materials in wall construction of freezers and coolers that are less than 1,000 sf (92.9 m²) when the walls are lined on both sides with noncombustible materials and the building is protected throughout with an automatic sprinkler system.

TYPE III CONSTRUCTION

Type III buildings are a mix of noncombustible and combustible elements, having noncombustible exterior walls and combustible interior construction. These building types arose in the U.S. at the end of the 19th century out of a desire to end the kind of conflagrations that struck congested business districts such as in Chicago. The buildings were designed to prevent a fire from spreading from building to building by requiring noncombustible exterior walls of buildings.

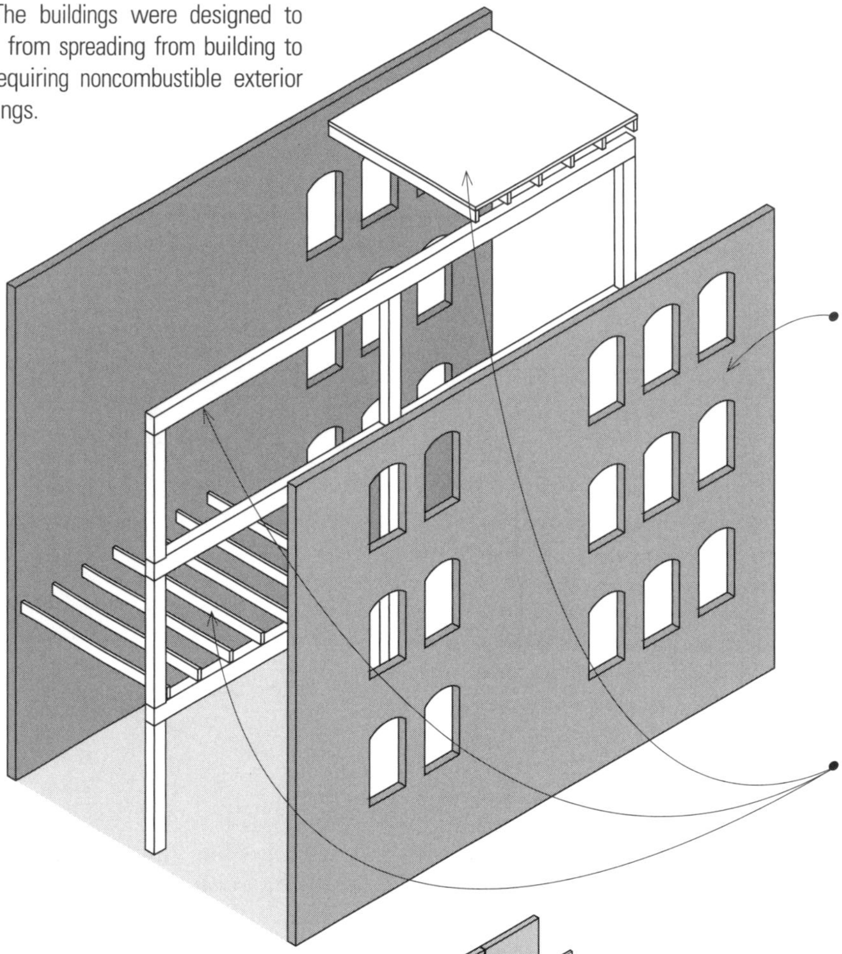

- *The construction materials on the exterior of a Type III building are required to be of noncombustible materials. Fire-retardant treated wood is allowable in exterior walls where the required fire-resistance rating is 2 hours or less. Table 601 requires 2-hour walls for Type III-A buildings; thus fire-retardant-treated wood is acceptable except where this is superseded by the requirements of Table 602 based on fire-separation distance. This would only occur in Group H occupancies with a fire-separation distance of less than 5' (1524).*

- *Type III buildings are considered combustible since the code allows their interior building elements to be of combustible materials and also to be of unprotected construction if allowed by the building height and area allowances based on occupancy.*

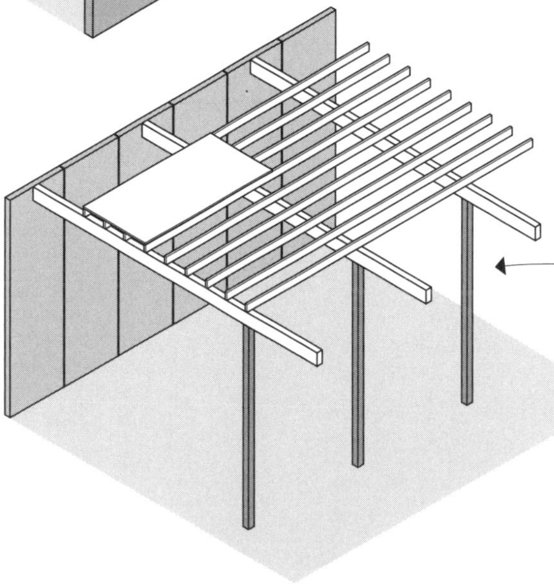

- *A very common example of a Type III-B building is the tilt-up warehouse. This building type has concrete exterior walls, with a wood-framed roof supported on unprotected steel pipe columns at the interior of the building.*

Type IV buildings came about to address fire-safety conditions for traditional methods of building manufacturing and storage buildings, as Type III buildings did for office and residential occupancies. The type of construction used in Type IV buildings is known as "mill construction" or "heavy timber" construction. These buildings utilize heavy timber structural members and heavy wood floor decking inside exterior walls of noncombustible construction. Many of these buildings also have movable heavy metal shutters to close off exterior openings to prevent a fire outside the building from propagating into the building through unprotected openings.

New types of large dimensional-wood construction materials are now recognized in the code as heavy timber. "Structural composite lumber" (SCL) comprises engineered products which include laminated veneer lumber (LVL), parallel strand lumber (PSL), laminated strand lumber (LSL), and oriented strand lumber (OSL). SCL is a family of engineered wood products created by layering dried and graded wood veneers, strands, or flakes with moisture-resistant adhesive into blocks of material that can be used for structural framing. There is now an equivalency in Table 602.4 for member sizes between solid sawn timber "nominal" (cut prior to drying and milling) sizes, glue-laminated timber "net" (actual) sizes, and SCL "net" sizes.

Table 602.4: Wood Member Size Equivalencies

Minimum Nominal Wood	Minimum Glue-Laminated	Minimum Structural Composite Lumber
[Typical actual size shown] / Sawn size	Net size shown	Net size shown
8" (203); 8" (203); [7¹/₄" (184)]; [7¹/₄" (184)]	8¹/₄" (210); 6³/₄" (171)	7¹/₂" (191); 7" (178)
6" (152); 10" (254); [9¹/₄" (235)]; [5¹/₂" (140)]	10¹/₂" (267); 5" (127)	9¹/₂" (241); 5¹/₄" (133)
6" (152); 8" (203); [7¹/₄" (184)]; [5¹/₂" (140)]	8¹/₄" (210); 5" (127)	7¹/₂" (191); 5¹/₄" (133)
6" (152); 6" (152); [5¹/₂" (140)]; [5¹/₂" (140)]	6" (152); 5" (127)	5¹/₂" (140); 5¹/₄" (133)
4" (102); 6" (152); [5¹/₂" (140)]; [3¹/₂" (89)]	6⁷/₈" (175); 3" (76)	5¹/₂" (140); 3¹/₂" (89)

The criteria for "heavy timber" (HT) construction are based on the past performance of historical construction, not on the scientific rationales contained in ASTM E 136 and E 119. These buildings have a good empirical performance record in fires. The insurance industry promoted construction of these types of buildings during the late 1800s and into the 1900s to limit their fire losses.

Type IV buildings generally burn slowly under fire conditions. The heavy timber members begin to flame and char at about 400°F (204.4°C). As the charring continues, it retards further deterioration of the wood members by insulating the interior of the wood members from the fire.

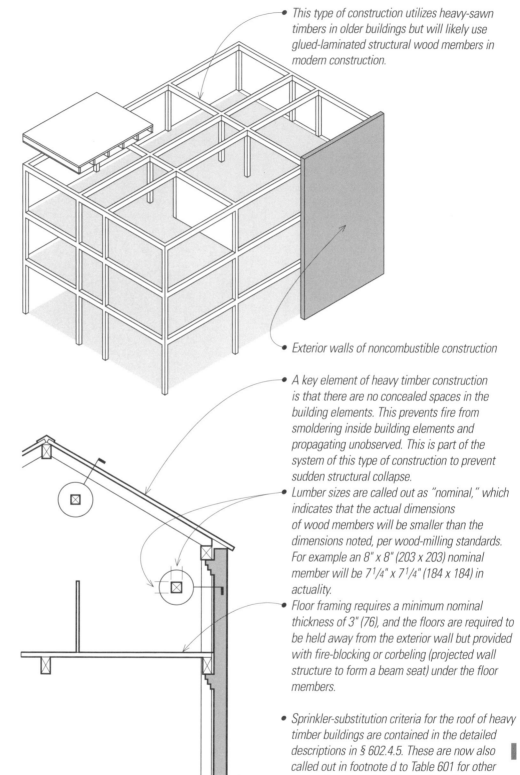

• This type of construction utilizes heavy-sawn timbers in older buildings but will likely use glued-laminated structural wood members in modern construction.

• Exterior walls of noncombustible construction

• A key element of heavy timber construction is that there are no concealed spaces in the building elements. This prevents fire from smoldering inside building elements and propagating unobserved. This is part of the system of this type of construction to prevent sudden structural collapse.

• Lumber sizes are called out as "nominal," which indicates that the actual dimensions of wood members will be smaller than the dimensions noted, per wood-milling standards. For example an 8" x 8" (203 x 203) nominal member will be 7 1/4" x 7 1/4" (184 x 184) in actuality.

• Floor framing requires a minimum nominal thickness of 3" (76), and the floors are required to be held away from the exterior wall but provided with fire-blocking or corbeling (projected wall structure to form a beam seat) under the floor members.

• Sprinkler-substitution criteria for the roof of heavy timber buildings are contained in the detailed descriptions in § 602.4.5. These are now also called out in footnote d to Table 601 for other types of construction where 1-hour fire resistance is required.

• Note that many other separation criteria for heavy timber buildings are noted in § 602.4, not in Table 602 as for other types of construction.

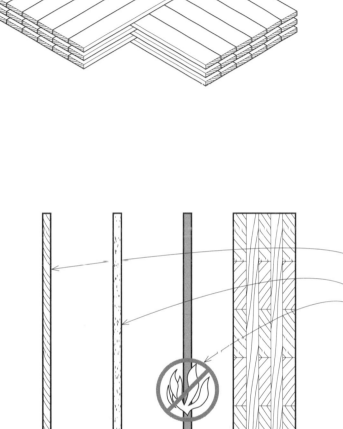

There is a new wood-based construction material now included in Type IV construction for use in exterior walls. The material is "cross laminated timber" (CLT). It is defined as:

"A prefabricated engineered wood product consisting of not less than three layers of solid-sawn lumber or structural composite lumber where the adjacent layers are cross oriented and bonded with structural adhesive to form a solid wood element."

It is intended to be used for walls, roofs, or floor/ceiling assemblies. Standards for the materials are included in Chapter 23. The material is required to be protected with prescribed materials.

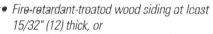

- Fire-retardant-treated wood siding at least 15/32" (12) thick, or
- 1/2" (12.7 mm) minimum gypsum board, or
- A noncombustible material

or   or

Siding   CLT

TYPE V CONSTRUCTION

Type V construction is the least restrictive construction type. It allows the use of any materials permitted by the code. A typical example of Type V construction is the conventional light-wood-framed single-family residence.

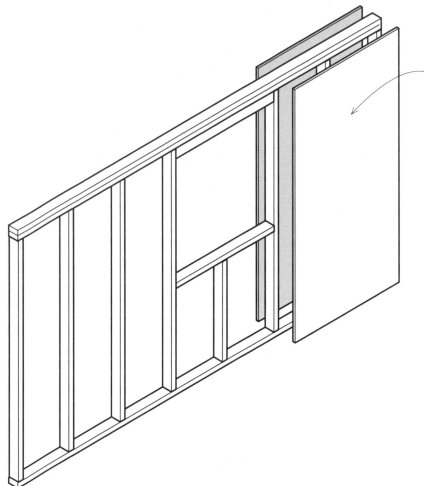

- Because any element of Type V construction may be combustible, the fire-resistance of building elements is typically provided by the application of fire-resistant materials, such as gypsum board, to the building parts.

- Type V-A construction is protected construction and all major building elements must therefore have a 1-hour fire-resistance rating. The only exception to this is for non-bearing interior walls and partitions contained in Table 601.
- Type V-B construction is unprotected and requires no fire-resistance ratings, except Table 602 requires exterior-wall protection.

7

Fire-Resistive Construction

Fire resistance is the major factor in determining classification of construction types. Structural materials are broadly classified as combustible or noncombustible. Noncombustible materials provide greater resistance to fire by their nature. But even noncombustible structural materials can be weakened by exposure to fire. Materials that have capabilities to resist fire of a designated intensity for a length of time as determined by fire tests can be applied to structural materials to achieve required fire resistance. As we saw in the discussion of types of construction, there is a direct relationship between fire-resistance requirements by construction type to occupancy type and to the allowable number of occupants.

The code recognizes two basic methods for providing fire-resistive protection to ensure life safety in buildings. These can be classified as either passive or active protection. The differences between these approaches lie in the way they respond to the effects of fire on a building structure. Passive protection is built into the building structure and provides a barrier between the structure and the fire. Active protection such as fire sprinklers responds to fire by activation of systems to contain or suppress fire and smoke to allow the structure to remain intact for a longer period of time than without protection, thus allowing the occupants to escape. The code allows trade-offs between the provision of active versus passive fire protection. For example, 1-hour structural protection requirements may be offset by provision of fire sprinklers under certain circumstances in certain occupancies. Note that this may occur only under very limited circumstances.

In this chapter, we consider code requirements for passive fire resistance; Chapter 9 discusses active measures of fire resistance. For designers and owners, the trade-offs between passive and active fire resistance are part of the design and economic analyses that go into deciding which systems are most suitable for a given project. The consideration of passive versus active systems is part of the iterative process of comparing occupancy and site requirements to allowable heights and areas for various construction types. Again, as noted in previous chapters, design goals typically involve using the most economical construction type that meets the needs of the occupancy.

The code recognizes the efficacy of trade-offs between types of construction and types of fire protection. It also recognizes that there are limits to the value of the trade-offs between active and passive fire-resistance as they relate to types of construction and uses. Where active systems are required by the code in relationship to given criteria, such as to increase heights and areas, then the provision of active systems in lieu of passive protection is generally not allowed. The idea of a trade-off implies a voluntary selection by the designer of how to provide the required degree of fire resistance. When code provisions otherwise require active systems, they are thus not available to offset passive requirements.

Fire-Resistance Ratings

Definitions used in Chapter 7 are listed in § 702, but the texts of the definitions themselves are contained in Chapter 2. The 2012 edition of the code moved all of the definitions, except for those of the appendices, into Chapter 2. § 202 defines fire-resistance rating as "the period of time a building element, component or assembly maintains the ability to confine a fire, continues to perform a given structural function, or both," as determined by tests or methods prescribed in § 703. Building Element is defined as: "A fundamental component of building construction, listed in Table 601, which may or may not be of fire-resistance-rated construction and is constructed of materials based on the building type of construction." The time-rating in hours indicates how long a building material, element or assembly can maintain its structural integrity and/or heat-transfer resistance in a fire, and corresponds to the construction type designations in Chapter 6 of the code.

§ 703.2 prescribes that fire-resistance ratings be assigned on the basis of a fundamental fire test promulgated by ASTM International (formerly known as the American Society for Testing and Materials) or Underwriters Laboratories (UL). For example, ASTM Test E 119 exposes materials and assemblies to actual fire tests. UL 263 is also listed as another set of criteria. The material or assembly being tested is installed in a furnace in a condition similar to the anticipated exposure—i.e., vertical for walls, horizontal for floors or ceilings—and then exposed to a fire of a known intensity. The fire exposure is governed by a standard time-temperature curve whereby the fire grows in intensity over a given period of time, reaching a predetermined temperature at a given rate and maintaining that temperature thereafter. The sample is then exposed to the fire until failure occurs or until the maximum desired duration of protection is exceeded. This determines the fire-resistance rating in hours for the material or assembly in question.

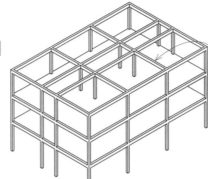

- Fire-resistive construction, whether passive or active, has two primary purposes.
- The first is the protection of the building structure. Where passive protection is provided such protection is typically applied directly to structural members.

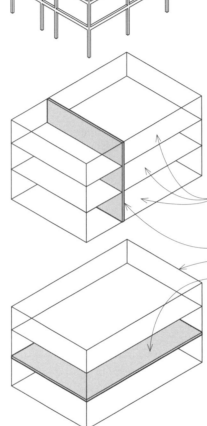

- The second is the separation of spaces to prevent the spread of fire or smoke within a building and the spread of fire between buildings. The protection of spaces addresses fire or smoke impacts on larger-scale building systems such as floors, walls and ceilings, as well as openings in these systems.

- § 202 defines a fire area as the aggregate floor area enclosed and bounded by
  - fire walls;
  - exterior walls; or
  - fire-resistance-rated horizontal assemblies of a building.

- Fire-resistance ratings are based on the performance of various materials and construction assemblies under fire-test conditions as defined by ASTM International or Underwriters Laboratories. Tests typically are based on assumptions about the side of the assembly where the fire is likely to occur.

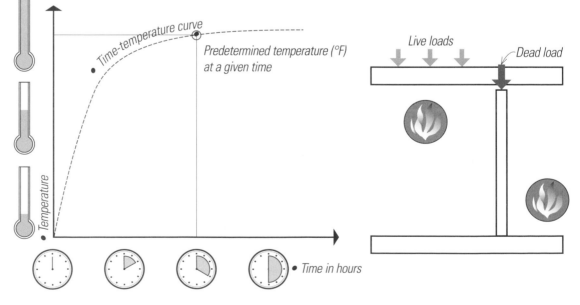

Time-temperature curve

Predetermined temperature (°F) at a given time

Temperature

Time in hours

Live loads

Dead load

§ 703.2.5 allows exterior bearing-wall rating requirements to equal those for nonbearing walls when all factors such as fire separations and occupancy are considered. This exception recognizes that fire-resistance in exterior walls is concerned with stopping the spread of fire beyond the structure as well as protecting the structure. Since the governing criteria for this condition is preventing the spread of fire outside the building, the code recognizes that there is no point in protecting the structure to a higher level than is required for the walls enclosing the space.

§ 703.2.3 assumes that tested assemblies are not restrained under the definitions contained in ASTM E 119 or UL 263. "Restrained" refers to the ability of structural members to expand or contract under fire conditions. Assemblies considered as restrained typically have a higher hourly rating with less application of fire protection and are thus attractive to use in design. However, the code requires that such assemblies be identified on the plans. The difficulty of designing and proving that assemblies are truly restrained very often outweighs any advantages gained in reducing the quantities of fire-protection materials used. We recommend that designers follow the lead of the code section and assume all assemblies to be unrestrained when determining fire-resistance requirements.

Methods for Determining Fire Resistance

While fire ratings are fundamentally based on the ASTM E 119 or UL 263 tests to determine hourly ratings, § 703.3 allows designers to use several methods to demonstrate compliance with fire-resistive criteria. One method allows the use of ratings determined by such recognized agencies as Underwriters Laboratory or Factory Mutual. The code itself contains a "cookbook" of prescriptive assemblies in Table 721, which gives the designer a list of protection measures that can be applied to structural members, to floor and roof construction, and to walls to achieve the necessary ratings. § 722 allows the designer to calculate the fire-resistance of assemblies by combining various materials. This gives much greater flexibility to meet actual design conditions than does the very specific set of assemblies listed in Table 721.

§ 703.3 also allows engineering analysis based on ASTM E 119 or UL 263 to be used to determine projected fire resistance. This typically requires use of a consultant familiar with extrapolations from data acquired from similar fire tests to pre-

dict the performance of systems without the time and expense of performing a full-scale fire test.

§ 703.3 also acknowledges the testing measures prescribed in § 104.11, which allows the building official to approve alternate ways of meeting the code when new technologies or unusual situations are encountered. The reality of using this clause is that the building official will require testing or a consultant's verification of the efficacy of a proposed fire assembly rating in order to grant approval to alternate fire-resistance systems. The designer will need to offer convincing evidence in some form to allow the building official to determine if the proposed system is code-compliant.

Test criteria appear in § 703.4 to clarify that fire tests for rated assemblies may not include fire supression. The assemblies must pass the tests without additional coooling from fire supression water. This section reiterates that the requirements for passive and active protection are to be considered separately.

§ 703.5 defines noncombustibility in terms of test criteria. The characteristics that determine noncombustibility must not be affected by exposure to age, moisture, or atmospheric conditions. The code also recognizes that certain combinations of combustible and noncombustible materials may be considered as noncombustible if they meet test criteria.

Chapter 7 analyzes various construction components and conditions in light of their fire-resistance capabilities. Once again, as in other chapters, the code sections take the form of statements and exceptions. The code is organized to move from the exterior of the building to areas inside the building and then to the structure. The first set of assemblies can best be thought of as planes, both vertical and horizontal, arranged around the structural system. These planes may be bearing walls and part of the structural system, or they may be curtain walls or interior partitions independent of the structure.

Various interrelated conditions impact the fire-resistance requirements of the systems considered. Openings (and their protection), location on the property, relationships of exterior walls facing each other (as in courts), separations of interior spaces by fire walls, vertical circulation, vertical openings, protection of egress paths, smoke barriers, penetrations by utility systems, the abutment

of floor systems with curtain-wall systems, and fire-resistive protection of structural systems—all must be considered. We will explore each of these sets of requirements in the same order they are presented in the code.

Per § 703.6, fire-resistance-rated glazing, when tested per ASTM E119 or UL 263 and complying with the Fire Barrier requirements contained in § 707, may be used. Such glazing is to have a permanently attached label identifying that the glazing is fire-resistant and indicating its fire-resistance-rating in minutes. Labels are to appear on the glass per the requirements of Table 716.3.

Per § 703.7, fire walls, fire barriers, fire partitions, smoke barriers, and smoke partitions—or any other wall that requires protected openings or penetrations—are to be identified with a permanent sign or stencil marking. The marking may be in concealed spaces when they are accessible. The markings are to occur at intervals not exceeding 30' (9144) and the lettering is to be at least 3" (76) high and read: "FIRE AND/OR SMOKE BARRIER–PROTECT ALL OPENINGS" or similar wording. The markings are required in concealed areas where access is possible. If there is no access to a concealed space, or if there is no ceiling to form concealed spaces, then markings are not required.

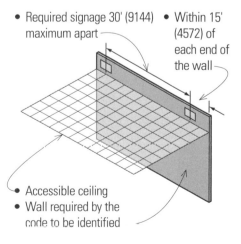

- Required signage 30' (9144) maximum apart
- Within 15' (4572) of each end of the wall
- Accessible ceiling
- Wall required by the code to be identified

FIRE-RESISTANCE OF STRUCTURAL MEMBERS

§ 704 requires that the fire-resistance ratings of structural members and assemblies comply with the requirements for type of construction as set forth in Chapter 6 and Table 601. The ratings should be complementary in that the structure supporting a fire-resistance-rated assembly should have at least the rating of the assembly supported.

§ 704.8 prohibits inclusion of service elements such as pipes or conduits into the fire-protection covering. This recognizes that such elements can conduct heat through the fire protection to the structural member and thus potentially compromise the time rating for fire-resistance.

§ 704.10 addresses the protection of structural members located on the exterior of a building. The protection of such members is set forth in Table 601 and must be as required for exterior bearing walls, for the structural frame, or as required for exterior walls based on fire separation distance per Table 602, whichever is greater.

§ 704.2 and § 704.3 require individual structural members such as columns or beams to be fully protected on all sides for their entire length if they are required to have a fire-resistance rating. This applies to members other than columns that either support a direct load from more than two floors or a floor and a roof, or support a load-bearing wall or a non-load-bearing wall more than two stories in height. All rated columns must be individually encased regardless of loading conditions. Per § 704.4, these requirements also apply to "secondary members" that are required to have a fire-resistance rating.

The code recognizes that attachment elements project out from structural members and that reinforcing ties may be located closer to the surface of a concrete element than the main reinforcing. § 704.6 allows these elements to be closer to the surface of the fire protection than the thickness required for the main members.

Secondary members can be fire-protected by a membrane or ceiling when they provide protection with a horizontal assembly complying with § 711.

§ 704.2. requires the full height of a column to be protected, including its connection to beams and girders, even if it extends through a rated ceiling assembly.

§ 704.13 clarifies the requirements for sprayed fire-resistant materials (SFRM). These materials are typically applied by pressure-spray on steel members to achieve the required fire-resistance rating for the steel members. The fire-resistance-rating duration is dependent on the thickness of the materials. The in-place performance of SFRM depends on it remaining in place during a fire so this section sets forth criteria for surface conditions of the steel members and for proper application to ensure that the materials will perform adequately under actual fire conditions. While it is acceptable per § 704.13.5 for the SFRM to have surface irregularities it is not acceptable for SFRM to have cracks, voids, spalls, or delamination in the surface that would allow fire to penetrate the protection layer and heat the steel underneath. Note that per § 704.11. It is acceptable to have unprotected steel shelf angles if they span not more than 6'-4" (1931).

Fire-protection materials, especially spray-applied fire protection, are subject to impact damage that could knock off the fire protection and compromise the fire-resistance of the structural member. § 704.9 requires impact protection for elements subject to damage. The protection is to extend to a height of at least 5' (1524) above the floor.

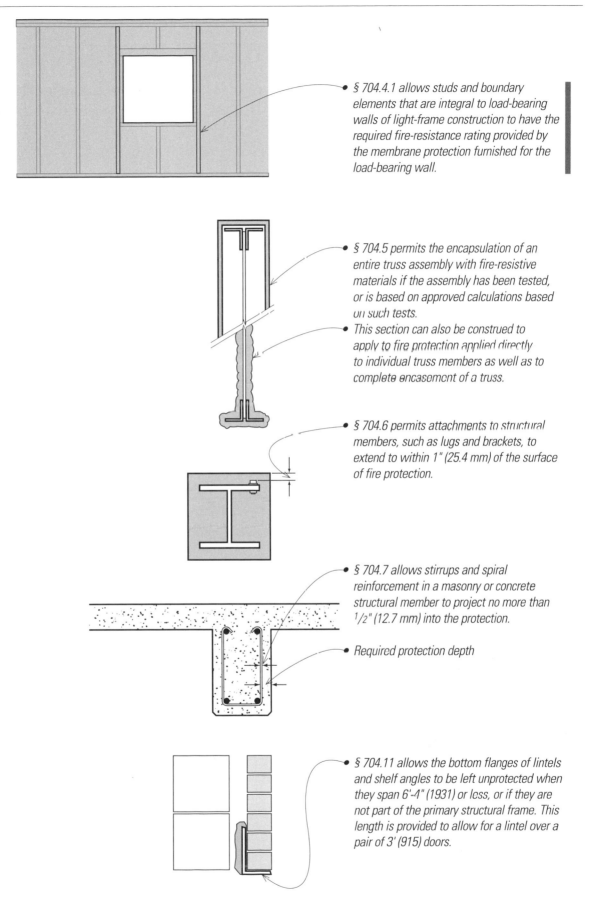

- § 704.4.1 allows studs and boundary elements that are integral to load-bearing walls of light-frame construction to have the required fire-resistance rating provided by the membrane protection furnished for the load-bearing wall.

- § 704.5 permits the encapsulation of an entire truss assembly with fire-resistive materials if the assembly has been tested, or is based on approved calculations based on such tests.
- This section can also be construed to apply to fire protection applied directly to individual truss members as well as to complete encasement of a truss.

- § 704.6 permits attachments to structural members, such as lugs and brackets, to extend to within 1" (25.4 mm) of the surface of fire protection.

- § 704.7 allows stirrups and spiral reinforcement in a masonry or concrete structural member to project no more than 1/2" (12.7 mm) into the protection.

- Required protection depth

- § 704.11 allows the bottom flanges of lintels and shelf angles to be left unprotected when they span 6'-4" (1931) or less, or if they are not part of the primary structural frame. This length is provided to allow for a lintel over a pair of 3' (915) doors.

The contents of § 705 apply more broadly than its title would suggest. The relationship to the property line of exterior walls as well as openings within and projections from the walls are covered in this section. The wall criteria also interact with the type of construction to dictate the fire resistance of the elements of the wall. This section should be read in conjunction with § 1406, which governs the use of combustible materials on the exterior face of exterior walls. Exterior egress balconies are to comply with § 1021 and exterior egress stairs are to comply with § 1027.

Projections

§ 705.2 governs the extent of allowable projections according to their relationship to the property line. The combustibility of the projections is governed by the wall construction type (which as we have seen is related to heights, areas, and occupancy types). Combustible projections extending to within 5 feet (1524) of the line used to determine the fire separation distance are to be of not less than 1-hour fire-resistance-rated construction, Type IV construction, fire-retardant-treated wood, or as required by § 1406.3.

Older IBC editions had a complicated set of standards for determining the extent of allowable projections based on how far beyond the wall the projection extended. The code now relates the extent of an allowable projection to the fire separation distance of the exterior wall at the projection location and expresses it as the minimum distance from the line used in determining the fire separation distance.

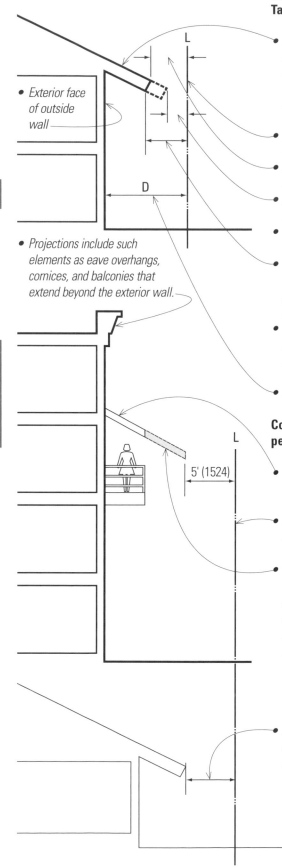

- Exterior face of outside wall

- Projections include such elements as eave overhangs, cornices, and balconies that extend beyond the exterior wall.

Minimum Distance of Projection per Table 705.2

- Projections from walls of Types I and II construction are to be of noncombustible construction. Projections from walls of other types of construction may be of any approved materials.

- Line used to determine fire separation distance (L).

- Projection distances are based on fire separation distance per Table 705.2

- 24" (610) minimum distance where D is between 2' (610) and 3' (914)

- No projections are allowed when D is less than 2' (610).

- For distances from 3' (914) to 30' (9144) the projection may be 2' (610) + 8" (203) per foot in the range from 3' (914) to 30' (9144) from line L.

- Where D is greater than 30' (9144) projections can only extend to within 20' (6096) of line L.

- Fire-separation distance (D)

Combustible Projection Protection per § 705.2.3

- Unrated projection if more than 5' (1524) from line L.

- Line used to determine fire separation distance (L).

- Combustible projections extending to within 5' (1524) of the lot line are to be of at least 1-hour fire-resistance-rated construction, Type IV construction, fire-retardant-treated wood, or as required by § 1406.3.

- Note that R-3 and U occupancies may have unrated Type V-B projections with D > 5' (1524).

Multiple Buildings on the Same Property

§ 705.3 assumes that, when determining the protection requirements for multiple buildings on the same property, an imaginary line exists between the buildings or elements. The code does not specify that the imaginary line be located midway between the elements, so the designer is free to locate the property line at any point between the elements in question as long as the wall protection requirements are met based on the distance to the assumed property line. The intent of § 705.3 is to prevent the spread of fire by radiant heating or convection. The impact of these conditions may be diminished by distance or by wall treatments, such as having openings in one wall face a solid wall on the opposite side of the assumed property line.

Where an S-2 parking garage of construction Type I or II-A is erected on the same lot as a Group R-2 building and there is no fire-separation distance between these buildings, then the adjoining exterior walls between the buildings are permitted to have occupant-use openings in accordance with § 705.8. However, opening protectives in such openings shall only be required in the exterior wall of the S-2 parking garage, not in the exterior wall openings in the R-2 building, and these opening protectives in the exterior wall of the S-2 parking garage shall be not less than 1-1/2 hour fire protection rating per § 705.3.

Fire-Resistance Ratings

§ 705.5 requires that the fire-resistance ratings for exterior walls be as prescribed by Tables 601 and 602. Based on the intent of the code to prevent the spread of fire from one property to another, when an exterior wall is located more than 10' (3048) from the property line the fire exposure is assumed to be from the inside. When an exterior wall is located 10' (3048) or less from the property line, the exposure must be assumed to come from either inside or outside the building. This recognizes that another building may be built on the lot line on the adjacent property.

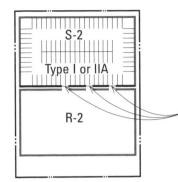

- There is a special case in Exception 2 to § 705.3 for an S-2 parking garage located on the same lot with an R-2 residential building with no fire-separation distance between the buildings. The S-2 building must be of I or II-A construction.
- 1-1/2 hour opening protectives on exterior garage wall only; none required at R-2 building.

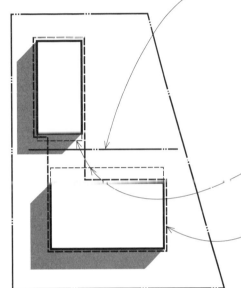

- Two or more buildings on the same property may be treated as separate buildings with an imaginary line between. Note that the distances from each building to this imaginary line need not be equal. By choosing the line location carefully and applying the rules consistently, one wall of a set of buildings relatively close to each other could have unprotected openings as long as the opposite wall was treated as required for being near the assumed location of the imaginary line.
- Projections on buildings located on the same lot with an imaginary line between them are to conform to the requirements regarding projections contained in § 705.2
- The buildings may be treated as portions of a single building if the aggregate area of the buildings are within the limits specified in Chapter 5 for the intended occupancies.

- Per § 705.6 the exterior wall is to extend to the height required by § 705.11 (parapets).
- Structural elements that brace the exterior wall and are located outside of the plane of the wall are to conform to the fire-resistance rating requirements of Table 601 for structural elements and Table 602 for wall ratings.
- § 705.5 specifies that exterior walls having a fire-separation distance greater than 10' (3048) be rated for exposure to fires from the inside.
- Exterior walls having a fire-separation distance of 10' (3048) or less must be rated for exposure to fire from both sides.

Openings

While § 705.7 contains detailed calculations (Equation 7-1) for determining the fire-resistance rating of protected openings, we will focus on the simpler calculation contained in § 705.8 and Table 705.8. (See page 89.) These relate location on the property to the percentage of wall openings and whether the openings are protected or not. For windows in exterior walls to be protected they must comply with the opening protection requirements of § 716, which we will discuss later.

Protected Openings

Where openings are required to be "protected" the code considers them to be protected per § 705.8.2 if fire doors and fire shutters comply with § 716.5 and fire window assemblies comply with § 716.6. Additional active fire-protection measures can also allow increases in the area of openings. For example, the provision of a fire-sprinkler system (adding an active fire-protection system to passive measures) is built into Table 705.8 to allow more unprotected openings in sprinklered buildings under most conditions.

Vertical Separation of Openings

§ 705.8.5 regulates the vertical relationship of openings to each other. These requirements <u>do not apply</u> to buildings less than three stories in height, or when fire sprinklers are provided. Again, provision of an active system allows more freedom in determining whether passive systems must also be incorporated.

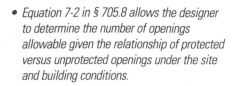

- *Equation 7-2 in § 705.8 allows the designer to determine the number of openings allowable given the relationship of protected versus unprotected openings under the site and building conditions.*

$$A_p/a_p + A_u/a_u \leq 1.0$$
where:
A_p = *actual area of protected openings or equivalent area per § 705.7*
a_p = *allowable area of protected openings per Table 705.8*
A_u = *actual area of unprotected openings*
a_u = *allowable area of unprotected openings per Table 705.8*

- *In other than Group H occupancies, exceptions to § 705.8.1 allow unlimited unprotected openings in the first floor of exterior walls if the exterior walls face a public street and have a fire-separation distance of more than 15' (4572), or if they face an unoccupied space that is at least 30' (9144) wide and has access from a street to a posted fire lane.*

- *If openings in adjacent stories are within 5' (1524) of each other and the lower one is not protected by at least a 1-hour fire-resistance rating, § 705.8.5 requires that they be separated:*
- *vertically at least 3' (914) by an assembly having at least a 1-hour fire-resistive rating rated for exposure to fire from both sides, or*
- *by a flame barrier that extends horizontally at least 30" (762) beyond the exterior wall.*

- *These requirements do not apply to buildings that are 3 stories tall or less, when fire sprinklers are provided, or in open parking garages.*

Excerpt from IBC Table 705.8

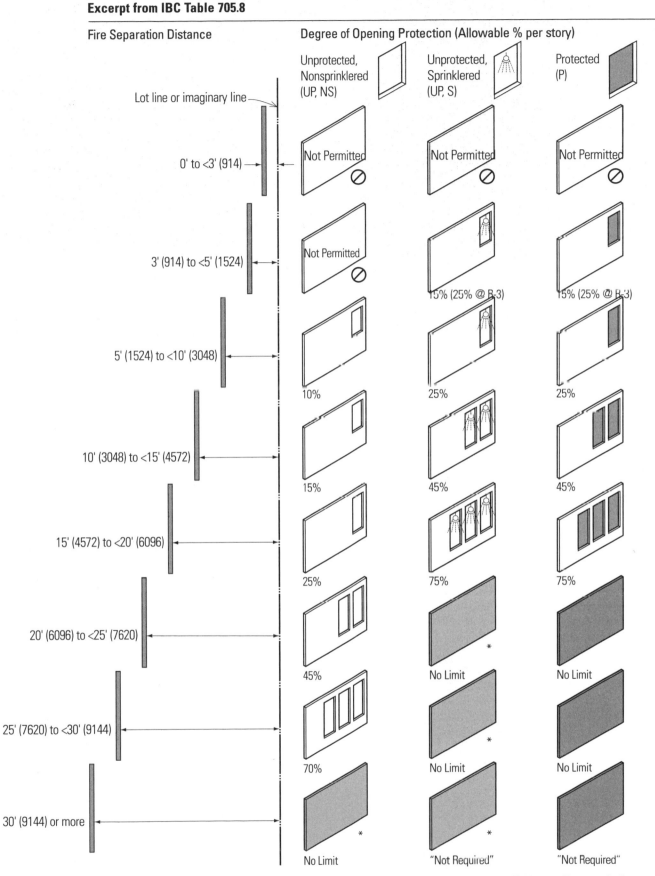

Fire Separation Distance

Degree of Opening Protection (Allowable % per story)

Unprotected, Nonsprinklered (UP, NS)

Unprotected, Sprinklered (UP, S)

Protected (P)

Lot line or imaginary line

0' to <3' (914)

Not Permitted — Not Permitted — Not Permitted

3' (914) to <5' (1524)

Not Permitted — 15% (25% @ R-3) — 15% (25% @ R-3)

5' (1524) to <10' (3048)

10% — 25% — 25%

10' (3048) to <15' (4572)

15% — 45% — 45%

15' (4572) to <20' (6096)

25% — 75% — 75%

20' (6096) to <25' (7620)

45% — No Limit* — No Limit

25' (7620) to <30' (9144)

70% — No Limit* — No Limit

30' (9144) or more

No Limit* — "Not Required"* — "Not Required"

*   Nonbearing walls may be unprotected when the area of unprotected openings is not limited per Table 602, Footnote "g."

Vertical Exposure

For multiple buildings on the same property, § 705.8.6 requires the protection of openings in any wall that extends above an adjacent roof. This protection can be provided in various ways: by distance, by opening protectives, or by protection of the roof framing and its supporting structure. The principle is one of reduction of the likelihood of fire spreading from one location to another. The buildings must be separated by a minimum distance, some method of fire protection applied to the openings, or the construction facing the openings must be protected.

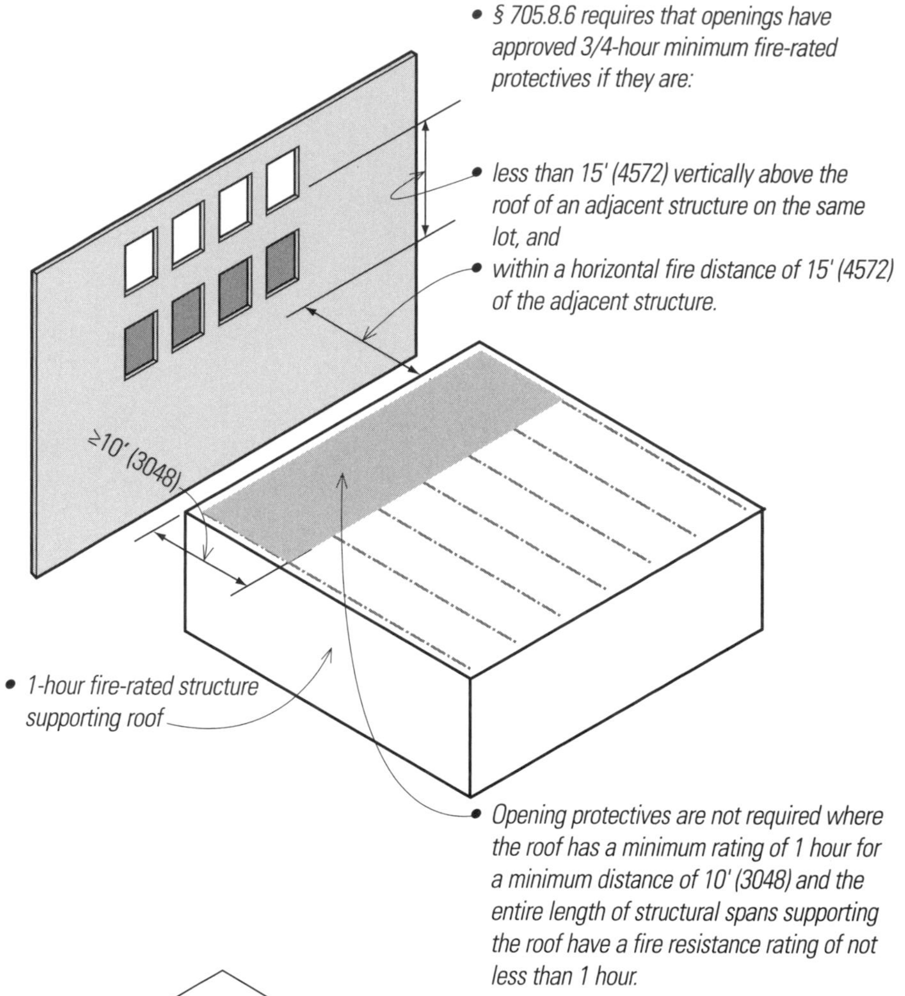

Fire protection of openings in exterior walls other than windows and doors must be addressed as part of the design as well. Expansion and seismic joints, wall and floor intersections, ducts, louvers and similar air-transfer openings must comply with the detailed requirements of sections discussed later in this chapter.

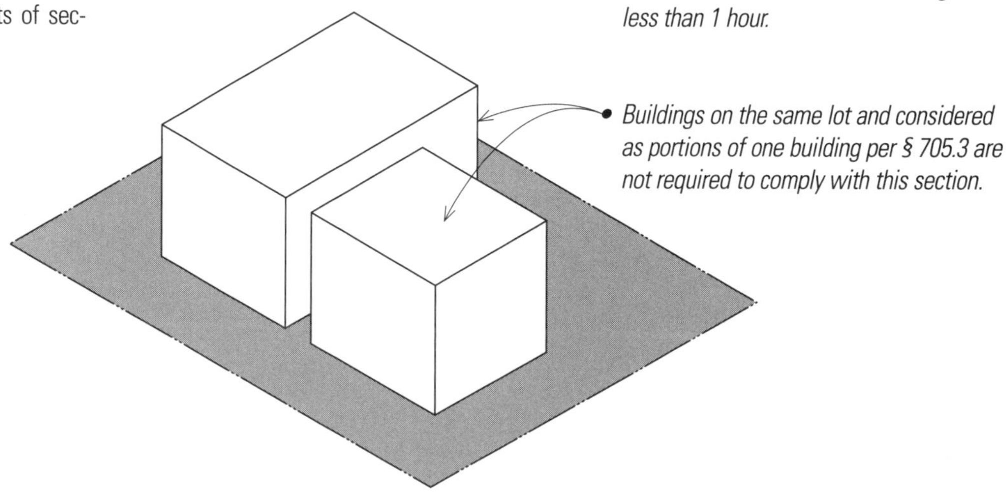

- § 705.8.6 requires that openings have approved 3/4-hour minimum fire-rated protectives if they are:

- less than 15' (4572) vertically above the roof of an adjacent structure on the same lot, and
- within a horizontal fire distance of 15' (4572) of the adjacent structure.

≥10' (3048)

- 1-hour fire-rated structure supporting roof

- Opening protectives are not required where the roof has a minimum rating of 1 hour for a minimum distance of 10' (3048) and the entire length of structural spans supporting the roof have a fire resistance rating of not less than 1 hour.

- Buildings on the same lot and considered as portions of one building per § 705.3 are not required to comply with this section.

Parapets

§ 705.11 makes a general statement that parapets shall be provided at exterior walls of buildings. The purpose of parapets is to impede the spread of fire from one building to another by providing a barrier to fire and radiant heat transfer if fire breaks through the roof membrane.

The exceptions that follow reduce or eliminate the need for parapets if any of the conditions are met. The list of exceptions becomes the code criteria, not the more general opening statement that parapets will always occur. Note that there may be extensive construction work involved to avoid a parapet. The converse is also true that the provisions noted in the exception can be avoided by providing a parapet. The exceptions, where parapets are not required, can be summarized as follows. No parapets are needed where:

1. The wall satisfies the fire-separation distance criteria in accordance with Table 602.
2. The building area does not exceed 1,000 sf (93 m²) on any floor.
3. The roof construction is entirely noncombustible or of at least 2-hour fire-resistive construction.
4. The roof framing is protected against fire exposure from the inside, as illustrated to the right.
5. In residential occupancies, a fire barrier is provided by sheathing the underside of the roof framing, or the roof sheathing is of noncombustible materials for 4' (1219) back from the roof/wall intersection and the entire building has a Class C or better roof covering.
6. § 705.8 allows the wall to have 25% or more of its openings unprotected due to the building's location from a property line.

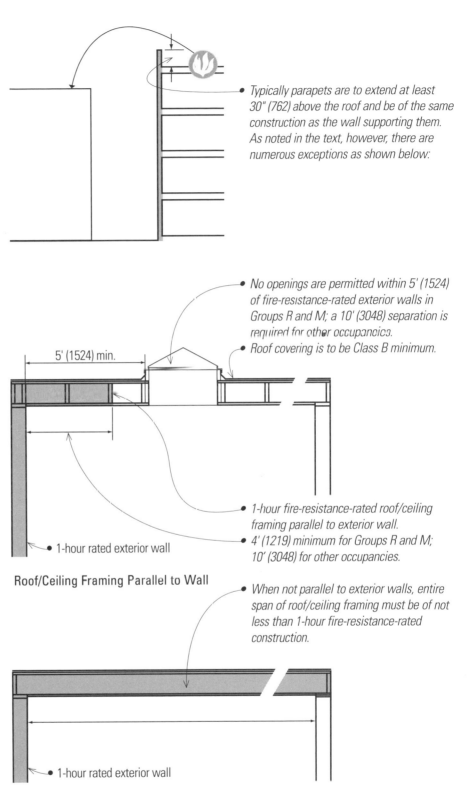

- Typically parapets are to extend at least 30" (762) above the roof and be of the same construction as the wall supporting them. As noted in the text, however, there are numerous exceptions as shown below:

- No openings are permitted within 5' (1524) of fire-resistance-rated exterior walls in Groups R and M; a 10' (3048) separation is required for other occupancies.
- Roof covering is to be Class B minimum.

5' (1524) min.

- 1-hour fire-resistance-rated roof/ceiling framing parallel to exterior wall.
- 4' (1219) minimum for Groups R and M; 10' (3048) for other occupancies.

- 1-hour rated exterior wall

Roof/Ceiling Framing Parallel to Wall

- When not parallel to exterior walls, entire span of roof/ceiling framing must be of not less than 1-hour fire-resistance-rated construction.

- 1-hour rated exterior wall

Roof/Ceiling Framing Not Parallel to Wall

§ 202 defines a fire wall as a fire-resistance-rated wall whose purpose is to restrict the spread of fire. To perform this function, a fire wall must extend continuously from the building foundation to or through the roof, and have sufficient structural stability to withstand collapse if construction on either side of it collapses.

Structural Stability

§ 706.2 requires that a fire wall have a structural configuration that allows for structural collapse on either side while the wall stays in place for the time required by the fire-resistance rating. Walls constructed per the requirements of NFPA 221 will be deemed to comply with this section. Using a double wall is the clearest way to comply with the structural collapse requirements.

The interrelated requirements of seismic design and sound control must be carefully considered along with the structural stability criteria, as all of these requirements are integrated into a project. This should be discussed early in the design process with the AHJ.

Materials

§ 706.3 requires fire walls to be constructed of noncombustible materials, except in Type V construction, where they can be of fire-protected combustible construction.

Fire-Resistance Ratings

§ 706.4 bases the required fire-resistance ratings of fire walls on occupancy. For most occupancies, fire walls are required to have 3-hour fire-resistance ratings. Table 706.4 allows 2-hour ratings in Type II or V buildings for certain occupancies. Where different occupancies or groups are separated by a fire wall, the more stringent requirements for separation rating will apply.

Horizontal Continuity

§ 706.5 specifies that fire walls are to be continuous horizontally from exterior wall to exterior wall, and extend at least 18" (457) beyond the exterior surface of the exterior walls.

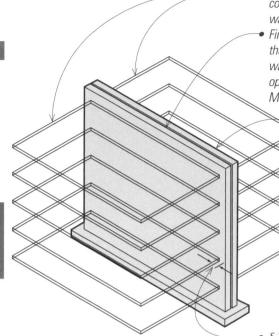

- § 706.1 considers each portion of a building completely separated by one or more fire walls to be a separate building.
- Fire wall. If located on a property line and thus considered to be serving as a party wall, the fire wall is not permitted to have openings. Note that this is different for Malls. See § 402.4.2.2.
- Double wall with minimum clearance between walls per NFPA 221: "Standards for High Challenge Fire Walls, Fire Walls and Fire Barrier Walls." The only connection between the walls is to be flashing at top of wall. Note that each wall may be allowed to have a lower fire rating to achieve the overall fire rating required for the total set of fire walls when considered as a complete assembly of all of the walls.

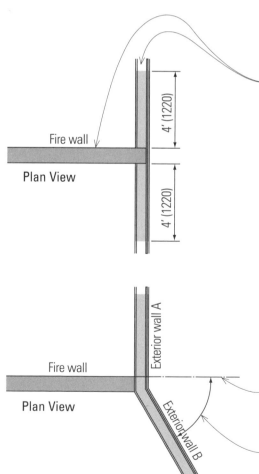

Fire wall

Plan View

4' (1220)

4' (1220)

Fire wall

Plan View

Exterior wall A

Exterior wall B

- § 706.5 requires fire walls to extend at least 18" (457) beyond the exterior surface of exterior walls. There are exceptions to this requirement, based on the provision of additional fire-resistive construction at the exterior wall to provide a barrier to heat and flame propagation.
- A fire wall may terminate at the interior surface of exterior sheathing, siding or other finish if fire-rated protection forms a "T" and extends a horizontal distance of at least 4' (1220) on both sides of the fire wall.
- The fire-rated protection may be provided by exterior-wall construction having a fire-resistance rating of at least 1 hour, or by the use of noncombustible exterior sheathing, siding or other finish.
- § 706.5 also allows a fire wall to terminate at the interior surface of noncombustible exterior sheathing if the building on each side of the fire wall is protected with an automatic sprinkler system.
- Note that exterior-wall intersections at fire walls that form an angle equal to or greater than 180° (3.14 rad) do not need fire protection.
- Where fire walls intersect an exterior wall that forms an angle of less than 180° (3.14 rad), an imaginary line is to be extended beyond the face of the exterior wall.
- The opening protection criteria of § 705.5 and § 705.8 are to be applied to Exterior Wall "B."

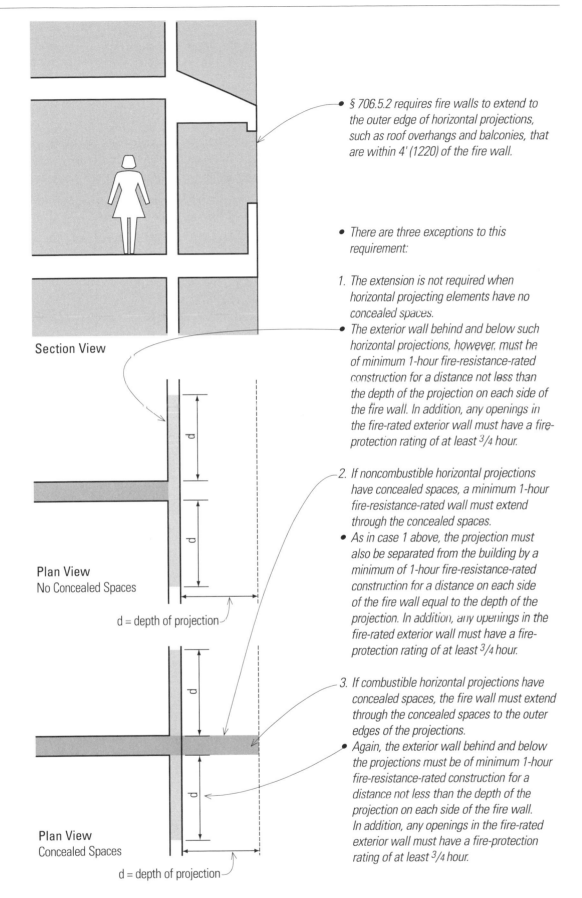

Section View

Plan View
No Concealed Spaces

d = depth of projection

Plan View
Concealed Spaces

d = depth of projection

• § 706.5.2 requires fire walls to extend to the outer edge of horizontal projections, such as roof overhangs and balconies, that are within 4' (1220) of the fire wall.

• There are three exceptions to this requirement:

1. The extension is not required when horizontal projecting elements have no concealed spaces.
• The exterior wall behind and below such horizontal projections, however, must be of minimum 1-hour fire-resistance-rated construction for a distance not less than the depth of the projection on each side of the fire wall. In addition, any openings in the fire-rated exterior wall must have a fire-protection rating of at least $3/4$ hour.

2. If noncombustible horizontal projections have concealed spaces, a minimum 1-hour fire-resistance-rated wall must extend through the concealed spaces.
• As in case 1 above, the projection must also be separated from the building by a minimum of 1-hour fire-resistance-rated construction for a distance on each side of the fire wall equal to the depth of the projection. In addition, any openings in the fire-rated exterior wall must have a fire-protection rating of at least $3/4$ hour.

3. If combustible horizontal projections have concealed spaces, the fire wall must extend through the concealed spaces to the outer edges of the projections.
• Again, the exterior wall behind and below the projections must be of minimum 1-hour fire-resistance-rated construction for a distance not less than the depth of the projection on each side of the fire wall. In addition, any openings in the fire-rated exterior wall must have a fire-protection rating of at least $3/4$ hour.

FIRE WALLS

Vertical Continuity

§ 706.6 requires that fire walls be continuous vertically from the building foundation to a point at least 30" (762) above adjacent roofs.

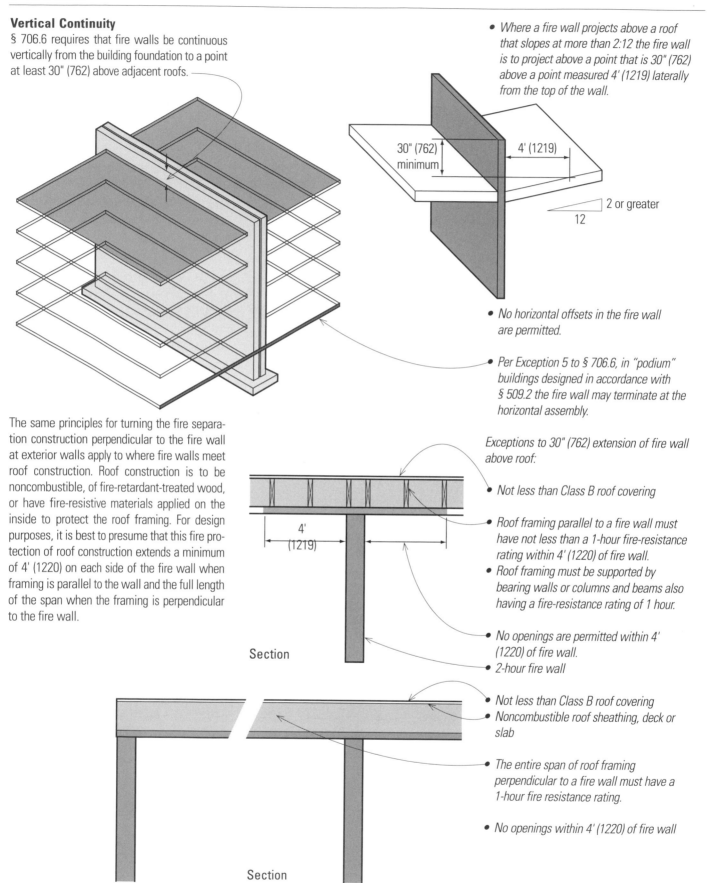

The same principles for turning the fire separation construction perpendicular to the fire wall at exterior walls apply to where fire walls meet roof construction. Roof construction is to be noncombustible, of fire-retardant-treated wood, or have fire-resistive materials applied on the inside to protect the roof framing. For design purposes, it is best to presume that this fire protection of roof construction extends a minimum of 4' (1220) on each side of the fire wall when framing is parallel to the wall and the full length of the span when the framing is perpendicular to the fire wall.

- Where a fire wall projects above a roof that slopes at more than 2:12 the fire wall is to project above a point that is 30" (762) above a point measured 4' (1219) laterally from the top of the wall.

30" (762) minimum

4' (1219)

2 or greater

12

- No horizontal offsets in the fire wall are permitted.

- Per Exception 5 to § 706.6, in "podium" buildings designed in accordance with § 509.2 the fire wall may terminate at the horizontal assembly.

Exceptions to 30" (762) extension of fire wall above roof:

- Not less than Class B roof covering

- Roof framing parallel to a fire wall must have not less than a 1-hour fire-resistance rating within 4' (1220) of fire wall.
- Roof framing must be supported by bearing walls or columns and beams also having a fire-resistance rating of 1 hour.

- No openings are permitted within 4' (1220) of fire wall.
- 2-hour fire wall

4' (1219)

Section

- Not less than Class B roof covering
- Noncombustible roof sheathing, deck or slab

- The entire span of roof framing perpendicular to a fire wall must have a 1-hour fire resistance rating.

- No openings within 4' (1220) of fire wall

Section

Penetrations and Joints

Openings, penetrations, and joints are required to have fire protection per sections occurring later in Chapter 7. Per § 706.11, ducts are not allowed to penetrate fire walls on property lines. Exceptions allow ducts at fire walls not located at lot lines where fire assemblies per § 717 protect the duct penetrations and the aggregate area of openings does not exceed that permitted under § 706.8.

Stepped Roofs

When a fire wall serves as the exterior wall of a building and separates buildings having different roof levels, the criteria of § 706.6.1 apply to the lower roof. This may also apply to construction of the wall for a designated height and opening protection. The lower roof allowance is one option available.

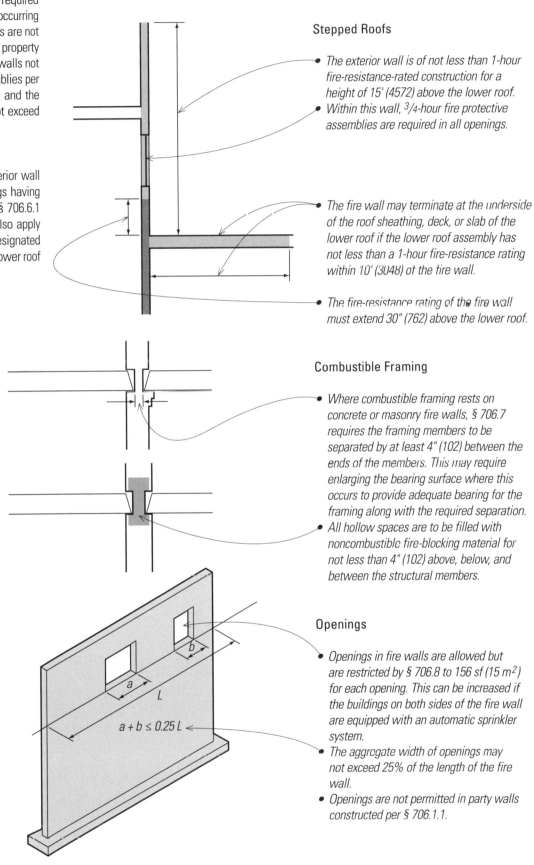

Stepped Roofs

- *The exterior wall is of not less than 1-hour fire-resistance-rated construction for a height of 15' (4572) above the lower roof.*
- *Within this wall, 3/4-hour fire protective assemblies are required in all openings.*

- *The fire wall may terminate at the underside of the roof sheathing, deck, or slab of the lower roof if the lower roof assembly has not less than a 1-hour fire-resistance rating within 10' (3048) of the fire wall.*

- *The fire-resistance rating of the fire wall must extend 30" (762) above the lower roof.*

Combustible Framing

- *Where combustible framing rests on concrete or masonry fire walls, § 706.7 requires the framing members to be separated by at least 4" (102) between the ends of the members. This may require enlarging the bearing surface where this occurs to provide adequate bearing for the framing along with the required separation.*
- *All hollow spaces are to be filled with noncombustible fire-blocking material for not less than 4" (102) above, below, and between the structural members.*

Openings

- *Openings in fire walls are allowed but are restricted by § 706.8 to 156 sf (15 m²) for each opening. This can be increased if the buildings on both sides of the fire wall are equipped with an automatic sprinkler system.*
- *The aggregate width of openings may not exceed 25% of the length of the fire wall.*
- *Openings are not permitted in party walls constructed per § 706.1.1.*

$$a + b \leq 0.25\,L$$

FIRE BARRIERS

Fire barriers are similar to fire walls but with simpler criteria. They are used to separate interior exit stairways from other egress components, to separate different occupancies, or to divide a single or mixed occupancy into different fire areas. Required fire-resistance ratings for fire barriers are determined by their use. Barriers used in means of egress protection are rated per the applicable sections in Chapter 10. Occupancy separation ratings are per Table 508.4. Fire resistance ratings between fire areas are to be per Table 707.3.10.

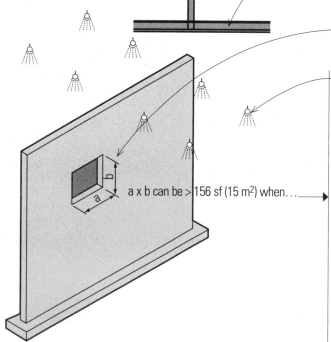

• *Fire barriers serve to separate interior exit stairways from other egress components, set apart different occupancies,*

or divide a single occupancy into different fire areas.

• *Fire-resistance-rated glazing is permitted in fire barriers but must be tested and listed.*

• *Note that walls located on the outside of the building at rated enclosures may have a different rating than the walls facing the interior of the building. Exterior-wall and opening ratings are determined by exterior criteria per § 705 in concert with the opening requirements in § 716 and exit requirements of § 1023.7.*

• *Fire barriers are to be continuous between floor levels and extend to abut adjacent interior or exterior walls. The intent is that the barriers prevent the spread of smoke or fire for the duration of the time rating. Penetrations and openings are permitted but must be protected to maintain the integrity of the barrier.*

• *Fire barrier should extend from the top of the floor assembly below to the underside of the floor or roof deck or slab above.*

• *Fire barrier should be continuous through concealed ceiling spaces.*

• *Supporting floor should have the same fire rating as the fire barrier supported.*

• *Per § 707.6, openings in fire barriers are limited to 156 sf (15 m^2) and an aggregate width of 25% of the length of the fire barrier wall. The requirements for fire barriers are less stringent than those for fire walls. Several exceptions are allowed:*

1. *Openings are not limited to 156 sf (15 m^2) when the adjoining floor areas have an automatic sprinkler system.*
2. *Openings are not limited to 156 sf (15 m^2) or to 25% of the length where the opening protective is a fire door serving an enclosure for an interior exit stairway.*
3. *Openings are not limited to 156 sf (15 m^2) when there is a tested opening protective assembly that has a fire-resistance rating equal to that of the wall.*
4. *Fire window assemblies in atrium walls are not limited to an aggregate length of 25% of the length of the wall.*
5. *Openings are not limited to 156 sf (15 m^2) or to 25% of the length where the opening protective is a fire-door assembly in a fire barrier separating an enclosure for an interior exit stairway from an exit passageway in accordance with § 1023.3.1.*

a x b can be > 156 sf (15 m^2) when...

Fire partitions are the next level of fire-resistive wall construction below fire walls and fire barriers. They typically have 1-hour fire-resistance ratings and are primarily used for separations between listed building elements.

Fire partitions have the same relationship to exterior walls as fire walls and fire barriers. They also have similar requirements for penetrations, openings, and ductwork as for the other groups of partition types.

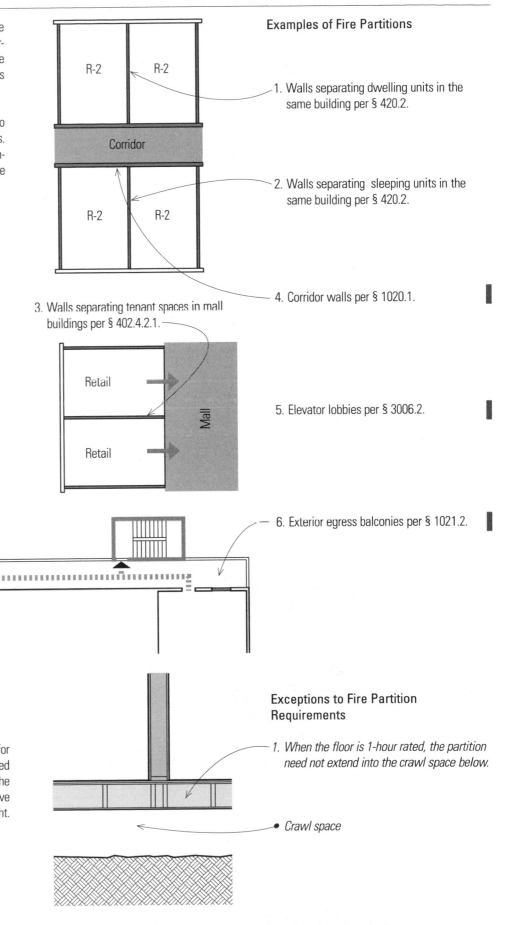

Examples of Fire Partitions

1. Walls separating dwelling units in the same building per § 420.2.

2. Walls separating sleeping units in the same building per § 420.2.

4. Corridor walls per § 1020.1.

3. Walls separating tenant spaces in mall buildings per § 402.4.2.1.

5. Elevator lobbies per § 3006.2.

6. Exterior egress balconies per § 1021.2.

Exceptions to Fire Partition Requirements

The exceptions with the most relevance for designers are contained in § 708.4, related to the extent and continuity of partitions. The partitions are to extend to the structure above and below with exceptions as listed on the right.

1. *When the floor is 1-hour rated, the partition need not extend into the crawl space below.*

• *Crawl space*

Exceptions to Fire Partition
Requirements

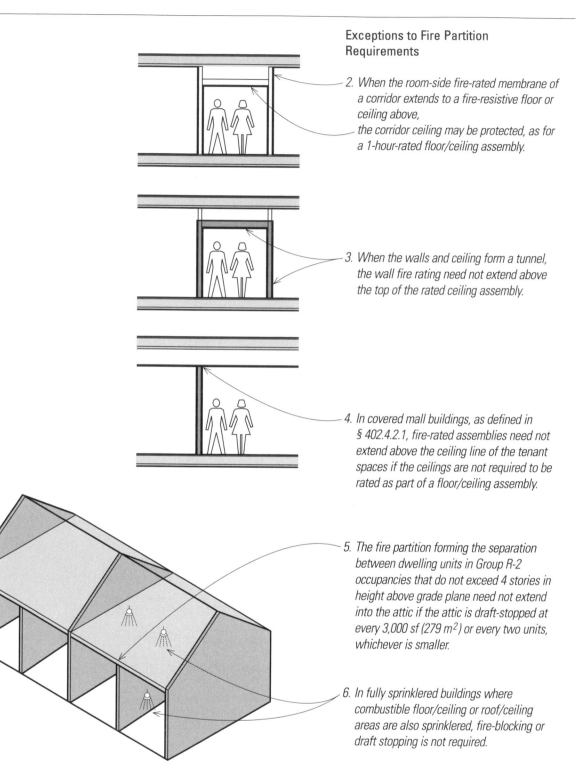

2. When the room-side fire-rated membrane of
    a corridor extends to a fire-resistive floor or
    ceiling above,
    the corridor ceiling may be protected, as for
    a 1-hour-rated floor/ceiling assembly.

3. When the walls and ceiling form a tunnel,
    the wall fire rating need not extend above
    the top of the rated ceiling assembly.

4. In covered mall buildings, as defined in
    § 402.4.2.1, fire-rated assemblies need not
    extend above the ceiling line of the tenant
    spaces if the ceilings are not required to be
    rated as part of a floor/ceiling assembly.

5. The fire partition forming the separation
    between dwelling units in Group R-2
    occupancies that do not exceed 4 stories in
    height above grade plane need not extend
    into the attic if the attic is draft-stopped at
    every 3,000 sf (279 m²) or every two units,
    whichever is smaller.

6. In fully sprinklered buildings where
    combustible floor/ceiling or roof/ceiling
    areas are also sprinklered, fire-blocking or
    draft stopping is not required.

Smoke Barriers and Smoke Partitions

§ 709 and § 710 treat smoke barriers as fire barriers, but with emphasis on restricting the migration of smoke. Smoke barriers are required to have a 1-hour rating with 20-minute-rated opening protectives. Smoke partitions are required to restrict smoke movement but are not required to have a fire-resistance rating.

Openings in smoke barriers are to be protected per § 716. There are exceptions for opposite-swinging and sliding doors in I-2 occupancies.

Horizontal Assemblies

§ 711 describes the requirements for floor/ceiling assemblies and roof/ceiling assemblies that require a fire resistance rating. Their required fire-resistance rating is determined by their use. The rating is primarily determined by the fire-resistance rating based on type of construction as dictated by Table 601. When separating occupancies or dividing a single or mixed occupancy into fire areas, the fire-resistance rating of the horizontal assembly must also be examined against the requirements of Table 508.4 and Table 707.3.10.

The criteria for penetrations of horizontal assemblies are more stringent than those for vertical assemblies, as the passage of smoke and gases vertically between floors of a building is of great concern and is facilitated by natural convective forces.

Where ducts are not required to have fire or smoke dampers complying with § 717 they are required to be treated as penetrations, and the spaces around the penetrations to be sealed per this section.

Horizontal assemblies have the same continuity requirements as for vertical assemblies. Penetrations, joints, and ducts are to be protected as for vertical assemblies; refer to § 707, § 712, and § 713.

- Smoke barriers are intended to provide separations to prevent smoke migration. Smoke-barrier walls are subdivided into two categories for continuity in § 709.4.
- § 709.4.1 addresses smoke barriers separating smoke compartments in uses such as hospitals and requires the smoke barrier to extend continuously from outside wall to outside wall.
- § 709.4.2 covers smoke barriers for smaller areas on a floor, such as an area of refuge or elevator lobby and allows the smoke-barrier walls to terminate at a 1-hour-rated fire barrier, another smoke-barrier wall, or at an exterior wall.
- Smoke barriers need to be continuous through concealed spaces unless they abut assemblies that will resist the passage of smoke, such as walls meeting fire-rated ceiling assemblies.
- Smoke partitions need not be fire-resistance rated.

- In 1-hour fire-resistance-rated floor construction, § 711.2.6 permits lower membranes to be omitted over unusable crawl spaces and upper membranes to be omitted below unusable attic spaces.

- Any structural members or walls supporting a horizontal assembly must have at least the same fire-resistance rating as the horizontal assembly.

Proportional Examples of Fire-Resistance-Rated Construction at Interior Walls

Not all types of the fire-resistance barriers illustrated below apply in all occupancies. Those that do not apply in Group E or Group B occupancies are noted. The drawings are not to scale; they are for comparison and reference purposes only.

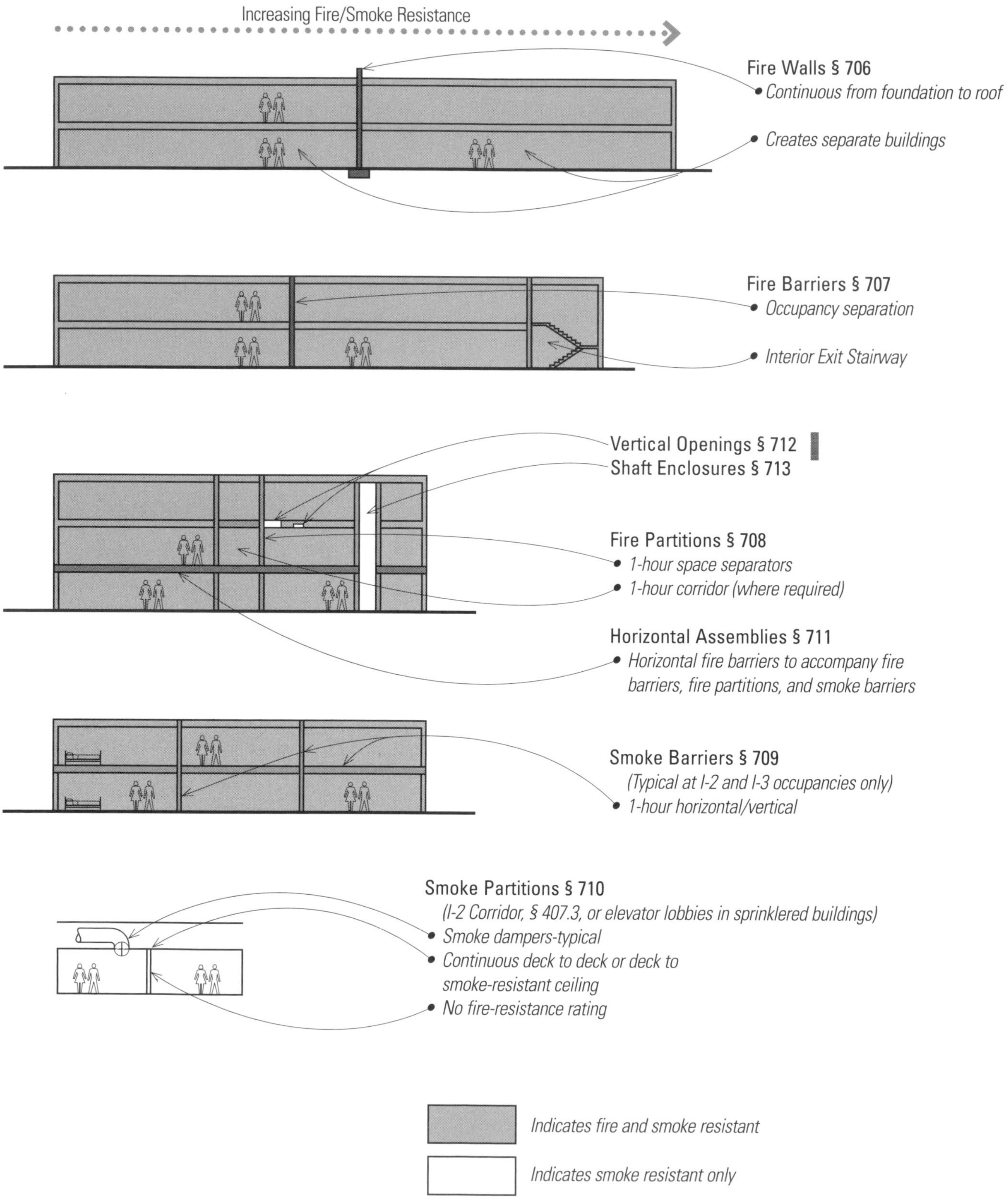

Increasing Fire/Smoke Resistance

Fire Walls § 706
- Continuous from foundation to roof
- Creates separate buildings

Fire Barriers § 707
- Occupancy separation
- Interior Exit Stairway

Vertical Openings § 712
Shaft Enclosures § 713

Fire Partitions § 708
- 1-hour space separators
- 1-hour corridor (where required)

Horizontal Assemblies § 711
- Horizontal fire barriers to accompany fire barriers, fire partitions, and smoke barriers

Smoke Barriers § 709
(Typical at I-2 and I-3 occupancies only)
- 1-hour horizontal/vertical

Smoke Partitions § 710
(I-2 Corridor, § 407.3, or elevator lobbies in sprinklered buildings)
- Smoke dampers-typical
- Continuous deck to deck or deck to smoke-resistant ceiling
- No fire-resistance rating

Indicates fire and smoke resistant

Indicates smoke resistant only

Vertical openings through floors can allow the movement of fire or smoke between floors. This represents a clear hazard to life safety that must be addressed in the design of the building. The code addresses treatments for various types of vertical openings. One of these treatments is the enclosure of openings in shafts. This is covered in § 713. Other provisions for treatment of openings are contained in § 712.

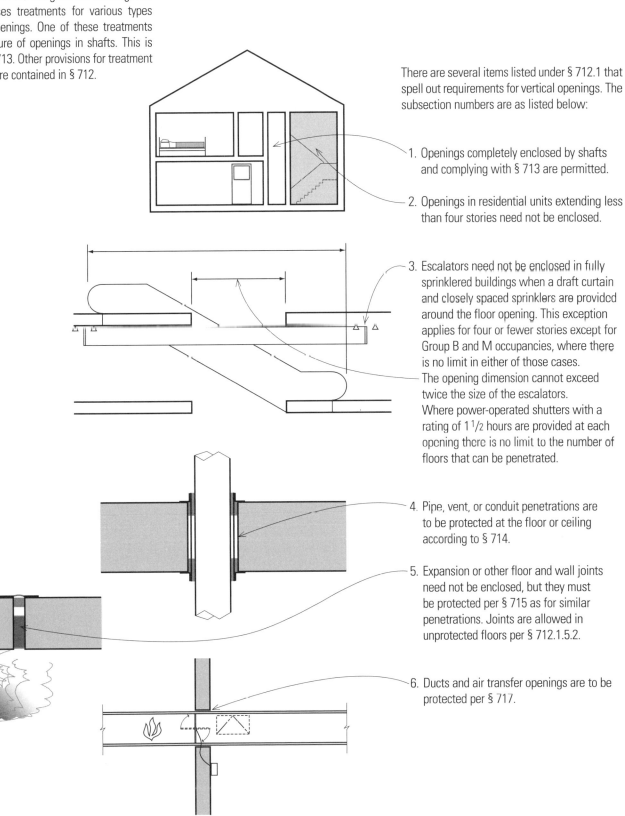

There are several items listed under § 712.1 that spell out requirements for vertical openings. The subsection numbers are as listed below:

1. Openings completely enclosed by shafts and complying with § 713 are permitted.

2. Openings in residential units extending less than four stories need not be enclosed.

3. Escalators need not be enclosed in fully sprinklered buildings when a draft curtain and closely spaced sprinklers are provided around the floor opening. This exception applies for four or fewer stories except for Group B and M occupancies, where there is no limit in either of those cases.
The opening dimension cannot exceed twice the size of the escalators.
Where power-operated shutters with a rating of 1 1/2 hours are provided at each opening there is no limit to the number of floors that can be penetrated.

4. Pipe, vent, or conduit penetrations are to be protected at the floor or ceiling according to § 714.

5. Expansion or other floor and wall joints need not be enclosed, but they must be protected per § 715 as for similar penetrations. Joints are allowed in unprotected floors per § 712.1.5.2.

6. Ducts and air transfer openings are to be protected per § 717.

(§ 712.1 items continued)

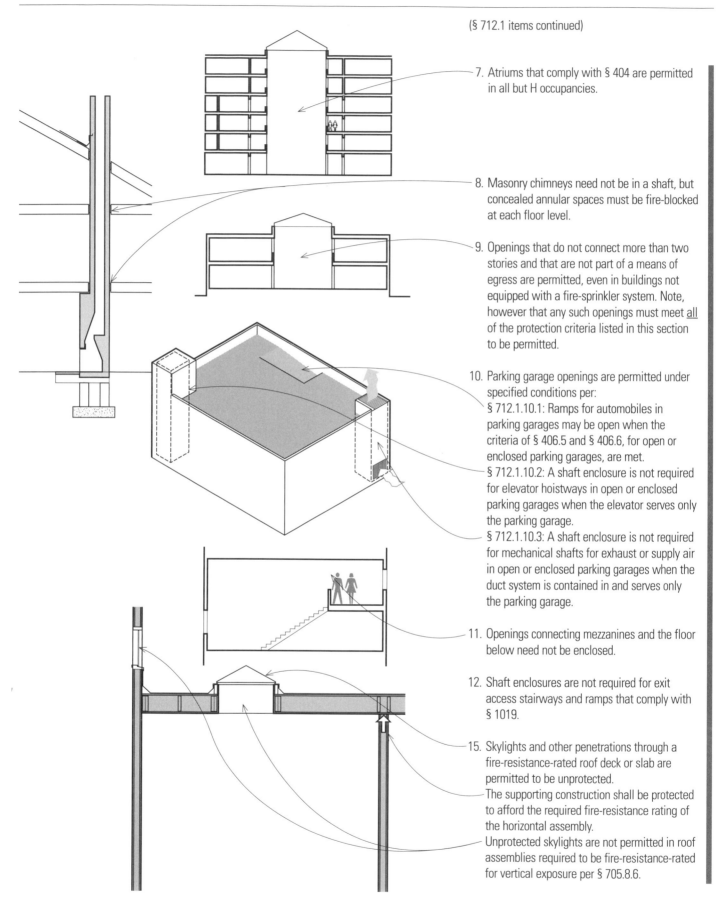

7. Atriums that comply with § 404 are permitted in all but H occupancies.

8. Masonry chimneys need not be in a shaft, but concealed annular spaces must be fire-blocked at each floor level.

9. Openings that do not connect more than two stories and that are not part of a means of egress are permitted, even in buildings not equipped with a fire-sprinkler system. Note, however that any such openings must meet <u>all</u> of the protection criteria listed in this section to be permitted.

10. Parking garage openings are permitted under specified conditions per:
    § 712.1.10.1: Ramps for automobiles in parking garages may be open when the criteria of § 406.5 and § 406.6, for open or enclosed parking garages, are met.
    § 712.1.10.2: A shaft enclosure is not required for elevator hoistways in open or enclosed parking garages when the elevator serves only the parking garage.
    § 712.1.10.3: A shaft enclosure is not required for mechanical shafts for exhaust or supply air in open or enclosed parking garages when the duct system is contained in and serves only the parking garage.

11. Openings connecting mezzanines and the floor below need not be enclosed.

12. Shaft enclosures are not required for exit access stairways and ramps that comply with § 1019.

15. Skylights and other penetrations through a fire-resistance-rated roof deck or slab are permitted to be unprotected.
    The supporting construction shall be protected to afford the required fire-resistance rating of the horizontal assembly.
    Unprotected skylights are not permitted in roof assemblies required to be fire-resistance-rated for vertical exposure per § 705.8.6.

Shaft enclosures differ from fire barriers in that they typically enclose openings extending through several floors. Shafts are to be constructed of the same materials as fire barriers or horizontal assemblies, and the required ratings for shafts and interior exit stairways are usually determined by the number of floors they interconnect. Shafts are to be of 2-hour construction if extending four stories or more and 1-hour otherwise. When determining the number of stories connected by shafts, basements are to be included as stories, but not mezzanines. Shaft ratings are to equal those of the floor assembly, but need not be greater than 2 hours.

The code requires that shafts not have multiple purposes. Penetrations in shaft walls are limited to those related to the purpose of the shaft. For example, ducts serving occupied spaces should not run through interior exit stairways, but ducts supplying air to the enclosure may be provided as long as penetration protection requirements are met to maintain the fire rating of the enclosure.

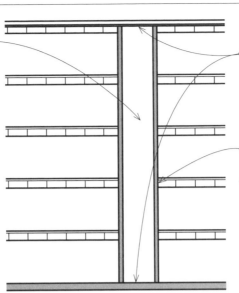

- *Shaft enclosures should be continuous from the top of the floor assembly below to the underside of the floor or roof deck or slab above, including concealed spaces such as those above suspended ceilings.*

- *Vertical spaces within shaft enclosures should be fire-blocked at each floor level.*
- *See below for guidance on enclosing shafts at the top and bottom when they do not extend to the top or bottom of the building or structure.*

- *Shaft continuity and rating requirements at exterior walls are similar to those for fire barriers. Exterior walls serving as shaft enclosures must satisfy the requirements of § 705.*

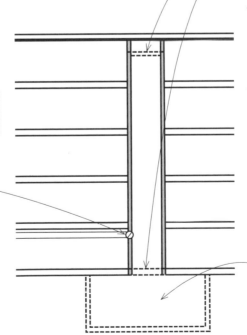

- *Note that fire dampers, smoke dampers, or fire/smoke dampers are typically required where ducts enter or exit shafts under most conditions. The integrity of the shaft is to be maintained continuously around all surfaces of the shaft.*

- *Shafts must be fully contained. Thus, a shaft that does not fully extend to the floor below, or to the floor or roof above, must be enclosed at the top or bottom.*
- *Shafts may be enclosed at the top or bottom with construction having the same fire-resistance rating as the last floor penetrated but not less than the required rating of the shaft.*
- *These enclosures must match the fire rating of the shaft wall. The designer must pay careful attention in these circumstances as assemblies respond to test fires of the same intensity much differently based on their orientation in relation to heat flows. It may not be possible to achieve equivalent ratings when a wall assembly tested vertically is installed horizontally. The code requires equal fire ratings as verified by testing in the actual horizontal or vertical orientation.*
- *Shafts may also terminate in a room related to the purpose of the shaft where the room is enclosed by construction having the same fire-resistance rating of the shaft enclosure.*

SHAFT ENCLOSURES

§ 713.13 addresses refuse and laundry chutes. The code recognizes that these shafts may interconnect many floors of a building. Requirements are included to provide a shaft, but also included are requirements to separate the chutes from the rest of the building with 1-hour-rated access rooms on each floor and 1-hour-rated termination rooms at the bottom of the shaft. Active fire protection is also required for these shafts per § 903.2.11.2.

§ 713.14 requires that elevator, dumbwaiter, and other hoistway enclosures be constructed in accordance with § 713 and Chapter 30. The requirements for elevator, dumbwaiter, and similar hoistways have been moved from §713.14 to Chapter 30, which covers elevators.

Refuse and laundry chutes must be separated from the rest of the building by 1-hour-rated access rooms at each floor level. These rooms are to be constructed as for Fire Barriers per § 707 or horizontal assemblies per § 711, or both.

§ 903.2.11.2 requires an automatic sprinkler system at the top of a chute, in the terminal rooms and on alternate floors when the chute passes through three or more floors.

Penetrations

§ 714 requires that penetrations be protected to maintain the fire-resistive integrity of the assembly being penetrated.

The governing criteria for penetration protection systems are that they prevent the passage of flame and hot gasses into or through the assembly. Penetration treatment requirements are based on the size and quantity of penetrations. The requirements for through-penetration fire stops call for tested assemblies meeting minimum criteria for resistance to the passage of flame and hot gases. The basic criteria are that the required fire-resistance of the penetrated assembly not be compromised or reduced. Certain limited penetrations by small pipes or electrical components of specified sizes are allowed by exceptions.

Penetration firestop systems are given "F" and "T" ratings. An F-rating is related to the time period that a through-penetration firestop system limits the movement of fire through a rated assembly. This rating should be nominally equal to the rating of the building assembly where the penetration is located. A T-rating applies to any penetration, not just through penetrations, and measures how long it takes to raise the temperature of an assembly by 325°F (163°C) on the opposite side of the assembly from a fire of specified size. Since the 2012 edition, the IBC also addresses "L" ratings (air leakage) for penetrations of smoke barriers.

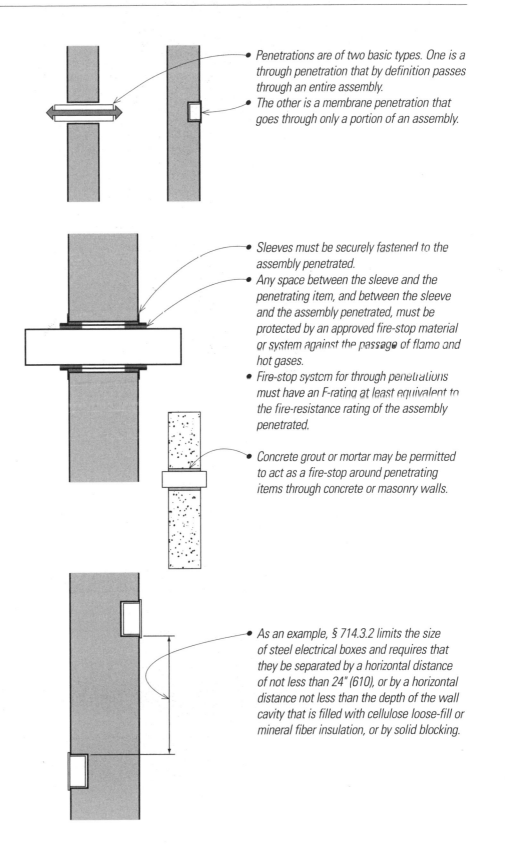

• Penetrations are of two basic types. One is a through penetration that by definition passes through an entire assembly.

• The other is a membrane penetration that goes through only a portion of an assembly.

• Sleeves must be securely fastened to the assembly penetrated.

• Any space between the sleeve and the penetrating item, and between the sleeve and the assembly penetrated, must be protected by an approved fire-stop material or system against the passage of flame and hot gases.

• Fire-stop system for through penetrations must have an F-rating at least equivalent to the fire-resistance rating of the assembly penetrated.

• Concrete grout or mortar may be permitted to act as a fire-stop around penetrating items through concrete or masonry walls.

• As an example, § 714.3.2 limits the size of steel electrical boxes and requires that they be separated by a horizontal distance of not less than 24" (610), or by a horizontal distance not less than the depth of the wall cavity that is filled with cellulose loose-fill or mineral fiber insulation, or by solid blocking.

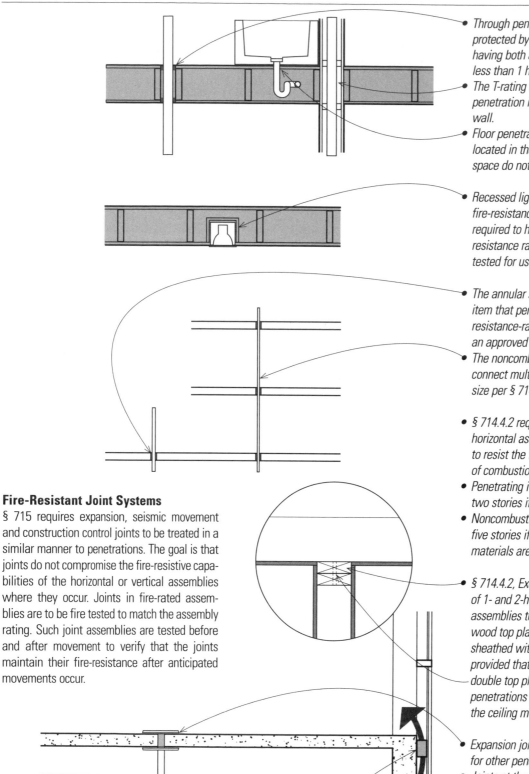

- Through penetrations in a floor must be protected by an approved fire-stop system having both an F-rating and a T-rating of not less than 1 hour.
- The T-rating may be omitted if the floor penetration is contained within the cavity of a wall.
- Floor penetrations for sink, tub, or shower drains located in the concealed horizontal assembly space do not require a T-rating.

- Recessed lighting fixtures shall not reduce the fire-resistance rating of floor/ceiling assemblies required to have a minimum 1-hour fire-resistance rating. Fixtures are to be boxed out or tested for use in fire-rated assemblies.

- The annular space around a noncombustible item that penetrates only a single fire-resistance-rated floor need only be filled with an approved material.
- The noncombustible penetrating item may connect multiple fire-rated floors if limited in size per § 714.4.1.

- § 714.4.2 requires that even non-rated horizontal assemblies have annular spaces filled to resist the free passage of flame and products of combustion.
- Penetrating items may connect no more than two stories if so treated.
- Noncombustible items may penetrate up to five stories if approved noncombustible sealing materials are used.

- § 714.4.2, Exc. 7, allows the ceiling membrane of 1- and 2-hour fire-resistance-rated horizontal assemblies to be interrupted with the double wood top plate of a wall assembly that is sheathed with Type X gypsum wallboard, provided that all penetrating items through the double top plates are protected as through-penetrations per § 714.4.1.1 or § 714.4.1.2 and the ceiling membrane is tight to the top plates.

- Expansion joints are to have fire-resistance as for other penetrations.
- Joints at the intersection of floor assemblies and exterior curtain walls are included in § 715.4. These intersections are to be sealed with approved materials tested for such applications. The materials are to be installed to prevent the spread of flame and hot gases at the intersection.

Fire-Resistant Joint Systems

§ 715 requires expansion, seismic movement and construction control joints to be treated in a similar manner to penetrations. The goal is that joints do not compromise the fire-resistive capabilities of the horizontal or vertical assemblies where they occur. Joints in fire-rated assemblies are to be fire tested to match the assembly rating. Such joint assemblies are tested before and after movement to verify that the joints maintain their fire-resistance after anticipated movements occur.

§ 716 addresses the requirements for protection of openings in fire-resistance rated walls. The openings may be either doors or glazed openings (windows). A glazed opening may occur in either a wall or within a door. It is permissible to have openings in fire-resistance rated walls, but the protection provided at the opening must provide some specified level of fire resistance so that the fire resistance of the wall is not compromised by the presence of the opening. Clearly doors are required to get into spaces, including rated exits. Also, it is often desired that vision panels occur in doors, or that windows occur in rated walls. This section provides the requirements for the various types of "opening protectives" that may be used in various circumstances.

The requirements of § 716 for the protection of openings in fire-resistive construction often allow the opening protectives to have lower ratings than those for the wall where they are located. For example, a 2-hour-rated fire wall typically requires a 1½-hour-rated opening protection assembly. Opening protectives are typically tested assemblies, so the designer can select compliant protection assemblies based on their tested performance.

Fire-rated glazing is a defined term in § 202. The definition contains two other defined terms. The first is "fire protection rating," which is defined as "The period of time that an opening protective will maintain the ability to confine a fire...." The second term is "fire resistance rating," the relevant portion of which is "The period of time a building element, component or assembly maintains the ability to confine a fire...." These terms allow the use of glazing that can either be tested as an opening protective or be of more robust transparent or translucent fire-resistant materials, such as ceramics or glass block that are tested as building materials and not just as glazing.

Glazing materials are often tested and rated to a higher degree of protection than the code requires for a given situation. The code allows the use of glazing that exceeds the minimum requirements as long as the assembly meets the applicable minimum requirements as well. For example, glazing may meet the hose stream test when it is not needed, but such glazing would also need to meet the applicable time limits for fire-rated glazing.

- The code typically requires that opening protectives, including fire doors and glazing materials, be labeled for test compliance and for their fire rating.

- Tables 716.5 and 716.6 specify the minimum opening protective fire-protection ratings, in hours, based on:
  - type of assembly
  - required assembly rating

- Glazing materials are to have markings on the materials to allow identification of which criteria the material was tested for. Table 716.3 lists the various criteria for marking fire-rated glazing assemblies. The requirements of this table are used in Table 716.5, which lists assemblies for opening fire protection. Our commentary on Table 716.3 is shown below:

Marking	Marking Definition	Commentary
W	Meets wall assembly criteria	This will be a material, such as glass block or transparent ceramic material, that is more a transparent wall than a glass window.
OH	Meets fire window criteria including the hose stream test	This is a window assembly that can take the force of a fire department hose stream and withstand both the hydraulic pressure from the hose and the thermal shock of water cooling after heating due to fire exposure.
D	Meets fire door assembly criteria	Glazing to occur at fire doors
H	Meets fire door assembly hose stream test	Similar to "OH," but for fire doors
T	Meets 450°F temperature rise criteria for 30 minutes	Called out for certain specific instances in various parts of § 716
XXX	Time in minutes of either the fire protection or fire resistance rating of the glazing assembly	e.g., a 1-hour rating would be "60" and a 1½-hour rating would be "90."

OPENING PROTECTIVES

Fire doors are to be self-closing. They typically require a latch as well. These requirements are based on maintaining the integrity of the assembly where the fire door is located. The doors should be closed under most circumstances and should be latched to prevent them from being forced open by air currents generated by fire.

Fire-rated glazing may also occur at exterior walls where dictated by fire separation distances. Fire ratings of window protection at exterior walls requiring more than a 1-hour rating per Table 602 must be at least 1½ hours. Other window openings where a 1-hour rating is required may have a ¾-hour rating. Where window-opening protection is required in otherwise unrated walls by proximity of building elements or for vertical or lateral exposure per § 705.8.5 or 705.8.6, the windows must have a fire-resistance rating of at least ¾-hour.

Fire-resistance-rated glazing that is tested as part of a fire-resistance-rated wall assembly per ASTM E119 or UL 263 is permitted in fire doors and fire window assemblies in accordance with their listing and need not otherwise comply with § 716.

4 (w x h) ≤ 25% of common wall area, including the area of any doorways

- Fire barrier wall at exit stair

- Fire barrier at corridor

Per § 716.6.7, fire-protection-rated glazing in fire-window assemblies may be used in fire partitions or fire barriers with a maximum fire rating of 1 hour. The total area of such windows cannot exceed 25 % of the area of a common wall with any room.

Doors and Sidelights (Table 716.5)

Wall Assembly	Required Wall Rating (hrs.)	Minimum Fire Door Rating (hrs.)	Door Vision Panel Size	Door Vision Panel Glazing Marking	Minimum Sidelight Rating (hours) FP*	FR**	Sidelight Fire-rated Glazing Marking FP*	FR**
Exit Enclosure	2	1½	100 in.²	D-H-T-90 or D-H-W-90	NP***	2	NP***	W-120
Corridor Fire Partition	½	⅓	Max. size tested	D-20	⅓	—	D-H-OH-20	—

Windows (Table 716.6)

Wall Assembly	Required Wall Rating (hrs.)	Fire Window Assembly Rating (hrs.)	Fire-rated Glazing Marking
Fire Partition	½	⅓	OH-20 or W-30

FP*	= Fire protection rating
FR**	= Fire resistance rating
NP***	= Not permitted for type of glazing rating

Ducts and air-transfer openings going through fire-rated assemblies must be treated in some way to prevent compromising the fire-resistance of the assemblies that the ducts pass through. Note also that there are some duct penetration provisions in this section that apply to ducts in nonfire-resistance rated floor assemblies. Ducts without dampers are treated as penetrations per § 714. Where ducts must remain operational during a fire or smoke emergency—for example, in an atrium smoke-control system—they cannot have dampers. Alternate protection must be provided to maintain the integrity of fire protectives. Fire and smoke dampers must be tested and listed assemblies. Dampers must be provided with access for maintenance, testing and resetting the assemblies when they close. These access panels must not compromise the fire rating of the fire assembly where they are located.

The fire resistive requirements for fire and smoke dampers are based on the type of assembly penetrated. Requirements are stated in the familiar pattern of basic requirements followed by exceptions. The assembly types are organized in the same hierarchy as in other parts of this chapter.

- *Fire dampers are listed mechanical devices installed in ducts and air-transfer openings and designed to close automatically on detection of heat to restrict the passage of flame.*
- *Smoke dampers are similar to fire dampers but are intended to resist the passage of air and smoke. They are controlled either by a smoke-detection system or by a remote-control station.*
- *Both fire and smoke dampers require access for inspection and maintenance. The access panels must not compromise the integrity of the fire-resistant assembly.*

- *Fire Walls: § 717.5.1 requires ducts that penetrate fire walls be provided with fire dampers per the exception to § 706.11.*
- *Fire Barriers: § 717.5.2 requires fire dampers where ducts or air transfer openings penetrate fire barriers. The exceptions to this requirement are:*
  1. *The penetrations are listed in accordance with ASTM E 119 or UL 263 as part of the fire-resistance-rated assembly.*
  2. *The ducts are part of a smoke-control system.*
  3. *The HVAC system is ducted, the wall is rated at 1-hour or less, the building is not an H occupancy and is fully sprinklered.*

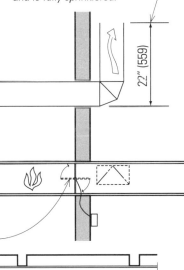

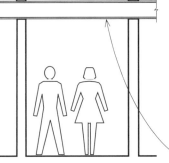

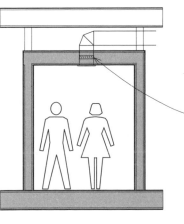

- *The opening language of § 717.5.3 states that shaft enclosures that are permitted to be penetrated by ducts and air transfer openings are to be protected with fire and smoke dampers.*

- *The exceptions then go on to state that fire and smoke dampers are not required where:*
  1.1 *The duct turns up 22" (559) in exhaust ducts in the direction of a continuous upward air flow.*
  1.2 *The penetrations are listed in accordance with ASTM E 119 or UL 263 as part of the fire-resistance-rated assembly.*
  1.3 *The ducts are part of a smoke-control system.*
  1.4 *The penetrations are in a parking garage shaft separated from other shafts by not less than 2-hour construction.*
  2. *In Group B and R occupancies with automatic sprinkler systems for kitchen, bath, and toilet room exhaust enclosed in steel ducts that extend vertically 22" (559) in the shaft, have an exhaust fan at the upper termination of the shaft to maintain a continuous upward air flow.*

- *Fire Partitions: § 717.5.4 requires duct penetrations in fire partitions to have fire dampers except in the following conditions:*
  1. *The partitions penetrated are tenant separation or corridor walls in buildings with sprinkler systems.*
  2. *Tenant partitions in malls.*
  3. *The ducts are steel, less than 100 square inches (0.06 m^2) in cross-section, do not connect the corridor with other spaces, are above a ceiling and do not have a wall register in the fire-resistance-rated wall.*
  4. *Ducted systems with min. 26 ga. steel ducts may penetrate walls of 1-hour or less fire-resistance rating in sprinklered buildings.*

- *Corridors: § 717.5.4.1 requires smoke dampers at corridors except where:*
  1. *There is a smoke-control system.*
  2. *The duct is steel and passes through the corridor with no openings into it.*

- *Smoke Barriers: § 717.5.5 requires that smoke dampers be provided when a duct penetrates a smoke barrier except when the duct is steel and serves only a single smoke compartment.*

- *At "tunnel corridors" provided per Exception 3 to § 708.4, if air is supplied to the corridor, a "corridor damper" is to be provided at the duct penetration in the ceiling per § 717.5.4.1.*

CONCEALED SPACES

Fire can spread rapidly inside concealed spaces in combustible construction if the spread of fire or movement of hot gases is not restricted. § 718 sets out requirements for fire-blocking and draft-stopping. Note that these provisions apply only to concealed locations in combustible construction or in areas containing combustible construction.

The purpose of each requirement is to restrict or eliminate the spread of fire or the movement of hot gases in order to prevent the spread of fire within concealed spaces. These criteria typically apply to buildings with combustible construction, but they also apply where combustible decorative materials or flooring is installed in buildings of noncombustible construction.

Sprinklers are often a mitigation measure for draft-stopping of concealed spaces. However, it should be noted that in such circumstances the concealed spaces must usually be sprinklered as well as the occupied spaces.

Combustible construction materials are not allowed in concealed spaces in Type I or II buildings except when permitted by § 603, when Class A finish materials are used, or when combustible piping is installed in accordance with the International Mechanical and Plumbing Codes.

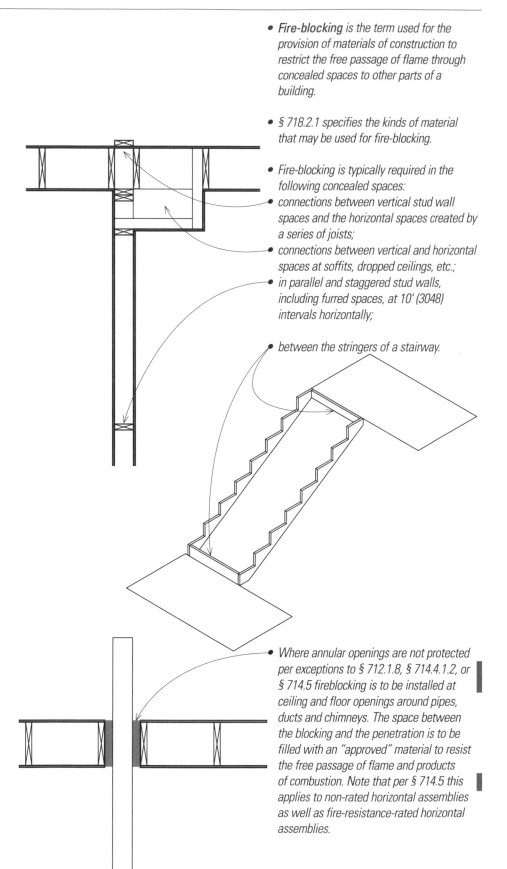

- *Fire-blocking* is the term used for the provision of materials of construction to restrict the free passage of flame through concealed spaces to other parts of a building.

- § 718.2.1 specifies the kinds of material that may be used for fire-blocking.

- Fire-blocking is typically required in the following concealed spaces:
- connections between vertical stud wall spaces and the horizontal spaces created by a series of joists;
- connections between vertical and horizontal spaces at soffits, dropped ceilings, etc.;
- in parallel and staggered stud walls, including furred spaces, at 10' (3048) intervals horizontally;

- between the stringers of a stairway.

- Where annular openings are not protected per exceptions to § 712.1.8, § 714.4.1.2, or § 714.5 fireblocking is to be installed at ceiling and floor openings around pipes, ducts and chimneys. The space between the blocking and the penetration is to be filled with an "approved" material to resist the free passage of flame and products of combustion. Note that per § 714.5 this applies to non-rated horizontal assemblies as well as fire-resistance-rated horizontal assemblies.

- *Draft-stopping* is the term used for the provision of materials or devices to restrict the movement of air within open spaces concealed in combustible construction, such as floor and ceiling cavities and attics. Draft-stopping in floors is to be per § 718.3 and draft-stopping in attics is to be per § 718.4.

- Draft-stopping is required to subdivide attics and other concealed roof spaces.
- In Group R-1 and R-2 occupancies, this draft-stopping is to be installed in attics above and in line with the walls that separate one dwelling unit from another where they do not already extend to the underside of the roof sheathing above.
- In other than residential occupancies, draft-stopping must subdivide attics and other concealed roof spaces into areas of less than 3,000 sf (279 m²) unless the building is fully sprinklered.

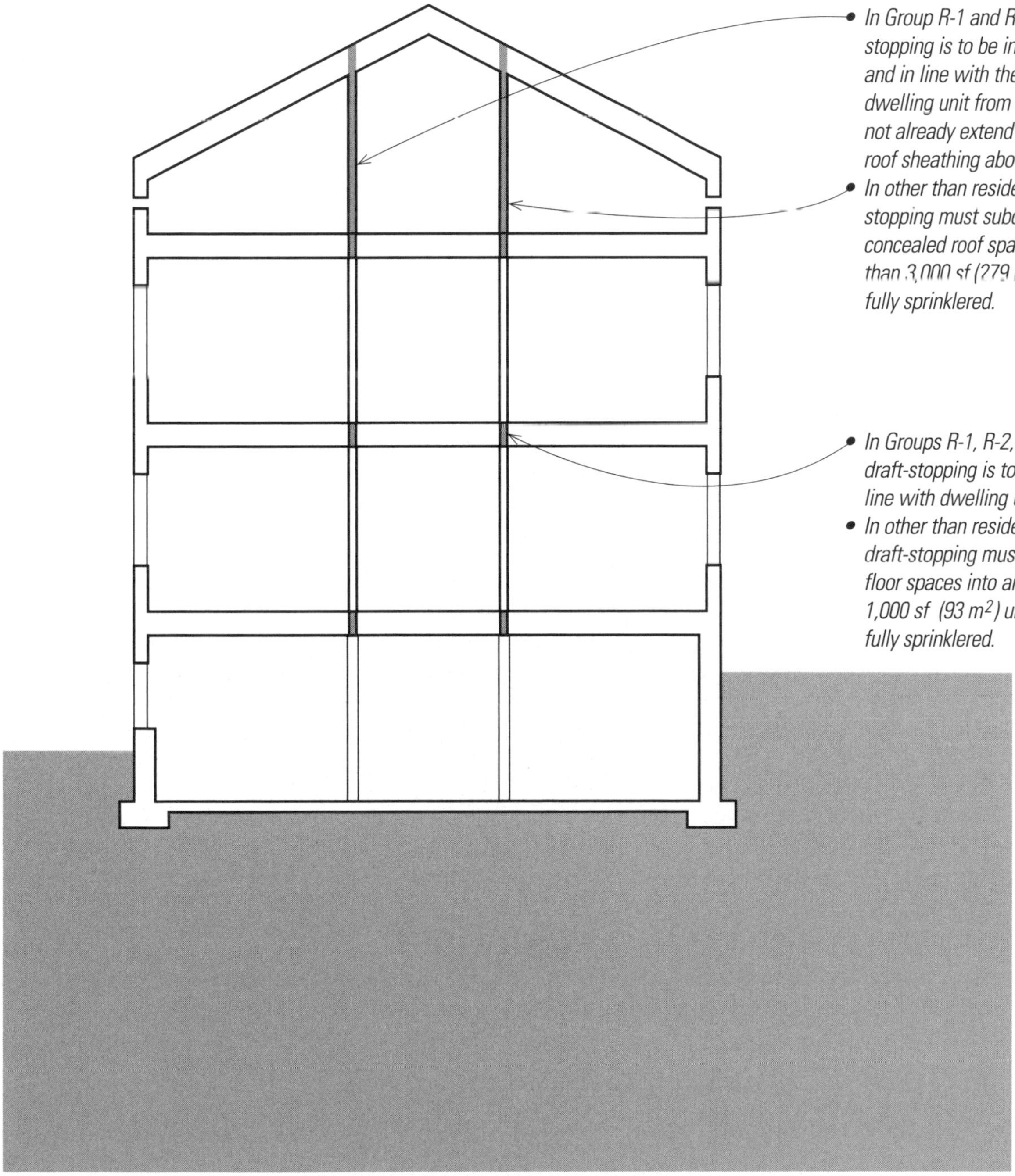

- In Groups R-1, R-2, R-3 and R-4 occupancies, draft-stopping is to be located above and in line with dwelling unit separations.
- In other than residential occupancies, draft-stopping must subdivide horizontal floor spaces into areas of less than 1,000 sf (93 m²) unless the building is fully sprinklered.

Plaster

Plaster is accepted as a fire-resistance-rated material when applied as prescribed in § 719. Plaster assemblies must be based on tested assemblies. Plaster may be used to substitute for 1/2" (12.7 mm) of the required overall assembly thickness when applied over concrete. Minimum concrete cover of 3/8" (9.5 mm) at floors and 1" (25.4 mm) at reinforced columns must still be maintained.

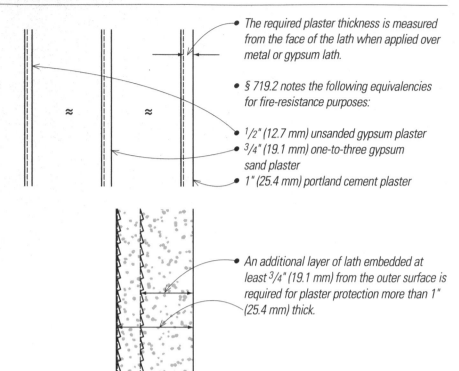

- The required plaster thickness is measured from the face of the lath when applied over metal or gypsum lath.

- § 719.2 notes the following equivalencies for fire-resistance purposes:

- 1/2" (12.7 mm) unsanded gypsum plaster
- 3/4" (19.1 mm) one-to-three gypsum sand plaster
- 1" (25.4 mm) portland cement plaster

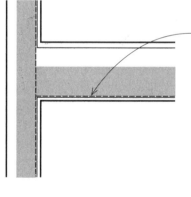

- An additional layer of lath embedded at least 3/4" (19.1 mm) from the outer surface is required for plaster protection more than 1" (25.4 mm) thick.

Thermal- and Sound-Insulating Materials

§ 720 recognizes that thermal and acoustical insulating materials often have paper facings or contain combustible materials. When installed in concealed spaces, the materials must have a flame-spread index of not more than 25 and a smoke-developed index of not more than 450. Per an exception, cellulosic fiber loose-fill insulation with the requirements of § 720.6 are not required to meet a flame-spread index requirement but shall be required to meet a smoke-developed index of not more than 450.

- Per § 720.2.1 flame spread and smoke developed limitations do not apply in Type III, IV, or V construction when the facing is turned toward and is in substantial contact with the unexposed surface of the wall, ceiling, or floor.

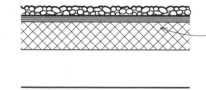

- Roof insulation may be combustible and need not meet the flame-spread and smoke-generation limits when it is covered with approved roof coverings.

The tables in § 721 provide a laundry list of assemblies deemed to comply with fire-resistance requirements for the times noted when installed at the thickness indicated. There are tables for various elements:

- Table 721.1(1) for Structural Elements
- Table 721.1(2) for Wall and Partition Assemblies
- Table 721.1(3) for Floor and Roof Systems

The assemblies listed are by no means an exhaustive list. The designer will often refer to other testing agencies that are acceptable to the code, such as Underwriters Laboratory or Factory Mutual, to find assemblies that meet the needs of the project. The designer must use these assemblies with care and identify where they are used in a project. Modifications to assembly designs should be done with caution as this may negate their approval and necessitate fire testing to prove their efficacy.

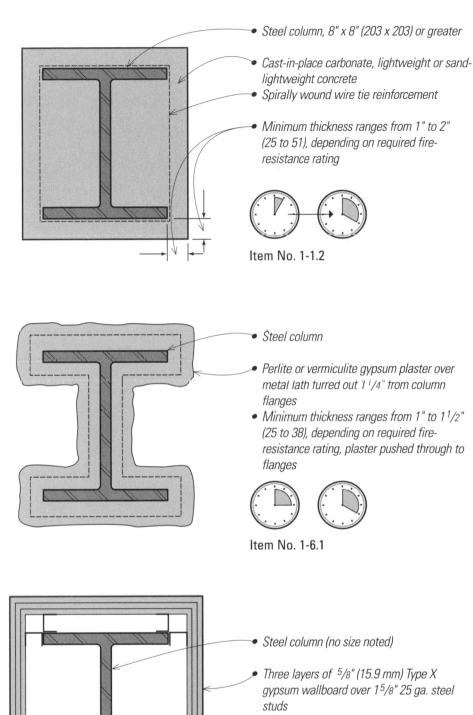

- Steel column, 8" x 8" (203 x 203) or greater

- Cast-in-place carbonate, lightweight or sand-lightweight concrete
- Spirally wound wire tie reinforcement

- Minimum thickness ranges from 1" to 2" (25 to 51), depending on required fire-resistance rating

Item No. 1-1.2

- Steel column

- Perlite or vermiculite gypsum plaster over metal lath turred out 1 1/4" from column flanges
- Minimum thickness ranges from 1" to 1 1/2" (25 to 38), depending on required fire-resistance rating, plaster pushed through to flanges

Item No. 1-6.1

- Steel column (no size noted)

- Three layers of 5/8" (15.9 mm) Type X gypsum wallboard over 1 5/8" 25 ga. steel studs
- 1 5/8" 25 ga. steel studs

Structural Elements

Item No. 1-7.3

Structural Elements

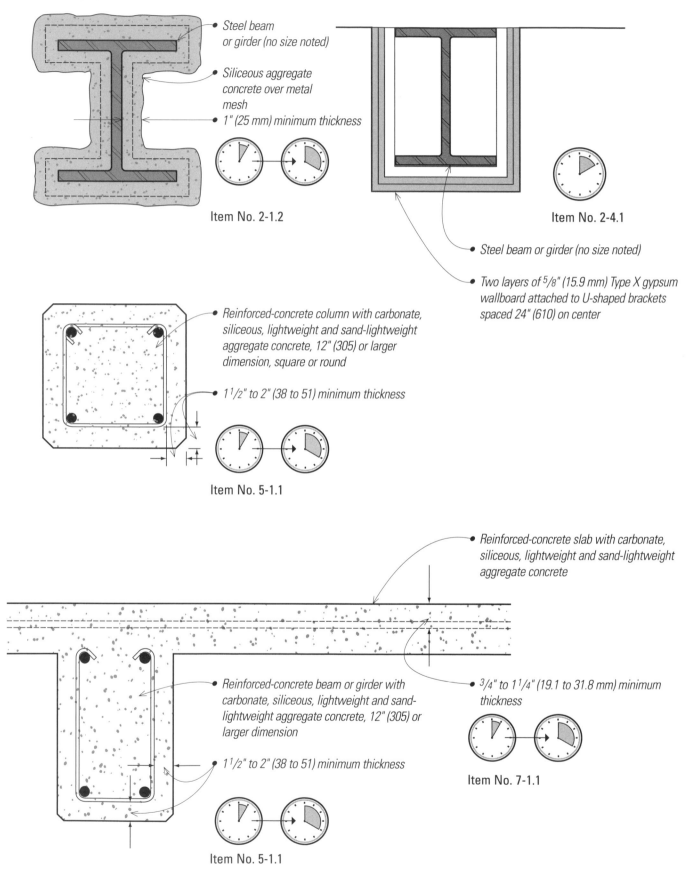

• Steel beam
  or girder (no size noted)

• Siliceous aggregate
  concrete over metal
  mesh

• 1" (25 mm) minimum thickness

Item No. 2-1.2

Item No. 2-4.1

• Steel beam or girder (no size noted)

• Two layers of ⁵⁄₈" (15.9 mm) Type X gypsum
  wallboard attached to U-shaped brackets
  spaced 24" (610) on center

• Reinforced-concrete column with carbonate,
  siliceous, lightweight and sand-lightweight
  aggregate concrete, 12" (305) or larger
  dimension, square or round

• 1¹⁄₂" to 2" (38 to 51) minimum thickness

Item No. 5-1.1

• Reinforced-concrete slab with carbonate,
  siliceous, lightweight and sand-lightweight
  aggregate concrete

• Reinforced-concrete beam or girder with
  carbonate, siliceous, lightweight and sand-
  lightweight aggregate concrete, 12" (305) or
  larger dimension

• 1¹⁄₂" to 2" (38 to 51) minimum thickness

• ³⁄₄" to 1¹⁄₄" (19.1 to 31.8 mm) minimum
  thickness

Item No. 7-1.1

Item No. 5-1.1

Wall and Partition Assemblies

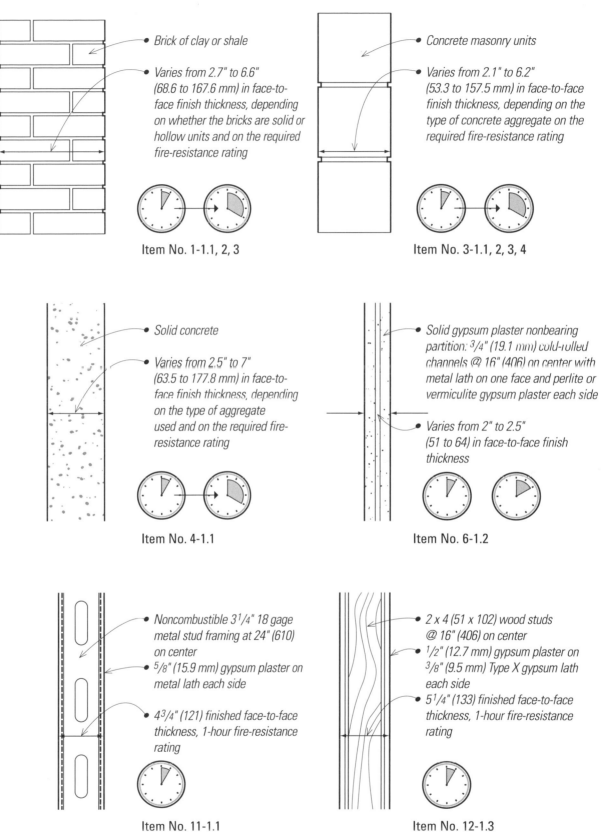

- Brick of clay or shale

- Varies from 2.7" to 6.6" (68.6 to 167.6 mm) in face-to-face finish thickness, depending on whether the bricks are solid or hollow units and on the required fire-resistance rating

Item No. 1-1.1, 2, 3

- Concrete masonry units

- Varies from 2.1" to 6.2" (53.3 to 157.5 mm) in face-to-face finish thickness, depending on the type of concrete aggregate on the required fire-resistance rating

Item No. 3-1.1, 2, 3, 4

- Solid concrete

- Varies from 2.5" to 7" (63.5 to 177.8 mm) in face-to-face finish thickness, depending on the type of aggregate used and on the required fire-resistance rating

Item No. 4-1.1

- Solid gypsum plaster nonbearing partition: 3/4" (19.1 mm) cold-rolled channels @ 16" (406) on center with metal lath on one face and perlite or vermiculite gypsum plaster each side

- Varies from 2" to 2.5" (51 to 64) in face-to-face finish thickness

Item No. 6-1.2

- Noncombustible 3 1/4" 18 gage metal stud framing at 24" (610) on center

- 5/8" (15.9 mm) gypsum plaster on metal lath each side

- 4 3/4" (121) finished face-to-face thickness, 1-hour fire-resistance rating

Item No. 11-1.1

- 2 x 4 (51 x 102) wood studs @ 16" (406) on center

- 1/2" (12.7 mm) gypsum plaster on 3/8" (9.5 mm) Type X gypsum lath each side

- 5 1/4" (133) finished face-to-face thickness, 1-hour fire-resistance rating

Item No. 12-1.3

Wall and Partition Assemblies

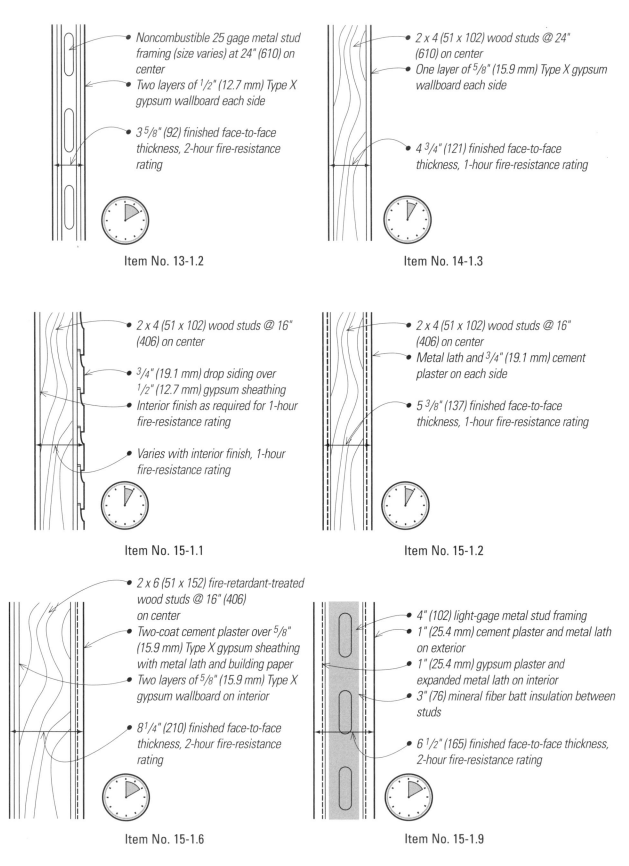

- Noncombustible 25 gage metal stud framing (size varies) at 24" (610) on center
- Two layers of 1/2" (12.7 mm) Type X gypsum wallboard each side

- 3 5/8" (92) finished face-to-face thickness, 2-hour fire-resistance rating

Item No. 13-1.2

- 2 x 4 (51 x 102) wood studs @ 24" (610) on center
- One layer of 5/8" (15.9 mm) Type X gypsum wallboard each side

- 4 3/4" (121) finished face-to-face thickness, 1-hour fire-resistance rating

Item No. 14-1.3

- 2 x 4 (51 x 102) wood studs @ 16" (406) on center

- 3/4" (19.1 mm) drop siding over 1/2" (12.7 mm) gypsum sheathing
- Interior finish as required for 1-hour fire-resistance rating

- Varies with interior finish, 1-hour fire-resistance rating

Item No. 15-1.1

- 2 x 4 (51 x 102) wood studs @ 16" (406) on center
- Metal lath and 3/4" (19.1 mm) cement plaster on each side

- 5 3/8" (137) finished face-to-face thickness, 1-hour fire-resistance rating

Item No. 15-1.2

- 2 x 6 (51 x 152) fire-retardant-treated wood studs @ 16" (406) on center
- Two-coat cement plaster over 5/8" (15.9 mm) Type X gypsum sheathing with metal lath and building paper
- Two layers of 5/8" (15.9 mm) Type X gypsum wallboard on interior

- 8 1/4" (210) finished face-to-face thickness, 2-hour fire-resistance rating

Item No. 15-1.6

- 4" (102) light-gage metal stud framing
- 1" (25.4 mm) cement plaster and metal lath on exterior
- 1" (25.4 mm) gypsum plaster and expanded metal lath on interior
- 3" (76) mineral fiber batt insulation between studs

- 6 1/2" (165) finished face-to-face thickness, 2-hour fire-resistance rating

Item No. 15-1.9

Floor and Roof Systems

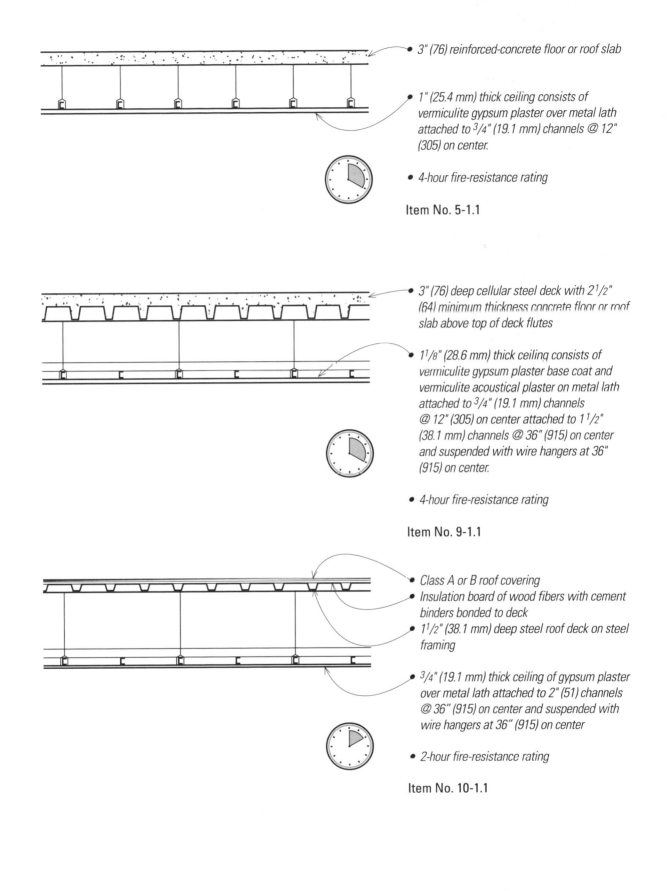

- *3" (76) reinforced-concrete floor or roof slab*

- *1" (25.4 mm) thick ceiling consists of vermiculite gypsum plaster over metal lath attached to 3/4" (19.1 mm) channels @ 12" (305) on center.*

- *4-hour fire-resistance rating*

Item No. 5-1.1

- *3" (76) deep cellular steel deck with 2 1/2" (64) minimum thickness concrete floor or roof slab above top of deck flutes*

- *1 1/8" (28.6 mm) thick ceiling consists of vermiculite gypsum plaster base coat and vermiculite acoustical plaster on metal lath attached to 3/4" (19.1 mm) channels @ 12" (305) on center attached to 1 1/2" (38.1 mm) channels @ 36" (915) on center and suspended with wire hangers at 36" (915) on center.*

- *4-hour fire-resistance rating*

Item No. 9-1.1

- *Class A or B roof covering*
- *Insulation board of wood fibers with cement binders bonded to deck*
- *1 1/2" (38.1 mm) deep steel roof deck on steel framing*

- *3/4" (19.1 mm) thick ceiling of gypsum plaster over metal lath attached to 2" (51) channels @ 36" (915) on center and suspended with wire hangers at 36" (915) on center*

- *2-hour fire-resistance rating*

Item No. 10-1.1

Floor and Roof Systems

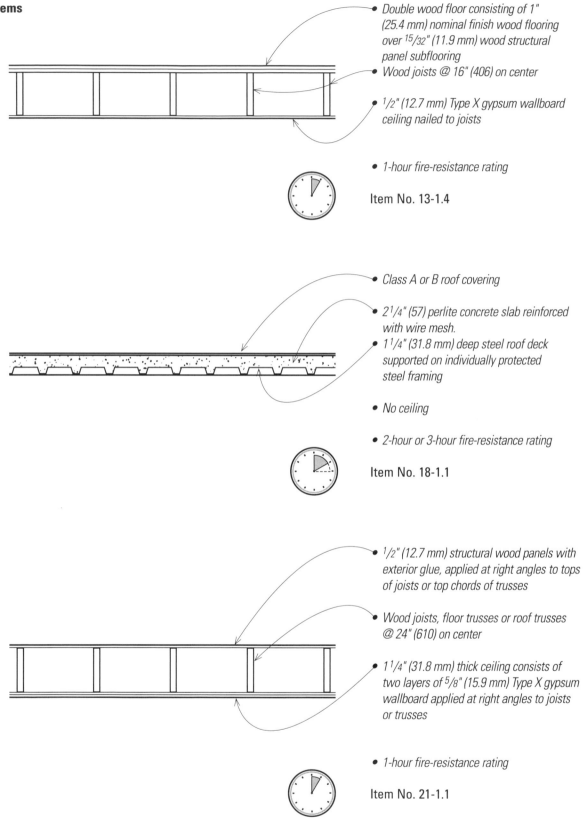

- Double wood floor consisting of 1" (25.4 mm) nominal finish wood flooring over $^{15}/_{32}$" (11.9 mm) wood structural panel subflooring
- Wood joists @ 16" (406) on center

- $^{1}/_{2}$" (12.7 mm) Type X gypsum wallboard ceiling nailed to joists

- 1-hour fire-resistance rating

Item No. 13-1.4

- Class A or B roof covering

- 2$^{1}/_{4}$" (57) perlite concrete slab reinforced with wire mesh.
- 1$^{1}/_{4}$" (31.8 mm) deep steel roof deck supported on individually protected steel framing

- No ceiling

- 2-hour or 3-hour fire-resistance rating

Item No. 18-1.1

- $^{1}/_{2}$" (12.7 mm) structural wood panels with exterior glue, applied at right angles to tops of joists or top chords of trusses

- Wood joists, floor trusses or roof trusses @ 24" (610) on center

- 1$^{1}/_{4}$" (31.8 mm) thick ceiling consists of two layers of $^{5}/_{8}$" (15.9 mm) Type X gypsum wallboard applied at right angles to joists or trusses

- 1-hour fire-resistance rating

Item No. 21-1.1

When project conditions cannot be met using prescriptive assemblies, § 722 provides a methodology to calculate the fire-resistive performance of specific materials or combinations of materials. These calculations are developed for use in the code and meant to apply only to the section in which they are contained. They are designed to facilitate design and documentation of fire assemblies so that the designer and the building official will have reasonable assurance of the performance of the calculated assembly under actual fire conditions. The formulas are based on data for heat transfer in structural members, thermal conductance of insulating materials, conduction in materials, fire-test data of the fire-resistance of various building materials; individually and in concert with each other, along with anticipated loads on assemblies in place.

The designer can use the data contained in this section to determine fire-resistance for assemblies that do not fit neatly into the prescriptive, pretested categories contained in § 721.

On the following pages are several examples for both structural protection and assembly calculations to illustrate the principles at work in this section.

There are several fundamental precepts for the calculation of fire-resistance.

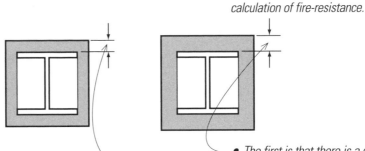

• *The first is that there is a quantifiable relationship between the thickness of fire-protection materials applied to building elements and the resulting time of fire resistance. In short, thicker fire protection yields longer fire-resistance duration.*

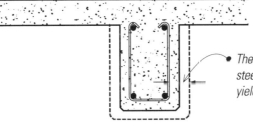

• *The second precept is that more cover on steel reinforcing in concrete construction yields a longer fire-resistance duration.*

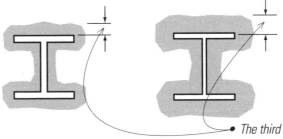

• *The third precept is that there is a relationship between the overall exterior surface dimension of a steel structural member (referred to as the "heated perimeter"), the thickness of the parts of the member and the thickness of the fire-protection materials necessary to achieve a certain fire rating. For example, compact steel wide flange sections with thick webs and flanges usually require thinner layers of fire-protective materials to achieve a given fire-resistance duration than a larger-dimension beam made up of thinner steel.*

§ 722.2 Concrete Assemblies

Typical concrete has either siliceous or carbonate aggregate; for our example, we will assume the use of siliceous aggregate.

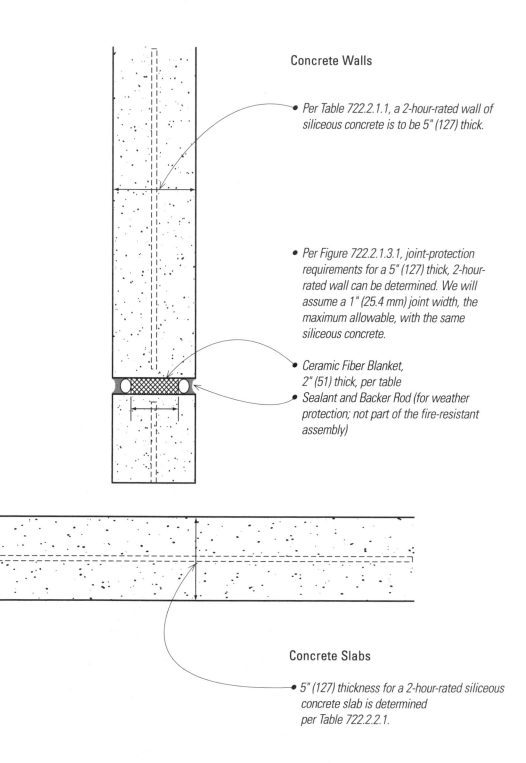

Concrete Walls

- *Per Table 722.2.1.1, a 2-hour-rated wall of siliceous concrete is to be 5" (127) thick.*

- *Per Figure 722.2.1.3.1, joint-protection requirements for a 5" (127) thick, 2-hour-rated wall can be determined. We will assume a 1" (25.4 mm) joint width, the maximum allowable, with the same siliceous concrete.*

- *Ceramic Fiber Blanket, 2" (51) thick, per table*
- *Sealant and Backer Rod (for weather protection; not part of the fire-resistant assembly)*

Concrete Slabs

- *5" (127) thickness for a 2-hour-rated siliceous concrete slab is determined per Table 722.2.2.1.*

§ 722.5 Steel Assemblies

Fire protection for steel columns is dependent on the weight per lineal foot (W) of the column and the heated perimeter (D) of the column, which is related to the physical dimensions of the column.

Table 722.5.1(1) shows W/D ratios for typical columns. We will assume a W12 x 96 column.

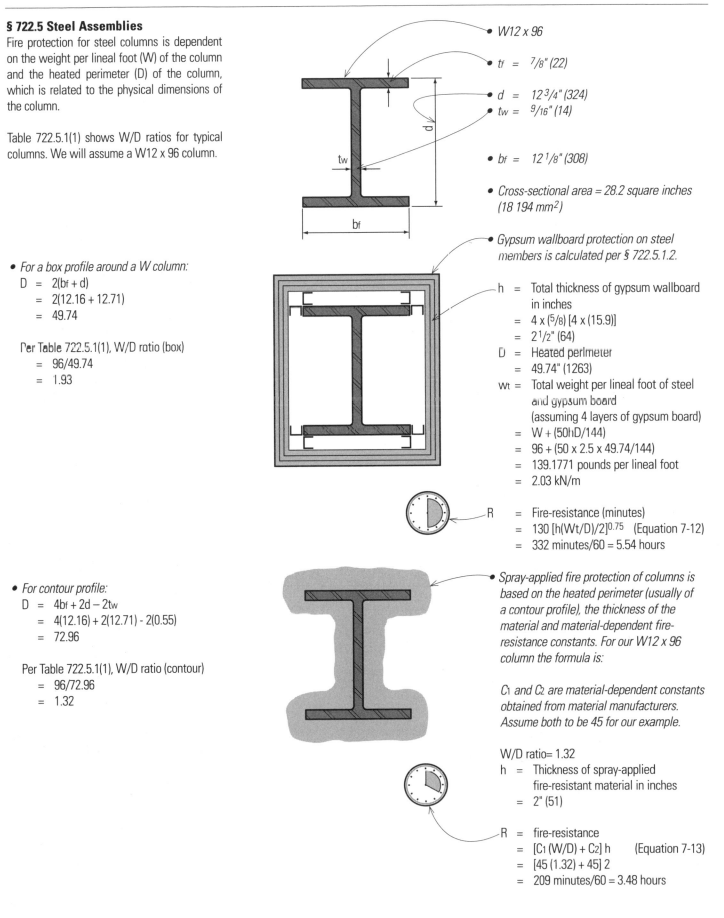

- W12 x 96

- t_f = ⁷/₈" (22)

- d = 12³/₄" (324)
- t_w = ⁹/₁₆" (14)

- b_f = 12¹/₈" (308)

- Cross-sectional area = 28.2 square inches (18 194 mm²)

- For a box profile around a W column:
  $$D = 2(b_f + d)$$
  $$= 2(12.16 + 12.71)$$
  $$= 49.74$$

  Per Table 722.5.1(1), W/D ratio (box)
  $$= 96/49.74$$
  $$= 1.93$$

- Gypsum wallboard protection on steel members is calculated per § 722.5.1.2.

  h = Total thickness of gypsum wallboard in inches
  $$= 4 \times (⁵/₈) [4 \times (15.9)]$$
  $$= 2¹/₂" (64)$$

  D = Heated perimeter
  $$= 49.74" (1263)$$

  W_t = Total weight per lineal foot of steel and gypsum board (assuming 4 layers of gypsum board)
  $$= W + (50hD/144)$$
  $$= 96 + (50 \times 2.5 \times 49.74/144)$$
  $$= 139.1771 \text{ pounds per lineal foot}$$
  $$= 2.03 \text{ kN/m}$$

  R = Fire-resistance (minutes)
  $$= 130 [h(W_t/D)/2]^{0.75} \quad \text{(Equation 7-12)}$$
  $$= 332 \text{ minutes}/60 = 5.54 \text{ hours}$$

- For contour profile:
  $$D = 4b_f + 2d - 2t_w$$
  $$= 4(12.16) + 2(12.71) - 2(0.55)$$
  $$= 72.96$$

  Per Table 722.5.1(1), W/D ratio (contour)
  $$= 96/72.96$$
  $$= 1.32$$

- Spray-applied fire protection of columns is based on the heated perimeter (usually of a contour profile), the thickness of the material and material-dependent fire-resistance constants. For our W12 x 96 column the formula is:

  C_1 and C_2 are material-dependent constants obtained from material manufacturers. Assume both to be 45 for our example.

  W/D ratio= 1.32
  h = Thickness of spray-applied fire-resistant material in inches
  $$= 2" (51)$$

  R = fire-resistance
  $$= [C_1 (W/D) + C_2] h \quad \text{(Equation 7-13)}$$
  $$= [45 (1.32) + 45] 2$$
  $$= 209 \text{ minutes}/60 = 3.48 \text{ hours}$$

§ 722.6 Wood Assemblies

These calculations may be used only for 1-hour rated assemblies. We will assume a wall located more than 10' (3048) from the property line. Thus the fire side is presumed to be on the interior of the building, per § 722.6.2.3.

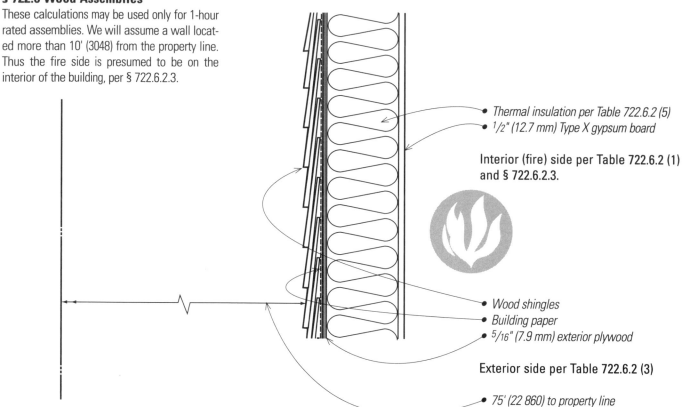

- Thermal insulation per Table 722.6.2 (5)
- 1/2" (12.7 mm) Type X gypsum board

Interior (fire) side per Table 722.6.2 (1) and § 722.6.2.3.

- Wood shingles
- Building paper
- 5/16" (7.9 mm) exterior plywood

Exterior side per Table 722.6.2 (3)

- 75' (22 860) to property line

Tabulation

Material	Time (minutes)	Alternate assembly*	Reference
Exterior	0		Excluded; not on fire-exposed side; see § 722.6.2.1.
Insulation	15	0	Table 722.6.2 (5)
Wood studs @ 16" (406) o.c.	20	20	Table 722.6.2 (2)
1/2" (12.7 mm) Type X gypsum board	25	40	Table 722.6.2 (1)
Total	60	60	

* Alternatively a 1-hour rating may be achieved without insulation by using two layers of 1/2" (12.7 mm) Type X gypsum wallboard (25 minutes x 2 = 50 minutes of fire-resistance assigned) or one layer of 5/8" (15.9 mm) Type X gypsum wallboard (40 minutes of fire-resistance assigned). Compliance may thus be achieved in several different ways.

8

Interior Finishes

Chapter 8 of the code governs the use of materials for interior finishes, trim, and decorative materials. The primary consideration of this chapter is the flame-spread and smoke-generation characteristics of materials when they are applied to underlying surfaces. These regulations are meant to govern those decorative finishes that are exposed to view. The regulations include all interior surfaces—floors, walls, and ceilings. Trim applied to finish surfaces is also included in these regulations. Note that § 801.5 requires finishes to be flood-damage-resistant when located below design flood elevation in buildings in flood hazard areas.

Classification

Materials are classified by their flame spread and smoke generation as tested on the test protocols of ASTM E 84 or UL 723. This test sets a standard for the surface-burning characteristics of building materials. The materials are placed in a test furnace and exposed to a flame of a calibrated size and the ignition, spread of flame, and generation of smoke are noted and assigned values based on a standard scale. The standard material against which other materials are measured for flame spread and smoke generation is Red Oak.

Typically the lower the number for each measurement, the slower the flames spread and the less smoke is generated. Once interior finish materials are tested, they are classified as A, B or C. The classifications, per § 803.1.1 are: ─────▶

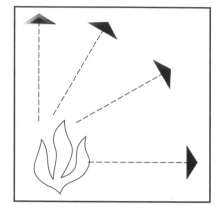 

	Flame-Spread Index	Smoke-Developed Index
Class A	0–25	0–450
Class B	26–75	0–450
Class C	76–200	0–450

The exception allows compliance with NFPA 286 instead of using ASTM E 84 or UL 723. This test is known as a "room corner" fire test. Many materials are tested using this standard test, which probably gives a better indication of actual performance in the field than does the ASTM test. § 803.1.2.1 lists the acceptance criteria for using NFPA 286 data.

§ 803.9 requires use of the UL 286 test for materials that contain high-density polyethylene (HDPE) or polypropylene (PP). This gives a more accurate basis for assessing the performance of these materials in actual fire conditions. The primary impact this has for designers and code officials is that when these materials are to be used in a project, they should ascertain that their manufacturers can demonstrate that the materials have been tested using the specific criteria established by the code.

The required classes of finish materials are determined by occupancy. The requirements are further subdivided into sprinklered and unsprinklered occupancies. The final consideration is whether the finish occurs in exits, in exit-access areas or in rooms. Per Table 803.11, unsprinklered buildings require higher classifications of finish materials. Also, egress paths require higher finishes than rooms or occupied spaces. This is consistent with the general philosophy of the code to offset active fire-protection measures with passive measures and to hold egress paths to higher standards than for occupied rooms.

Note that in Table 803.11 the most restrictive flame-spread and smoke-developed classifications are required for:

- *Interior exit stairways, interior exit ramps, and exit passageways*

- *Group A (assembly), H (high-hazard) and I (institutional) occupancies*

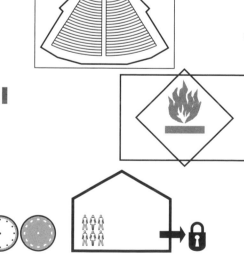

Application

§ 803.13 governs the application of materials over walls or ceilings required to be fire-resistance rated or of noncombustible construction.

Where materials are set off from fire-resistive construction by more than the distances noted, the finish materials must be Class A except where sprinklers protect both the visible and the concealed side of the finish materials.

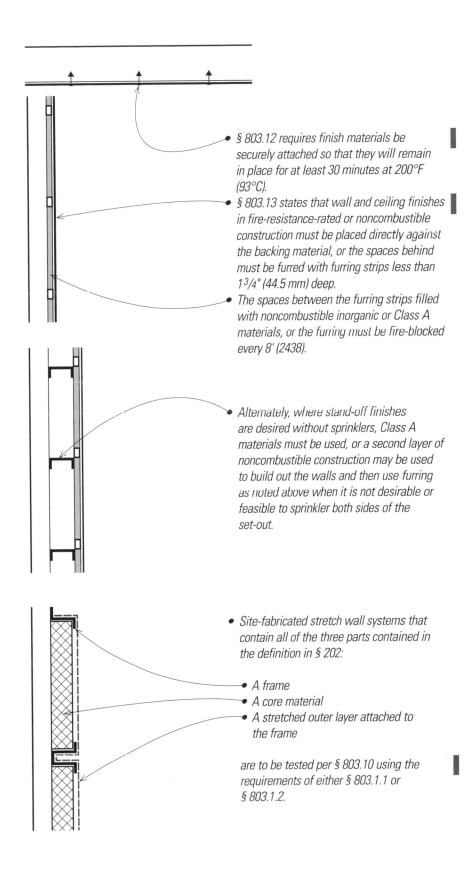

- *§ 803.12 requires finish materials be securely attached so that they will remain in place for at least 30 minutes at 200°F (93°C).*
- *§ 803.13 states that wall and ceiling finishes in fire-resistance-rated or noncombustible construction must be placed directly against the backing material, or the spaces behind must be furred with furring strips less than 1³/4" (44.5 mm) deep.*
- *The spaces between the furring strips filled with noncombustible inorganic or Class A materials, or the furring must be fire-blocked every 8' (2438).*

- *Alternately, where stand-off finishes are desired without sprinklers, Class A materials must be used, or a second layer of noncombustible construction may be used to build out the walls and then use furring as noted above when it is not desirable or feasible to sprinkler both sides of the set-out.*

- *Site-fabricated stretch wall systems that contain all of the three parts contained in the definition in § 202:*
  - *A frame*
  - *A core material*
  - *A stretched outer layer attached to the frame*

  are to be tested per § 803.10 using the requirements of either § 803.1.1 or § 803.1.2.

§ 804 deals primarily with carpets or similar fibrous flooring materials. Traditional-type flooring—such as wood, vinyl, linoleum, or terrazzo—are excepted. Flooring is to be classified into two categories, Class I or II, per the results of fire testing done per NFPA 253, with Class I materials being the more resistant to flame spread than Class II materials. This test records the fire and smoke response of flooring assemblies to a radiant heat source. Carpets are to be tested in configurations similar to how they are to be installed, including pads and adhesives or fasteners. Flooring materials are to be tagged with test results.

§ 804.4 governs the interior floor finish in enclosures for stairways and ramps, exit passageways, corridors, and rooms not separated from corridors by full-height partitions extending from the floor to the underside of the ceiling. The finishes in these conditions are to withstand a minimum critical radiant flux as specified in § 804.4.2.

Note that this section applies to all occupancies and introduces one additional test criteria, the Department of Commerce FF-1 Pill Test (per Consumer Product Safety Commission 16, Code of Federal Regulations 1630). This criteria is similar to, but less stringent than the NFPA test. The requirements for interior floor finishes are thus based on occupancy, construction type, and sprinklering, and can be summarized as follows:

§ 805 addresses the use of combustible materials in floors of Type I and II construction.

- *There are provisions allowing use of wood flooring in Type I or II buildings. In these conditions wood floors are to be installed over fire-blocked sleepers with blocking under walls.*

- *§ 805.1.1 regulates subfloor construction and prohibits combustible sleepers and nailing blocks unless the space between the fire-resistance-rated floor construction and the subfloor is solidly filled with noncombustible material or fire-blocked per § 718.*

- *§ 805.1.2 permits wood flooring to be attached directly to embedded or fire-blocked wood sleepers, or to be cemented directly to the top surface of fire-resistance-rated construction, or to a wood subfloor attached to sleepers per § 805.1.1.*
- *Another stipulation of § 805.1.1 prohibits spaces from extending under or through permanent walls and partitions.*

	Unsprinklered		Sprinklered	
	Enclosures for Stairways and Ramps; Exit Passageways; Corridors	All Areas	Enclosures for Stairways and Ramps; Exit Passageways; Corridors	All Areas
Occupancy	Critical Radiant Flux		Critical Radiant Flux	
I-1, I-2, I-3	Class I	FF-1	Class II	FF-1
A, B, E, H, I-4 M, R-1, R-2, S	Class II	FF-1	FF-1	FF-1

§ 806 regulates the flame-resistance of combustible decorative materials. This section was extensively revised in the 2015 IBC. Many of the references in this section are taken from the International Fire Code (IFC) and there are references to IFC code sections in this IBC section. Decorative materials, such as curtains, draperies, and hangings, must be flame-resistant per NFPA 701, NFPA 289, or be noncombustible. In I-3 occupancies, all combustible decorations are prohibited.

§ 806.7 requires all interior trim other than foam plastic to have minimum Class C flame-spread and smoke-developed indices (FS = 76–200 and S–D = 0–450 per § 803.1). The amount of combustible trim, excluding handrails and guardrails, may not exceed 10% of the specific wall or ceiling area where it is located.

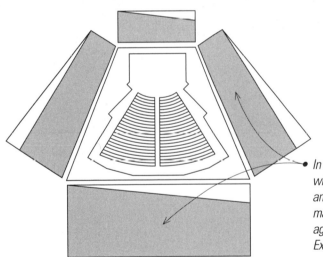

Noncombustible trim and decorations are not limited in quantity. Flame-resistant combustible materials are limited to 10% of the area of the specific wall or ceiling to which they are attached.

Fixed or movable walls and partitions, paneling, wall pads applied structurally or for decorative or acoustical treatment, and surface insulation are not to be considered decorative materials or furnishings. They are to be considered interior finishes and are to comply with § 803.

In auditoriums of Group A occupancy, when equipped with sprinklers, the amount of flame-resistant decorative materials may not exceed 75% of the aggregate area of walls and ceiling per Exception 1 to § 806.3.

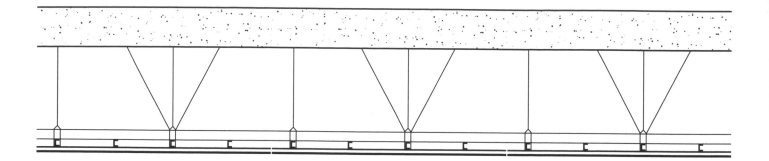

§ 808 regulates the quality, design, fabrication, and installation of acoustical tile and lay-in panel ceiling systems. The suspension systems must meet general engineering principles for vertical and lateral load capabilities. The acoustic materials must comply with the classification ratings noted for the occupancy and configuration in relation to the interior finish requirements per § 808.1.1. Where the ceiling suspension system is part of the fire-resistance-rated construction, the assembly must be installed consistent with the tested assemblies and must conform to the fire-resistance-rating requirements of Chapter 7.

9

Fire-Protection Systems

As we have seen in Chapter 7, the code recognizes the effectiveness of active fire-protection systems. The provision of an automatic sprinkler system allows trade-offs with passive fire-resistance in numerous sections of the code. The code also requires that active systems be provided in buildings above a certain height and above certain occupancy loadings. Thus the code recognizes the efficacy of active systems in concert with passive fire-protection to provide a balanced approach to fire and life safety for building occupants.

Active systems, especially fire sprinklers, are very effective but subject to interruption of water supplies unless emergency water sources with backup pressure systems are provided. At the same time, passive systems are subject to failure due to construction defects, poor maintenance, remodeling, failure of attachments, and damage from building movement or building use. The designer should consider the integration of both passive and active systems while developing the building design. The best designs do not rely on just one set of systems to provide fire protection but use an overall holistic approach to provide maximum protection.

We will touch on those active systems that integrate most effectively with passive fire-resistive strategies. The primary systems considered are fire sprinklers, smoke-control systems, and smoke and heat vents. These systems respond to hazards with defined actions designed to suppress fires or provide for occupant safety and egress. Other systems—fire alarms, fire extinguishers, and stand-pipe systems—provide notification for egress or auxiliary fire-fighting capabilities for the fire service. The code requires their presence for certain occupancies but does not allow balancing their use with alternate design considerations. The systems that interact with design decisions, especially fire sprinkler systems, are the ones discussed here.

FIRE-PROTECTION SYSTEMS

The design and installation of automatic sprinkler systems is typically governed by rules developed by the National Fire Protection Association and promulgated as NFPA 13. An automatic sprinkler system is designed to respond to a fire when the sprinkler heads are activated by a fire or by heat. The systems are designed to function without intervention by the building occupants to cause their operation. The history of fire sprinklers as fire-suppression devices has been a good one, and they have been required under a greater range of circumstances in each new edition of model codes.

Residential sprinkler systems may be installed under the provisions of NFPA 13D or 13R, which are subsets of the provisions of NFPA 13. These may be acceptable as sprinkler systems in specific instances, but the code does not recognize these as fully equivalent to NFPA 13 systems for the trade-offs contained in exceptions or reductions unless they are specifically allowed. See the requirements for Group R occupancies for allowable uses for these sprinkler-system classes.

When reading sections of the code that refer to Chapter 9, the designer should go to the section referred to in Chapter 9 to verify which type of sprinkler system is required by the IBC. These systems are described in § 903.3. This is where the code draws distinctions between NFPA 13, 13D, 13R and alternative sprinkler systems. Do not assume that all automatic sprinkler systems are per NFPA 13 without referring to Chapter 9.

Fire-protection systems consist of:

- *Detection systems that sense heat, fire, or smoke (particles of combustion) and activate an appropriate alarm.*

- *Alarm systems that alert occupants of an emergency in a building by the sense of hearing, sight, or, in some cases, touch, as by such things as vibrations.*

- *Automatic fire-extinguishing or sprinkler systems that are activated by heat from a fire and discharge either an approved fire-extinguishing agent or water over the fire area in order to extinguish or control a fire.*

- *Automatic sprinkler systems that consist of underground and overhead piping from a suitable water supply, to which automatic sprinklers are attached in a regular pattern designed to provide even coverage for water discharge. Upon activation by heat from a fire, the systems discharge water over the fire area.*

A fire-protection system may also include equipment to control or manage smoke and combustion products of a fire.

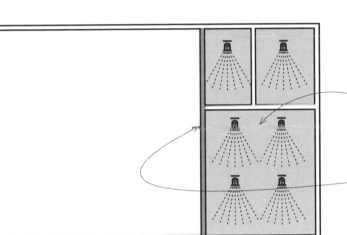

Various occupancies are required to have automatic sprinkler systems by § 903. These requirements are based on several factors:

- Occupancy type
- Occupant load
- Area of occupied space
- Locations not providing ready egress or ready fire-department access

The requirements are listed by occupancy group. Carefully note that an automatic sprinkler system may be required:

- *Throughout an entire building*
  because of a code requirement or because the sprinkler system is used as a substitute for other fire-protection features

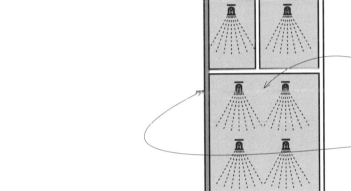

- *Throughout a fire area*
  that may exceed a certain size or occupant load, or one that is located in a specific portion of a building

  Per the definitions contained in Chapter 2, fire areas are enclosed and bounded by fire walls, fire barriers, exterior walls or fire-resistance-rated horizontal assemblies.

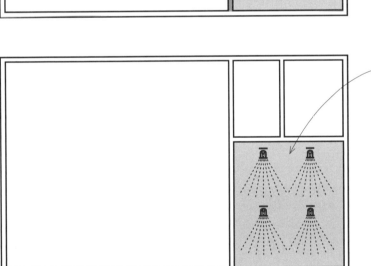

- *In specific rooms or areas*
  to protect against a specific hazard

Note also that the increases for building heights and areas allowed in Chapter 5 for provision of sprinkler systems apply only when those systems are installed throughout a building.

In addition to the requirements contained in § 903.2, Table 903.2.11.6 is a useful cross reference for sprinkler requirements contained in other code chapters.

Group A: § 903.2.1 requires that when any of the conditions listed on this and the following page exist, an automatic sprinkler system be installed:

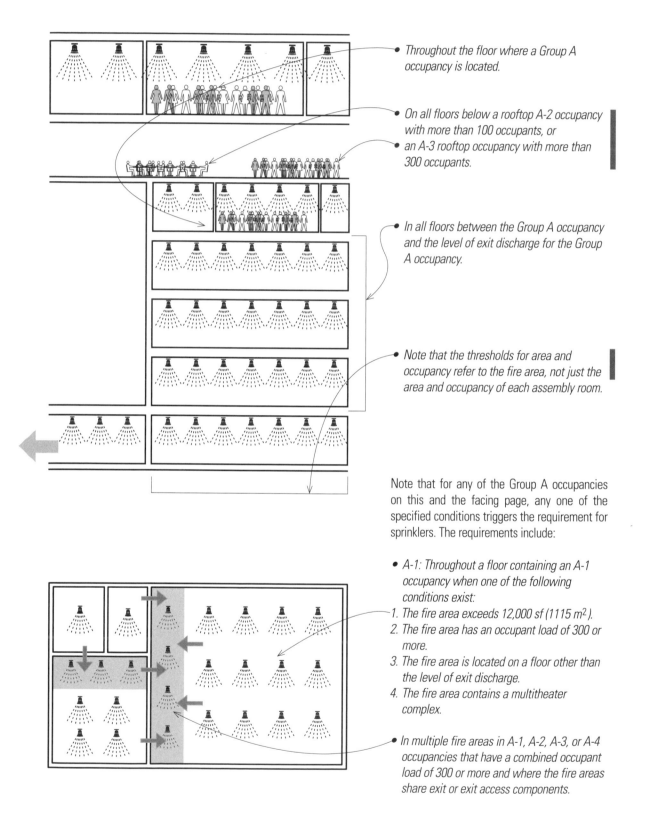

• Throughout the floor where a Group A occupancy is located.

• On all floors below a rooftop A-2 occupancy with more than 100 occupants, or
• an A-3 rooftop occupancy with more than 300 occupants.

• In all floors between the Group A occupancy and the level of exit discharge for the Group A occupancy.

• Note that the thresholds for area and occupancy refer to the fire area, not just the area and occupancy of each assembly room.

Note that for any of the Group A occupancies on this and the facing page, any one of the specified conditions triggers the requirement for sprinklers. The requirements include:

• A-1: Throughout a floor containing an A-1 occupancy when one of the following conditions exist:
1. The fire area exceeds 12,000 sf (1115 m²).
2. The fire area has an occupant load of 300 or more.
3. The fire area is located on a floor other than the level of exit discharge.
4. The fire area contains a multitheater complex.

• In multiple fire areas in A-1, A-2, A-3, or A-4 occupancies that have a combined occupant load of 300 or more and where the fire areas share exit or exit access components.

Any one of the specified conditions below triggers the requirement for sprinklers in Group A occupancies:

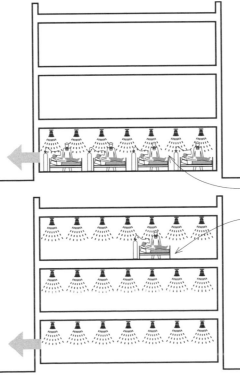

- *Fire area exceeds 5,000 sf (465 m²) for Group A-2 occupancies.*

- *For Group A occupancies other than A-2 or A-5, the occupant threshold is 300 for the entire floor area, not just the assembly room. For A-2 occupancies, the threshold is 100 occupants.*

- *A-2: Throughout a floor containing an A-2 occupancy when one of the following conditions exist:*
1. *The fire area exceeds 5,000 sf (465 m²).*
2. *The fire area has an occupant load of 100 or more.*
3. *The fire area is located on a floor other than the level of exit discharge.*

- *A-3: Throughout a floor containing an A-3 occupancy when one of the following conditions exist:*
1. *The fire area exceeds 12,000 sf (1115 m²).*
2. *The fire area has an occupant load of 300 or more.*
3. *The fire area is located on a floor other than the level of exit discharge.*

- *A-4: Throughout a floor containing an A-4 occupancy when one of the following conditions exist:*
1. *The fire area exceeds 12,000 sf (1115 m²).*
2. *The fire area has an occupant load of 300 or more.*
3. *The fire area is located on a floor other than the level of exit discharge.*

- *A-5: A sprinkler system is to be provided in concession stands, retail areas, press boxes, and other accessory use areas larger than 1,000 sf (93 m²) in A-5 occupancies, such as outdoor stadiums.*

Group B: There are increasing numbers of "ambulatory care facilities," which are usually classified as B occupancies. The sprinkler provisions in § 902.2.2 are based on the use description of ambulatory care, not on the occupancy classification. Sprinklers are required on the entire floor where there are more than four care recipients incapable of self-preservation on the level of exit discharge, or when one or more such persons are located at other than the level of exit discharge. When there are incapacitated care recipients above the level of exit discharge then the floors supporting that level must also be sprinklered.

Group B occupancies

- *Four or more care recipients incapable of self-preservation: sprinkler entire floor.*
- *One or more care recipients incapable of self-preservation and located at other than the level of exit discharge: sprinkler entire floor and floors below to level of exit discharge.*

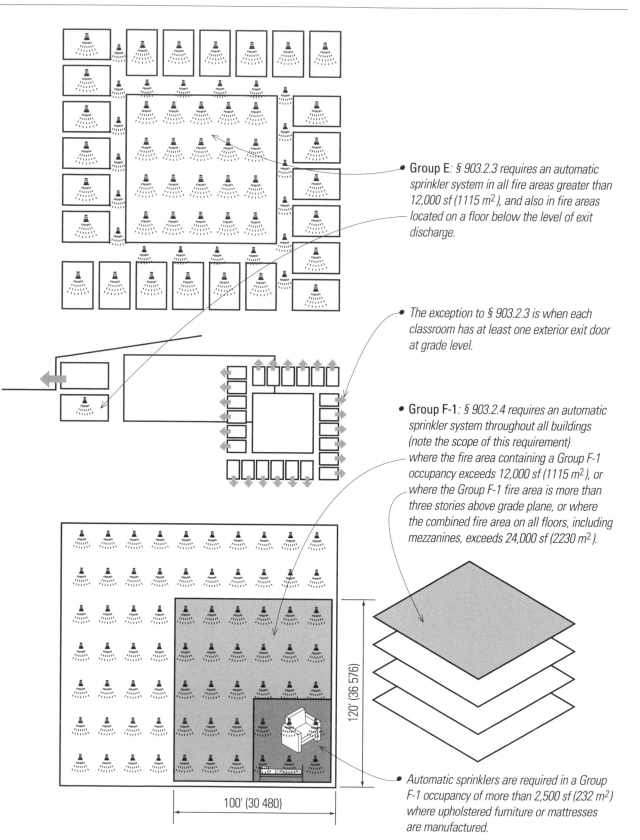

- Group E: *§ 903.2.3 requires an automatic sprinkler system in all fire areas greater than 12,000 sf (1115 m².), and also in fire areas located on a floor below the level of exit discharge.*

- *The exception to § 903.2.3 is when each classroom has at least one exterior exit door at grade level.*

- Group F-1: *§ 903.2.4 requires an automatic sprinkler system throughout all buildings (note the scope of this requirement) where the fire area containing a Group F-1 occupancy exceeds 12,000 sf (1115 m².), or where the Group F-1 fire area is more than three stories above grade plane, or where the combined fire area on all floors, including mezzanines, exceeds 24,000 sf (2230 m².).*

- *Automatic sprinklers are required in a Group F-1 occupancy of more than 2,500 sf (232 m².) where upholstered furniture or mattresses are manufactured.*

120' (36 576)

100' (30 480)

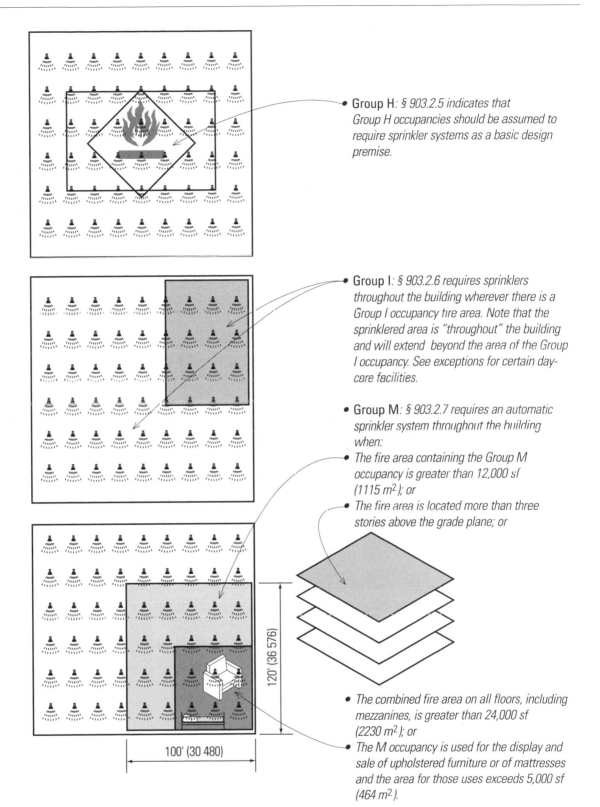

- **Group H**: *§ 903.2.5 indicates that Group H occupancies should be assumed to require sprinkler systems as a basic design premise.*

- **Group I**: *§ 903.2.6 requires sprinklers throughout the building wherever there is a Group I occupancy fire area. Note that the sprinklered area is "throughout" the building and will extend beyond the area of the Group I occupancy. See exceptions for certain day-care facilities.*

- **Group M**: *§ 903.2.7 requires an automatic sprinkler system throughout the building when:*
- *The fire area containing the Group M occupancy is greater than 12,000 sf (1115 m²); or*
- *The fire area is located more than three stories above the grade plane; or*

- *The combined fire area on all floors, including mezzanines, is greater than 24,000 sf (2230 m²); or*
- *The M occupancy is used for the display and sale of upholstered furniture or of mattresses and the area for those uses exceeds 5,000 sf (464 m²).*

- *Where merchandise is stored in high-piled or rack storage, sprinklers shall be provided at those areas per the International Fire Code.*

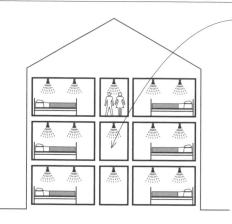

- **Group R**: § 903.2.8 requires an automatic sprinkler system throughout buildings with an R fire area. This includes all R occupancies as noted. Verify with the local AHJ regarding the adoption of the International Residential Code to see what is applicable for one- and two-family dwellings as well as when an NFPA "13R" sprinkler system may be used in Type R-4 buildings.

- **Group S-1**: § 903.2.9 requires an automatic sprinkler system throughout all buildings where:

- *The S-1 fire area exceeds 12,000 sf (1115 m²), or*
- *The S-1 fire area is more than 3 stories above grade plane, or*
- *The combined fire area on all floors, including mezzanines, exceeds 24,000 sf (2230 m²), or*
- *The S-1 fire area used for the storage of commercial trucks or buses is larger than 5,000 sf (464 m²), or*
- *The area used to store upholsted funiture or matresses exceeds 2,500 sf (232 m²).*

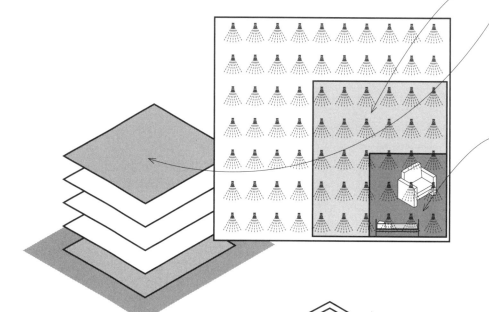

- *Where S-1 occupancies are used as repair garages, § 903.2.9.1 requires an automatic sprinkler system thoughout the building when:*
- *The fire area containing the repair garage exceeds 10,000 sf (929 m²) and the building is two or more stories above grade plane; or*
- *The S-1 fire area containing a repair garage in a building no more than one story above grade plane exceeds 12,000 sf (1115 m²); or*
- *The repair garage service area is located in a basement; or*
- *There is an S-1 fire area used for the commercial repair of trucks or buses and the fire area exceeds 5,000 sf (464 m²).*

- **Group S-2**: § 903.2.10 requires an automatic sprinkler system throughout buildings with enclosed S-2 occupancies that are:
- *located beneath other occupancy groups, or*
- *classified as enclosed parking garages per § 406.4 and the fire area of the enclosed parking garage exceeds 12,000 sf (1115 m²).*

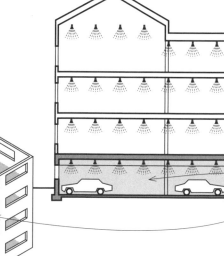

- *Excepted are enclosed parking garages under Group R-3 occupancies. Note that this exception also includes the requirement that the area of the garage be less than or equal to 12,000 sf (1115 m²).*

§ 903.2.11.1 requires that in buildings other than U occupancies, sprinklers are required at floors below grade or with limited fire-fighting access. Any floor area exceeding 1,500 sf (139.4 m²) must be provided with one type or the other of exterior wall openings noted to the right, or automatic sprinklers must be provided for the story.

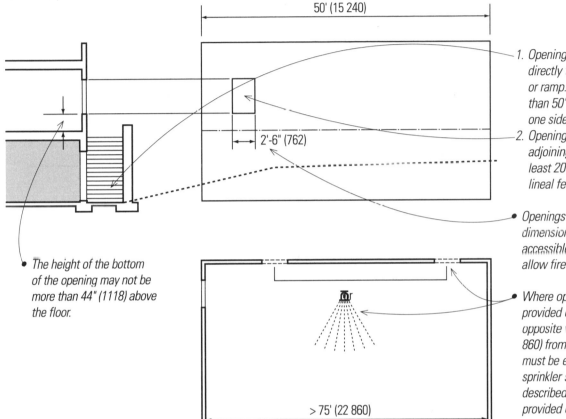

50' (15 240)

2'-6" (762)

1. *Openings below grade must lead directly to the ground floor via a stair or ramp. Openings must be no more than 50' (15 240) apart on at least one side of the space.*

2. *Openings that are entirely above the adjoining ground level must total at least 20 sf (1.86 m²) for every 50 lineal feet (15 240) of exterior wall.*

• *Openings must have a minimum dimension of at least 30" (762) and be accessible to the fire department to allow fire-fighting or rescue.*

• *The height of the bottom of the opening may not be more than 44" (1118) above the floor.*

> 75' (22 860)

• *Where openings in a story are provided on one side only and the opposite wall is more than 75' (22 860) from such openings, the story must be equipped with an automatic sprinkler system, or openings as described in 1 and 2 above must be provided on at least two sides of the story.*

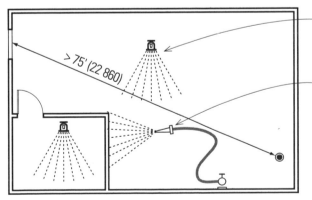

> 75' (22 860)

• *Where any portion of a basement (even with openings as noted above) is more than 75' (22 860) from openings required by § 903.2.11.1, or where walls, partitions, or other obstructions occur that would restrict the application of water from hose streams, then the basement must be equipped with an automatic sprinkler system.*

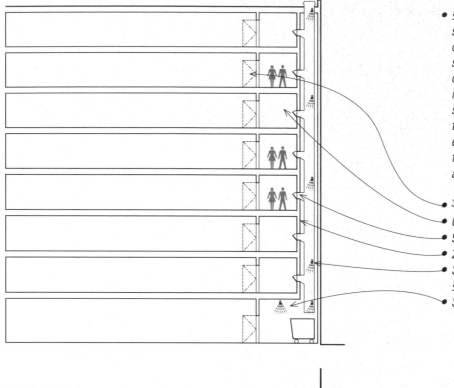

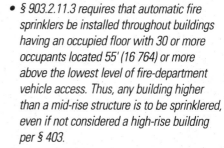

- § 903.2.11.2: Trash and linen chutes merit special sprinkler protection. They typically occur in residential buildings where people sleep. They are also accessible for use by occupants and thus may not be maintained in a safe condition by users. Therefore sprinklers are to be provided in addition to the passive protection provided by shaft enclosures and fire-rated rooms separating the chutes from circulation spaces and adjacent uses.

- 3/4-hour door in 1-hour wall (typical)
- Chute access room
- 90-minute chute door (typical)
- 2-hour shaft @ chute (typical)
- Sprinklers @ top and alternate floors per § 903.2.11.2 and NFPA 13
- Sprinklers @ terminal room

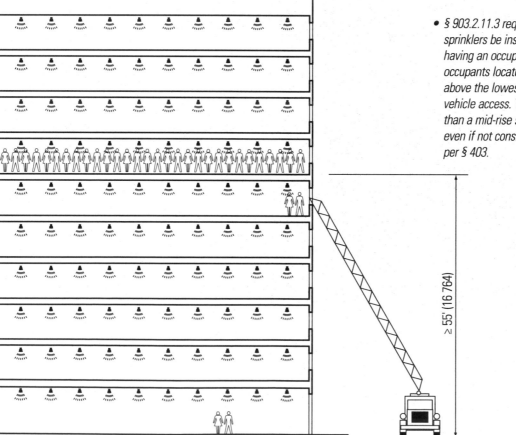

- § 903.2.11.3 requires that automatic fire sprinklers be installed throughout buildings having an occupied floor with 30 or more occupants located 55' (16 764) or more above the lowest level of fire-department vehicle access. Thus, any building higher than a mid-rise structure is to be sprinklered, even if not considered a high-rise building per § 403.

≥ 55' (16 764)

§ 905 contains the requirements for the installation of standpipe systems. Standpipes are permanent pipes rising through a building that provide hose connections for use in interior firefighting. Standpipes are designated as Class I, II, or III per the definitions in Chapter 2, based on the hose connections they furnish.

- Class I standpipes provide large, 2¹/₂" (64) hose connections for use by firefighters who are trained in the use of the heavy flow of water these connections provide.
- Class II standpipes provide 1¹/₂" (38) hose connections that are lower volume and pressure and can conceivably be used either by untrained building occupants or first responders to help fight a fire inside the building.
- Class III standpipe systems provide access to both sizes of connections to allow use by either building occupants or firefighters with the choice of which connection to use based on the ability and training of the responders.
- Standpipes are to have approved standard threads for hose connections that are compatible with fire department hose threads. These connections should be verified and approved by the AHJ.

Standpipe types are classified as either wet or dry and automatic or manual. Dry standpipes contain air that is displaced by water when they are put to use. Wet standpipes contain water at all times. The use of these is often determined by location. For example, dry standpipes can be on open landings in cold climates, where the water in wet standpipes would freeze.

Standpipe classifications for automatic standpipes presume that the water supply for the standpipe can meet the system demand. Manual standpipes depend on additional pressure and water supply to meet the demand. Hooking up a fire-department pumper truck to the standpipe typically provides such additional supply.

Standpipes are often referred to as *fire risers*, a term also applied to vertical fire-sprinkler supply lines. Avoid confusion in language by determining to which pipes the term applies.

Standpipes are permitted to be combined with automatic sprinkler systems. Thus a single riser pipe may supply both the sprinkler system and the hose connections. However, such a single pipe will be larger in diameter than two separate pipes since it must meet the demand of both the sprinkler and hose connection systems. Typically the systems are combined since a single riser, even if somewhat larger in diameter, is easier to locate in the building than two such risers.

- Water pressure for a standpipe or sprinkler system may be provided by a municipal water main or a pumper truck, augmented by a fire pump or a rooftop water tank.

Required Installations

Triggers for standpipe requirements have different thresholds depending on building height, occupancy type, provision of sprinklers, and building area.

Class III Standpipes Required

§ 905.3.1 requires that buildings having a floor level >30' (9144) above or below the lowest level of fire vehicle access are to have Class III standpipes.

Exceptions to § 905.3.1 are:

1. Class I standpipes are allowed in buildings that are fully sprinklered per § 903.3.1.1 or § 903.3.1.2.
2. Class I manual standpipes are allowed in open parking garages where the highest floor is not more than 150' (45 720) above the lowest level of fire-department access.
3. Class I manual dry standpipes are allowed in open parking garages subject to freezing as long as the standpipes meet spacing and location criteria per § 905.5.
4. Class I standpipes are allowed in basements that have automatic sprinklers.
5. Determining the lowest level of fire department access does not require consideration of recessed loading docks for four or fewer vehicles and topographic conditions that make fire department vehicle access impractical or impossible.

§ 905.3.4 requires Class III wet standpipes be provided at stages larger than 1,000 sf (93 m²) in area, with 1½" (38) and 2½" (64) hose connections located on each side of the stage. If there is an automatic sprinkler system a 1½" (38) hose connection is to be provided. § 905.3.4.1 requires a hose cabinet or rack and the hose to be equipped with an adjustable fog nozzle.

Class I Standpipes Required

§ 905.3.2 requires that Class I automatic wet standpipes be provided in nonsprinklered Group-A occupancies having an occupant load of more than 1,000 people. This is not required for open-air seating spaces without enclosed spaces.

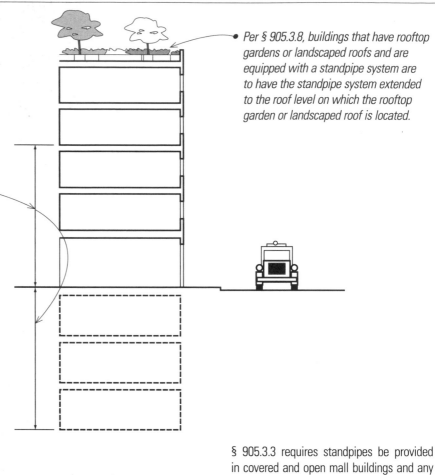

Per § 905.3.8, buildings that have rooftop gardens or landscaped roofs and are equipped with a standpipe system are to have the standpipe system extended to the roof level on which the rooftop garden or landscaped roof is located.

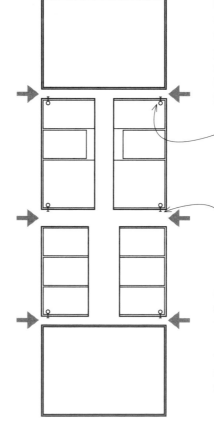

§ 905.3.3 requires standpipes be provided in covered and open mall buildings and any building connected to them where otherwise required in § 905.3.1. This translates into requirements for Class I standpipes located per § 905.4 as illustrated to the left. When other types of standpipes are not required by § 905.3.1, Class I hose connections are to be located:

- *Within the mall at the entrance to each exit corridor;*
- *At each floor level landing in enclosed exit stairways opening directly to the mall;*
- *At exterior public entrances to the mall of a covered mall building or at public entrances at the perimeter line of an open mall building.*

It is to be presumed that these requirements are supplementary and complementary with those for malls contained in § 905.4.

§ 905.3.5 requires Class I automatic wet or manual wet standpipes be provided in all underground buildings.

Standpipe Locations

Locations are described for hose connections for the various standpipe classes. Class III standpipes, having components of both other classes, must comply with both sets of regulations.

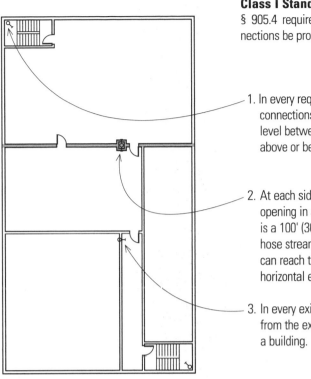

Class I Standpipe Hose Connections

§ 905.4 requires Class I standpipe hose connections be provided at the following locations:

1. In every required stairway. The hose connections are to be at the intermediate level between floors at every floor level above or below grade.

2. At each side of the wall adjacent to an exit opening in a horizontal exit unless there is a 100' (30 480) hose with a 30' (9144) hose stream in an adjacent exit stair that can reach the floor areas adjacent to the horizontal exit.

3. In every exit passageway at the entrance from the exit passageway to other areas of a building.

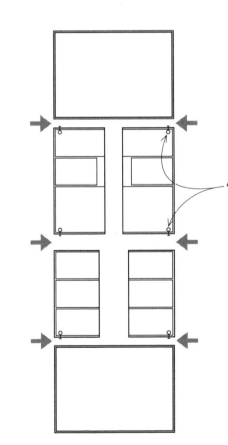

4. In covered mall buildings, adjacent to each exterior public entrance to the mall and adjacent to each entrance from an exit passageway or exit corridor to the mall. In open mall buildings, adjacent to each public entrance to the mall at the perimeter line and adjacent to each entrance from an exit passageway or exit corridor to the mall.

Class I Standpipe Hose Connections
(continued from page 171)

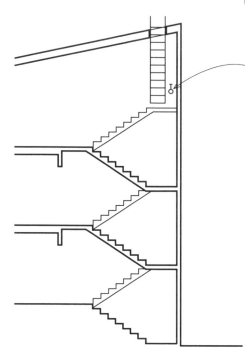

5. Where a roof has a slope of less than 4:12 (33.3% slope), a standpipe is to have a connection on the roof or at the highest landing of stairs with access to the roof per § 1009.16. There is also to be a connection at the most hydraulically remote standpipe for testing purposes.

6. The building official is authorized to require additional hose connections where the most remote portion of a nonsprinklered building is more than 150' (45 720) from a hose connection, or the most remote part of a sprinklered building is more than 200' (60 960) from a hose connection.

When risers and laterals of Class I standpipes are not located in an enclosed stairway or pressurized enclosure, § 905.4.1 requires the piping to be protected by fire-resistant materials equal to those required in the building for vertical enclosures. Protection is not required for laterals in fully sprinklered buildings.

Class II Standpipe Hose Connections

Where Class II standpipes are required, § 905.5 requires the standpipe hose connections to be located so that all portions of the building are within 30' (9144) of a nozzle attached to a 100' (30 480) hose.

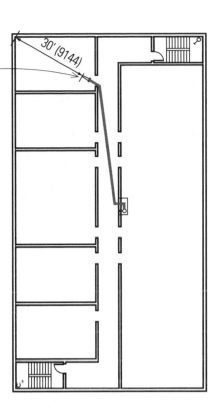

Class III Standpipe Hose Connections

Class III standpipe hose connections, by definition, have both Class I and II hose connections. Therefore, § 905.6 refers back to § 905.4 for the location of Class I connections and to § 905.5 for the location of Class II hose connections. The laterals and risers are to be protected as for Class I systems per § 905.4.1. Where there is more than one Class III standpipe, they are to be hydraulically interconnected at the bottom.

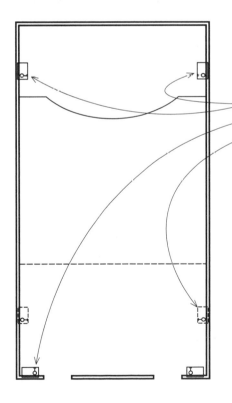

In Group A-1 and A-2 occupancies having loads larger than 1,000 people, Class II hose connections are to be located:

- *on each side of any stage,*
- *on each side of the rear of the auditorium,*
- *on each side of any balcony, and*
- *on each tier of dressing rooms.*

- *Class II standpipe laterals and risers do not require fire-resistance-rated protection.*
- *For light-hazard occupancies, the hose for Class II systems may be minimum 1" (25.4 mm) hose where approved by the building official.*

§ 906 is excerpted from sections contained in the International Fire Code. It is included in the IBC since the requirements have design implications for building planning. We will discuss the typical requirements for buildings without sprinkler systems or with conventional sprinkler systems. Note that per the Exception to § 906.1, buildings of Group R-2 occupancy have less extensive extinguisher requirements when each dwelling unit is provided with a fire extinguisher with a minimum 1-A:10-B:C rating. Note also that Table 906.1 contains a number of additonal requirements for portable fire extinguishers based on specific building operations.

Extinguishers are assumed to be available for use by building occupants who have little or no training in their use. They are intended as a first line of defense against a developing fire until trained fire fighters can respond to the scene of the fire. The requirements are based on the type of fires anticipated; the extent of flammable materials, which determines the hazard-class; the size of the potential floor area in which a fire may occur; and the travel distance for a building occupant to get to an extinguisher's location.

Extinguishers are rated A, B, C or D, depending on the type of fire they are designed to suppress. See the discussion at right for an explanation of their ratings. Their rating also gives an indication of the size of fire they are designed to fight. Many extinguishers have chemicals in them that are designed to respond to multiple types of fires. Thus, one will often see extinguishers noted as "2A-10B-C." This extinguisher would be usable on ordinary combustibles, flammable liquids, or an electrical fire. The basic code requirements are determined by the expectation that fires will generally require Class A or B extinguishers. The requirements for Class C extinguishers, per § 906.3.3, are tied to those for Classes A and B. Class D extinguishers are related to the specific type of metals anticipated for use and their quantities. These specialized requirements are contained in the reference standard, NFPA 10.

The determination of the type of extinguishers required will be based on the anticipated use of the facility. These assumptions should be confirmed with the AHJ early in the design process to set extinguisher spacing and size criteria. We interpret the requirements for mulitple-class exstinguishers to be complementary. Thus, for multiple-class extinguishers, the most strigent requirements for extinguisher spacing will apply for multiple classifications.

Ordinary Combustibles

- Class A extinguishers are intended for use with "ordinary combustibles," such as wood or paper. Water is the primary extinguishing agent.

Flammable Liquids

- Class B extinguishers are intended for use with spilled flammable liquids, such as grease, oil, or gasoline, in shallow depths. The exinguishing agents are designed to smother the fire and not spread the burning liquid.

Electrical Equipment

- Class C extinguishers are intended for use in electical fires. The extinguishing agent is designed to be non-conductive so as not to spread the influence of an energized conductor on the fire.

- Class D extinguishers are intended for use on flammable metals and are often specific for the type of metal in question. There is no picture designator for Class D extinguishers. These extinguishers generally have no multi-purpose rating for use on other types of fires.

Fire Extinguisher Size and Spacing

Class **A**	Light (Low) Hazard	Ordinary (Moderate) Hazard	Extra (High) Hazard
Minimum Class Rating	2-A	2-A	4-A
Max. Floor Area per Unit of A	3000 sf / A (279 m²)	1500 sf / A (139 m²)	1000 sf / A (93 m²)
Max. Floor Area per Extinguisher	11,250 sf (1045 m²)	11,250 sf (1045 m²)	11,250 sf (1045 m²)
Max. Travel Distance to Extinguisher (Distance between Extinguishers)	75' (22.8 m) | 75' (22.8 m) — 150' (45.7 m)	75' (22.8 m) | 75' (22.8 m) — 150' (45.7 m)	75' (22.8 m) | 75' (22.8 m) — 150' (45.7 m)

B

Basic Extinguisher Rating

	Light (Low) Hazard	Ordinary (Moderate) Hazard	Extra (High) Hazard
5-B, Max. Travel Distance to Extinguisher (Distance between Extinguishers)	30' (9144) | 30' (9144) — 60' (18.2 m)	NA	NA
10-B, Max. Travel Distance to Extinguisher (Distance between Extinguishers)	50' (15.2 m) | 50' (15.2 m) — 100' (30.5 m)	30' (9144) | 30' (9144) — 60' (18.2 m)	NA
20-B, Max. Travel Distance to Extinguisher (Distance between Extinguishers)	50' (15.2 m) | 50' (15.2 m) — 100' (30.5 m)	50' (15.2 m) | 50' (15.2 m) — 100' (30.5 m)	NA
40-B, Max. Travel Distance to Extinguisher (Distance between Extinguishers)	50' (15.2 m) | 50' (15.2 m) — 100' (30.5 m)	50' (15.2 m) | 50' (15.2 m) — 100' (30.5 m)	30' (9144) | 30' (9144) — 60' (18.2 m)
80-B, Max. Travel Distance to Extinguisher (Distance between Extinguishers)	50' (15.2 m) | 50' (15.2 m) — 100' (30.5 m)	50' (15.2 m) | 50' (15.2 m) — 100' (30.5 m)	50' (15.2 m) | 50' (15.2 m) — 100' (30.5 m)

◄- - - - - - - - - -►   Larger extinguisher in lower Hazard Class for Class B

Fire alarms are audible and visual devices to alert occupants and responders of emergencies. Detectors are automatic devices that usually sound an audible and visual alarm to alert occupants and also trigger other responses in systems such as sprinklers, smoke-control systems, or HVAC controls. Systems to notify building occupants of an emergency can be either manually or automatically actuated.

The code requires differing types of alarms or detectors, and different levels of actuation in various occupancies and types of buildings. When buildings are sprinklered and the sprinklers connected to the alarm system, automatic heat detection is not required. Sprinklers are heat-actuated and thus are a type of heat detector themselves. Fire detectors are to be smoke detectors as well, except in areas like boiler rooms where products of combustion would tend to set off smoke detectors. In those rooms alternative types of fire detectors may be used. Alarms are to be per NFPA 72.

The code offers trade-offs between manual alarms and automatic detection systems under certain conditions. There are instances where having manual alarms may result in a large number of false alarms, so providing automatic detection may be a desirable alternative.

Detailed requirements are grouped by occupancy or use. The table on the following pages gives general requirements; it does not provide for every nuance of conditions.

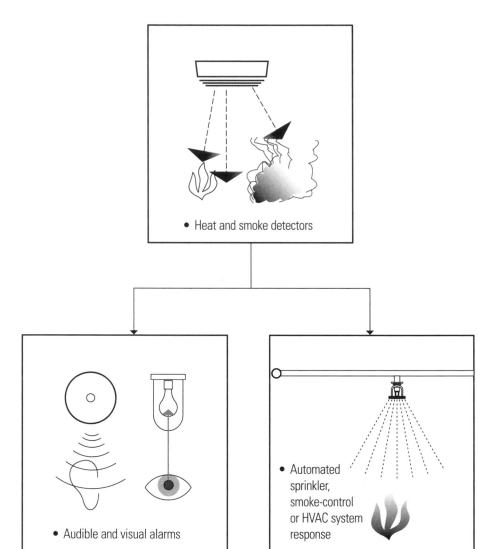

- Heat and smoke detectors

- Audible and visual alarms

- Automated sprinkler, smoke-control or HVAC system response

Section 907.2.x	Occupancy or Building Type	Occupant Load or Condition	Device Type	Exceptions	Notes
.1	A	≥ 300 " due to assembly occupancy"	Manual fire alarm	Not required if sprinklered & w/ water-flow alarm	E Assembly per Group E requirements; captioned systems for hearing impaired to be provided if required per § 1108.2.7.3.
.1.1	A	≥ 1,000	Voice/alarm		
.2	B	≥ 500, or > 100 occ. above/below exit discharge, or B ambulatory health facility	Manual fire alarm	Not required if sprinklered & w/ water-flow alarm	
.3	E	> 50	Manual fire alarm	Manual pull boxes are not required if all of a long criteria list for detection are met or if the building is fully sprinklered with automatic notification to a normally occupied location.	When installed, sprinklers & smoke detectors must interconnect to alarm system; system must accommodate communication between secure areas and a central location when the school is under lockdown conditions.
		>100	Voice/alarm		
.4	F	≥ 2 stories and ≥ 500 occupants above/ below exit discharge	Manual fire alarm	Not required if sprinklered & w/ water flow alarm	
.5	H-5 and manufacturing of organic coatings	All	Manual fire alarm		Smoke detection required for toxic gas, peroxides, and oxidizers per International Fire Code
.6	All I	All	Manual fire alarm	Manual pull boxes not required at sleeping rooms if at staff stations in I-1 and I-2 occupancies	
.6.1	I-1	Corridors, habitable spaces	Auto smoke detection	In Condition 1, not required if fully sprinklered	Smoke alarms to be installed per § 907.2.11
.6.2	I-2	Corridors in nursing homes and hospitals	Auto smoke detection and alarm activation per § 907.4	Not required if smoke compartments containing rooms have smoke detectors or auto closing doors	
.6.3	I-3	All	Manual fire alarm and auto smoke detection		Alarms to alert staff
.6.3.3	I-3	Housing area	Smoke detectors	Alternate detector location and size limits for small groups	Not required for sleeping units with 4 or fewer occupants in sprinklered smoke compartments
.7	M	≥ 500 occupants on all floors, or > 100 above/below exit discharge	Manual fire alarm	Not required if a covered or open mall per § 402, or fully sprinklered & w/ water-flow alarm	When occupied, alarm may notify attended station that will activate voice/alarm system

FIRE-ALARM AND DETECTION SYSTEMS

Section 907.2.x	Occupancy or Building Type	Occupant Load or Condition	Device Type	Exceptions	Notes
.8	R-1	All	Manual fire alarm & auto fire detection	1. No alarm if ≤ 2 stories with 1-hour separations and direct exit 2. No alarm if sprinklered and local alarm and one manual pull box at approved location	
.9	R-2	1. 3 or more stories 2. Dwelling units > 1 level below exit discharge 3. > 16 dwelling units	Manual fire-alarm system	1. Not required if ≤ 2 stories with 1-hour separations and direct exit 2. No manual alarm box if sprinklered and local alarm	
.9.3	R-2	College and university buildings	Automatic smoke detection that activates occupant-notification system	Not required if there are no interior corridors, and sleeping rooms have direct exit access	At common, laundry, and storage areas, and interior corridors serving sleeping units. When required, the smoke detection devices are to be interconnected to the building fire alarm system.
.10	R-4	All	1. Manual fire-alarm system w/ occupant notification per § 907.5 2. Automatic smoke detection in corridors, waiting areas, and habitable spaces other than sleeping rooms	1. Not required in ≤ 2 stories w/ 1-hour separations and direct exit 2. Automatic sprinkler system w/ notification appliances : one manual pull box at approved location 3. Not required if pull boxes at attended staff locations	
.11			Smoke alarms		Where indicated below
.11.1	R-1	1. Sleeping areas 2. Every room in means of egress path 3. Each story in multistory units			
.11.2	R-2, R-3, R-4, I-1	1. Near each separate sleeping area 2. In each sleeping room 3. In each story of dwelling units			Not required in sleeping rooms of I-1 with smoke detectors in sleeping rooms as part of an automatic smoke detection system
.11.3		To cut down on false alarms from cooking or from water vapor, the location of smoke alarms near cooking appliances and bathrooms is dependent on the type of smoke alarm (ionization or photoelectric) used. The location is to be per NFPA 72.			
.11.4			Smoke-alarm power		From electrical source w/ battery backup in new construction; battery power OK in retrofit

Section 907.2.x	Occupancy or Building Type	Occupant Load or Condition	Device Type	Exceptions	Notes
.11.5			Smoke-alarm interconnection		Where more than one smoke detector is required in dwelling or sleeping units the smoke alarms are to be interconnected such that the activation of one alarm will activate all the smoke alarms in the unit. Interconnection may be wireless if listed system.
.12	Special amusement buildings		Automatic smoke detection	Alternates where smoke detectors will be activated by ambient conditions	Detection system sounds alarm at attended location
.12.2, .12.3	Special amusement buildings		System response (See notes at right)		1. Illuminate means of egress with 1 foot-candle (11 lux) minimum. 2. Stop sounds and distractions. 3. Activate exit markings. 4. Activate voice message.
.13	High-rise buildings		Automatic smoke detection system per § 907.2.13.1, fire department communication systems per § 907.2.13.2, and emergency voice/alarm communication systems per § 907.5.2.2		
.13.1	High-rise buildings		Automatic smoke detection		
.13.2	High-rise buildings		Fire-department communication	Fire-department radios may be used in lieu of two-way communication when approved by the fire department.	Two-way fire-department communication per NFPA 72 from central command to elevators, elevator lobbies, emergency power rooms, fire-pump rooms, areas of refuge, and on each floor inside enclosed stairways
.14	Atrium connecting more than 2 stories		Smoke detection per § 907.5 by automatic alarm, fire flow, or manual alarm		Emergency voice/alarm system in Group A, E, or M occupancies per § 907.5.2.2
.15		High-piled combustible storage	Automatic smoke-detection system		Where required by International Fire Code
.16		Aerosol storage uses	Manual fire alarm		When required by International Fire Code

FIRE-ALARM AND DETECTION SYSTEMS

Section 907.2.x	Occupancy or Building Type	Occupant Load or Condition	Device Type	Exceptions	Notes
.17		Lumber, wood structural panel, & plywood veneer mills	Manual fire alarm		
.18		Underground buildings with smoke exhaust	Automatic smoke detectors		Similar conditions to high-rise buildings; also activation of smoke exhaust activates audible alarm in attended location
.19	Underground buildings > 60 below lowest exit discharge		Manual fire alarm		Emergency voice/alarm system per § 907.5.2.2
.20	Covered and open mall buildings > 50,000 sf (4645 m²)		Emergency voice/alarm system per § 907.5.2.2		System to be accessible to fire department
.21	Residential aircraft hangars		Smoke alarm		Interconnected with sleeping-area smoke alarms
.22	Airport control towers		Automatic smoke-detection system		Activates occupant notification system per § 907.5
.23	Battery rooms, lead-acid batteries, liquid capacity > 50 gal. (189.3 L)		Automatic smoke-detection system		

Emergency Voice/Alarm Communication

§ 907.5.2.2	Device Type	Notes
	Emergency voice/alarm communication system	Voice/alarm system per NFPA 72 Activation of detector, fire flow, or manual pull station will sound tone and activate alert instructions per International Fire Code at: 1. Elevator groups 2. Exit stairways 3. Each floor 4. Areas of refuge per this code In stadiums, arenas, and grandstands required to caption audible public announcements per § 1108.2.7.3, the emergency/voice alarm system is also to be captioned.

Manual Alarm Boxes

§ 907.4.2 requires manual alarm boxes be located no more than 5' (1524) from the entrance to each exit. Travel distance to the nearest box is not to exceed 200' (60 960).

Visual Alarms

§ 907.5.2.3 specifies where visual alarms are to be provided to notify persons with hearing impairments of alarm conditions. These are white strobe lights mounted on the wall of certain areas. Accessibility criteria, such as ICC/ANSI A117.1, require that wall-mounted visual alarms be located at least 80" (2032) but no more than 96" (2438) above the floor.

Visual alarms are to be provided in the following locations:

1. Public and common areas
2. Make provisions for visual alarms to be added in employee work areas.
3. I-1 and R-1 sleeping accommodations per the quantities noted in Table 907.5.2.3.2.
4. R-2 occupancies that are required by § 907 to have a fire-alarm system. (All dwelling units are required to be adaptable to accommodate visual alarm appliances per accessibility requirements of ICC/ANSI A117.1.)

Audible Alarms

§ 907.5.2.1 requires audible alarms to have a distinctive sound not used for any other purpose. They are to be loud enough to provide a sound-pressure level at least 15 decibels (dBA) above the ambient sound or 5 dBA above the maximum sound level.

Emergency Alarms

§ 908.7 requires carbon monoxide detectors in Group E, I, and R occupancies located in buildings with potential sources of CO, such as a fuel-burning appliance or an attached garage.

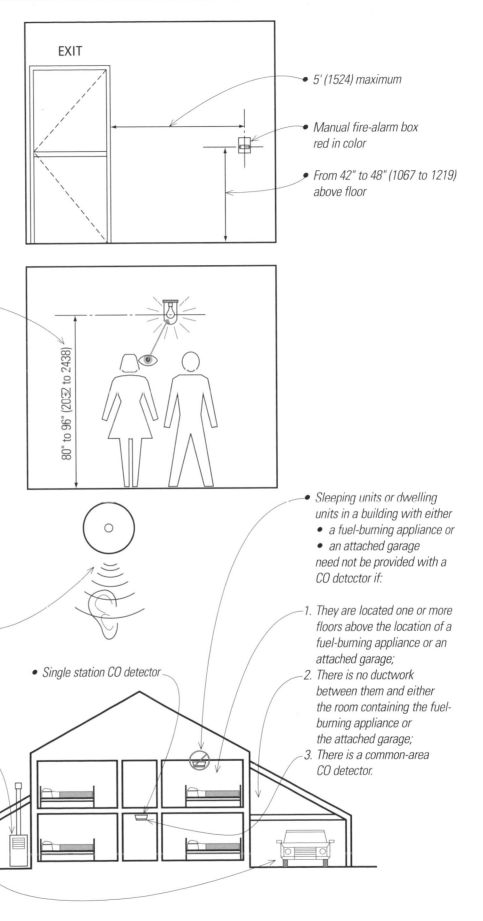

EXIT

- 5' (1524) maximum

- Manual fire-alarm box red in color

- From 42" to 48" (1067 to 1219) above floor

80" to 96" (2032 to 2438)

- Sleeping units or dwelling units in a building with either
  - a fuel-burning appliance or
  - an attached garage
  need not be provided with a CO detector if:

- Single station CO detector

1. They are located one or more floors above the location of a fuel-burning appliance or an attached garage;
2. There is no ductwork between them and either the room containing the fuel-burning appliance or the attached garage;
3. There is a common-area CO detector.

The purpose of smoke-control systems as stated in § 909 is to provide a tenable environment for the evacuation or relocation of occupants. The provisions are not intended for the preservation of contents, the timely restoration of operations, or for assistance in fire suppression or overhaul activities.

Smoke-control systems are classified as active fire-protection systems for our discussion in that they actively perform their basic function for life safety. They respond to fire not by their presence as barriers to fire or heat but by activating a sequence of operations to safeguard the building's occupants. These systems are referred to in the code as either of the active or passive type. This refers to whether the systems exhaust smoke through natural convection or by the use of mechanical ventilation. All smoke-control systems rely on automatic activation, whether the exhaust mechanisms are passive or active.

The systems are provided in certain building types such as malls or atriums to contain or evacuate smoke to allow building occupants to leave areas where smoke might hinder their egress. Buildings with smoke-control systems are typically those having large areas with interconnected air spaces where smoke cannot be contained by barriers but must be moved or exhausted for occupant protection. The design criteria for smoke-control systems require detailed calculations and modeling. They are almost invariably designed with the aid of a consultant experienced in design and construction of such systems.

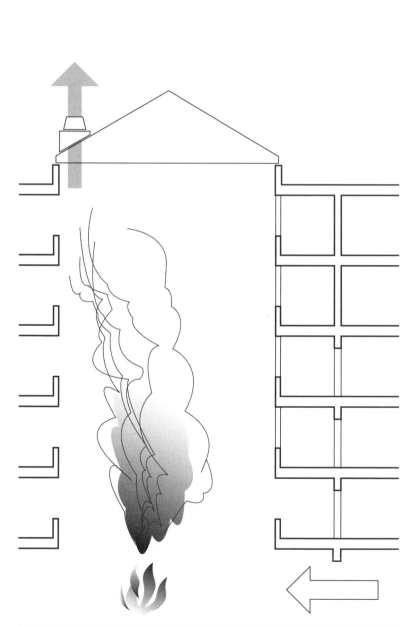

§ 909.20 requires that smoke-proof enclosures required by § 1023.11 consist of an enclosed interior stairway accessed by way of an outside balcony or a ventilated vestibule. This requirement refers back to the requirements of § 403 and § 405 for high-rise buildings and underground buildings.

- Smoke-proof enclosure for interior exit stairways accessible by way of a vestibule or an open exterior balcony.

- Smoke-proof enclosure ventilation systems are to be independent of other building ventilation systems for location and controls, and have standby power.

- Vestibule must be separated from the smoke-proof enclosure by a 2-hour fire barrier.

- Per § 909.20.5, where the building is equipped with an automatic sprinkler system, vestibules are not required when the exit stairways are pressurized with a minimum of 0.10 inches of water (25 Pa) and a maximum of 0.35 inches of water (87 Pa) in the shaft with the pressures measured relative to the building.

- Vestibule must be at least 44" (1118) wide and 72" (1829) long in the direction of egress travel.

- Natural ventilation may be provided by a minimum net area of 16 sf (1.5 m²) opening in a wall facing an outer court, yard, or public way at least 20' (6096) in width.

- Smoke-proof enclosure is to be separated from the remainder of the building by a 2-hour fire barrier constructed per § 707 or a horizontal boundary per § 711, or both, except for the required egress door, which must be self-closing or automatic-closing by actuation of a smoke detector.

- Fire door per § 716.5.

- Mechanical ventilation may be provided by supply and exhaust ducts.
- Tightly constructed duct must exhaust at least 150% of the supply air.
- No more than 6" (152) below top of smoke trap

- Space serves as a smoke and heat trap.
- 20" (508) minimum

- Tightly constructed supply duct must provide at least one air change per minute.
- No more than 6" (152) above the floor

- Door in open position must not obstruct either of the duct openings.

SMOKE AND HEAT REMOVAL

§ 910 covers the requirements for smoke and heat removal, which have functions similar to smoke-control systems. They typically use simpler technology to actively respond to fire conditions. Smoke and heat vents allow products of combustion or explosion to vent from the building and minimize the damage they can cause.

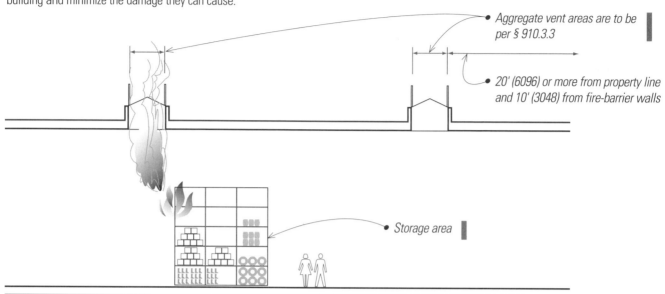

Aggregate vent areas are to be per § 910.3.3

20' (6096) or more from property line and 10' (3048) from fire-barrier walls

Storage area

Smoke and heat vents are used in industrial and commercial occupancies where high-piled storage, manufacturing, or warehousing activities have high fuel loads or large quantities of hazardous materials. There is a potential for large catastrophic fires in such occupancies. The occupancy groups covered by this section are Group F-1 and S-1 occupancies larger than 50,000 sf (4645 m²) in undivided area as well as in buildings with high-piled combustible storage per § 3206.7 of the International Fire Code.

Smoke and heat vents are to operate automatically, either tied to sprinkler activation in sprinklered buildings or by response to heat in unsprinklered buildings. Engineered smoke-exhaust systems, similar in principle to a smoke-control system, may be substituted for prescriptive systems.

Under revisions to this code section, the design of mechanical smoke-removal systems is now allowed to be a designer's option without prior approval of the fire code official. Designers now have broader options to use active systems in lieu of the passive systems that have been in the code for many years. This is a significant and extensive change to this section that is beyond the scope of this introductory text.

10
Means of Egress

Chapter 10 of the International Building Code contains the requirements for designing exiting systems known as "means of egress." The fundamental purpose for a means of egress is to get all of the occupants out of a building in a safe and expeditious manner during a fire or other emergency. A means of egress must therefore provide a continuous and unobstructed path of exit travel from any occupied point in a building to a public way, which is a space such as a street or alley, permanently dedicated for public use.

The term "means of egress" is a general one describing ways of getting out of a building. *Webster's Third New International Dictionary* defines "egress" as "1. the act or right of going or coming out." This term has been chosen to encompass all system components used for getting people out of a building in an emergency. The emphasis is on emergency egress, not convenience or function. However, access for persons with disabilities is also a consideration in designing a means of egress.

In the definitions used in this chapter but spelled out in Chapter 2, such common terms as exit access, exit, and exit discharge take on more specific, code-defined meanings as components of a means of egress, which is the complete system for escape. Pay close attention to code-specific nomenclature as you familiarize yourself with this chapter.

Note that this chapter was completely renumbered in 2003 and subsequent revisions relocated sections in this chapter in the change from the 2006 IBC to the 2009 edition of the code. Many sections were again renumbered and relocated in the 2012 and 2015 editions as well. Those familiar with the 2012 IBC will need to study the new arrangement carefully. This is yet another reason not to memorize the code, but to use the index or an electronic file where you can do a keyword search to locate information.

§ 1002 refers to Chapter 2, which defines "means of egress" as a continuous, unobstructed path of vertical and horizontal exit travel from any occupied portion of a building or structure to a public way. The means of egress for every occupancy in a building must meet the provisions of Chapter 10. The requirements are driven by the occupancy type of the area to be provided with egress and the occupant load calculated per Table 1004.1.2.

A building may contain several different types of occupancies. The designer must consider all of the uses, present or contemplated, so that adequate numbers and capacities of exits are provided. The occupant load is typically calculated as if each area is occupied at the same time to determine the maximum possible number of occupants to be accommodated by the means of egress. The code presumes that means of egress components themselves are generally not occupied spaces but serve the occupants of the building. There are specific and narrow exceptions to the requirements for calculating occupant load that will be discussed later.

Egress widths determine the number of occupants that may egress. In other words, the "capacity" of the means of egress is dependent on the width of the various components of the means of egress system. The code uses the terms "width" and "capacity" somewhat interchangeably since they are so closely related.

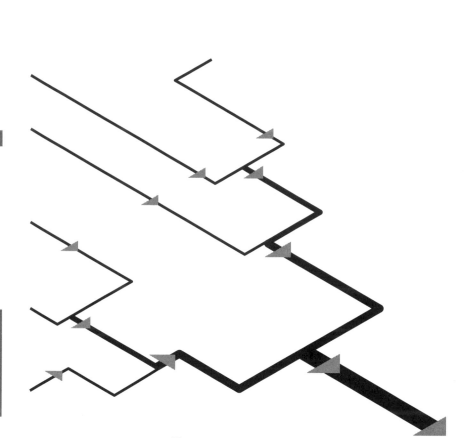

Egress Concepts

The general objective of egress, that of providing a continuous, unobstructed, and protected path to the outside of a building, is fundamental to the code and must be thoroughly understood. It must also be understood that when the egress path from a major occupancy of the building passes through an area containing another occupancy, possibly a public assemblage or a garage area, the egress path retains the occupancy-class designation and fire-protection requirements of the main use. Protection should never be reduced as the occupants proceed downstream in the means-of-egress system.

Flow

- There is a presumed direction of flow to every means of egress, leading from an occupied space to a final safe outside area, away from any hazard or emergency in the building. The best analogy for means-of-egress design is that of watercourses. Small streams lead to creeks, which feed rivers, which then lead to the sea. Rivers get larger and carry more water as they go downstream as tributaries feed into them; so too should the conceptual design of a means of egress. Exit paths must remain the same size or get larger as the building occupants proceed downstream from areas of lesser safety to areas of greater safety and ultimately out of the building through the exit discharge.

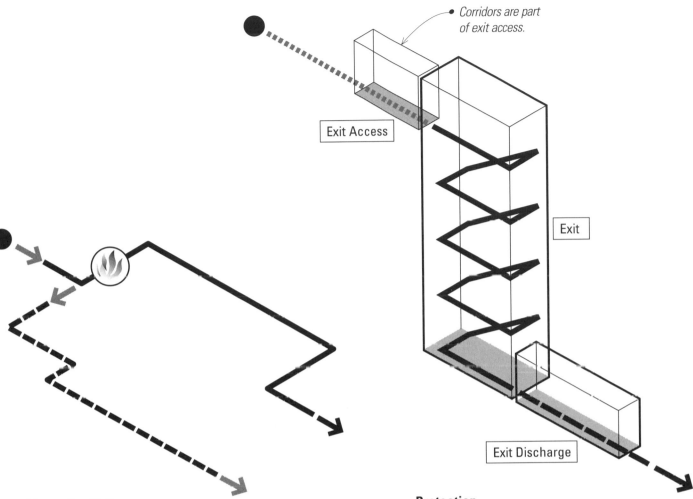

Corridors are part of exit access.

Exit Access

Exit

Exit Discharge

Alternative Paths

- Another basic exiting principle is that at least two different egress paths should lead from the interior of a building to the outside at ground level. The rationale is that if one path is blocked or endangered by a hazard, then the other path will be available. There are exceptions to this rule for situations involving relatively small numbers of occupants, but the designer should always begin with the basic design concept that two ways out of each space should typically be provided in case of an emergency.

Protection

- Various sections of the egress path may be required to provide fire-resistive protection for the occupants. Exit access begins in any occupied part of the building, which in turn can connect to a corridor or to an exit, extend in the exit enclosure down through the building, and then to the exit discharge leading to the exterior. Note that often corridors will not be required to be of fire-resistive construction.

Once in a rated corridor, exit stairway, or similar protected egress path, the occupant is to remain protected until the building exterior is reached. In the process of exiting, the occupant should not be required to move out of a protected environment into adjacent occupied spaces or unprotected egress paths to get to the next portion of the protected egress path or to the exterior, because doing so would necessitate removing the protection the exit enclosure is required to provide.

There are three basic components to a means of egress: the exit access, the exit, and the exit discharge. It is important to clearly understand how the code defines these components so that one can apply the requirements of Chapter 10.

It is important that components of a means of egress be integrated with the requirements for accessible means of egress contained in Chapter 11. The egress requirements of Chapter 10 must also be considered together along with the Americans with Disabilities Act (ADA) and local accessibility regulations.

1. EXIT ACCESS is that portion of the means-of-egress system that leads from any occupied portion in a building or structure to an exit.

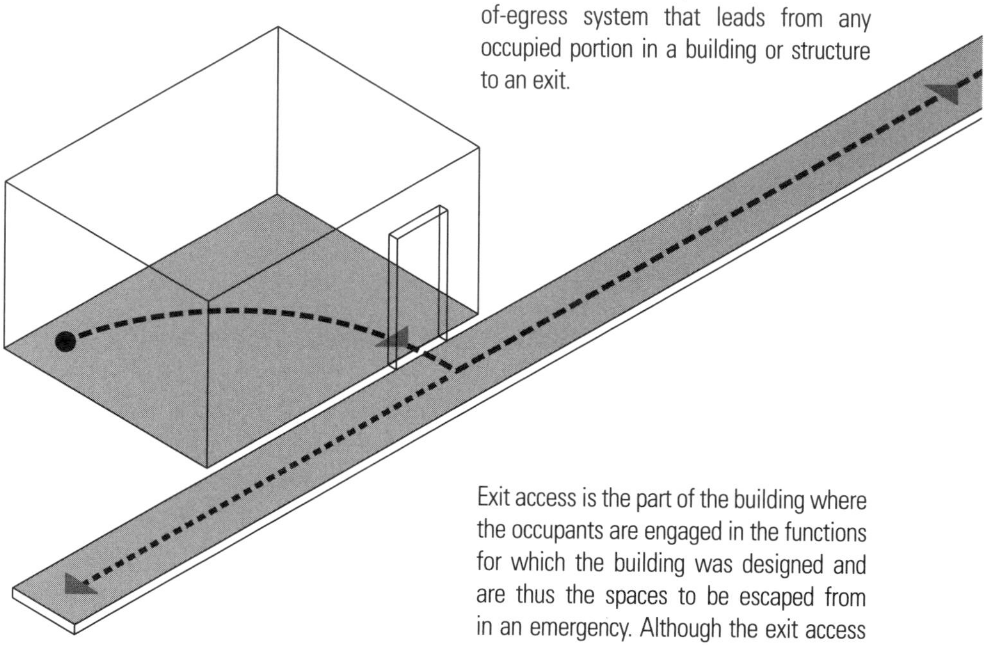

Exit access is the part of the building where the occupants are engaged in the functions for which the building was designed and are thus the spaces to be escaped from in an emergency. Although the exit access allows the occupants the most freedom of movement, it also offers the lowest level of life-safety protection of any of the components of the means of egress.

In the typical exit access path from a room or space one may encounter aisles, passages, corridors, or other intervening rooms before entering a protected fire-rated enclosure called the exit. The distance to be traversed is limited by the code as will be covered in this analysis.

- *It is important to remember that the distance one may travel in the exit access, from the most remote point in the room or space to the door of an exit, is regulated by the code. It may be necessary to provide a fire-rated passage, such as an exit passageway, for larger floor areas that may exceed the travel distances for various other means-of-egress components.*
- *Travel distances are not restricted in exits or in the exit discharge.*

2. EXIT is that portion of the means-of-egress system between the exit access and the exit discharge or the public way. The exit may be separated from other interior spaces by fire-resistive construction, but this may not be the case for each and every exit. Separation used to be part of the definition of "exit," but that is no longer the case.

The exit portion of the means of egress allows the occupants of a building to move inside or toward a protected enclosure from the area where a hazardous event is occurring to a place where they may finally escape the building. Exits are typically separated from other interior spaces of a building or structure by fire-resistance-rated construction and opening protectives as required to provide a protected path-of-egress travel from the exit access to the exit discharge.

Exits include interior exit stairways and ramps, exit passageways, exterior exit stairways, exterior exit ramps, horizontal exits, and exterior exit doors at ground level. The distance one may travel within an exit is not limited by the code. This part of the egress path can be very long, as in the case of the stairways in a high-rise building.

Note that an unenclosed exit access stair may be permitted as part of the means of egress at certain locations within a building, even though it is a part of the exit access and not an "exit." See the discussion about open stairs later in this chapter.

3. EXIT DISCHARGE is that portion of the means-of-egress system between the termination of an exit and a public way. The exit discharge may include exit courts and yards, and stairways and ramps within them. Many of these are building-related components, but an exit discharge may also include site elements.

This portion of the means of egress is basically assumed to be at or near grade and open to the atmosphere. The occupants are presumed to be able to clearly see where an area of safety outside the building lies and are able to move toward it.

The code defines "public way" as any street, alley or other parcel of land open to the outside air leading to a street that has been deeded, dedicated or otherwise permanently appropriated to the public for public use and having a clear width and height of not less than 10' (3048).

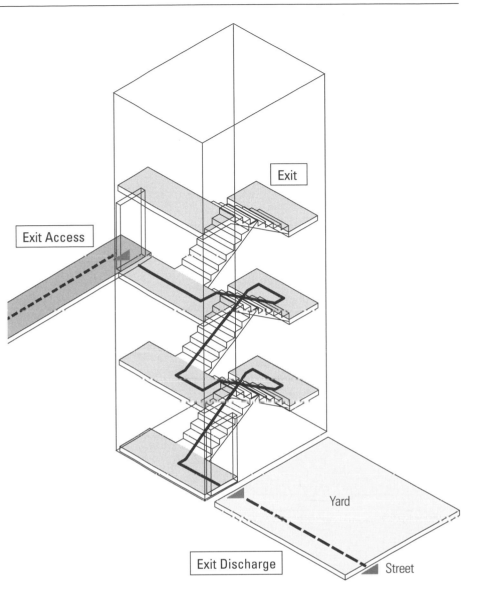

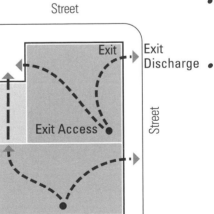

- *The means of egress for a small single-story building is usually simple, because the second and third components of the exit path are often combined.*
- *In many one-story buildings, such as retail stores and banks, only the first portion of the means of egress is obvious, but there will still be an "exit" and an "exit dischage." A corridor may extend to the exterior wall and open onto a street, yard, or other public space. This simultaneously provides the exit access, the exit, and the exit discharge to the exterior public way of the building at ground level. The room or space opens directly to the building's exterior without the need of protected egress pathways or stairways.*

§ 1003 through § 1015 specify the requirements that apply to all three portions of the means of egress. Thus, requirements for doors, stairs, ramps, and similar egress components apply to all three parts of the means of egress when included in these sections. Note also that there may be additional modifications to conditions in this section contained in the specific sections applicable to the three parts of a means of egress.

Ceiling Height

§ 1003.2 requires that egress paths have a ceiling height of not less than 7'-6" (2286), although it is acceptable to have some projections that reduce the minimum headroom to 80" (2032) for any walking surface.

Means-of-egress ramps may have a minimum headroom of 80" (2032) per § 1012.5.2. Pedestrian and vehicular areas in public parking garages may have egress paths with a minimum clear height of 7' (2134) per § 406.4.1. Egress areas above and below mezzanine floors are to have clear heights of at least 7' (2134) per § 505.2.

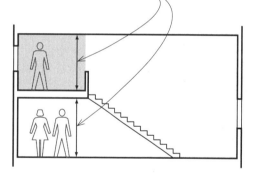

Protruding Objects

§ 1003.3 governs how much objects may project into the required ceiling height and required egress widths.

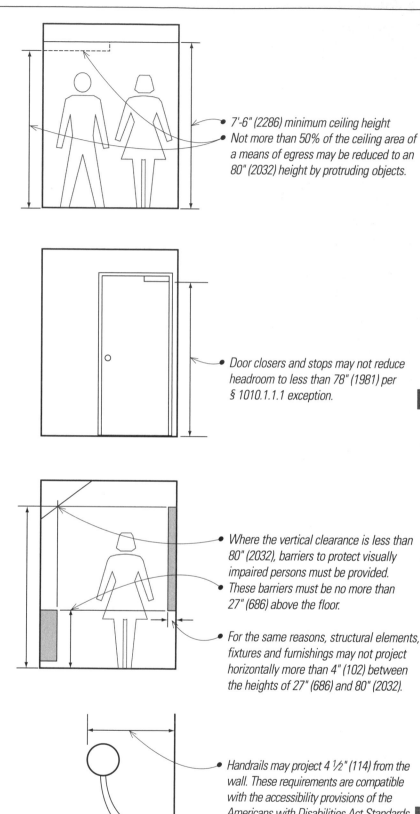

- 7'-6" (2286) minimum ceiling height
- Not more than 50% of the ceiling area of a means of egress may be reduced to an 80" (2032) height by protruding objects.

- Door closers and stops may not reduce headroom to less than 78" (1981) per § 1010.1.1.1 exception.

- Where the vertical clearance is less than 80" (2032), barriers to protect visually impaired persons must be provided.
- These barriers must be no more than 27" (686) above the floor.

- For the same reasons, structural elements, fixtures and furnishings may not project horizontally more than 4" (102) between the heights of 27" (686) and 80" (2032).

- Handrails may project 4 ½" (114) from the wall. These requirements are compatible with the accessibility provisions of the Americans with Disabilities Act Standards (ADAS).

Elevation Changes

§ 1003.5 restricts elevation changes in the means of egress. If the elevation change is less than 12" (305), it must be sloped.

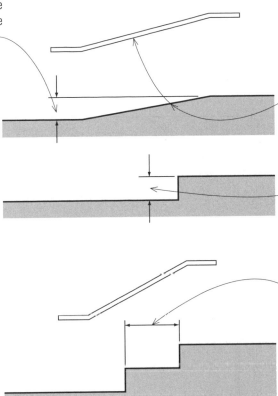

- *When the slope exceeds 1 in 20, then the transition should be made by a ramp. We recommend also reviewing the ramp requirements in Chapter 11 related to accessibility.*
- *Slopes rising less than 6" (152) must be equipped with handrails or a floor finish that contrasts with adjacent flooring. This is to provide visual cues for a shallow ramp, which may not be readily visible.*
- *In stepped aisles serving seating areas not required to be accessible by Chapter 11, exceptions allow for steps with a minimum riser height of 4" (102) and a maximum riser height of 8" (178) per § 1029.13.2.2 and provision of a handrail per § 1029.15.*
- *A stair having up to two risers must comply with § 1011.5, with a minimum tread depth of 13" (330) and one handrail complying with § 1014 within 30" (762) of the center-line of the normal path-of-egress travel on the stair.*

Maintaining Width and Capacity of the Means of Egress

§ 1003.6 emphasizes that when objects, such as brackets or columns, occur in a means of egress, they shall not decrease the required width or capacity of the means of egress. Where these obstructions or projections do occur, additional width is needed to maintain the required egress capacity.

- *It is not recommended to use single steps or short stairways in any passageway, as such steps may be overlooked by occupants and present a severe tripping hazard in daily use. They are to be avoided whenever possible.*

- *Maintain minimum width of egress travel around obstructions.*

Elevators, Escalators, and Moving Walks

§ 1003.7 does not permit any of these modes of transportation to be used as components of a means of egress. The only exception is for elevators used as an accessible means of egress per § 1009.4, where they are provided with standby power and also with operation and signal devices per § 2.27 of ASME A17.1.

Design Occupant Load

§ 1004.1 specifies that means-of-egress facilities for a building are to be designed to accommodate the number of occupants as computed in accordance with § 1004.1.2 and Table 1004.1.2. The occupant load is to be based on actual occupant loads when it can be determined, as for the number of seats in a theater, or by using Table 1004.1.2, where occupant-load factors are assigned to determine occupant loads based on use. These factors are based on past history of anticipated occupant loads for various uses. The code does not state requirements regarding rounding. We suggest rounding all fractional calculations up to the next whole number in typical cases.

The floor-area allowances in the table are based not on the actual physical situation within any building but for code purposes, on probabilities and observation. The values are codified so that they can be used uniformly by everyone in determining the exit details; i.e., the number and width of the exit components. They are not intended as design program guidelines. It is not necessary that every office worker have a 100 sf (9.3 m²) office even though the occupant load factor is 100.

Per § 1004.2 occupant loads may be increased beyond those listed in Table 1004.1.2 as long as the means of egress system is sized to accommodate the occupant load. In no case may the occupant load calculated under this provision exceed one occupant per 7 sf (0.65 m²) of occupiable floor area.

Where there are mixed uses in a building, some of which use "gross" floor area calculations per Table 1004.1.2 and others use "net" floor areas, the occupant load factors should be applied consistently, based on the use of the areas. When areas such as toilet rooms are used by both assembly areas (net) and office areas (gross), we recommend that the toilet rooms be treated as a part of the net area occupant load and thus they may be excluded from occupied floor area calculations per the definitions referenced in § 1002. This interpretation should be confirmed with the AHJ.

Actual Number

- § 1004.1.2 states that the design occupant load shall be based on the number of occupants determined by assigning one occupant per unit of area from Table 1004.1.2. For areas with fixed seating, however, the actual number of fixed seats in a theater will determine the occupant load for that space, per § 1004.4.
- Per § 1004.4, occupant loads for areas such as waiting areas or wheelchair areas for persons with disabilities are to be calculated using Table 1004.1.2.

- 30' × 40' (9144 × 12 192) room
- Fixed seating for 46 occupants
- No standing room, fixed walls
- Two wheelchair locations for accessibility
- Occupant load = 48
- This example is based on § 1004.4 as referenced in Table 1004.1.2.

Number by Table 1004.1.2

- § 1004 uses a table to prescribe the design occupant load, computed on the basis of one occupant per unit of area.

- 30' × 40' (9144 × 12 192) room
- Standing assembly area
- From Table 1004.1.2, allow 5 sf (0.46 m²) of floor area per occupant.
- Occupant load = 1200/5 = 240

- Note that the words **net** and **gross** used in the table are referenced in § 1002, but are defined in Chapter 2. It is expected that the interpretation of these terms will be that **net** refers to the actual area where occupants may stand, less the space occupied by building elements and not including accessory areas such as corridors, stairways, or toilet rooms. **Gross** would be expected to apply to large areas defined by the perimeter walls, excluding vent shafts.
- Note also that there are no occupant-load factors for such service spaces as restrooms where it can be anticipated that the users of those spaces are already occupants of the building. It is anticipated that these spaces will be considered a part of the gross area per the discussion above, and may not be deducted from the area used to determine occupant loads.

- 30' × 40' (9144 × 12 192) room
- Business area
- From Table 1004.1.2, allow 100 sf (9.29 m²) of floor area per occupant.
- Occupant load = 1200/100 = 12

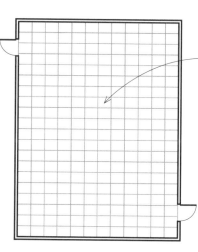

Number by Combination

§ 1004.1.1.1 states that occupants from accessory spaces who exit through a primary area are to be added to the design occupant load. This section addresses such areas as conference rooms or alcoves, and adheres to the principle that each tributary area adds to the occupant load "downstream" of the areas being served by a means of egress.

Total Design Occupant Load = 32 + 20 + 9 = 61

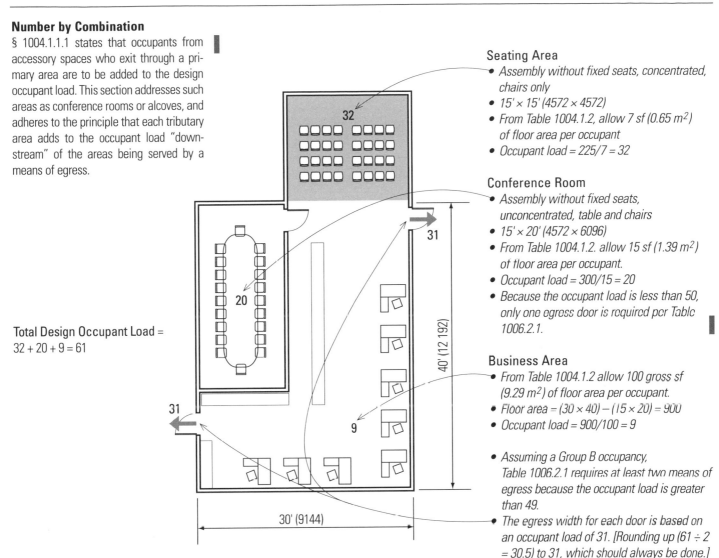

Seating Area
- *Assembly without fixed seats, concentrated, chairs only*
- *15' × 15' (4572 × 4572)*
- *From Table 1004.1.2, allow 7 sf (0.65 m²) of floor area per occupant*
- *Occupant load = 225/7 = 32*

Conference Room
- *Assembly without fixed seats, unconcentrated, table and chairs*
- *15' × 20' (4572 × 6096)*
- *From Table 1004.1.2. allow 15 sf (1.39 m²) of floor area per occupant.*
- *Occupant load = 300/15 = 20*
- *Because the occupant load is less than 50, only one egress door is required per Table 1006.2.1.*

Business Area
- *From Table 1004.1.2 allow 100 gross sf (9.29 m²) of floor area per occupant.*
- *Floor area = (30 × 40) − (15 × 20) = 900*
- *Occupant load = 900/100 = 9*

- *Assuming a Group B occupancy, Table 1006.2.1 requires at least two means of egress because the occupant load is greater than 49.*
- *The egress width for each door is based on an occupant load of 31. [Rounding up (61 ÷ 2 = 30.5) to 31, which should always be done.]*

§ 1004.1.1.2 applies the principle of convergence to the means of egress from a mezzanine, based on the assumption that some of the occupants of the mezzanine will pass through the floor below to get to a common set of exit paths and thus are added to the occupant load. When other egress paths are provided, those occupants need not be added.

Note that other than times when egress paths converge on a story, which is to be considered per § 1005.6, the occupant loads from stories separate from the one under consideration are not to be added to the occupant load for that story.

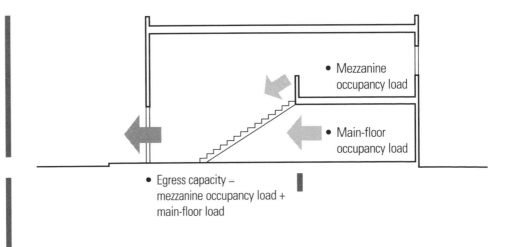

- Mezzanine occupancy load
- Main-floor occupancy load
- Egress capacity – mezzanine occupancy load + main-floor load

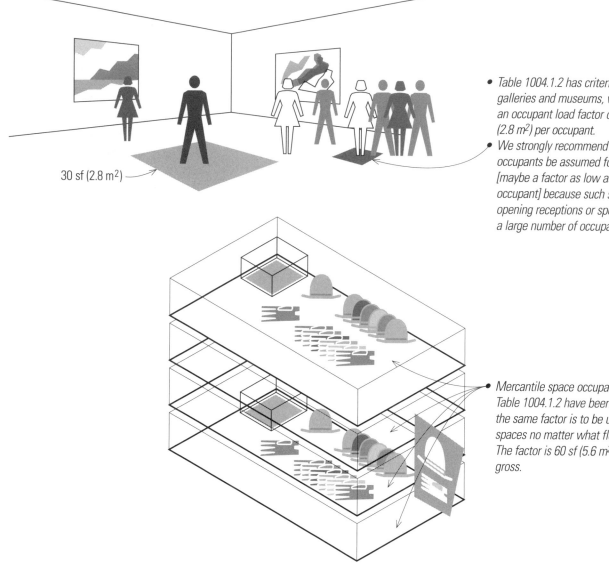

30 sf (2.8 m²)

- Table 1004.1.2 has criteria for exhibit galleries and museums, which establishes an occupant load factor of 30 square feet (2.8 m²) per occupant.
- We strongly recommend that more occupants be assumed for gallery uses [maybe a factor as low as 7 sf (0.7 m²) per occupant] because such spaces often have opening receptions or special events with a large number of occupants.

- Mercantile space occupant load factors in Table 1004.1.2 have been revised so that the same factor is to be used for these spaces no matter what floor they are on. The factor is 60 sf (5.6 m²) per occupant, gross.

§ 1004.3 requires assembly occupancies to have signs posted in a conspicuous place showing the occupant load. This is to prevent overloading of the spaces, which could impair exiting in a panic situation.

Maximum Occupant Load

75

persons

Sign to remain posted

§ 1004.4 states that for areas having fixed seating, the occupant load is to be determined by the number of fixed seats.

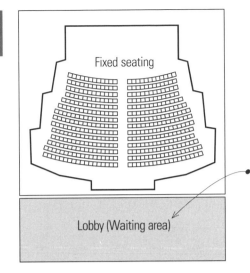

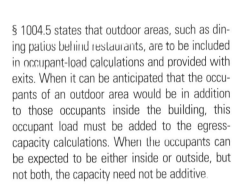

If there are waiting areas, such as theater lobbies where patrons for the next show may gather, the occupant load for that space is to be determined for that area without fixed seats per Table 1004.1.2 and added to the occupant load assciated with the fixed seats. However, if the lobby is a "pre-function" area where the patrons in the lobby will be the same users as those to be seated, we believe the occupant load may be determined by only the number of fixed seats. This asssumption should be verified with the Authority Having Jurisdiction early in the design process.

§ 1004.5 states that outdoor areas, such as dining patios behind restaurants, are to be included in occupant-load calculations and provided with exits. When it can be anticipated that the occupants of an outdoor area would be in addition to those occupants inside the building, this occupant load must be added to the egress-capacity calculations. When the occupants can be expected to be either inside or outside, but not both, the capacity need not be additive.

The designer should make assumptions about uses of spaces with great caution. For example, even when a courtyard serves an office area for the office occupants only, it is conceivable that there could be a public event in the office that would have guests and employees occupying both spaces. Such special events with crowded conditions can be the most conducive to panic in an emergency, and egress systems should take such possibilities into account.

Multiple Occupancies

§ 1004.6 covers the means-of-egress requirements that apply to buildings housing multiple occupancies. When there are special egress requirements based on occupancy, they apply in that portion of the building housing that occupancy. When different occupancies share common egress paths, the most stringent requirements for each occupancy will govern the design of the means-of-egress system.

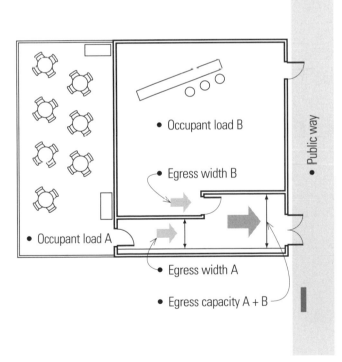

Egress Sizing

§ 1005 specifies that the capacity of exit pathways be governed by: the occupant load, the hazard of the occupancy, whether the building is sprinklered, and whether the path is a stair or other component of a means of egress.

* Note that a reduction in stair widths and the width of other egress components (in other than H and I-2 occupancies) for sprinklered buildings is allowed by Exception 1 to § 1005.3.1 when an emergency voice/alarm system is also provided. For stairs the factor is 0.2" (5.1 mm) per occupant and for other egress components the factor is 0.15" (3.8 mm) per occupant. Since most buildings are sprinklered per the IBC and provision of a voice/alarm system is relatively low-cost, these will probably be the sizing factors used by most designers.

The required egress width in unsprinklered buildings is based on the occupant load served by an egress component multiplied by an egress width factor. For stairs the factor is 0.3" (7.62 mm) per occupant and for other egress components it is 0.2" (5.08 mm) per occupant.

§ 1005.3.1 states that stairs are to be sized based on the occupant load of the invidual story served by the stair. Thus the highest occupant load of any story served by a stair will determine the minimum size of the stair. This is based on observations of the time factor, along with their directional nature, in determining how people move through egress systems. The occupants of the floor below are assumed to exit that level before those behind them get to the same point in the egress system.

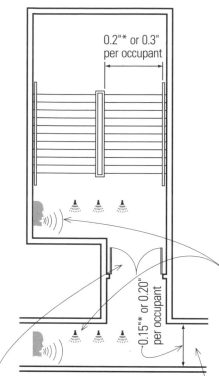

0.2"* or 0.3" per occupant

0.15"* or 0.20" per occupant

* = reduced width in sprinklered buildings

- A pair of doors may be necessary to satisfy egress width requirements. See egress door requirements on pg. 203.
- The calculated width of other egress components, such as corridors, will be less than the required width calculated for egress stairways because of their differing egress width factors per § 1005.

- Stairs are required to provide more width than corridors since people move more slowly in stairways than in corridors or passages. Thus a corridor with a given occupant capacity will be narrower than a stair in the same egress system.

- Based on the principle of maintaining capacity, not width, it should be permissible to have a narrower egress passage width downstream of a stairway as long as the required capacity is provided. This may be subject to interpretation and negotiation between the building official and the designer.

- Egress width reductions are tied to provision of both sprinklers and a voice/alarm system.

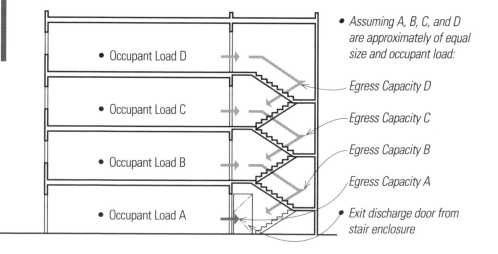

- Occupant Load D
- Occupant Load C
- Occupant Load B
- Occupant Load A

- Assuming A, B, C, and D are approximately of equal size and occupant load:

Egress Capacity D

Egress Capacity C

Egress Capacity B

Egress Capacity A

- Exit discharge door from stair enclosure

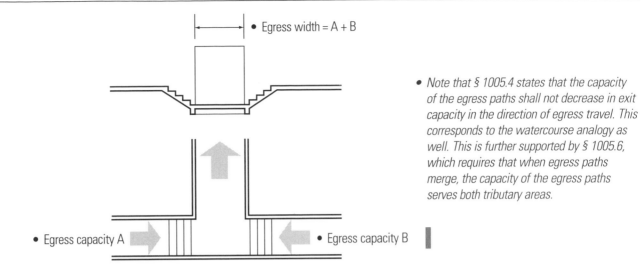

• Egress width = A + B

• Egress capacity A

• Egress capacity B

• Note that § 1005.4 states that the capacity of the egress paths shall not decrease in exit capacity in the direction of egress travel. This corresponds to the watercourse analogy as well. This is further supported by § 1005.6, which requires that when egress paths merge, the capacity of the egress paths serves both tributary areas.

The code requires that in buildings or spaces needing two means of egress that occupant loads be distributed more or less equally between exits, not weighted based on proximity to an exit. Per § 1005.5 the means of egress system is to be configured such that the loss of any one exit or access to one exit will not reduce the available capacity to less than 50 percent of the required capacity. This means in effect that the egress widths are to be sized to make the smallest capacity greater than or equal to 50 percent of the anticipated occupant load.

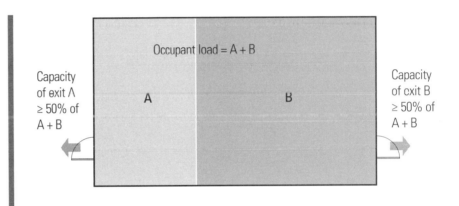

Occupant load = A + B

Capacity of exit A ≥ 50% of A + B

A

B

Capacity of exit B ≥ 50% of A + B

Because exit doors typically swing in the direction of exit travel, doors from rooms will often swing into paths of egress travel, such as corridors. § 1005.7 requires that in such situations:

• The door should project a maximum of 7" (178) into the required width when fully opened against the wall of the passage, and
• The opening of the door should not reduce the required width by more than one-half.

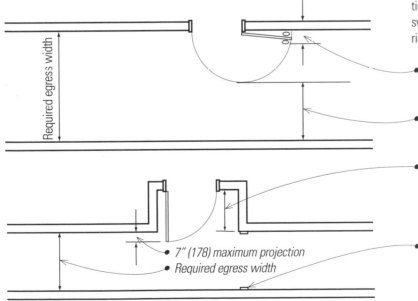

Required egress width

• 7" (178) maximum projection
• Required egress width

• Along narrow corridors, doors should be recessed. Minimum recess for a 36" (914) door would be:
36" − 7" = 29" (914 − 178 = 736)

• Nonstructural provisions, such as trim and similar decorative features, can project into the required corridor width a maximum of 1 1/2" (38) on each side. Handrail projections are to be per § 1014.8.

§ 1015 and § 1021 from the previous edition of the code have been moved forward to § 1006 and § 1007 in Chapter 10 of the 2015 edition. The provisions for the number of exits and exit access doorways and their configuration are now gathered together in a more rational flow for code users to determine how the various portions of the means of egress system are to be arranged. After occupant loads are determined using § 1004 the capacities of the means of egress system are determined using § 1005. § 1006 then is used to establish the number of means of egress required and § 1007 is used to determine their arrangement.

Exit-Access Components

The criteria contained in § 1006 and § 1007 apply to those components that occur within the exit access. Some common terminology may also occur in the exit and exit discharge portions of the means of egress, but their application must be viewed in the context of which parts of the means of egress are being described by the various code sections.

Number of Exits and Exit-Access Doorways

§ 1006 sets the requirements for the number of exit or exit-access doorways required from any space. Two exits or exit-access doorways are required when the occupant load exceeds the values in Table 1006.2.1 or when the conditions of the common path-of-egress travel distance exceed the requirements of the table.

Table 1006.2.1 [including information from Table 1006.3.2 (2)]

Occupancy	Maximum Occupant Load with 1 Exit	Minimum No. of Occupants with 2 Exits	No. of Occupants Requiring 3 Exits (§1006.2.1.1)	No. of Occupants Requiring 4 Exits (§1006.2.1.1)	Length of Common Path-of-Egress Travel** before 2 Paths of Egress Travel are Required	
All	See § 1006.3.2	Up to 500	501–1,000	> 1,000	Nonsprinklered	Sprinklered
A, E	49	50–500	"	"	75 (22 860)	75
B, F	49 (29 @ 2nd story)	50–500	"	"	75*	100
H-1, 2, 3	3	4–500	"	"	Not permitted	25
H-4, 5	10	11–500	"	"	75	75
I-1	10	11–500	"	"	75	75
I-2	10	11–500	"	"	75	75
I-3	10	11–500	"	"	100 (30 480)	100
I-4	10	11–500	"	"	75	75
M	49 (29 @ 2nd story)	50–500	"	"	75	75
R-1	10	11–500	"	"	75	75
R-2, R-3	10	11–500	"	"	75	125 (R-3 in mixed occ.)
S	29	30–500	"	"	75*	100
U	49	50–500	"	"	75*	75*

* Tenant spaces in occupancy groups B, S, & U with an occupant load of not more than 30 may have a common path-of-egress travel up to 100 feet (30 480).

** See illustration on page 199.

Common-Path-of-Egress Travel

Chapter 2 defines a common-path-of-egress travel as that portion of the exit-access travel distance measured from the most remote point within a story to that point where the occupants have separate access to two exits or exit-access doorways. Common-paths-of-egress travel are limited per § 1006.2.1 and Table 1006.2.1.

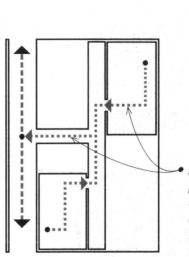

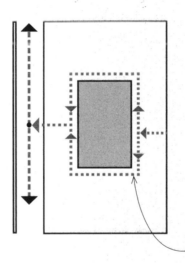

A common-path-of-egress travel is any portion of an exit access offering an occupant no choice between separate and distinct paths of egress travel to two exits. It is measured from the most remote point in a room to that point where multiple paths to separate exits become available to occupants.

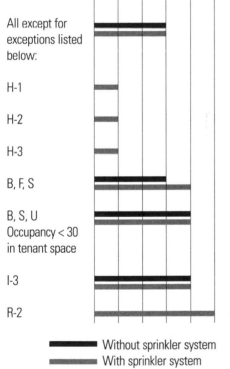

| | 0 | 25 | 50 | 75 | 100 | 125 | Feet |
| | 0 | 7.8 | 15.2 | 22.9 | 30.5 | 38.1 | Meters |

Occupancy

All except for exceptions listed below:

H-1

H-2

H-3

B, F, S

B, S, U Occupancy < 30 in tenant space

I-3

R-2

━━━ Without sprinkler system
▓▓▓ With sprinkler system

Common-paths-of-egress travel include paths that split and merge within the exit access prior to the location where multiple paths lead to separate exits.

The basic provision for egress is to provide two means of egress for each story except under certain circumstances where single exits are permitted. The basic egress requirements per story appear in Table 1006.3.1. This table leads the code user to believe that two means of egress are required but subsequent tables allow several conditions where a single exit is allowable.

Table 1006.3.1: Minimum Number of Exits or Access to Exits per Story

Occupant Load Per Story	Minimum Number of Exits or Access to Exits from Story
1–500	2
501–1,000	3
More than 1,000	4

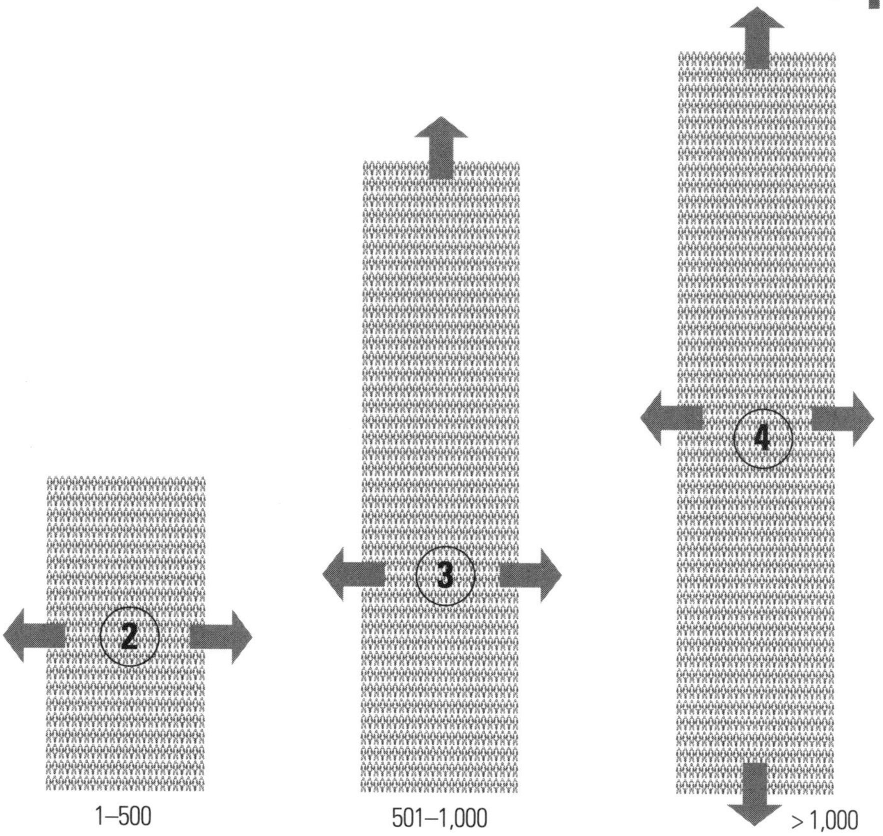

Basic Number of Exits per Story Based on Occupant Load per Story

Stories with One Exit per Tables 1006.3.2(1) and 1006.3.2(2)

Story	Occupancy	Maximum Occupants (or Dwelling Units) per Floor / Travel Distance
First Story or Basement	A, B[1], E, F, M, U[1], S[1]	49 / 75' (22 860) [[1] 100' (30 480) in sprinklered buildings]
	H-2, H-3	3 / 25' (7620)
	H-4, H-5, I, R-1, R-2, R-4[2]	10 / 75' (22 860) [[2] R-3 needs only one exit]
Second Story	B, F, M, S	29 / 75' (22 860)
	R-2 with sprinklers and escape windows *	4 dwelling units / 125' (38 100) *
Third Story	R-2 with sprinklers and escape windows	4 dwelling units / 125' (38 100)

* These limits apply above the first story and basement, and are limited to R-2 occupancies with dwelling units, such as apartments.

Exits and Exit-Access Doorway Arrangement

§ 1007 requires that all exits be arranged for ease of use and be separated as prescribed by this section.

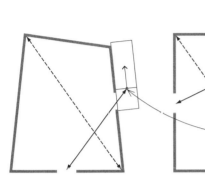

- When two exits are required, they are to be placed a distance apart equal to one-half the diagonal dimension of the space.
- The diagonal measurement line can go outside the building footprint. See below for reductions allowed at sprinklered buildings.
- The separation distance required in § 1007.1.1 is to be measured from:
1. Any point along the width of the doorway. [We recommend using the door centerline to be conservative.]
2. The closest riser at exit access stairs.
3. The start of the ramp run at exit access ramps.

- There are exceptions to the exit layout for corridors and for sprinklered buildings.

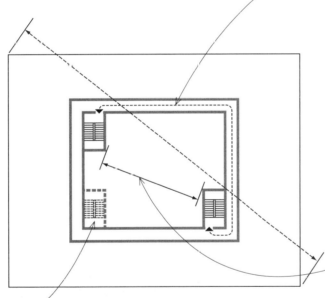

- When a 1-hour fire-rated corridor connecting interior exit stairways is provided, the exit separation may be measured along a direct path of travel within the corridor. No minimum distance is required between stair enclosures except in high-rise buildings as noted below, but interlocking or "scissor" stairs that touch can only be counted as one exit stairway per § 1007.1.1. This provision addresses the required separation of interior exit stairways in the core of office buildings.
- In such instances, the corridor configuration connecting the tenant spaces to the interior exit stairways allows placement of the interior exit stairways closer together than half the diagonal distance of the floor without a corridor.

- Note that in high-rise buildings having floor levels above 420' (128 m), stair separations of 30' (9144) apply. See § 403.5.1. Also, additional stairs are required in such buildings per § 403.5.2.

- Third egress stairway in buildings taller than 420' (128 m) per § 403.5.2.
- An additional exit stair is not required if elevators used for occupant self-evacuation are provided per § 3008. See the elevator section in Chapter 17 for a discussion of the requirements for such elevators.

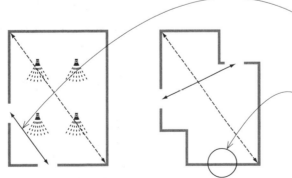

- In sprinklered buildings, the exits may be more closely spaced. Exit doors or exit-access doorways may be a minimum of one-third the diagonal dimension of the area served.
- When three exits are required, two are to be placed to comply with the separation requirements for two exits and the third is to be arranged a reasonable distance apart so that if one becomes blocked, the other two will be available. Determination of the location of the third exit is thus open to interpretation by the building official.

Means-of-Egress Illumination

§ 1008.2 requires that the illumination level for a means of egress be not less than 1 foot-candle (11 lux) at the walking surface level. The areas to be illuminated should include all three parts of the means-of-egress system to be certain that occupants can safely exit the building to the public way. In assembly areas such as movie theaters, the illumination may be dimmed during a performance but should be automatically restored in the event of activation of the premises' fire-alarm system. Emergency-power requirements are intended to apply to those buildings that require two or more exits, thus exempting small structures and residences.

Emergency-lighting requirements for means of egress require an average of 1 foot-candle (11 lux) of illumination within means of egress with a minimum of 0.1 foot-candle (1 lux) upon initial operation. Such systems are allowed to dim slightly over the 90-minute life of the emergency operations but must not fall below 0.6 foot-candle (6 lux) average and 0.06 foot-candle (0.6 lux) minimum. In Group I-2 occupancies, failure of any single lighting unit shall not reduce the illumination level to less than 0.2 foot-candle (22 lux).

Accessible Means of Egress

§ 1009 addresses the egress requirements for people with disabilities. The basic requirement is that accessible spaces in a building must have an accessible means of egress. Where more than one means of egress is required, based on occupancy or occupant load, then at least two accessible means of egress are to be provided. Note that this requirement for two accessible means of egress applies even when three or more exits may be required based on occupant load. This provision applies only to new construction; it is not required for alterations to existing buildings, although work in altered areas must comply with code requirements for the altered area.

For buildings with four or more stories, one accessible means of egress is to be provided by elevator with standby power and signal devices per § 1009.2.1. Note that Exception 1 to this section allows the use of a horizontal exit in fully sprinklered buildings in lieu of providing emergency power to the elevator.

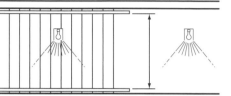

- Stairways in an accessible means of egress must be at least 48" (1219) wide between handrails. This is to provide sufficient width to carry people with disabilities between two other people. This requirement does not apply to exit access stairways or exit stairs in fully sprinklered buildings.

- Area of Refuge. The code defines "area of refuge" as an "area where persons unable to use stairways can remain temporarily to await instructions or assistance during emergency evacuation." Temporary is not further defined, so the duration of stay is not set. When required, the area of refuge must be on an accessible path of travel from the area served. The area of refuge must be in a stairway or have direct access to an enclosed stairway or to an elevator with emergency power.

- Because an area of refuge is defined as being a place to await instruction, two-way communications are required between the area of refuge and a central control point, or via a public telephone if the central control is not continuously attended. The communications shall be both visual and audible.

- The area of refuge must provide space for one 30" x 48" (762 x 1219) wheelchair space for each 200 occupants of the space served. These spaces must not reduce the egress width. Smoke barriers per § 709 are required at areas of refuge except when they are located in a stairway enclosure.

- Areas of refuge are not required when an automatic sprinkler system is provided per Exception 5 to § 1009.3. This also applies to open stairs and enclosed exit stairways per the Exceptions to § 1009.3. Areas of refuge are also not required in R-2 occupancies, all of which are required to be sprinklered and also are generally more compartmented than other buildings.

- Exterior areas for assisted rescue have the same space requirements for wheelchairs as for areas of refuge.
- They are to be open to the outside air and be separated by walls of 1-hour construction with ¾-hour doors.
- The protection must extend beyond the area laterally and vertically for 10' (3048).
- An exterior area of refuge must be at least 50% open with guards distributed to prevent the accumulation of smoke or toxic gases.
- Two-way communication systems are to be provided either at the elevator landing per § 1009.8 or at the area of refuge per § 1009.6.5.

Doors, Gates, and Turnstiles

§ 1010 is a general section that applies to all doors, gates, and turnstiles that are part of any of the three parts of the means of egress.

Egress Doors

§ 1010.1 requires that egress doors be readily distinguishable from adjacent construction. They should never be blind doors, hidden by decorative materials.

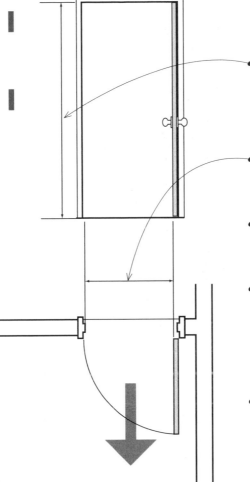

Revolving Doors

Where egress doors are power-operated, they shall be openable in the event of a power failure. Doors with access controls must also have a failsafe mechanism to allow egress in the event of power failure. The operation of any egress door shall be obvious and not require special knowledge or effort on the part of the user.

§ 1010.1.4.1. Revolving doors may be used as egress doors when the leaves of the door collapse in the direction of egress and provide an aggregate width of egress of at least 36" (914). For practical purposes, it is desirable that each opening be at least the 32" (813) minimum required for typical doors.

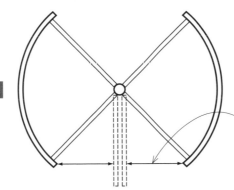

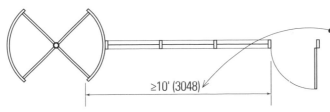

- *Egress doors should be not less than 80" (2032) high.*

- *Egress doors must have a minimum clear width of 32" (813), measured from the face of the door to the stop when the door is open 90° (1.57 rad).*
- *Practically speaking this means that egress doors should always be 3'- 0" × 6'- 8" (914 × 2032) doors to provide the required minimum opening clearances.*
- *There are minor exceptions for doors in small closets or in residences, but these should be avoided by the designer. This width criteria should also be applied to all doors in residential occupancies, even when not strictly required by access standards.*

- *Egress doors should typically be side-hinged swinging doors. Per § 1010.1.2.1, they must swing in the direction of exit travel when serving a room having an occupant load of 50 or more in a typical occupancy, or when serving any occupant load in a high-hazard occupancy. Note that the requirement is based on the occupant load of the space, not on the occupant load at each door.*
- *Access criteria limit the force that must be exerted on doors to open them. The maximum force is 5 pounds (22 N) at interior doors and 15 pounds (67 N) at exterior doors.*

- *The capacity and use of revolving doors is limited. Revolving doors may be credited for no more than 50% of the required egress capacity, each door may have no more than a 50-occupant capacity, and the collapsing force can be no greater than 130 pounds (578 N) in a revolving door used as an egress component.*
- *Each revolving door must have a side-hinged swinging door complying with § 1010.1 in the same wall and withing 10 feet (3048) of the revolving door.*

Landings

§ 1010.1.5. There should be a landing or floor on each side of a door, and the elevation of the floor or landing should be the same. There are exceptions in residential occupancies for screen doors and at interior stairways to allow doors to swing over landings.

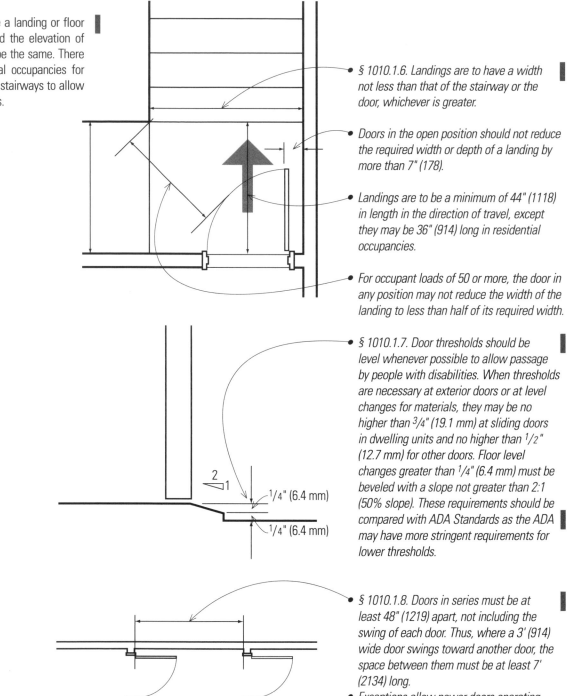

§ 1010.1.6. Landings are to have a width not less than that of the stairway or the door, whichever is greater.

Doors in the open position should not reduce the required width or depth of a landing by more than 7" (178).

Landings are to be a minimum of 44" (1118) in length in the direction of travel, except they may be 36" (914) long in residential occupancies.

For occupant loads of 50 or more, the door in any position may not reduce the width of the landing to less than half of its required width.

§ 1010.1.7. Door thresholds should be level whenever possible to allow passage by people with disabilities. When thresholds are necessary at exterior doors or at level changes for materials, they may be no higher than 3/4" (19.1 mm) at sliding doors in dwelling units and no higher than 1/2" (12.7 mm) for other doors. Floor level changes greater than 1/4" (6.4 mm) must be beveled with a slope not greater than 2:1 (50% slope). These requirements should be compared with ADA Standards as the ADA may have more stringent requirements for lower thresholds.

§ 1010.1.8. Doors in series must be at least 48" (1219) apart, not including the swing of each door. Thus, where a 3' (914) wide door swings toward another door, the space between them must be at least 7' (2134) long.

Exceptions allow power doors operating in tandem and storm or screen doors in residential occupancies to be closer together.

Locks and Latches

§ 1010.1.9 requires egress doors to be readily openable from the egress side without the use of a key or special knowledge or effort. The unlatching of any door or leaf should not require more than one operation. This recognizes the directional nature of the egress path and that the path serves to make exiting clear and simple for the least familiar building occupant.

Exceptions to the basic rule recognize the special nature of detention centers and of time-limited occupancies in such facilities as stores, assembly areas with fewer than 300 occupants, and churches. Key lock devices may be used when occupancies have exits that are unlocked during times of use, and signs are posted requiring that the exit doors are to remain unlocked when the building is occupied.

Power-operated locks are permissible under certain conditions. The space layout must not require an occupant to pass through more than one access-controlled door before entering an exit. Door locks must be deactivated upon actuation of the sprinkler system or automatic detection system. Also, locks must have a fail-safe mechanism to allow egress in the event of power failure. Mechanisms that open the door upon application of a constant force to the egress mechanism for a maximum of 15 seconds are also allowed.

Panic Hardware

§ 1010.1.10 contains the provisions for panic and fire exit hardware. Panic hardware is typically a bar that opens a door when depressed. It is named panic hardware based on experience in assembly occupancies where people may crush against doors in panic situations such that normal hardware is jammed by pressure, even if the door opens outward. Panic hardware is designed to open the door if a person is pressed against it. This hardware is always used in conjunction with doors opening in the direction of egress.

Panic hardware is required in Group A or E occupancies having occupant loads of 50 or more and in Group H occupancies with any occupant load. Panic hardware is not required in very large assembly occupancies such as stadiums, where the gates are under constant, immediate supervision, as is usually the case.

Electrical rooms with electrical equipment rated at 1,200 amperes or more must have panic hardware or fire-exit hardware, and the doors to such spaces must swing in the direction of exit travel.

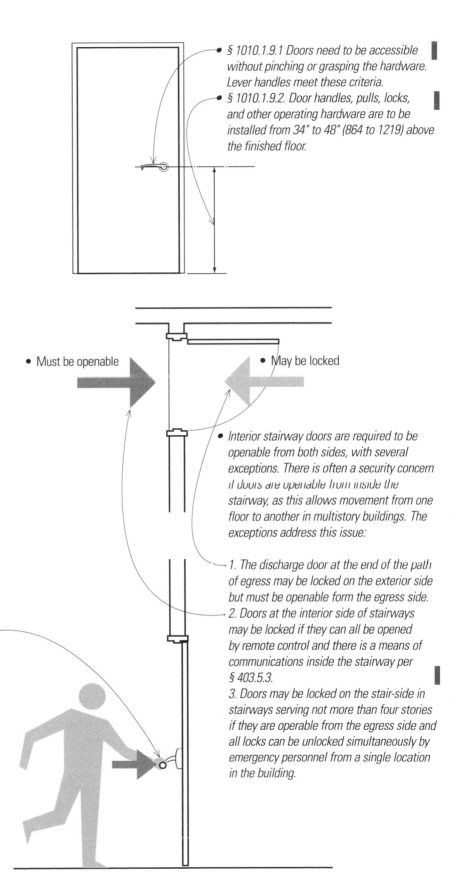

§ 1010.1.9.1 Doors need to be accessible without pinching or grasping the hardware. Lever handles meet these criteria.

§ 1010.1.9.2. Door handles, pulls, locks, and other operating hardware are to be installed from 34" to 48" (864 to 1219) above the finished floor.

• Must be openable

• May be locked

Interior stairway doors are required to be openable from both sides, with several exceptions. There is often a security concern if doors are openable from inside the stairway, as this allows movement from one floor to another in multistory buildings. The exceptions address this issue:

1. The discharge door at the end of the path of egress may be locked on the exterior side but must be openable form the egress side.
2. Doors at the interior side of stairways may be locked if they can all be opened by remote control and there is a means of communications inside the stairway per § 403.5.3.
3. Doors may be locked on the stair-side in stairways serving not more than four stories if they are operable from the egress side and all locks can be unlocked simultaneously by emergency personnel from a single location in the building.

Stairways

§ 1011 covers requirements for the design of stairs and stairways. Note that per § 1011.1, it is the intent of the code that all stairs serving occupied portions of a building comply with Chapter 10 regardless of whether they are part of a means of egress or not.

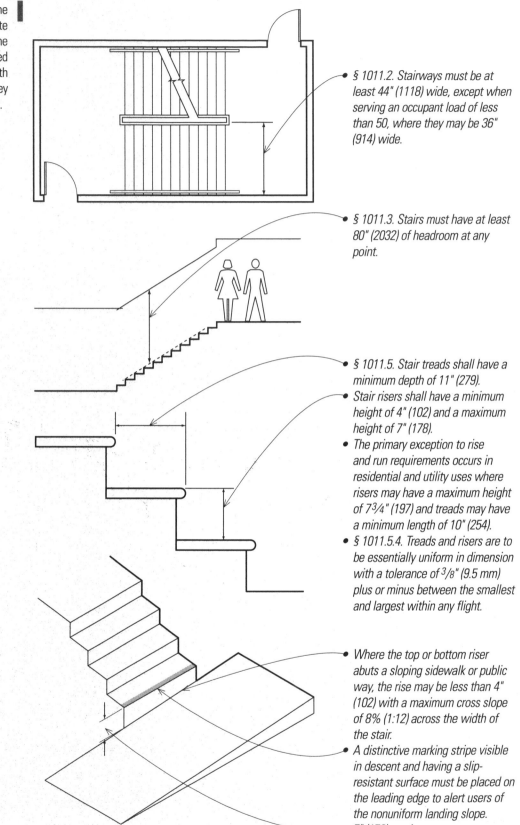

• § 1011.2. Stairways must be at least 44" (1118) wide, except when serving an occupant load of less than 50, where they may be 36" (914) wide.

• § 1011.3. Stairs must have at least 80" (2032) of headroom at any point.

• § 1011.5. Stair treads shall have a minimum depth of 11" (279).

• Stair risers shall have a minimum height of 4" (102) and a maximum height of 7" (178).

• The primary exception to rise and run requirements occurs in residential and utility uses where risers may have a maximum height of 7¾" (197) and treads may have a minimum length of 10" (254).

• § 1011.5.4. Treads and risers are to be essentially uniform in dimension with a tolerance of ³/₈" (9.5 mm) plus or minus between the smallest and largest within any flight.

• Where the top or bottom riser abuts a sloping sidewalk or public way, the rise may be less than 4" (102) with a maximum cross slope of 8% (1:12) across the width of the stair.

• A distinctive marking stripe visible in descent and having a slip-resistant surface must be placed on the leading edge to alert users of the nonuniform landing slope.

• 7" (178) maximum

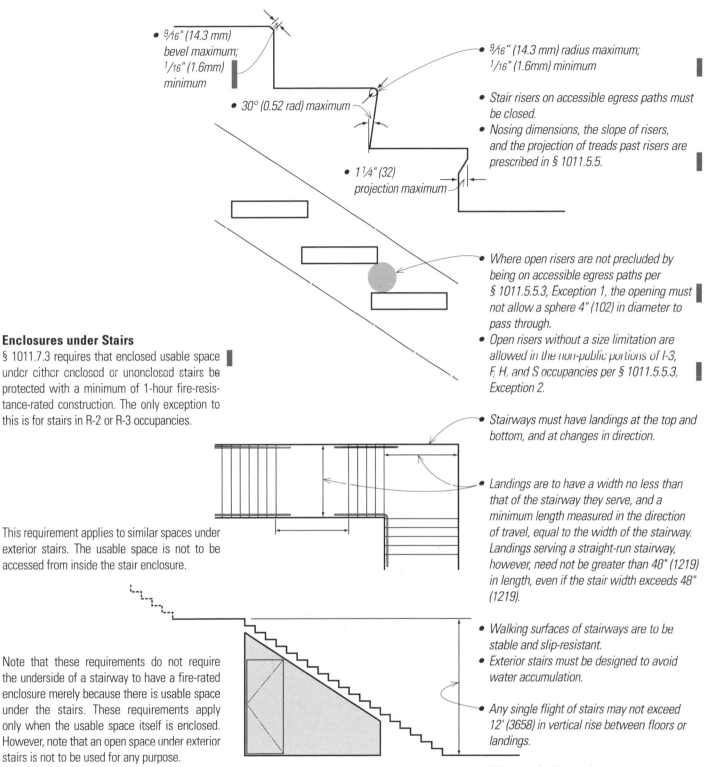

- 9/16" (14.3 mm) bevel maximum; 1/16" (1.6mm) minimum

- 30° (0.52 rad) maximum

- 1 1/4" (32) projection maximum

- 9/16" (14.3 mm) radius maximum; 1/16" (1.6mm) minimum

- Stair risers on accessible egress paths must be closed.
- Nosing dimensions, the slope of risers, and the projection of treads past risers are prescribed in § 1011.5.5.

- Where open risers are not precluded by being on accessible egress paths per § 1011.5.5.3, Exception 1, the opening must not allow a sphere 4" (102) in diameter to pass through.
- Open risers without a size limitation are allowed in the non-public portions of I-3, F, H, and S occupancies per § 1011.5.5.3, Exception 2.

- Stairways must have landings at the top and bottom, and at changes in direction.

- Landings are to have a width no less than that of the stairway they serve, and a minimum length measured in the direction of travel, equal to the width of the stairway. Landings serving a straight-run stairway, however, need not be greater than 48" (1219) in length, even if the stair width exceeds 48" (1219).

- Walking surfaces of stairways are to be stable and slip-resistant.
- Exterior stairs must be designed to avoid water accumulation.

- Any single flight of stairs may not exceed 12' (3658) in vertical rise between floors or landings.

- Where stairs have a rise greater than 12' (3658), then intermediate landings are required.

Enclosures under Stairs

§ 1011.7.3 requires that enclosed usable space under either enclosed or unenclosed stairs be protected with a minimum of 1-hour fire-resistance-rated construction. The only exception to this is for stairs in R-2 or R-3 occupancies.

This requirement applies to similar spaces under exterior stairs. The usable space is not to be accessed from inside the stair enclosure.

Note that these requirements do not require the underside of a stairway to have a fire-rated enclosure merely because there is usable space under the stairs. These requirements apply only when the usable space itself is enclosed. However, note that an open space under exterior stairs is not to be used for any purpose.

Curved stairs, winding stairs, and spiral stairs are allowable as egress elements in limited use, primarily in residential occupancies.

Circular stairs may be part of a means-of-egress system when they comply with the following dimensional requirements.

- *The treads and risers of curved stairs must comply with § 1011.9.*
- *The smaller radius of a circular stairway must be no less than twice the required width of the stairway.*
- *The treads of a circular stairway shall be no less than 10" (254) at the narrow end, and not less than 11" (279) when measured at a point 12" (305) from the narrower end of the tread.*
- *In residential occupancies, the treads may be no less than 6" (152) at the narrow end.*

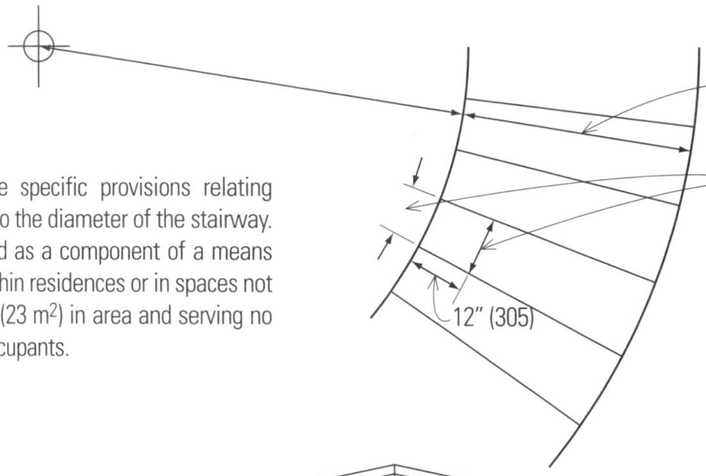

Spiral stairs have specific provisions relating stair tread width to the diameter of the stairway. They may be used as a component of a means of egress only within residences or in spaces not more than 250 sf (23 m²) in area and serving no more than five occupants.

12" (305)

- *The treads of a spiral stair shall be no less than 7 1/2" (191) at a point 12" (305) from the narrow end.*
- *The minimum width of a spiral stairway is 26" (660).*

12" (305)

- *The risers of a spiral stair shall have a height sufficient to provide a minimum headroom of 78" (1981), but in no case should they be more than 9 1/2" (241) in height.*

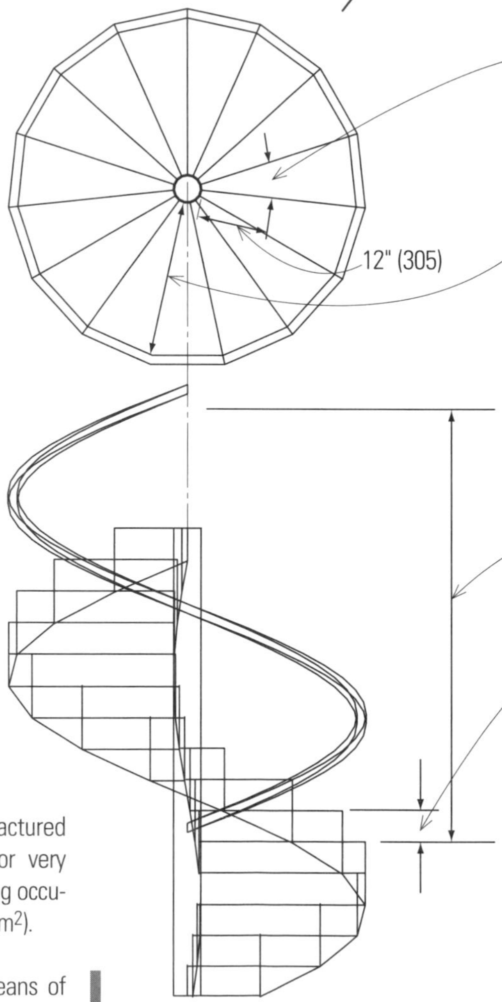

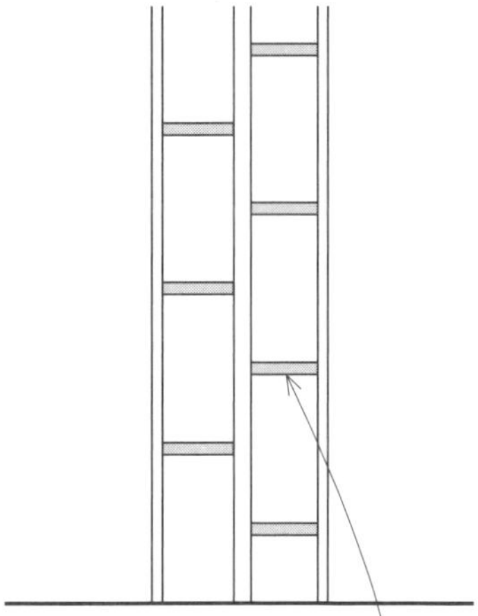

Alternating tread devices are manufactured stairs that are allowable as egress for very limited access in storage or manufacturing occupancies for areas of less than 250 sf (23 m²).

Alternating tread devices used as a means of egress may not have a rise greater than 20 feet (6096) between floor levels or landings.

Roof Access

§ 1010.12 requires that, in buildings four or more stories in height above grade plane, at least one stairway must extend to the roof, unless the roof is sloped at more than a 4-in-12 pitch. An exception allows access to unoccupied roofs by a hatch not less than 16 sf (1.5 m²) in area and having a minimum dimension of 2' (610).

Ramps

§ 1012 contains provisions that apply to all ramps that are part of a means of egress, except when amended by other provisions where indicated. For example, § 1029 governs ramps in assembly areas. As for stairs, all interior exit ramps are to be enclosed per the applicable provisions of § 1023. Exit access ramps are to be enclosed in accordance per the provisions of § 1019.3 for enclosure of stairways.

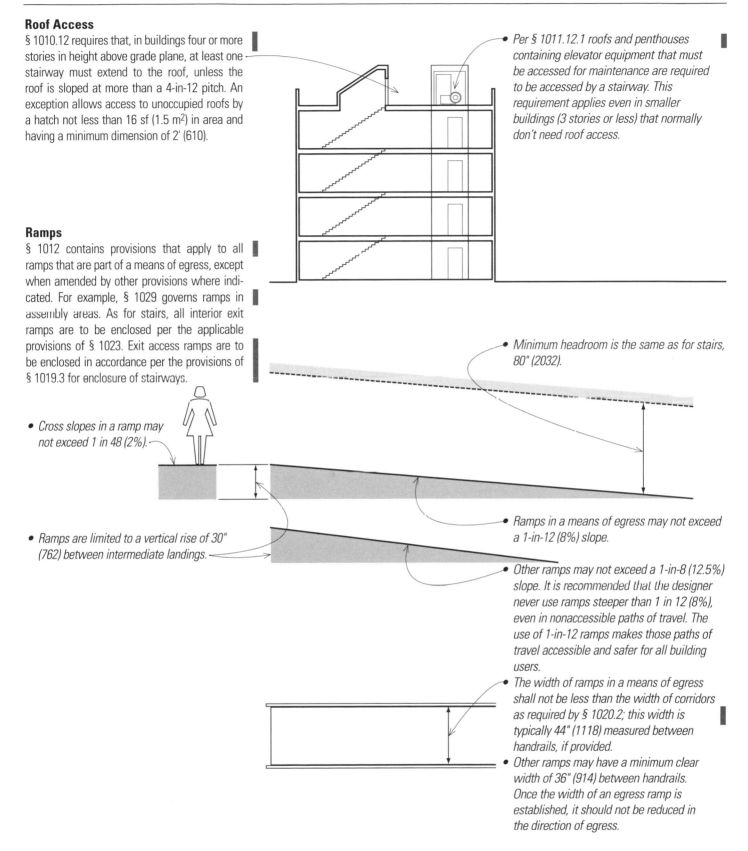

- Per § 1011.12.1 roofs and penthouses containing elevator equipment that must be accessed for maintenance are required to be accessed by a stairway. This requirement applies even in smaller buildings (3 stories or less) that normally don't need roof access.

- Minimum headroom is the same as for stairs, 80" (2032).

- Cross slopes in a ramp may not exceed 1 in 48 (2%).

- Ramps are limited to a vertical rise of 30" (762) between intermediate landings.

- Ramps in a means of egress may not exceed a 1-in-12 (8%) slope.

- Other ramps may not exceed a 1-in-8 (12.5%) slope. It is recommended that the designer never use ramps steeper than 1 in 12 (8%), even in nonaccessible paths of travel. The use of 1-in-12 ramps makes those paths of travel accessible and safer for all building users.

- The width of ramps in a means of egress shall not be less than the width of corridors as required by § 1020.2; this width is typically 44" (1118) measured between handrails, if provided.

- Other ramps may have a minimum clear width of 36" (914) between handrails. Once the width of an egress ramp is established, it should not be reduced in the direction of egress.

Ramps (continued)

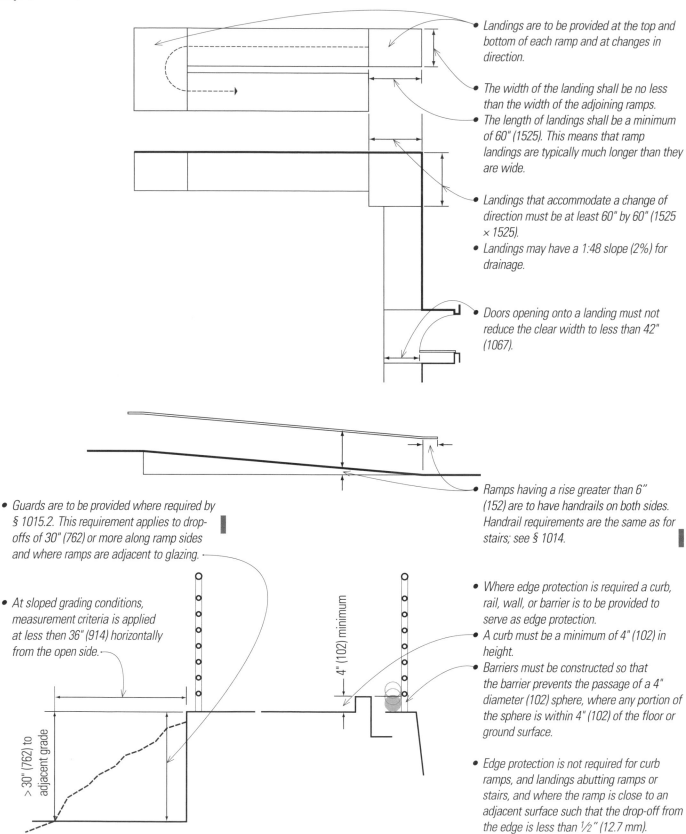

Landings are to be provided at the top and bottom of each ramp and at changes in direction.

The width of the landing shall be no less than the width of the adjoining ramps.

The length of landings shall be a minimum of 60" (1525). This means that ramp landings are typically much longer than they are wide.

Landings that accommodate a change of direction must be at least 60" by 60" (1525 × 1525).

Landings may have a 1:48 slope (2%) for drainage.

Doors opening onto a landing must not reduce the clear width to less than 42" (1067).

Ramps having a rise greater than 6″ (152) are to have handrails on both sides. Handrail requirements are the same as for stairs; see § 1014.

Guards are to be provided where required by § 1015.2. This requirement applies to drop-offs of 30" (762) or more along ramp sides and where ramps are adjacent to glazing.

At sloped grading conditions, measurement criteria is applied at less then 36" (914) horizontally from the open side.

> 30" (762) to adjacent grade

4" (102) minimum

Where edge protection is required a curb, rail, wall, or barrier is to be provided to serve as edge protection.

A curb must be a minimum of 4" (102) in height.

Barriers must be constructed so that the barrier prevents the passage of a 4" diameter (102) sphere, where any portion of the sphere is within 4" (102) of the floor or ground surface.

Edge protection is not required for curb ramps, and landings abutting ramps or stairs, and where the ramp is close to an adjacent surface such that the drop-off from the edge is less than ½″ (12.7 mm).

Exit Signs

§ 1013.1 calls for exit signs to be provided at exits and exit-access doors. Exit signs may be omitted in some residential occupancies and in cases where the exit pathway is obvious to occupants. Such conditions where signs are to be omitted should be reviewed and approved by the building official.

- *Exit signs must be of an approved design, be illuminated by internal or external means, and have the capability to remain illuminated for up to 90 minutes after power is cut off, either by battery, internal illumination, or connection to an emergency power source.*

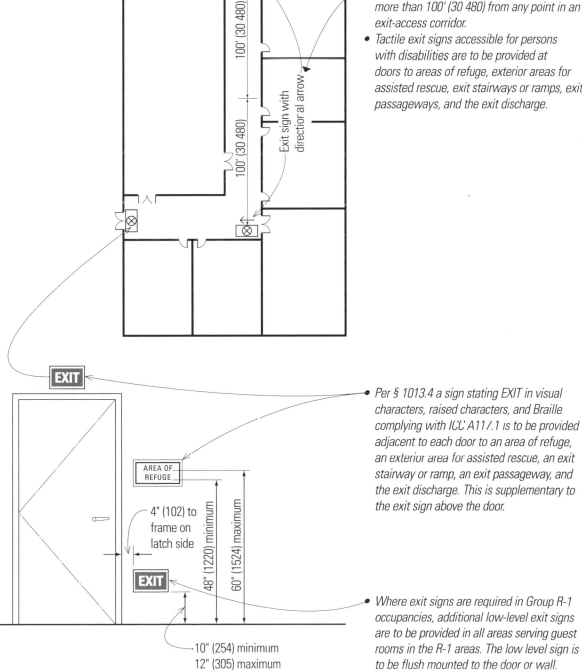

- *Exit signs must be clearly visible and be not more than 100' (30 480) from any point in an exit-access corridor.*
- *Tactile exit signs accessible for persons with disabilities are to be provided at doors to areas of refuge, exterior areas for assisted rescue, exit stairways or ramps, exit passageways, and the exit discharge.*

- *Per § 1013.4 a sign stating EXIT in visual characters, raised characters, and Braille complying with ICC A117.1 is to be provided adjacent to each door to an area of refuge, an exterior area for assisted rescue, an exit stairway or ramp, an exit passageway, and the exit discharge. This is supplementary to the exit sign above the door.*

- *Where exit signs are required in Group R-1 occupancies, additional low-level exit signs are to be provided in all areas serving guest rooms in the R-1 areas. The low level sign is to be flush mounted to the door or wall.*

Handrails

§ 1011.11 specifies that stairways are to have handrails on each side complying with § 1014, except in certain limited cases, mostly dwellings. Handrails are not required on decks having a single-level change between two areas that are equal to or greater than a landing dimension and in residences where there is only one riser.

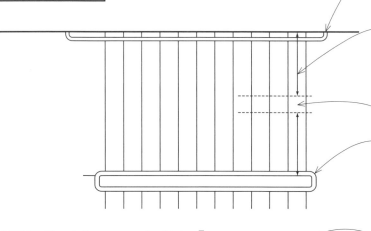

- Handrails are to be between 34" and 38" (864 and 965) above the stair-tread nosing.
- Handrails must extend horizontally for 12" (305) beyond the top riser of a stairway.
- Handrails must also continue their slope for the depth of one tread beyond the bottom riser. Bends or transitions that occur between flights or to transition to a guard are permitted to exceed the maximum height of 38" (965).
- Note that ADA Standards require an additional 12" (305) horizontal extension at the bottom of a stairway. In no case should the designer use less than the ADA Standards dimensions, except where the stairway is in a residence and not on an accessible path.
- When handrails do not continue to the handrail of an adjacent flight, they are required to return to a wall or to the walking surface.
- Only portions of a stairway width within 30" (762) of a handrail may count toward the width required for egress capacity. This means that intermediate handrails may be required for stairways that are required by occupant load to be more than 60" (1524) wide.
- Stair width more than 30" (762) from handrails does not count toward required egress capacity.
- Railings are to be continuous except in residences where newel posts and turnouts are acceptable.
- Handrail extensions are not required where the handrails are continuous between flights.

Per § 1014.3 all handrails are to comply with the requirements for Type I handrails as described in § 1014.3.1 except at R-3 occupancies, the inside of dwelling units in R-2 occupancies, and in U occupancies, where Type II handrails per § 1014.3.2 or handrails with equivalent graspability may be used.

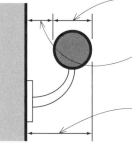

Type I Circular Rail

- Circular handrails are to have a minimum diameter of 1 1/4" (32) and a maximum diameter of 2" (51).
- Handrails require a minimum clearance from the wall of 1 1/2" (38) to allow for grasping.
- There are to be no sharp or abrasive elements to interfere with the ability of the stair user to grasp the handrail. Edges must have a minimum radius of 0.01" (0.25 mm).
- Projections, such as stringers and baseboards, are allowed at and below each handrail, but they cannot project more than a total of 4 1/2" (114) into the required width of the stairway.

Type I Non-Circular Handrail

- Railings that do not have a circular profile shall have a perimeter dimension of at least 4" (102) but no greater than 6 1/4" (159), a maximum cross-sectional dimension of 2 1/4" (57), and a minimum cross sectional dimension of 1" (25).

Type II Non-Circular Handrail

- Type II handrails with a perimeter greater than 6 1/4" (159) shall provide a 5/16" (8) graspable finger recess on both sides of the profile.
- 3/4" (19) maximum crown.
- 1 3/4" (44) maximum extent of finger recess.
- Other shapes of equivalent graspability are acceptable. Note that the definition of graspability is subject to interpretation by the building official.

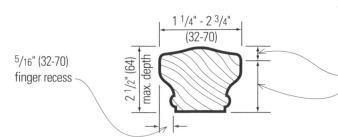

5/16" (32-70) finger recess

1 1/4" - 2 3/4" (32-70)

2 1/2" (64) max. depth

Guards

§ 1015 requires that railings or similar protective elements be provided where any grade change of 30" (762) or more occurs in a means of egress. This also applies when a means of egress is adjacent to glazing elements that do not comply with the strength requirements for railings and guards per § 1607.8.

- Height of guards is measured from the leading edge of treads on a stairway.
- Guards are typically 42" (1067) high except in R-2 or R-3 occupancies, where they may be 36" (914) in height when not more than 3 stories above grade in height.
- Bends or transitions in handrails that occur between flights or transition to a guard in R-2 and R-3 occupancies are permitted to exceed the maximum handrail height of 38" (965).

- Guards are to be designed with a pattern from the floor up to 34" (864) such that a sphere 4" (102) in diameter cannot pass through. [Openings in R-2 and R-3 sleeping units at the open sides of stairs may allow passage of a 4.375" (111) sphere.]
- From a height of 36" to 42" (864 to 1067), the pattern may be more open, allowing a sphere up to 4 3/8" (111) in diameter to pass.

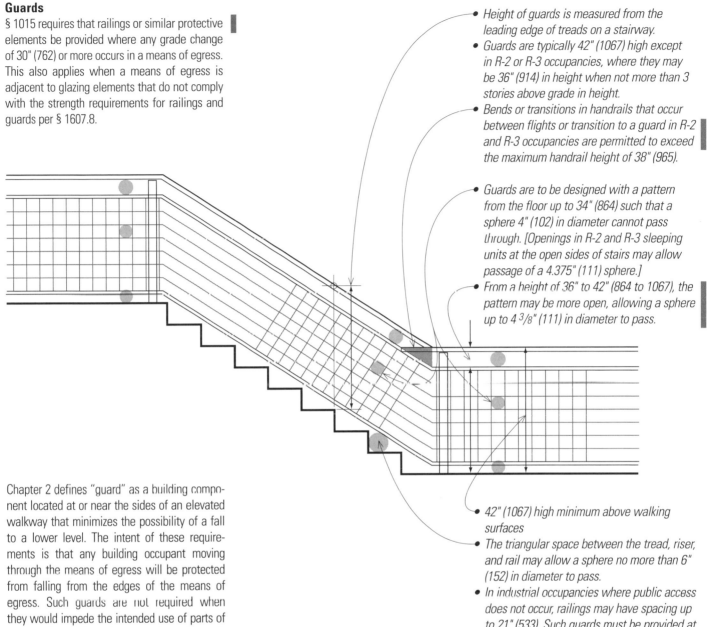

Chapter 2 defines "guard" as a building component located at or near the sides of an elevated walkway that minimizes the possibility of a fall to a lower level. The intent of these requirements is that any building occupant moving through the means of egress will be protected from falling from the edges of the means of egress. Such guards are not required when they would impede the intended use of parts of occupancies, such as in areas where the audience is viewing a stage, or at service pits and loading docks.

- 42" (1067) high minimum above walking surfaces
- The triangular space between the tread, riser, and rail may allow a sphere no more than 6" (152) in diameter to pass.
- In industrial occupancies where public access does not occur, railings may have spacing up to 21" (533). Such guards must be provided at rooftop mechanical equipment or roof access openings located closer than 10' (3048) from the roof edge.

Window Sill Height

Window sill heights for operable windows are regulated in residential occupancies R-2 and R-3 by § 1015.8. We recommend that these criteria be applied to R-1 transient lodging as well, to protect children in all types of residential occupancies.

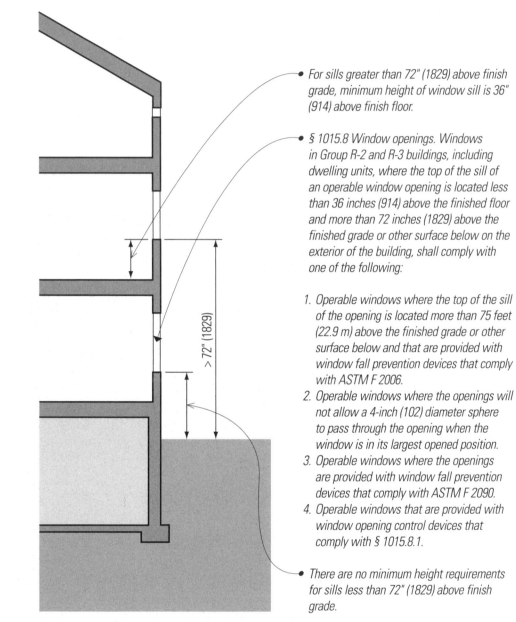

For sills greater than 72" (1829) above finish grade, minimum height of window sill is 36" (914) above finish floor.

§ 1015.8 Window openings. Windows in Group R-2 and R-3 buildings, including dwelling units, where the top of the sill of an operable window opening is located less than 36 inches (914) above the finished floor and more than 72 inches (1829) above the finished grade or other surface below on the exterior of the building, shall comply with one of the following:

1. Operable windows where the top of the sill of the opening is located more than 75 feet (22.9 m) above the finished grade or other surface below and that are provided with window fall prevention devices that comply with ASTM F 2006.
2. Operable windows where the openings will not allow a 4-inch (102) diameter sphere to pass through the opening when the window is in its largest opened position.
3. Operable windows where the openings are provided with window fall prevention devices that comply with ASTM F 2090.
4. Operable windows that are provided with window opening control devices that comply with § 1015.8.1.

There are no minimum height requirements for sills less than 72" (1829) above finish grade.

§ 1016 through § 1021 cover the exit-access portion of the means of egress that leads from any occupied portion of a building to any component of an exit—an exterior exit door at grade, interior exit stairways and passageways, horizontal exits, and exterior exit stairways. Exit access therefore includes the functional areas of the building along with various levels of egress pathways that will be discussed in detail.

As will become clear as we proceed through the analysis, there is a hierarchy of protection requirements for various elements of the exit access. As the number of occupants increases or as occupants get closer to an exit these requirements become more stringent.

Exit-Access Design Requirements
§ 1006 and § 1007 contain the key design requirements for exits and exit-access doorways, addressing such issues as the number and arrangement of exit paths. Exit access travel distances, as well as travel through intervening rooms and spaces, are addressed in § 1016 and § 1017.

- *Per § 1016.2 Exception 1, exit access through an enclosed elevator lobby is permitted when access to not less than one of the required exits is provided without travel through the enclosed elevator lobbies required by § 3006. Where the path of exit access travel passes through an enclosed elevator lobby, the level of protection required for the enclosed elevator lobby is not required to be extended to the exit unless direct access to an exit is required by other sections of this code.*

EXIT
- *The exit portion of a means of egress may include any of the following components: an exterior exit door at grade, interior exit stairways and ramps, exit passageways, exterior exit stairs or ramps, and horizontal exits.*
- *Exits mark the end of the exit access and the beginning of the exit portion of a means of egress system.*

EXIT ACCESS
- *The exit-access portion of a means of egress leads from any occupied point in a building to an exit.*
- *Exit-access doorways lead from one component of the exit access to another exit-access component. Note that an exit-access doorway refers to the opening and may or may not actually have a door.*
- *Note also that the terms exit and exit access doorway are used without distinction in the general sections of § 1005, 1006, and 1007.*
- *Note too that exit access stairways are part of the exit access.*

- *§ 1016.2 does not allow egress from a room or space to pass through intervening spaces unless they are accessory to each other and there is a discernible path of egress travel to an exit. These adjacent spaces may not be high-hazard occupancies unless the rooms are of the same occupancy group.*
- *There is no hierarchy of size for rooms that are accessory to each other. A larger room may egress through a smaller room if they are functionally related.*
- *Egress paths are not to lead through kitchens, storerooms, closets, or similar spaces; through rooms that can be locked to prevent egress; or through sleeping areas or bathrooms in dwelling units.*

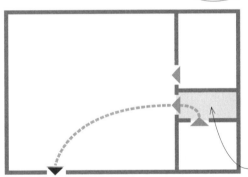

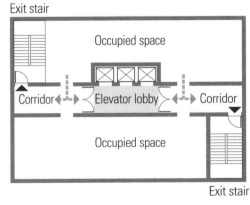

Exit stair

Occupied space

Corridor | Elevator lobby | Corridor

Occupied space

Exit stair

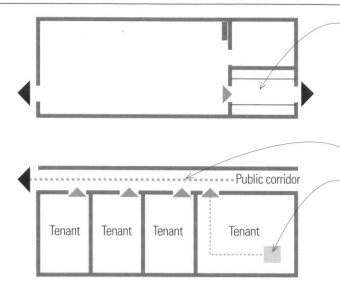

• *Egress paths may pass through kitchens that are part of the same dwelling unit or guestroom.*

• *Occupants should not be required to exit through a space controlled by another tenant or owner. For example, egress paths may not pass through adjacent tenant spaces, dwelling units, or sleeping units. Each occupant's access to the means of egress should be under their own control to the maximum extent possible.*

Public corridor

Tenant   Tenant   Tenant   Tenant

• *Note that a provision allows tenant spaces within other larger tenant spaces to exit through the space they are contained within if they occupy less than 10% of the larger area. This allows separate tenancies such as coffee bars to exit through a larger retail store under the control of a different tenant.*

Exit-Access Travel Distance

§ 1017 and Table 1017.2 provide the maximum length of exit-access travel distances, measured from the most remote point in the exit-access space to the entrance to an exit along a "natural and unobstructed path of egress travel."

Egress distances are measured in the exit-access space under consideration. They are not the total length of the means of egress but rather the distance an occupant must travel within the exit-access portion of the means of egress before entering the next higher level of protection in the means of egress, the exit. Thus these distances would apply on the upper floor of a high-rise building, but only until the occupant entered the exit stair enclosure and began moving through the exit portion of the means of egress.

See § 1019 for a discussion of how to treat open stairways, which are now considered by the Exceptions to § 1017.3.1 to be part of exit access.

• *Group I-2 occupancies are those where the occupants are not capable of self-preservation without assistance, such as in hospitals and nursing homes. In these occupancies, § 407.4.1 requires that hospital rooms or suites have an exit-access door leading directly to an exit-access corridor. The exceptions apply to detailed hospital design considerations that we will not consider here.*

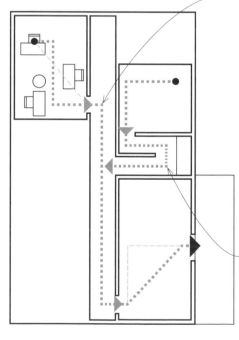

• *The path length is to be measured along the natural and unobstructed path of egress travel. The determination of the natural path must take fixed obstacles and obvious pathways into account. The potential location of furniture, especially large fixed furniture, such as library shelving, should be taken into account when measuring distances.*

• *On the other hand, in speculative office or commercial buildings, the designer may not have any idea of the ultimate use of the space and must use the 90° method. The designer should use common sense and care in determining travel distances.*

• *The measurement of exit-access travel distance must include the central path along unenclosed stairs and ramps and be measured from the most remote part of the building that makes use of the egress pathway.*

For most occupancies, the allowable exit-access travel distance is 200' (60 960) without a sprinkler system and from 250' to 300' (76 200 to 91 440) with a sprinkler system. The table below graphically represents the relative lengths of exit-access travel allowable for various occupancies.

Note that allowable exit access travel distances are increased in buildings with automatic sprinkler systems. This provision acknowledges the increased level of safety for occupants in sprinklered buildings. Note also that there are numerous footnotes to Table 1017.2 regarding occupancy-specific travel distances in such specialized building types as covered malls, atriums, and assembly spaces.

See § 1006.3.2 for stories with one exit.

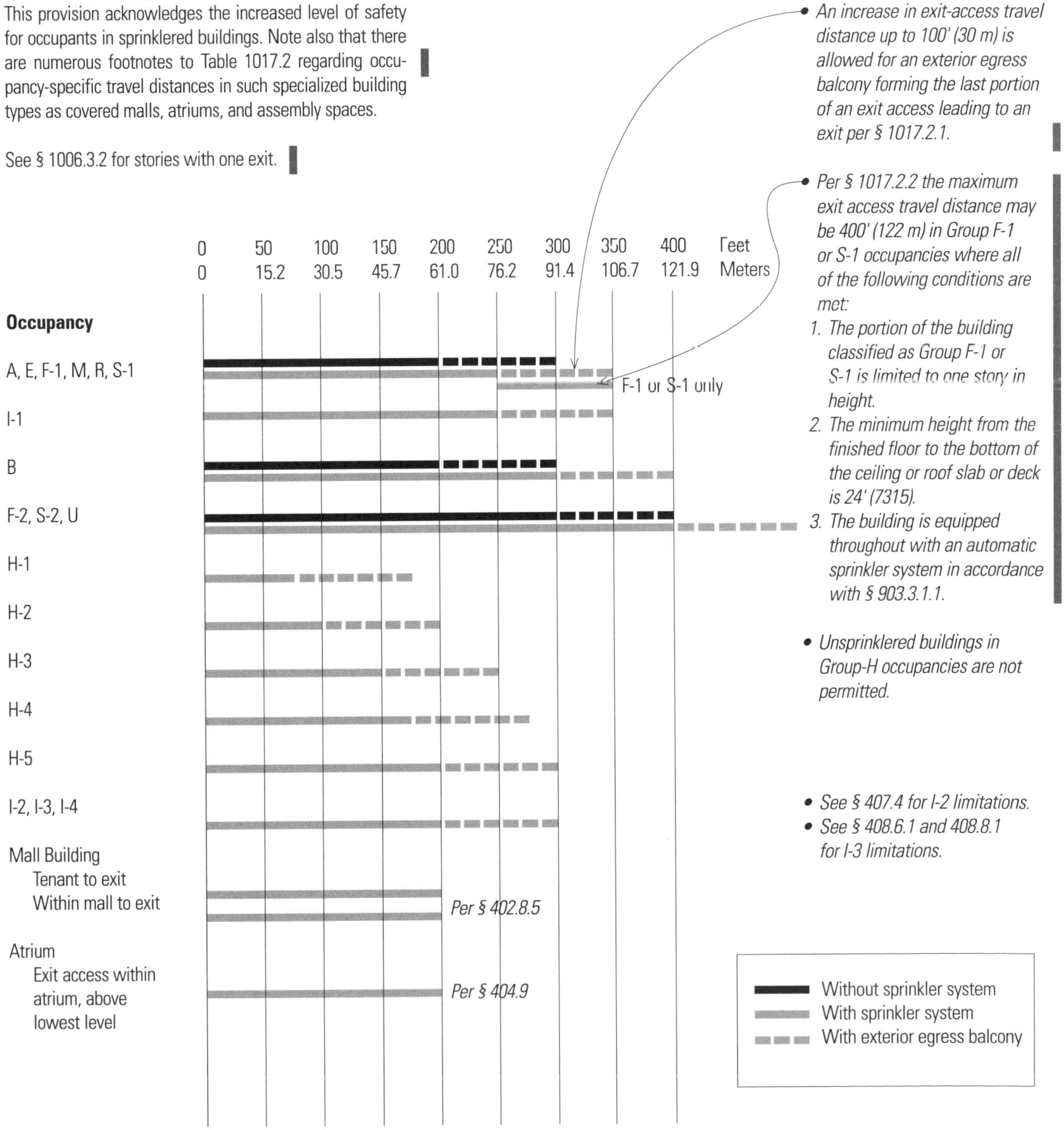

An increase in exit-access travel distance up to 100' (30 m) is allowed for an exterior egress balcony forming the last portion of an exit access leading to an exit per § 1017.2.1.

Per § 1017.2.2 the maximum exit access travel distance may be 400' (122 m) in Group F-1 or S-1 occupancies where all of the following conditions are met:

1. *The portion of the building classified as Group F-1 or S-1 is limited to one story in height.*
2. *The minimum height from the finished floor to the bottom of the ceiling or roof slab or deck is 24' (7315).*
3. *The building is equipped throughout with an automatic sprinkler system in accordance with § 903.3.1.1.*

- *Unsprinklered buildings in Group-H occupancies are not permitted.*

- *See § 407.4 for I-2 limitations.*
- *See § 408.6.1 and 408.8.1 for I-3 limitations.*

	0	50	100	150	200	250	300	350	400	Feet
	0	15.2	30.5	45.7	61.0	76.2	91.4	106.7	121.9	Meters

Occupancy

A, E, F-1, M, R, S-1 — F-1 or S-1 only

I-1

B

F-2, S-2, U

H-1

H-2

H-3

H-4

H-5

I-2, I-3, I-4

Mall Building
  Tenant to exit
  Within mall to exit — Per § 402.8.5

Atrium
  Exit access within atrium, above lowest level — Per § 404.9

Legend	
▬▬▬	Without sprinkler system
▬▬▬	With sprinkler system
▬ ▬ ▬	With exterior egress balcony

Aisles

§ 1018 applies not just to the conventional definition of aisles in assembly areas with fixed seats, but also to any occupied portions of the exit access. Components may be fixed or movable, such as tables, furnishings or chairs. Assembly-area aisles for fixed seats, grandstands or bleachers are governed by § 1029.

The aisle is the simplest defined component in the exit access, with the most flexibility. The intent of aisle requirements is to provide clear pathways so that building occupants can easily find egress pathways to exits in an emergency.

Aisle requirements relate to unobstructed widths; there are no fire-resistive construction requirements for aisles. Indeed, most aisle requirements apply to non-fixed building elements, such as tables, chairs, or merchandise display racks. It should also be recognized that the designer does not have day-to-day control over how spaces with non-fixed elements are used by the building occupants. However, the means-of-egress design should be based on delineated design assumptions as to occupant load and furniture layout to justify the design of the means-of-egress system. Such design should be rationally based on quantified determinations of how the space is anticipated to be used.

- *The required widths of aisles must be unobstructed, except for doors, handrails, and trim as noted below. These exceptions mirror those for hallways and corridors.*

- *Doors, in any position, may not reduce the required aisle width by more than one-half.*
- *Doors may not reduce the required width of aisles by more than 7" (178) when fully open.*

- *Rails and trim may protrude into aisles 1½" (38), which leads to a puzzle of how to apply such requirements to furniture or chairs.*

- *§ 1018.3 specifies that aisle requirements in Group B office and Group M mercantile occupancies are to be determined by occupant loads per § 1005.1 and must have a minimum width as would be required for a corridor serving that occupant load.*

- *Per the exception to § 1018.3, aisles in nonpublic areas having fewer than 50 occupants and not required to be accessible may be 28" (711) wide. Due to the difficulty of determining exactly what is nonpublic as well as what may need to be accessible, especially in office uses, we recommend always using the criteria for public aisles for design purposes. This is also more likely to be compliant with accessibility regulations that may apply in both public and employee areas.*

- *§ 1018.4 addresses "merchandise pads," which is defined as a display area for merchandise surrounded by aisles, permanent fixtures, or walls.*
- *There is to be an aisle accessway provided on at least one side of the merchandise pad. Where the aisle accessway is not required to be accessible, it is to be 30" (762) wide. The common path of travel shall not exceed 30' (9144) from any point in the merchandise pad.*

- *Aisles in other than assembly spaces and Groups B and M occupancies are also to have minimum clear aisle capacity as determined by § 1005.1 for the occupant load served. The width may not be less than that required for corridors by § 1020.2.*

Exit Access Stairways and Ramps

§ 1009 was heavily revised in the 2012 IBC to try and standardize interpretation and enforcement of egress requirements for enclosed "exit" stairs and unenclosed "exit access" stairs. Both may be components of the means of egress. The primary design difference is that exit access stairs, as part of the exit access, have travel distance restrictions, whereas exit stairs do not. Only enclosed stairs are to be considered to be "exits." The requirements for open exit access stairways have now been relocated to § 1019.

"Interior Exit Stairways," discussed in § 1023, are defined as being an exit component that serves to meet such egress design requirements as number of means of egress or exit access travel distance (by ending the travel distance where the exit enclosure begins). They are to provide a protected (rated) path of egress travel to an exit discharge or a public way.

Exit Access Stairs

§ 1019.3 calls for exit access stairs to be enclosed, but provides numerous exceptions that may be applied for other than Group I-2 and I-3 occupancies. Among the most relevant for designers are:

1. Exit access stairways that connect only two stories and do not open to other stories are not required to be enclosed.
2. Exit access stairways within a single residential dwelling unit or sleeping unit in Group R-1, R-2, or R-3 occupancies and connecting four or fewer stories are not required to be enclosed.
3. Exit access stairway openings are not required to be enclosed provided that the building is equipped with an automatic sprinkler system, the area of the floor opening between stories does not exceed twice the horizontal projected area of the exit access stairway, and the opening is protected by a draft curtain and closely spaced sprinklers.
4. In other than Group B and M occupancies, this provision is limited to openings that do not connect more than four stories. Exit access stairway openings are not required to be enclosed provided that the building is equipped throughout with an automatic sprinkler system, the floor opening does not connect more than four stories, the area of the floor opening between stories does not exceed twice the horizontal projected area of the exit access stairway, and the opening is protected by a draft curtain and closely spaced sprinklers.
5. Exit access stairways within an atrium complying with the provisions of § 404 are not required to be enclosed.
6. Exit access stairways and ramps in open parking garages that serve only the parking garage are not required to be enclosed.
7. Vertical exits need not be enclosed in Group A-5 buildings, such as outdoor stadiums, where the entire means of egress is essentially open.

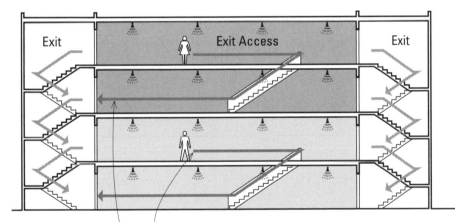

- Exit access travel distance is measured from the most remote point to an exit using unenclosed exit access stairways.
- Note that per § 1006.3 the path of egress travel to an exit may not pass through more than one adjacent story. This could be seen as limiting the use of open exit access stairways connecting up to four stories per Exceptions 3 and 4 to § 1019.3, unless the criteria for added protection at the stairs using those exceptions are met.

Corridors

§ 1020 provides for the design of corridors, which comprise the next level of occupant protection in the exit access above the aisle. Corridor is now a defined term in the code as an enclosed exit access component that defines and provides a path of egress travel to an exit. It is important to note and remember that corridors are not exits; they are a component of the exit access.

The table on the facing page, based on Tables 1020.1 and 1020.2, provides information about the occupant load, fire-resistance rating, and dimensions of corridors. Widths shown are minimums, which should be compared with width requirements calculated per § 1005.3.2.

• *In exit-access systems with multiple components, it can be visualized that aisles lead to corridors that, in turn, lead to exits.*

• *While layouts are subject to interpretation by the building official, a corridor typically is a space longer than it is wide, separated from adjacent spaces by walls, and having two clear choices of egress leading to two exits. There may be variations in the details of this arrangement but the basic components will almost always be present in a corridor.*

• *Corridors usually have a fire-resistance rating of at least 1 hour, based on the occupancy group where they occur. Several occupancies allow the use of unrated corridors in sprinklered buildings.*

• *Corridors at exterior walls may have unprotected openings when the walls are allowed to be unrated per Table 602 and unprotected openings are allowed per Table 705.8.*

Table based on Tables 1020.1 and 1020.2

Occupancy	Corridor Required for Occupant Load	Fire-Resistance Rating Without Sprinklers	Fire-Resistance Rating With Sprinklers	Notes	Dead-End Distance [20' (6096) typical]	Minimum Corridor Width Per Table 1020.2 [44" (1118) typical]
A, B, F, M, S, U	>30	1	0	No rating required in open parking garages per § 1020.1, Exc. 3 ▌	50' (15 240) @ B, E, F, I-1, M, R-1, R-2, R-4, S & U when sprinklered	72" (1829) in corridors serving gurney traffic in outpatient medical occupancies where patients are not capable of self-preservation
B	>30 ≤49	1 0 (only 1 exit required per §1006.2)	0			
E	>30	1	0	No rating if at least one door in each room used for instruction opens directly to the outside and if used for assembly, room has at least one-half of the required means-of-egress doors opening directly to the exterior per § 1020.1, Exc. 1 ▌		72" (1829) when occupant capacity >100
R	>10	Not permitted	1/2 hour	No rating at corridors inside dwelling unit or sleeping unit per § 1020.1, Exc. 2 ▌		36" (914) within dwelling unit
H-1, H-2, H-3	All	Not permitted	1			
H-4, H-5	>30	Not permitted	1			
I-2[1], I-4	All	Not permitted	0	1. See § 407.4 for I-2		72" (1829) when serving stretcher traffic in ambulatory care; 96" (2438) in I 2 when required for bed movement
I-1, I-3	All	Not permitted	1 [2]	2. See § 408.8 for I-3	50' (15 240); see § 1020.4, Exception 1 (only @ I-3) ▌	I-occupants not capable of self-preservation
All					Unlimited when dead-end is less than 2 1/2 times least corridor width	24" (610) typical for mechanical access; 36" (914) with < 50 occupants

Dead Ends

§ 1020.4 prescribes a maximum length for dead-end corridors. This is to avoid having occupants backtrack after they have gone some distance down a corridor before discovering that there is no exit or exit-access doorway at its end. Note that per the preceding table based on IBC Table 1020.1, the allowable length of dead-end corridors may be modified in certain occupancies if an automatic sprinkler system is provided.

- Dead ends in corridors are generally limited to 20' (6096) in length. See the table on page 221 for exceptions where the distance may be 50' (15 240) in sprinklered buildings.

- Dead-end provisions apply where there are corridors that branch off the main egress path and may thus lead an occupant to proceed to the end of a side corridor which does not have an exit, before having to return to the main egress path.

- When only one exit is required, the provisions for dead-end corridors do not apply. Single exits have relatively low occupant loads and the premise of a single exit assumes a directional nature to the egress path where the way to the exit will be clear.

Air Movement in Corridors

§ 1020.5 prohibits corridors from being used as part of the air-supply or return system. This is to allow the corridor to remain a separate atmosphere from the spaces it serves to the maximum extent possible. There are several exceptions to the corridor air-supply requirements:

1. Corridors may be used for makeup air exhaust systems for rooms such as toilet rooms, dressing rooms, or janitors' closets if the corridor is directly supplied with outdoor air at a rate to keep a positive pressure in the corridor.
2. Corridors in dwelling units may be used to convey return air.
3. Corridors in tenant spaces of less than 1,000 sf (93 m²) may be used to convey return air.
4. Corridors may have incidental air movement resulting from abutting pressurized rooms in health care facilities, but the corridor cannot be the primary source of supply or return air.

width (w)

< 2½ w

- Dead-end corridors are not limited in length when their length is less than 2½ times the least width of the dead end.

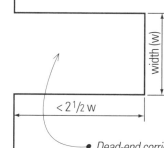

- Per § 1020.5.1 corridor ceilings may be used as a return-air plenum if one of the following conditions apply. (These are not listed as exceptions, and all need not apply at once):

1. The corridor is not required to be of fire-resistance-rated construction.
2. The corridor is separated from the plenum by fire-resistance-rated construction.
3. The air handlers serving the corridor are shut down by smoke detectors at the units.
4. The air handlers serving the corridor are shut down upon detection of sprinkler waterflow.
5. The plenum space is a component of an engineered smoke control system.

Corridor Continuity

§ 1020.6 stipulates that when a fire-resistance-rated corridor is required, the fire rating is to be maintained throughout the egress path from the point that an occupant enters the corridor in the exit access until they leave the corridor at the exit.

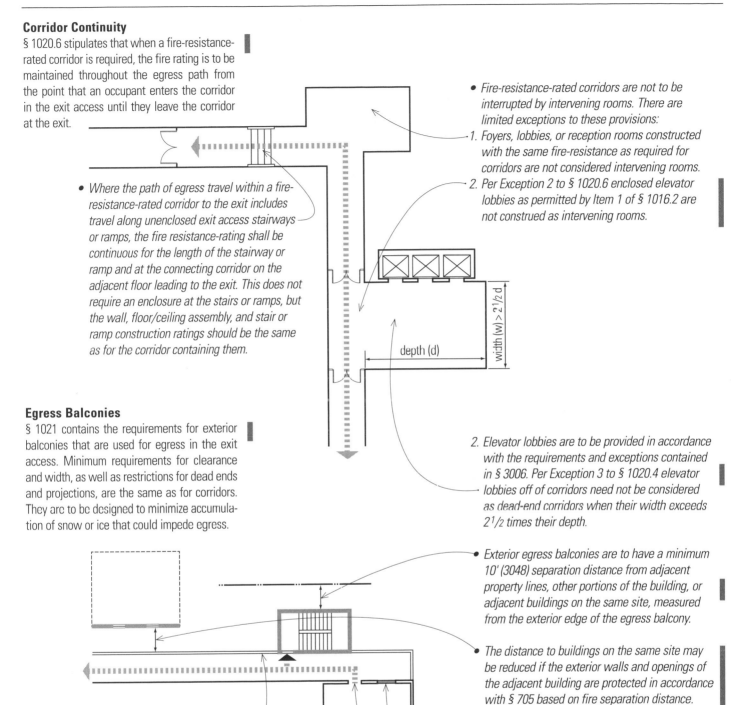

- *Where the path of egress travel within a fire-resistance-rated corridor to the exit includes travel along unenclosed exit access stairways or ramps, the fire resistance-rating shall be continuous for the length of the stairway or ramp and at the connecting corridor on the adjacent floor leading to the exit. This does not require an enclosure at the stairs or ramps, but the wall, floor/ceiling assembly, and stair or ramp construction ratings should be the same as for the corridor containing them.*

- *Fire-resistance-rated corridors are not to be interrupted by intervening rooms. There are limited exceptions to these provisions:*
1. *Foyers, lobbies, or reception rooms constructed with the same fire-resistance as required for corridors are not considered intervening rooms.*
2. *Per Exception 2 to § 1020.6 enclosed elevator lobbies as permitted by Item 1 of § 1016.2 are not construed as intervening rooms.*

depth (d)

width (w) > 2¹/₂ d

2. *Elevator lobbies are to be provided in accordance with the requirements and exceptions contained in § 3006. Per Exception 3 to § 1020.4 elevator lobbies off of corridors need not be considered as dead-end corridors when their width exceeds 2¹/₂ times their depth.*

Egress Balconies

§ 1021 contains the requirements for exterior balconies that are used for egress in the exit access. Minimum requirements for clearance and width, as well as restrictions for dead ends and projections, are the same as for corridors. They are to be designed to minimize accumulation of snow or ice that could impede egress.

- *Exterior egress balconies are to have a minimum 10' (3048) separation distance from adjacent property lines, other portions of the building, or adjacent buildings on the same site, measured from the exterior edge of the egress balcony.*

- *The distance to buildings on the same site may be reduced if the exterior walls and openings of the adjacent building are protected in accordance with § 705 based on fire separation distance.*

- *The long side of exterior egress balconies must be at least 50% open and arranged to minimize the accumulation of smoke or toxic gases.*

- *Since occupants may pass by doors or windows in getting to the exits, wall and opening protectives may be required as for corridors. The wall and all openings are to be protected if there is only one means of egress from the balcony.*

- *When two means of egress are provided, then only those openings in the dead ends will require protectives.*

EXITS

The requirements of § 1022 through § 1027 apply to the level of fire-resistance, the quantities, the dimensions, and the occupant capacity of exits. The exit is the intermediate portion of a means of egress, located between the exit access and the exit discharge. Unlike the exit access, where building functions share the occupied spaces with egress uses, exits are generally single-purpose spaces that function primarily as a means of egress. Once a certain level of occupant protection is achieved in the exit, it is not to be reduced until arrival at the exit discharge.

Exit Design Requirements

§ 1022 through § 1027 set out the general design requirements for exits. The requirements for spaces with single exits that used to be located with exit provisions have been moved to § 1006.

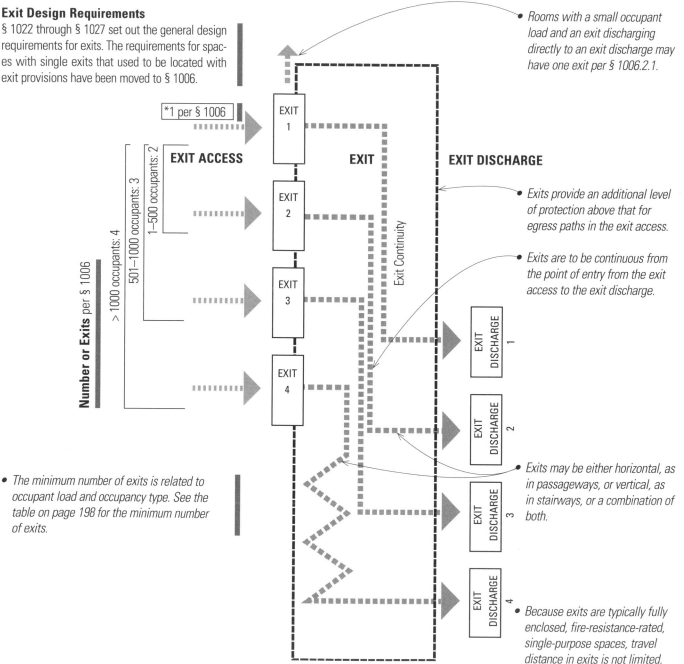

*1 per § 1006

EXIT ACCESS   EXIT   EXIT DISCHARGE

EXIT 1
EXIT 2
EXIT 3
EXIT 4

EXIT DISCHARGE 1
EXIT DISCHARGE 2
EXIT DISCHARGE 3
EXIT DISCHARGE 4

Exit Continuity

Number or Exits per § 1006

> 1000 occupants: 4
501–1000 occupants: 3
1–500 occupants: 2
occupant capacity: 2

• Rooms with a small occupant load and an exit discharging directly to an exit discharge may have one exit per § 1006.2.1.

• Exits provide an additional level of protection above that for egress paths in the exit access.

• Exits are to be continuous from the point of entry from the exit access to the exit discharge.

• Exits may be either horizontal, as in passageways, or vertical, as in stairways, or a combination of both.

• Because exits are typically fully enclosed, fire-resistance-rated, single-purpose spaces, travel distance in exits is not limited.

• The minimum number of exits is related to occupant load and occupancy type. See the table on page 198 for the minimum number of exits.

Exit Components

Various elements of the Exit are described in the following sections:

- § 1022.2. Exterior exit doors that lead directly to an exit discharge or public way
- § 1023. Interior exit stairways and ramps
- § 1024. Exit passageways
- § 1025. Luminous egress path markings
- § 1026. Horizontal exits
- § 1027. Exterior exit ramps and stairways

Interior Exit Stairways and Ramps

§ 1023.1 presumes per the definition in Chapter 2 and the text in the section that all interior exit stairways are enclosed interior exit stairways that provide for a protected path of egress travel. Interior exit stairways connecting four stories or more shall have a 2-hour fire-resistance rating. Per § 1023.2 Interior exit stairways connecting less than four stories are to have a 1-hour rating. Enclosures at exit ramps have the same requirements as for stairways. The number of stories connected includes basements, but mezzanines are not counted as additional stories.

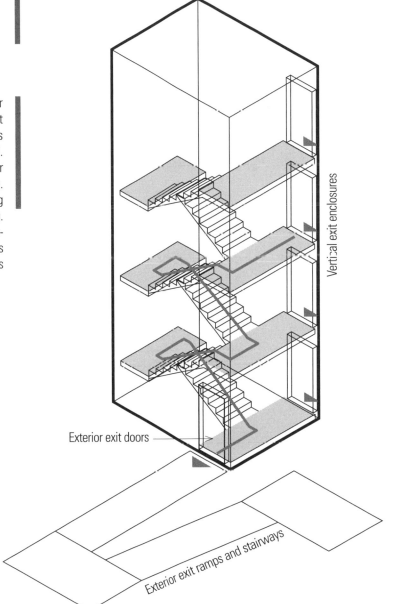

Vertical exit enclosures

Exterior exit doors

Exterior exit ramps and stairways

EXIT DESIGN REQUIREMENTS

Openings and Penetrations

§ 1023.5 and § 1024.5 limit openings and penetrations in interior exit stairways and exit passageways to those necessary for exit access to the enclosure from normally occupied spaces and for egress from the enclosure. This recognizes the primary use of exit components as pathways for egress.

Opening protectives for both exit passageways and interior exit stairways shall be as required by § 716. Thus 1-hour fire-rated walls will require 1-hour-rated doors per Table 716.5. Where higher fire ratings for interior exit stairways are required, the rating of exit-passageway construction and opening protectives should match as well.

§ 1023.3 requires interior exit stairways to terminate at an exit discharge or a public way. Per the Exception to this section, an exit passageway may extend the interior exit stairway to an exit discharge or to a public way. When an exit passageway is provided, it must be separated from the interior exit stairway by a fire barrier per § 707, by a horizontal assembly per § 711, or both.

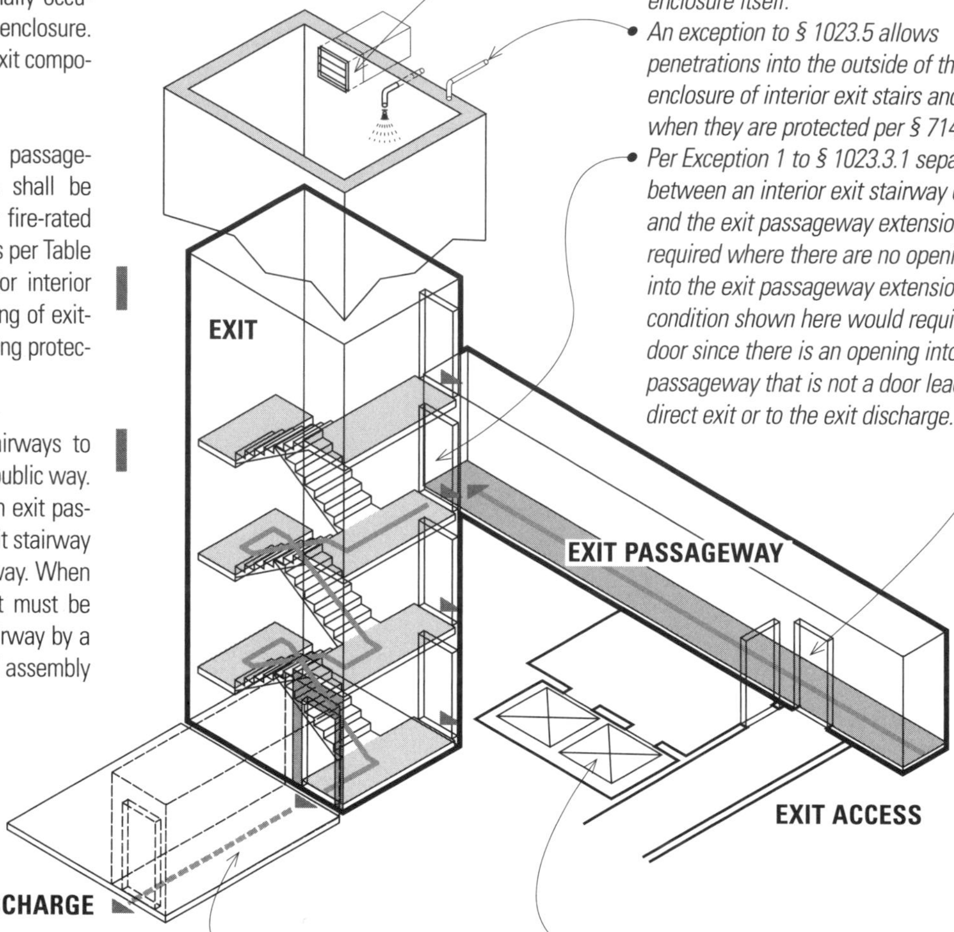

EXIT

EXIT PASSAGEWAY

EXIT ACCESS

EXIT DISCHARGE ▶

- *Penetrations into the inside of enclosures are to be limited to those items such as sprinklers or ventilation ducts that serve the enclosure itself.*
- *An exception to § 1023.5 allows penetrations into the outside of the enclosure of interior exit stairs and ramps when they are protected per § 714.3.2.*
- *Per Exception 1 to § 1023.3.1 separation between an interior exit stairway or ramp and the exit passageway extension is not required where there are no openings into the exit passageway extension. The condition shown here would require a door since there is an opening into the exit passageway that is not a door leading to a direct exit or to the exit discharge.*
- *Optional exit passageway extending an exit to an exit discharge or public way*
- *Elevators are not permitted to open into exit passageways per § 1023.4.*
- *Penetrations are limited to those providing exit access to the passageway and to mechanical systems serving the exit passageway.*
- *Ventilation for exit enclosures is to be served directly from outside or from ductwork enclosed in fire protection as required for shafts.*
- *The intent of these requirements is that vertical and horizontal exit enclosures should be as separate from the occupied spaces as possible to provide a safe means of egress from those spaces.*
- *In malls, areas such as mechanical and electrical rooms may open onto the exit passageway per § 402.8.7 if they are provided with 1-hour fire-resistance-rated doors.*

Penetrations

§ 1023.5 prohibits penetrations into or through interior exit stairways and ramps except for equipment and ductwork necessary for independent ventilation or pressurization, sprinkler piping, standpipes, electrical raceways for fire department communication systems, and electrical raceways serving the interior exit stairway and ramp and terminating at a steel box not exceeding 16 in^2 (0.010 m^2). Such penetrations shall be protected in accordance with § 714. There shall not be penetrations or communication openings, whether protected or not, between adjacent interior exit stairways and ramps. Exception: Membrane penetrations shall be permitted on the outside of an interior exit stairway and ramp. Such penetrations shall be protected in accordance with § 714.3.2.

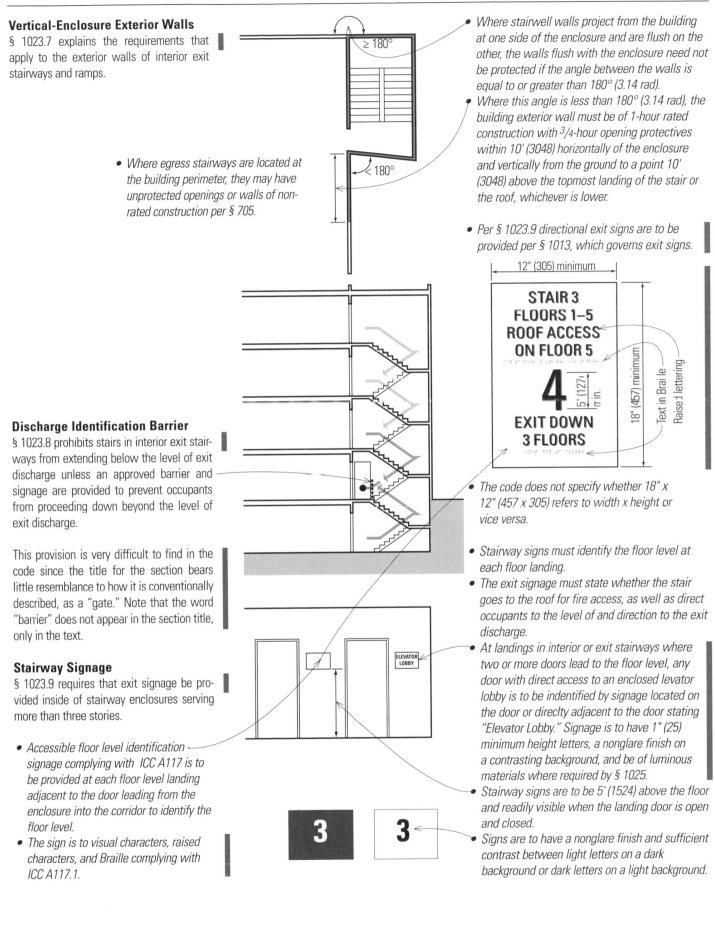

Vertical-Enclosure Exterior Walls

§ 1023.7 explains the requirements that apply to the exterior walls of interior exit stairways and ramps.

• Where egress stairways are located at the building perimeter, they may have unprotected openings or walls of non-rated construction per § 705.

• Where stairwell walls project from the building at one side of the enclosure and are flush on the other, the walls flush with the enclosure need not be protected if the angle between the walls is equal to or greater than 180° (3.14 rad).

• Where this angle is less than 180° (3.14 rad), the building exterior wall must be of 1-hour rated construction with ³/₄-hour opening protectives within 10' (3048) horizontally of the enclosure and vertically from the ground to a point 10' (3048) above the topmost landing of the stair or the roof, whichever is lower.

• Per § 1023.9 directional exit signs are to be provided per § 1013, which governs exit signs.

STAIR 3
FLOORS 1–5
ROOF ACCESS
ON FLOOR 5

4

EXIT DOWN
3 FLOORS

12" (305) minimum

18" (457) minimum

Text in Braille

Raised lettering

5" (127) min.

Discharge Identification Barrier

§ 1023.8 prohibits stairs in interior exit stairways from extending below the level of exit discharge unless an approved barrier and signage are provided to prevent occupants from proceeding down beyond the level of exit discharge.

This provision is very difficult to find in the code since the title for the section bears little resemblance to how it is conventionally described, as a "gate." Note that the word "barrier" does not appear in the section title, only in the text.

• The code does not specify whether 18" x 12" (457 x 305) refers to width x height or vice versa.

• Stairway signs must identify the floor level at each floor landing.

• The exit signage must state whether the stair goes to the roof for fire access, as well as direct occupants to the level of and direction to the exit discharge.

• At landings in interior or exit stairways where two or more doors lead to the floor level, any door with direct access to an enclosed elevator lobby is to be indentified by signage located on the door or direclty adjacent to the door stating "Elevator Lobby." Signage is to have 1" (25) minimum height letters, a nonglare finish on a contrasting background, and be of luminous materials where required by § 1025.

Stairway Signage

§ 1023.9 requires that exit signage be provided inside of stairway enclosures serving more than three stories.

• Accessible floor level identification signage complying with ICC A117 is to be provided at each floor level landing adjacent to the door leading from the enclosure into the corridor to identify the floor level.

• The sign is to visual characters, raised characters, and Braille complying with ICC A117.1.

ELEVATOR LOBBY

3   **3**

• Stairway signs are to be 5' (1524) above the floor and readily visible when the landing door is open and closed.

• Signs are to have a nonglare finish and sufficient contrast between light letters on a dark background or dark letters on a light background.

Smoke-proof Enclosures

§ 1023.11 requires smoke-proof enclosures for each of the required exits in high-rise buildings (§ 403), where floor surfaces are more than 75' (22 860) above the lowest level of fire-department vehicle access, and in underground buildings (§ 405), where floor surfaces are more than 30' (9144) below the level of exit discharge.

The stairway enclosures are to comply with the requirements of § 909.20 for smoke-control systems in smoke-proof enclosures.

Exit Passageways

§ 1024 contains the requirements for exit passageways, which are similar to corridors in the exit access, but have more restrictions placed on their use since they are part of the exit. They are not to be used for any other purpose than as a means of egress. They are similar to vertical stairway enclosures but are used for the horizontal movement portions of exits.

> 75' (22 860) above the lowest level of fire-department vehicle access

> 30' (9144) for underground buildings

- *If an exit passageway occurs at other than the level of exit discharge it is to terminate in an exit.*

- *The stairways shall exit into a public way or an exit passageway, yard, or open space having direct access to a public way.*
- *The exit passageway is to have no other opening, which implies it is not used for any other purpose except for egress.*
- *Exceptions allow other openings into the exit passageway when they too are pressurized and protected as for the smoke-proof enclosure or the pressurized stairway.*
- *There are no limits on travel distance in interior-exit-stairway and exit-passageway enclosures, so they could be many stories high or very long in horizontal distance. The intent is that occupants have the protection necessary to give them time in an emergency to safely traverse the egress travel distance.*

- *Width requirements for exit passageways are similar to other parts of the egress system, with a 44" (1118) minimum width for typical exit passageways and 36" (914) for those serving fewer than 50 occupants.*
- *Doors may not project more than 7" (178) into the passageway when fully open, nor reduce the required width by more than one-half in their fully open position.*
- *Exit passageways are to be of at least 1-hour fire-rated construction, or more if connected to an interior exit stairway with a higher fire rating. Opening protectives in exit passageways are to comply with § 716.*

Luminous Egress Path Markings

§ 1025 applies to high-rise buildings with A, B, E, I, M or R-1 occupancies. This requirement applies to interior exit stairways, interior exit ramps, and exit passageways, as well as where transfer exit passageways occur between sections of stairs that are part of the exit. Note that it does not apply to R-2 occupancies. The markings required by § 1024 may be photoluminescent materials, which give off light after being excited by another light source, or self-luminescent materials, which give off light from a self-contained power source other than batteries. Either source must operate without external power so that they are available in an emergency, when power to building systems is not available.

- *1"(25) marking for handrails and extensions at top of rail, continuous except for 4" (102) max. gaps.*

- *All steps are to have stripes 1" to 2" (25 to 51) wide along their leading edge and extend for their full length.*
- *1/2" (13) maximum back from edge of tread; lap down maximum 1/2" (13) onto face of riser.*

- *Obstacles such as standpipes or structural elements at or below 6'-6" (1981) and projecting more than 4" (102) into the egress path are to be outlined in marking tape with 45-degree alternating dark and luminous patterns. We recommend outlining the projection on the floor and on the object.*

- *The leading edges of landings are to have stripes with the same size and location criteria as for stair treads.*
- *Stair landings are to have 1" to 2" (25 to 51) wide demarcation lines. They may be mounted on the floor or wall. Where wall mounted and coming to a stair, they must drop vertically within 2" (51) of the stair tread or riser. When wall mounted, their bottom edge must be within 4" (102) of the floor.*

- *2" (51) max. gap*

- *Doors where occupants of exit enclosure leave the exit enclosure are to have:*
- *Top and side of door frame to be marked with 1" to 2" (25 to 51) wide stripes;*
- *Door hardware area marked with at least 16 square inches (406 mm²) of luminous material; panic hardware bars to be marked with a 1" (25) min. wide stripe;*
- *"Running Man" exit sign per NFPA 170 Standard for Fire Safety and Emergency Symbols, mounted at centerline of door, no more than 18" (457) from finish floor level to top of sign.*

- *Exceptions apply to marking widths when they are listed per UL 1994 Low Level Path Marking and Lighting Systems.*
- *In egress system arrangements where there is an exit passageway for transfer between interior exit stairways, egress path marking should be provided in the exit passageway as well as in the interior exit stairways.*

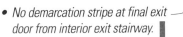

- *No demarcation stripe at final exit door from interior exit stairway.*

Minimum 4" (102) high

Horizontal Exits

§ 1026 provides for horizontal exits, a unique concept for exiting because they provide an intermediate area of escape rather than a complete means of egress to grade. The concept is based on the assumption that, by providing a high degree of fire-resistive separation between two segments of a building, occupants can pass through the separation, which is essentially a fire-compartment wall, and be safe from the danger that caused the need to egress.

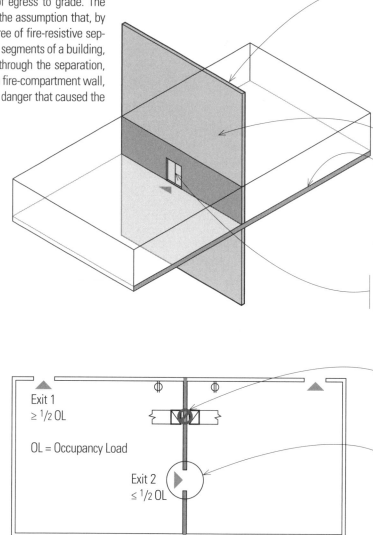

• A horizontal exit is a wall that completely divides a floor of a building into two or more separate exit-access areas in order to afford safety from fire and smoke in the exit-access area of incident origin. The horizontal exit essentially creates separate buildings on each floor level to allow exiting to occur from one protected area into another without entering exit enclosures or exit passageways.

• Horizontal exit separations must extend vertically through all levels of a building...

• ...unless horizontal floor assemblies having a fire-resistance rating of not less than two hours with no unprotected openings are provided.

• The essential characteristics of a horizontal exit are as follows:

• The separation must be of at least 2-hour construction.

• Opening protectives are based on the fire-rating of the wall.

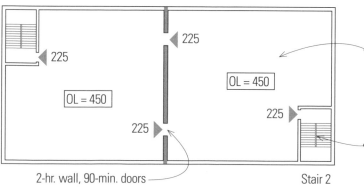

• Interconnection by ductwork between the sides of the horizontal exit is not allowed unless the duct or air transfer opening is provided with fire/smoke dampers.

• Horizontal exits may not serve as the only exit from a portion of a building. Where two or more exits are required, not more than one-half of the exits may be in the form of a horizontal exit. The previous edition of the IBC required that no more than one-half of the number of exits and the exit width _provided_ be at the horizontal exit. The 2015 edition states "not more than one-half of the total number of exits or total exit _minimum width or required capacity_ shall be horizontal exits."

• For many buildings, using this concept enables the omission of at least one stairway or egress pathway. Only one stairway need be provided for each segment, and the horizontal exit can be used as the second exit for each segment.

• At least one refuge area exit must lead directly to the exterior or to an interior exit stair or ramp.

§ 1026.4 specifies that the refuge area to which a horizontal exit leads shall be of sufficient size to accommodate 100% of the occupant load of the exit access from which refuge is sought, plus 100% of the normal occupant load of the exit access serving as the refuge area. The capacity of such refuge floor area shall be determined by allowing 3 sf (0.28 m²) of net clear floor area per occupant, not including aisles, hallways, and corridors. The area of stairs, elevators, and other shafts shall not be counted.

Note that the anticipated occupant load from the adjoining compartment is to be based on the capacity of the horizontal exit doors entering the refuge area. In cases where there is a relatively small occupant load but minimum door widths are specified elsewhere in Chapter 10, this provision may be interpreted as requiring a larger refuge area based on door egress capacity as opposed to the actual anticipated occupant load at the horizontal exit. The interpretation of this provision should be discussed with the AHJ early in the design process since it has floor plan implications for the size of the refuge area.

In Group I-3 occupancies, the capacity of the refuge area shall be determined by allowing 6 sf (0.6 m²) of net clear floor area per occupant. In Group I-2 occupancies, the capacity of the refuge area shall be determined by allowing 15 sf (1.4 m²) of net clear floor area per ambulatory occupant and 30 sf (2.8 m²) of net clear floor area per nonambulatory occupant.

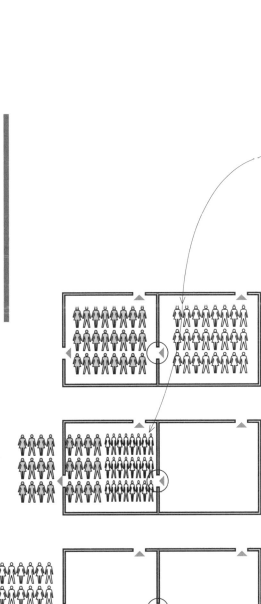

- The theory underlying the horizontal exit involves moving occupants from an area impacted by an emergency to another safe area of refuge. A building designed with a horizontal exit has two adjacent areas that may serve as both exit access and horizontal exit. To accommodate the anticipated number of occupants, the area to be considered as a horizontal exit must accommodate its own occupant load plus 100% of the load of the area being exited.

This additional load is calculated at 3 sf (0.28 m²) per occupant of net clear area for other than hospitals. This recognizes that in an emergency people can be in tighter quarters and still egress safely. Where there may be nonambulatory patients the floor area requirements are 30 sf (2.8 m²) per occupant to allow more space for beds and wheelchairs.

The application of the design criteria takes into account the direction of exit flow. The downstream area receiving the occupants from upstream must be able to accommodate both its normal occupant load and that of the occupants from the adjacent space.

Only in cases where a horizontal exit may function in both directions must both areas have more exit capacity than is normally required for the area itself. A two-way exit is allowed when the exit-access design requirements are independently satisfied for each exit-access area.

- The design of the exit-access capacity for the building segment serving as the refuge area shall be based on the normal occupant load served and need not consider the increased occupant load imposed by persons entering such refuge area through horizontal exits.

Exterior Exit Stairways

§ 1027 contains the requirements for exterior exit ramps and stairways that serve as a component of a required means of egress. Except for Group I-2 occupancies, exterior exit stairways may be used in a means of egress for occupancies less than 7 stories (6 or less) or 75' (22 860) in height.

• *Exterior exit stairways serving as part of a required means of egress must be open on one side, with an aggregate open area of at least 35 sf (3.3 m²) at each floor level and at each intermediate landing.*

• *Each opening must be a minimum of 42" (1067) high above the adjacent walking surface.*

• *The open areas must face yards, courts, or public ways.*

• To second stairway

Exterior exit ramps and stairways are to be separated from the building interior per § 1027.6, with openings limited to those necessary for exit access. The exceptions to this protection requirement are:

1. In other than Group R-1 or R-2 occupancies, in buildings no more than two stories above grade, and where the exit discharge is at the first story, no protection is required. The path of travel is only one story high and is considered short enough not to need protection.

2. When there is an exterior egress balcony that connects two remote exterior ramps or stairways with a 50% open balcony and openings at least 7' (2134) above the balcony, protection is not required. This recognizes the inherent safety of having two means of egress from the balcony as well as the protection afforded by the openings, which minimize the chance of heat or toxic gases being trapped in the egress path.

Open-Ended Corridors

The third exception to § 1027.6 is used where there are open-ended corridors that are by their nature not separated from exit stairways. Additional separation from the interior to the stairways is not required if several conditions (not exceptions) are met.

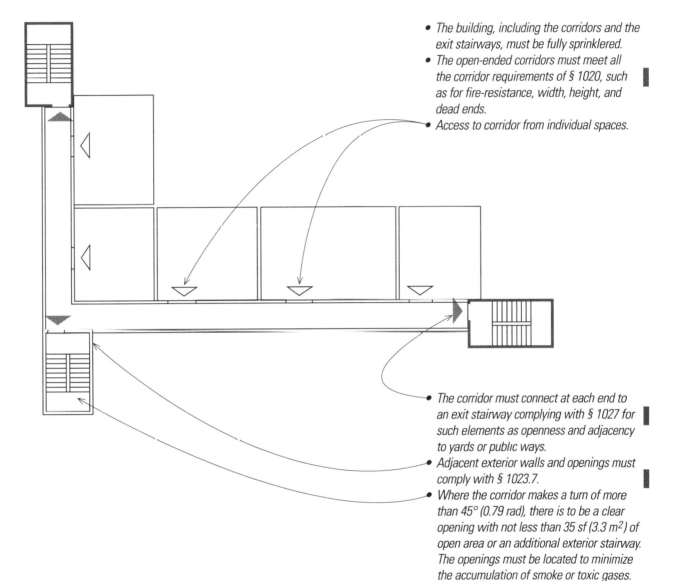

- The building, including the corridors and the exit stairways, must be fully sprinklered.
- The open-ended corridors must meet all the corridor requirements of § 1020, such as for fire-resistance, width, height, and dead ends.
- Access to corridor from individual spaces.

- The corridor must connect at each end to an exit stairway complying with § 1027 for such elements as openness and adjacency to yards or public ways.
- Adjacent exterior walls and openings must comply with § 1023.7.
- Where the corridor makes a turn of more than 45° (0.79 rad), there is to be a clear opening with not less than 35 sf (3.3 m²) of open area or an additional exterior stairway. The openings must be located to minimize the accumulation of smoke or toxic gases. (This provision is subject to interpretation by the building official.)

§ 1028 contains the provisions for the design of the exit discharge. The exit discharge is the third and final portion of the means of egress. It begins where building occupants leave the exit portion of the means of egress and ends when they reach the public way. There is some flexibility on the part of the building official to determine when occupants have gone far enough from the structure in question to be safe, and in these cases, the exit discharge may lead through an egress court. Egress courts are defined as a court or yard that provides access to a public way.

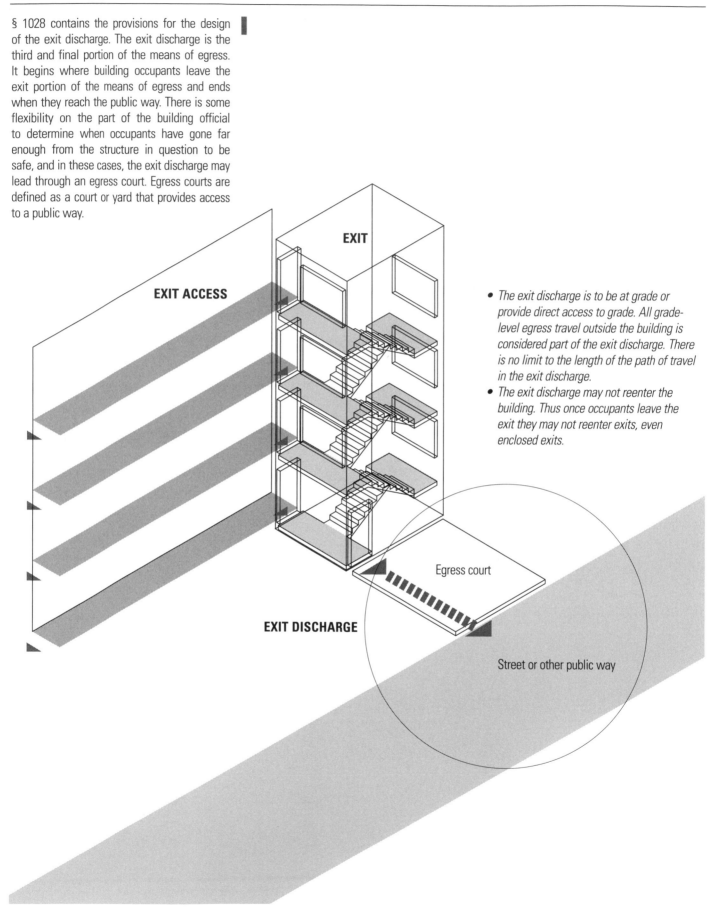

EXIT

EXIT ACCESS

- *The exit discharge is to be at grade or provide direct access to grade. All grade-level egress travel outside the building is considered part of the exit discharge. There is no limit to the length of the path of travel in the exit discharge.*
- *The exit discharge may not reenter the building. Thus once occupants leave the exit they may not reenter exits, even enclosed exits.*

Egress court

EXIT DISCHARGE

Street or other public way

Exit Discharge through Intervening Spaces

The exit discharge path must connect the exit to the public way without intervening spaces except under specific conditions. Note that per § 1027.1, the combined use of Exceptions 1 and 2 may not exceed 50% of the number and minimum width or required capacity of the required exits.

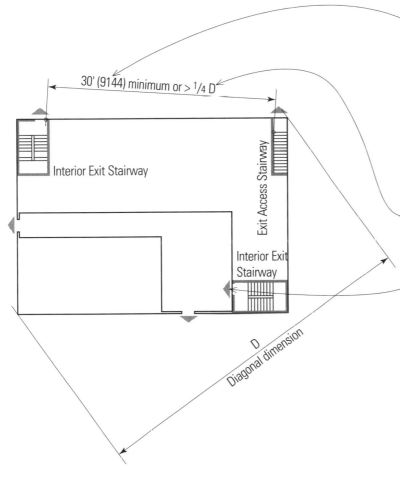

30' (9144) minimum or > 1/4 D

Interior Exit Stairway

Exit Access Stairway

Interior Exit Stairway

D
Diagonal dimension

• It is expected that one exit discharge will be direct to the building exterior.

• Where a required interior exit stairway or ramp and an exit access stairway or ramp serve the same floor level and terminate at the same level of exit discharge, the termination of the exit access stairway or ramp and the exit discharge door of the interior exit stairway or ramp shall be separated by a distance of not less than 30' (9144). The distance is to be:

• Measured in a straight line between the exit discharge door and the last tread of the exit access stairway or end of the ramp slope.

• Or, be not less than one-fourth the length of the maximum overall diagonal dimension (D) of the building, whichever is less.

1. Up to 50% of the number and capacity of the required enclosed exits may exit through areas on the level of exit discharge when all of the following conditions are met:

1.1. Such interior exit stairways egress to a free and unobstructed way to the exterior of the building.

1.2. The entire level of exit discharge is separated from the area below by fire-resistive construction complying with the required fire rating for the exit enclosure. (It is not clear why this applies only to levels below, nor what is to be done when no levels below exist.)

1.3. The egress path from the interior exit stairway is protected throughout by a sprinkler system.

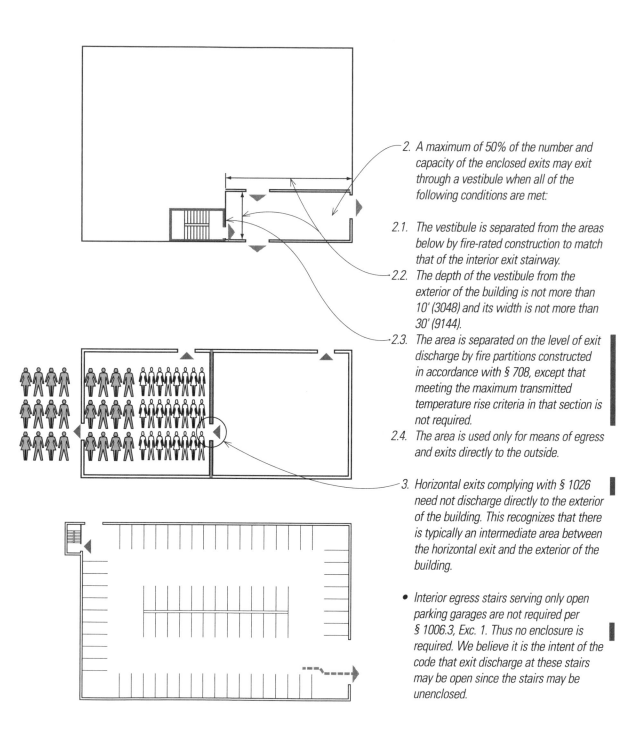

2. A maximum of 50% of the number and capacity of the enclosed exits may exit through a vestibule when all of the following conditions are met:

2.1. The vestibule is separated from the areas below by fire-rated construction to match that of the interior exit stairway.

2.2. The depth of the vestibule from the exterior of the building is not more than 10' (3048) and its width is not more than 30' (9144).

2.3. The area is separated on the level of exit discharge by fire partitions constructed in accordance with § 708, except that meeting the maximum transmitted temperature rise criteria in that section is not required.

2.4. The area is used only for means of egress and exits directly to the outside.

3. Horizontal exits complying with § 1026 need not discharge directly to the exterior of the building. This recognizes that there is typically an intermediate area between the horizontal exit and the exterior of the building.

• Interior egress stairs serving only open parking garages are not required per § 1006.3, Exc. 1. Thus no enclosure is required. We believe it is the intent of the code that exit discharge at these stairs may be open since the stairs may be unenclosed.

Exit-Discharge Capacity

§ 1028.2 requires that the capacity of an exit discharge be not less than the minimum width or required capacity of the exits being served.

Access to Public Way

Exit discharge is to provide direct access to a public way. If that is not possible a safe dispersal area may be provided if all of these conditions are met: 5 sf (0.46m²) per person; 50' (15 240) clear from building; permanently maintained; and identified as a safe dispersal area, with safe path of travel from the building.

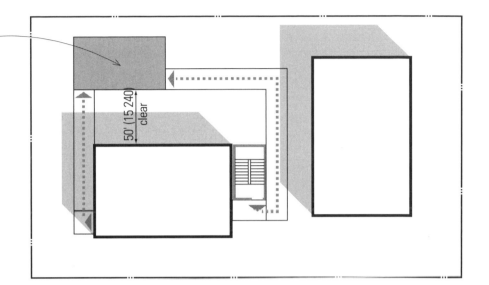

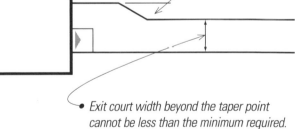

• When the egress court is wider than the required egress width, any reductions in width should be gradual and at an angle of less than 30° (0.52 rad). This is to prevent having inside corners where occupants could be trapped by the press of large groups of people exiting the building in an emergency. This is another example of the water-flow analogy for exiting.

• Exit court width beyond the taper point cannot be less than the minimum required.

Exit-Discharge Components

Per § 1028.3 exit-discharge components are presumed to be outside the building envelope and are thus required to be sufficiently open to prevent the accumulation of smoke or toxic gases.

Egress Courts

§ 1028.4 requires egress courts to comply with corridor and exit-passageway requirements for clear width and door encroachment.

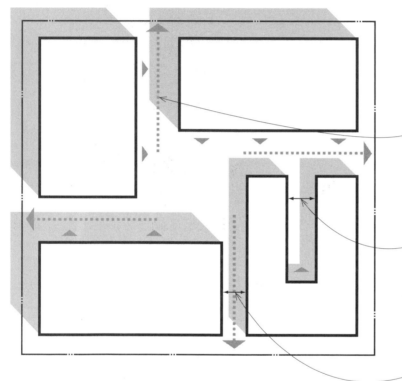

- Egress courts are open spaces that provide access to a public way from one or more exits.
- Doors may encroach into this space but must be compliant with § 1005 in not reducing the required width or capacity of the means of egress.
- Egress courts less than 10' (3048) wide are to be of 1-hour-rated construction for 10' (3048) above the floor of the court.
- Openings in such conditions are to have ³/₄-hour-rated opening protectives that are fixed or self-closing, except in Group R-3 occupancies or where the court serves an occupant load of less than ten.
- Per § 1028.4.1 the required capacity of egress courts is to be as specified in § 1005.1, but the minimum width shall be not less than 44" (1118), except for egress courts serving Group R-3 and U occupancies, which are to be not less than 36" (914) in width. The required capacity and width of egress courts is to be unobstructed to a height of 7' (2134).

§ 1029 contains egress requirements specific to assembly occupancies that supplement the general requirements located elsewhere in Chapter 10. Very large assembly occupancies typically provide smoke-protected seating to avoid having excessive egress widths. The number of such large assembly occupancies that are designed and constructed every year are so small as not to warrant treatment in this book. However, there are several basic principles that apply to assembly occupancies that should be understood.

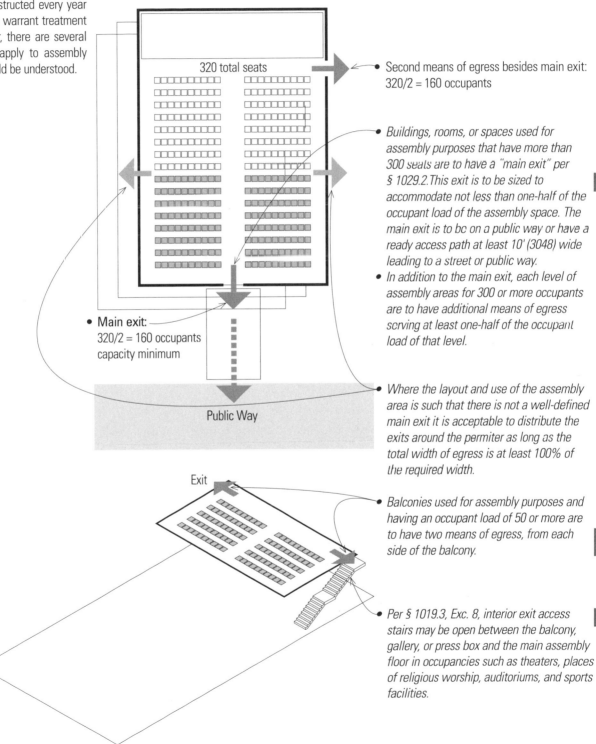

320 total seats

Second means of egress besides main exit: 320/2 = 160 occupants

Buildings, rooms, or spaces used for assembly purposes that have more than 300 seats are to have a "main exit" per § 1029.2. This exit is to be sized to accommodate not less than one-half of the occupant load of the assembly space. The main exit is to be on a public way or have a ready access path at least 10' (3048) wide leading to a street or public way.

- *In addition to the main exit, each level of assembly areas for 300 or more occupants are to have additional means of egress serving at least one-half of the occupant load of that level.*

• **Main exit:**
320/2 = 160 occupants
capacity minimum

Public Way

Where the layout and use of the assembly area is such that there is not a well-defined main exit it is acceptable to distribute the exits around the perimeter as long as the total width of egress is at least 100% of the required width.

Exit

Balconies used for assembly purposes and having an occupant load of 50 or more are to have two means of egress, from each side of the balcony.

Per § 1019.3, Exc. 8, interior exit access stairs may be open between the balcony, gallery, or press box and the main assembly floor in occupancies such as theaters, places of religious worship, auditoriums, and sports facilities.

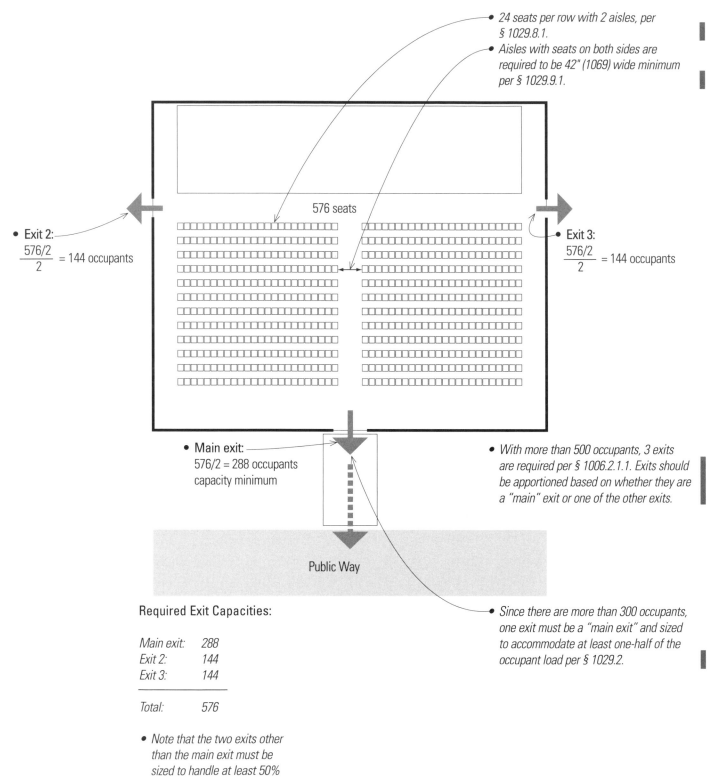

- *24 seats per row with 2 aisles, per § 1029.8.1.*
- *Aisles with seats on both sides are required to be 42" (1069) wide minimum per § 1029.9.1.*

576 seats

- Exit 2:
$$\frac{576/2}{2} = 144 \text{ occupants}$$

- Exit 3:
$$\frac{576/2}{2} = 144 \text{ occupants}$$

- Main exit:
  576/2 = 288 occupants
  capacity minimum

- *With more than 500 occupants, 3 exits are required per § 1006.2.1.1. Exits should be apportioned based on whether they are a "main" exit or one of the other exits.*

Public Way

- *Since there are more than 300 occupants, one exit must be a "main exit" and sized to accommodate at least one-half of the occupant load per § 1029.2.*

Required Exit Capacities:

Main exit:	*288*
Exit 2:	*144*
Exit 3:	*144*
Total:	*576*

- *Note that the two exits other than the main exit must be sized to handle at least 50% of the occupant load.*

§ 1029.12.1 addresses seating at tables and chairs, whether loose or fixed.

Aisle Accessways

§ 1029.12.1 divides areas with tables and chairs into aisles and aisle accessways.

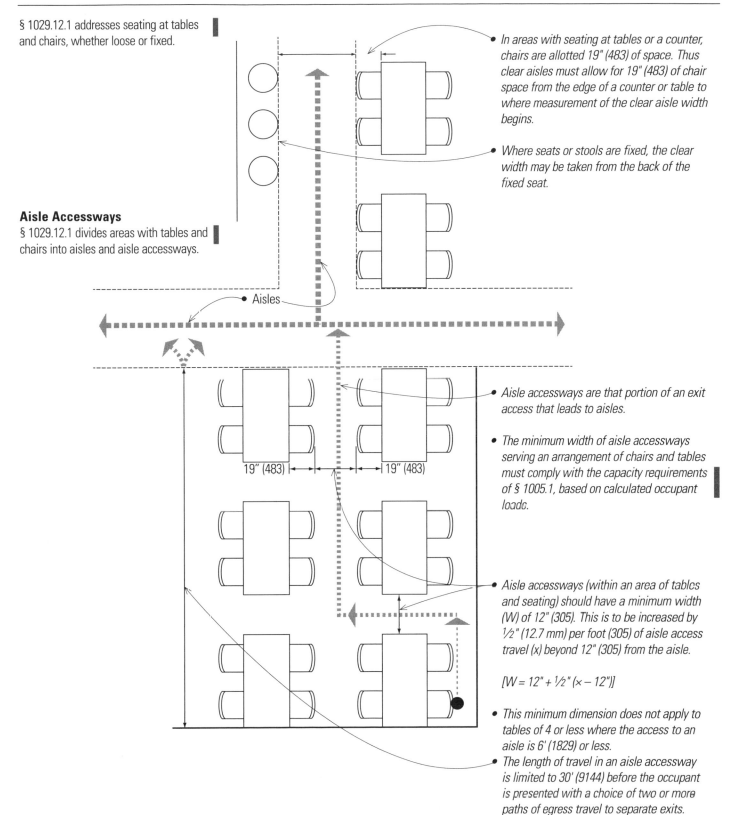

Aisles

19" (483)   19" (483)

- In areas with seating at tables or a counter, chairs are allotted 19" (483) of space. Thus clear aisles must allow for 19" (483) of chair space from the edge of a counter or table to where measurement of the clear aisle width begins.

- Where seats or stools are fixed, the clear width may be taken from the back of the fixed seat.

- Aisle accessways are that portion of an exit access that leads to aisles.

- The minimum width of aisle accessways serving an arrangement of chairs and tables must comply with the capacity requirements of § 1005.1, based on calculated occupant loads.

- Aisle accessways (within an area of tables and seating) should have a minimum width (W) of 12" (305). This is to be increased by ½" (12.7 mm) per foot (305) of aisle access travel (x) beyond 12" (305) from the aisle.

  $$[W = 12" + \tfrac{1}{2}" (x - 12")]$$

- This minimum dimension does not apply to tables of 4 or less where the access to an aisle is 6' (1829) or less.

- The length of travel in an aisle accessway is limited to 30' (9144) before the occupant is presented with a choice of two or more paths of egress travel to separate exits.

Residential R-2 occupancies that make use of the single exit provisions of Tables 1006.3.2(1) and 1006.3.2(2) and Group R-3 occupancies (which require only a single means of egress) are required by § 1030 to have egress openings for emergency escape and rescue. These are in addition to normal paths of egress leading out of rooms in such occupancies. These are to provide a way out of sleeping rooms for the occupants and a way into those rooms for rescue personnel in emergencies.

We construe § 1006.3 and § 1030, when read together, to not require emergency escape and rescue windows in fully sprinklered R-2 buildings that have two exits on floors below the fourth story where dwelling sleeping units are located.

Basements and all sleeping rooms below the fourth story in buildings that have only a single exit are to have at least one emergency escape and rescue opening in each sleeping room. These are to open directly onto a public street, public alley, yard, or court. There are exceptions to this requirement applicable to certain occupancies, but we recommend provision of such openings in all residential occupancies where it is practical.

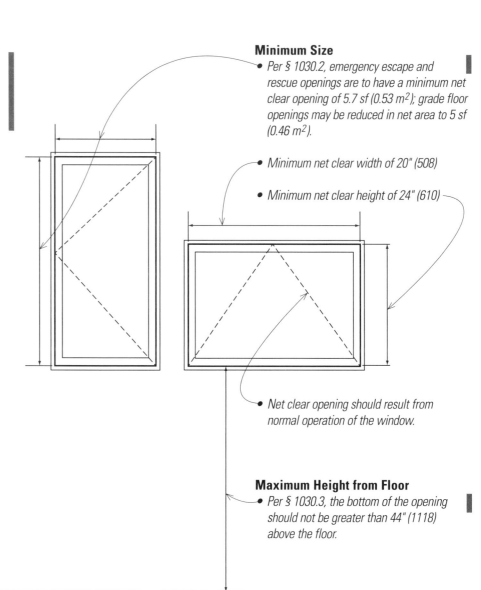

Minimum Size
- Per § 1030.2, emergency escape and rescue openings are to have a minimum net clear opening of 5.7 sf (0.53 m^2); grade floor openings may be reduced in net area to 5 sf (0.46 m^2).

- Minimum net clear width of 20" (508)

- Minimum net clear height of 24" (610)

- Net clear opening should result from normal operation of the window.

Maximum Height from Floor
- Per § 1030.3, the bottom of the opening should not be greater than 44" (1118) above the floor.

11
Accessibility

Chapter 11 regulates the design and construction of "facilities for accessibility to individuals with disabilities." The terms of federal law and of state code modifications often expand coverage of local codes far beyond the basic code requirements. The designer must understand that many states have significantly different, locally developed accessibility requirements; in some cases, states have rewritten Chapter 11 completely. The basic code provisions should therefore be reviewed carefully against federal criteria as well as state and local amendments. The likelihood of significant and extensive local variation from the basic IBC is higher for this chapter than for any other in the code. The designer must be certain to use the correct accessibility code for a specific project.

The provisions for existing buildings, which used to be in Chapter 34 of the IBC, have been removed from the IBC. The provisions for accessibility to existing buildings are now found in the *International Existing Building Code* (IEBC). The existing building provisions are therefore not examined in this chapter. Also, we believe that several portions of the "Supplementary Accessibility Requirements" of the Code Appendix E apply in most conditions covered by the ADA or local amendments; we will therefore discuss Appendix E as part of this chapter. The designer should verify that status of the adoption of this Appendix by the local AHJ. Because of the interrelationship of scoping provisions, the authors assume that Appendix E will be adopted. We will therefore treat Chapter 11 as containing both the body of the Code and the Appendix.

Making buildings accessible to persons with disabilities is an increasingly important design requirement. It has become an even greater issue since the passage of the Americans with Disabilities Act (ADA) in 1990.

The model codes have long incorporated requirements for accessibility that are intended to be coordinated with the requirements of the ADA. However, the designer must remember that plan review by the building official is only for compliance with the provisions of the building code. The model codes are typically not considered to be equivalent substitutions for the ADA and compliance with the code is no guarantee of compliance with the ADA. Therefore, no designer should rely solely on the code to determine access-compliance requirements. Every project should also be carefully reviewed against the provisions of the ADA to assure compliance with federal law. Remember that any approval by the building official has no bearing on the applicability of the ADA. The building official does not review for ADA compliance and has neither authority nor responsibility to enforce this federal law. The ADA is enforced only through legal action and obtaining a permit is no guarantee of ADA compliance.

Note also that a new version of the ADA Accessibility Guidelines [2010 ADA Standards for Accessible Design (2010 ADA Standards)] has been published by the Department of Justice and the Access Board, which went into effect for mandatory application on March 15, 2012. The new technical criteria contained in the 2010 ADA Standards are generally well-coordinated with the aplicable reference standard, ICC A117.1. However, we recommend designers carefully review the IBC, ICC A117.1, and the 2010 ADA Standards to help assure accessibility compliance both for scoping and for technical requirements.

The code basis for access clearances and reach ranges is primarily for people who use wheelchairs. It is important to remember that the definition of disability also includes sensory and cognitive impairments, not just mobility impairments. Designers must also accommodate people with visual impairments and people with hearing impairments. Provision for access by mobility-impaired people will accommodate most disabilities, but the designer must also be certain to accommodate other disabled groups, such as people of short stature, in a coordinated fashion. A design solution for one group of disabled people should not adversely impact another group with different disabilities.

Accessibility to buildings is monitored closely by a large number of advocacy groups. They review the provision of, or lack of access to, buildings on an ongoing basis. A challenge to the accessibility of a building is among the most likely post-occupancy code reviews that can happen after the completion of a project. Any decisions that lead to a lack of access are subject to scrutiny over the life of the project. Our advice is: If the applicability of accessibility requirements is in doubt, the designer and building owner should opt to provide the access.

The basic accessibility requirements in the code have been developed from the predecessor model codes and scoping criteria. The code requires that buildings and facilities be designed and constructed to be accessible in accordance with the code and the detailed dimensional requirements contained in the referenced standard, ICC A117.1, referenced hereafter simply as A117.1.

The provisions of Chapter 11 focus on scoping, telling the designer and building official where provisions are to apply and in what quantities. For example, scoping sets forth such items as the number of required accessible rooms in hotel accommodations. The dimensions and technical requirements for such accessible hotel rooms are contained in A117.1. The designer must therefore have a current reference copy of A117.1 to be able to comply with the access requirements of the code. It is critical that you are using the currently referenced 2009 version of A117.1 as it is much changed from prior editions.

While designers should read and familiarize themselves thoroughly with the detailed requirements of A117.1, we will only touch on small areas of that standard here. A117.1 has a strong resemblance to the 2010 ADA Standards. However, we reiterate that the designer must consult both the locally modified code and the ADA to be certain of compliance.

The designer must also be completely familiar with the Americans with Disabilities Act (ADA), particularly the 2010 ADA Standards for Accessible Design (2010 ADA Standards). The 2010 ADA Standards set forth the fundamental federal design criteria for access. The ADA is a civil-rights law and applies under different circumstances than the code. It also may be applied retroactively under different circumstances than the code as well. It should be presumed from the beginning of a design project that both the 2010 ADA Standards and the code, as amended by local code modifications, apply to the project. A detailed comparison of the applicability and potential conflicts between the federal guidelines, local modifications and the code is beyond the scope of this book, but the designer must not only review the application of the code to projects but also the 2010 ADA Standards and local modifications as well.

Designers should pay particular attention to the requirements for door clearances and landings contained in A117.1. The requirements for clear and level landings and for clearances at the latch side of doors depend on the direction of approach to the door by persons with mobility impairments. The provision of space in the floor plan for these clearances is essential during the initial design phases of a project.

The designer must consider the approach configuration and the side of approach to determine which criteria to apply. If these clearances are not provided at the outset of planning it will be very difficult to provide such clearances later without major revisions to the floor plans. It is essential that such clearance criteria for doors and for Type A and B dwelling units, designed and constructed to be in accordance with A117.1, be understood early and incorporated into the plans.

- *Study the diagrams in A117.1 to understand the criteria for provision of required clearances. The clearances are to allow wheelchairs to clear door swings, to allow maneuvering around obstacles, and to allow wheelchairs to pivot and turn.*
- *It is acceptable to demonstrate alternative means of providing such maneuvering room, but the designer must understand wheelchair movements and design criteria in the same way one understands how a car moves through a parking lot or a truck approaches a loading dock. The same understanding should be gained of reach ranges for people seated in wheelchairs to allow the designer to correctly place operating switches or equipment.*

- *Be especially conscious of ranges of dimensions for accessible reach to things like light switches and door handles [e.g., side reach range is 15" (380) to 48" (1229)]. Items located beyond the reach range are considered code violations, even if only by a fraction of an inch. There are no construction tolerances that allow placing things outside of a permitted dimensional range.*

Accessible Route

The intent of an accessible route is to allow persons with disabilities to enter a building, get into and out of spaces where desired functions occur, and then exit the building. It is also necessary that support functions such as toilets, telephones, and drinking fountains be accessible. The goal is the integration of people with disabilities into the full function of a facility with a minimum of atypical treatment. Such unequal treatment could be considered to include provision of separate routes or auxiliary aids such as wheelchair lifts.

The concept of universal design is useful to keep in mind. The goal of universal design is to make facilities accessible to the widest possible range of people, regardless of mobility, physical ability, size, age, or cognitive skills.

The designer should bear in mind all types of disabilities when designing accessible routes. Projections may affect people with visual impairments and, of course, changes in grade, such as ramps or steps, impact people in wheelchairs.

The requirements for areas of refuge, discussed in Chapter 10, recognize that getting people with disabilities into a building under normal conditions may not allow them to exit under emergency circumstances. See the provisions for areas of refuge in § 1009. ▌

- The basis of accessible design is the idea of an accessible route. The definition of **accessible route** in Chapter 2 uses the words **continuous** and **unobstructed**. Any usable path for people with disabilities must not cut them off from the spaces or elements of the building that they have a right to use. This route is often referred to in other code sections or access documents as the path of travel.

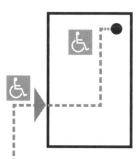

- Ramps shallower than 1:12 and complying with the technical requirements of A117.1 are acceptable for use in accessible routes.
- A sloped surface with a pitch shallower than 1:20 is not considered a ramp. It is acceptable to use such slopes in accessible routes if level landing areas are provided at doors or changes in direction, as required by A117.1.

- The path of travel extends to the edge of the project site. People with disabilities often rely on public transit, and it must be possible to traverse the site and reach the building from pedestrian access points.

Dwelling Unit Types

There are three broad categories of accessible dwelling units addressed in the code. The definitions for these units are contained in Chapter 2. The definitions all refer back to ICC A117.1 for the descriptions of the detailed requirements for each type of unit. The units can be generally described, in descending order of accessibility as follows:

- Accessible units (with the "A" always capitalized), which are fully wheelchair accessible at the time of first occupancy;
- "Type A" units, which are adaptable units, with clearances for wheelchair access built-in and provisions such as blocking for grab bars to allow them to be modfied into Accessible units;
- "Type B" units, which match Fair Housing Act requirements and are wheelchair friendly but not accessible. They generally allow tighter spaces than Accessible or Type A units.

These requirements impact the space requirements for single-level multi-family housing and multiple-level buildings where elevators are provided. Designers of Group-R occupancies should study the scoping requirements carefully. Note also that while these code revisions are intended to conform to Federal Fair Housing ACT requirements, those requirements should be reviewed as well, so that the designer may be assured of compliance with both federal and local requirements.

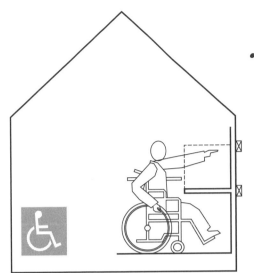

Type A dwelling unit

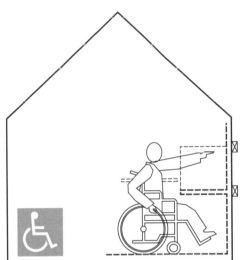

Type B dwelling unit

- Definitions and requirements for Type A and B dwelling units have been incorporated into the code to bring the code requirements in line with the Federal Fair Housing Act Guidelines (FFHA). The designer has the option under given conditions of providing fully accessible units per A117.1 (Accessible units) or adaptable units (Type A or B) in residential projects. The scoping requirements for these dwelling units are contained in § 1107. The plan dimension requirements are essentially the same for both Accessible and Type A units, as clearances must be provided for future accessibility in adaptable units. Type D units are intended to match the Fair Housing requirements and are not held to the higher levels that Accessible and Type A units must meet.

- Certain accessibility features, such as grab bars, lowered counters, and clear space under cabinets, may be provided later in adaptable units. Construction features, such as convertible cabinetry and wall blocking for grab bars, are necessary so that the conversion to an accessible unit may be made readily, without major remodeling.

§ 1103.1 states that the requirements for accessibility apply both to buildings and to the sites where they are located. The accessible route is typically considered to extend to the boundaries of the site. Every path of travel may not need to be accessible, but a readily located accessible route must be provided inside and outside of the building and on the site.

Exceptions

§ 1103.2 specifies the exceptions to access requirements, and these exceptions are distributed among sections in other chapters of the code. The exceptions apply in general to low occupancy spaces and those where provision of access would be disproportionate to the utility of the space. However, it is also worth noting once again that the exceptions noted in the code may not correspond to federal or local laws and regulations, and must be carefully reviewed.

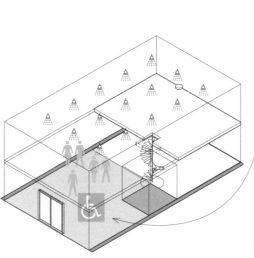

Specific exceptions to accessibility in the IBC include the following items:

- Individual workstations are not required to be accessible but must be on an accessible route. Thus aisles leading to individual workstations must be of accessible width. Note that typically areas under 300 sf (30 m²) in area and more than 7" (178) above adjacent areas are exempt. This exception does not apply to raised courtroom stations in accordance with § 1108.4.1.4.
- Raised or lowered areas in places of religious worship that are less than 300 sf (30 m²) in area and located 7" (178) or more above or below the finished floor and used primarily for the performance of religious ceremonies are not required to comply with this chapter.
- Detached residences, such as single-family homes and duplexes, along with their sites and facilities, are not required to be accessible.
- Utility buildings (Group-U occupancies) not open to the general public or required to have accessible parking are exempt from accessibility requirements.
- Where a day-care facility is part of a dwelling unit, only the portion of the structure used for day care is required to be accessible. The converse, however, is also that where day-care facilities are provided in dwelling units the day-care portion must be accessible.

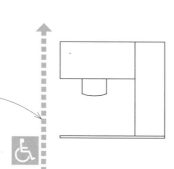

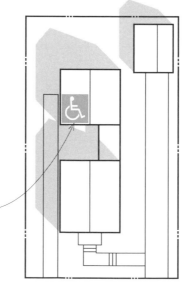

- Construction sites need not be accessible.
- Raised areas, areas with limited access, equipment spaces, and single-occupant structures, such as guard stations, catwalks, crawl spaces, elevator pits, and tollbooths, are not required to be accessible.
- R-1 occupancies with 5 or fewer sleeping rooms that are also the residence of the proprietor are not required to be accessible.
- Per § 1107.6.2.1, live/work units constructed per § 419 the nonresidential portion of the unit is to be accessible. The residential portion of the unit is to be evaluated as a residential unit in accordance with § 1107.6.2 and § 1107.7.
- Walk-in coolers and freezers are not required to be accessible where they are intended for employee use only. Local access requirements should be verified with the local AHJ.

When dealing with accessibility requirements, especially for new construction, the designer's first assumption should be that all areas and all functions used by the public should be accessible. It is also a prudent assumption that all employee areas should be accessible to people with disabilities, except for specific service areas not typically occupied by either the public or employees.

- Because of the potential for local or federal variations, use the exceptions with great caution!
- Note that many temporary facilities, such as tents or public-use facilities, are not exempt from access requirements. These are covered by the wording of the first scoping paragraph, § 1103.1, that mentions buildings and structures, temporary or permanent.

§ 1104 requires that at least one accessible route be provided at site arrival points, from public transportation stops, accessible parking and loading zones, public streets, and sidewalks within the site. The only exception to this requirement is for a large site where elements are spread out along a vehicular access route that is not in itself accessible. This assumes that all people on the site are moving from one location to another by vehicle and that there is not a separate inaccessible pedestrian route for people without disabilities. The wording seems to require that an accessible route must be provided where a pedestrian path is included as part of the site path-of-travel system. This is consistent with the idea that persons with disabilities receive equal treatment as pedestrians. Note that this exception does not apply to buildings where there are Type B units; in such cases, an accessible route from site arrival points would need to be provided. Note that § 1110 has been added to Chapter 11, covering access to recreational facilities.

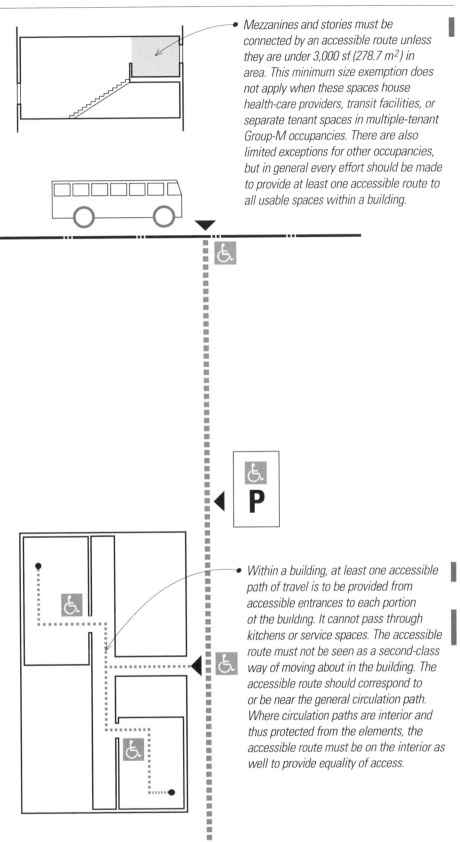

Mezzanines and stories must be connected by an accessible route unless they are under 3,000 sf (278.7 m²) in area. This minimum size exemption does not apply when these spaces house health-care providers, transit facilities, or separate tenant spaces in multiple-tenant Group-M occupancies. There are also limited exceptions for other occupancies, but in general every effort should be made to provide at least one accessible route to all usable spaces within a building.

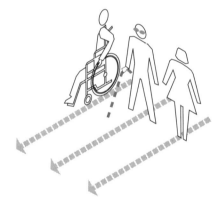

Within a building, at least one accessible path of travel is to be provided from accessible entrances to each portion of the building. It cannot pass through kitchens or service spaces. The accessible route must not be seen as a second-class way of moving about in the building. The accessible route should correspond to or be near the general circulation path. Where circulation paths are interior and thus protected from the elements, the accessible route must be on the interior as well to provide equality of access.

ACCESSIBLE ENTRANCES

§ 1105 requires that at least one main entrance, and at least 60% of the total of all entrances, to a building must be accessible. Where there are separate tenant space entries the same criteria apply to each tenant space. The only exceptions are entrances not required to be accessible and service entrances or loading docks that are not the only entry to a building or tenant space. Where service entrances are the only entrance they are to be accessible.

When entrances to the building serve accessible adjunct facilities, such as accessible parking areas, passenger loading zones, transit facilities, or public streets, then at least one of each of the entries serving those functions must be accessible. The design of the accessible route and entrance systems cannot require people with disabilities to traverse long distances to get from one accessible facility to another.

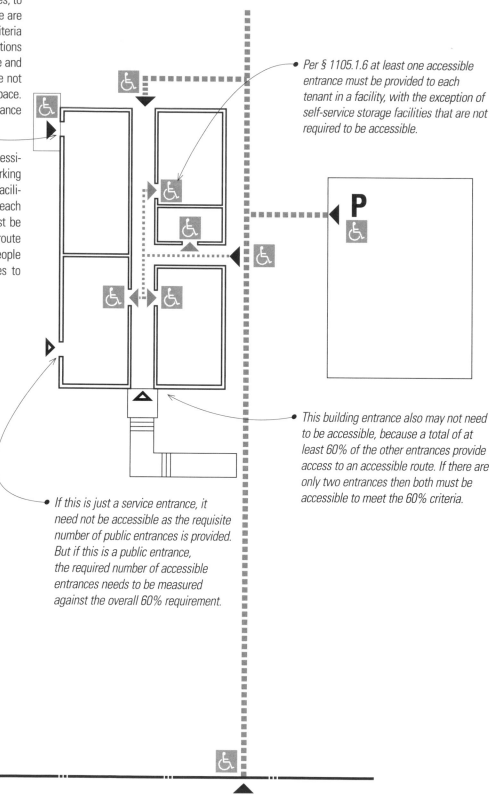

Per § 1105.1.6 at least one accessible entrance must be provided to each tenant in a facility, with the exception of self-service storage facilities that are not required to be accessible.

This building entrance also may not need to be accessible, because a total of at least 60% of the other entrances provide access to an accessible route. If there are only two entrances then both must be accessible to meet the 60% criteria.

If this is just a service entrance, it need not be accessible as the requisite number of public entrances is provided. But if this is a public entrance, the required number of accessible entrances needs to be measured against the overall 60% requirement.

The requirements of § 1106 highlight the nature of how Chapter 11 operates. The requirements for parking are stated in terms of quantities, not as criteria for how to lay out accessible stalls. The stall dimensions are contained in the reference standard, A117.1. The scoping requirements for parking are per Table 1106.1, which stipulates the number of accessible parking stalls to be provided based on the total number of parking spaces provided.

- The accessible stalls are to be included in the total parking count, but they must be set aside for use by people with disabilities. The basic criterion for residential occupancies is that at least 2% of parking spaces be accessible. Other occupancies vary significantly. Parking requirements at rehabilitation and outpatient facilities are higher, being 20% of the total. This recognizes that the population of users of such facilities is much more likely to have disabilities that would require accessible parking.
- For every 6 accessible spaces, or fraction thereof, one space is to be a van-accessible space. This is a space with a larger access aisle than the typical accessible parking space. For small parking areas, where only one space is provided, it must be van accessible. The van space counts toward the total of required accessible spaces. All accessible parking counts in the grand total of parking spaces, both accessible and nonaccessible.

- § 1106.2 sets out requirements for accessible parking for Groups I-1, R-1, R-2, R-3, and R-4.

1. In Group R-2, R-3, and R-4 occupancies that are required to have "Accessible," "Type A," or "Type B" dwelling units or sleeping units, at least 2% but not less than one of each type of parking space provided must be accessible. By "type" we presume that if spaces are associated with each type of unit, then accessible spaces must be provided for each group of parking spaces assigned to each unit type. This is more clearly explained in Item 3 below.
2. In Group I-1 and R-1 occupancies, accessible parking is to be provided in accordance with Table 1106.1.
3. Where at least one parking space is provided for each dwelling unit or sleeping unit, at least one accessible parking space is to be provided for each "Accessible" and "Type A" unit.
4. Where parking is provided within or beneath a building, accessible parking spaces shall also be provided within or beneath the building. This is an expression of the idea of equal treatment for all persons regardless of disability, which is fundamental to how accessibility requirements are meant to be applied.

8' (2440) minimum width for access aisles adjacent to van-accessible spaces; may be 5' (1525) wide if the van parking space is 11' (3350), which results in the same overall width.

8' (2440) minimum width for parking spaces

5' (1525) minimum width for access aisles

Access aisles are considered part of the accessible route.

Parking is to be located such that the accessible route of travel is the shortest possible path from the parking area to the nearest accessible building entrance. Note that this requirement can be construed to place accessible parking immediately adjacent to an entrance no matter how the circulation in the parking area is configured. The definition of "possible" can be the subject for debate and subject to non-uniform interpretation by building officials and disabled access advocates. For buildings with multiple accessible entrances and adjacent parking, accessible parking is to be dispersed in such a way as to have accessible parking nearby each accessible entrance.

- *Example: Parking for 400 vehicles; 8 accessible spaces minimum; 2 of the 8 must be van-accessible since there are more than 6 accessible spaces required. When the triggering number is exceeded by any fractional amount the requirement rounds to the next whole number of spaces.*

Accessible passenger loading zones are to be provided at medical facilities where people stay longer than 24 hours, whether as long-term residents or as medical patients. Loading zones are also required when valet parking services are provided.

Accessible passenger loading zones must have a minimum overhead clearance of 114" (3658).

5' (1525) minimum width for adjacent access aisle at passenger loading zones.

DWELLING UNITS AND SLEEPING UNITS

The intent of the dwelling unit and sleeping unit requirements is that hotels, motels, multifamily dwellings, and Group I institutional uses be accessible to the maximum extent that is practical, and in quantities that will serve the anticipated demand by people with disabilities. The determination of the quantities required is not always empirically based, but the designer must use the scoping required by the code to design the facility. Common-use and recreational facilities open to all residents or to the public are to be accessible as well.

Accessible Dwelling Units and Sleeping Units

§ 1107.2 divides accessible dwelling units and sleeping units into Accessible, Type A, and Type B units. We will use the word "units" here to include both dwelling and sleeping units unless indicated otherwise. Sleeping units are defined in Chapter 2 as rooms or spaces in which people sleep. This could include dormitory, hotel or motel guest rooms or suites, or nursing home rooms.

Accessible Spaces

The requirements of § 1107.3 arise from the requirements for accessible routes. Rooms and spaces that serve accessible units and that are available to the general public, or for the use of the residents in general, are to be accessible. This includes such areas as toilet and bathing rooms, kitchens, living and dining areas, and exterior spaces, including patios, terraces, and balconies. There is an exception related to recreational facilities that we will discuss later in commentary about § 1110.2.

Accessible Route

§ 1107.4 requires that at least one accessible route connect the primary building or site entrance with the front entry to each accessible dwelling unit. An accessible route should also connect the accessible units to areas that serve the units, such as laundry rooms or community rooms. One exception to this provision applies on steep sites where buildings with dwelling units are connected by nonaccessible vehicular routes, similar to the provisions of § 1104.1. In such cases, accessible parking at each accessible facility is acceptable.

There are a number of exceptions to § 1107.4 which exempt certain upper-level areas from access requirements when accessible elements are available on an accessible level.

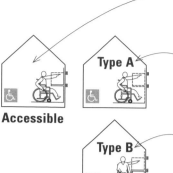

Accessible

Type A

Type B

- Accessible units are described in detail in ICC A117.1. They are to be laid out and constructed to be wheelchair accessible at the time of first occupancy.
- "Type A" units are also described in detail in A117.1. They are "adaptable" units, with clearances for wheelchair access built-in and provisions, such as blocking for grab bars, to allow them to be modified into Accessible units.
- "Type B" unit criteria in A117.1 are intended to be consistent with the intent of the criteria of the U.S. Department of Housing and Urban Development (HUD) Fair Housing Accessibility Guidelines. Type B units are intended to supplement, not replace, Accessible units or Type A units. These units are wheelchair friendly, but not as fully accessible as the other two types of units.

- Decks and patios in Type B units that are usually dropped at exterior doors for drainage and weather protection need not be accessible if the step is less than 4" (102) and the exterior area has an impervious paving surface.

  Note that this exception does not apply to Type A dwelling units. Type A units are to be accessible; Type B units are adaptable. The code assumes that when a Type B unit is adapted the access can be provided at the time of adaptation.

- Per § 1107.4, in Group I-3 facilities, an accessible route is not required to connect stories or mezzanines where Accessible units, all common-use areas serving Accessible units, and all public-use areas are on an accessible level.
- **In other than Group R-2 dormitory housing provided by places of education**, in Group R-2 facilities with Accessible units complying with § 1107.6.2.3.1, an accessible route is not required to connect stories or mezzanines where Accessible units, all common-use areas serving Accessible units, and all public-use areas are on an accessible route.
- In Group R-1, an accessible route is not required to connect stories or mezzanines within individual units, provided the accessible level meets the provisions for Accessible units and sleeping accommodations for two persons minimum and a toilet facility are provided on that level.
- In congregate residences in Groups R-3 and R-4, an accessible route is not required to connect stories or mezzanines where Accessible or Type B units, all common-use areas serving Accessible and Type B units, and all public-use areas serving Accessible and Type B units are on an accessible route.

Group I Occupancies

Group I occupancies have detailed special requirements in § 1107.5 that recognize the institutional nature of this occupancy group. Typically, the requirements for the number of accessible spaces are higher than for other occupancies as these facilities have a higher proportion of people with disabilities than other occupancies. Where facilities specialize in treatment of conditions affecting mobility, up to 100% of the rooms may be required to be accessible. The designer should verify the percentage of Accessible and Type B units required by § 1107.5 based on the prospective use of an I occupancy.

Building with more than 50 dwelling units

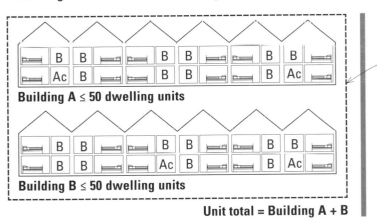

Building A ≤ 50 dwelling units

Building B ≤ 50 dwelling units

Unit total = Building A + B

Group R Occupancies

The trigger for various scoping requirements in Group R occupancies is the number of sleeping spaces and the number of dwelling units. A percentage of each type of multi-unit residential facility must be accessible, with the number and diversity of the types of accommodation increasing with the size and type of the residential facility. These provisions do not apply to individual single-family residences, but do apply to single family residences where there are 4 or more such units per building.

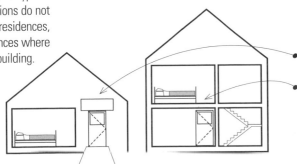

- *§ 1107.6.1.2 requires every dwelling unit to be a Type B dwelling unit in residential occupancies, such as Group R-2 and R-3 occupancies, where there are more than four dwelling units. See also the comment at left regarding I occupancies.*

- *As buildings get larger, Type A dwelling units are required. For example, in Group R-2 occupancies containing more than 20 dwelling units, at least 2%, but not less than one, of the dwelling units must be a Type A dwelling unit. Because they have a higher degree of accessibility, Type A units may be substituted for Type B units, but not vice-versa.*

- *Per § 1107.6.1.1, as the number of units increases, the number of required Accessible units increases.*

- *Accessible dwelling and sleeping units are to be provided per Table 1107.6.1.1. Where a building contains **more** than 50 dwelling units or sleeping units, the number of Accessible units are to be determined per building.*

- *Where each building in a group of buildings contains 50 or fewer dwelling units or sleeping units, **all** dwelling units and sleeping units on the site are to be considered together when determining the total number of Accessible units. Accessible units are to be dispersed among the various classes of units.*

- *Note that additional accessible features such as roll-in showers are required as the number of units increases. Thus Table 1007.6.1.1 requires 2 Accessible units for up to 50 total units, with no roll-in shower requirements. However, when there are between 51 and 75 units, a roll-in shower is to be provided in one of the 4 required accessible units; the other 3 units cannot be provided with a roll-in shower.*

- *To apply the numerous exceptions to these requirements, the designer must further understand the distinction for Type B dwelling unit requirements, based on whether the units in question are ground-floor units or multistory units.*

- *A ground-floor dwelling unit has a primary entrance and habitable space at grade.*

- *A multistory unit refers to a single dwelling unit with multiple floors where there is habitable space or a bathroom space (which is not normally considered habitable space) on more than one floor level. Note that the definition of **multistory** does not refer to a single-level dwelling unit located above grade in a multistory building.*

General Exceptions

The exceptions for accessible dwelling units depend on specific circumstances and do not apply equally to Type A and B dwelling units. The exceptions are:

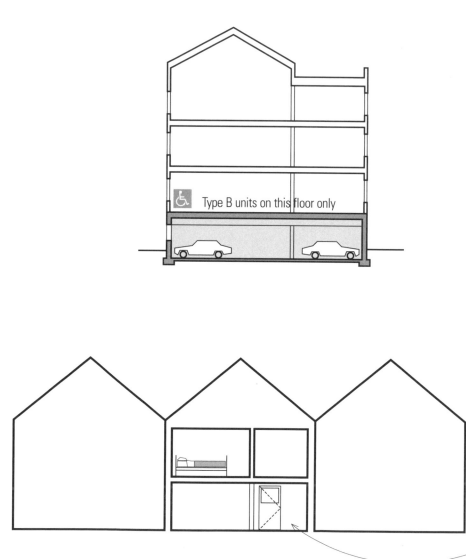

Type B units on this floor only

1. In walk-up type buildings, where no elevator is provided, neither Type A nor Type B dwelling units need be provided on floors other than the ground floor. The number of Type A dwelling units is to be provided based on the total of all units in the building, not just at the ground floor. It should be assumed that in buildings with more than 4 and less than 20 units, the ground-floor units should all be Type B units.

2. In podium-type buildings without elevators, where the dwelling units occur only above the ground floor, only the dwelling units on the lowest floor need comply with the requirements of this section. Thus, on the lowest level of a building with 4 to 20 units, all of the units on the lowest level of dwelling units need be Type B units, but only on that level. When the total dwelling unit count exceeds 20, then Type A dwelling units would need to be provided as required in this section, but again only on the lowest dwelling unit level.

3. A multilevel dwelling unit without an elevator is not required to comply with the requirements for Type B dwelling units. Thus, townhouse-style multilevel dwelling units are not required to be Type B units. When elevator service is provided to one floor of the unit, however, that floor must meet Type B requirements and a toilet facility provided. It is not stated that this facility requires access, but it should be designed as such. If an elevator accesses any level serving a multilevel unit, that level must meet the requirements noted above.

• To meet the intent of accessibility provisions, we recommend that the ground floors of townhouses that are on an accessible route be made adaptable, and that an adaptable, or fully accessible, powder room be provided for use by guests on the ground floor.

4. Where there are multiple buildings on a site that do not have elevators, and the site has varying grades, then the need to provide Type B dwelling units should be examined in the context of the entire site.

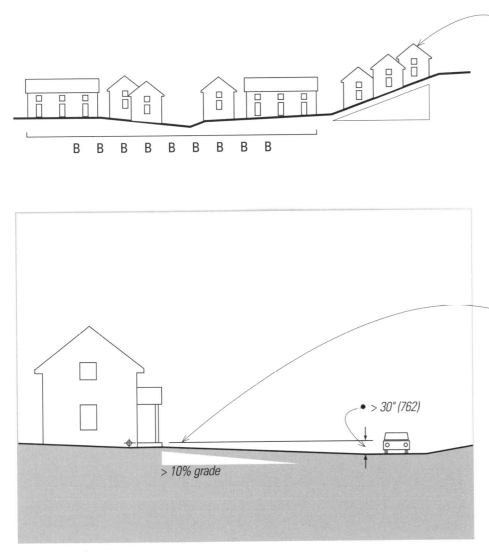

B B B B B B B B B

> 30" (762)

> 10% grade

- Where site grades prior to development are 10% or steeper, then the units on that slope are exempt from the ground-floor Type B dwelling unit requirement. This recognizes that under such site conditions, it is unlikely that an accessible route can be easily provided.
- In no case, however, should the total number of Type B dwelling units be less than 20% of the total number of ground-floor dwelling units on the entire site. So even where the site is steeply sloped throughout, accessible route provisions must be made to satisfy the 20% minimum requirement.

5. Neither Type A nor Type B dwelling units need be provided where a site is susceptible to flooding and an accessible route cannot be provided such that the grade cannot be within 30" (762) of the floor within 50' (15 240) of the entry, or the grade exceeds 10% between the pedestrian or vehicular arrival point and the primary entrances of the units. This is very specific site criteria. This exception should be used with great caution as the conditions may be subject to design solution by site grading.

- The arcane and somewhat ambiguous nature of these and most other exceptions to accessibility provisions in this code and ADA Standards only reinforce our basic recommendation regarding provision of access in buildings. If it seems that access may be required by the code, then it should be provided. Provision of access does the building and occupants no harm, while its absence can lead to lack of access and legal problems that are best avoided.

§ 1108 establishes supplemental accessibility requirements for special occupancies. The wording "special occupancies" is somewhat misleading in that the occupancies discussed in this section are the same as those described throughout the code, and their occurrence in buildings is not unusual or special in most cases. However, the occupancies described in this section do not necessarily correspond to the conventional occupancy groups discussed in other parts of the code.

Assembly Areas

In assembly areas with fixed seating, the following provisions are required:

- *§ 1108.2.1 requires that services be accessible either by providing an accessible route or providing equal services on the accessible route as in nonaccessible areas.*
- *§ 1108.2.2–§ 1108.2.4 require wheelchair spaces to be provided based on the number of seats in the assembly occupancy per Table 1108.2.2.1, or as described in the noted sections.*
- *§ 1108.2.4 requires the wheelchair seating to be dispersed. The purpose of the dispersal is to provide a variety of sightlines and a variety of seating prices for people with disabilities to choose from.*
- *At least one companion seat complying with A117 shall be provided for each required wheelchair space.*

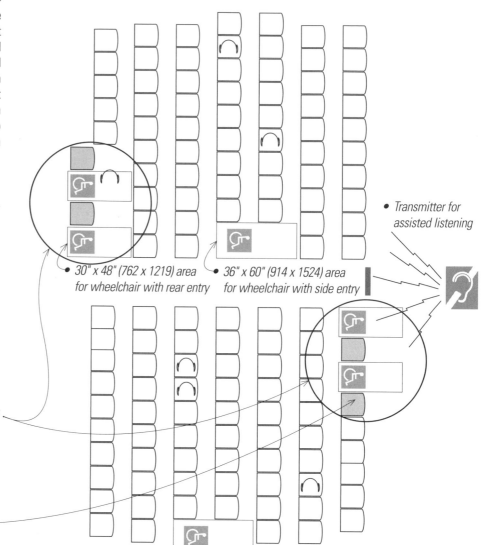

- *30" x 48" (762 x 1219) area for wheelchair with rear entry*
- *36" x 60" (914 x 1524) area for wheelchair with side entry*
- *Transmitter for assisted listening*

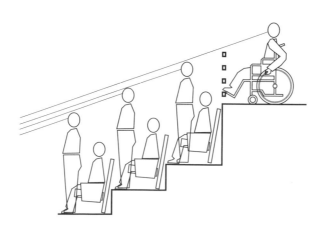

- *Sightlines should be carefully studied to allow wheelchair patrons to see the event. Sightlines for patrons in wheelchairs are the subject of much controversy. Especially at issue is providing views for wheelchair patrons over patrons who may be standing at their seats at sporting events, where fans often jump up in excitement during the event. This has been the subject of review by the courts in several cases. It is worth the designer's attention to the current legal status of seating dispersal and sightline access criteria as the design is prepared.*

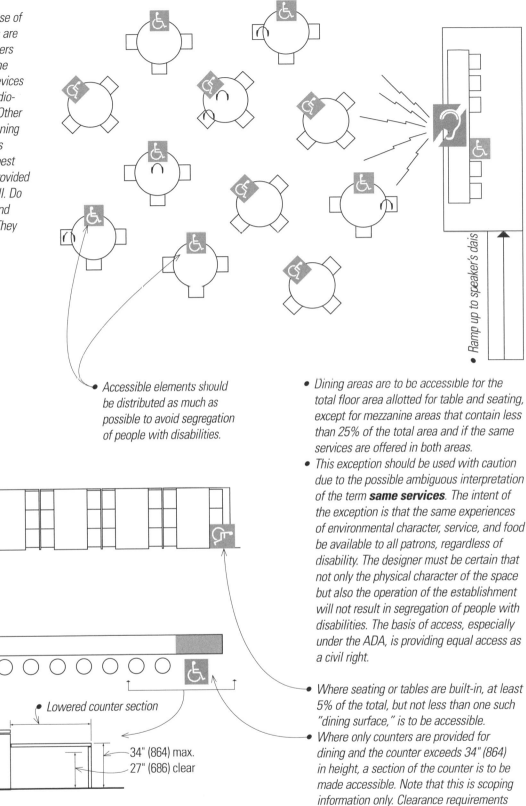

- In assembly areas where audible communications are integral to the use of the space, assistive listening devices are to be provided. The number of receivers is based on the seating capacity in the assembly area. Assistive listening devices are required for all spaces where audio-amplification systems are installed. Other than in courtrooms, an assistive listening system is not required where there is no audio amplification system. The best guideline is that if amplification is provided for some, it should be provided for all. Do not assume that assisted listening and wheelchair access always overlap. They often do not.

- Ramp up to speaker's dais

- Accessible elements should be distributed as much as possible to avoid segregation of people with disabilities.

- Dining areas are to be accessible for the total floor area allotted for table and seating, except for mezzanine areas that contain less than 25% of the total area and if the same services are offered in both areas.

- This exception should be used with caution due to the possible ambiguous interpretation of the term **same services**. The intent of the exception is that the same experiences of environmental character, service, and food be available to all patrons, regardless of disability. The designer must be certain that not only the physical character of the space but also the operation of the establishment will not result in segregation of people with disabilities. The basis of access, especially under the ADA, is providing equal access as a civil right.

- Lowered counter section

34" (864) max.

27" (686) clear

- Where seating or tables are built-in, at least 5% of the total, but not less than one such "dining surface," is to be accessible.
- Where only counters are provided for dining and the counter exceeds 34" (864) in height, a section of the counter is to be made accessible. Note that this is scoping information only. Clearance requirements for aisles between tables and chairs and at counters are contained in the reference standard A117.1.

Self-Service Storage Facilities

Self-service storage facilities are to provide accessible spaces per Table 1108.3. This requires that at least 5% of the spaces be accessible up to 200 spaces, and that 10 spaces plus 2% of the total over 200 spaces be accessible in larger facilities. The accessible units are to be dispersed among various classes of space provided, but the units may be located all in a single building or in multiple buildings. These requirements are similar in principle and application to the requirements for accessible parking, accessible seating, and accessible dwelling units in multiple-unit dwellings.

Other Features and Facilities

§ 1109 sets forth scoping provisions for access to various building parts and functions. These provisions apply to all areas except Accessible, Type A, and Type B dwelling units, which are to comply with A117.1. Where facilities for people without disabilities are provided, then essentially equal facilities are to be provided for people with disabilities. It is also possible and permissible to make all facilities usable by almost all potential users whether disabled or not. This is the underlying principle of what is called "universal design." Where there are multiple facilities, then percentages apply to determine the total number of such facilities to be provided. But in almost every case, at least one such facility is to be accessible as a base requirement. Where there is a distinctive use for facilities, such as bathing versus toilet facilities, or express checkout lines in addition to normal lines, then accessible facilities should be provided for each different function. The criteria in this section usually do not determine if the facility in question needs to be accessible, but only what criteria apply if accessibility is required by other parts of the code.

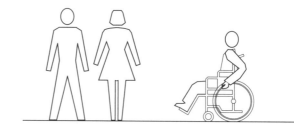

Equal access to facilities

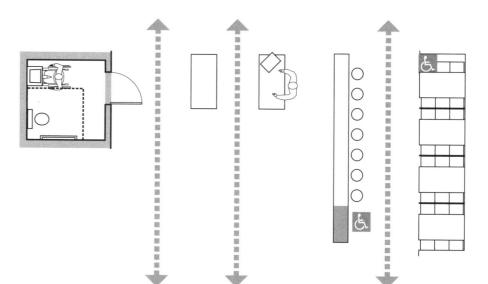

Toilet and Bathing Facilities

§ 1109.2 requires all toilet rooms and bathing facilities to be accessible. Where there are inaccessible floors that otherwise comply with the code, the only available toilet and bathing facilities should not be located on that level. At least one of each type of fixture, element, control, or dispenser in each toilet room is to be accessible. The facilities are to provide equal access to all of the functions provided in them.

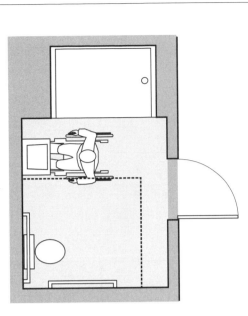

The exceptions for accessible toilet rooms and bathing facilities are very focused and very minimal:

1. *In private offices not meant for public use and meant for a single occupant, the toilet facilities need not be accessible, but provisions must be made for them to be adapted for use by a person with disabilities. Thus, the space layout must accommodate access in the initial floor plan.*

2. *These provisions do not apply to dwelling or sleeping units that are not required to be accessible in § 1107.*

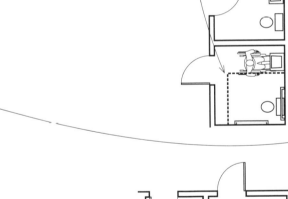

3. *Where multiple instances of single-user toilet facilities occur that are in excess of the plumbing requirements, then at least 50%, but not less than one in each cluster of such facilities, must be accessible. This is an instance of provision of equal access at each location of a group of facilities.*

4. *Where not more than one urinal is provided in a toilet room or bathing room, the urinal is not required to be accessible.*

5. *Toilet rooms that are part of a critical-care or intensive-care patient sleeping room need not be accessible. (This is on the theory that the patient will not be using the toilet room.)*

Family or Assisted-Use Toilet and Bathing Rooms

§ 1109.2.1 requires an accessible unisex toilet in assembly and mercantile occupancies when six or more water closets in total are required in the facility. This also applies to all recreational facilities where separate-sex facilities are provided, regardless of the count of water closets. This does not apply in facilities where there is only one bathing fixture in each separated-sex bathing room. These unisex facilities can be counted as part of the total number of fixtures to satisfy fixture-count requirements. Per § 1009.2.2 at least 5% of toilet compartments are to be accessible. For very large toilet rooms (>20 stalls) this will result in needing to provide two accessible stalls in such toilet rooms.

Sinks

§ 1109.3 requires 5% of sinks to be accessible, except for service sinks.

Kitchens

§ 1109.4 requires that, when provided in accessible space or rooms, kitchens, kitchenettes and wet bars must be accessible per the space criteria of A117.1.

Drinking Fountains

§ 1109.5 requires that 50% of the drinking fountains be accessible on floors where they are provided. Note that, given the wording of this section, this requirement will also apply for floors not otherwise considered or required to be accessible. Note also that each drinking fountain location has two fountains; one located at a low elevation for persons using wheelchairs and one higher for standing persons. A single drinking fountain with two separate spouts that complies with the requirements for people who use a wheelchair and for standing persons is permitted to be substituted for two separate drinking fountains.

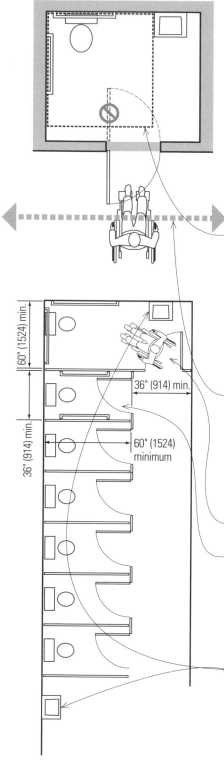

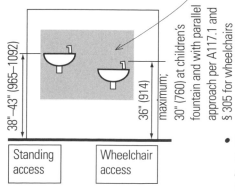

- Unisex facilities are to meet the criteria of A117.1 for space layout. Each facility is to contain only one water closet and one lavatory; however, in unisex bathing facilities, a shower or bathtub may be in the same room. Where lockers or similar storage units are provided in separate-sex bathing facilities, then accessible storage facilities are to be provided in the unisex bathing facilities as well.

- Separate-sex toilets with only two sanitary fixtures in each—one water closet and a lavatory or one water closet, a lavatory, and a urinal—may be considered as unisex toilet rooms.

- Unisex toilets will need to be larger than under previous editions of A117.1 and the old ADAAG. The new provisions of § 604 in both documents require a clear space of 60" x 56" (1525 x 1420) at the water closet. The lavatory may not be located in the clear space and the door swing should not impinge on this clear space unless a 30" x 48" (762 x 1219) clear floor space is provided beyond the arc of the door.

- Unisex facilities are to be on an accessible route. They are to be reasonably close to the separate-sex facilities, no more than one floor above or below them, and with the accessible route no more than 500' (15 m) in length. Practically speaking, in most instances, all of these facilities should be located adjacent to one another.

- When water closet compartments are provided, at least one should be accessible.

- When there are six or more toilet compartments in a toilet facility, then at least one compartment is to be an ambulatory-accessible stall per A117.1, in addition to the wheelchair-accessible compartment.

- Where an accessible lavatory is located within the accessible water closet compartment at least one additional accessible lavatory must be provided in the multicompartment toilet room outside the water closet compartment.

- Where plumbing fixtures and drinking fountains are designed primarily for use by children, the fixtures may be located using the children's provisions from A117.1.

Elevators

§ 1109.7 requires passenger elevators on an accessible route to be accessible and to comply with IBC Chapter 30.

5'-8" (1730) minimum

4'-3" (1295) minimum

3'-0" (915) minimum

Lifts

§ 1109.8 prohibits the use of platform (wheelchair) lifts for accessibility in new buildings except under certain specific conditions. Lifts are often not well maintained and are often nonfunctional in real-world applications. They should be avoided by designers and used only in these specific applications or in the retrofitting of older buildings when other modifications to provide access are not feasible.

Storage

Where fixed or built-in storage facilities, such as cabinets, lockers, and medicine cabinets are provided, § 1109.9 requires that 5% or at least one of each type of storage be accessible. When items such as coat hooks and folding shelves are provided in inaccessible facilities, then at least one of each shall also be provided in an accessible facility as well.

The allowable uses for lifts for accessibility are:
1. At stages, other raised performing areas, or speaker's platforms in Group A occupancies. This should be applied sparingly only where use of ramps or elevators is not feasible.
2. In assembly areas to provide accessible wheelchair seating required under § 1108.2.2. Again, this should be applied sparingly only where use of ramps or elevators is not feasible.
3. To provide an accessible route to spaces not accessible to the general public and with fewer than five occupants.
4. For an accessible route within a dwelling or sleeping unit that is required to be an Accessible unit, Type A unit, or Type B unit.
5. In courtrooms to provide access to such items as jury boxes, witness stands, and judge's benches.

6. For access to amusement rides.
7. To provide access to play structures or soft contained play structures.
8. An accessible route to team or player seating areas serving areas of sport activity.
9. An accessible route instead of gangways serving recreational boating facilities and fishing piers and platforms.
10. An accessible route where existing exterior site constraints make use of a ramp or a stair infeasible.

Detectable Warnings

A detectable warning is a defined term, typically meaning a pattern of raised truncated domes of specified size and spacing. § 1109.10 requires passenger transit platforms without guards to have detectable warnings at the edge to warn people with visual impairments of the falling hazard at that edge.

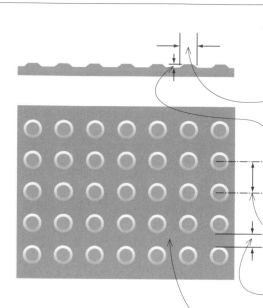

A117.1 regulates detectable warnings as follows:

- *§ 705.5 Truncated Domes. Detectable warning surfaces shall have truncated domes complying with § 705.5.*
- *§ 705.5.1 Size. Truncated domes shall have a base diameter of 0.9" (23 mm) minimum and 1.4 " (36 mm) maximum, and a top diameter of 50 percent minimum and 65 percent maximum of the base diameter.*
- *§ 705.5.2 Height. Truncated domes shall have a height of 0.2" (5.1 mm).*
- *§ 705.5.3 Spacing. Truncated domes shall have a center-to-center spacing of 1.6" (41 mm) minimum and 2.4" (61 mm) maximum, and a base-to-base spacing of 0.65" (16.5 mm) minimum, measured between the most adjacent domes on the grid.*
- *§ 705.5.4 Alignment. Truncated domes shall be aligned in a square grid pattern.*

- *Note that this provision does not apply to bus stops as they typically abut a curb rather than have the kind of drop that occurs at a train or subway platform.*

Seating at Tables, Counters, and Work Surfaces

§ 1109.11 is to be read in concert with § 1108.2.9.1. The scoping requires 5% of seats at fixed or built-in tables or work surfaces to be accessible if they are on an accessible route. As is typical for such provisions, these accessible facilities are to be dispersed in the building or the space containing these features.

Customer-Service Facilities

§ 1109.12 provides for customer-service facilities for public use on accessible routes. These facilities include dressing rooms, locker rooms, check-out aisles in stores, point-of-sales stations, food service lines, and waiting lines. They should be dispersed, and they should provide the same diversity of service facilities as those for nonaccessible facilities.

Controls, Operating Mechanisms, and Hardware

Where controls such as light switches, thermostats, window hardware, and convenience outlets are intended for operation by the occupant, § 1109.13 requires that they be accessible per the reach-range criteria contained in A117.1. These requirements apply to accessible spaces and along accessible routes. Only one window need be accessible in each space under these requirements. Also, accessible windows are not required in kitchens or bathrooms, recognizing the small size of these rooms and the potential access restrictions posed by fixtures and cabinets.

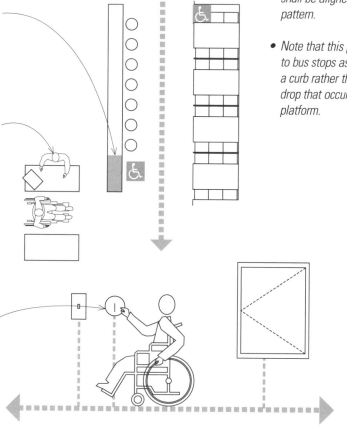

Recreational Facilities

To coordinate with the 2010 ADA Standards, a new section, §1110, has been created to gather together the prior and new provisions for accessibility to recreational facilities.

Illustrations of technical requirements are taken from ICC A117.1–09, the applicable technical reference for use with IBC Chapter 11. Note that there are sections of A117.1–09 that are not scoped in the IBC. One example of this are play structures. A117.1–09 has technical requirements for accessible play structures, but there is no reference to play structures in the IBC, even in this new section for recreational facilities.

The examples here illustrate the variety of facilities that are to be accessible to some degree. See the code for detailed descriptions of access requirements.

General

Recreational facilities are to be provided with accessible features in accordance with the requirements of § 1110.

Recreational Facilities for Dwellings

Recreational facilities that serve Group R-2, R-3, and R-4 occupancies are to be accessible.

- All recreational facilities serving Accessible units are to be accessible.
- 25% of each type of recreational facility serving Type A and Type B units are to be accessible.

Other Occupancies

Recreational facilities serving other than R-2, R-3, and R-4 occupancies are to be accessible per § 1110.

Areas of Sport Activity

Each area of sport activity is to be on an accessible route but is not required to be accessible except as provided for in § 1110.4.2 through § 1110.4.14, which set forth specific requirements or exclude some areas from accessibility requirements.

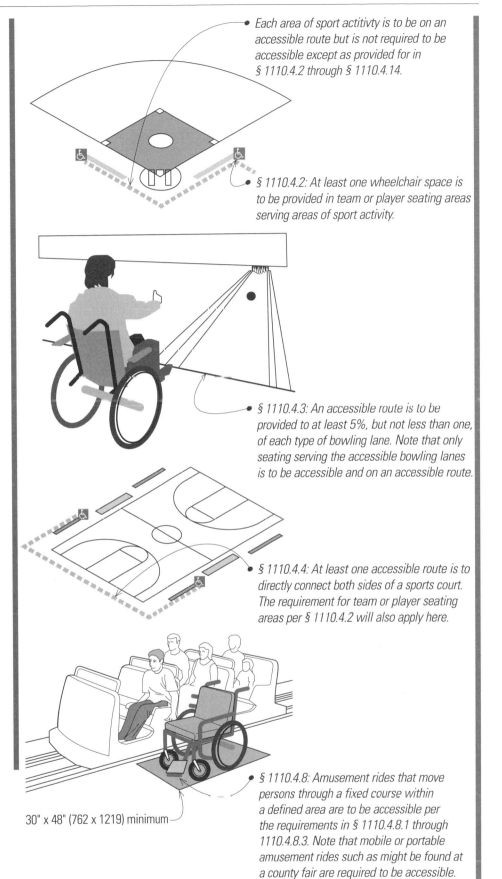

Each area of sport actitivty is to be on an accessible route but is not required to be accessible except as provided for in § 1110.4.2 through § 1110.4.14.

§ 1110.4.2: At least one wheelchair space is to be provided in team or player seating areas serving areas of sport activity.

§ 1110.4.3: An accessible route is to be provided to at least 5%, but not less than one, of each type of bowling lane. Note that only seating serving the accessible bowling lanes is to be accessible and on an accessible route.

§ 1110.4.4: At least one accessible route is to directly connect both sides of a sports court. The requirement for team or player seating areas per § 1110.4.2 will also apply here.

30" x 48" (762 x 1219) minimum

§ 1110.4.8: Amusement rides that move persons through a fixed course within a defined area are to be accessible per the requirements in § 1110.4.8.1 through 1110.4.8.3. Note that mobile or portable amusement rides such as might be found at a county fair are required to be accessible.

Areas of Sport Activity (continued)

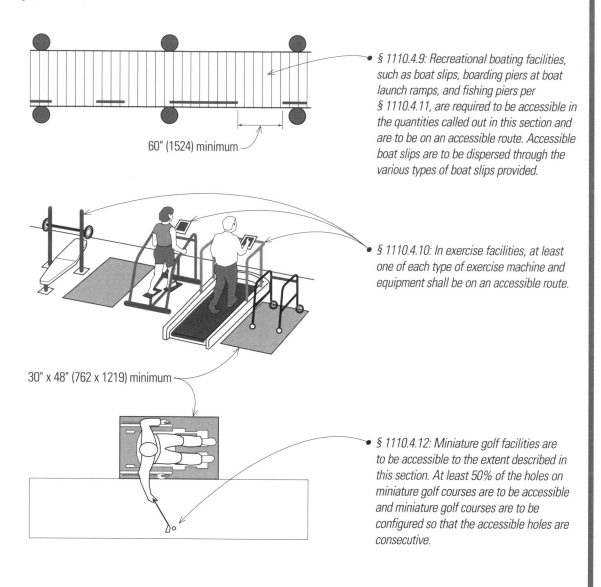

60" (1524) minimum

30" x 48" (762 x 1219) minimum

§ 1110.4.9: Recreational boating facilities, such as boat slips, boarding piers at boat launch ramps, and fishing piers per § 1110.4.11, are required to be accessible in the quantities called out in this section and are to be on an accessible route. Accessible boat slips are to be dispersed through the various types of boat slips provided.

§ 1110.4.10: In exercise facilities, at least one of each type of exercise machine and equipment shall be on an accessible route.

§ 1110.4.12: Miniature golf facilities are to be accessible to the extent described in this section. At least 50% of the holes on miniature golf courses are to be accessible and miniature golf courses are to be configured so that the accessible holes are consecutive.

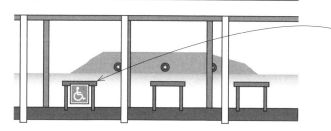

§ 1110.4.14: Where shooting facilities with firing positions are dseigned and constructed at a site, at least 5% but not less than one of each type of firing position is to be accessible and be on an accessible route.

Recreational Facilities that need <u>NOT</u> be Accessible

The following areas shown here are not required to be accessible or be on an accessible route, except for some areas that serve facilities which have a percentage of uses accessible, such as team or player seating for accessible bowling lanes per § 1110.4.3.

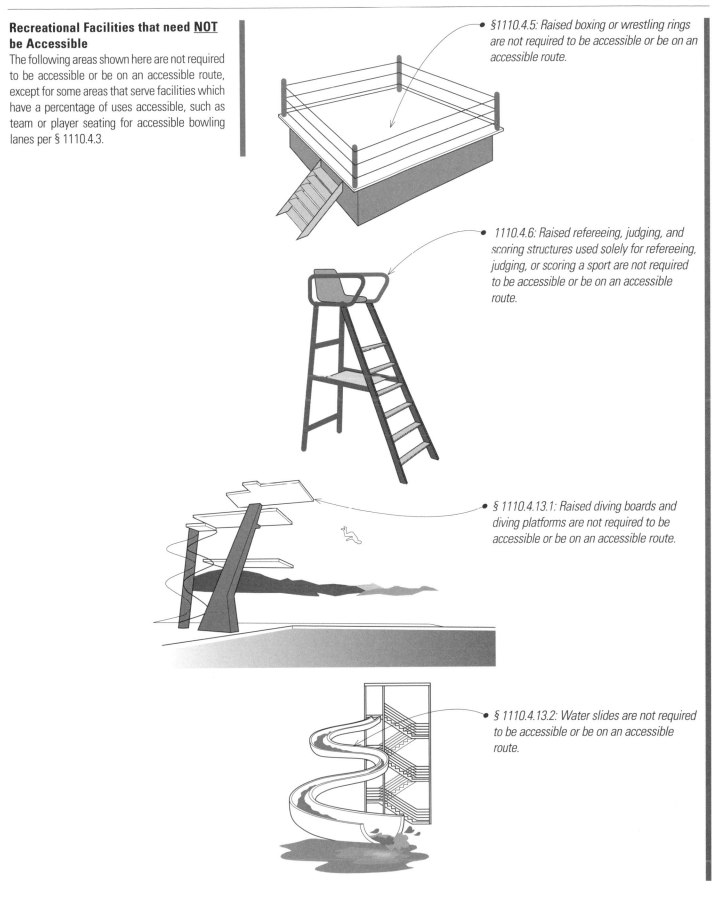

§1110.4.5: Raised boxing or wrestling rings are not required to be accessible or be on an accessible route.

1110.4.6: Raised refereeing, judging, and scoring structures used solely for refereeing, judging, or scoring a sport are not required to be accessible or be on an accessible route.

§ 1110.4.13.1: Raised diving boards and diving platforms are not required to be accessible or be on an accessible route.

§ 1110.4.13.2: Water slides are not required to be accessible or be on an accessible route.

§ 1111 contains the requirements for signage, such as for the international symbol of accessibility used to identify required accessible elements.

Signs

§ 1111.1 requires the international symbol of accessibility to be located at accessible parking spaces per § 1106.1 and 1106.2, accessible areas of refuge per § 1007.9, at accessible toilet locations, at accessible entries, accessible checkout aisles, and at accessible dressing and accessible locker rooms.

The 2010 ADA Standards requires permanent room signage to be located in a prescribed location. Signs are also to have tactile raised lettering and Braille symbols. These requirements apply even if not stated in the body of the code since the 2010 ADA Standards are to be applied as well. This is a good example of why designers must review ADA requirements along with code requirements. See signage requirements in the commentary on Appendix Chapter E, on page 236.

Directional Signage

Where not all elements are accessible, § 1111.2 requires there be signage to direct people with disabilities to the nearest accessible element. These signs must have the international symbol of accessibility. Directional signage is required at inaccessible building entrances, inaccessible toilet facilities, inaccessible bathing facilities, and elevators not serving an accessible route. Directions to the nearest accessible unisex toilet are to be provided where there are unisex facilities per § 1109.2.1.

Other Signs

When special access provisions are made, then § 1111.3 requires signage be provided to highlight those provisions. The specific requirements noted in the code are:

1. When assistive listening devices are provided per § 1108.2.7, signs to that effect are to be provided at ticket offices or similar locations.
2. Each door to an exit stairway is to have a sign in accordance with § 1013.4. This section requires a tactile exit sign complying with A117.1.
3. At areas of refuge and areas for assisted rescue, signage shall be provided in accordance with § 1009.11.
4. At areas for assisted rescue, signage is to be provided per § 1009.11.

Signs for assitive listening devices are to comply with ICC A117.1 requirements for visual characters and include the International Symbol of Access for Hearing Loss.

Appendix E

Provisions in the appendices of the IBC do not have any force or effect in local jurisdictions unless the local authority having jurisdiction specifically adopts them. We have included the supplementary accessibility provisions in this chapter as an example of how appendices work. The access section is included because the provisions in this appendix closely parallel ADA and local modifications made to access regulations. In our opinion, most of these requirements should be applied based on common sense or compliance with the ADA, whether the appendix is adopted locally or not. Note that the referenced standards in the appendix include the ADA and various federal publications related to access and access regulations in addition to A117.1. Although the code refers to the old ADAAG we suggest the reader follow the 2010 ADA Standards, since March 15, 2012 was the effective date for the new ADA standards.

Designers should be familiar with these provisions as it is likely that these requirements or similar ones will be encountered in the course of design work. Appendix requirements are typically ones that are not universally accepted or that are still under development. These provisions are placed in the appendix to give local authorities the option to adopt them or not without compromising the basic code.

Appendix E uses the same reference criteria as the basic code, A117.1. The provisions of the appendix are designed to coordinate the basic code with supplemental requirements. If adopted, the section numbers are placed in the basic code in the numerical sequences noted in the appendix. The appendix requirements form an overlay with the basic code to add requirements for specific occupancies or functions beyond the requirements of the basic code.

Definitions

§ E102 contains definitions of accessible elements.

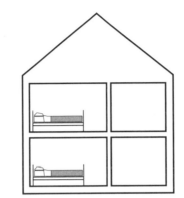

• *Transient Lodging: This is the primary additional term introduced in Appendix E. This function is typically a Group I or Group R occupancy. The major distinction is that the residents of these facilities are not long-term residents and thus are less familiar with their surroundings and may require supplementary services, clearances, or devices to use the transient lodging functions. Longer-term residents may adapt their spaces or have personal or programmatic supplements to their activities to accommodate their disabilities.*

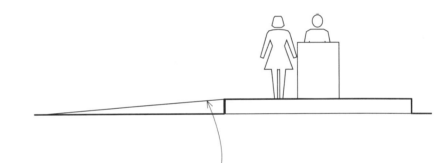

Accessible Routes

§ E103 adds requirements for access to raised speaker's platforms or lecterns in banquet areas. (Note that this is an ADA requirement.)

Special Occupancies

§ E104 adds requirements for transient lodging facilities as defined.

Communication Features

§ E104.2 provides for accessible communication features at sleeping accommodations in transient lodging per Table E104.2.1, based on the number of rooms. These features are to accommodate people with hearing disabilities and include visual notification of telephone rings, door knocks or bells. These functions are to be separate from the visual emergency alarm notifications. There is also to be an electrical receptacle near the phone to allow plugging in of a portable TTY for phone access. Telephones are also required to have volume controls.

It is not stated whether these rooms are to be combined with rooms made accessible for other disabilities, or separate. It is best to assume that the provision of mobility and auditory access is separate, and the requirements for numbers of rooms are additive. However, it is also reasonable to assume that the idea of dispersal and diversity of access will require certain rooms to provide both types of access in the same room. People with multiple disabilities should be accommodated. Also, rooms that are accessible for people with mobility impairments are usable by people without those disabilities. If adopted in the project's jurisdiction, then these requirements should be reviewed with the building official.

Other Features and Facilities

The facilities noted in § E105 are temporary in nature or equipment added after the construction of the building is complete. As such, they may not be under the control of the designer, but designers should be aware of these requirements in order to make physical layouts that can accommodate them.

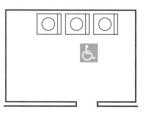

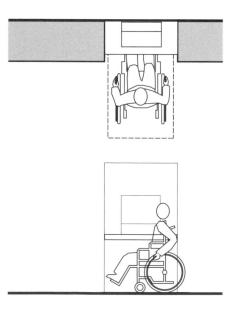

- *Portable Toilet and Bathing Rooms: Where portable facilities are clustered together, § E105.1 requires that at least 5%, or at least one, of the facilities must be accessible. This provision does not apply to construction sites.*
- *Laundry Equipment: When laundry equipment is provided in spaces that are required to be accessible, § E105.2 requires that at least one of each type of equipment should be accessible per A117.1.*
- *Depositories, Vending Machines, and Other Equipment: § E105.3 requires that spaces containing vending machines be accessible per A117.1. At least one of each type of depository, vending machine, change machine, and similar equipment is to be accessible.*
- *Mailboxes: § E105.4 requires that when mailboxes are provided at an interior location that at least 5% of them be accessible per A117.1. Where mailboxes are provided at each unit then accessible mailboxes are to be provided at accessible units.*
- *Automatic Teller Machines and Fare Machines: § E105.5 requires that at least one of each type of these machines be accessible. Also, where bins for materials such as envelopes or writing surfaces are provided, at least one of each of these facilities should be accessible as well.*
- *Two-way communication systems: Where communication systems are provided, such as those located at apartment entrances to gain admittance, the system is to be accessible.*

Telephones

The telephone access requirements contained in § E106, although in the appendix, should be applied in almost all cases. In addition, these detailed access requirements should be reviewed with the 2010 ADA Standards and local code adoptions.

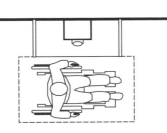

- *The access requirements illustrated are from A117.1. Note that while phones may be accessible from the front or the side as illustrated, the general rule to apply is that where pay phones are provided, they should be accessible per Table E106.2.*
- *Each public phone is to have accessible volume controls.*

Phones per Floor or Level	Wheelchair-Accessible Phones
1	1 per floor or level
1 bank*	1 per floor or level
2 or more banks	1 per bank

* Bank consists of a row of two or more phones.

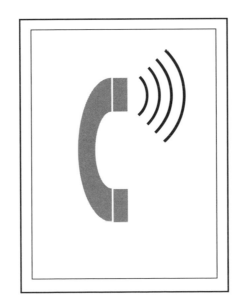

- *TTY's: § E106.4 requires that TTY's, telephone devices for hearing-impaired people using text or other nonverbal communication, are to be provided when there are more than four public telephones in a bank. The only exception applies to multiple banks of phones on one floor that are less than 200' (60 960) apart; then only one such bank need have a TTY. TTY locations are to be indicated by the international symbol of TTY and directional signs are to be provided to TTY locations. In addition to the TTY requirements, a shelf for portable TTY's along with an electrical receptacle is to be provided at each interior bank of three or more telephones.*

Signage

Where permanent signs for rooms or spaces are provided at doors, § E107 requires that the visual characters, raised characters, and braille comply with ICC A117.1. Where pictograms are provided as permanent designations of permanent interior rooms, the pictograms are to have tactile text descriptors. Directional signs for permanent interior locations except for building directories and personnel names and temporary signs should also be accessible. This is another instance where these requirements should be followed regardless of local adoptions. The 2010 ADA Standards should be reviewed along with A117.1 for signage requirements.

• *International TTY/TDD Symbol*

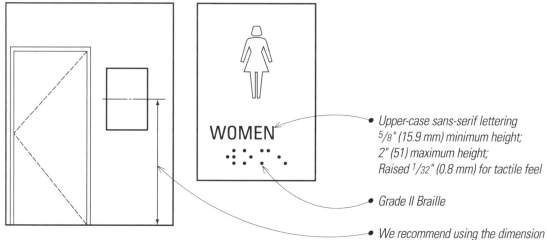

• *Upper-case sans-serif lettering $5/8$" (15.9 mm) minimum height; 2" (51) maximum height; Raised $1/32$" (0.8 mm) for tactile feel*

• *Grade II Braille*

• *We recommend using the dimension of 60" (1524) to centerline of sign on strike side of door. This should result in location compliance for the raised and Braille lettering.*

Transit Facilities

The last three sections of the Appendix contain requirements for transit facilities and airports. The specialized requirements for these uses are beyond the scope of our discussion. However, designers should be aware of the special requirements for these facilities placed on them by the ADA, the Code and the Appendix, and apply them when appropriate.

12

Interior Environment

The quality of interior environments is one of the primary factors in code development outside of the considerations of structural safety, fire resistance, and egress. Many of the environmental considerations in model codes came into being as a response to deplorable living conditions in buildings at the turn of the 20th century. Tenement housing and factory conditions often contributed to serious public health problems for occupants. Tenants were often crowded together in tiny rooms with little light or ventilation and with inadequate sanitation or maintenance of facilities. Also, unregulated building materials, especially decorative materials, led to installation of highly flammable materials in egress paths, often making egress passages more dangerous than the spaces occupants were leaving in an emergency. Code provisions were written to address these quality-of-life issues for occupants. Recently, indoor air quality has become increasingly important, as buildings become more energy efficient and more airtight. The need to prevent accumulations of molds or toxic gases while at the same time achieving energy efficiency has been a challenge for recent code development.

The considerations for interior environment address several primary factors. Chapter 8 considers the flame-resistance and smoke-generation capacities of various building materials used in interior spaces; Chapter 12 addresses the remaining environmental considerations.

These include air quality, both for human health and also for building durability, which is governed by regulations for the ventilation of building and occupied spaces. Another consideration is the quality of the occupants' experience in a space, which is regulated by provisions for temperature controls, natural or artificial lighting levels, and air and sound isolation between spaces. Also covered are the sizes of the spaces to be occupied, access to unoccupied spaces, and ongoing sanitation and maintenance issues for building interiors, including the materials that can be readily maintained in toilet and bathing facilities. Chapter 12 is therefore something of a catchall chapter in the code, with many provisions having only slight relationship to the chapter title.

This chapter has many disparate parts. One part governs quality-of-life issues for interiors and also includes measures to assist in mitigating the impact of climate on buildings. The standards set forth in this chapter also relate to how spaces work and feel for occupants, and how buildings can be maintained. This is in contrast to Chapter 8, which deals primarily with the fire safety of the occupants of interior spaces. The chapter title is somewhat misleading in that requirements of the chapter also pertain to spaces not normally occupied, although they are inside the building envelope.

Ventilation

§ 1203 deals with the ventilation of concealed attic and rafter spaces as well as with the ventilation of occupied spaces. The section is therefore divided among requirements for ventilation of building material areas and for ventilation of spaces used by building occupants.

Where building materials are enclosed on both the exterior and interior side of spaces, the concealed spaces, whether attics or rafter spaces, become susceptible to moisture intrusion.

Building Ventilation

Where houses are found to be relatively airtight, which means for code purposes that a blower door test finds the air infiltration rate in a dwelling to be less than 5 air changes per hour when tested at a pressure of 0.2 inch of water at 4°C (50 Pa) in accordance with the International Energy Conservation Code, the dwelling must be ventilated by mechanical means in accordance with the International Mechanical Code. If the house is found to allow 5 or more air changes per hour, then natural ventilation is still allowed. However, the IECC typically does not permit a house to have more than 5 air changes per hour, so if it is adopted, mechanical ventilation will typically be mandated. As houses become more energy efficient and thus more airtight, it will become more likely that blower door tests will be required for residences and mechanical ventilation will be required more often than in the past.

No matter what number of air changes per hour are anticipated, ambulatory care facilities and Group I-2 occupancies are to be ventilated by mechanical means in accordance with § 407 of the International Mechanical Code.

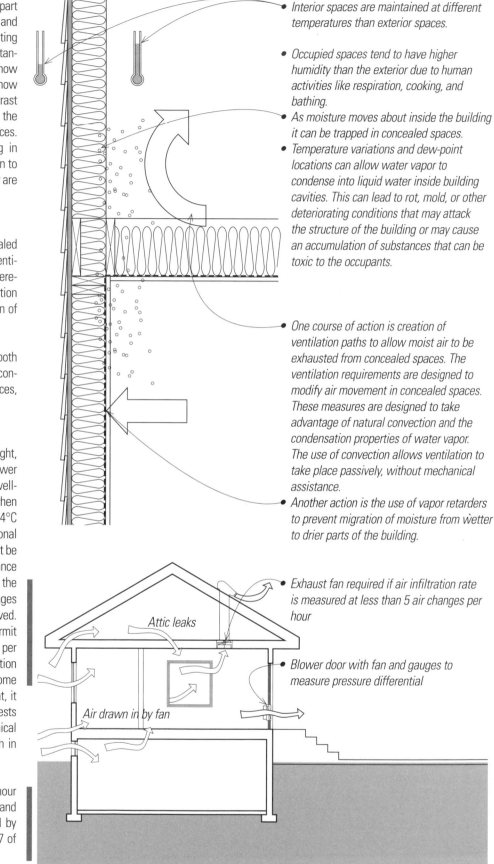

- Interior spaces are maintained at different temperatures than exterior spaces.

- Occupied spaces tend to have higher humidity than the exterior due to human activities like respiration, cooking, and bathing.

- As moisture moves about inside the building it can be trapped in concealed spaces.

- Temperature variations and dew-point locations can allow water vapor to condense into liquid water inside building cavities. This can lead to rot, mold, or other deteriorating conditions that may attack the structure of the building or may cause an accumulation of substances that can be toxic to the occupants.

- One course of action is creation of ventilation paths to allow moist air to be exhausted from concealed spaces. The ventilation requirements are designed to modify air movement in concealed spaces. These measures are designed to take advantage of natural convection and the condensation properties of water vapor. The use of convection allows ventilation to take place passively, without mechanical assistance.

- Another action is the use of vapor retarders to prevent migration of moisture from wetter to drier parts of the building.

- Exhaust fan required if air infiltration rate is measured at less than 5 air changes per hour

- Blower door with fan and gauges to measure pressure differential

Attic leaks

Air drawn in by fan

Attic Spaces

§ 1203.2 requires that ventilation openings be provided at the bottom and top of sloped roof conditions to allow for convection in attic spaces and cathedral ceilings.

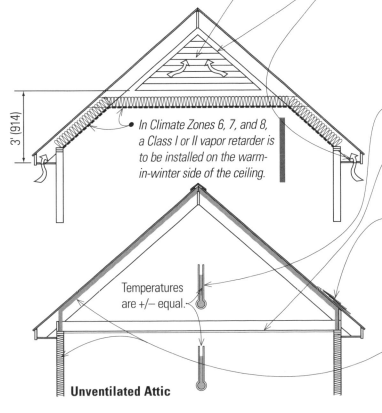

Closer to exterior temperature

Conditioned space temperature

Ventilated Attic

Ventilation opening requirements are expressed in terms of fractions of the area to be ventilated. Note that ventilation area requirements refer to free area. Free area is the amount of space allowing actual airflow. Vent louvers and screened openings do not provide 100% free area. A good rule of thumb for louvers at vent openings is to assume 50% free area. Consult manufacturers' data for actual free areas of any vent coverings selected to be certain of their actual free area.

3' (914)

In Climate Zones 6, 7, and 8, a Class I or II vapor retarder is to be installed on the warm-in-winter side of the ceiling.

Temperatures are +/– equal.

Unventilated Attic

- With this provision the code assumes that ventilation for insulation will be above the insulation. Designs should make this assumption as well. Vents are to be distributed to promote convection, with half high and half low in sloped conditions.

- The basic net free ventilation area requirement for attics is to be 1/150 of the space being ventilated. There is no guidance or set requirement for vertical offsets between the vent locations.

- Blocking and bridging must be arranged to not interfere with the flow of ventilation.
- A minimum of 1" (25.4 mm) of space is to be provided between insulation and roof sheathing.
- The net free cross-ventilation area is permitted to be reduced to 1/300 where a Class I or II vapor retarder is installed on the warm-in-winter side of the ceiling.
- Insulation between conditioned space and attic space.

- Ventilation may be reduced to 1/300 of the area to be ventilated when at least 40% and up to 50% of the required ventilating area is provided by ventilators located in the upper portion of the space.
- Upper ventilators are to be located not more than 3' (914) below the ridge or highest point of the space, with the balance of the ventilation provided by eave or cornice vents.

- Vents are to be covered with screens to keep out vermin and birds as well as be protected from the entry of rain and snow.

- Per § 1203.3 unvented attics and unvented enclosed roof framing assemblies are permitted where all of the following conditions are met:
1. The unvented attic space is completely within the building thermal envelope (i.e., attic is conditioned interior space, as is the space below.)
2. No interior Class I vapor retarders are installed on the ceiling side (attic floor) of the unvented attic assembly or on the ceiling side of the unvented enclosed roof framing assembly.
3. Where wood shingles or shakes are used, a minimum 1/4" (6.4 mm) vented air space separates the shingles or shakes from the roofing underlayment above the structural sheathing.
4. In Climate Zones 5, 6, 7, and 8, any air-impermeable insulation shall be a Class II vapor retarder or shall have a Class III vapor retarder coating or covering in direct contact with the underside of the insulation.
5. A continuous envelope of insulation is applied per the requirements of Item 5 of this section depending on whether the insulation is air-permeable or air-impermeable.

Under-Floor Ventilation

§ 1203.4 requires that, in buildings that are not slab-on-grade structures, the space between the underside of floor joists and the earth below be ventilated.

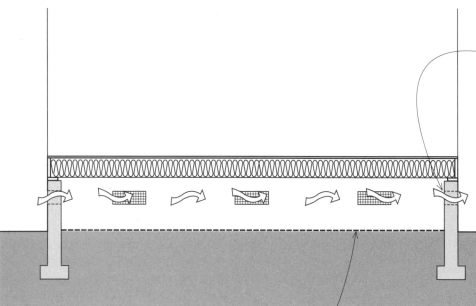

- *Vents are to have a net (free) area of 1 sf for each 150 sf (0.67 m² for each 100 m²) of crawl space. The vents should be vermin proof to prevent animals getting into the crawl-space area.*
- *The vent openings should be placed to allow cross-ventilation of the under-floor area. Thus openings should be distributed around the building perimeter to the maximum extent possible.*

Exceptions allow under-floor ventilation to be reduced or replaced with mechanical ventilation. The ventilation area may be reduced to 1/500 of the under-floor area when a vapor retarder is placed on the ground surface of the crawl space. The ventilation is also not required when the space is insulated, climate conditioned, and provided with a vapor retarder. Any of these measures is considered equivalent protection from vapor intrusion and collection when combined with a given quantity of passive or mechanical ventilation.

Temperature Control

§ 1204 states that all habitable spaces are to be provided with space heating. The heating system must be capable of sustaining a temperature of 68°F (20°C) at a point 36" (914) above the floor of the space. This capability is to be available on the coldest anticipated design day of the year.

Space heating systems are not required for interior spaces whose primary purpose is not associated with human comfort, or in Group F, H, S, or U occupancies.

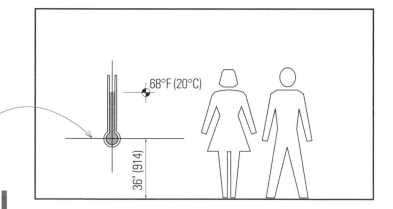

68°F (20°C)

36" (914)

Natural Ventilation

§ 1203.1 requires natural ventilation when mechanical ventilation is not provided. Mechanical ventilation is to be per the International Mechanical Code. The intent of these requirements is that habitable spaces be provided with light and air, even when those interior spaces are windowless and adjoin another room.

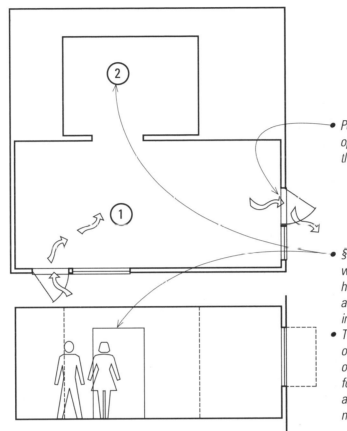

• Per § 1203.4.1 rooms are to have an area openable to the outdoors of at least 4% of the floor area of the space being ventilated.

• § 1203.4.1.1 states that adjoining rooms without openings to the outdoors must have an opening of at least 8% of the floor area, or 25 sf (2.3 m²), whichever is larger, into the adjacent room with the window.

• The openable area in the room facing the outdoors shall be based on the total area of all of the rooms relying on the window for ventilation. Thus in this example, area number 2 is considered part of room number 1.

Where there are additional contaminants in the air in naturally ventilated spaces, then additional mechanical ventilation may be required by the code.

In all cases, the code requires mechanical ventilation of rooms containing bathtubs, showers, spas, and similar bathing fixtures. Note that natural ventilation is not considered an alternate to mechanical ventilation in bathrooms. This recognizes the need for positive ventilation of interior moisture to prevent moisture buildup in the structure. Many times, especially in cold climates, natural ventilation is not used and moisture can build up in buildings when mechanical ventilation is not provided.

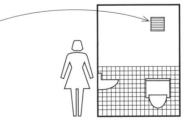

§ 1205 requires all habitable spaces to have natural or artificial light. Note that while artificial light is to provide 10 foot-candles (107 lux) over the area of the room at a height of 30" (762), no specific light-quantity criteria is set for natural light. While highly unlikely, it is thus possible under a literal interpretation of the code to have a building that could be occupied only during daylight as long as there were no internal rooms lacking natural light.

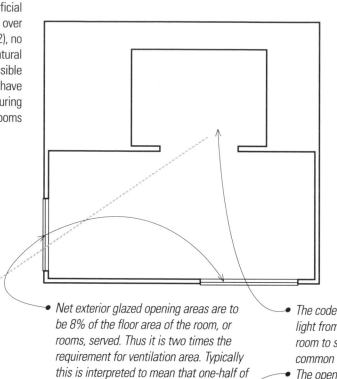

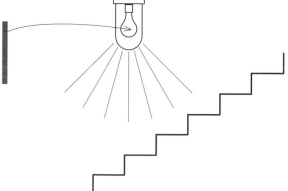

• Net exterior glazed opening areas are to be 8% of the floor area of the room, or rooms, served. Thus it is two times the requirement for ventilation area. Typically this is interpreted to mean that one-half of the window area is to be openable.

• The code allows for interior rooms to borrow light from adjacent rooms. For an adjoining room to serve another, at least half of the common wall between them must be open.

• The opening must be at least 10% of the floor area of the interior room, or 25 sf (2.3 m²), whichever is larger.

Stairways in dwelling units must have specified light levels, measured at the nosing of every stair tread. The basic light level is to be 1 foot-candle (11 lux) at the tread run. Stairs in other occupancies are to be lit per Chapter 10. See § 1008 for emergency lighting requirements at means of egress. The requirements in Chapter 10 are essentially the same as for residential stairs as noted above.

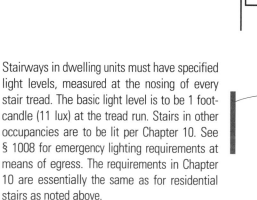

Yards or Courts

Exterior openings are to open to the outdoors to yards and courts of sizes specified in § 1206. Yard and court sizes are set to provide minimum dimensions for light wells and backyards of multistory buildings so that these areas provide real light and air to the spaces they serve.

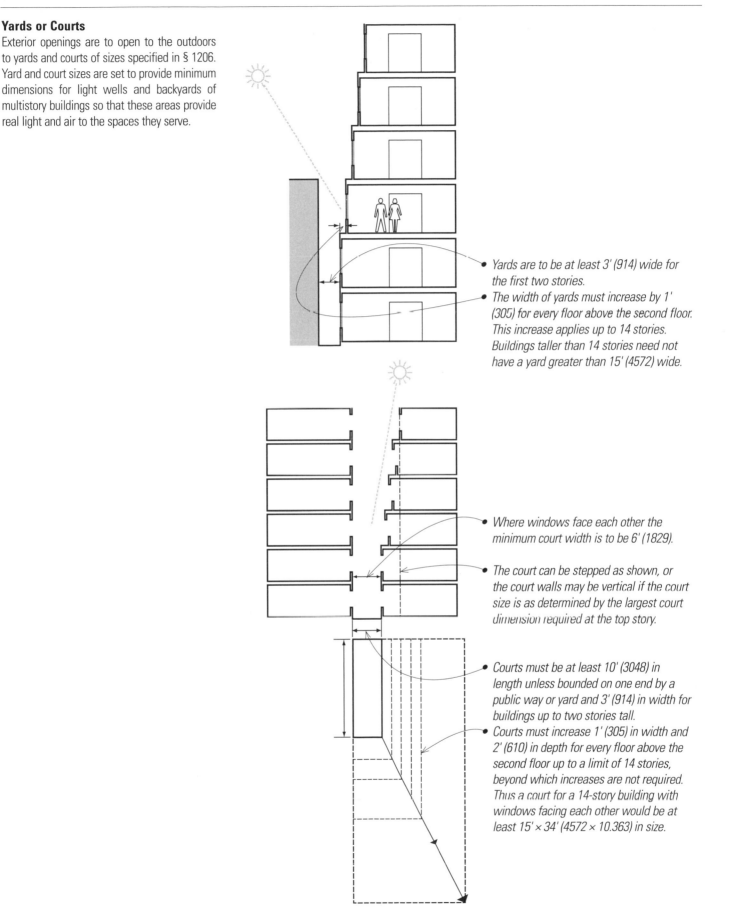

- *Yards are to be at least 3' (914) wide for the first two stories.*
- *The width of yards must increase by 1' (305) for every floor above the second floor. This increase applies up to 14 stories. Buildings taller than 14 stories need not have a yard greater than 15' (4572) wide.*

- *Where windows face each other the minimum court width is to be 6' (1829).*

- *The court can be stepped as shown, or the court walls may be vertical if the court size is as determined by the largest court dimension required at the top story.*

- *Courts must be at least 10' (3048) in length unless bounded on one end by a public way or yard and 3' (914) in width for buildings up to two stories tall.*
- *Courts must increase 1' (305) in width and 2' (610) in depth for every floor above the second floor up to a limit of 14 stories, beyond which increases are not required. Thus a court for a 14-story building with windows facing each other would be at least 15' × 34' (4572 × 10.363) in size.*

Sound transmission can severely impact the quality of life in multitenant buildings, especially in residential occupancies. § 1207 sets standards for sound-transmission reduction at walls and floor/ceiling assemblies between adjoining units. These criteria apply at the perimeter of dwelling units where they abut other units, public areas or service areas.

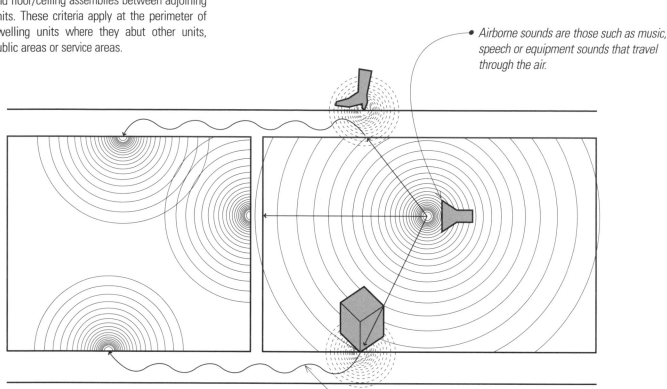

Airborne sounds are those such as music, speech or equipment sounds that travel through the air.

Structure-borne sounds are those such as footfalls, dropped items or equipment vibrations that are conducted by the structure and resonate in other spaces than the space of origin.

Criteria are established using ASTM test criteria. The code sets a higher standard for design criteria based on test data versus field-testing. These criteria recognize that test conditions are difficult to achieve in the field, and thus the expected minimum criteria are established such that field-measured conditions will meet the minimum necessary criteria. Criteria are established for both airborne sound (ASTM E 90) and for structure-borne sound (ASTM E 492).

Based on the abuses of tenement housing during the early part of the industrial revolution, model codes as well as § 1208 of this code set minimum room dimensions for each anticipated use of a dwelling.

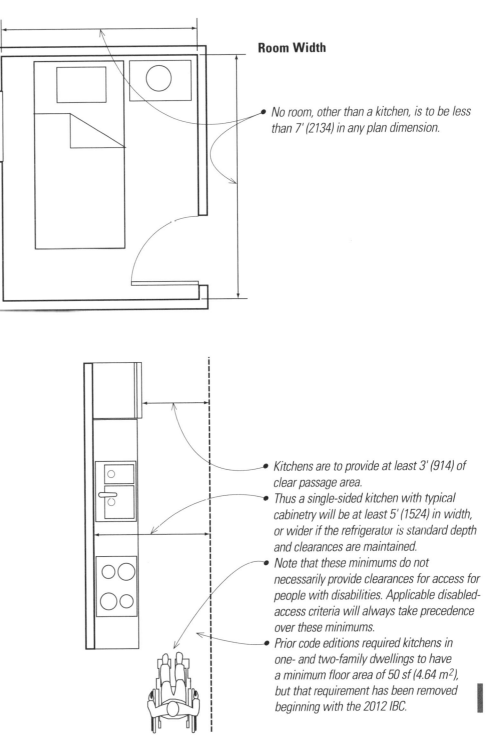

Room Width

- *No room, other than a kitchen, is to be less than 7' (2134) in any plan dimension.*

- *Kitchens are to provide at least 3' (914) of clear passage area.*
- *Thus a single-sided kitchen with typical cabinetry will be at least 5' (1524) in width, or wider if the refrigerator is standard depth and clearances are maintained.*
- *Note that these minimums do not necessarily provide clearances for access for people with disabilities. Applicable disabled-access criteria will always take precedence over these minimums.*
- *Prior code editions required kitchens in one- and two-family dwellings to have a minimum floor area of 50 sf (4.64 m²), but that requirement has been removed beginning with the 2012 IBC.*

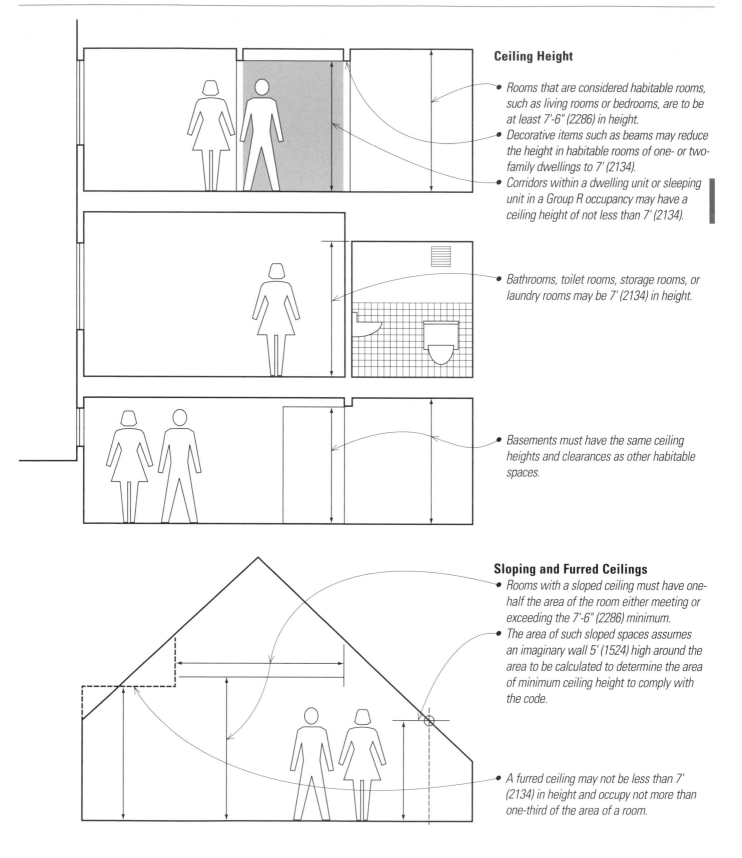

Ceiling Height

- *Rooms that are considered habitable rooms, such as living rooms or bedrooms, are to be at least 7'-6" (2286) in height.*
- *Decorative items such as beams may reduce the height in habitable rooms of one- or two-family dwellings to 7' (2134).*
- *Corridors within a dwelling unit or sleeping unit in a Group R occupancy may have a ceiling height of not less than 7' (2134).*

- *Bathrooms, toilet rooms, storage rooms, or laundry rooms may be 7' (2134) in height.*

- *Basements must have the same ceiling heights and clearances as other habitable spaces.*

Sloping and Furred Ceilings

- *Rooms with a sloped ceiling must have one-half the area of the room either meeting or exceeding the 7'-6" (2286) minimum.*
- *The area of such sloped spaces assumes an imaginary wall 5' (1524) high around the area to be calculated to determine the area of minimum ceiling height to comply with the code.*

- *A furred ceiling may not be less than 7' (2134) in height and occupy not more than one-third of the area of a room.*

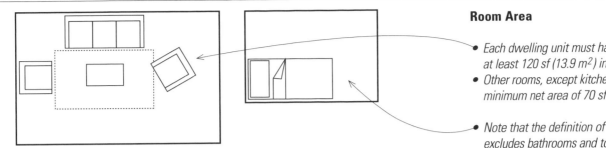

Room Area

- Each dwelling unit must have one room of at least 120 sf (13.9 m²) in net area.
- Other rooms, except kitchens, are to have a minimum net area of 70 sf (6.5 m²).

- Note that the definition of habitable spaces excludes bathrooms and toilet rooms, but includes spaces for cooking, living, sleeping, or eating. Thus, bedrooms must be at least 10' x 7' (3048 x 2134) to meet the space criteria of this section.

Efficiency Dwelling Units

§ 1208.4 covers low- and moderate-income housing and senior housing, which have special needs that can often be accommodated by small units meeting minimum space and layout criteria. These are often called studio, efficiency, or single-room-occupancy units.

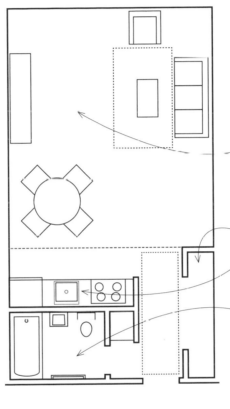

Based on the criteria of § 1208.4, a single-person unit would contain:

- A living/dining sleeping room of 220 sf (20.4 m²). An additional 100 sf (9.3 m²) of area is required for each occupant in excess of two.

- A separate closet (of undefined size).

- A cooking area with a sink, cooking appliances, and refrigerator with 30" (762) of clear space in front.

- There is also to be a separate bathroom with a water closet, lavatory, and bathtub or shower.

- The unit is to meet all of the ventilation and natural-light requirements contained in the code.

- Note that access criteria must also be examined regarding doorway and path-of-travel clearances.

Access to Unoccupied Spaces

Per § 1209 access is to be provided to mechanical appliances installed in crawl spaces, in attics or on roofs. Equipment must be provided with maintenance access both as a good design practice and per the International Mechanical Code.

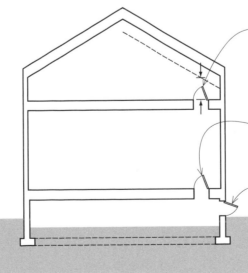

- Attic spaces that have more than 30" (762) of clear height inside the attic are to have an access opening of at least 22" x 30" (559 x 762). The opening is to be located such that there is at least 30" (762) of headroom above the opening.
- Crawl spaces under a building must have an access opening of at least 18" x 24" (457 x 610). This is of sufficient size to allow a person to get into the crawlspace.
- The access opening may be either inside or outside of the building.

Surrounding Materials

These provisions in § 1210 apply to toilet and bathing facilities in uses other than dwelling units. They are to address the maintenance, cleanliness, and health issues associated with public toilet and bathing facilities. Note that while these provisions do not apply to dwelling units except as indicated, their application should be carefully considered by the designer for all types of buildings as good design practice.

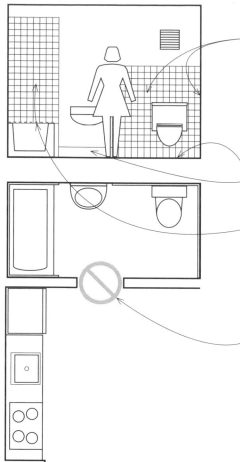

• Walls and partitions within 2' (610) of service sinks, urinals, and water closets must have a smooth, hard, nonabsorbent surface at least 4' (1219) high. The wall materials, apart from the structure, must also be of materials not adversely affected by moisture. Items such as grab bars and dispensers must be sealed to protect the underlying structure from moisture.

• Floors are to be smooth, hard, and nonabsorbent.

• The surface treatment must extend up the wall at least 4" (102).

• Shower compartments and walls above tubs must be finished with a hard, nonabsorbent finish to a height of 72" (1829) above the drain inlet elevation. Built-in tubs with showers are to have sealant joints between the tub and the adjacent walls.

• Per § 2902.3.6 of the International Plumbing Code, toilet rooms are not to open directly into a room used for preparation of food for the public. This obviously would include commercial kitchens but would also include serving areas or food-preparation stations outside the kitchen in a food-service venue. A vestibule or hallway needs to be provided in such circumstances.

This requirement has moved from § 1210 but it still seems appropriate to refer to it in this section as well as in Chapter 29.

Privacy at Toilet Rooms

Provisions for privacy at water closet compartments and urinals in multi-accommodation toilet rooms used by the public or employees have been moved into § 1210.3 from § 2903.

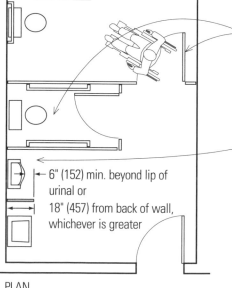

6" (152) min. beyond lip of urinal or
18" (457) from back of wall, whichever is greater

• Each water closet is to have a separate compartment with walls or partitions and a door enclosing the fixtures to ensure privacy. Enclosures are not required in single-accomodation toilet rooms where there is a lockable door.

• Each urinal is to have a separate area with walls or partitions to provide privacy. The walls or partitions are to start at a height no more than 12" (305) from the floor and extend to at least 60" (1524) above the floor surface. The walls or partitions shall extend from the wall surface at each side of the urinal not less than 18" (457) or to a point not less than 6" (152) beyond the outermost front lip of the urinal measured from the finished back wall surface, whichever is greater.

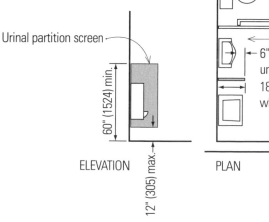

Urinal partition screen

60" (1524) min.

12" (305) max.

ELEVATION

PLAN

13

Energy Efficiency

The requirements for energy-efficient design are contained in a separate companion code, the International Energy Conservation Code (IECC). This code volume must be adopted by local jurisdictions to allow its enforcement to accompany the International Building Code. Similar correlations occur with several other I-codes, such as the International Mechanical Code and the International Plumbing Code. For the purposes of this very short chapter, when we refer to "the code" we mean the IECC.

The building-design implications of energy conservation are contained in the International Energy Conservation Code. The energy conservation requirements for mechanical and plumbing installations are typically contained in the mechanical and plumbing codes rather than in the energy code. Discussions of the energy-efficiency design requirements of the energy code, mechanical code, or plumbing code are outside the scope of this book.

Note that many states and local jurisdictions have adopted their own energy codes. These local codes may have quite different standards than this model code. As is the case for other possible local modifications, the designer should always verify the status of local code adoptions.

The calculations for energy use are inherently site specific. They depend heavily upon geography, climate, and local environmental conditions. Obviously a building that performs well in a hot, humid climate near sea level, such as in Florida, will have quite different environmental-control and energy-use patterns than a building in the hot, dry high-desert climate of central Arizona. In order to clearly discuss the concepts of the energy conservation calculation methods and criteria in the code, one must know where the building is, what its function is, and what type of construction it uses.

14

Exterior Walls

Chapter 14 establishes requirements for exterior walls. It also sets standards for wall materials and wall coverings, as well as for wall components such as windows, doors and trim. The provisions of this chapter are meant to apply primarily to weather protection and moisture control. The definition of "exterior wall" specifically excludes fire walls, which have additional fire-resistive requirements.

It is the intent of the code that exterior-wall requirements for weather protection and moisture control not supersede or compromise the overriding structural bearing and fire-resistance requirements for walls. On the other hand, the code does not intend for fire walls or structural bearing walls not to provide the required degree of weather resistance. As we will see as we proceed through the chapter, the intent is that weather resistance be built into exterior wall systems and that bearing walls need not have added envelope protection if they are designed as both load-bearing and weather-resistant systems.

EXTERIOR-WALL ENVELOPE

§ 1403.2 requires an "exterior wall envelope" to protect the structural members of a building, including framing and sheathing materials, as well as conditioned interior spaces from detrimental effects of the exterior environment.

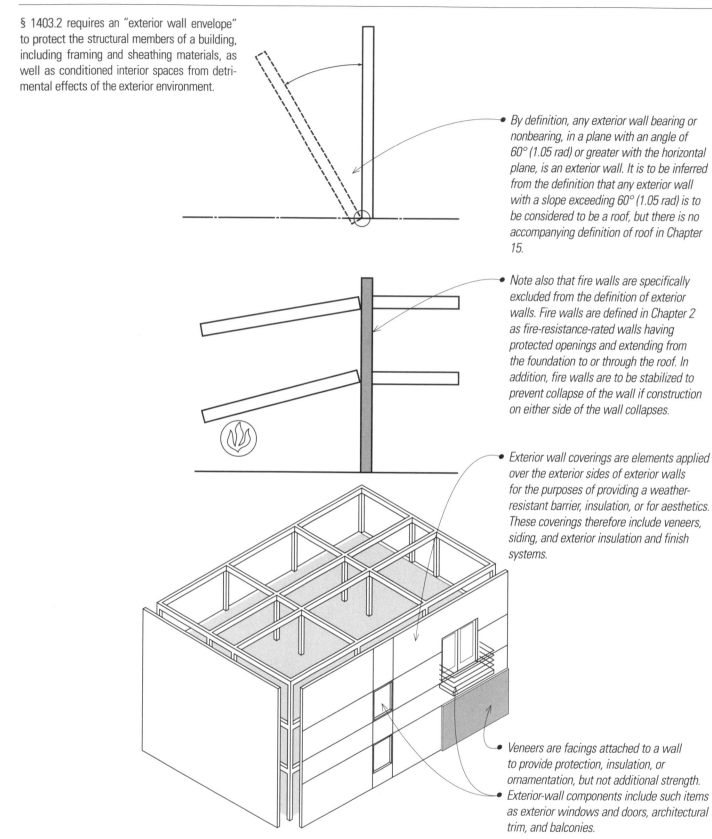

• By definition, any exterior wall bearing or nonbearing, in a plane with an angle of 60° (1.05 rad) or greater with the horizontal plane, is an exterior wall. It is to be inferred from the definition that any exterior wall with a slope exceeding 60° (1.05 rad) is to be considered to be a roof, but there is no accompanying definition of roof in Chapter 15.

• Note also that fire walls are specifically excluded from the definition of exterior walls. Fire walls are defined in Chapter 2 as fire-resistance-rated walls having protected openings and extending from the foundation to or through the roof. In addition, fire walls are to be stabilized to prevent collapse of the wall if construction on either side of the wall collapses.

• Exterior wall coverings are elements applied over the exterior sides of exterior walls for the purposes of providing a weather-resistant barrier, insulation, or for aesthetics. These coverings therefore include veneers, siding, and exterior insulation and finish systems.

• Veneers are facings attached to a wall to provide protection, insulation, or ornamentation, but not additional strength.

• Exterior-wall components include such items as exterior windows and doors, architectural trim, and balconies.

§ 1403 sets out the performance criteria for exterior walls, wall coverings and components.

Weather Protection

§ 1403.2 states that the basic performance criterion for exterior walls is providing an exterior-wall envelope that is weather-resistant. Exterior-wall systems must therefore be designed to prevent water penetration, the accumulation of water behind exterior veneers, and to provide drainage for any moisture that does enter the wall assemblies to the exterior of the veneer. The systems must also protect against condensation inside wall assemblies as required by § 1405.4, which describes flashing requirements.

- Exception 1: Weather-resistant systems are not required when exterior concrete walls or exterior masonry walls are designed for weather resistance per Chapters 19 and 21, respectively.
- Exception 2: Drainage requirements for wall assemblies (§ 1404.2 for water-resistive barriers and § 1405.4 for flashing) may be waived when acceptable testing is performed on envelope assemblies including joints, penetrations, and intersections per the test procedures of ASTM E-331. The basic criteria for this test require that a 4' by 8' (1219 by 2438) wall section be tested. The test section must contain a typical opening control joint, wall/eave intersection, control joint, and wall sill. The test must simulate pressure differentials of 6.24 psf (0.297 kN/m^2) and last for at least 2 hours. These criteria are established to require that the tested wall assembly with all of its typical parts be exposed to simulations of wind-driven rain conditions that can be reasonably anticipated in actual installations.
- Exception 3: Exterior insulation and finish systems (EIFS) that comply with the drainage requirements of § 1408.4.1.

Other Requirements

Exterior walls are to be designed to resist structural loads per Chapter 16, and meet the applicable fire-resistance and opening-protection requirements of Chapter 7. In flood-hazard areas, designated per § 1612.3, exterior walls extending below the design flood elevation are to be resistant to water damage. Any wood used in these areas is to be pressure-treated or naturally decay resistant.

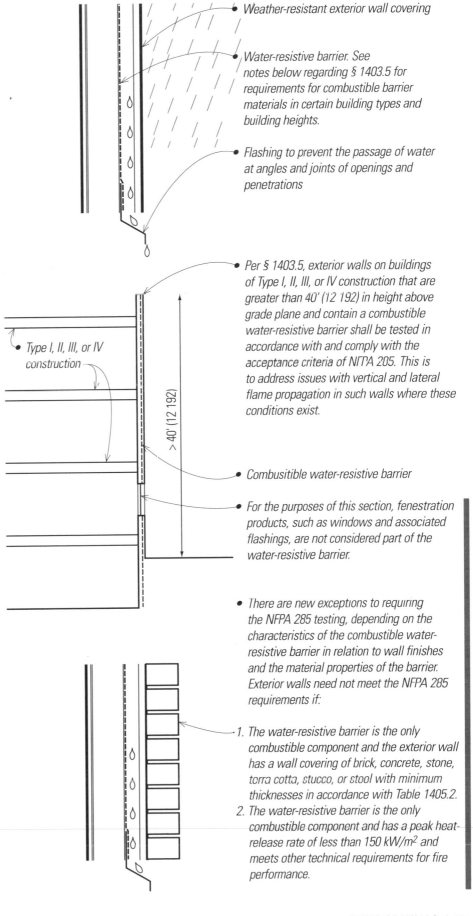

Weather-resistant exterior wall covering

Water-resistive barrier. See notes below regarding § 1403.5 for requirements for combustible barrier materials in certain building types and building heights.

Flashing to prevent the passage of water at angles and joints of openings and penetrations

Per § 1403.5, exterior walls on buildings of Type I, II, III, or IV construction that are greater than 40' (12 192) in height above grade plane and contain a combustible water-resistive barrier shall be tested in accordance with and comply with the acceptance criteria of NFPA 285. This is to address issues with vertical and lateral flame propagation in such walls where these conditions exist.

Type I, II, III, or IV construction

> 40' (12 192)

Combustible water-resistive barrier

For the purposes of this section, fenestration products, such as windows and associated flashings, are not considered part of the water-resistive barrier.

There are new exceptions to requiring the NFPA 285 testing, depending on the characteristics of the combustible water-resistive barrier in relation to wall finishes and the material properties of the barrier. Exterior walls need not meet the NFPA 285 requirements if:

1. The water-resistive barrier is the only combustible component and the exterior wall has a wall covering of brick, concrete, stone, terra cotta, stucco, or stool with minimum thicknesses in accordance with Table 1405.2.
2. The water-resistive barrier is the only combustible component and has a peak heat-release rate of less than 150 kW/m^2 and meets other technical requirements for fire performance.

§ 1403 and § 1404 require that all materials used in exterior walls are to meet the structural criteria contained in Chapter 16, as well as the detailed provisions for specific materials contained in Chapters 19 through 26.

- Concrete: Chapter 19
- Aluminum: Chapter 20. Aluminum siding must satisfy the requirements of AAMA 1402.
- Masonry and Glass Unit Masonry: Chapter 21
- Steel: Chapter 22
- Wood: Chapter 23
- Glass: Chapter 24
- Gypsum Board and Plaster: Chapter 25
- Plastics: Chapter 26
- Vinyl siding must conform to the requirements of ASTM D 3679.
- Fiber-cement siding is to comply with ASTM C1186, Type A.
- Exterior Insulation and Finish Systems (EIFS) are to comply with § 1408.

- *All walls are to have a continuous water-resistive barrier attached over exterior wall sheathing and behind the exterior wall veneer. The minimum barrier allowed is a single layer of No. 15 asphalt felt or equivalent complying with ASTM D 226, with flashing per § 1405.4. The water-resistive barrier is intended to resist liquid water that has penetrated behind the exterior covering from further intruding into the exterior wall assembly.*

- § 1405.2 requires exterior wall coverings to provide weather protection for the building. The minimum thicknesses of weather coverings are specified in Table 1405.2. These thicknesses range from thin steel (0.0149" or 0.38 mm) to anchored masonry veneer (2.625" or 66.67 mm).
  The minimum thicknesses are based on conventional construction techniques and recorded performance of these materials in actual installations. These are minima, not maxima. Thicker assemblies or thicker individual components should be acceptable to the AHJ as long as the assemblies are designed to hold the weight of the covering materials.

- *Full-size comparison of relative thicknesses of steel and stone weather coverings*

Vapor Retarders

§ 1405.3 describes the requirements for vapor retarders that are required in buildings to prevent the condensation of moisture inside of wall cavities. Moisture tends to migrate from the warmer and more moist interior of a building toward the exterior. If moisture is allowed to collect in wall cavities, it can lead to mold, mildew, or decay of the materials. The code requires different classes of vapor retarders, based on the location of the building in relation to the Climate Zones described in the International Energy Conservation Code (IECC).

Vapor retarder class is determined by the manufacturer's certified testing of assemblies. Certain materials, as described at right, are deemed by the code to meet the classes noted. The lowest class of vapor retarders is paint, which is Class III. This lowest level of vapor retarder is permitted in a specific group of assemblies in the Climate Zones listed in Table 1405.3.2.

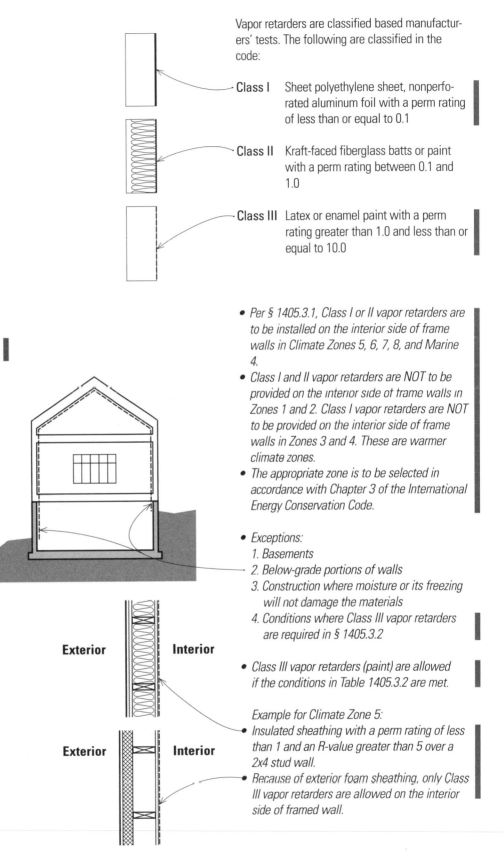

Vapor retarders are classified based manufacturers' tests. The following are classified in the code:

Class I — Sheet polyethylene sheet, nonperforated aluminum foil with a perm rating of less than or equal to 0.1

Class II — Kraft-faced fiberglass batts or paint with a perm rating between 0.1 and 1.0

Class III — Latex or enamel paint with a perm rating greater than 1.0 and less than or equal to 10.0

- *Per § 1405.3.1, Class I or II vapor retarders are to be installed on the interior side of frame walls in Climate Zones 5, 6, 7, 8, and Marine 4.*
- *Class I and II vapor retarders are NOT to be provided on the interior side of frame walls in Zones 1 and 2. Class I vapor retarders are NOT to be provided on the interior side of frame walls in Zones 3 and 4. These are warmer climate zones.*
- *The appropriate zone is to be selected in accordance with Chapter 3 of the International Energy Conservation Code.*

- *Exceptions:*
  1. *Basements*
  2. *Below-grade portions of walls*
  3. *Construction where moisture or its freezing will not damage the materials*
  4. *Conditions where Class III vapor retarders are required in § 1405.3.2*

- *Class III vapor retarders (paint) are allowed if the conditions in Table 1405.3.2 are met.*

Example for Climate Zone 5:
- *Insulated sheathing with a perm rating of less than 1 and an R-value greater than 5 over a 2x4 stud wall.*
- *Because of exterior foam sheathing, only Class III vapor retarders are allowed on the interior side of framed wall.*

Exterior   Interior

Exterior   Interior

Flashing

§1405.4 requires the installation of flashing to prevent moisture from entering at locations such as those illustrated to the right. The intent of the list that contains examples, not just the conditions to be satisfied, is that flashing be provided at any condition where it would prevent moisture from entering the structure.

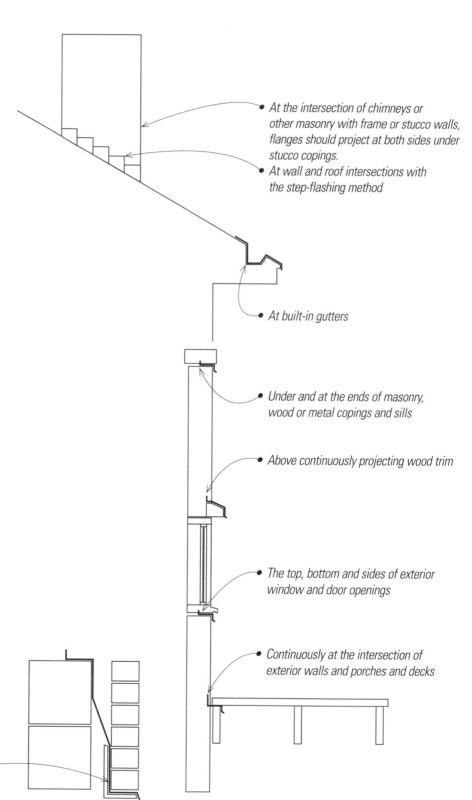

- *At the intersection of chimneys or other masonry with frame or stucco walls, flanges should project at both sides under stucco copings.*
- *At wall and roof intersections with the step-flashing method*

- *At built-in gutters*

- *Under and at the ends of masonry, wood or metal copings and sills*

- *Above continuously projecting wood trim*

- *The top, bottom and sides of exterior window and door openings*

- *Continuously at the intersection of exterior walls and porches and decks*

- *Flashing is also to be provided at wall pockets or crevices where moisture can accumulate.*
- *Flashing is also to be provided, along with weep holes in masonry walls, at the first course above the finished grade level and at support points such as floors, shelf angles, and lintels.*

Wood Veneers

§ 1405.5 prescribes the requirements for installing wood veneers.

Notwithstanding the requirements of Table 1405.2 for the minimum thickness of weather coverings, wood veneer used in Type I, II, III, and IV construction is to be of thickness called out in § 1405.5.

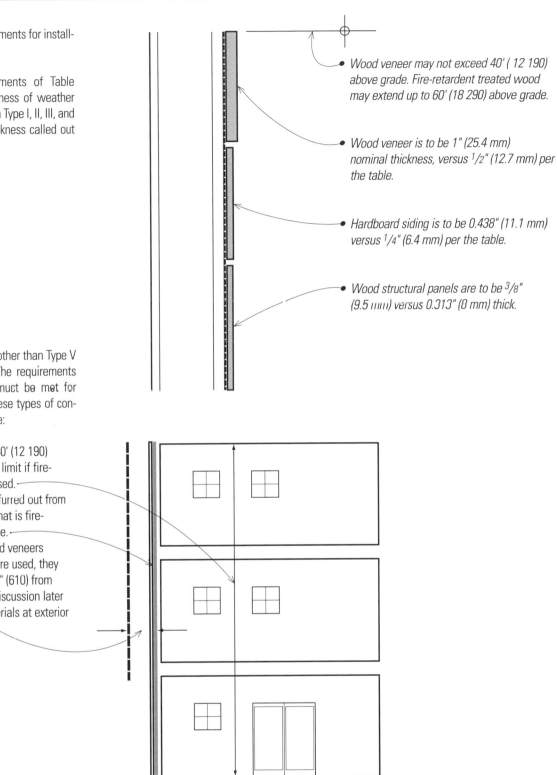

- Wood veneer may not exceed 40' (12 190) above grade. Fire-retardent treated wood may extend up to 60' (18 290) above grade.

- Wood veneer is to be 1" (25.4 mm) nominal thickness, versus ¹/₂" (12.7 mm) per the table.

- Hardboard siding is to be 0.438" (11.1 mm) versus ¹/₄" (6.4 mm) per the table.

- Wood structural panels are to be ³/₈" (9.5 mm) versus 0.313" (8 mm) thick.

The extent of wood veneer in other than Type V construction is also limited. The requirements are not exceptions, and all must be met for wood veneer to be used in these types of construction. The requirements are:

1. The veneer cannot exceed 40' (12 190) in height; 60' (18 290) is the limit if fire-retardant treated wood is used.
2. The wood is attached to or furred out from a noncombustible backing that is fire-resistance rated per the code.
3. Where open or spaced wood veneers without concealed spaces are used, they do not project more than 24" (610) from the building wall. See the discussion later regarding combustible materials at exterior walls contained in § 1406.

Anchored Masonry Veneer

§ 1405.6 prescribes specific requirements for the use of anchored veneers, whether of masonry, stone, or terra-cotta. These provisions apply to materials anchored to backing materials using mechanical fasteners. This is distinct from adhered veneers that are attached to the backing by adhesives. These requirements are broken down by material into separate sections.

§ 1405.6 also requires anchored masonry veneers to comply with the standards contained in § 6.1 and § 6.2 of TMS 402/ACI 530/ASCE 5, but the text applies these requirements to several types of veneers: masonry, stone, slab-type, and terra-cotta.

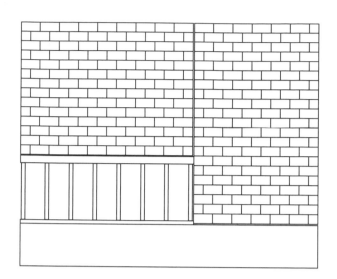

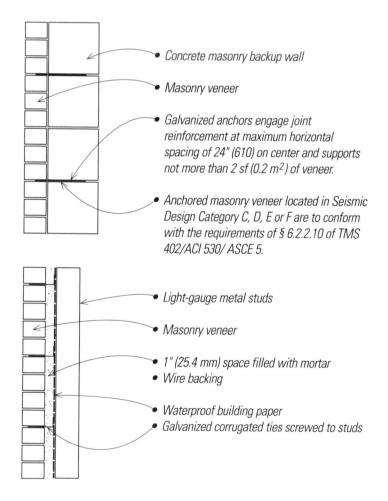

- Concrete masonry backup wall

- Masonry veneer

- Galvanized anchors engage joint reinforcement at maximum horizontal spacing of 24" (610) on center and supports not more than 2 sf (0.2 m^2) of veneer.

- Anchored masonry veneer located in Seismic Design Category C, D, E or F are to conform with the requirements of § 6.2.2.10 of TMS 402/ACI 530/ ASCE 5.

- Light-gauge metal studs

- Masonry veneer

- 1" (25.4 mm) space filled with mortar
- Wire backing

- Waterproof building paper
- Galvanized corrugated ties screwed to studs

Stone Veneer

§ 1405.7 requires stone veneer units up to 10" (254) thick to be anchored to masonry, stone, or wood construction by any one of the following methods. The methods are based on the structural system backing the veneer.

1. With concrete or masonry backing, anchor ties of dimension and spacing as indicated on the illustration are to be provided. These ties are to be laid in mortar joints and are to be located in such a manner that no more than 2 sf (0.2 m^2) of the wall is unsupported by the backing. In addition to the anchor ties in mortar joints attached to the backing with mechanical fasteners there is to be a minimum of 1" (25.4 mm) of continuous grout between the backing and the stone veneer.

2. With stud backing, wire mesh and building paper are to be applied and nailed as indicated on the illustration. Anchors similar to those required at concrete or masonry backing are to installed in the mortar joints and anchored to the backing to support every 2 sf (0.2 m^2) of veneer. Here too a minimum of 1" (25.4 mm) of grout is to fill the cavity between the backing and the stone veneer.

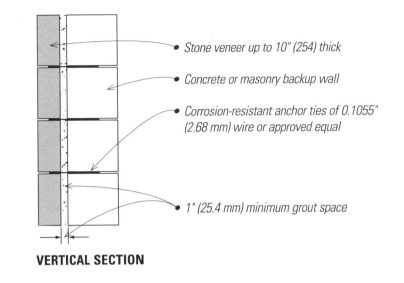

- Stone veneer up to 10" (254) thick
- Concrete or masonry backup wall
- Corrosion-resistant anchor ties of 0.1055" (2.68 mm) wire or approved equal
- 1" (25.4 mm) minimum grout space

VERTICAL SECTION

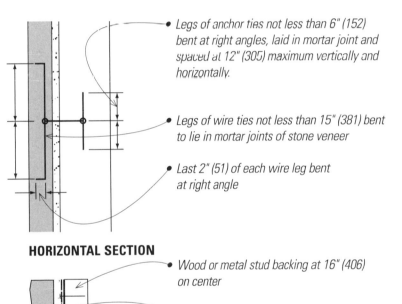

- Legs of anchor ties not less than 6" (152) bent at right angles, laid in mortar joint and spaced at 12" (305) maximum vertically and horizontally.
- Legs of wire ties not less than 15" (381) bent to lie in mortar joints of stone veneer
- Last 2" (51) of each wire leg bent at right angle

HORIZONTAL SECTION

- Wood or metal stud backing at 16" (406) on center
- 2" by 2" (51 x 51) 0.0625" (1.59 mm) corrosion-resistant wire mesh, attached with 2" (51) long corrosion-resistant steel wire furring nails at 4" (102) on center into studs, and 8d common nails at 8" (203) on center into top and bottom plates
- Two layers of waterproof paper backing
- One 0.1055" (2.68 mm) corrosion-resistant wire tie for every 2 sf (0.2 m^2), looped through wire mesh, with legs embedded in mortar joints of stone veneer as illustrated above

HORIZONTAL SECTION

Slab-Type Veneer

§ 1405.8 covers marble, travertine, granite, and other stone veneer units in slab form. These units are to be not more than 2" (51) in thickness and are to be anchored directly to concrete or masonry backings, or to wood or metal studs. Dowels are to be placed in the middle third of the slab thickness, a maximum of 24" (610) apart with a minimum of four per unit. The slab units are to be no larger than 20 sf (1.9 m²) in area. They are to have wire ties to the backing materials of size and spacing to resist a force in tension or compression of two times the weight of the attached veneer.

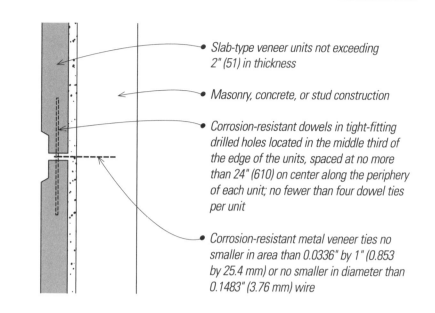

- Slab-type veneer units not exceeding 2" (51) in thickness

- Masonry, concrete, or stud construction

- Corrosion-resistant dowels in tight-fitting drilled holes located in the middle third of the edge of the units, spaced at no more than 24" (610) on center along the periphery of each unit; no fewer than four dowel ties per unit

- Corrosion-resistant metal veneer ties no smaller in area than 0.0336" by 1" (0.853 by 25.4 mm) or no smaller in diameter than 0.1483" (3.76 mm) wire

Terra-cotta

§ 1405.9 specifies anchoring terra-cotta veneers in a manner similar to that for slab veneers. The terra-cotta must be at least 1.625" (41) in thickness with projecting dovetail webs on 8" (203) centers. Metal anchors are to be placed at 12" to 18" (305 to 457) spacing in the joints between units and tied to the backing materials by pencil rods passing through loops in the wire ties and embedded in at least 2" (51) of grout.

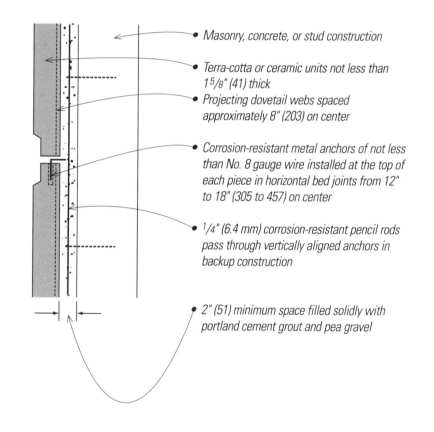

- Masonry, concrete, or stud construction

- Terra-cotta or ceramic units not less than 1⅝" (41) thick
- Projecting dovetail webs spaced approximately 8" (203) on center

- Corrosion-resistant metal anchors of not less than No. 8 gauge wire installed at the top of each piece in horizontal bed joints from 12" to 18" (305 to 457) on center

- ¼" (6.4 mm) corrosion-resistant pencil rods pass through vertically aligned anchors in backup construction

- 2" (51) minimum space filled solidly with portland cement grout and pea gravel

Adhered Masonry Veneer

§ 1405.10 considers adhered masonry veneer units to be held to the backing by the adhesion of bonding materials to the substrate. Exterior veneer is to comply with the applicable portions of § 6.1 and § 6.3 of the reference standards: TMS 402/ ACI 530/ ASCE 5.

Exterior Veneers

Water-resistive barriers shall be installed as required in § 2510.6.

There is to be flashing at the foundation, using a corrosion-resistant screed or flashing of a minimum dimension. The water-resistive barrier is to lap over the exterior of the attachment flange of the screed or flashing.

Porcelain tile is considered to be an adhered masonry veneer. Adhered porcelain tile units are not to exceed $5/8$" (15.8 mm) in thickness, 24" (610) in any face dimension, nor be more than 3 sf (0.28 m²) in total face area. Each tile may not weigh more than 9 psf (0.43 kN/m²). Porcelain tile must be adhered to an approved backing system.

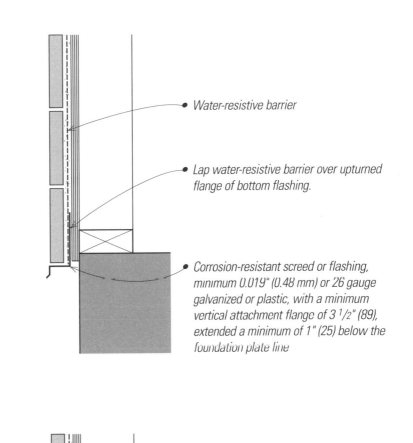

Water-resistive barrier

Lap water-resistive barrier over upturned flange of bottom flashing.

Corrosion-resistant screed or flashing, minimum 0.019" (0.48 mm) or 26 gauge galvanized or plastic, with a minimum vertical attachment flange of 3 1/2" (89), extended a minimum of 1" (25) below the foundation plate line

Minimum of 2"(102) above paved area or 1/2" (12) above exterior walking surface that is an extension of the foundation

4" (102) minimum above earth

Interior Veneers

§ 1405.10.3 applies only to the installation of interior masonry veneers, which must comply with the same installation requirements and weigh no more than 20 pounds per square foot (0.958 kg/m2). Where supported by wood framing, the supporting members are limited to deflection to 1/600 of the span of the supporting members.

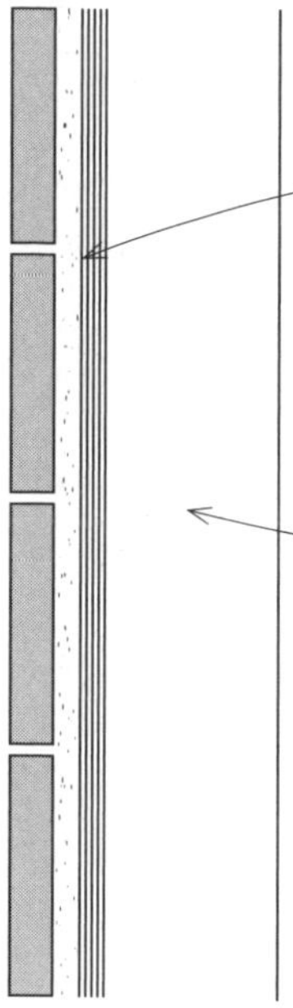

- Adhesive material must have a shear strength of at least 50 pounds per square inch (0.34 MPa).

- Interior masonry veneers should have a maximum weight of 20 psf (0.958 kg/m^2).

- Supporting members of wood construction should be designed to limit deflection to $^1/_{600}$ of the span of the supporting members.

Metal Veneers

§ 1405.11 states that metal veneers must be of noncorrosive materials or must be coated with anticorrosive coatings such as porcelain enamel. Connections to the backing are to be made with corrosion-resistant fasteners. Wood supports for metal veneers are to be of pressure-treated wood. Joints are to be caulked or sealed to prevent penetration of moisture. Masonry backing is not required for metal veneers except as may be necessary for fire resistance per other code sections.

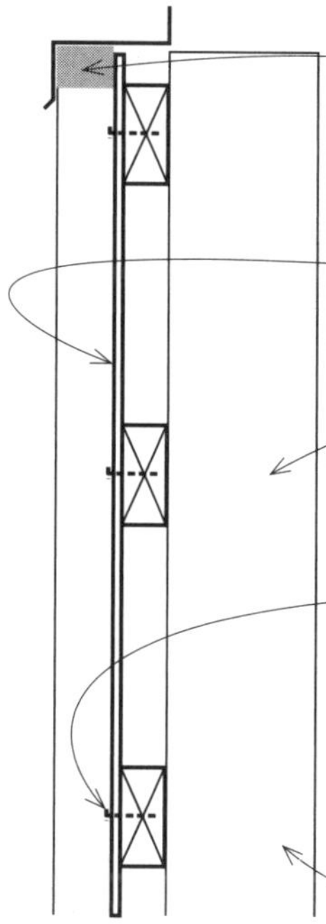

- Joints and edges exposed to weather must be caulked or otherwise protected against the penetration of moisture.

- Exterior metal veneer must be protected by painting, galvanizing, or equivalent coating or treatment.

- Wood studs, furring strips, or wood supports must be of pressure-treated wood or protected as required by § 1403.2.

- Corrosion-resistant fastenings spaced not more than 24" (610) on center vertically and horizontally.

- Units exceeding 4 sf (0.4 m^2) in area must have no fewer than four attachments per unit.

- Masonry backup not required except when necessary to meet fire-resistance requirements.

- Metal-veneer walls need to be grounded for lightning and electrical discharge protection per Chapter 27 of the IBC and per NFPA 70.

Glass Veneers

§ 1405.12 permits glass panels to be used as thin exterior structural glass veneer. The pieces of such glass, used as finish and not as glazing, may not exceed 10 sf (0.93 m^2) in areas up to 15' (4572) above grade and may not be larger than 6 sf (0.56 m^2) above that height. The glass is to be bonded to the substrate with a bond coat material that effectively seals the backing surface. Over this, mastic cement is to be applied to at least 50% of the glass surface to adhere it directly to the backing.

Where the glass veneer is installed at sidewalk level it is to be held above the adjacent paving by at least 1/4" (6.4 mm) and the joint thus created is to be sealed and made watertight. When located more than 36" (914) above grade, glass units are to be supported with shelf angles. When installed at a height above 12' (3658), the glass units are to be fastened at each vertical and horizontal edge in addition to the required adhesive mastic and shelf angles. Edges of the glass panels are to be ground square and are to be flashed at exposed edges.

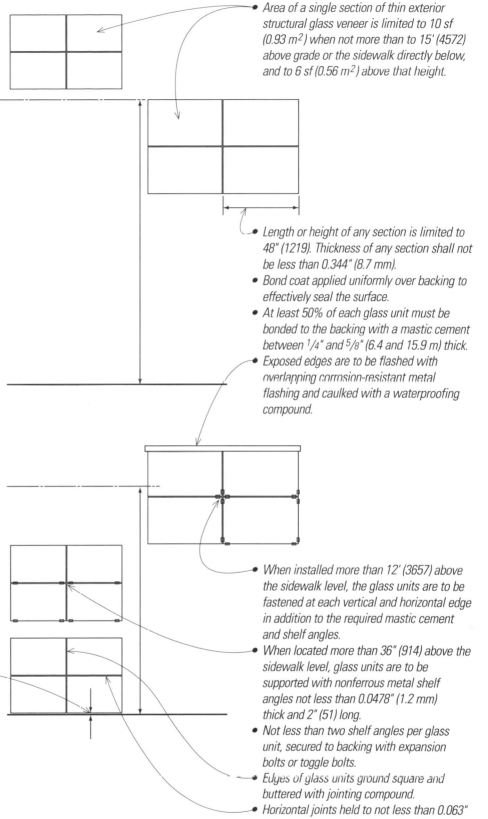

- Area of a single section of thin exterior structural glass veneer is limited to 10 sf (0.93 m^2) when not more than to 15' (4572) above grade or the sidewalk directly below, and to 6 sf (0.56 m^2) above that height.

- Length or height of any section is limited to 48" (1219). Thickness of any section shall not be less than 0.344" (8.7 mm).
- Bond coat applied uniformly over backing to effectively seal the surface.
- At least 50% of each glass unit must be bonded to the backing with a mastic cement between 1/4" and 5/8" (6.4 and 15.9 m) thick.
- Exposed edges are to be flashed with overlapping corrosion-resistant metal flashing and caulked with a waterproofing compound.

- Glass veneer installed at sidewalk level is to be held by an approved metal molding at least 1/4" (6.4 mm) above the highest point of the adjacent paving.
- The joint thus created is to be caulked and made watertight.

- When installed more than 12' (3657) above the sidewalk level, the glass units are to be fastened at each vertical and horizontal edge in addition to the required mastic cement and shelf angles.
- When located more than 36" (914) above the sidewalk level, glass units are to be supported with nonferrous metal shelf angles not less than 0.0478" (1.2 mm) thick and 2" (51) long.
- Not less than two shelf angles per glass unit, secured to backing with expansion bolts or toggle bolts.
- Edges of glass units ground square and buttered with jointing compound.
- Horizontal joints held to not less than 0.063" (1.6 mm) by nonrigid substance or device.

Vinyl Siding

Per § 1405.14, vinyl siding is to conform with that section and with ASTM D 3679. It is permitted for use on exterior walls where the wind speed does not exceed 100 mph (45 m/s) and the building height does not exceed 40' (12 192) in Exposure C (See § 1609.3.1). Where buildings exceed these requirements, calculations or test data demonstrating compliance must be submitted. The siding is to be applied per the requirements of § 1405.14.1. The siding must meet the water-resistive barrier requirements of § 1403.

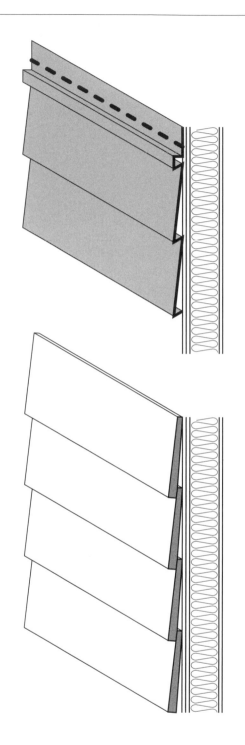

Fiber-Cement Siding

Fiber-cement siding is permitted per § 1405.16 on any type of construction. It is to meet the water-resistive barrier requirements of § 1403. The siding is to be applied per the manufacturer's instructions with fastenings per § 1405.16.

Polypropylene Siding

Per § 1405.18 use of polypropeylene siding is to be limited to exterior walls of Type VB construction located in areas where the wind speed does not exceed 100 miles per hour (45 m/s) and the building height is less than or equal to 40' (12 192) in Exposure C. For construction located in areas where the basic wind speed exceeds 100 miles per hour (45 m/s), or building heights are in excess of 40' (12 192), tests or calculations indicating compliance with Chapter 16 shall be submitted.

§ 1406 applies not only to building materials but also to appendages that project beyond the plane of the exterior wall. Such appendages include balconies, bay windows, and oriel windows. The criteria for plastics in this application are contained in Chapter 26. The standards for ignition resistance of exterior materials are set forth in NFPA 268. Note, however, that the exceptions to § 1406.2.1.1 cover such broad areas that the criteria from NFPA 268 may not apply in many cases. The exceptions include: wood or wood-based products, combustible materials other than vinyl siding, and aluminum at least 0.019" (0.48 mm) thick and at exterior walls of Type V construction. Thus these requirements apply to classes of construction other than Type V.

Table 1406.2.1.1.2 shows the relationship of combustible veneers to fire-separation distance from a lot line. When located closer than 5' (1524) to a lot line, materials (those not covered by the exceptions) shall not exhibit sustained flaming per NFPA 268. As the distance to the lot line increases, the radiant-heat energy flux decreases. Thus the heat impact on the materials decreases with distance and the types of material that will not exhibit sustained flaming increases.

Combustible Materials in Construction Types I, II, III, and IV

Per § 1406.2.1, exterior wall coverings may be of wood where permitted by § 1405.5 in buildings of Types I, II, III, and IV construction if the buildings are no more than three stories or 40' (12 192) in height. Where such buildings have a fire-separation distance of less than 5' (1524), no more than 10% of the exterior wall may be of combustible materials unless of fire-retardant-treated wood. Where such exterior wall coverings are located more than 40' (12 192) above grade they must be of noncombustible materials and attached with noncombustible fasteners. Note that combustible exterior wall coverings constructed of fire-retardant-treated wood are permitted up to 60' (18 288) in height above grade plane regardless of the fire separation distance.

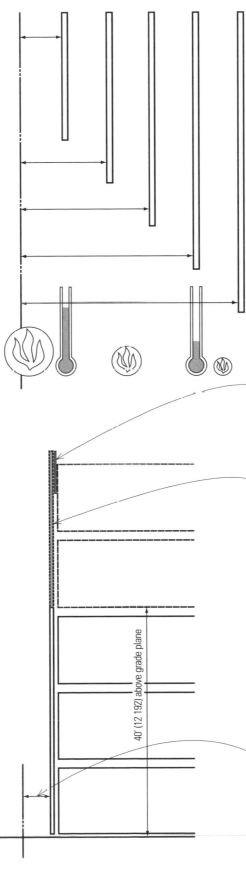

- As fire-separation distance increases, the tolerable level of incident radiant-heat energy decreases.

- Per § 1406.2.2, combustible exterior wall coverings located along the top of exterior walls are to be completely backed up by the exterior wall and not extend over or above the top of the exterior wall.

- Exterior wall coverings more than 40' (12 192) above grade plane must be constructed of noncombustible materials. (May be combustible up to 60' (18 288) if of fire-retardant-treated wood.)

- Architectural items such as trim or balconies may be constructed of wood or other equivalent combustible material where combustible wall coverings are allowed.

- Where the fire-separation distance is less than 5' (1524), combustible exterior-wall covering, except for fire-retardant-treated wood, shall not exceed 10% of exterior wall surface.

- Combustible exterior wall coverings constructed of fire-retardant-treated wood per § 2303.2 shall not be limited in area when the fire-separation distance is 5' (1524) or less and may be used up to 60' above grade regardless of the fire-separation distance.

40' (12 192) above grade plane

Fire-Blocking

When combustible wall coverings are furred from the wall and form a solid surface, § 1406.2.3 requires the space between the back of the covering and the wall to not exceed $1^5/8"$ (41), and the space must be fire-blocked per § 718 so that no open space exceeds 100 sf (9.3 m²). Note that Exception 3 to § 1405.5 allows open or spaced veneers to project up to 24" (610) from the backing wall. Fire-blocking may be omitted in certain circumstances, but good practice should dictate its inclusion in almost every condition where feasible.

- $1^5/8"$ (41) maximum between back of exterior wall covering and wall.

- Fire-blocking per § 718 with no open space exceeding 100 sf (9.3 m²).

- Fire-blocking is not required where the exterior wall covering is installed over noncombustible framing and the face of the exterior wall finish exposed to the concealed space is faced with aluminum, corrosion-resistant steel or other approved noncombustible material.

- Aggregate length of balconies not to exceed 50% of building perimeter on each floor.

Balconies and Similar Projections

§ 1406.3 requires balconies to meet the requirements of Table 601 for floor construction or to be of Type IV construction. The aggregate length of balconies may not exceed 50% of the building perimeter on each floor. This applies to all construction types. The exceptions again have a significant impact on how this section is applied in practice. The exceptions are:

1. On buildings of Type I or II construction that are three stories or less in height, fire-retardant-treated wood may be used for elements such as balconies or exterior stairs that are not used as required exits.
2. Untreated wood may be used for pickets and rails at guardrails that are under 42" (1067) in height.
3. Balconies and similar appendages on buildings of Type III, IV, or V construction may be of Type V construction. Also fire sprinklers may be substituted for fire-resistance ratings when sprinklers are extended to these areas.

- Fire-retardant-treated wood may be used for balconies, decks, and porches on buildings of Types I and II construction that are three stories or less in height.

- On buildings of Types III, IV, and V construction, balconies and similar appendages may be of Type V construction.

Metal composite materials (MCM) are a recently developed type of exterior finish material combining metal skin panels with plastic cores. These materials are regulated in two ways, both as exterior finishes under § 1407 and as plastics under Chapter 26. They are required to meet all of the water-resistance and durability criteria set forth in this chapter for other finish materials. Their installation in rated construction is controlled by testing and approval data establishing flame spread and smoke generation. A gypsum wall board thermal barrier may be required under the assemblies to limit heat transfer from exterior fire exposure into the building. This barrier is not required when test data support its removal.

The use of this material will be governed by tests and approvals for individual materials. These tests and approvals must be examined in light of the detailed requirements for generic types of exterior enclosure. As new materials are tested and approved, they must be compared to the code requirements to determine detailed responses to their installation. An example of a typical exterior MCM assembly is illustrated. Note that per § 1407.11.3, installations of MCM may go up to 75' (22 860) in height if the installation meets a more stringent list of criteria in this section. Note also that per the Exception to this section, buildings with automatic sprinkler systems are exempt from the height limitation.

Successful installations of innovative materials such as MCM will be dependent on close conformance with manufacturers' recommendations. This is true of other innovations as well. The code endeavors to incorporate new materials and new ways of assembling familiar materials such as the composite of aluminum and plastics to create MCMs. Innovations usually precede code development, so such innovative materials must be incorporated into buildings using manufacturers' data in concert with close consultation with the AHJ.

Exterior Insulation and Finish Systems

Exterior insulation and finish (EIFS) systems are to conform to the requirements of § 1408. They are to be designed to comply with ASTM E 2568, conform to the structural requirements of Chapter 16, and meet the weather resistance requirements of § 1403. Installation is to be in accordance with the EIFS manufacturer's instructions.

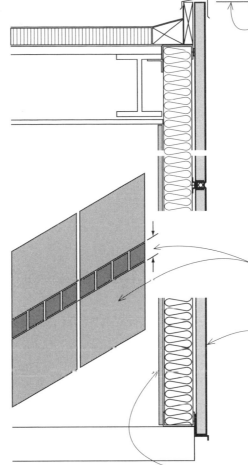

- Per § 1407.11.1, MCM may not be installed more than 40' (12 190) above grade when the fire-separation distance at the building exterior is less than 5' (1524), in which case the MCM may not exceed 10% of the exterior wall surface. Where there is a fire-separation distance of more than 5' (1524), there is no limit to MCM surface area [up to the 40' (12 190) maximum above grade].

- Per § 1407.11.2, MCM may be installed up to 50' (15 240) in height if the self-ignition temperature is 650°F (343°C) or more. Sections shall not exceed 300 sf (27.9 m²) and shall be separated by a minimum of 4' (1219) vertically.

- MCM is to have a flame-spread index of 75 or less and a smoke developed index of 450 or less, except:
- when installed on a building of Type I, II, III or IV construction;
- the flame-spread index is to be not more than 25 with a smoke-developed index of not more than 450.

- The MCM is to be separated from the interior of the building by an approved thermal barrier of 1/2" (12.7 mm) gypsum board or an equivalent thermal barrier that meets prescribed temperature-rise criteria. This barrier may be omitted if the MCM assembly complies with specified test criteria which are applicable to the proposed installation.

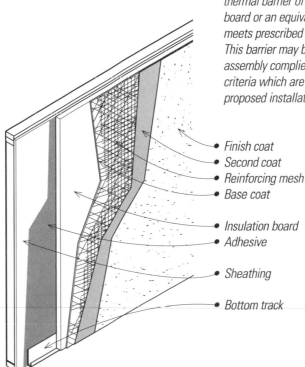

- Finish coat
- Second coat
- Reinforcing mesh
- Base coat

- Insulation board
- Adhesive

- Sheathing

- Bottom track

§ 1409 High-Pressure Decorative Exterior-Grade Laminates (HPL)

These exterior wall covering systems use panels made of layers of cellulose fibrous material impregnated with thermosetting resins and bonded together by a high-pressure process to form a homogeneous, nonporous core suitable for exterior use. They are usually applied as panels over a metal-channel backing system. These are often used in "rain screen" systems.

Per §1409.8, where HPL systems are used on exterior walls required to have a fire-resistance rating, evidence is to be submitted to the building official that the required fire-resistance rating is maintained.

Per the Exception, this requirement does not apply to HPL systems that do not contain foam plastic insulation and are installed on the outer surface of a fire-resistance-rated exterior wall in a manner such that the attachments do not penetrate through the entire exterior wall assembly.

Unless otherwise specified, HPL shall have a maximum flame spread index of 75 or less (25 or less in Types I, II, III, and IV construction) and a smoke-developed index of 450 or less when tested in the minimum and maximum thicknesses intended for use in accordance with ASTM E 84 or UL 723.

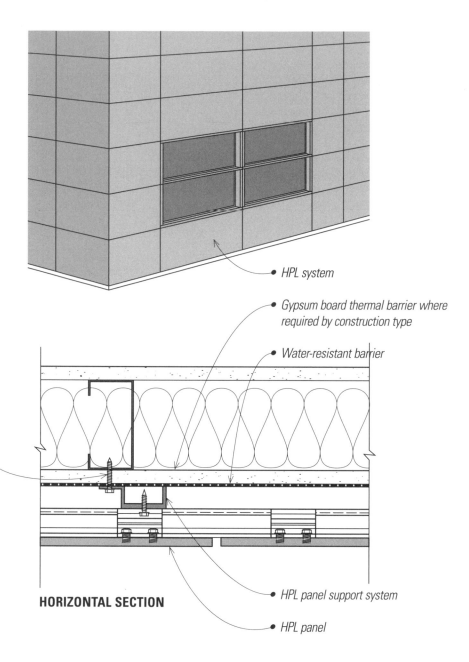

- HPL system
- Gypsum board thermal barrier where required by construction type
- Water-resistant barrier

HORIZONTAL SECTION

- HPL panel support system
- HPL panel

15

Roof Assemblies

This chapter establishes requirements for the design and construction of roofing assemblies for buildings. It also establishes requirements for rooftop structures, those that are built on or projecting from building roofs.

§ 1502 contains references to definitions located in Chapter 2 that describe different types of roofing. The most common types are illustrated in this chapter to accompany the requirements for roof coverings.

GENERAL REQUIREMENTS

Minimum Slope

The roofing criteria include minimum slope requirements for the installation of various roof coverings. In no case are dead-flat roofs allowed for any roofing material.

Weather Protection

The general criteria in § 1503 require that roofing materials and assemblies be installed in accordance with code requirements and manufacturers' recommendations.

- Flashing and underlayments are to be installed to provide a tight weather-resistant covering and to prevent moisture from entering the wall through joints or at intersections between building elements.
- Drainage is to be installed per the International Plumbing Code.
- Attic spaces at roof assemblies are to be ventilated as required by § 1203.2.

- *Roof drainage is to comply with the International Plumbing Code. Secondary (emergency overflow) roof drains or scuppers are to be provided where the roof perimeter extends above the roof such that water will be trapped if the primary drains are blocked. The need and sizing for secondary drains is to be per § 1106 and 1108 of the International Plumbing Code.*

- *Where scuppers are used they are to be sized to prevent ponding that will exceed the roof's design capacity. Scuppers are to have a minimum dimension of 4" (102).*

- *The tops of parapet walls are to be topped with coping of noncombustible weatherproof materials. The width of this material (typically sheet metal) is to be no less than the width of the parapet.*

- *Attic and rafter ventilation is to be provided where required by § 1203.2.*

- *The minimum slope allowable is for coal-tar built-up roofs that can be installed with a slope of $1/8$ vertical in 12 units (1% slope). We recommend that roofs typically be installed with a minimum slope of $1/4$ vertical in 12 units (2% slope) at the shallowest diagonal slope.*

- *At roofs with multiple drainage slopes—that is, with a series of high and low points—the slopes, which are expressed as minimums, should be measured at the shallowest slope of the roof. This usually occurs along a diagonal intersection of two slopes.*
- *If minimum slopes are measured along the fall line of intersecting slopes, the roof geometry will dictate that the slope of the longer intersection will be less than the allowable minimum. This is to be avoided.*

- *Flashings are to be installed at wall and roof intersections, at gutters, at changes in roof slope or direction, and around roof openings.*

- *Gutters and drains are to be provided to conduct water off the roof and prevent ponding and leaking.*

Performance Requirements

§ 1504 requires roofing to be securely fastened to the building to prevent damage in wind exposure. Roofs are to resist wind loads per Chapter 16 of the code and per requirements spelled out in test criteria for specific types of roofing materials, as called out in § 1504.2, 1504.3, and 1504.4.

- When low-slope roofs (defined as having a roof slope of less than 2:12) are installed, the roof materials must be tested to verify that they will maintain their physical integrity over the life of the roof. The tests are to cover physical properties such as sun and wind exposure, flexure of membranes in wind-load conditions, and impact-resistance of the roof coverings.

Fire Classification

§ 1505 divides roofing assemblies into fire-resistance classifications: A, B, C, and Nonclassified in descending order of effectiveness against fire exposure. Nonclassified roofing is material not listed as Class A, B, or C and must be approved by the building official. The ratings are determined based on the performance of roof coverings in fire tests.

- The fire classification of roof coverings is related to construction type in Table 1505.1.
- Class A roofing assemblies are permitted in all types of construction.
- Class B or better roofing assemblies are required for all types of construction other than IIB, IIIB, and VB.
- There is a general exception for R-3 occupancies when the roof edges are separated from other buildings by at least 6' (1829).
- There is also an exception for buildings that normally require a Class C roof, allowing the use of No. 1 cedar or redwood shakes and shingles on buildings two stories or less in height with a roof area of less than 6,000 sf (557.4 m²) and with a minimum 10' (3048) fire-separation distance to a lot line on all sides, except for street fronts or public ways.

Type of Construction

	IA	IB		IIA	IIB		IIIA	IIIB		IV		VA		VB
Allowable Fire Classifications of Roof Coverings (Minimums in *italics*)	A *B*	A *B*		A *B*	A *B* *C*		A *B*	A *B* *C*		A *B*		A *B*		A *B* *C*

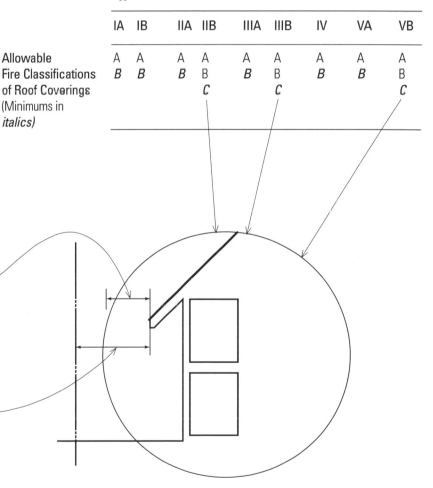

REQUIREMENTS FOR ROOF COVERINGS

Roof coverings are to be installed in accordance with § 1507 and the manufacturer's installation instructions. The building official may require testing for unusual roofing assemblies where standards are unclear or the suitability of installation criteria may be in question for a proposed application.

Asphalt Shingles

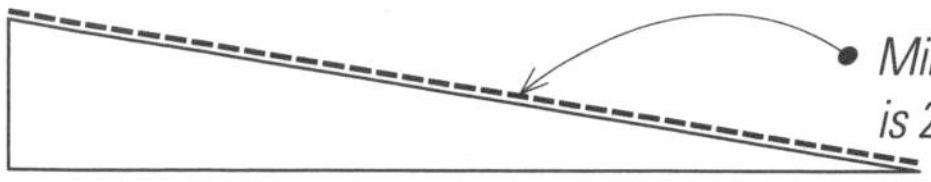

- Minimum roof slope for asphalt shingles is 2:12.

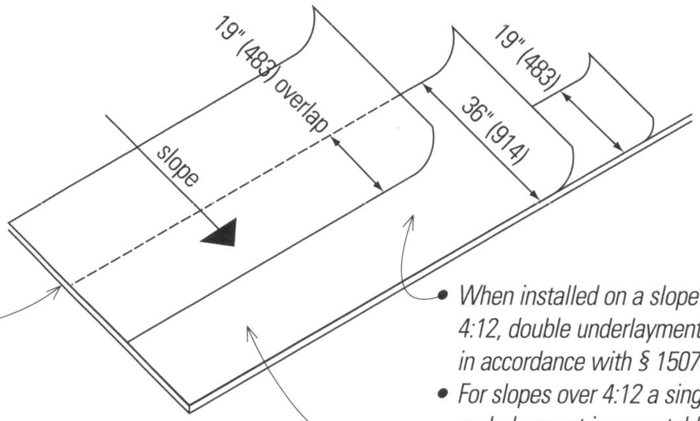

19" (483) overlap

19" (483)

36" (914)

slope

- § 1507.2 specifies that asphalt shingles are to be installed over solidly sheathed decks.

- Typical shingles are to have at least 2 nails per individual shingle or 4 per shingle strip unless more nailing is called for in the manufacturers' installation instructions.
- Special fastening methods with increased numbers of fasteners are required for very steep roofs or in areas where high basic wind speeds are noted in Chapter 16 of the code.

- When installed on a slope of less than 4:12, double underlayment is to be applied in accordance with § 1507.2.8.
- For slopes over 4:12 a single layer of underlayment is acceptable.
- Per § 1507.2.8.1, there are additional underlayment type, nailing size, and spacing requirements in high wind areas with wind speeds above 110 mph (49 m/s).

- Asphalt shingles are to have self-seal strips or be interlocking.
- They are to be nailed with galvanized steel, stainless-steel, aluminum, or copper 12-gauge headed roofing nails that must penetrate into the sheathing at least $^3/_4$" (19.1 mm), or through sheathing of lesser thickness.
- Asphalt shingles are to meet the classification requirements of Tables 1507.2.7.1 (1) or (2) for resistance to maximum basic wind speeds, depending on which criteria they are tested under.

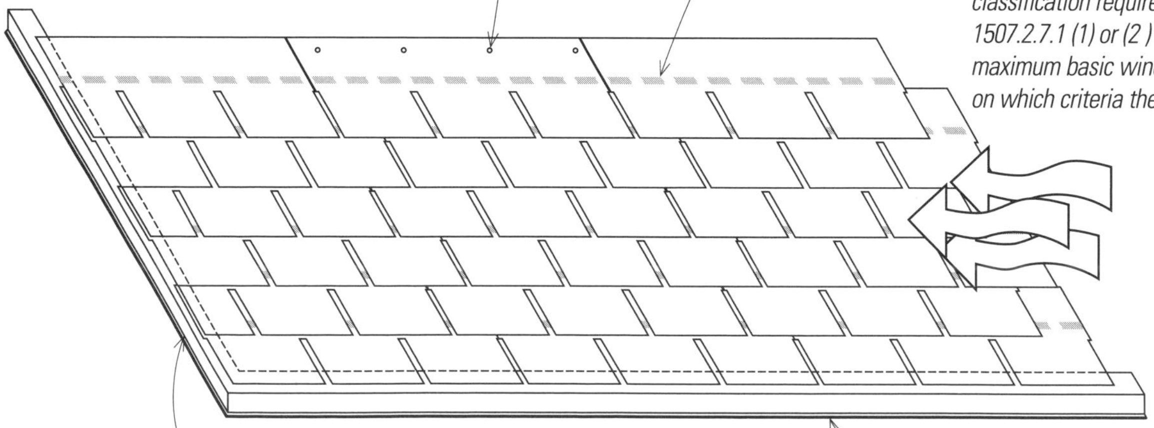

- Eaves and gables of shingle roofs are to receive drip edges extending below the roof sheathing and extending back under the roof.

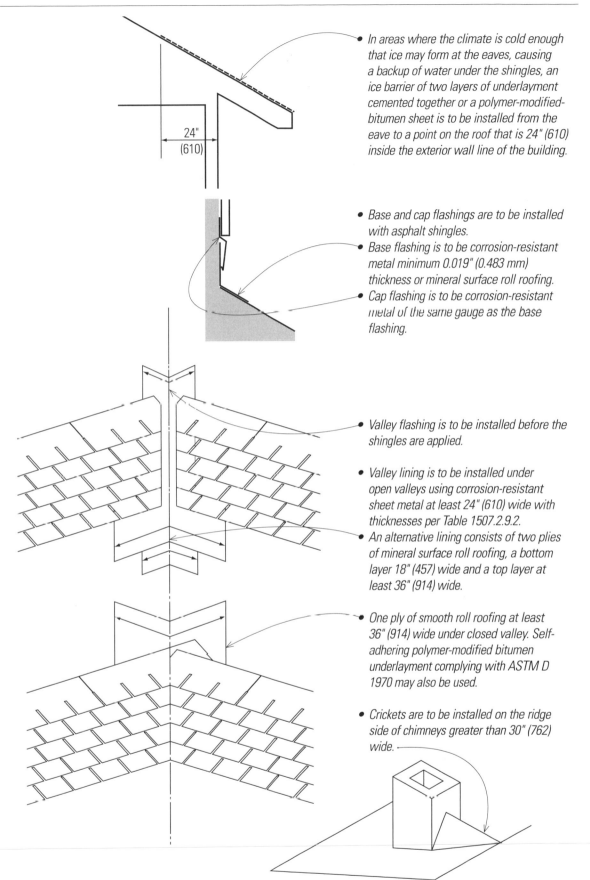

- In areas where the climate is cold enough that ice may form at the eaves, causing a backup of water under the shingles, an ice barrier of two layers of underlayment cemented together or a polymer-modified-bitumen sheet is to be installed from the eave to a point on the roof that is 24" (610) inside the exterior wall line of the building.

- Base and cap flashings are to be installed with asphalt shingles.
- Base flashing is to be corrosion-resistant metal minimum 0.019" (0.483 mm) thickness or mineral surface roll roofing.
- Cap flashing is to be corrosion-resistant metal of the same gauge as the base flashing.

- Valley flashing is to be installed before the shingles are applied.

- Valley lining is to be installed under open valleys using corrosion-resistant sheet metal at least 24" (610) wide with thicknesses per Table 1507.2.9.2.
- An alternative lining consists of two plies of mineral surface roll roofing, a bottom layer 18" (457) wide and a top layer at least 36" (914) wide.

- One ply of smooth roll roofing at least 36" (914) wide under closed valley. Self-adhering polymer-modified bitumen underlayment complying with ASTM D 1970 may also be used.

- Crickets are to be installed on the ridge side of chimneys greater than 30" (762) wide.

Clay tiles and concrete tiles are to meet strength and durability requirements supported by testing. Concrete tiles are also required to be tested for freeze-thaw resistance, absorption, and transverse breaking strength.

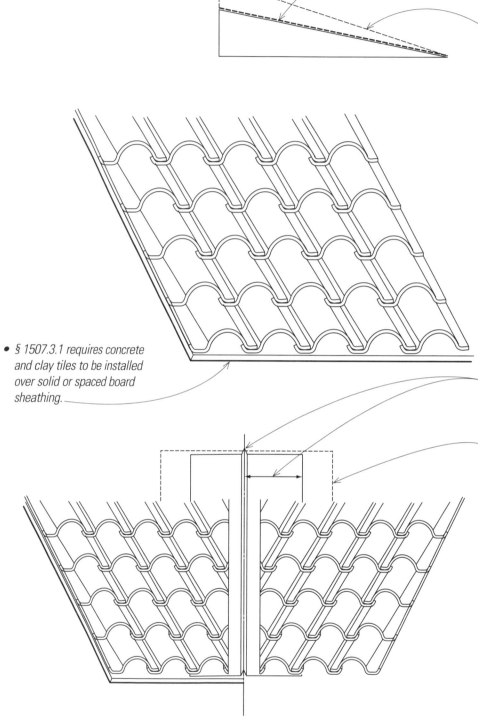

- § 1507.3.1 requires concrete and clay tiles to be installed over solid or spaced board sheathing.

- The slope of the roof deck is to be at least 2¹/₂ vertical in 12 units horizontal (21% slope).
- When the slope is less than 4:12, double underlayment is to be installed per § 1507.3.3.1.
- At slopes greater than 4:12, one layer of interlayment installed shingle fashion per § 1507.3.3.2 is acceptable.

- Fasteners for these tiles are to be corrosion-resistant and of a length to penetrate at least ³/₄" (19.1 mm) into or through the sheathing.
- The number and configuration of fasteners is spelled out in Table 1507.3.7.
- Tile is to be installed in accordance with the manufacturer's installation instructions based on climatic conditions, roof slope, underlayment system, and the type of tile being installed.

- Flashings are to be corrosion resistant and at least 26 galvanized sheet gage (0.019-inch).
- Flashings are to be installed at the juncture of roof tiles to vertical surfaces, and at valleys.
- Flashing to extend 11" (280) to each side of valley centerline and have a splash diverter rib 1" (25.4 mm) high.
- Overlap flashing 4" (102) at ends.
- 36" (914) wide underlayment for roof slopes of 3:12 and over.

- In cold climates where there is a possibility of ice forming along the eaves and causing backups of water and the roof is under 7:12 slope, the metal valley flashing underlayment is to be solidly cemented to the roofing underlayment.

Chapter 2 defines metal roof panels as being interlocking metal sheets having a minimum installed weather exposure of at least 3 sf (0.28 m²) per sheet. Smaller panels are defined as being metal roof shingles.

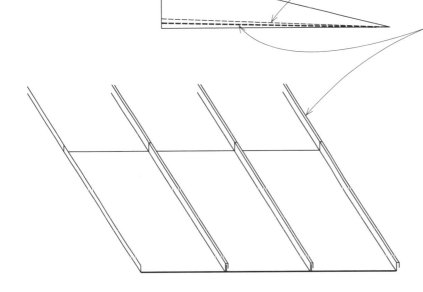

- The minimum slope for lapped, nonsoldered seam metal roofs without applied lap sealant is to be 3:12.
- With lap sealant the minimum slope is $1/2$ vertical in 12 units horizontal (4% slope).
- For standing seam roofs, the minimum slope is $1/4$ vertical in 12 units horizontal (2% slope).

- When the roof covering incorporates supporting structural members, the system is to be designed in accordance with Chapter 22.
- Metal-sheet roof coverings installed over structural decking are to comply with Table 1507.4.3 (1). The table sets testing standards, application rates, and thicknesses for various types of metal roofing system ranging from galvanized steel to copper, aluminum, and terne-coated stainless steel. Metal roofs must be of a naturally corrosion-resistant material or be provided with corrosion resistance per Table 1507.4.3(2).

- Fastenings must match the type of metal to avoid corrosion caused by galvanic electrical activity between dissimilar metals.
- Panels are to be installed per the manufacturer's instructions. In the absence of such instructions, the fastenings are to be galvanized fasteners for galvanized roofs and hard copper or copper alloy for copper roofs. Stainless-steel fasteners are acceptable for all types of metal roofs.

- Note that underlayment requirements are not spelled out in the code for metal roof panel installations. Many manufacturers recommend the use of underlayment. This is a reminder that the code is only the minimum standard for construction quality, not the maximum standard.

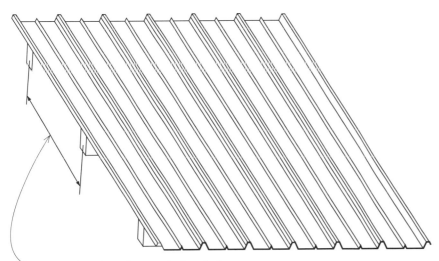

- Metal roof panels are to be installed over solid or closely spaced decking unless specifically designed to be installed over spaced supports.

Metal roof shingles are smaller in size than metal roof panels, being by definition less than 3 sf (0.28 m²) in weather exposure.

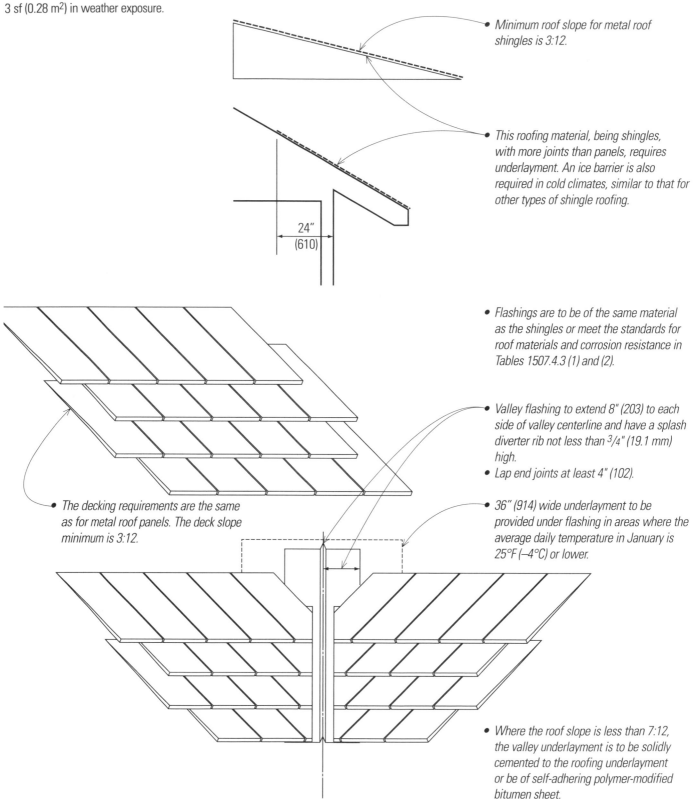

- Minimum roof slope for metal roof shingles is 3:12.

- This roofing material, being shingles, with more joints than panels, requires underlayment. An ice barrier is also required in cold climates, similar to that for other types of shingle roofing.

24" (610)

- Flashings are to be of the same material as the shingles or meet the standards for roof materials and corrosion resistance in Tables 1507.4.3 (1) and (2).

- Valley flashing to extend 8" (203) to each side of valley centerline and have a splash diverter rib not less than ³/4" (19.1 mm) high.
- Lap end joints at least 4" (102).

- 36" (914) wide underlayment to be provided under flashing in areas where the average daily temperature in January is 25°F (–4°C) or lower.

- The decking requirements are the same as for metal roof panels. The deck slope minimum is 3:12.

- Where the roof slope is less than 7:12, the valley underlayment is to be solidly cemented to the roofing underlayment or be of self-adhering polymer-modified bitumen sheet.

Mineral-Surfaced Roll Roofing

- Mineral-surfaced roll roofing is to be applied only over solidly sheathed roofs.
- The roof slope must be at least 1:12.
- A single layer of underlayment is typically required.
- Two layers are required to serve as an ice barrier in cold climates.

Slate Shingles

- *Slate shingles are to be applied only over solidly sheathed roofs.*

- *The minimum roof slope is to be 4:12.*
- *Underlayment requirements are the same as for metal roof shingles and roll roofing.*

- *Minimum headlap at shingles is per Table 1507.7.6.*
- *2" (51) for slopes equal to or greater than 20:12*
- *3" (76) for slopes greater than 8:12 but less than 20:12*
- *4" (102) for slopes from 4:12 up to 8:12*

- *Slates are to be secured with two fasteners per slate.*

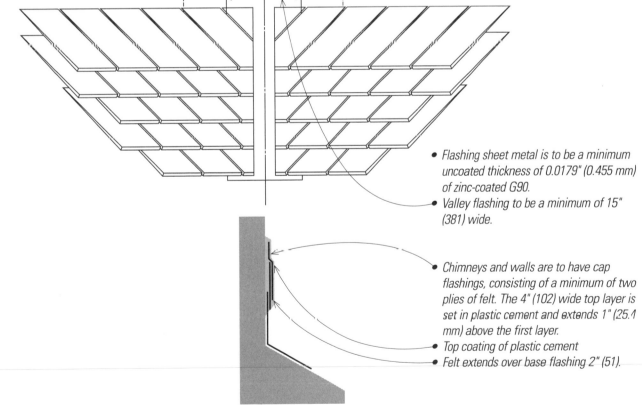

- *Flashing sheet metal is to be a minimum uncoated thickness of 0.0179" (0.455 mm) of zinc-coated G90.*
- *Valley flashing to be a minimum of 15" (381) wide.*

- *Chimneys and walls are to have cap flashings, consisting of a minimum of two plies of felt. The 4" (102) wide top layer is set in plastic cement and extends 1" (25.4 mm) above the first layer.*
- *Top coating of plastic cement*
- *Felt extends over base flashing 2" (51).*

WOOD SHINGLES

The installation requirements for both wood shakes and shingles are summarized in Table 1507.8.

- Wood shingles may be installed over either spaced or solid sheathing.
- Spaced sheathing shall not be less than 1x4 (nominal) boards, spaced equal to exposure.
- Solid sheathing is required in areas where the average daily temperature in January is 25°F (-4°C) or lower.

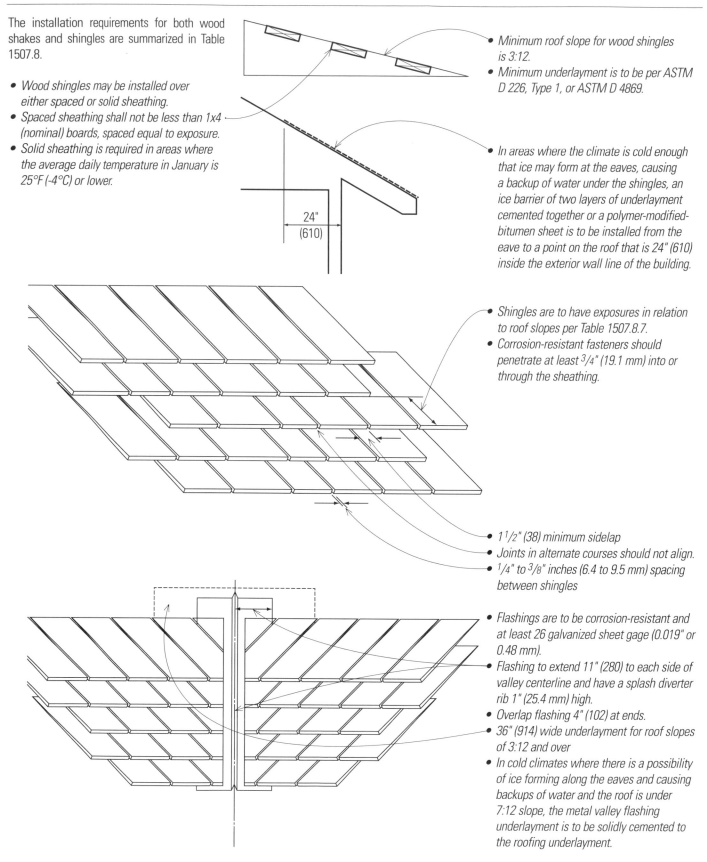

- Minimum roof slope for wood shingles is 3:12.
- Minimum underlayment is to be per ASTM D 226, Type 1, or ASTM D 4869.

- In areas where the climate is cold enough that ice may form at the eaves, causing a backup of water under the shingles, an ice barrier of two layers of underlayment cemented together or a polymer-modified-bitumen sheet is to be installed from the eave to a point on the roof that is 24" (610) inside the exterior wall line of the building.

24" (610)

- Shingles are to have exposures in relation to roof slopes per Table 1507.8.7.
- Corrosion-resistant fasteners should penetrate at least $3/4$" (19.1 mm) into or through the sheathing.

- $1 1/2$" (38) minimum sidelap
- Joints in alternate courses should not align.
- $1/4$" to $3/8$" inches (6.4 to 9.5 mm) spacing between shingles

- Flashings are to be corrosion-resistant and at least 26 galvanized sheet gage (0.019" or 0.48 mm).
- Flashing to extend 11" (280) to each side of valley centerline and have a splash diverter rib 1" (25.4 mm) high.
- Overlap flashing 4" (102) at ends.
- 36" (914) wide underlayment for roof slopes of 3:12 and over
- In cold climates where there is a possibility of ice forming along the eaves and causing backups of water and the roof is under 7:12 slope, the metal valley flashing underlayment is to be solidly cemented to the roofing underlayment.

- *While wood shingles are sawn, wood shakes are formed by splitting a short log into a number of tapered radial sections, resulting in at least one texture face.*
- *Wood shakes may be installed over either spaced or solid sheathing.*
- *Spaced sheathing shall not be less than 1x4 (nominal; 25 x 102) boards, spaced equal to weather exposure.*
- *Solid sheathing is required in areas where the average daily temperature in January is 25°F (-4°C) or lower.*

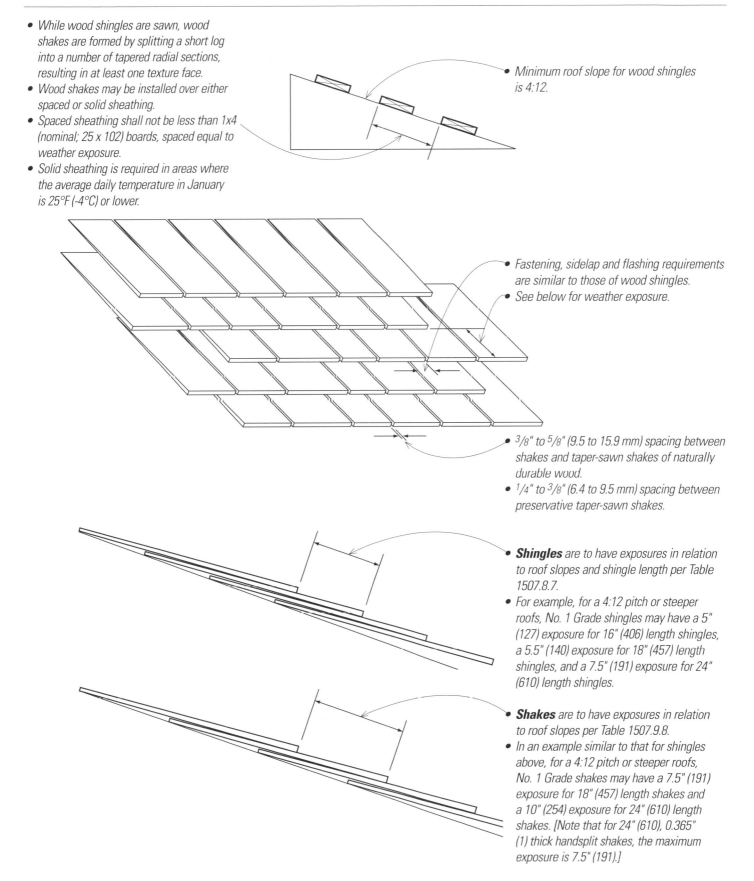

- *Minimum roof slope for wood shingles is 4:12.*

- *Fastening, sidelap and flashing requirements are similar to those of wood shingles.*
- *See below for weather exposure.*

- *³/₈" to ⁵/₈" (9.5 to 15.9 mm) spacing between shakes and taper-sawn shakes of naturally durable wood.*
- *¹/₄" to ³/₈" (6.4 to 9.5 mm) spacing between preservative taper-sawn shakes.*

- ***Shingles*** *are to have exposures in relation to roof slopes and shingle length per Table 1507.8.7.*
- *For example, for a 4:12 pitch or steeper roofs, No. 1 Grade shingles may have a 5" (127) exposure for 16" (406) length shingles, a 5.5" (140) exposure for 18" (457) length shingles, and a 7.5" (191) exposure for 24" (610) length shingles.*

- ***Shakes*** *are to have exposures in relation to roof slopes per Table 1507.9.8.*
- *In an example similar to that for shingles above, for a 4:12 pitch or steeper roofs, No. 1 Grade shakes may have a 7.5" (191) exposure for 18" (457) length shakes and a 10" (254) exposure for 24" (610) length shakes. [Note that for 24" (610), 0.365" (1) thick handsplit shakes, the maximum exposure is 7.5" (191).]*

BUILT-UP ROOFS

Built-up roof coverings are defined as two or more layers of felt cemented together and topped with a cap sheet, aggregate, or similar surfacing material. Although not stated in the code, the intent of this section is that materials for such roofs must be complementary and work together in accordance with the manufacturer's written installation instructions. The designer should verify the compatibility of the various components of such roofs to be certain they work together chemically and mechanically in accordance with the test criteria and standards cited in § 1507.10.2 and § 1507.11.2.

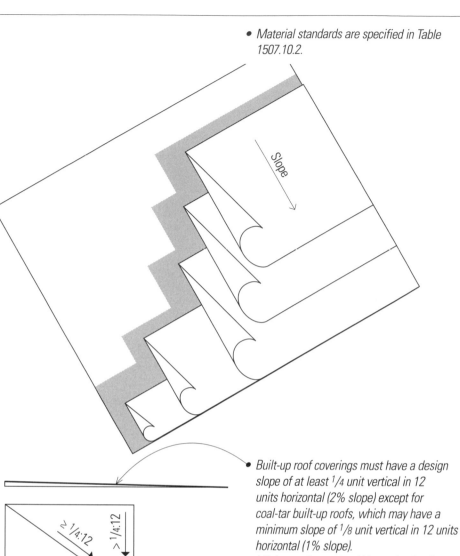

- Material standards are specified in Table 1507.10.2.

- Built-up roof coverings must have a design slope of at least $1/4$ unit vertical in 12 units horizontal (2% slope) except for coal-tar built-up roofs, which may have a minimum slope of $1/8$ unit vertical in 12 units horizontal (1% slope).
- Minimum slopes should be maintained along the shallowest slope at intersecting valleys. Thus typical roof slopes will be slightly greater than $1/4$:12.

Modified Bitumen Roofing

Modified Bitumen Roofing consists of one or more layers of polymer-modified asphalt sheets.

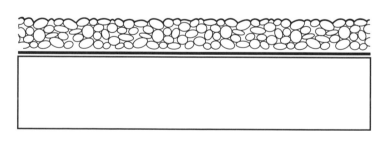

- Modified bitumen roofing is similar to built-up roofing in application. The sheets are fully adhered or mechanically attached to the substrate or held in place with a layer of ballast.
- These roofing materials are to be installed with a minimum slope of at least $1/4$:12.

Single-Ply Roofing Membranes

Single-ply roofing membranes are field applied using one layer of a homogeneous or composite material rather than multiple layers.

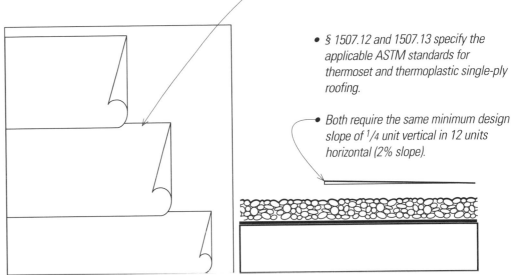

- The membrane material is seamed together with heat or adhesives or a combination of seaming methods.

- § 1507.12 and 1507.13 specify the applicable ASTM standards for thermoset and thermoplastic single-ply roofing.

- Both require the same minimum design slope of $1/4$ unit vertical in 12 units horizontal (2% slope).

Sprayed Polyurethane Foam Roofing

This type of roof covering is applied by spraying a layer of polyurethane foam onto the roof deck and then applying a liquid-applied protective coating over the foam membrane after it has been chemically cured.

- Application is to be per the manufacturer's installation instructions. The foam plastic materials must also comply with the code requirements for plastics contained in Chapter 26. Note that the only portion of the chapter that seems to apply is § 2603.6, which is contained in the section pertaining to foam plastic insulation and not roofing as such.

- The design slope is to be at least $1/4$ unit vertical in 12 units horizontal (2% slope).

Liquid-Applied Coatings

Liquid-applied coatings are not defined in this chapter. Typically such coatings form a membrane by sealing the surface to which they are applied after the liquid congeals or dries.

- Liquid-applied roofing must have a minimum design slope of $1/4$ unit vertical in 12 units horizontal (2% slope).

Vegetative Roofs, Roof Gardens, and Landscaped Roofs

§ 1507.16 addresses the requirements for vegetated roofs. IBC Chapter 2 defines a vegetative roof as "an assembly of interacting components designed to waterrpoof and normally insulate a building's top surface that includes, by design, vegetation and related landscape elements." There are requirements contained in the International Fire Code (IFC) that are referenced in this chapter, but not restated in the IBC. They are illustrated here. In this instance the International Fire Code contains requirements that impact project design.

§ 1507.16.1. states that the the structural frame and roof construction supporting the load imposed upon the roof by the roof gardens or landscaped roofs is to comply with the requirements of Table 601. This is intended to prevent the use of Footnote "a" to that table where structural elements are permitted to be reduced by 1 hour "where supporting a roof only." It is the intent that roof gardens and landscape elements on the roof constitute more than only a roof.

Vegetation is to be maintained, with supplemental irrigation provided to maintain levels of hydration necessary to keep green roof plants alive and to keep dry foliage to a minimum. Excess biomass, such as overgrown vegetation, leaves, and other dead and decaying material, is to be removed at regular intervals, but not less than two times per year.

Photovoltaic Shingle Systems

The increased popularity of photovoltaic (PV) roof assemblies has led to a need for regulation of their installation. § 1507.17 addresses requirements for installation of photovolatic shingle systems.

Photovoltaic modules/shingles are flat-plate PV modules that resemble three-tab composite shingles. They are typically installed as shingles would be, integrated into a field of other PV shingles modules along with conventional shingles.

IFC § 317 states that rooftop gardens and landscaped roofs are to be installed and maintained in accordance with § 317.2 through § 317.5 of the IFC. Any single area of a rooftop garden or landscaped roof areas is not to exceed 15,625 sf (1,450 m2) in size for any single area with a maximum dimension of 125 feet (39 m) in length or width.

A minimum 6' wide (1800) clearance consisting of a Class A-rated roof system is to be provided between adjacent rooftop gardens or landscaped roof areas. We believe it is the intent of the IFC that 6' (1800) wide buffer zones be provided around all of the items listed in this section, both for fire protection and for maintenance access.

IFC § 317.3 calls for all vegetated roofing systems abutting combustible vertical surfaces to provide a Class A-rated roof system for a minimum 6' wide (1800) continuous border around rooftop structures and all rooftop equipment including mechanical and machine rooms, penthouses, skylights, roof vents, solar panels, antenna supports, and building service equipment. Many of the items listed would not necessarily be considered to have combustible vertical surfaces.

125' (39 m) max.

125' (39

6' (1800) min.

Per IFC § 905.3.8, buildings or structures that have rooftop gardens or landscaped roofs and that are equipped with a standpipe system shall have the standpipe system extended to the roof level on which the rooftop garden or landscaped roof is located.

- *Photovoltaic modules/shingles are to be listed and labeled in accordance with UL 1703.*
- *The installation of photovoltaic modules/shingles is to comply with the provisions of § 1507.17.*
- *Photovoltaic modules/shingles are to be attached in accordance with the manufacturer's installation instructions.*
- *Per § 1507.17.2, photovoltaic shngles are not to be installed on roof slopes less than 3 units vertical in 12 units horizontal (25% slope).*

Roof Insulation

Per § 1508.1, thermal insulation may be installed above the roof deck if it is protected by a roof covering complying with the fire-resistance ratings of NFPA 276 or UL 1256, or a concrete roof deck is used and the above-deck thermal insulation is covered with an approved roof covering.

- Foam plastic roof insulation shall conform to the material and installation requirements of Chapter 26.
- Cellulosic fiber insulation shall comply with the applicable requirements for wood contained in Chapter 23.

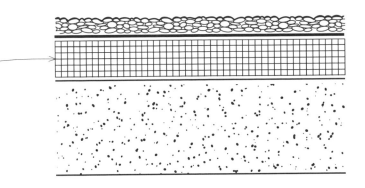

Radiant Barriers Installed Above Deck

§ 1509.1 adds new provisions for radiant barriers, which are reflective low-emittance layers in attics or similar spaces to reflect heat from roofs. Any radiant barrier installed above a roof deck shall comply with § 1509.2 through § 1509.4.

Fire Testing

Radiant barriers shall be permitted for use above decks where the radiant barrier is covered with an approved roof covering and the system consisting of the radiant barrier and the roof covering complies with the requirements of either FM 4550 or UL 1256.

Installation

§ 1509.3: The low-emittance surface of the radiant barrier shall face the continuous air space between the radiant barrier and the roof covering.

Material Standards

§ 1509.4: A radiant berrier installed above a deck shall comply with ASTM C 1313/1313M.

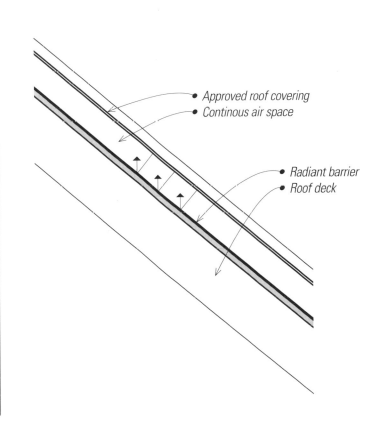

- Approved roof covering
- Continous air space
- Radiant barrier
- Roof deck

Penthouses

Rooftop structures include such items as penthouses for elevators, water tanks, cooling towers, and spires. In the 2012 code, all of § 1509, the section regarding rooftop structures along with some technical modifications, was reorganized. In the 2015 code, the section on rooftop structures is now renumbered as § 1510. The change bars shown here for this section relate to modifications to text from prior editions of this book.

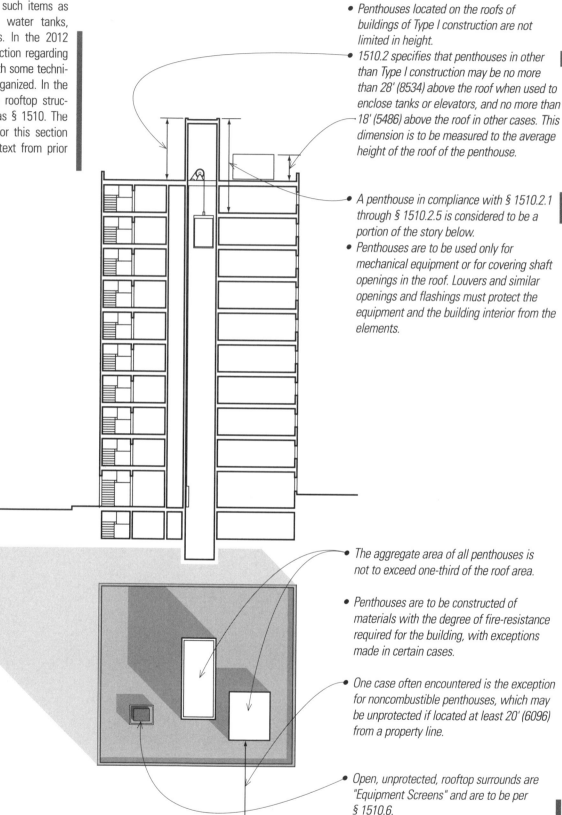

- Penthouses located on the roofs of buildings of Type I construction are not limited in height.

- 1510.2 specifies that penthouses in other than Type I construction may be no more than 28' (8534) above the roof when used to enclose tanks or elevators, and no more than 18' (5486) above the roof in other cases. This dimension is to be measured to the average height of the roof of the penthouse.

- A penthouse in compliance with § 1510.2.1 through § 1510.2.5 is considered to be a portion of the story below.

- Penthouses are to be used only for mechanical equipment or for covering shaft openings in the roof. Louvers and similar openings and flashings must protect the equipment and the building interior from the elements.

- The aggregate area of all penthouses is not to exceed one-third of the roof area.

- Penthouses are to be constructed of materials with the degree of fire-resistance required for the building, with exceptions made in certain cases.

- One case often encountered is the exception for noncombustible penthouses, which may be unprotected if located at least 20' (6096) from a property line.

- Open, unprotected, rooftop surrounds are "Equipment Screens" and are to be per § 1510.6.

Tanks

Tanks on the roof are often used for supplying water for fire sprinklers or fire fighting. When having a capacity larger than 500 gallons, they must be supported on masonry, reinforced concrete or steel, or be of Type IV construction.

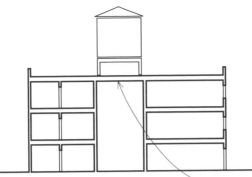

- When such tanks are above the lowest story, supports are to be of Type I-A construction. Thus one could construe § 1510.3 to say that all roof-mounted tanks are to be on supports of Type I-A construction.

Cooling Towers

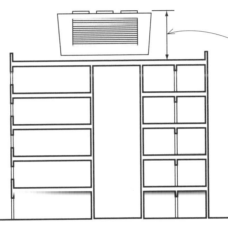

- Cooling towers that are larger than 250 sf (23.2 m²) in area or over 15' (4572) high and located on buildings more than 50' (15 240) high are to be of noncombustible construction.

- If the cooling tower is located on a lower part of a roof of a building that is more than 50' (15 240) in height, this provision could be construed to apply in this case as well.

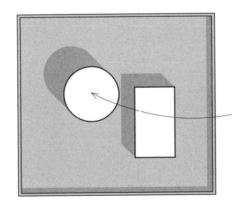

- Cooling towers, as for penthouses, may not exceed one-third of their supporting roof area. This is to be measured at the "base area" of the cooling tower. This would allow the cooling tower to extend beyond the base area below the cooling tower.

Towers, Spires, Domes, and Cupolas

Towers, spires, domes, and cupolas are considered to be rooftop structures that are not occupied. § 1510.5 requires these structures to at least match the fire-resistance of the building supporting them, with the exceptions noted to the right.

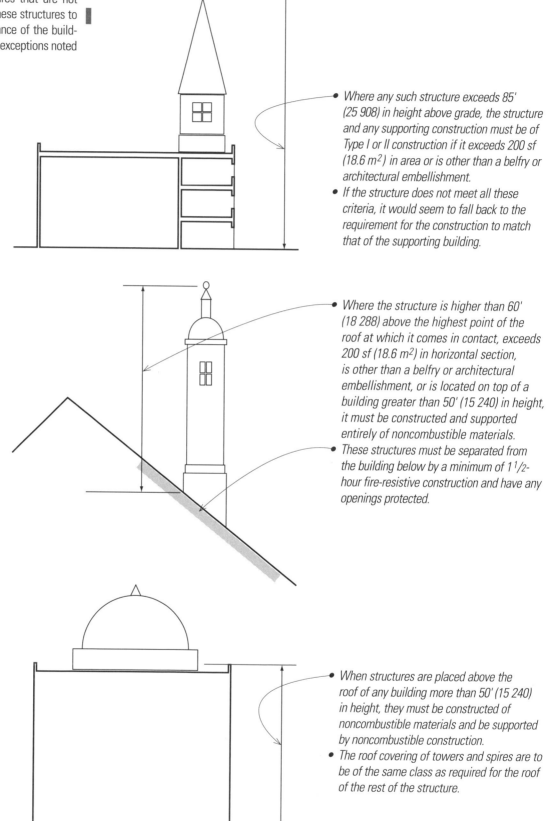

- Where any such structure exceeds 85' (25 908) in height above grade, the structure and any supporting construction must be of Type I or II construction if it exceeds 200 sf (18.6 m²) in area or is other than a belfry or architectural embellishment.
- If the structure does not meet all these criteria, it would seem to fall back to the requirement for the construction to match that of the supporting building.

- Where the structure is higher than 60' (18 288) above the highest point of the roof at which it comes in contact, exceeds 200 sf (18.6 m²) in horizontal section, is other than a belfry or architectural embellishment, or is located on top of a building greater than 50' (15 240) in height, it must be constructed and supported entirely of noncombustible materials.
- These structures must be separated from the building below by a minimum of 1¹/₂-hour fire-resistive construction and have any openings protected.

- When structures are placed above the roof of any building more than 50' (15 240) in height, they must be constructed of noncombustible materials and be supported by noncombustible construction.
- The roof covering of towers and spires are to be of the same class as required for the roof of the rest of the structure.

Mechanical Equipment Screens

Mechanical equipment screens are typically walls placed around rooftop-mounted mechanical equipment to screen equipment from the view of persons looking at a building from a distance. These screens are to be constructed of the same types of materials used for the exterior walls of the building, in accordance with the type of construction of the building.

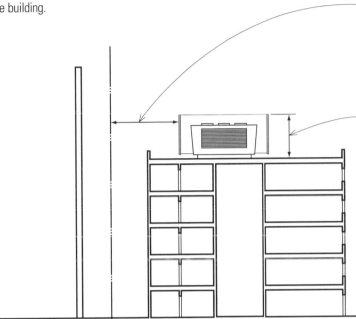

- Where the fire separation distance is greater than 5' (1524), mechanical equipment screens are not required to comply with the building's fire-resistance rating requirements.

- Mechanical equipment screens are not to exceed 18' (5486) in height above the roof deck, as measured to the highest point on the mechanical equipment screen.
- However, when located on buildings of Type IA construction, the height of mechanical equipment screens is not limited.

- Per § 1510.6.2, on buildings of Types I, II, III, and IV construction, regardless of the requirements in § 1510.6, mechanical equipment screens are permitted to be constructed of combustible materials if they are in accordance with a defined set of limitations based on fire separation distance and combustibility of the screening materials.

- Per § 1510.6.3, the height of mechanical equipment screens located on the roof decks of buildings of Type V construction is permitted to exceed the maximum building height as measured to the highest point on the mechanical equipment screen from grade plane if the screen complies with the criteria contained in this section.

Height of equipment screen above grade plane

Allowable building height for Type V construction

Photovoltaic Systems

Rooftop-mounted photovoltaic systems are to be designed in accordance with § 1510.7.

Rooftop mounted photovoltaic systems are to have the same fire classification as the roof assembly as required by § 1505.9.

Photovoltaic panels and modules mounted on top of a roof are to be listed and labeled in accordance with UL 1703 and shall be installed in accordance with the manufacturer's installation instructions.

• *Rooftop-mounted photovoltaic systems are to be designed for wind loads for components and cladding in accordance with Chapter 16, using an effective wind area based on the dimensions of a single unit frame.*

• *Two unit frames, each with multiple solar panels*

• *Rooftop-mounted photovoltaic systems shall be installed in accordance with the manufacturer's installation instructions.*

• *Per § 1512.1, photovoltaic panels and modules installed upon a roof or as an integral part of a roof assembly are to comply with the requirements of the International Building Code and the International Fire Code.*

Other Rooftop Structures

Per § 1510.8, those rooftop structures not regulated by the other sections in 1510, which are § 1510.2 through § 1510.7 are to comply with § 1510.8.1 through § 1510.8.5.

Aerial Supports

Supports for rooftop antennas and aerials are to be per § 1510.8.1. Aerial supports are to be constructed of noncombustible materials, except that aerial supports not greater than 12' (3658) in height as measured from the roof deck to the highest point on the aerial support are permitted to be constructed of combustible materials.

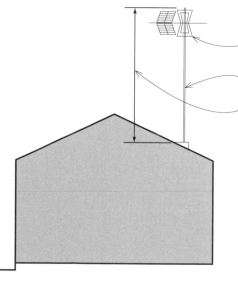

• *Rooftop antennas or aerials*

• *Aerial support*

• *Aerial supports not greater than 12' (3658) in height above the roof deck are permitted to be constructed of combustible materials. If the support is taller than 12' (3658) then it must be constructed of noncomustible materials.*

Bulkheads

Per § 1510.8.2, bulkheads used for the shelter of mechanical or electrical equipment or vertical shaft openings in the roof assembly shall comply with § 1510.2 as penthouses. Bulkheads used for any other purpose shall be considered as an additional story of the building.

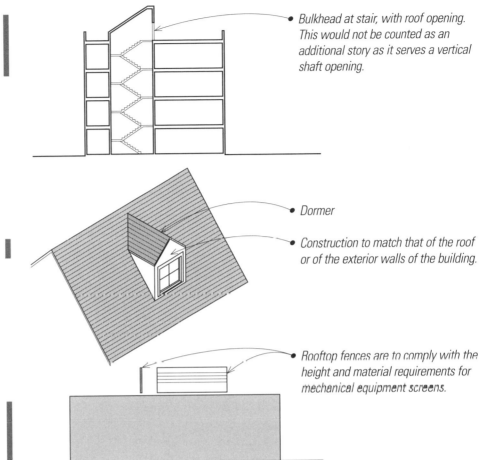

• *Bulkhead at stair, with roof opening. This would not be counted as an additional story as it serves a vertical shaft opening.*

• *Dormer*

• *Construction to match that of the roof or of the exterior walls of the building.*

Dormers

Per § 1510.8.3, dormers are to be of the same type of construction as required for the roof in which such dormers are located or the exterior walls of the building.

Fences

Per § 1510.8.4, fences and similar vertical structures located on roofs are to comply with the requirements for mechanical equipment screens contained in § 1510.6.

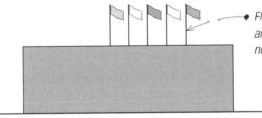

• *Rooftop fences are to comply with the height and material requirements for mechanical equipment screens.*

Flagpoles

Per § 1510.8.5, flagpoles and similar structures are not required to be constructed of noncombustible materials and are not limited in height or number.

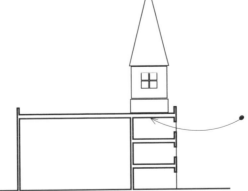

• *Flagpoles are unlimited in height and number, and need not be of noncombustible construction.*

Supporting Structures

Per § 1510.9 the structural frame and roof construction supporting imposed loads upon the roof by any rooftop structure are to comply with the requirements of Table 601.

• *Fire-resistance reduction permitted by Table 601, Note (a), is not to be applied to structural frames supporting roof structures.*

Roofs are typically replaced to comply with the requirements for new roofing materials.

- Per the exception in § 1511.1, where a roof has positive roof drainage (i.e., a slope sufficient to ensure drainage within 48 hours of precipitation, taking into consideration all loading deflections), a reroofing need not meet the minimum design slope requirement of $1/4$ unit vertical in 12 units horizontal (2% slope).

Reroofing requirements are concerned with not overloading existing roof structures by allowing multiple roof layers of heavy or combustible materials. Roof structures must be capable of supporting the loads for the new roofing system along with the weight of any existing materials that may remain. Also, the roof structure must be able to support the loads imposed by materials and equipment used during the reroofing process.

Applying new roofing without removing the old roof is allowed in limited circumstances. Existing roofing must be removed when any of the following conditions occur:

1. The roof or roof covering is water-soaked or deteriorated such that the existing roof is not an adequate base for added roofing.
2. If the existing roof covering is wood shakes, slate, or tiles.

- Note that an exception allows metal or tile roofs to be applied over wood shakes if combustible concealed spaces are avoided by applying gypsum board, mineral fiber or glass fiber over the shakes.

3. Where there are already two or more roof applications of any type of roof covering. This is to avoid overloading the roof structure with multiple layers of roofing.

Existing durable materials such as slate or clay tiles may be reapplied if in good condition and undamaged. Aggregate surfacing materials are not to be removed and reinstalled. Flashing may be reinstalled if in good condition.

16

Structural Provisions

This chapter is a summary of structural design requirements, which begin with Chapter 16 of the code. Chapter 16 sets forth general design criteria for structural loads to be accommodated by the structural system of a building. Detailed criteria for building materials are contained in the code chapters devoted to specific materials, such as wood (Chapter 23), concrete (Chapter 19), and steel (Chapter 22). Chapter 17 of the code governs the testing and inspection of construction materials. Chapter 18 of the code applies to the requirements for soils, site grading, and foundation design.

STRUCTURAL DESIGN

The structural design requirements contained in Chapter 16 apply to all buildings and structures. The chapter focuses on the engineering principles that underlie the requirements and design of structural systems to accommodate anticipated loads, such as the weight of the building, the weight of occupants and materials in the building, and loads imposed by nature such as wind, snow, floods and earthquakes.

Chapter 16 contains numerous tables and criteria that are to be applied in specific situations based on building use, occupancy, construction type and geographic location. Detailed analysis must be undertaken by the designer in concert with appropriate engineering consultants as needed to supplement the designer's training and expertise to prepare a code-compliant design.

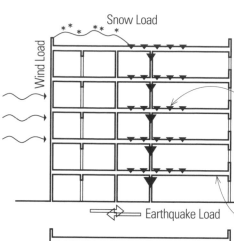

Wind Load
Snow Load
Earthquake Load

Definitions

Many of the terms in Chapter 16 are listed in § 1602 but are actually defined in Chapter 2. Other basic structural terms may not be defined, but also need to be understood. Terms include:

- *Dead Load: The weight of construction materials incorporated into a building, including architectural elements, such as walls, floors, roofs and ceilings, stairs, and finishes, as well as equipment attached to the structure.*

- *Note that many definitions in the IBC are derived from reference standards and are updated when the definitions in the reference standards change. For example, the definitions of rigid and flexible diaphragms have changed in the base reference standard, ASCE 7, and have also been updated in the IBC.*

- *Live Loads: Loads produced by the use and occupancy of a building and not including dead loads or environmental loads such as wind, snow, floods, or earthquakes.*

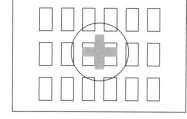

- *Essential Facilities: Buildings and other structures intended to remain operational in the event of extreme environmental loading, such as from wind, snow, floods, or earthquakes.*

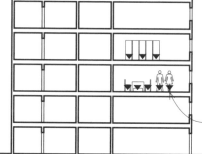

- *Stress is the internal resistance or reaction of an elastic body to external forces applied to it, expressed in units of force per unit of cross-sectional area.*

- *Nonductile Element: An element having a failure mode that results in an abrupt loss of resistance when the element is deformed beyond the deformation corresponding to its nominal strength. Such elements lose their strength when deformed beyond their load ranges.*

- *Ductile Element: An element capable of sustaining large cyclic deformation without any significant loss of strength. Such elements can deform and still maintain structural strength.*

- *Strain is the deformation of a body under the action of an applied force, equal to the ratio of the change in size or shape to the original size or shape of a stressed element.*

Construction Documents

Construction documents must have sufficient information to allow the AHJ to review the documents for code compliance. The documents are to show the size, section dimensions and relative locations of structural members. Design loads are to be indicated to verify compliance with structural design requirements for various types of loading. Light-frame buildings, such as houses and small commercial buildings constructed under the conventional framing provisions of § 2308, have a separate, shorter set of design requirements for floor and roof live loads, ground snow load, basic wind speed, seismic design category, and site class.

The construction documents are to show the loads and information for specified items. The detailed requirements for these items will be elaborated on later in this chapter.

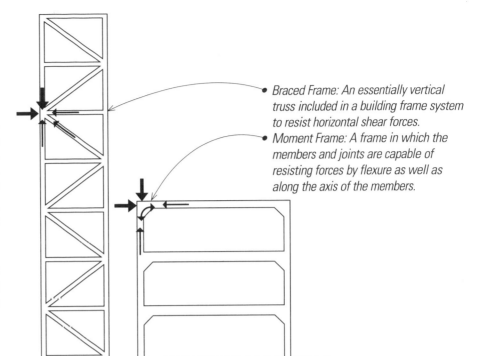

- *Braced Frame: An essentially vertical truss included in a building frame system to resist horizontal shear forces.*
- *Moment Frame: A frame in which the members and joints are capable of resisting forces by flexure as well as along the axis of the members.*

- *Shear Wall: A wall designed to resist lateral forces applied parallel to the plane of the wall.*
- *Wall, Load Bearing: Defined as any metal or wood stud wall that supports more than 100 pounds per lineal foot (1459 N/m). Also, any masonry or concrete wall that supports more than 200 pounds per lineal foot (2919 N/m). The basic concept is that bearing walls support the weight of the structure above them in a way that their removal would compromise the structural stability of the building. Non-load-bearing walls could be removed with no impact on the building's structural system.*

General Design Requirements

Buildings are to be designed in accordance with one of several defined and approved structural design methods, such as the strength design method, the load and resistance factor design method, the allowable stress method, and so forth. The structure is to support the factored loads in load combinations as defined in the code.

Serviceability

The structure is to be designed to limit deflections and lateral drift under anticipated loading. Load effects on the structure are to be determined by application of a rational analysis taking into account equilibrium of the structure, general stability, and short-term and long-term material properties.

Risk Category

Table 1604.5 classifies buildings into risk categories by importance. Factors noted in the structural chapters are for typical buildings. Values for loads and strengths are to be increased by the factors based on the anticipated consequences of the failure of the structure being categorized.

- Buildings with low occupancy loads and with little hazard to human life in the event of failure, such as agricultural buildings or minor storage facilities, fall into Risk Category I.
- Typical buildings not classified as any other category are classified as Category II.
- Category III buildings are those where structural failures would be a substantial hazard to human life. These include structures such as assembly areas having more than 300 occupants, schools, health-care facilities, and detention facilities.
- Essential facilities, such as hospitals with surgery or emergency facilities, fire stations, police stations, water and power stations that need to be relied on in emergencies, have the highest importance, Category IV.
- Note that the presence of quantities of hazardous materials sufficient to pose a threat to the public if they are released can place a structure in either Risk Category III or IV, depending on the quantities of such materials, as governed by the hazardous materials tables in § 307.

Calculation formulas apply different factors for each category, taking into account the relative importance of each facility. Thus "essential facilities" may have factors of up to 1.5 applied to loading criteria to provide additional strength to such structures in the event of such events as hurricanes, earthquakes, or floods. Note that these factors are applied to external loading, not other effects such as fires or loads imposed by use. These other load factors are addressed in live load tables.

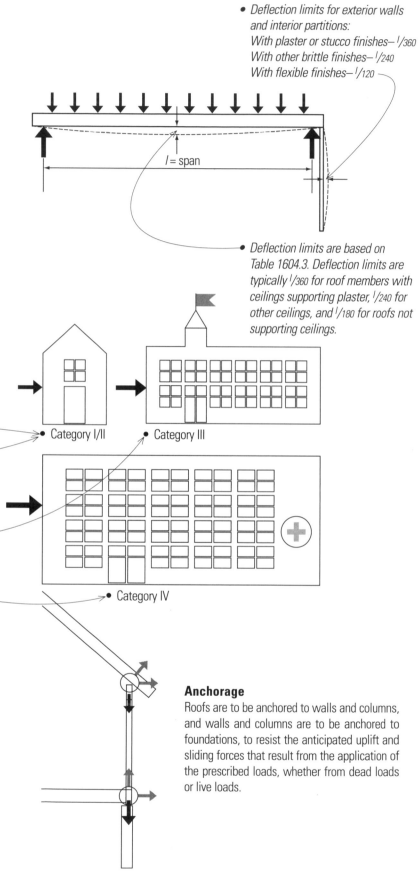

- Deflection limits for exterior walls and interior partitions:
  With plaster or stucco finishes—$l/360$
  With other brittle finishes—$l/240$
  With flexible finishes—$l/120$

l = span

- Deflection limits are based on Table 1604.3. Deflection limits are typically $l/360$ for roof members with ceilings supporting plaster, $l/240$ for other ceilings, and $l/180$ for roofs not supporting ceilings.

Category I/II

Category III

Category IV

Anchorage

Roofs are to be anchored to walls and columns, and walls and columns are to be anchored to foundations, to resist the anticipated uplift and sliding forces that result from the application of the prescribed loads, whether from dead loads or live loads.

Load Combinations

Various combinations of dead loads, live loads, seismic loads, and wind loads are to be applied in the design of structural systems. The load factors for each combination depend on the type of analysis used. Various combinations of loading are to be examined and the design is to resist the most critical effects of the combinations specified. We will examine the detailed descriptions for each load category.

Dead Loads

Actual weights of materials and construction are to be used to determine dead loads. Fixed service equipment is to be considered as dead load. These fixed elements include plumbing, electrical feeders, HVAC systems, and fire sprinklers. Dead loads are to be considered as permanent loads.

Live Loads

As defined in Chapter 2, live loads are those produced by the use or occupancy of the building. Table 1607.1 defines minimum uniformly distributed live loads and concentrated loads for various occupancies. Per § 1607.2, live loads not designated in Table 1607.1 shall be determined in accordance with a method approved by the building official. Thus live loads not noted in the table must be evaluated by an approved method.

Concentrated loads are to be determined either by the table or the approved methods, and the design is to use the method producing the greatest load effect. Concentrated loads are to be applied over an area of $2\frac{1}{2}$ feet square [$6\frac{1}{4}$ sf (0.58 m²)], located so as to produce the maximum load effect on the structural members being designed.

Where partitions may be installed and later moved, a uniformly distributed partition live load of 15 psf (0.74 kN/m²) is to be assumed unless the specified floor live load is 80 psf (3.8 kN/m²) or greater.

To the right is a summary of examples from Table 1607.1. The numbers alongside the occupancy correspond to the location of the examples in the complete table.

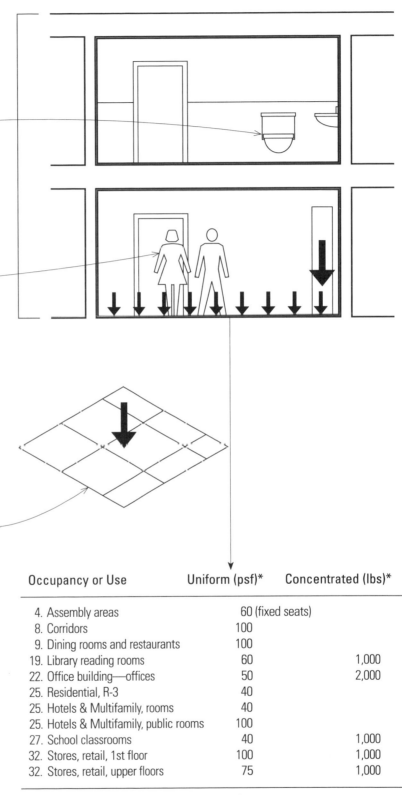

Occupancy or Use	Uniform (psf)*	Concentrated (lbs)*
4. Assembly areas	60 (fixed seats)	
8. Corridors	100	
9. Dining rooms and restaurants	100	
19. Library reading rooms	60	1,000
22. Office building—offices	50	2,000
25. Residential, R-3	40	
25. Hotels & Multifamily, rooms	40	
25. Hotels & Multifamily, public rooms	100	
27. School classrooms	40	1,000
32. Stores, retail, 1st floor	100	1,000
32. Stores, retail, upper floors	75	1,000

* 1 pound per square foot (psf) = 0.0479 kN/m²; 1 pound = 0.004448 kN

STRUCTURAL DESIGN

Loads on Handrails and Guards

Handrails and guards are to be designed to resist a load of 50 pounds per lineal foot (0.73 kN/m) applied in any direction at the top and to transfer this load through the supports to the structure supporting the rail or guard.

- Handrail assemblies are also to be able to resist a single concentrated load of 200 pounds (0.89 kN) applied in any direction at any point along the top. This load can be considered independently of the uniform load noted previously.

- Intermediate rails, that is, those not the handrail, are to be able to resist a load of 50 pounds (0.22 kN) on an area not to exceed 1 sf (0.09 m²) including the openings and spaces between rails. These are not required to be superimposed with the other railing loads noted above.

- Grab bars are to be designed to resist a single concentrated load of 250 pounds (1.11 kN) applied in any direction at any point.

Roof Loads

Roof loads acting on a sloping surface are to be assumed to act vertically on the horizontal projection of that surface.

- Minimum roof live loads are determined based on roof slopes per § 1607.12.2.1 through 1607.12.3.

- Landscaped roofs are to have a uniform design live load of 20 psf (0.958 kN/m²). The weight of the landscaping materials is to be considered as dead load, and the weight is to be calculated based on saturation of the soil.

Interior Walls and Partitions

Walls that exceed 6' (1829) in height are to be designed to resist loads to which they are subjected, but not less than a horizontal load of 5 psf (0.240 kN/m²).

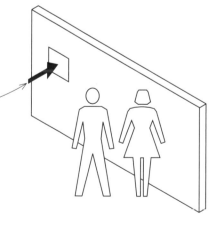

Snow Loads

Snow loads are to be determined in accordance with a reference standard: Chapter 7 of ASCE 7. Snow loads in the contiguous United States are shown in Figure 1608.2. Snow loads are determined based on historical data and are correlated to geographic location and to elevations.

- For example, the snow load in northcentral Kansas is 25 psf (1.19 kN/m²).
- In northeast Arizona, the load varies from zero up to the 3000' (914 m) elevation; 5 psf up to the 4500' elevation (0.24 kN/m² load up to the 1372 m elevation); 10 psf up to the 5400' elevation (0.48 kN/m² load up to the 1645 m elevation); and 15 psf up to the 6300' elevation (0.72 kN/m² load up to the 1920 m elevation).
- In heavy snow areas, such as the Sierra Nevada and the Rocky Mountains, the snow load is to be determined by case studies that are based on 50-year recurrence data and must be approved by the building official.

Roofs are to be designed in accordance with ASCE 7 to accommodate snow loads under varying conditions, such as:

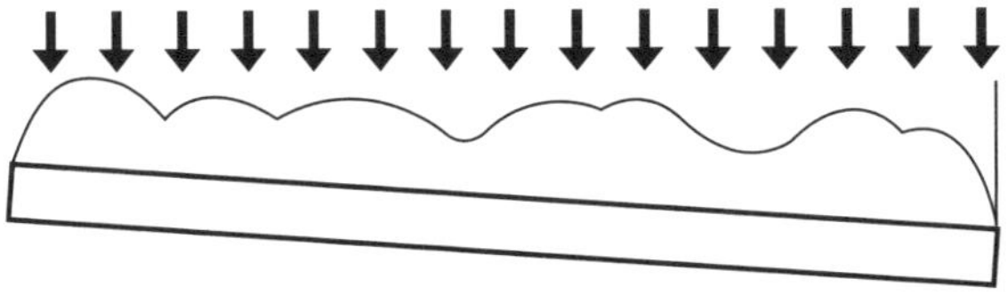

- *Snow loads on flat roofs (≤ 5°; 0.09 rad), taking into account such factors as exposure and rain-on-snow surcharge*

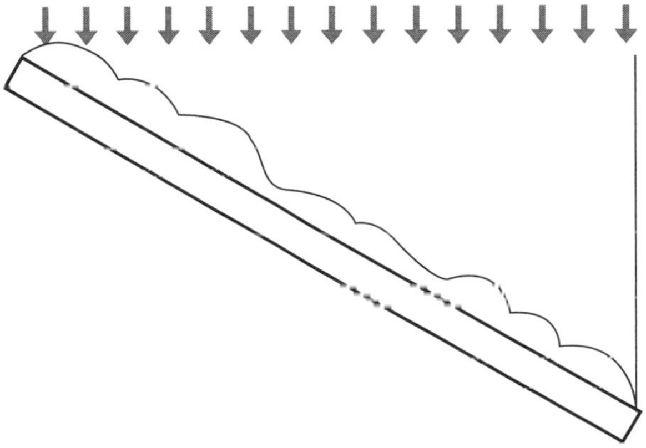

- *Snow loads on sloped roofs (> 5°; 0.09 rad)*

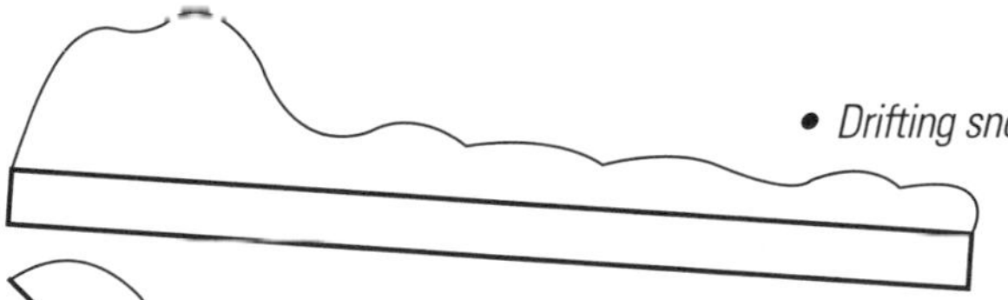

- *Drifting snow on low roofs*

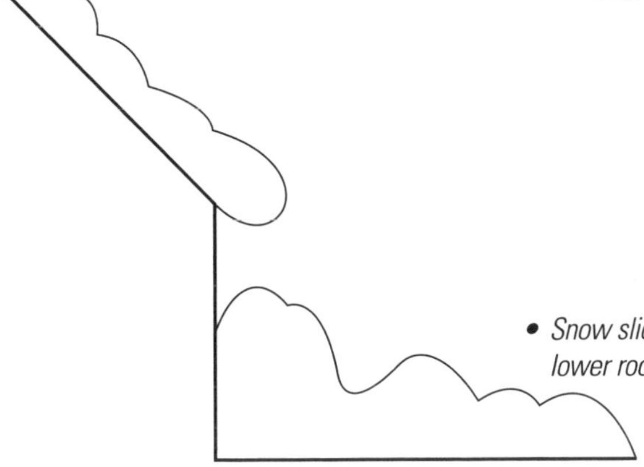

- *Snow sliding from higher sloped roofs onto lower roofs*

STRUCTURAL DESIGN

Wind Loads

Buildings and portions of buildings are to be designed to withstand, at a minimum, the wind loads included in the code in accordance with Chapters 26–30 of ASCE 7. The wind is assumed to come from any horizontal direction, and no reduction is to be taken for the effect of shielding by other structures. This is in keeping with the principle that the code applies to the building in question and is affected neither positively nor negatively by adjacent buildings. There are, however, portions of § 1609 where adjacent site and topographic conditions may impact wind loads. See § 1609.4.

- Total wind loads are determined by taking the product of the wind load per square foot multiplied by the area of building or structure projected on a vertical plane normal to the wind direction.
- Wind is to be assumed to come from any horizontal direction and wind pressures are to be assumed to act normal to the surface considered.
- Because wind can create suction as well as pressure effects on a building, the force is to be resisted in either direction normal to the surface.

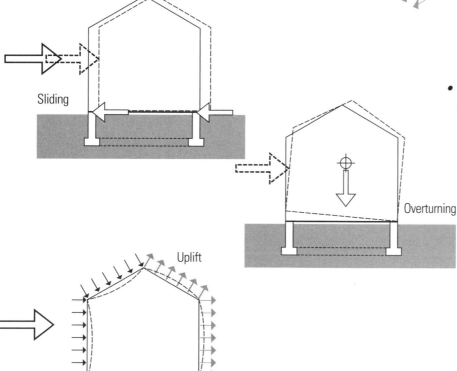

- Structural members and systems as well as building cladding must be anchored to resist overturning, uplift, or sliding caused by wind forces. Continuous load paths for these forces are to be provided to the foundation.

Sliding

Overturning

Uplift

Wind Speed

Wind speeds are designated as "ultimate design" or "nominal design" wind speeds and are used for either strength design or allowable stress designs respectively. The ultimate design wind speeds are indicated in Figures 1609.3 (1), (2), and (3), and vary based on the building's risk category and location. The ultimate design wind speeds for a Risk Category II building vary from 110 mph (49 m/s) on the West Coast of the U.S. to 180 mph (80 m/s) in hurricane-prone areas in southern Florida. These wind speeds would convert to a nominal design wind speed, or what was previously called the "basic wind speed," of 85 mph (38 m/s) for the West Coast and 139 mph (61m/s) for southern Florida when using allowable stress design (ASD).

Exposure Category

The exposure category reflects the how ground surface irregularities affect design wind pressure. The exposure conditions vary from the most protected to the least protected wind exposures. Where buildings have multiple exposures, the condition that results in the highest wind force shall apply. The exposures are determined by applying a "surface roughness" category to wind calculations over each 45° (0.79 rad) sector from which wind can impact the building. The factors roughly increase with each surface roughness category:

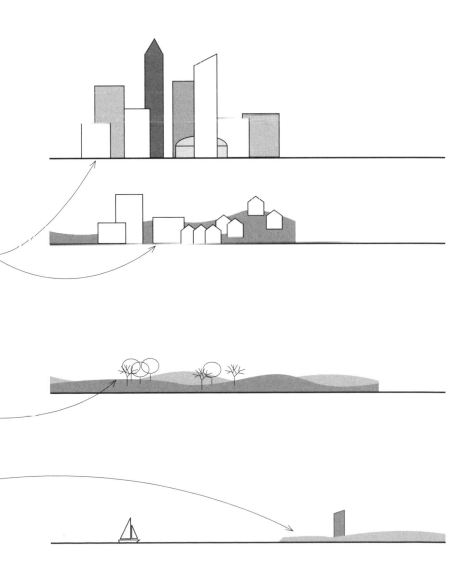

- Surface Roughness B in urban and suburban residential areas; this is the assumed basic exposure. For buildings more than 30' (9140) tall, Exposure B occurs when the surface roughness prevails in the upwind direction for a distance of at least 2,600' (792 m) or 20 times the height of the building, whichever is greater. For buildings less than or equal to 30' (9140) in height, the distance is 1,500' (457 m).
- Surface Roughness C in open terrain with scattered obstructions, including areas in flat open country and grasslands. Exposure C occurs when Exposure B or D does not apply.
- Surface Roughness D in flat, unobstructed areas and water surfaces. Exposure D occurs when surface roughness D prevails upwind for at least 5,000' (1524 m) or 20 times the height of the building, whichever is greater. Exposure D extends inland from the shoreline for 600' (183 m) or 20 times the height of the structure, whichever is greater.

Soil Lateral Load

§ 1610 requires basement walls and retaining walls to be designed to resist lateral loads imposed by soils behind the walls. These walls are to be designed to be stable against overturning, sliding, excessive foundation pressure and water uplift. The soil loads are to be per Table 1610.1 and range from 30 psf per foot of depth (4.7 kPa/m) for gravels to 60 psf per foot of depth (9.4 kPa/m) for relatively dense inorganic clay soils.

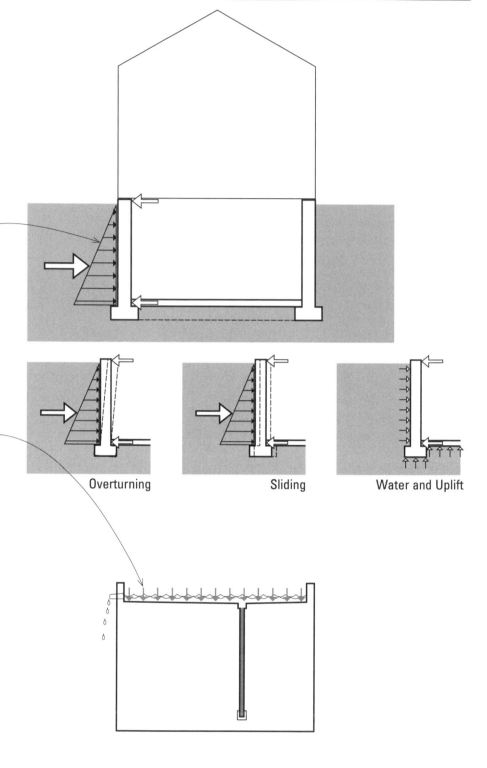

Overturning   Sliding   Water and Uplift

Rain Loads

§ 1611 specifies that roofs are to be designed to accommodate the load of accumulated water when roof drains are clogged. Roofs with a slope less than a $1/4$ unit vertical in 12 units horizontal (2% slope) must be analyzed to determine if ponding will result in progressive deformation of the roof members, leading to potential roof instability or failure in accordance with Section 8.4 of ASCE 7. The anticipated depth of water is based on the difference in elevation between the normal roof drain system and the outlet of the overflow system.

Flood Loads

§ 1612 requires that, in flood hazard areas established under the Federal Energy Management Agency Flood Insurance Study Program, all new buildings as well as major improvements or reconstruction projects must be designed to resist the effects of flood hazards or flood loads. Determination of whether a building falls under this requirement is based on locally adopted flood-hazard maps. These identify the anticipated flooding areas and elevations of flood waters for given anticipated return periods such as 50 or 100 years. The elevation and location of the building site must be compared to the flood-hazard maps to determine if this section is applicable.

Earthquake Loads

§ 1613 contains the provisions for the seismic design of building structures. Earthquake design must be investigated for every structure and included to varying degrees based on the location of the building and the anticipated seismicity of the location. Earthquake design can be quite complex and involve detailed calculations. Certain basic types of structure, notably those wood-frame residences and light commercial buildings using the Conventional Light-Frame Construction provisions of § 2308, are deemed to comply with the seismic requirements of the code. Other more complex buildings must undergo seismic analysis based on ASCE 7. This analysis takes into account several basic factors. While we will not go into the design calculation bases in detail, it is worth understanding the basic criteria that are to be addressed by seismic analysis and design. The 2006 edition of the code greatly shortened the earthquake section of Chapter 16 by adopting references to ASCE 7. Our discussion is conceptual, with the assumption that those seeking greater detail will refer to the design criteria contained in ASCE 7.

Chapter 16 requires that all structures be designed and constructed to resist the effects of earthquake motions and be assigned a Seismic Design Category based on anticipated earthquake acceleration, risk category, and seismic design of the building as outlined in § 1613.3.5 and Tables 1613.3.5 (1 and 2).

Seismic forces are produced in a structure by ground motions that cause a time-dependent response in the structure. The response generated by the ground motions depends on:

- the magnitude, duration, and harmonic content of the ground motions
- the dynamic properties of the structure (size, configuration, and stiffness)
- the type and characteristics of the soil supporting the structure

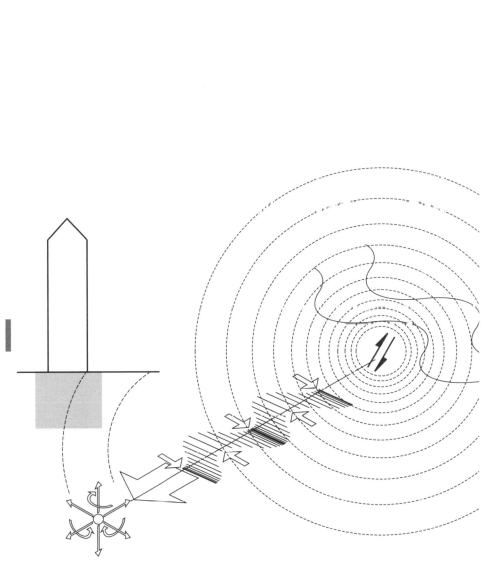

Site Ground Motion

§ 1613 provides procedures for determining design-earthquake ground motions.

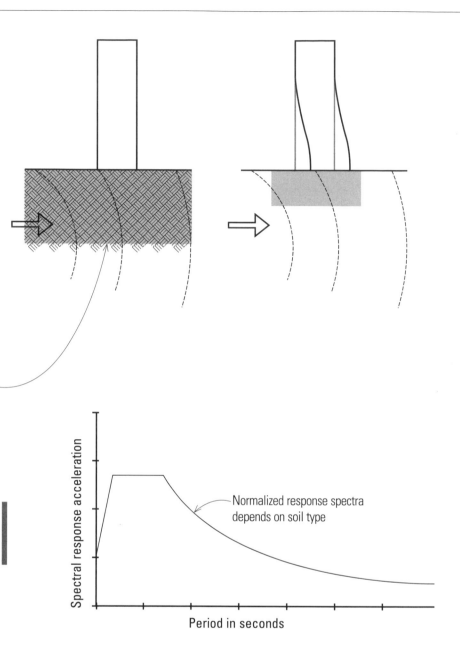

The magnitude of earthquake ground motions at a specific site depends on the proximity of the site to the earthquake source, the site's soil characteristics, and the attenuation of the peak acceleration. The dynamic response of a structure to earthquake ground motions can be represented by a graph of spectral response acceleration versus period.

Site class definitions are to be per § 1613.3.2. Based on the site soil properties, the site shall be classified as Site Class A, B, C, D, E, or F in accordance with Chapter 20 of ASCE 7.

Where the soil properties are not known in sufficient detail to determine the site class, Site Class D is to be used unless the building official or geotechnical data determines Site Class E or F soils are present at the site.

Figures 1613.3 (1) through (8) map the maximum spectral response accelerations for the United States and its territories, now including Guam and American Samoa, at short (0.2 second) and longer 1-second periods. The spectral response accelerations are given in percentages of gravity (g), assuming Site Class B (rock).

Normalized response spectra depends on soil type

Spectral response acceleration

Period in seconds

Structural Design Criteria

All structures require lateral-force-resisting and vertical-force-resisting systems having adequate strength, stiffness, and energy dissipation capacity to withstand the anticipated or design earthquake ground motions.

- These ground motions are assumed to occur along any horizontal direction of a structure.
- Continuous load paths are required to transfer forces induced by earthquake ground motions from points of application to points of resistance.

Seismic Design Categories (SDC)

The seismic design section requires that each structure be assigned a Seismic Design Category (A, B, C, D, E or F) based on the occupancy category and the anticipated severity of the earthquake ground motion at the site. This classification is used to determine permissible structural systems, limitations on height and irregularity, which components must be designed for seismic resistance, and the type of lateral force analysis required.

Risk Groups

Risk Groups are taken from the classification of buildings in § 1604.

- Risk Group I refers to low-hazard uses such as agricultural buildings and minor storage facilities.
- Risk Group II refers to most buildings that cannot be categorized into other groups.
- Risk Group III includes buildings whose failure would result in substantial risk due to use or occupancy.
- Risk Group IV comprises structures having essential facilities for post earthquake recovery or a substantial amount of hazardous substances.

Seismic Design Category

(short period used for illustration except as noted)*

Risk Category	I or II	III	IV
Short Period: < 0.167g	A	A	A
0.167g up to 0.33g	B	B	C
0.33g up to 0.50g	C	C	D
> 0.50g	D	D	D
*for 1-second period	E*	E*	F*

$S_I \geq 0.75g$ for noted occupancy category, set by § 1613.3.5

* Seismic Design Categories from Table 1613.3.5 (1) or (2)
* E, if 1-second period lateral acceleration greater than or equal to 0.75g for Risk Categories I, II, III
* F, if 1-second period lateral acceleration greater than or equal to 0.75g for Risk Category IV

Determination of Seismic Design Category

All structures must be assigned a Seismic Design Category based on its Seismic Use Group and the design spectral response acceleration coefficient, based on either its short or 1-second period response acceleration, whichever produces the most severe SDC.

The design criteria provide the design requirements for buildings in Seismic Design Category A because earthquakes are possible but rare. These structures must have all of their parts interconnected and be provided with a lateral-force-resisting system to resist 0.01 of the design lateral force.

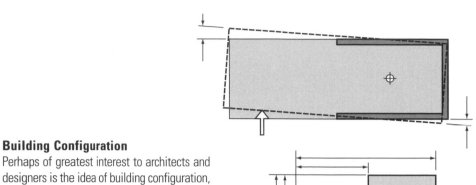

Building Configuration

Perhaps of greatest interest to architects and designers is the idea of building configuration, which classifies buildings into regular and irregular configurations. Irregularity in a building, either in its plan or its section configuration, can impact its susceptibility to damage in an earthquake.

Plan Irregularities

Plan irregularities include:

- Torsional irregularity existing when the maximum story drift at one end of a structure is 120–140% greater than the average of the story drifts at the two ends of the structure

- Reentrant corners where the projections are greater than 15% of the plan dimension in the given direction

- Discontinuous diaphragms, especially when containing cutouts or open areas greater than 50% of the gross enclosed diaphragm area

- Out-of-plane offsets creating discontinuities in lateral-force-resisting paths

- Nonparallel systems in which the vertical lateral-force-resisting systems are not parallel or symmetric about the major orthogonal axes of the lateral-force-resisting systems

Vertical Irregularities

Vertical or sectional irregularities include:

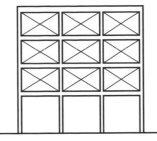

- *Soft story having a lateral stiffness significantly less than that in the story above*

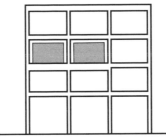

- *Weight or mass irregularity caused by the mass of a story being significantly heavier than the mass of an adjacent story*

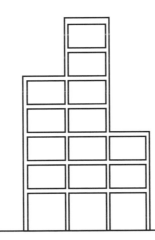

- *Geometric irregularity caused by one horizontal dimension of the lateral force-resisting system that is significantly greater than that of an adjacent story*

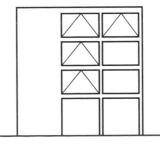

- *In-plane discontinuity in vertical lateral-force-resisting elements*

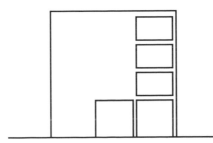

- *Weak story caused by the lateral strength of one story being significantly less than that in the story above*

Earthquake Loads:
Minimum Design Lateral Force and
Related Effects

The design criteria define the combined effect of horizontal and vertical earthquake-induced forces as well as the maximum seismic load effect. These load effects are to be used when calculating the load combinations of § 1605.

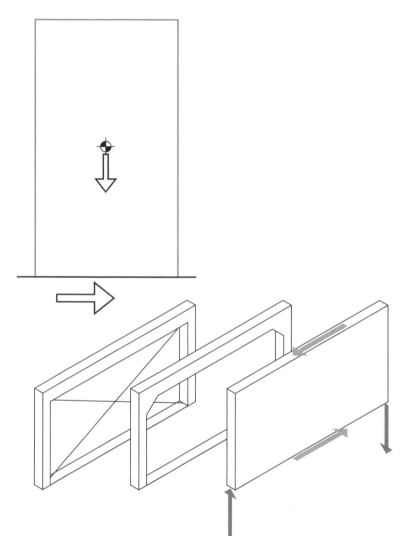

Redundancy

Redundancy provides multiple paths for a load to travel from a point of application to a point of resistance. The design criteria assign a redundancy coefficient to a structure based on the extent of structural redundancy inherent in its lateral-force-resisting system.

Deflection and Drift Limits

The design criteria specify that the design story drift not exceed the allowable story drift obtained from the criteria specifications. All portions of a building should act as a structural unit unless they are separated structurally by a distance sufficient to avoid damaging contact when under deflection.

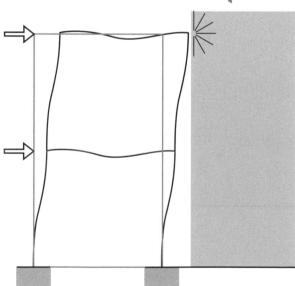

Equivalent Lateral Force Procedure

The equivalent lateral force procedure for the seismic design of buildings assumes that the buildings are fixed at their base.

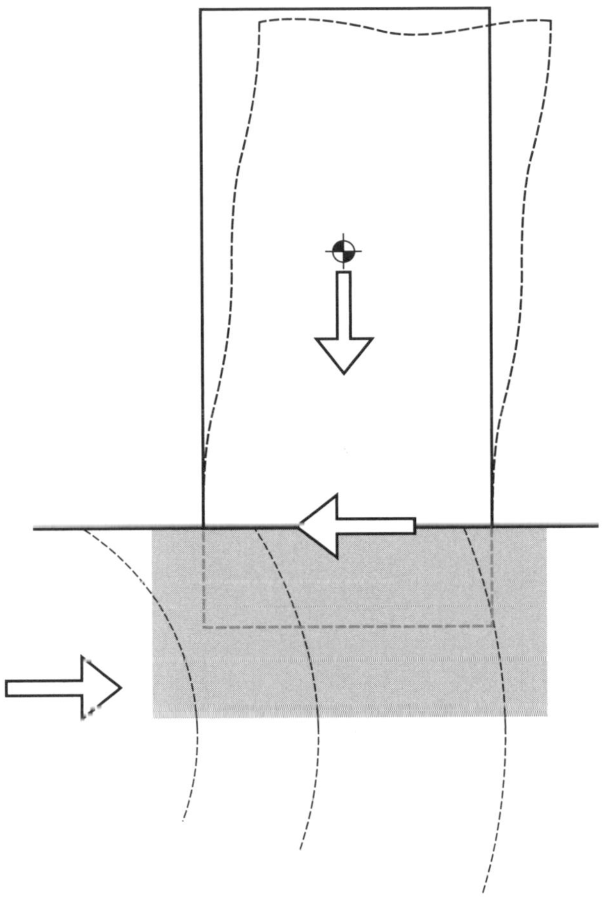

Seismic Base Shear

- The basic formula for determining seismic base shear (V) is:

$$V = C_s W$$

where:
C_s = the seismic response coefficient determined from the design criteria and
W = the effective seismic weight (dead load) of the structure, including partitions and permanent mechanical and electrical equipment.

- *The seismic response coefficient is equal to a design spectral response coefficient amplified by an occupancy importance factor and reduced by a response modification factor based on the type of seismic-force-resisting system used.*

$$\text{Seismic response coefficient} = \frac{\text{Design spectral response acceleration}}{(\text{Response modification factor} / \text{Seismic importance factor})}$$

Vertical Distribution of Seismic Forces

The design criteria specify how the seismic base shear is to be distributed at each story level.

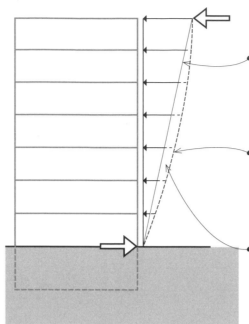

- The seismic base shear for buildings having a fundamental period not exceeding a specified period (around 0.5 second) are distributed linearly along the height with a zero value at the base and the maximum value at the top.
- The seismic base shear for buildings having a fundamental period exceeding a specified period (around 2.5 seconds) is distributed in a parabolic manner along the height with a zero value at the base and the maximum value at the top.
- The seismic base shear for buildings having a fundamental period between the specified low and high limits is distributed by linear interpolation between a linear and a parabolic distribution.

Horizontal Shear Distribution

Seismic design story shear is the sum of the lateral forces acting at all levels above the story. The design criteria specify how the seismic design story shear is distributed according to the rigidity or flexibility of horizontal diaphragms and torsion.

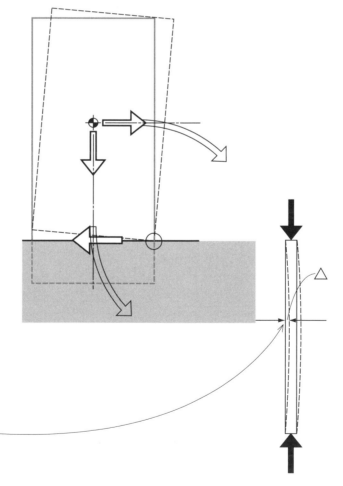

Overturning

A structure must be able to resist the overturning moments caused by the lateral forces determined to impact the structure.

Drift and P-delta Effects

Frames and columns are to be designed to resist both brittle fracture and overturning instability when building elements drift. They should also be able to resist the second-order effects on shear, axial forces and moments introduced during displacement. These forces are defined as the "P-delta effects."

Dynamic Analysis Procedure for the Seismic Design of Buildings

The static analysis contained in the design criteria may only be used for buildings with a lower Seismic Design Category, or buildings with a regular configuration that meet height limitations and are assigned a higher Seismic Design Category. There are basically three types of dynamic analysis procedures that may be used for the seismic design of all buildings: modal response spectra analysis, linear time-history analysis, and nonlinear time-history analysis.

Seismic-Force-Resisting Systems

There are several basic types of seismic-force-resisting systems:

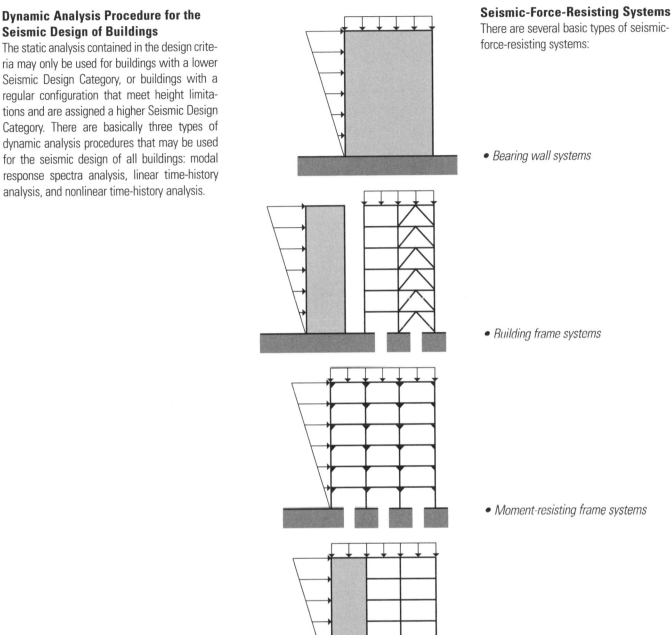

- *Bearing wall systems*

- *Building frame systems*

- *Moment-resisting frame systems*

- *Dual systems with special moment frames*
- *Dual systems with intermediate moment frames*

- *Inverted pendulum systems*

Detailing of Structural Components

There are requirements for the design and detailing of the components making up the seismic-force-resisting system of a building.

After a building is analyzed by calculations to determine its dynamic and static responses to seismic loads, it must be detailed to implement the design requirements of its seismic-force-resisting system.

This analysis must determine the worst-case forces based on the direction of seismic load, and that maximum force is to be used as the design basis.

Among details to be considered are:

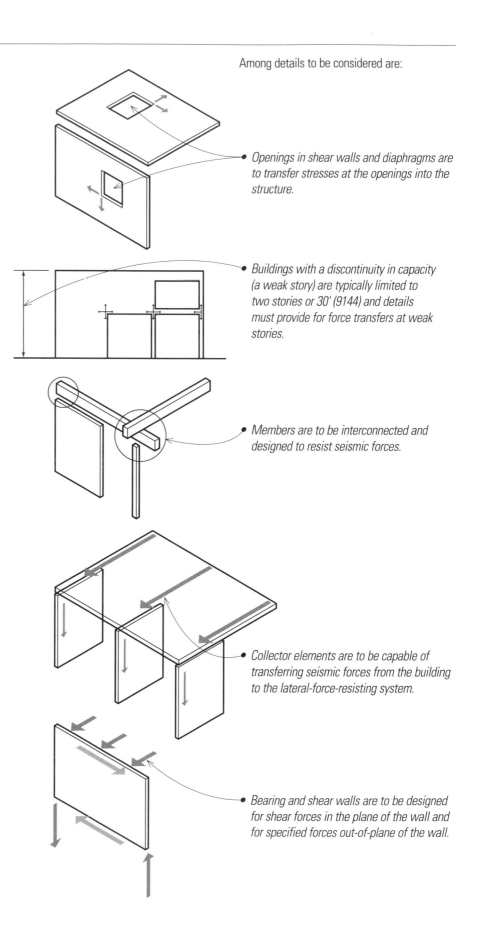

- Openings in shear walls and diaphragms are to transfer stresses at the openings into the structure.

- Buildings with a discontinuity in capacity (a weak story) are typically limited to two stories or 30' (9144) and details must provide for force transfers at weak stories.

- Members are to be interconnected and designed to resist seismic forces.

- Collector elements are to be capable of transferring seismic forces from the building to the lateral-force-resisting system.

- Bearing and shear walls are to be designed for shear forces in the plane of the wall and for specified forces out-of-plane of the wall.

Seismic Design of Architectural, Mechanical and Electrical Components

The seismic design of such non-structural elements as architectural, mechanical, and electrical components must also be considered. These components are typically not part of the structural system either for resisting conventional gravity loads or seismic forces. However, these components, when a permanent part of the building, must be seismically restrained. Failures of these systems result in a great deal of physical damage and are often a factor in casualties from earthquakes. Also, life safety systems, such as fire sprinklers and electrical systems, need to be functional after an earthquake.

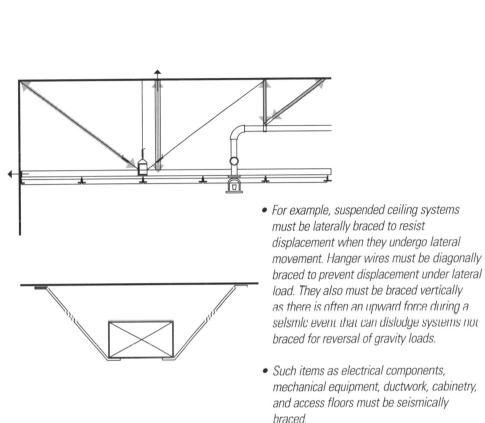

- *For example, suspended ceiling systems must be laterally braced to resist displacement when they undergo lateral movement. Hanger wires must be diagonally braced to prevent displacement under lateral load. They also must be braced vertically as there is often an upward force during a seismic event that can dislodge systems not braced for reversal of gravity loads.*

- *Such items as electrical components, mechanical equipment, ductwork, cabinetry, and access floors must be seismically braced.*

- *Also, such elements as exterior architectural veneers, cantilevered exterior elements, signs, and building ornament must be designed and detailed to resist seismic forces.*

17

Special Inspections and Tests

Construction materials and methods of construction are subject to approval and inspection for quality, workmanship, and labeling. The intent of the provisions and requirements contained in Chapter 17 is that materials should have the properties, strengths, and performance that are represented and used as the basis for design. For products, these criteria are applied at the factory. For construction, these criteria are applied either during fabrication for shop-fabricated items or at the job site during construction. Testing and approval agencies must be acceptable to the building official. The building official typically recognizes accreditation by national agencies that certify approval processes and inspection protocols.

Special inspections are required for the manufacture, installation, fabrication, erection, or placement of components where special expertise is required to ensure compliance with design documents and referenced standards. Such inspections may be required to be continuous or periodic, depending on the critical nature of the process and whether the inspector can determine compliance without being present during the entire process. Testing and sample gathering take place to be certain that materials that are to be covered by other construction, such as soils work, footings, or structural elements, are determined to meet design and code criteria before they are covered up. Special inspection does not take the place of structural observation, which is the visual observation of the construction process for the structural system. Conversely, such observation does not take the place of special inspection, as observations by their nature are periodic and not continuous. The definition of structural observation in Chapter 2 specifically states that it does not waive responsibilities for special inspections required by §1705.

Special Inspections

§1705 specifies certain types of work that require inspection by special inspectors, employed by the owner or the responsible design professional acting as the owner's agent. The special inspector is subject to the approval of the Building Official. The registered design professional is to prepare a statement of the types of special inspections required by § 1704. There are many areas of construction where special inspection may be required. Note that per Exception 2 to §1704.2, special inspections are not required in U occupancies accessory to a residential occupancy unless otherwise required by the building official. It is assumed by the International Building Code that 1- and 2-family dwellings and townhouses will be constructed and inspected under the International Residential Code. A representative list of inspections that can be anticipated on most relatively complex projects include the following. Note that criteria for some items, such as those for structural steel quality assurance, are contained in reference documents external to the code. Where that occurs we have included a note about the reference document, but we have not shown the specific sections from the reference document.

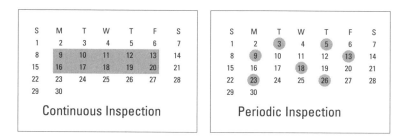

Continuous Inspection   Periodic Inspection

Verification and Inspection (External Reference Document)	Continuous Inspection	Periodic Inspection
Steel		
Material verification for high-strength bolts (ANSI/AISC 360-10)	—	calendar
Inspection of high-strength bolting with bearing type connections (ANSI/AISC 360-10)	—	
Inspection of high-strength bolting with pretensioned and slip-critical connections with matchmarking, twist-off bolts or direct tension indicator methods (ANSI/AISC 360-10)	calendar	calendar
Pretensioned and slip-critical joints with twist-off nuts, without matchmarking or calibrated wrench methods (ANSI/AISC 360-10)		
Material verification of structural steel (ANSI/AISC 360-10)	—	—
Material verification of weld filler materials (ANSI/AISC 360-10)	—	—

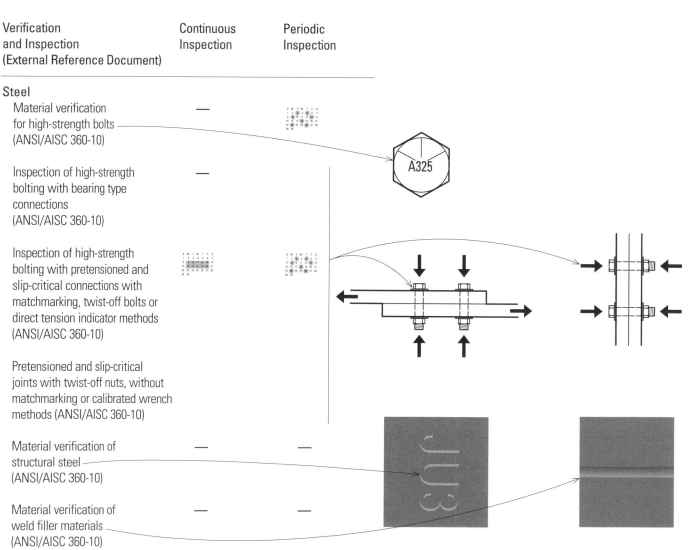

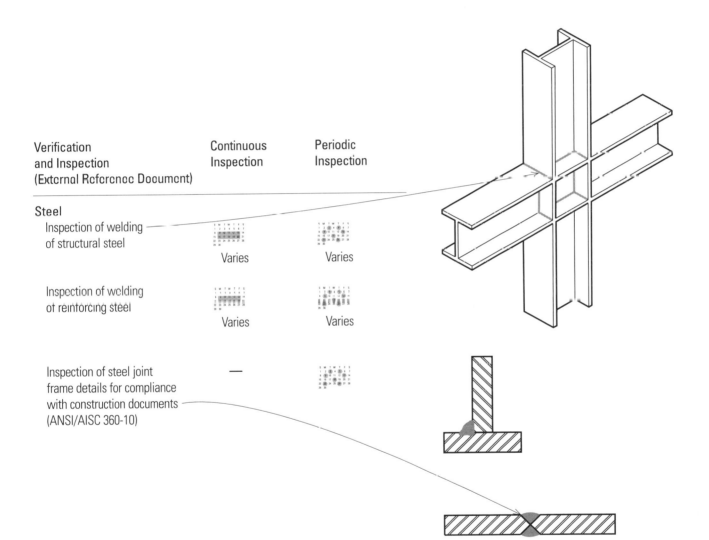

Verification and Inspection (External Reference Document)	Continuous Inspection	Periodic Inspection
Steel		
Inspection of welding of structural steel	Varies	Varies
Inspection of welding of reinforcing steel	Varies	Varies
Inspection of steel joint frame details for compliance with construction documents (ANSI/AISC 360-10)	—	

SPECIAL INSPECTIONS: CONCRETE

Verification and Inspection ACI 318	Continuous Inspection	Periodic Inspection
Concrete		
Inspection of reinforcing steel	—	
Inspection of reinforcing steel welding (AWS D1.4)	—	—
Inspection of anchors cast in concrete where allowable loads have been increased or where strength design is used	—	
Inspection of anchors installed in hardened concrete members	—	
Verifying use of required design mix	—	
Sample concrete during placement for subsequent strength testing		—
Inspection of concrete and shotcrete placement for proper techniques		—
Inspection for proper curing temperature and techniques	—	
Inspection of prestressed concrete, application of forces, and grouting of tendons		—
Erection of precast concrete members	—	
Verification of in-situ concrete strength prior to prestressing, or removal or shoring or forms	—	
Inspect formwork for shape, location, and dimensions of concrete members being formed	—	

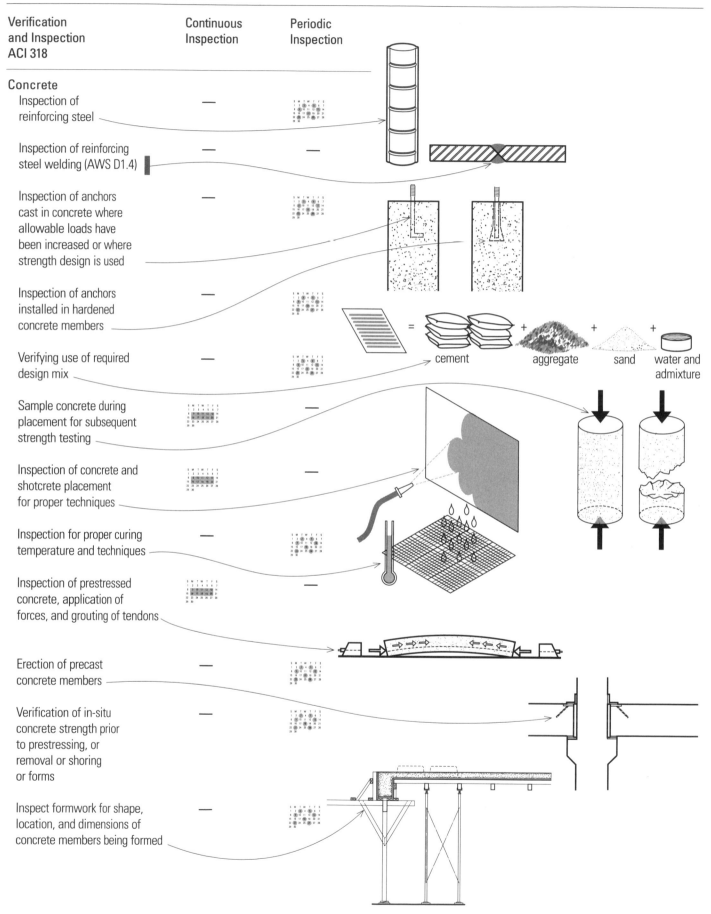

cement + aggregate + sand + water and admixture

Masonry construction sets criteria for special inspections depending on the Occupancy Category of the building. We will use a hospital with surgical facilities, Risk Category IV from Table 1604.5, as an example. Per § 1705.4.1, such a facility would require "Level B Quality Assurance" per TMS 402/ACI 530/ASCE 5, and TMS 602/ACI 530.1/ASCE 6. Examples of some of the quality assurance measures that may be needed are shown below.

Verification and Inspection (TMS 402/ACI 530/ASCE 5, TMS 602/ACI 530.1/ASCE 6) Level B Quality Assurance)	Continuous Inspection	Periodic Inspection
Masonry		
Verify compliance of special inspection provisions in the construction documents	—	☑
Verification of proportions of materials in premixed or preblended mortar or grout as delivered to site	—	☑
Verification of slump flow for self-consolidating grout	☑	—
From the beginning of masonry construction the following is to be verified to ensure compliance:	☑	
Proportions of site-mixed mortar, grout, and prestressing grout	—	☑
Placement of masonry units and construction of mortar joints	—	☑
Placement of reinforcement, connectors, and prestressing tendons and anchors	—	☑

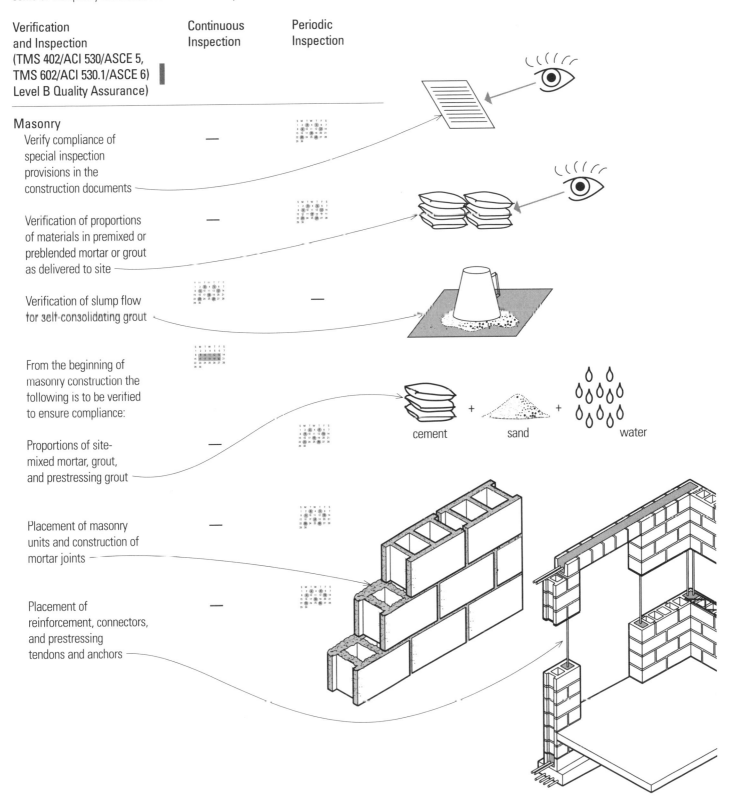

cement + sand + water

SPECIAL INSPECTIONS: MASONRY

Verification and Inspection	Continuous Inspection	Periodic Inspection
Masonry		
Grout space prior to grouting	▦	—
Placement of grout	▦	—
Placement of prestressing grout	▦	—
Size and location of structural elements	—	▦
Type, size, and location of anchors, including anchorage of masonry to structural members, frames, or other construction	▦	—
Specified size, grade, and type of reinforcement	—	▦
Welding of reinforcing bars	▦	—
Preparation and protection of masonry during cold or hot weather	—	▦
Application and measurement of prestressing force	▦	—
Preparation of any required grout or mortar specimens/prisms shall be observed by the special inspector	▦	—

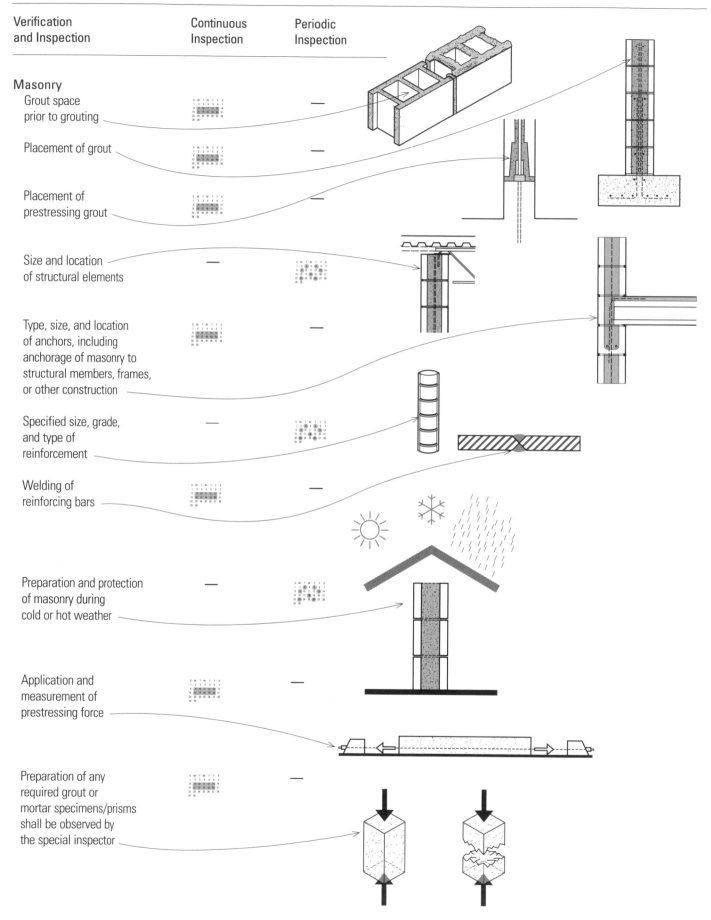

Special inspections are also required for soils work (Table 1705.6), driven deep foundation elements (Table 1705.7), and cast-in-place deep foundation elements (Table 1705.8) to determine that buildings with specialized design criteria for those systems meet code requirements. In addition, there are detailed special inspection requirements for special systems, of which the following are representative examples:

- High-load diaphragms in wood construction (§1705.5.1).

High-load diaphragms designed in accordance with § 2306.2 are to receive special inspections to ascertain whether the diaphragm is of the grade and thickness shown on the approved building plans.

Additionally, the special inspector must verify the nominal size of framing members at adjoining panel edges.

Verify the nail or staple diameter and length.
Verify the number of fastener lines and that the spacing between fasteners in each line and at edge margins agrees with the approved building plans.

- Sprayed fire-resistant materials: for surface conditions, application, thickness, density, and bond strength (§ 1705.14).

- Mastic and intumescent fire-resistant materials (§ 1705.15).

- Exterior insulation and finish systems (§ 1705.16).

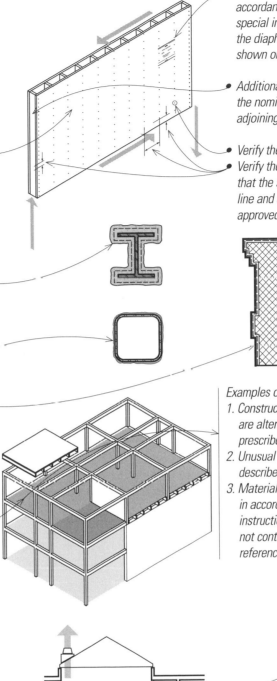

Examples of special cases could include:
1. *Construction materials and systems that are alternatives to materials and systems prescribed by the code.*
2. *Unusual design applications of materials described in this code.*
3. *Materials and systems required to be installed in accordance with additional manufacturer's instructions that prescribe requirements not contained in this code or in standards referenced by this code.*

- Special cases where there are alternate means and methods or unusual or new materials and special inspection is required by the building official (§ 1705.1.1).

- Special inspection for smoke control systems (found in atrium buildings, large covered malls, or high-rise construction) (§1705.18)

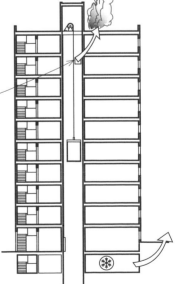

Where special inspections are required per § 1705, then the registered design professional in responsible charge of the project is to prepare a statement of the requirements for special inspections. The statement is to be in accord with the requirements of § 1704.3.

§ 1705.12 and § 1705.13 specify special inspection and testing requirements for seismic designs in Seismic design categories B, C, D, E, or F. § 1705.4.1 specifies testing and verification requirements for masonry materials and glass unit masonry based on their Risk Categories. For example, hospitals in Risk Category IV are to have Level B Quality Assurance for masonry.

The contractor is required by § 1704.4 to acknowledge their awareness of special design and inspection requirements for wind and/or seismic force resisting systems.

A new version of § 1704.5 contains the requirements for submittal of reports and certificates for items subject to special inspections and tests. Certificates are to be submitted by the owner or the owner's authorized agent to the building official for each of the following:

1. Certificates of compliance for the fabrication of structural, load-bearing, or lateral-load-resisting members or assemblies on the premises of a registered and approved fabricator.
2. Certificates of compliance for the seismic qualification of nonstructural components, supports, and attachments.
3. Certificates of compliance for designated seismic systems.
4. Reports of preconstruction tests for shotcrete.
5. Certificates of compliance for open-web joists and joist girders.

There are also requirements in § 1704.6 for structural observation by a registered design professional employed by the owner. These requirements come into play for buildings in Seismic Design Category D, E, or F per § 1704.6.1, or where wind speeds of more than 110 mph (49 m/sec) are anticipated per § 1704.6.2, when one or more of the seismic or wind condtions listed on the right exist.

The code makes provisions for innovative construction materials and techniques. Alternative test procedures and load tests of actual assemblies may be used to demonstrate compliance with the intent of the code for strength and durability. The code also has provisions for in-situ testing when there is reason to believe that construction already in place may not have the stability or load-bearing capacity to carry expected loads.

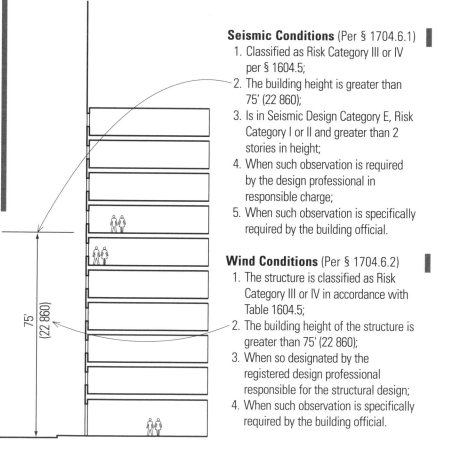

Seismic Conditions (Per § 1704.6.1)
1. Classified as Risk Category III or IV per § 1604.5;
2. The building height is greater than 75' (22 860);
3. Is in Seismic Design Category E, Risk Category I or II and greater than 2 stories in height;
4. When such observation is required by the design professional in responsible charge;
5. When such observation is specifically required by the building official.

Wind Conditions (Per § 1704.6.2)
1. The structure is classified as Risk Category III or IV in accordance with Table 1604.5;
2. The building height of the structure is greater than 75' (22 860);
3. When so designated by the registered design professional responsible for the structural design;
4. When such observation is specifically required by the building official.

75' (22 860)

18

Soils and Foundations

Chapter 18 contains the provisions to the design and construction of buildings and foundation systems. Chapter 16 regulates buildings and foundations subject to water pressure from wind and wave action; Chapter 33 governs excavations and fills made during the course of construction.

Soil and Foundation Investigations

The building official will normally require a soils investigation to determine the stability and bearing capacity of the site soils. The height of the groundwater table should also be part of the soils investigation, as any slabs or occupied spaces below grade will require either dampproofing or waterproofing, depending on the elevation of the groundwater table. The report should also classify the type of soil, recommend the type of footing, and design criteria for the footings. Where buildings are located in Seismic Design Categories C or above, then § 1803.5.11 and § 1803.5.12 require additional investigations for potential earthquake motion-related hazards such as slope instability, liquefaction, total and differential settlement, surface displacement due to faulting, or seismically induced lateral spreading or lateral flow.

Excavation, Grading, and Fill

§ 1804 governs excavations, placement of backfill, and site grading near footings and foundations.

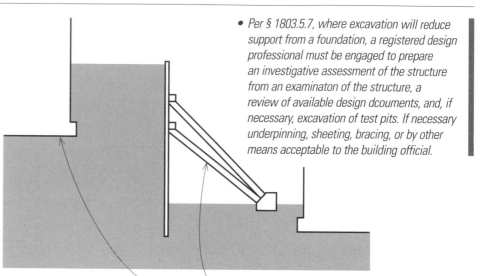

• Per § 1803.5.7, where excavation will reduce support from a foundation, a registered design professional must be engaged to prepare an investigative assessment of the structure from an examinaton of the structure, a review of available design dcouments, and, if necessary, excavation of test pits. If necessary underpinning, sheeting, bracing, or by other means acceptable to the building official.

• Cut-and-fill grading must not remove lateral support for the footings of the proposed building and any adjacent buildings. If there is a danger to adjacent footings, shoring or underpinning must be installed to stabilize the excavation.

• For the design of structures assigned to Seismic Design Category D, E, or F, the geotechnical investigation is to include the items listed in § 1803.5.12:
  1. The determination of lateral earth pressures on foundation walls and retaining walls supporting more than 6' (1828) of backfill.
  2. The potential for liquefaction and soil strength loss.
  3. An assessment of potential consequences of liquefaction and soil strength loss.
  4. Necessary mitigation measures for earthquake-related soils problems.

Height of retained earth 6' (1830) or greater

• The site grading must slope away from footings at a 5% minimum slope for at least 10' (3048) from the footing to prevent ponding of water against the footings. Swales with a longitudinal slope of 2% may be used if there is not sufficient space to provide this drainage. Also, impervious (paved) surfaces may be provided if they have a 2% or greater slope.

• Fills should be placed in lifts and compacted to prevent settlement or displacement.

• Alternate systems, such as drains, may be used in conditions where the building is built into a slope.

- When excavation takes place near existing foundations, it should not remove or reduce lateral support without first underpinning or protecting the foundation against settlement or detrimental lateral translation, or vertical movement, or both.
- Where underpinning is chosen to provide the protection or support, the underpinning system is to be designed and installed in accordance with Chapters 18 and 33.
- Underpinning is to be installed in a sequential manner that protects neighboring structures, existing building structures on site, and the working construction site

§ 1805 requires walls that retain earth and enclose interior spaces below grade to be waterproofed or dampproofed. The location of the water table determines whether dampproofing or more extensive waterproofing is required.

- Dampproofing is required when there may be moisture present, but not under hydrostatic pressure.
- § 1805.1.3 specifies that floors and walls are to be dampproofed when floors and walls are at least 6" (152) above the groundwater table.

- Walls requiring damp proofing are to be treated on the earth side of the wall. They are to receive a bituminous coating, acrylic modified cement, or any of the wall waterproofing treatments noted in the code.
- Slabs are to be protected with an under-slab polyethylene membrane at least 6 mil (0.006"; 0.152 mm) in thickness with joints lapped and sealed.
- Alternately a mopped-on bitumen layer or 4-mil (0.004"; 0.102 mm) polyethylene membrane may be applied to the top of the slab when other materials will cover it.

Subsoil Drainage System

When conditions requiring damp-proofing occur at below-grade rooms, § 1805.4 requires that additional subsoil drainage provisions be made. Such conditions are presumed not to have hydrostatic pressures.

- Floor slabs of basements are to be placed over a base course of not less than 4" (102) of gravel or crushed stone.
- A foundation drain is to be placed around the perimeter with gravel or crushed stone extending a minimum of 12" (305) beyond the outside edge of the footing.
- The drain gravel or pipe must be located with the water-flow line no higher than the floor slab.

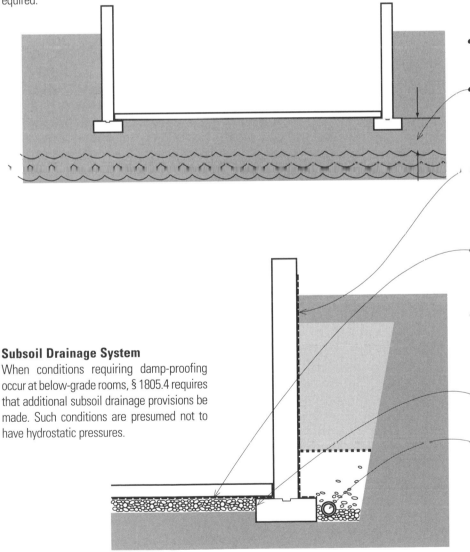

WATERPROOFING

Waterproofing is required when the site soils investigation indicates that there is water under hydrostatic pressure at the site. Waterproofing is to be installed unless a groundwater control system is installed that lowers the water table to 6" (152) below the lowest floor level.

Walls that are to be waterproofed must be of concrete or masonry construction. They must be designed to resist the anticipated hydrostatic pressures along with expected lateral and vertical loads.

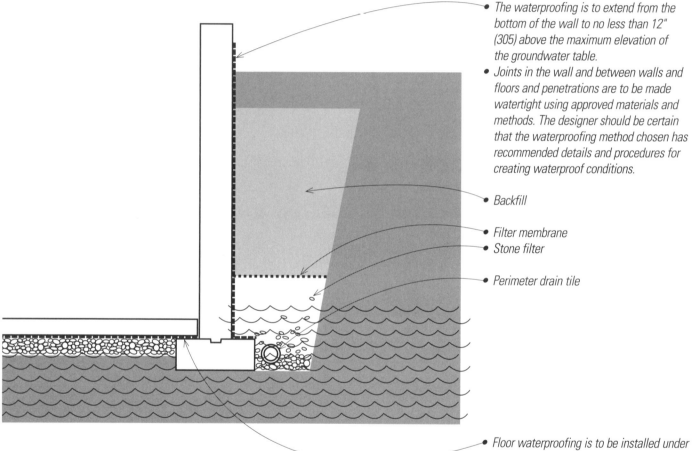

- The waterproofing is to extend from the bottom of the wall to no less than 12" (305) above the maximum elevation of the groundwater table.
- Joints in the wall and between walls and floors and penetrations are to be made watertight using approved materials and methods. The designer should be certain that the waterproofing method chosen has recommended details and procedures for creating waterproof conditions.

- Backfill

- Filter membrane
- Stone filter

- Perimeter drain tile

- Floor waterproofing is to be installed under the slab, consisting of a membrane of rubberized asphalt, butyl rubber, or a 6-mil (0.006"; 0.152 mm) polyethylene membrane. All joints are to be lapped and sealed.

Allowable Load-Bearing Values of Soils

Table 1806.2 contains presumptive load-bearing values for foundations and lateral pressure, based on the observed capacities for various types of rock and soils. The use of these allowable pressures for vertical and lateral loads determines the size of the footing, based on the weight of the structure bearing down on them.

The allowable vertical pressures vary from 12,000 psf (575 kN/m²) for bedrock to 1,500 psf (72 kN/m²) for clay soils.

- For example, a footing supported on clay soil will need to be eight times larger in plan area than one carried on bedrock.

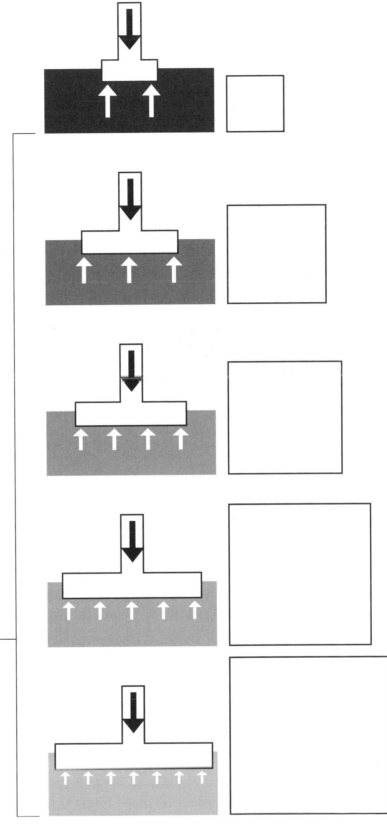

§ 1808 and § 1809 describe the requirements for
footings and for shallow foundations.

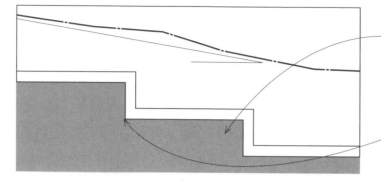

- Footings are to be placed on undisturbed soil
  or on properly compacted fill.
- Footing tops are to be level, whereas the
  bottom of footings may have a slope of up
  to 10%.

- Footings must be stepped when necessary
  to keep the footings in the ground when site
  slopes exceed 10%.

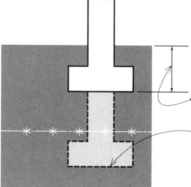

- Footings are to be at least 12" (305) below
  grade, except in conditions
  where frost occurs, in which case the
  footings must extend below the frost line of
  the locality.

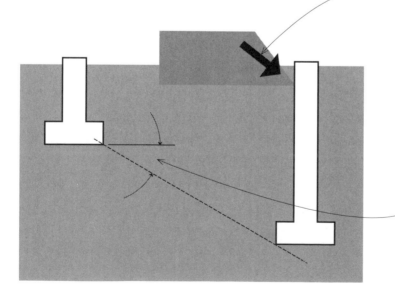

- Per § 1808.3.2 no fill or other surcharge
  loads are to be placed adjacent to any
  building or structure unless such building
  or structure is capable of withstanding
  the additional loads caused by the fill or
  surcharge. Existing footings or foundations
  which will be affected by any excavation
  shall be underpinned or otherwise protected
  against settlement and shall be protected
  against detrimental lateral or vertical
  movement, or both.

- Footings on granular soils must be located
  so that a line drawn between the lower
  edges of adjoining footings does not exceed
  a 30° (0.52 rad) angle with the horizontal.

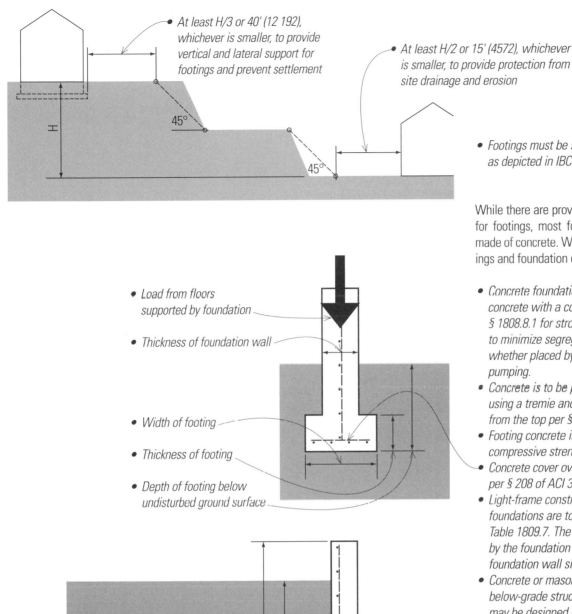

At least H/3 or 40' (12 192), whichever is smaller, to provide vertical and lateral support for footings and prevent settlement

At least H/2 or 15' (4572), whichever is smaller, to provide protection from site drainage and erosion

45°

45°

H

• Footings must be set back from slopes as depicted in IBC Figure 1808.7.1.

While there are provisions for alternate materials for footings, most footings and foundations are made of concrete. We will focus on concrete footings and foundation designs.

• Load from floors supported by foundation

• Thickness of foundation wall

• Width of footing

• Thickness of footing

• Depth of footing below undisturbed ground surface

• Concrete foundations are to be of reinforced concrete with a concrete mix designed per § 1808.8.1 for strength and per § 1808.8.3 to minimize segregation during placement, whether placed by funnel hopper or by pumping.
• Concrete is to be placed to avoid segregation using a tremie and not dropped in the pier from the top per § 1808.8.3.
• Footing concrete is to have a minimum compressive strength of 2,500 psi (17.2 MPa).
• Concrete cover over reinforcing steel is to be per § 208 of ACI 318.
• Light-frame construction footings and foundations are to be in accordance with Table 1809.7. The number of floors supported by the foundation determines the footing and foundation wall sizes.
• Concrete or masonry foundation walls for below-grade structures where earth is retained may be designed by using Tables 1807.1.6.2 through 1807.1.6.3 (4) or by calculation.
• The tables are based on the height and the thickness of the wall. They assume steel with 60,000 psi (414 MPa) yield strength and concrete with a compressive strength of 2,500 psi (17.2 MPa). Reinforcing steel is to be placed in the wall based on the tables. Alternate reinforcing from that called for in the tables may be used as long as an equivalent cross-sectional area is maintained and the rebar spacing does not exceed 72" (1829 mm) and the rebar sizes do not exceed No. 11.

DEEP FOUNDATIONS

When spread footings are not adequate or appropriate for a foundation system, pier and pile foundations are often used. Both systems use columnar structural elements either cast in drilled holes or driven into the ground to support foundations. § 1810 describes the requirements for such deep foundation systems.

Chapter 2 defines a Deep Foundation as a foundation element that cannot be considered a shallow foundation, or in other words, not a strip footing, a mat foundation, a slab-on-grade foundation, or similar elements that are installed relatively close to the ground surface.

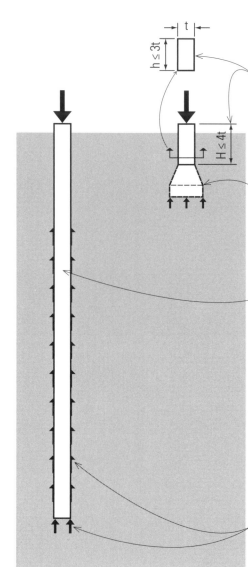

- Per the definition in Chapter 2, Foundation Piers are isolated vertical foundation members whose horizontal dimension (h) does not exceed three times their thickness (t) and whose height (H) is equal to or less than four times their thickness.

- Belled piers are cast-in-place concrete piers having a base that is larger than the diameter of the rest of the shaft. This enlarged base increases the load-bearing area of an end-bearing pier.

- Piles are relatively slender structural elements, having lengths exceeding 12 times their least horizontal dimension.

- § 1810 covers the design and construction of driven piles, such as timber piles and precast concrete piles.
- § 1810 also covers the design and construction of cast-in-place concrete pile foundations: auguered uncased piles, caisson piles, concrete-filled steel pipe and tube piles, driven uncased piles, and enlarged-base piles.

- Both piers and piles derive their load-carrying capacity through skin friction (friction between their surfaces and the surrounding soil), and through end-bearing on supporting material, or a combination of both.

Both pier and pile foundations are to be based on the recommendations of a soil investigation. Once the capacity of the soil is determined, a system design can be selected. The code contains detailed requirements for the design and configuration of pier and pile foundations.

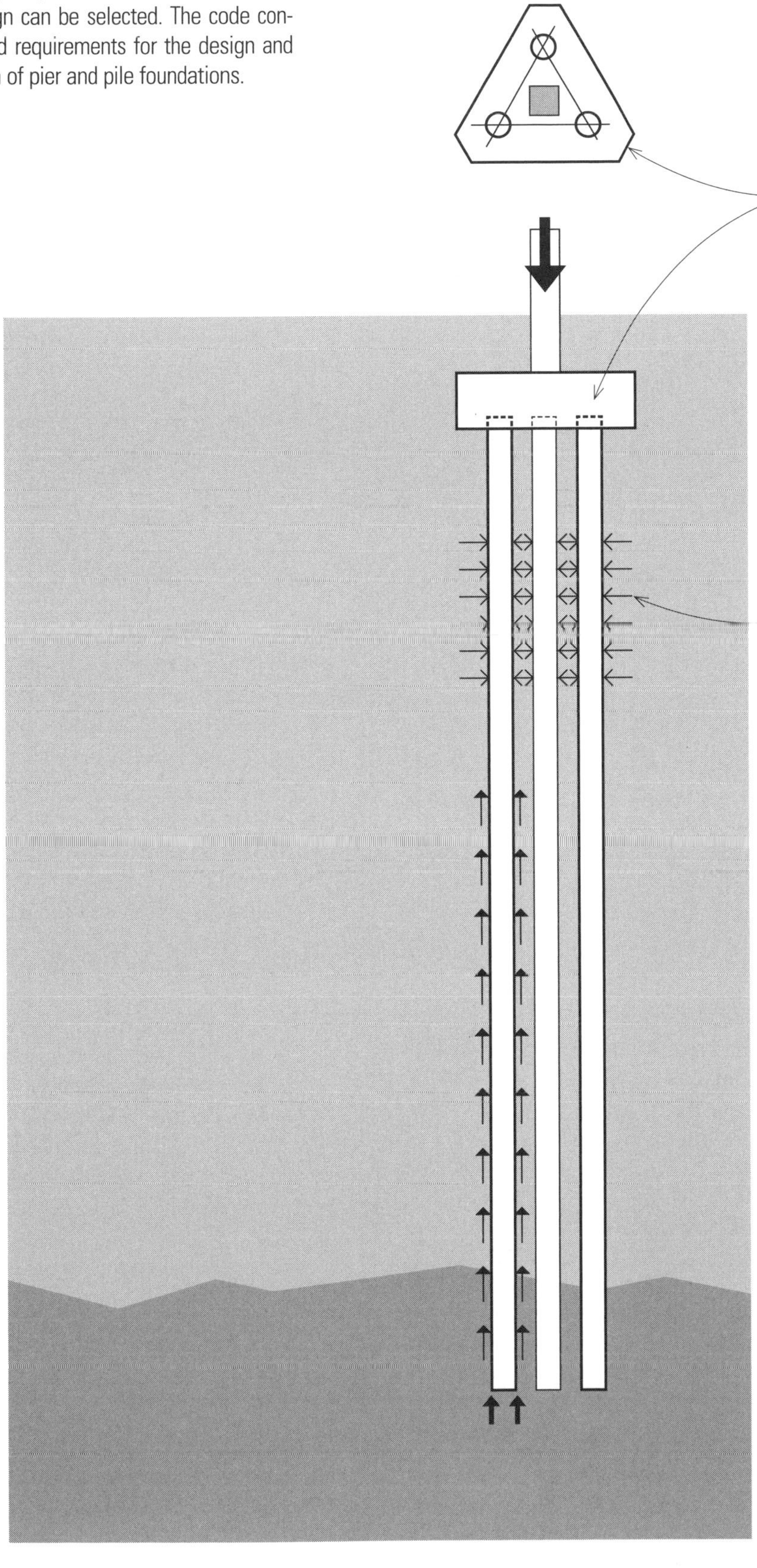

- Groups of piles or large-diameter piers are located in a quantity sufficient to transfer the weight of the structure into the underlying soil.

- Pile caps of reinforced concrete join the heads of a cluster of piles to distribute the load from a column or grade beam equally among the piles.

- Piles must be embedded at least 3" (76) into the pile cap; the pile cap itself must extend at least 4" (102) beyond the edges of the piles.

- Piers and piles must be braced to provide lateral stability in all directions.

- Reinforcement is to be tied together as a unit and placed in the pier. Reinforcement may be wet-set-in-place concrete in R-3 and U occupancies of light-frame construction and not exceeding two stories in height.

DEEP FOUNDATIONS

Driven Piles

Driven piles are piles that rely on either end-bearing or friction on the surface of the pile to provide support for the building. They are inserted into the ground and driven into place by impact of a hammer, similar to driving a nail into wood. Piles may also be driven by vibratory drives, subject to verification by load tests.

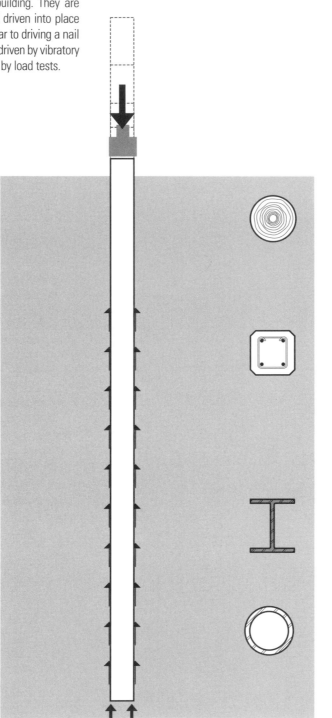

Driven piles may be of various materials:

- *Timber piles may be round or sawn. They must be preservative-treated unless the entire pile will be under water for its entire life of service. Timber piles should be capped or monitored closely as they are driven to ensure their shafts or tips are not split or shattered during driving.*

- *Precast concrete piles are to be reinforced with longitudinal rods tied in place with lateral or spiral ties. Concrete piles are to be designed to resist seismic forces as for concrete columns. Reinforcement for precast nonprestressed piles is to have a minimum cover of 2" (51). Reinforcement for precast prestressed piles should have a minimum cover as specified in ACI 318.*

- *Steel piles consist of either H-sections or sections fabricated from steel plates. They are to have a flange projection not exceeding 14 times the minimum thickness of either the flange or the web. Their nominal depth in the direction of the web is not to be less than 8" (203) and the flanges and webs are to have a minimum thickness of 3/8" (9.5 mm).*

- *Steel-pipe piles driven open-ended are to be at least 8" (203) in outside diameter. Wall thickness of the pipe sections depends on the driving force used.*

Cast-in-Place Deep Foundations
§ 1810.3.9. Cast-in-place deep foundations are usually constructed by drilling a hole to suitable bearing strata and placing concrete in the hole.

Drilled Shafts
A drilled shaft is defined in Chapter 2 as being a cast-in-place deep-foundation element constructed by drilling a hole and filling it with liquid concrete. It is considered "socketed" if a permanent pipe casing extends the full length of the pile to bedrock.

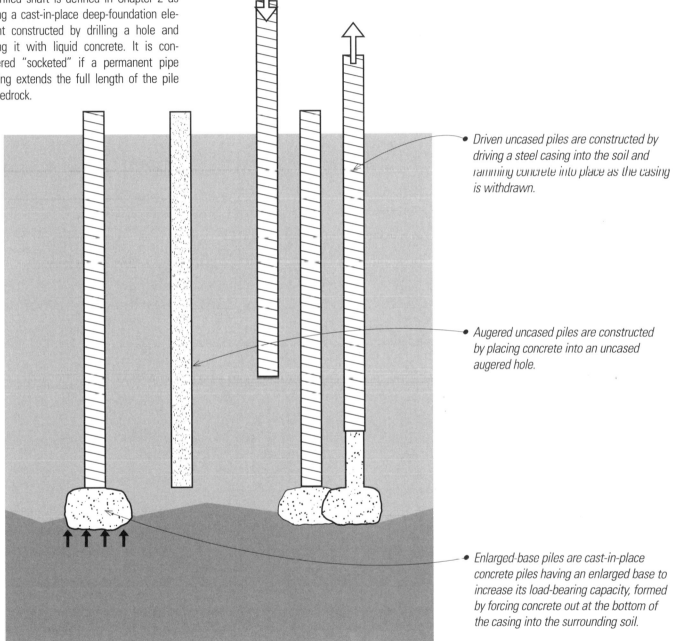

Driven uncased piles are constructed by driving a steel casing into the soil and ramming concrete into place as the casing is withdrawn.

Augered uncased piles are constructed by placing concrete into an uncased augered hole.

Enlarged-base piles are cast-in-place concrete piles having an enlarged base to increase its load-bearing capacity, formed by forcing concrete out at the bottom of the casing into the surrounding soil.

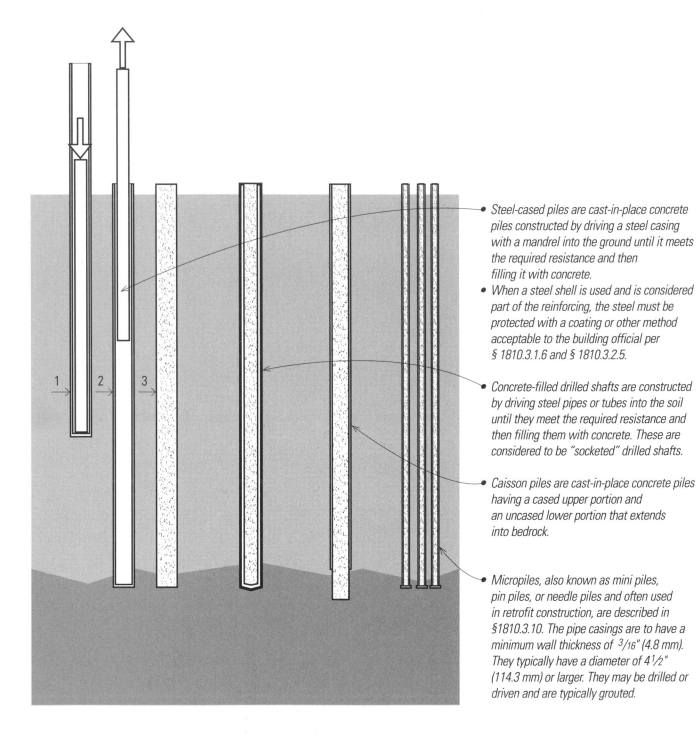

Steel-cased piles are cast-in-place concrete piles constructed by driving a steel casing with a mandrel into the ground until it meets the required resistance and then filling it with concrete.

When a steel shell is used and is considered part of the reinforcing, the steel must be protected with a coating or other method acceptable to the building official per § 1810.3.1.6 and § 1810.3.2.5.

Concrete-filled drilled shafts are constructed by driving steel pipes or tubes into the soil until they meet the required resistance and then filling them with concrete. These are considered to be "socketed" drilled shafts.

Caisson piles are cast-in-place concrete piles having a cased upper portion and an uncased lower portion that extends into bedrock.

Micropiles, also known as mini piles, pin piles, or needle piles and often used in retrofit construction, are described in §1810.3.10. The pipe casings are to have a minimum wall thickness of $3/16$" (4.8 mm). They typically have a diameter of $4\frac{1}{2}$" (114.3 mm) or larger. They may be drilled or driven and are typically grouted.

19

Building Materials and Systems

This chapter is a summary of design requirements contained in Chapters 19 through 33 of the code. Chapters 19 through 23 deal primarily with the structural requirements for building materials: concrete, masonry, steel, wood, and aluminum. We will touch on the implications of the structural design requirements for the physical form of the building. A detailed discussion of the mathematics of structural design is beyond the scope of this book.

Chapters 24 through 26 cover building materials used primarily for building-envelope construction and for finishes: glass and glazing, gypsum board and plaster, and plastics.

Chapters 27 through 30 cover building-code requirements for systems that are addressed in other related codes: electrical, mechanical, and plumbing systems. Chapters 30 through 33 deal with miscellaneous items not readily related to other code sections: elevator and conveying systems, special construction, encroachments on the public right of way, and safeguards during construction.

Our discussion will concentrate on the code chapters related to building design. These are grouped together into sections for construction materials, finish materials, and conveying systems. We will not touch on the other sections noted above, as most of the other items are addressed in other codes or by specialized constructors and are thus beyond the scope of this book.

The materials chapters of the code are based on standards developed by institutions that concentrate on developing industry standards for specific materials. These groups bring together materials experts, industry representatives, design professionals, testing agencies, and building officials to develop criteria for strength, material design calculations, testing, and quality assurance for various materials. These standards are developed through a consensus process similar to that for building-code development. Materials are also subjected to physical tests under controlled load or fire conditions to determine their performance and develop criteria to be incorporated into the standards. These criteria are continually updated to incorporate new knowledge learned from improvements in design techniques and analyses of building performance under actual conditions such as wind, fire and earthquake.

Chapter 19: Concrete

Chapter 19 is based on standard ACI 318, developed by the American Concrete Institute. There are certain detailed modifications to ACI 318 made in the code-development process. These modifications are shown in § 1905.1 and are revised sections. Because of these modifications, the code must be used for reference during concrete design in conjunction with ACI 318. ACI 318 should not be used alone for design work that will be undertaken under the purview of the IBC.

§ 1901.2 states that Chapter 19 governs design of all concrete, whether reinforced or unreinforced, except for slabs on grade that do not transfer vertical or lateral loads from the structure to the soil. Since most, if not all, slabs on grade contained in buildings typically meet these criteria in some if not all locations, it should be assumed that Chapter 19 effectively governs the design of all concrete except for stand-alone slabs on grade such as patios or paving. As for other materials, concrete is to be designed to resist wind and seismic loads in addition to anticipated live and dead loads.

Per § 1901.3, anchoring to concrete is to be in accordance with ACI 318 as amended in § 1905. The criteria apply to a wide range of anchors, including cast-in (headed bolts, headed studs, and hooked J- or L-bolts), post-installed expansion (torque-controlled and displacement-controlled), undercut, and adhesive anchors.

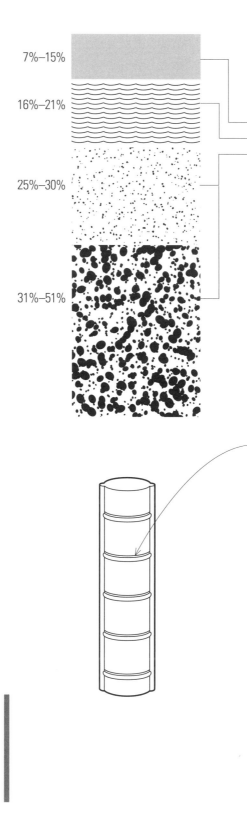

7%–15%

16%–21%

25%–30%

31%–51%

Definitions

§ 1902 2 refers to definitions from ACI 318 for concrete and related terms used in this chapter and in the rest of the IBC. See also § 1905.1.1 for IBC modifications to ACI 318.

- *Concrete is made up of cementitious materials that bind it and other aggregates together with a cementing action. Concrete is defined as a mixture of:*
  - *Portland or other hydraulic cement*
  - *water*
  - *fine aggregate and coarse aggregate with or without admixtures.*

- *Aggregate is a hard, inert, granular material, such as sand, gravel, crushed rock, and blast-furnace slag, added to a cement paste to form concrete or mortar.*
- *Lightweight aggregate has a dry, loose weight of not more than 70 pounds per cubic foot (pcf) (1120 kg/m³).*
- *Admixtures are added to concrete before or during its mixing to alter its properties or those of the hardened product.*

- *Concrete performs much better in compression than in tension, so reinforcing is introduced to produce a material with balanced performance. Reinforcing is usually steel, with deformations on the surface to increase the bonding between the concrete and the steel, placed in the concrete in such a location as to resist tension, shear and sometimes compressive stresses.*
- *Reinforced concrete is structural concrete reinforced with prestressing tendons or nonprestressed reinforcement.*
- *Plain concrete refers to structural concrete having no reinforcement or less reinforcement than the minimum specified for reinforced concrete.*

- *Cast-in-place concrete is deposited, formed, cured, and finished in its final position as part of a structure.*
- *Precast concrete elements are cast and cured in a place other than their final location in a structure.*

Strength and Durability

There are many factors that can affect the ultimate strength of the concrete. The first of these is the mix design, setting the ratios of the materials and water. The second is the time that passes between the initial introduction of water and the placement of the concrete. Concrete setting is a chemical reaction that has a very definite time component. The mixture must also be kept from segregating into its constituent parts by rotating the drum of the mixer prior to placement.

The temperature at the time of placement can also affect the strength of the concrete, with strengths declining at both high and low placement temperatures.

Air is entrained into the concrete for freeze/thaw protection based on the anticipated weathering severity. The probability of weathering, shown in ACI 318, places the majority of the continental U.S. in the moderate to severe weathering probability areas.

In cold weather areas where de-icing chemicals such as salts are used, steps must be taken to increase the strength of the concrete and also to protect reinforcing from corrosion to resist the long-term impacts of weathering and corrosion on the strength and durability of the concrete.

Cylinder Tests

Concrete is typically mixed in one location and placed in another. Because of this, concrete must be field tested to be certain that the material actually placed in the building meets the design criteria. Test cylinders are made as the material is placed. These cylinders are broken in a test machine to determine the strength of the concrete. Tests are typically done at 7 days to determine the strength trend for the concrete and at 28 days, which is the defined time when the design strength is to be achieved. Concrete mixes are proportioned to achieve workability, durability under expected exposure, and development of the desired design strength.

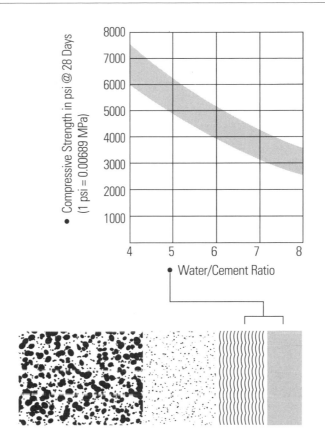

CONCRETE

Formwork

The design, fabrication and erection of formwork is to comply with ACI 318. Formwork is necessary to develop the required shape and dimensions of concrete members in a structure. Forms must be substantial and tight enough to prevent leakage of cement mortar, be properly braced to maintain their proper position and shape, and be supported so as not to damage previously placed concrete.

Note that items such as conduits and pipes may be embedded in concrete if they are not harmful to the concrete and comply with the limits set in ACI 318.

Joints

Refer to ACI 318 for provisions for construction joints between two successive placements of concrete.

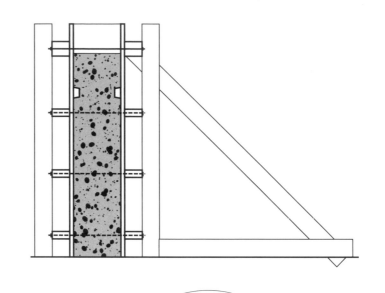

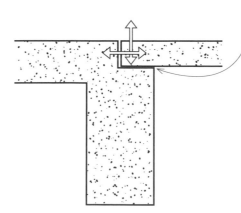

• Construction joints must provide for the transfer of shear and other forces through the joints, usually by means of mechanical keys or dowels.

• Construction joints must be located within the middle third of floor slabs, beams, and girders.

• Construction joints in girders must be offset a minimum distance of two times the width of intersecting beams.

• Contraction joints are formed, sawed, or tooled grooves in a concrete structure to create a weakened plane and regulate the location of cracking resulting from thermal stresses or drying shrinkage.

• Isolation joints separate adjoining parts of a concrete structure to allow relative movement in three directions to occur and to avoid formation of cracks elsewhere in the concrete. All or part of the bonded reinforcement may be interrupted at isolation joints, but the joints must not interfere with the performance of the structure.

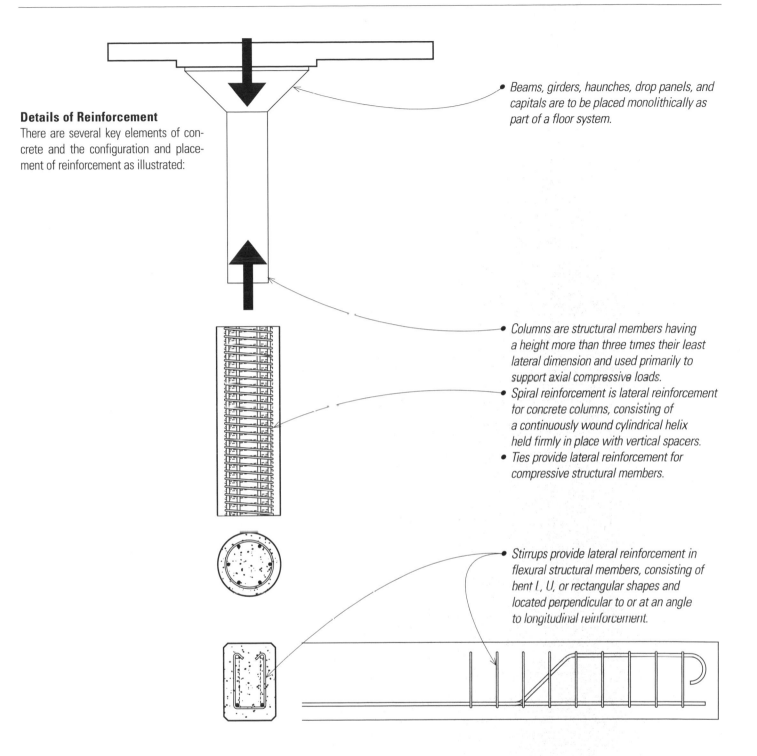

Details of Reinforcement
There are several key elements of concrete and the configuration and placement of reinforcement as illustrated:

• Beams, girders, haunches, drop panels, and capitals are to be placed monolithically as part of a floor system.

• Columns are structural members having a height more than three times their least lateral dimension and used primarily to support axial compressive loads.

• Spiral reinforcement is lateral reinforcement for concrete columns, consisting of a continuously wound cylindrical helix held firmly in place with vertical spacers.

• Ties provide lateral reinforcement for compressive structural members.

• Stirrups provide lateral reinforcement in flexural structural members, consisting of bent I, U, or rectangular shapes and located perpendicular to or at an angle to longitudinal reinforcement.

Details of Reinforcement

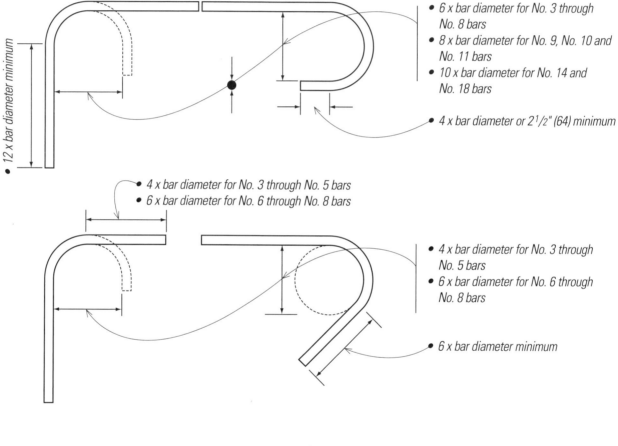

- Deformed reinforcement has surface deformations or a configuration to develop a greater bond with concrete.

Bend Diameters
- Minimum bend diameters are regulated by ACI 318.

- 6 x bar diameter for No. 3 through No. 8 bars
- 8 x bar diameter for No. 9, No. 10 and No. 11 bars
- 10 x bar diameter for No. 14 and No. 18 bars

- 4 x bar diameter or 2^1/$_2$" (64) minimum

- 12 x bar diameter minimum

- 4 x bar diameter for No. 3 through No. 5 bars
- 6 x bar diameter for No. 6 through No. 8 bars

- 4 x bar diameter for No. 3 through No. 5 bars
- 6 x bar diameter for No. 6 through No. 8 bars

- 6 x bar diameter minimum

Bar Spacing
- One bar diameter or 1" (25.4 mm) minimum for flexural members
- 1.5 x bar diameter or 1^1/$_2$" (38) minimum for compression members

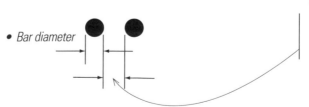

- Bar diameter

Concrete Cover for Weather, Moisture, and Fire Protection

ACI 318 specifies minimum concrete cover for reinforcing steel for several reasons. The cover may be to afford fire resistance as required by the classification of the structure. The cover may be specified in underground situations to provide protection for the reinforcing steel from moisture in the ground. The cover for above-grade concrete exposed to exterior weather conditions is to protect the reinforcing steel from rain or snow. Typical examples of depth and cover are shown in the illustrations below.

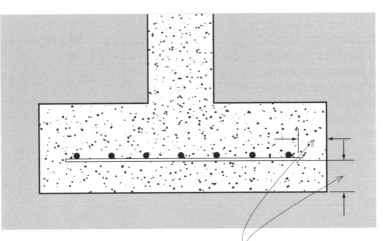

• *3" (76) minimum for concrete cast against and permanently exposed to earth*

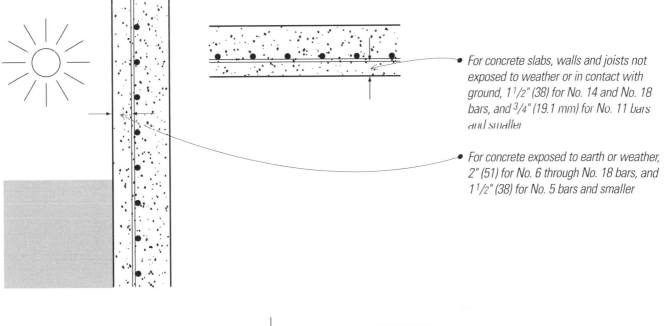

• *For concrete slabs, walls and joists not exposed to weather or in contact with ground, 1 1/2" (38) for No. 14 and No. 18 bars, and 3/4" (19.1 mm) for No. 11 bars and smaller*

• *For concrete exposed to earth or weather, 2" (51) for No. 6 through No. 18 bars, and 1 1/2" (38) for No. 5 bars and smaller*

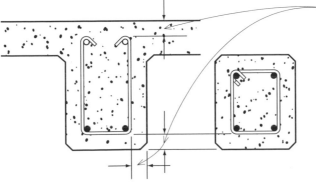

• *1 1/2" (38) for primary reinforcement, stirrups, ties and spirals in concrete beams, and columns for fire protection*

Structural Plain Concrete

Per § 1906, it is acceptable to use plain unreinforced concrete under certain conditions, but only for simple structures. The design and construction of structural plain concrete, both cast-in-place and precast, is comply with the minimum requirements of ACI 318, as modified in § 1905. In most circumstances the use of minimal reinforcing to address temperature changes and shrinkage cracking is recommended practice instead of using plain concrete.

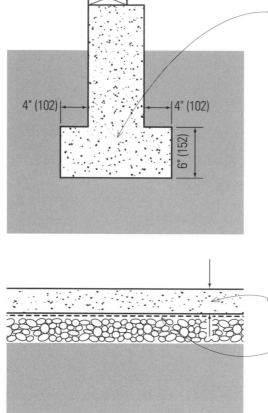

4" (102)   4" (102)

6" (152)

• *Per the Exception to § 1906 for Group R-3 occupancies and buildings of other occupancies less than two stories above grade plane and of light-frame construction, the required footing thickness of ACI 318 is permitted to be reduced to 6" (152), provided that the footing does not extend more than 4" (102) on either side of the supported wall. Note that some foundations in Seismic Design Categories D, E, and F may require reinforcement at the footings per § 1905.1.7.*

• *Per § 1907.1, ground-supported concrete floor slabs are to be a minimum of 3$\frac{1}{2}$" (89) thick, with a 6-mil (0.006"; 0.152 mm) polyethylene vapor retarder under the slab to prevent the transmission of vapor through the slab.*

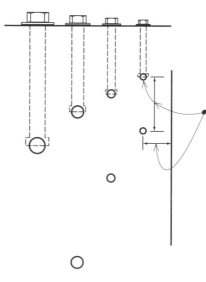

• *§ 1901.3 now specifies that anchoring to concrete is to be in accordance with ACI 318 as amended in § 1905. The criteria which used to be covered in Table 1908.2— interrelating bolt diameter, embedment length, edge distance, spacing, and concrete strength—is now addressed in ACI 318, which has more up-to-date criteria than the older standards found previously in the IBC.*

Chapter 20: Aluminum

Chapter 20 is based completely on AA ASM 35 and AA ADM 1, both published by the Aluminum Association. The code has adopted the industry standards for this material without modification. Aluminum structural design criteria are to conform to the design loads set forth in Chapter 16. § 1604.3.5 refers to AA ADM 1 for deflection limit criteria.

Aluminum members behave similarly to steel except that aluminum is more flexible and will exhibit greater deformation and deflection under the same stress and strain than will steel. Thus aluminum structural members are typically larger in thickness and/or section dimension than steel members under the same load conditions. Except under specialized conditions, where other materials may not be appropriate or durable, aluminum is used very infrequently as a primary structural material. Aluminum members are widely used in secondary structural elements such as windows, curtain walls, and skylights.

Aluminum structural elements may be readily made into many shapes by extrusion or fabrication. The illustrations show typical applications that are generally encountered by designers. They are consistent with the recommendations and requirements of the referenced standards.

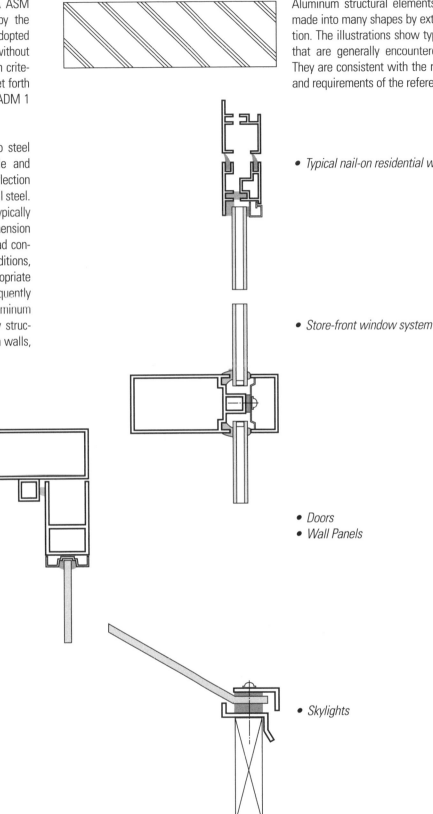

- *Typical nail-on residential window*

- *Store-front window system*

- *Doors*
- *Wall Panels*

- *Skylights*

Chapter 21: Masonry

Chapter 21 primarily uses standards developed by the Masonry Standards Joint Committee (MSJC): TMS 402/ACI 530/ASCE 5, or TMS 403. Masonry is defined as construction made up of units made of clay, shale, concrete, glass, gypsum, stone, or other approved units bonded together. Ceramic tile is also classified by the code as masonry.

The units may be mortared or not, and may be grouted or not, depending on the materials and the structural conditions. Typically, most masonry units are mortared together between units. There are some types of surface bonding mortar that hold the units together by covering the surface with a mixture of cementitious materials and glass fibers. These mortars consist of cementitious materials and fine aggregates. Cement lime mortar contains hydrated lime or lime putty.

Masonry is often grouted, especially in conditions where there are high seismic-resistive design criteria. Grout is similar in composition to concrete, but with smaller-size coarse aggregates.

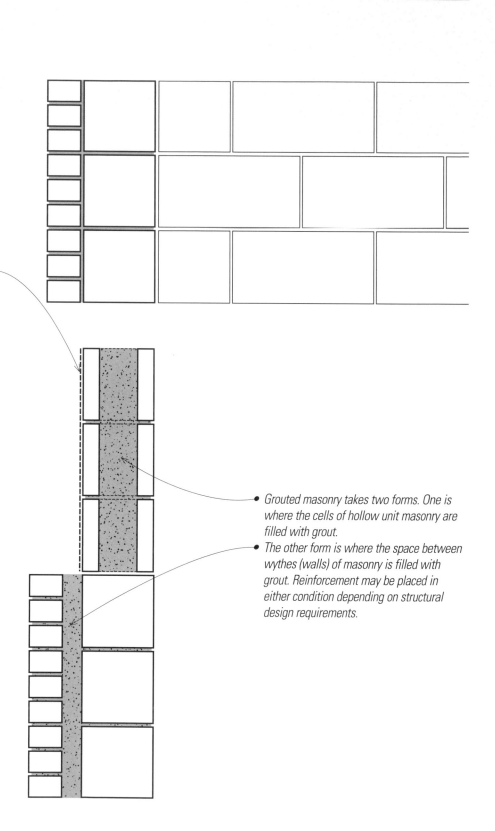

• Grouted masonry takes two forms. One is where the cells of hollow unit masonry are filled with grout.
• The other form is where the space between wythes (walls) of masonry is filled with grout. Reinforcement may be placed in either condition depending on structural design requirements.

Construction

§ 2104 provides references for masonry construction practices. Requirements are contained in the referenced standards: TMS 602/ACI 530.1/ASCE 6.

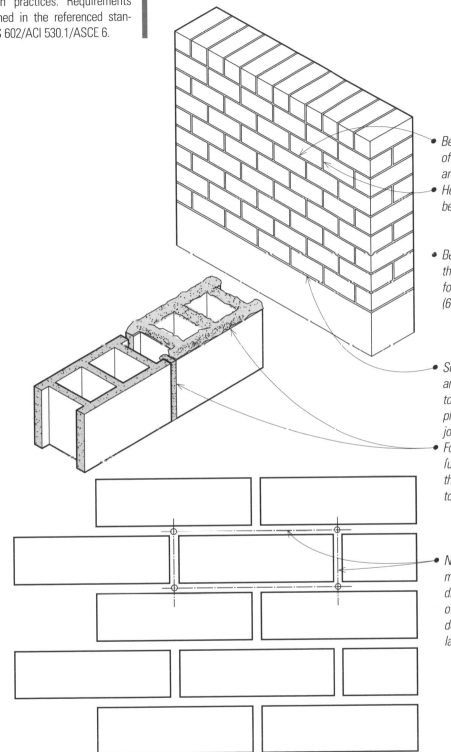

- Bed joints are defined as the horizontal layer of mortar on which masonry units are laid.
- Head joints are the vertical mortar joints between masonry units.

- Bed and head joints are to be $3/8$" (9.5mm) thick, except for starter courses over foundations, which may vary from $1/4$" to $3/4$" (6.4 mm to 19.1mm).

- Solid units are to have fully mortared bed and head joints. Mortar is to be applied to the mortared faces by buttering before placement. Mortar is not to be forced into joints after placement.
- For hollow units, block shells are to have fully mortared bed joints over the face of the unit and the head joints to be mortared to equal the thickness of the shell.

- Note that masonry units, especially concrete masonry units, are described in nominal dimensions where the actual dimension of the unit is typically less. This is usually done to account for the thickness of joints in laying out modular dimensions.

Code users are now to consult the reference standards TMS 402/ACI 530/ASCE 5, or TMS 403 for procedures for cold-weather and hot-weather construction. Wind factors are also included to address wind chill in cold weather and the drying effects of hot winds. The basic criteria for masonry units, as well as mortars and grouts, apply in cold weather when the temperature falls below 40°F (4°C) and in hot weather when the temperature is above 100°F (37.8°C) or when there is a wind velocity greater than 8 mph (12.9 km/hr) and the temperature is above 90°F (32.2°C).

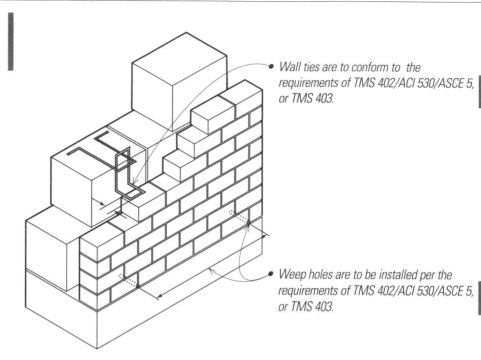

• Wall ties are to conform to the requirements of TMS 402/ACI 530/ASCE 5, or TMS 403.

• Weep holes are to be installed per the requirements of TMS 402/ACI 530/ASCE 5, or TMS 403.

Seismic Design

Seismic design of masonry, as for other materials, depends on the anticipated lateral forces in the locale of the building. It is acceptable to use masonry for seismic-resistant systems, as long as the criteria for seismic design are met. As for the other masonry design elements, these criteria are contained in external references, which are different than those referred to in other masonry sections: TMS 402/ACI 530/ASCE 5, or TMS 403, depending on the structure's seismic design category.

• A critical element for masonry concerns partition walls that are not designed to resist vertical or lateral loads other than that of their own mass. Such walls must be isolated from the building structural system by elements that accommodate anticipated movements in the structure. No seismic or wind loads are to be transmitted to or from these partitions.

Movement

Design Methods

Chapter 21 recognizes that there are several alternative structural design methodologies for masonry. Designers may choose which method to apply using the criteria specified in § 2107 for Allowable Stress Design, § 2108 for Strength Design or § 2109 for Empirical Design.

Allowable Stress Design of Masonry

Allowable stress design for masonry is to be per § 2107. Allowable stress design is a structural design method that is based on some of the oldest principals of structural eingineering. First, loads and forces acting on a structure are determined. Then the ability of the structural materials to resist those forces without encountering elastic deformations is determined, based on the sizes of the structural members and the allowable forces within them. Then a factor of safety is applied to the ability of the materials to resist the forces to determine the final design sizes of structural members. For masonry, allowable stress design is to be per the standards of TMS 402/ACI 530/ASCE 5, or TMS 403. Seismic design per § 2106 and the modifications contained in § 2107 are to be applied in concert with the standards.

Strength Design of Masonry

Strength design is based on the principle of the ability of materials to resist forces (the strength aspect of design) versus determining structural element properties based on the load (the stresses). The principle was first applied for concrete, which uses this method almost exclusively, and has moved into other material design criteria as well. The requirements of § 2106 for seismic design and the modifications contained in § 2108 are to be applied to the standards contained in the adopted standards: TMS 402/ACI 530/ASCE 5, or TMS 403.

Empirical Design

As discussed above, masonry structural design may use several alternate methods for determining dimensions, connections and reinforcement. The empirical design method described in § 2109 is the simplest and most direct. This method corresponds to the conventional framing provisions for wood-frame construction. It is based on customary field practices and familiar techniques. Its use is restricted to low-to-moderate seismic and wind-hazard areas and generally is used for buildings with walls constructed of surface-bonded, dry-stacked masonry such as adobe. The use of empirically designed masonry will be very limited. Where the very limited load or height criteria are exceeded, masonry structures are to be designed using allowable stress design, strength design, or as prestressed masonry.

Masonry Shear Walls

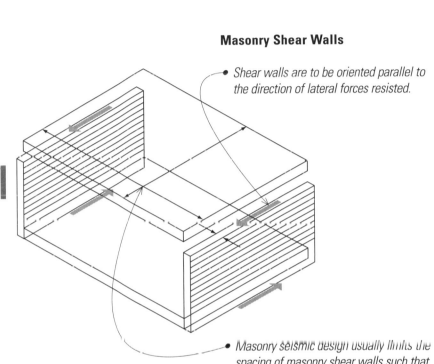

- *Shear walls are to be oriented parallel to the direction of lateral forces resisted.*

- *Masonry seismic design usually limits the spacing of masonry shear walls such that the length-to-width ratios of floor or roof diaphragms transferring lateral forces to the shear walls do not exceed specified ratios.*

Glass Unit Masonry

§ 2110 covers the requirements for nonload-bearing glass unit masonry elements in both interior and exterior walls. They are not to be used in fire walls, party walls, fire partitions, or smoke barriers. The exception to this section allows glass unit masonry having a minimum fire-resistance rating of 3/4 hour to be used as opening protectives or in fire partitions that are required to have a fire-resistance rating of 1 hour or less and do not enclose exit stairways or exit passageways. Detailed glass unit masonry design criteria are contained in the referenced standards: TMS 402/ ACI 530/ASCE 5, or TMS 403. The illustrations are for design principles. The precise requirements must be confirmed with the reference standards for detailed design criteria.

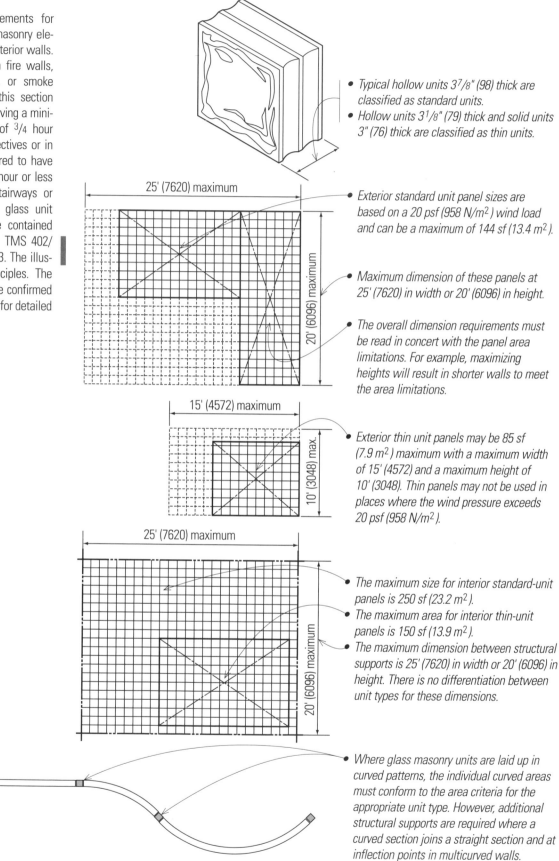

- Typical hollow units 3⁷/₈" (98) thick are classified as standard units.
- Hollow units 3¹/₈" (79) thick and solid units 3" (76) thick are classified as thin units.

25' (7620) maximum

20' (6096) maximum

- Exterior standard unit panel sizes are based on a 20 psf (958 N/m²) wind load and can be a maximum of 144 sf (13.4 m²).

- Maximum dimension of these panels at 25' (7620) in width or 20' (6096) in height.

- The overall dimension requirements must be read in concert with the panel area limitations. For example, maximizing heights will result in shorter walls to meet the area limitations.

15' (4572) maximum

10' (3048) max.

- Exterior thin unit panels may be 85 sf (7.9 m²) maximum with a maximum width of 15' (4572) and a maximum height of 10' (3048). Thin panels may not be used in places where the wind pressure exceeds 20 psf (958 N/m²).

25' (7620) maximum

20' (6096) maximum

- The maximum size for interior standard-unit panels is 250 sf (23.2 m²).
- The maximum area for interior thin-unit panels is 150 sf (13.9 m²).
- The maximum dimension between structural supports is 25' (7620) in width or 20' (6096) in height. There is no differentiation between unit types for these dimensions.

- Where glass masonry units are laid up in curved patterns, the individual curved areas must conform to the area criteria for the appropriate unit type. However, additional structural supports are required where a curved section joins a straight section and at inflection points in multicurved walls.

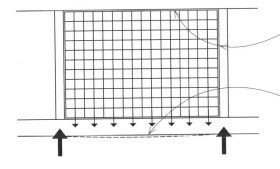

- Unit panels are to be isolated from the adjoining structure so that in-plane loads are not transferred to the panels.

- Also, unit panels are to be supported on structural members having a deflection of less than $^1/_{600}$.

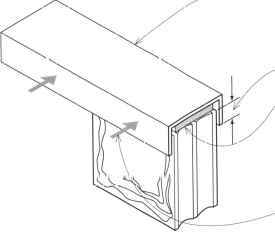

- Glass unit masonry panels are to be laterally supported along their tops and sides.
- Support is to be by panel anchors spaced not more than 16" (406) on center or by continuous channels with at least 1" (25.4 mm) overlap over the unit.

- The channels are to be oversized to allow expansion material in the opening and packing or sealant between the face of the unit and the channel. Panels are to have expansion joints along the top and sides of panels with at least 3/8" (9.5 mm) allowance for expansion.
- Channels are to resist applied loads or a minimum of 200 pounds per lineal foot (2919 N/m) of panel, whichever is greater.

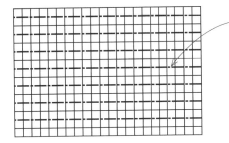

- Units are to be mortared together with mortar complying with § 2103.2.
- Unit panels are to have reinforcing in the horizontal mortar bed joints at not more than 16" (406) on center. Reinforcing is also required above and below openings in the panel. The reinforcing is to be a ladder type with two parallel wires of size W1.7 and welded cross wires of W1.7, and are to be lapped a minimum of 6" (152) at splices.

Masonry Fireplaces

§ 2111 describes the construction requirements for masonry fireplaces. The illustration and summary of requirements for masonry fireplaces are contained in § 2111.

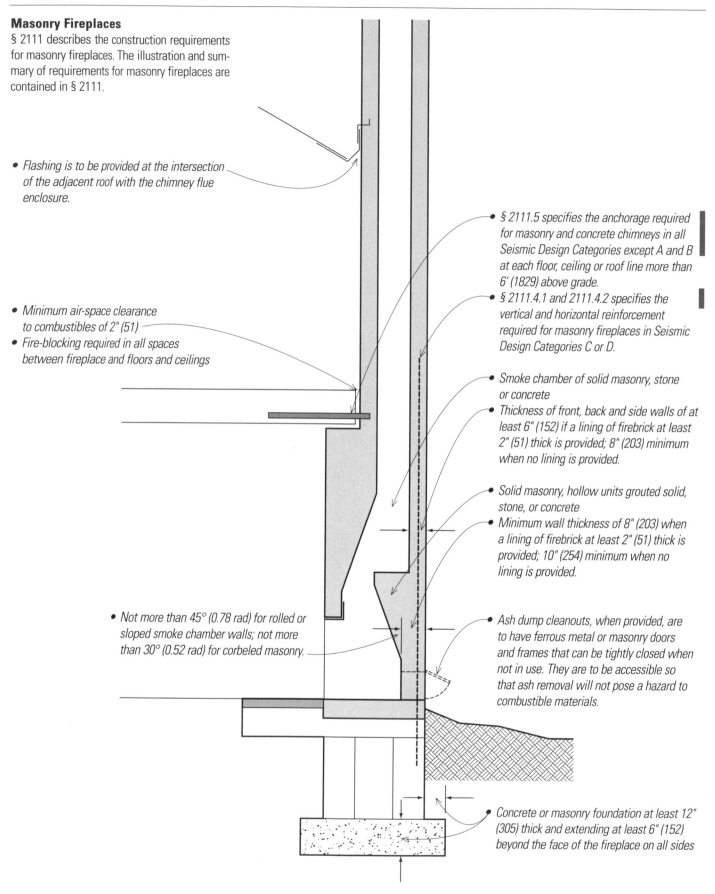

- Flashing is to be provided at the intersection of the adjacent roof with the chimney flue enclosure.

- Minimum air-space clearance to combustibles of 2" (51)
- Fire-blocking required in all spaces between fireplace and floors and ceilings

- Not more than 45° (0.78 rad) for rolled or sloped smoke chamber walls; not more than 30° (0.52 rad) for corbeled masonry.

- § 2111.5 specifies the anchorage required for masonry and concrete chimneys in all Seismic Design Categories except A and B at each floor, ceiling or roof line more than 6' (1829) above grade.
- § 2111.4.1 and 2111.4.2 specifies the vertical and horizontal reinforcement required for masonry fireplaces in Seismic Design Categories C or D.

- Smoke chamber of solid masonry, stone or concrete
- Thickness of front, back and side walls of at least 6" (152) if a lining of firebrick at least 2" (51) thick is provided; 8" (203) minimum when no lining is provided.

- Solid masonry, hollow units grouted solid, stone, or concrete
- Minimum wall thickness of 8" (203) when a lining of firebrick at least 2" (51) thick is provided; 10" (254) minimum when no lining is provided.

- Ash dump cleanouts, when provided, are to have ferrous metal or masonry doors and frames that can be tightly closed when not in use. They are to be accessible so that ash removal will not pose a hazard to combustible materials.

- Concrete or masonry foundation at least 12" (305) thick and extending at least 6" (152) beyond the face of the fireplace on all sides

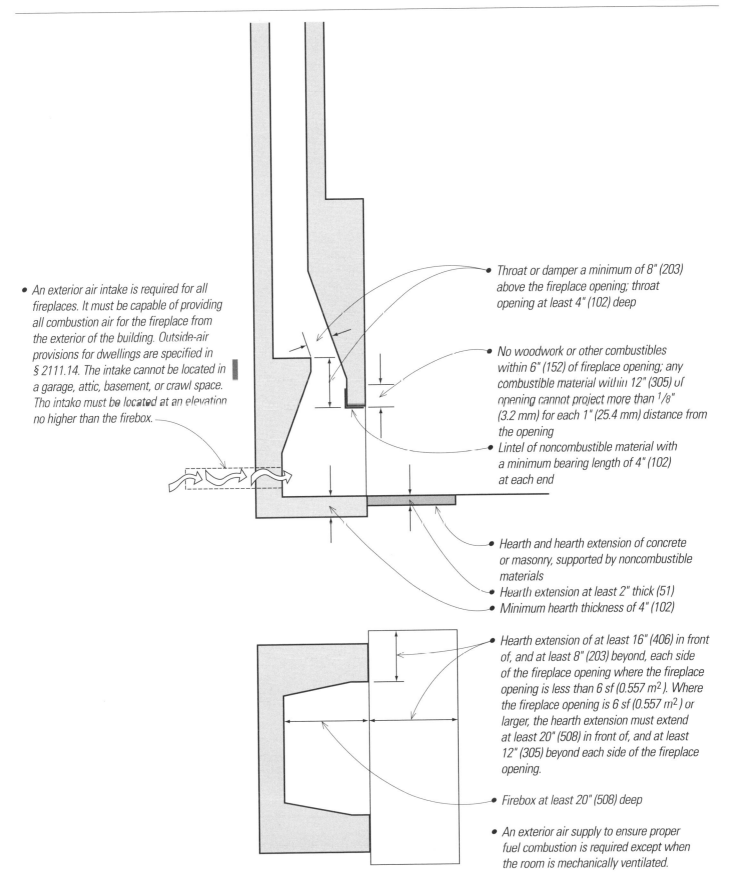

An exterior air intake is required for all fireplaces. It must be capable of providing all combustion air for the fireplace from the exterior of the building. Outside-air provisions for dwellings are specified in § 2111.14. The intake cannot be located in a garage, attic, basement, or crawl space. The intake must be located at an elevation no higher than the firebox.

Throat or damper a minimum of 8" (203) above the fireplace opening; throat opening at least 4" (102) deep

No woodwork or other combustibles within 6" (152) of fireplace opening; any combustible material within 12" (305) of opening cannot project more than $^1/8$" (3.2 mm) for each 1" (25.4 mm) distance from the opening

Lintel of noncombustible material with a minimum bearing length of 4" (102) at each end

Hearth and hearth extension of concrete or masonry, supported by noncombustible materials

Hearth extension at least 2" thick (51)

Minimum hearth thickness of 4" (102)

Hearth extension of at least 16" (406) in front of, and at least 8" (203) beyond, each side of the fireplace opening where the fireplace opening is less than 6 sf (0.557 m^2). Where the fireplace opening is 6 sf (0.557 m^2) or larger, the hearth extension must extend at least 20" (508) in front of, and at least 12" (305) beyond each side of the fireplace opening.

Firebox at least 20" (508) deep

An exterior air supply to ensure proper fuel combustion is required except when the room is mechanically ventilated.

Chapter 22: Steel

Chapter 22 divides steel construction materials into basically four broad classes. They are structural steel, composite steel/concrete, steel joists, and cold-formed steel members.

The first broad category is for structural steel members, which are rolled steel shapes, usually hot rolled, and not otherwise falling into the other two categories. The design of these members falls under the specifications of the American Institute of Steel Construction (AISC) 360. There are separate sets of specifications for structural steel design depending on the design method used, load and resistance factor design, or allowable stress design.

Bolts and welding of connections are governed by the applicable specifications for each type of steel construction. As for other materials, steel structures are to comply with seismic and wind-design requirements, where applicable.

The second category recognizes the use of steel and concrete framing for columns, beams, walls, floors, and roofs in buildings in many varied combinations. These types of buildings are known as composite steel and concrete structures. Systems of structural steel acting compositely with reinforced concrete are to be designed in accordance with both AISC 360 and ACI 318, but excluding ACI 318 Chapter 14. Where required by the seismic design category of the building, the seismic design of composite steel and concrete systems is to be in accordance with the additional provisions of § 2206.2, "Seismic requirements for composite structural steel and concrete construction." Where a response modification coefficient, R, in accordance with ASCE 7, Table 12.2-1, is used for the design of systems of structural steel acting compositely with reinforced concrete, the structures are to be designed and detailed in accordance with the requirements of AISC 341.

The third category is for steel joists, made of combinations of hot-rolled or cold-formed solid or open-web sections. Design of steel joists is governed by specifications from the Steel Joist Institute (SJI).

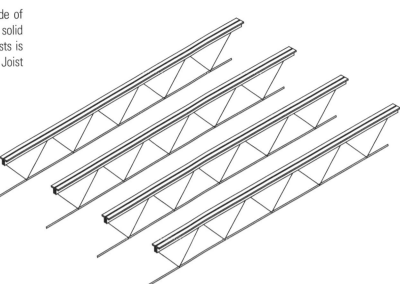

The fourth widely used category is cold-formed steel, made up of members bent from steel sheets or strips, including roof decks, floor and wall panels, studs, floor joists, and other structural members. The design of cold-formed members is governed by the American Iron and Steel Institute (AISI) Specifications for the Design of Cold-Formed Steel Structural Members.

§ 2211 governs the design of light-framed cold-formed steel walls. These requirements are analogous to those for conventional wood-framed construction in that the code sets design and configuration criteria for typical installations that are deemed to be code compliant when they meet the prescriptive criteria.

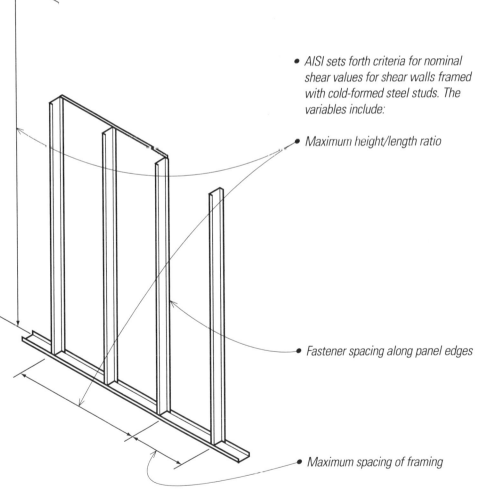

- AISI sets forth criteria for nominal shear values for shear walls framed with cold-formed steel studs. The variables include:

- Maximum height/length ratio

- Fastener spacing along panel edges

- Maximum spacing of framing

Chapter 23: Wood

Chapter 23 governs the materials, design, and construction of wood members and their fasteners. Wood structures are to be designed using one of the approved methods: allowable stress design per § 2304, § 2305, and § 2306; load and resistance factor design per § 2304, § 2305, and § 2307; or using conventional light-frame construction provisions per § 2304 and § 2308. Wood-frame construction is very prevalent, especially in home-building in the United States. The code contains a prescriptive approach for wood-frame construction as it is typically practiced. These criteria are termed as conventional light-frame wood construction. This is defined as a system where the primary structure is made up of repetitive wood framing members. We will use these conventional construction provisions for our illustrations of code-compliant wood-frame construction. We have not duplicated the illustrations contained in the code, as they are self-explanatory. Note that our discussion does not include the exceptions to the prescriptive requirements. Code-compliant design must take all of the code requirements and exceptions under consideration for the specific conditions of the project.

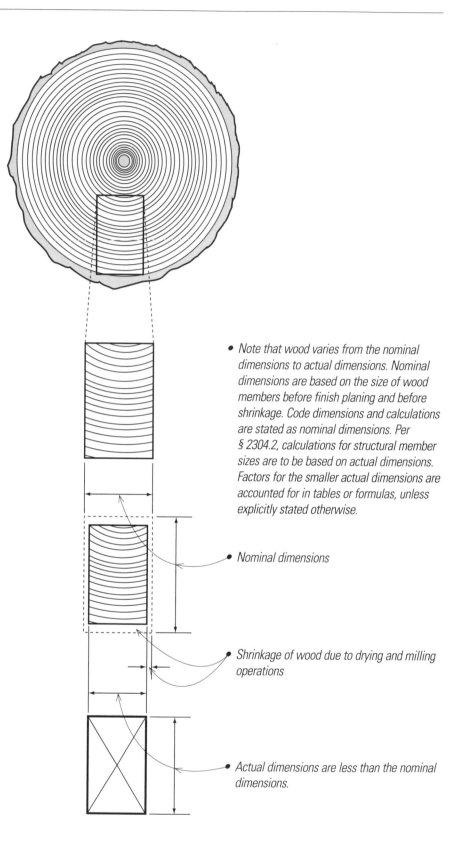

• Note that wood varies from the nominal dimensions to actual dimensions. Nominal dimensions are based on the size of wood members before finish planing and before shrinkage. Code dimensions and calculations are stated as nominal dimensions. Per § 2304.2, calculations for structural member sizes are to be based on actual dimensions. Factors for the smaller actual dimensions are accounted for in tables or formulas, unless explicitly stated otherwise.

• Nominal dimensions

• Shrinkage of wood due to drying and milling operations

• Actual dimensions are less than the nominal dimensions.

Minimum Standards and Quality

§ 2303 specifies minimum standards and quality for lumber, sheathing, siding, and other wood-based products. Lumber is to be graded per the standards of the Department of Commerce (DOC) American Softwood Lumber Standard, PS 20.

Lumber is to be stamped to indicate that it has been reviewed and graded according to species and grade. Calculations are based on the stress capabilities of the wood, depending on the grade and the lumber species.

Wood is also classified as to its natural durability. The heartwood for species such as redwood and cedar are classified as decay-resistant. Redwood and eastern red cedar are also classified as termite-resistant. The code requires the use of naturally durable woods or pressure-treated woods in certain situations, especially in conditions where wood members are close to adjacent soil.

Each of the criteria is specific to the type of wood materials they cover. Wood structural panels are to be per requirements of standards DOC PS 1, PS 2, or ANSI/APA PRP 210. Structural glued laminated timbers are to be manufactured and identified as required in ANSI/AITC A 190.1 and ASTM D 3737.

Wood structural panels, when permanently exposed in outdoor applications, are to be of Exterior Type, except that wood structural panel roof sheathing exposed to the outdoors on the underside is permitted to be Exposure Type 1.

New § 2303.1.4 addresses Structural Glued Cross-Laminated Timber. This material is new to the United States but is widely used in other countries. Cross-laminated timber materials are made of large boards cross-laminated into larger members and are used as large timbers. They are to be manufactured and identified as required in ANSI/APA PRG 320.

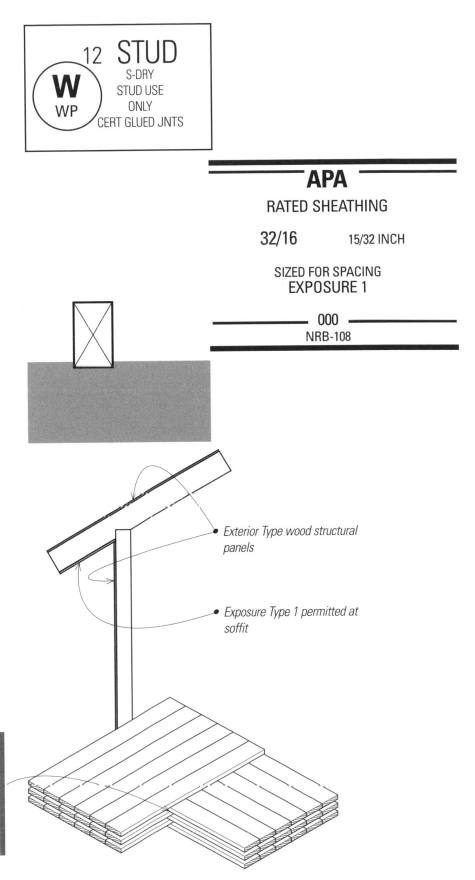

Exterior Type wood structural panels

Exposure Type 1 permitted at soffit

WOOD

General Construction Requirements

§ 2304 contains the construction requirements for structural elements and systems built of wood or wood-based products.

Roof Sheathing

- *Table 2304.8 (1) provides allowable spans for surface-dry lumber roof sheathing: 24" (610) span for 5/8" (15.9 mm) thick sheathing perpendicular to supports or 3/4" (19.1 mm) thick sheathing diagonal to supports.*
- *Table 2304.8 (3) provides examples for structural panels: 1/2" (12.7 mm) thick, 24/16 span rating: 24" (610) maximum span; 40 psf (1.92 kN/m2) roof live load, 10 psf (0.48 kN/m2) roof dead load; 3/4" (19.1 mm) thick, 48/24 span rating: 48" (1219) span, 35 psf (1.68 kN/m2) roof live load, 10 psf roof dead load.*

- *In the 2012 IBC, Table 2304.6 specified wall sheathing thicknesses. Since this table is really a prescriptive table, it has been relocated to § 2308.*
- *Table 2308.5.11 specifies wall sheathing to be of wood boards minimum 5/8" (15.9 mm) thick on studs 24" (610) on-center, maximum. Gypsum sheathing is to be minimum 1/2" (12.7 mm) thickness on studs 16" (406) on-center, maximum.*

- *§ 2304.3.1 requires studs to have full bearing on minimum 2x (nominal) thick bottom plates equal in width to the studs.*

Floor Sheathing

- *Table 2304.8 (1) provides allowable spans for surfaced-dry lumber floor sheathing: 24" (610) span, 3/4" (19.1 mm) thick, perpendicular or diagonal to supports; 16" (406) span, 5/8" (15.9 mm) thick, perpendicular or diagonal to supports.*
- *Table 2304.8 (3) provides examples for structural panels: 1/2" (12.7 mm) thick, 24/16 span rating: 16" (406) span, 100 psf (4.79 kN/m2) total floor load (l/360) deflection; 3/4" (19.1 mm) thick, 48/24 span rating: 24" (610) span, 65 psf (3.11 kN/m2) total floor load (l/360) deflection.*

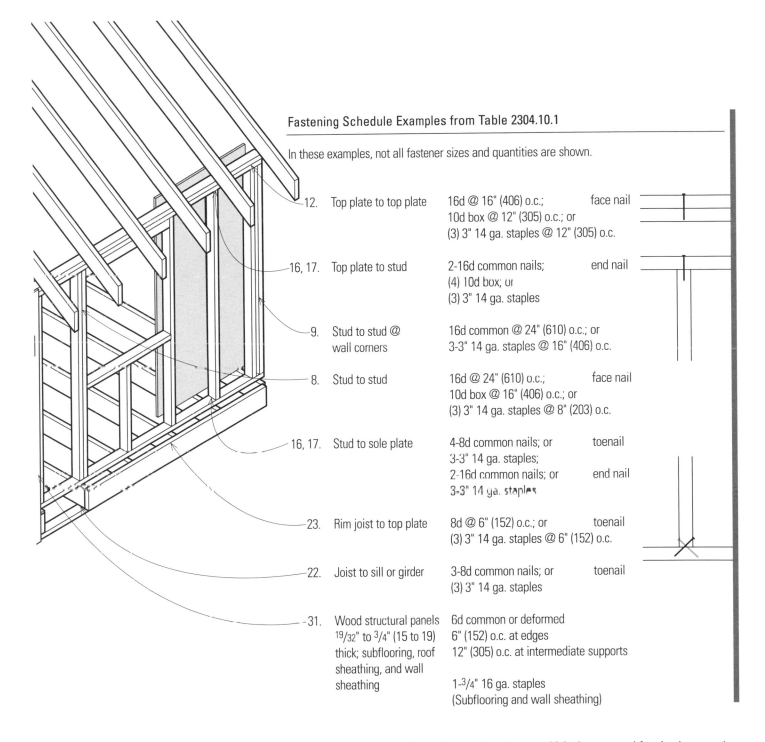

Fastening Schedule Examples from Table 2304.10.1

In these examples, not all fastener sizes and quantities are shown.

12.	Top plate to top plate	16d @ 16" (406) o.c.; 10d box @ 12" (305) o.c.; or (3) 3" 14 ga. staples @ 12" (305) o.c.	face nail
16, 17.	Top plate to stud	2-16d common nails; (4) 10d box; or (3) 3" 14 ga. staples	end nail
9.	Stud to stud @ wall corners	16d common @ 24" (610) o.c.; or 3-3" 14 ga. staples @ 16" (406) o.c.	
8.	Stud to stud	16d @ 24" (610) o.c.; 10d box @ 16" (406) o.c.; or (3) 3" 14 ga. staples @ 8" (203) o.c.	face nail
16, 17.	Stud to sole plate	4-8d common nails; or 3-3" 14 ga. staples; 2-16d common nails; or 3-3" 14 ga. staples	toenail end nail
23.	Rim joist to top plate	8d @ 6" (152) o.c.; or (3) 3" 14 ga. staples @ 6" (152) o.c.	toenail
22.	Joist to sill or girder	3-8d common nails; or (3) 3" 14 ga. staples	toenail
31.	Wood structural panels 19/32" to 3/4" (15 to 19) thick; subflooring, roof sheathing, and wall sheathing	6d common or deformed 6" (152) o.c. at edges 12" (305) o.c. at intermediate supports 1-3/4" 16 ga. staples (Subflooring and wall sheathing)	

Note that there are manufactured, tested, and approved joist hangers and framing hangers that perform the functions of the fasteners noted in Table 2304.10.1. These are acceptable if they are listed and approved, and used in the manner intended.

Protection against Decay and Termites

§ 2304.12 requires protection against decay and termites by the use of naturally durable or preservative-treated wood in the following conditions:

- § 2304.12.1.5 requires protection for wood siding that is less than 6" (152) to exposed earth.
- § 2304.12.1.3 requires protection for all framing, including wood sheathing, that is in contact with exterior walls that extend below grade.

- § 2304.12.2.1 requires a $1/2$" (12.7 mm) air space on the top, sides, and end of girders entering exterior masonry or concrete walls, unless preservative-treated or naturally durable wood is used.

- § 2304.12.1.1: If joists and subflooring are closer than 18" (457) to exposed ground in crawl space, or if girders are closer than 12" (305) to exposed ground, then the floor assembly—including posts, girders, joists, and subfloor—must be of naturally durable or preservative-treated wood.

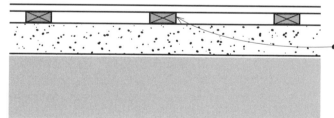

- § 2304.12.1.4 requires similar protection for sleepers and sills on a concrete slab that is in direct contact with the earth.

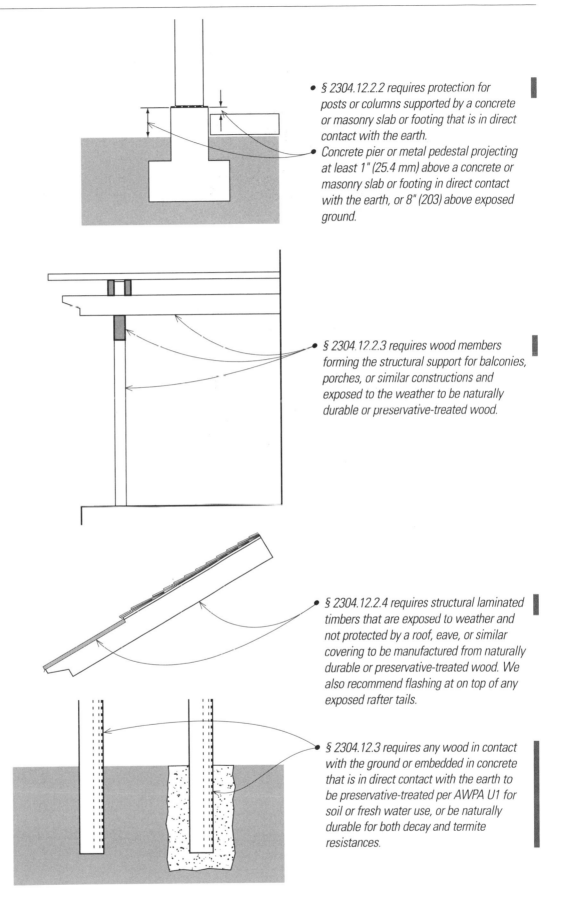

- *§ 2304.12.2.2 requires protection for posts or columns supported by a concrete or masonry slab or footing that is in direct contact with the earth.*
- *Concrete pier or metal pedestal projecting at least 1" (25.4 mm) above a concrete or masonry slab or footing in direct contact with the earth, or 8" (203) above exposed ground.*

- *§ 2304.12.2.3 requires wood members forming the structural support for balconies, porches, or similar constructions and exposed to the weather to be naturally durable or preservative-treated wood.*

- *§ 2304.12.2.4 requires structural laminated timbers that are exposed to weather and not protected by a roof, eave, or similar covering to be manufactured from naturally durable or preservative-treated wood. We also recommend flashing at on top of any exposed rafter tails.*

- *§ 2304.12.3 requires any wood in contact with the ground or embedded in concrete that is in direct contact with the earth to be preservative-treated per AWPA U1 for soil or fresh water use, or be naturally durable for both decay and termite resistances.*

Conventional Light-Frame Construction

The provisions of § 2308 are intended for use in residential and light commercial construction. Buildings are limited to three stories in height (depending on the Seismic Design Category); bearing wall heights are limited to 10' (3048); roof trusses and rafters are to span no more than 40' (12 192); and loads are limited. Braced walls are to be placed in the structure at maximum intervals to provide lateral bracing against lateral loads imposed by wind or seismic forces.

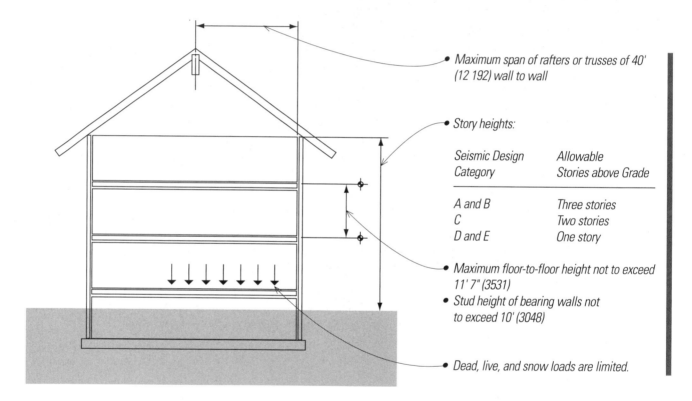

• Maximum span of rafters or trusses of 40' (12 192) wall to wall

• Story heights:

Seismic Design Category	Allowable Stories above Grade
A and B	Three stories
C	Two stories
D and E	One story

• Maximum floor-to-floor height not to exceed 11' 7" (3531)
• Stud height of bearing walls not to exceed 10' (3048)

• Dead, live, and snow loads are limited.

Foundation Plates or Sills

§ 2308.3 refers to the design and construction of foundations and footings prescribed in Chapter 18.

- Sills or plates are to be anchored to the footing with ¹/₂" (12.7 mm) diameter minimum steel bolts or approved anchors.
- Bolts are to extend 7" (178) into concrete or masonry and be spaced not more than 6' (1829) apart.
- Every plate must have at least two anchors; end anchors are to be no more than 12" (305) and no less than 4" (102) from the end of the member.

- Along braced wall lines in structures assigned to Seismic Design Category E, steel bolts with a minimum nominal diameter of ⁵/₈" (15.9 mm) or approved anchor straps load-rated in accordance with § 2304.10.3 and spaced to provide equivalent anchorage are to be used.
- Bolts in braced wall lines in structures over two stories above grade are to be spaced not more than 4' (1219) on center.

Girders

§ 2308.4.1 specifies that girders for single-story construction are to be minimum 4x6 (102 x 152) with a 6' (1829) maximum span on maximum 8' (2438) centers.

- Built-up girders made from 2x members are to be per Tables 2308.4.1.1 (1) or 2308.4.1.1 (2).

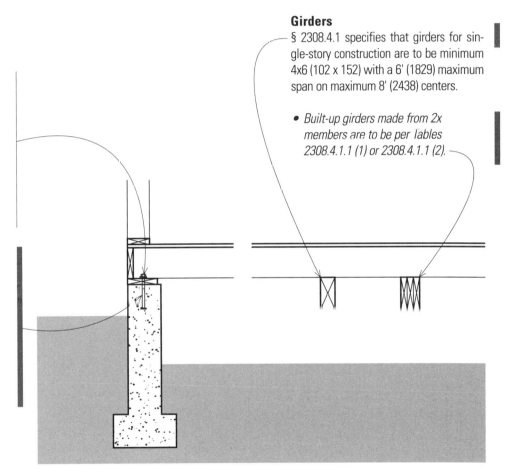

Floor Joists

§ 2308.4.2 prescribes that joists are to be per Table 2308.4.2.1 (1), Table 2308.4.2.1 (2), or the AWC STJR.

• For example, in residential areas, with l/360 maximum deflection, a live load of 40 psf, 10 psf dead load, 16" (406) spacing, a Douglas Fir-Larch #1 2x10 joist will span 16'-5" (5004).

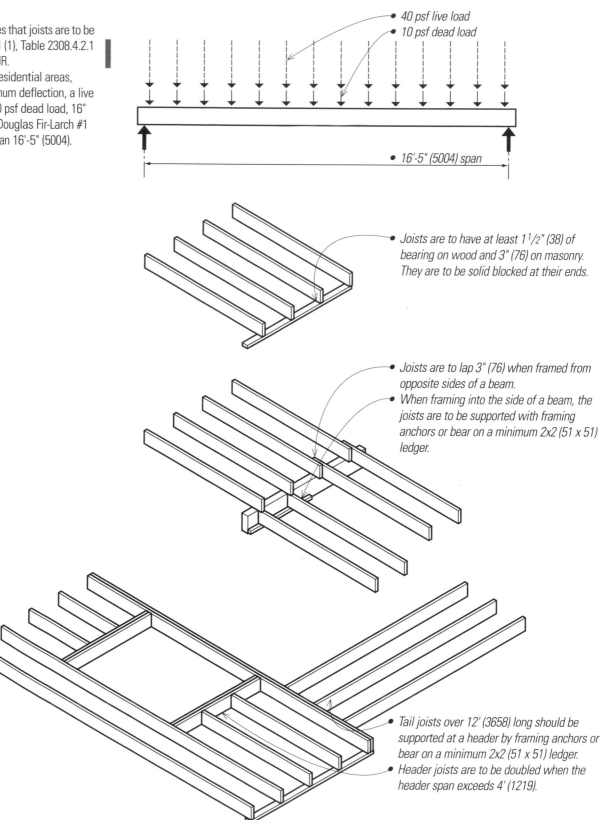

• 40 psf live load
• 10 psf dead load

• 16'-5" (5004) span

• Joists are to have at least 1 1/2" (38) of bearing on wood and 3" (76) on masonry. They are to be solid blocked at their ends.

• Joists are to lap 3" (76) when framed from opposite sides of a beam.
• When framing into the side of a beam, the joists are to be supported with framing anchors or bear on a minimum 2x2 (51 x 51) ledger.

• Tail joists over 12' (3658) long should be supported at a header by framing anchors or bear on a minimum 2x2 (51 x 51) ledger.
• Header joists are to be doubled when the header span exceeds 4' (1219).

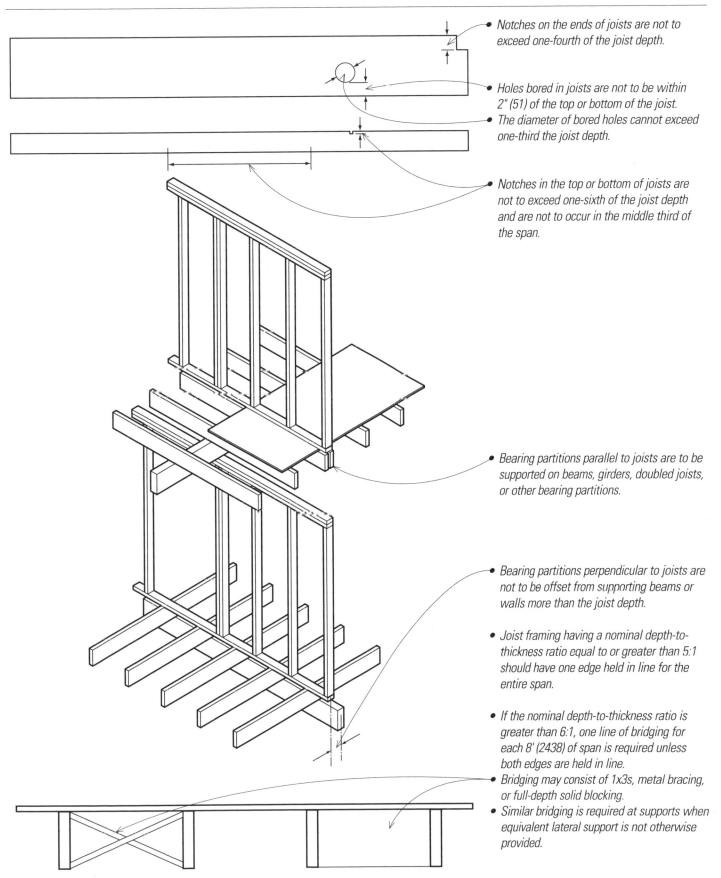

Notches on the ends of joists are not to exceed one-fourth of the joist depth.

Holes bored in joists are not to be within 2" (51) of the top or bottom of the joist.

The diameter of bored holes cannot exceed one-third the joist depth.

Notches in the top or bottom of joists are not to exceed one-sixth of the joist depth and are not to occur in the middle third of the span.

Bearing partitions parallel to joists are to be supported on beams, girders, doubled joists, or other bearing partitions.

Bearing partitions perpendicular to joists are not to be offset from supporting beams or walls more than the joist depth.

Joist framing having a nominal depth-to-thickness ratio equal to or greater than 5:1 should have one edge held in line for the entire span.

If the nominal depth-to-thickness ratio is greater than 6:1, one line of bridging for each 8' (2438) of span is required unless both edges are held in line.

Bridging may consist of 1x3s, metal bracing, or full-depth solid blocking.

Similar bridging is required at supports when equivalent lateral support is not otherwise provided.

Wall Framing

§ 2308.5.2 requires studs to be placed with their wide dimension perpendicular to the wall. The size, height, and spacing of wood studs are called out in Table 2308.5.1.

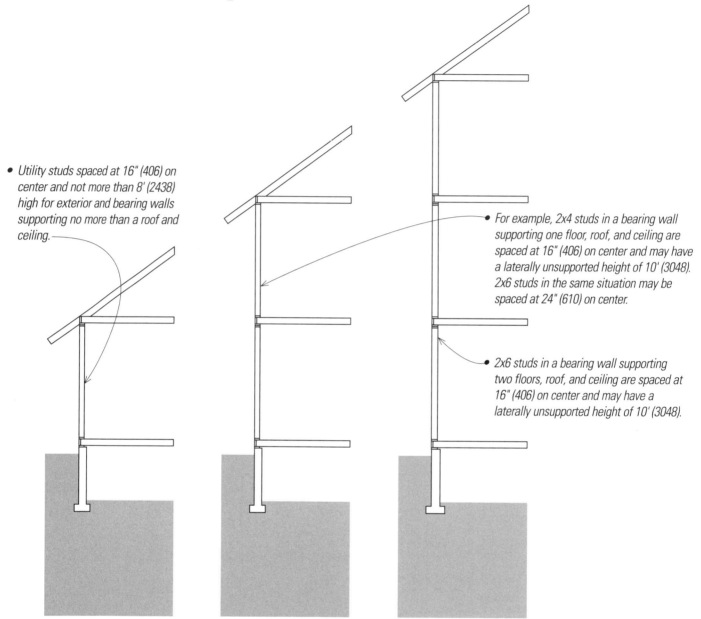

- Utility studs spaced at 16" (406) on center and not more than 8' (2438) high for exterior and bearing walls supporting no more than a roof and ceiling.

- For example, 2x4 studs in a bearing wall supporting one floor, roof, and ceiling are spaced at 16" (406) on center and may have a laterally unsupported height of 10' (3048). 2x6 studs in the same situation may be spaced at 24" (610) on center.

- 2x6 studs in a bearing wall supporting two floors, roof, and ceiling are spaced at 16" (406) on center and may have a laterally unsupported height of 10' (3048).

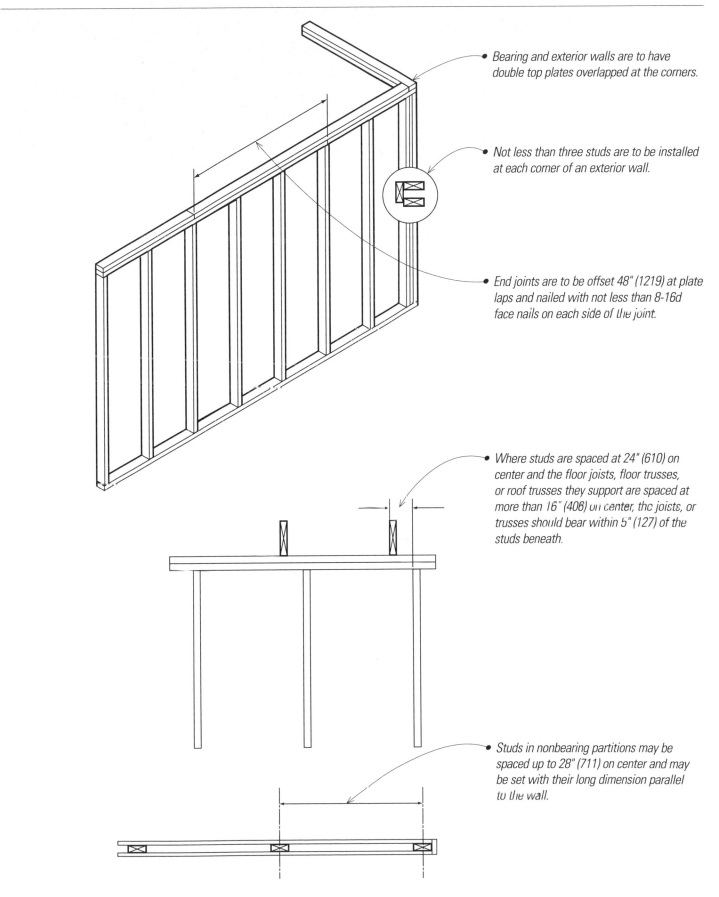

Bearing and exterior walls are to have double top plates overlapped at the corners.

Not less than three studs are to be installed at each corner of an exterior wall.

End joints are to be offset 48" (1219) at plate laps and nailed with not less than 8-16d face nails on each side of the joint.

Where studs are spaced at 24" (610) on center and the floor joists, floor trusses, or roof trusses they support are spaced at more than 16" (406) on center, the joists, or trusses should bear within 5" (127) of the studs beneath.

Studs in nonbearing partitions may be spaced up to 28" (711) on center and may be set with their long dimension parallel to the wall.

Cripple Walls

§ 2308.5.6 specifies that cripple walls—walls extending from the top of the foundation to the framing of the lowest floor level—are to be framed with the same size studs as the walls above. The studs must be 14" (356) or more in height; if they are not, the cripple wall must be of solid blocking. If the cripple wall studs are more than 4' (1219) high, the wall frame is considered to be a story. Cripple walls must be braced per § 2308.6.6 as for any other braced wall panel.

Headers

§ 2308.5.5.1 requires that headers be provided over each opening in exterior bearing walls. The size and spans in Table 2308.4.1.1 (1) are permitted to be used for one- and two-family dwellings. Headers for other buildings shall be designed in accordance with § 2301.2, Item 1 or 2. Headers shall be of two pieces of nominal 2" (51) framing lumber set on edge as permitted by Table 2308. 4.1.1 (1) and nailed together in accordance with Table 2304.10.1, or be of solid lumber of equivalent size.

Cutting, Notching, or Boring

Exterior wall studs and bearing partition studs may be partially cut, notched, or bored under certain conditions as prescribed in § 2308.5.9 and § 2308.5.10.

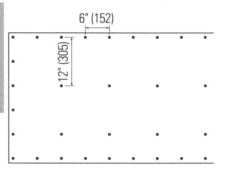

- Nailing at the foundation plate and the top plate is not to exceed 6" (152) on center.
- For example, nailing for $3/8$" (9.5 mm) plywood per Table 2304.10.1 would be 6d nails, 6" (152) on center at the edges and 12" (305) on center in the field of the panel.

6" (152)

12" (305)

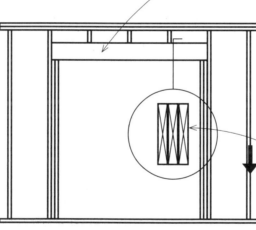

- Headers are to be of 2x material set on edge and nailed together per Table 2304.10.1 or lumber of equivalent size.
- For example, for a 36' (10 973) wide building with a 30 psf (1.44 kN/m²) snow load, a header supporting the roof, ceiling and one clear span floor, a 5'-1" (1549) opening would require a header of either 2-2x12s with two jack studs supporting each end or 3-2x8s with two jack studs supporting each end.
- Using three 2xs would require a wall depth of at least $4^1/2$" (114) to allow the jack studs to carry all three members of the built-up header.

$5/8$" (15.9 mm) minimum

- Bearing wall studs may be notched up to 25% of their width.

- Bearing wall studs may have bored holes up to 40% of their width and no closer than $5/8$" (15.9 mm) from their edges. When bored studs are doubled, holes may be up to 60% of the studs' width.

- Nonbearing wall studs may have notches of up to 40% of their width. Bored holes may be up to 60% of the stud width with the same edge clearance as for bearing wall studs.

$5/8$" (15.9 mm) minimum

Bracing

§ 2308.6 requires that bracing be provided per § 2308.6.1 through § 2308 6.10.2, depending on the type of bracing used, the seismic design category, and the height of the building.

- BWL = Braced wall line
- BWP = Braced wall panel

- Braced panels allowed up to 4' (1219) offset from braced wall line
- Maximum distance from end of BWL to braced panel per Table 2308.6.1

- RWL2 can be considered separate BWL from BWL 3 if it has braced panels per Table 2308.6.1.

- Braced panels allowed up to 4' (1219) offset from braced wall line

- Continuous foundation and braced cripple wall recommended under lower-story braced wall panels

- Maximum distance of BWP extending over opening below in seismic design categories D and E in accordance with § 2308.6.8.1

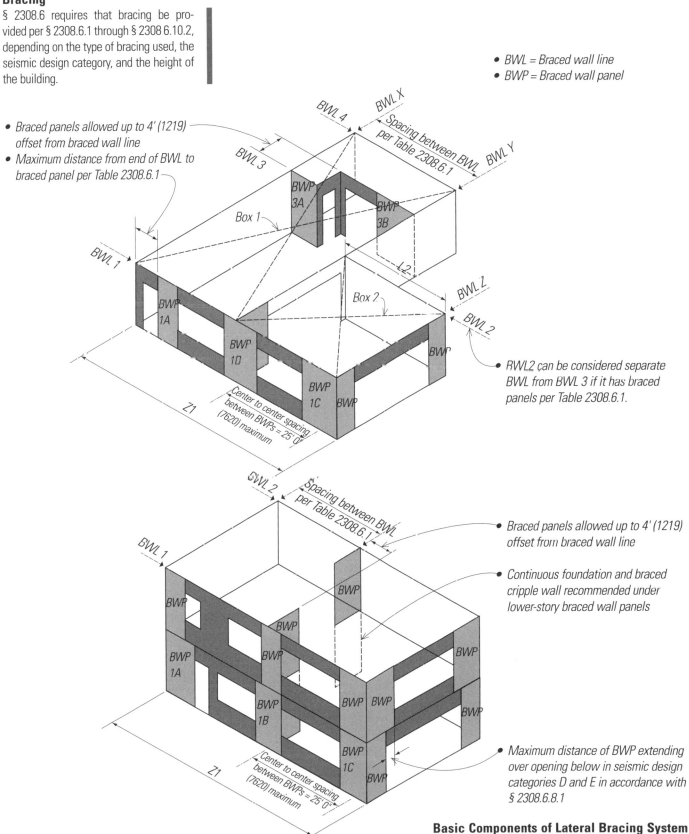

Basic Components of Lateral Bracing System

WOOD

Table 2308.6.1: Wall Bracing Requirements

Seismic Design Category	Story Condition (See § 2308.2)	Maximum Spacing of Braced Wall Lines	Braced Panel Location Spacing (o.c.) and minimum Percentage (X)			Maximum Distance of Braced Wall Panels from Each End of Braced Wall Lines
			Bracing Method[b]			
			LIB	DWB, WSP	SFB, PBS, PCP,HPS, GB[c,d]	
A and B		35'-0" (10.7 m)	Each end ≤ 25'-0" o.c.	Each end and ≤25'-0" o.c. (7.6 m)	Each end and ≤25'-0" o.c.	12'-6" (3.8 m)
		35'-0"	Each end ≤ 25'-0" o.c.	Each end and ≤25'-0" o.c.	Each end and ≤25'-0" o.c.	12'-6"
		35'-0"	NP	Each end and ≤25'-0" o.c.	Each end and ≤25'-0" o.c.	12'-6"
C		35'-0"	NP	Each end and ≤25'-0" o.c.	Each end and ≤25'-0" o.c.	12'-6"
		35'-0"	NP	Each end and ≤25'-0" o.c. (minimum 25% of wall length)	Each end and ≤25'-0" o.c. (minimum 25% of wall length)	12'-6"
D and E		25'-0"	NP	$S_{DS} < 0.50$: Each end and ≤ 25'-0" o.c. (min. 21% of wall length)	$S_{DS} < 0.50$: Each end and ≤ 25'-0" o.c. (min. 43% of wall length)	8'-0" (2.4 m)
				$0.50 < S_{DS} < 0.75$: Each end and ≤ 25'-0" o.c. (min. 32% of wall length)	$0.5 ≤ S_{DS} < 0.75$: Each end and ≤ 25'-0" o.c. (min. 59% of wall length)	
				$0.75 < S_{DS} < 1.00$: Each end and ≤ 25'-0" o.c. (min. 37% of wall length)	$0.75 ≤ S_{DS} < 1.00$: Each end and ≤ 25'-0" o.c. (min. 75% of wall length)	
				$S_{DS} > 1.00$: Each end and ≤ 25'-0" o.c. (min. 48% of wall length)	$S_{DS} > 1.00$: Each end and ≤ 25'-0" o.c. (min. 100% of wall length)	

- NP = Not permitted
a. This table specifies minimum requirements for braced wall panels along interior or exterior braced wall lines.
b. See § 2308.6.3 for full description of bracing methods. See also page 401 for illustrations.
c. For method GB, gypsum wallboard applied to framing supports that are spaced at 16" o.c.
d. The required lengths shall be doubled for gypsum board applied to only one face of a braced wall panel.
e. Percentage shown represents the minimum amount of bracing required along the building length (or wall length if the structure has an irregular shape).

Table 2308.6.3 (1) provides prescriptive requirements for types of braced wall panels. A typical braced panel, used in many types of construction and allowable in all bracing conditions, is wood structural panel sheathing with plywood or oriented strand board. Other types of bracing include let-in bracing, diagonal boards, fiberboard sheathing panels, gypsum board, particleboard, Portland cement plaster, and specialized portal frames with hold-downs.

Table 2308.6.3 (1): Bracing Methods

Methods, Materials	Minimum Thickness		Methods, Materials	Minimum Thickness	
LIB Let-in-bracing	1" x 4" wood or approved metal straps attached at 45° to 60° angles to studs at maximum of 16" o.c.		PBS Particleboard sheathing	$3/8$" or $1/2$" in accordance with Table 2308.6.3 (4) to studs at max. of 16" o.c.	
DWB Diagonal wood boards	$3/4$" thick (1" nominal) x 6" minimum width to studs at maximum of 24" o.c.		PCP Portland cement plaster	§ 2510 to studs at maximum of 16" o.c	
WSP Wood structural panel	$3/8$" in accordance with Table 2308.6.3 (2) or 2308.6.3 (3).		HPS Hardboard panel siding	$7/16$" in accordance with Table 2308.6.3 (5)	
SFB Structural fiberboard sheathing	$1/2$" in accordance with Table 2304.10.1 to studs at maximum of 16" o.c.		ABW Alternate braced wall	$3/8$"	
GB Gypsum board (Double sided)	$1/2$" or $5/8$" by a minimum of 4' wide to studs at maximum of 24" o.c.		PFH Portal frame with hold-downs	$3/8$"	

Roof and Ceiling Framing

§ 2308.7 contains the criteria for roofs having slopes 3:12 and steeper.

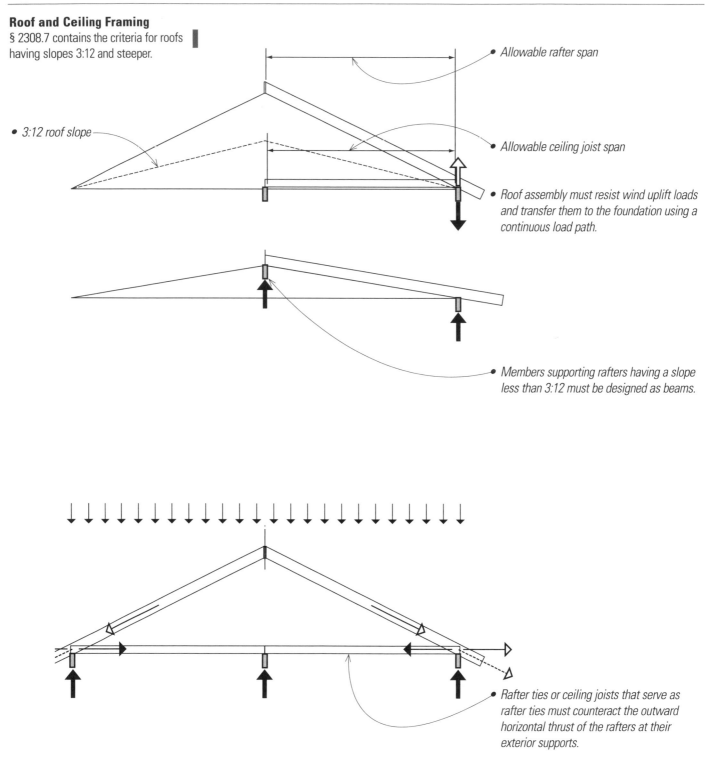

- Allowable rafter span

- 3:12 roof slope

- Allowable ceiling joist span

- Roof assembly must resist wind uplift loads and transfer them to the foundation using a continuous load path.

- Members supporting rafters having a slope less than 3:12 must be designed as beams.

- Rafter ties or ceiling joists that serve as rafter ties must counteract the outward horizontal thrust of the rafters at their exterior supports.

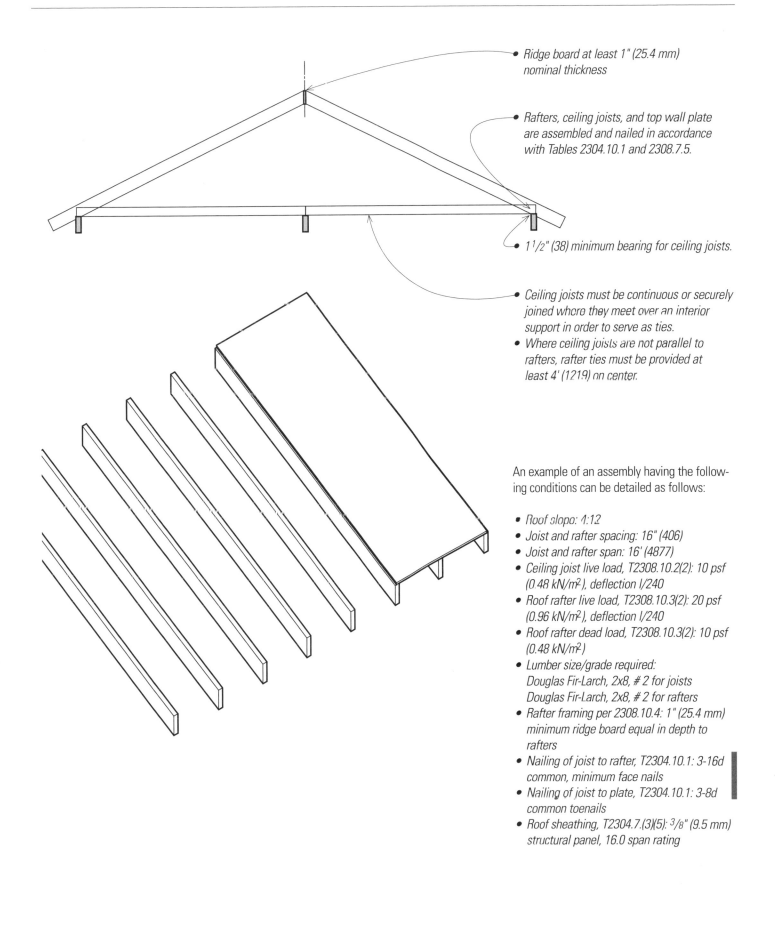

Ridge board at least 1" (25.4 mm) nominal thickness

Rafters, ceiling joists, and top wall plate are assembled and nailed in accordance with Tables 2304.10.1 and 2308.7.5.

$1^1/_2$" (38) minimum bearing for ceiling joists.

Ceiling joists must be continuous or securely joined where they meet over an interior support in order to serve as ties.

Where ceiling joists are not parallel to rafters, rafter ties must be provided at least 4' (1219) on center.

An example of an assembly having the following conditions can be detailed as follows:

- Roof slope: 4:12
- Joist and rafter spacing: 16" (406)
- Joist and rafter span: 16' (4877)
- Ceiling joist live load, T2308.10.2(2): 10 psf (0.48 kN/m²), deflection l/240
- Roof rafter live load, T2308.10.3(2): 20 psf (0.96 kN/m²), deflection l/240
- Roof rafter dead load, T2308.10.3(2): 10 psf (0.48 kN/m²)
- Lumber size/grade required: Douglas Fir-Larch, 2x8, # 2 for joists Douglas Fir-Larch, 2x8, # 2 for rafters
- Rafter framing per 2308.10.4: 1" (25.4 mm) minimum ridge board equal in depth to rafters
- Nailing of joist to rafter, T2304.10.1: 3-16d common, minimum face nails
- Nailing of joist to plate, T2304.10.1: 3-8d common toenails
- Roof sheathing, T2304.7.(3)(5): $^3/_8$" (9.5 mm) structural panel, 16.0 span rating

Chapter 24: Glass and Glazing

Chapter 24 contains the provisions governing the materials, design, and construction of glass, light-transmitting ceramic, and light-transmitting plastic panels used for glazing. The requirements apply to vertical and sloped applications such as for windows and skylights.

§ 2403 requires that glass bear a manufacturer's mark on each pane designating the thickness and type of glass or glazing material.

- *Glass is to be firmly supported in such a manner that the deflection of a pane of glass in a direction perpendicular to the pane must not exceed $1/175$ of the glass edge length or $3/4"$ (19.1 mm), whichever is less, when subjected to either positive or negative combined loads per § 1605, such as dead loads, live loads, wind loads, snow loads, or seismic loads.*

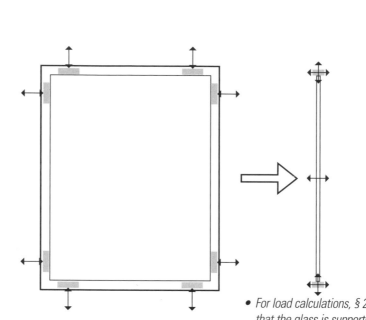

- *For load calculations, § 2404 assumes that the glass is supported on all four sides. Analysis or test data prepared by a registered design professional is required to verify that glass not supported on four sides will meet the code's safety criteria.*

- *Tempered glass is heat-treated to strengthen it. The treatment also makes the glass panes shatter into small granular pieces that are much less sharp and dangerous than shards from untreated glass. However, since the entire pane shatters, protection or limitation of the panes' sizes is required by the code.*
- *Laminated glass is made up of two panes of glass with a plastic layer between them. Glass fragments are contained by the plastic in the event of breakage of the glass panes, thus not having the panels fall out of their frames or rain glass pieces on the area below.*
- *Wired glass has pieces of wire embedded in the glass that act to contain glass fragments and keep the pane in place if the glass breaks.*

Sloped Glazing and Skylights

§ 2405 applies where glazing is installed at a slope more than 15° (0.26 rad) from the vertical plane. These requirements apply to all types of glazing materials, but the detailed requirements focus on the use of various types of glass. We will illustrate basic criteria and exceptions used in typical skylight designs glazed with glass. Because skylights often occur above walkways or occupied spaces, the code places special safety requirements on skylight glazing to protect building occupants. Special glazing materials or protective measures are required.

- *This section on sloped glazing and skylights applies to the installation of glazing materials at a slope greater than 15° (0.26 rad) from a vertical plane.*

- *§ 2405.3 requires screening of noncombustible material not thinner than No. 12 B&S gauge [0.0808" or 2 mm] with mesh no larger than 1" x 1" (25.4 mm x 25.4 mm) below heat-strengthened and fully tempered glass in monolithic glazing systems.*

- *Screen should be located a maximum of 4" (102) below the glazing.*
- *Screening should be securely fastened and be able to adequately support the weight of the falling glass.*

- *This screening is also required where heat-strengthened glass, fully tempered glass, or wired glass is used in multiple-layer glazing systems.*

- *These screens are intended to protect occupants below from falling chunks of glass, but they are not often seen in practice, due to use of the exceptions listed on the following page.*

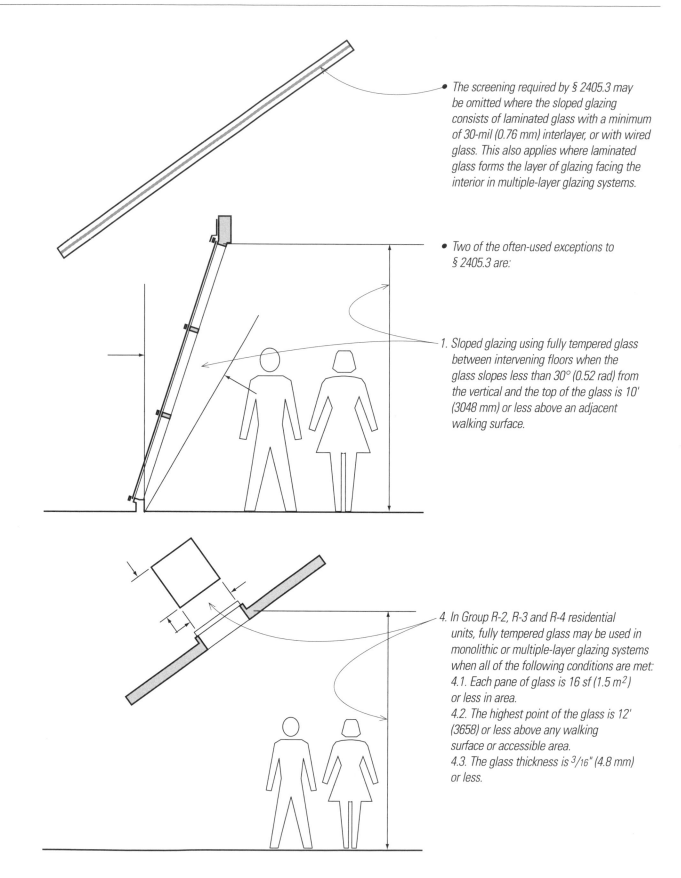

• The screening required by § 2405.3 may be omitted where the sloped glazing consists of laminated glass with a minimum of 30-mil (0.76 mm) interlayer, or with wired glass. This also applies where laminated glass forms the layer of glazing facing the interior in multiple-layer glazing systems.

• Two of the often-used exceptions to § 2405.3 are:

1. Sloped glazing using fully tempered glass between intervening floors when the glass slopes less than 30° (0.52 rad) from the vertical and the top of the glass is 10' (3048 mm) or less above an adjacent walking surface.

4. In Group R-2, R-3 and R-4 residential units, fully tempered glass may be used in monolithic or multiple-layer glazing systems when all of the following conditions are met:
4.1. Each pane of glass is 16 sf (1.5 m²) or less in area.
4.2. The highest point of the glass is 12' (3658) or less above any walking surface or accessible area.
4.3. The glass thickness is 3/16" (4.8 mm) or less.

Safety Glazing

A major design consideration is the use of safety glazing, primarily tempered glass, laminated glass, or impact-resistant plastic under certain circumstances. The basic criteria for safety glazing contained in § 2406 may be summarized as requiring safety glazing for glass panels subject to human impact under normal conditions of use.

Panes of glass in showers or baths, along corridors, at storefronts next to sidewalks, or in glass handrails need safety glazing. The criteria for safety glazing are set forth in 16 CFR 1201 by the Consumer Product Safety Commission. Glazing complying with ANSI Z97.1 may be used at locations where the code does not mandate compliance solely with the CPSC standard. Under most circumstances, this glazing is basically the same type as for skylights, tempered glass, or laminated glass. Typically, wired glass does not meet the CPSC criteria. There are many specific conditions where safety glazing is required. We will illustrate them, along with some common exceptions that are often applied. The locations in § 2406.4.1 through § 2406.4.7 are considered specific hazardous locations requiring safety glazing materials.

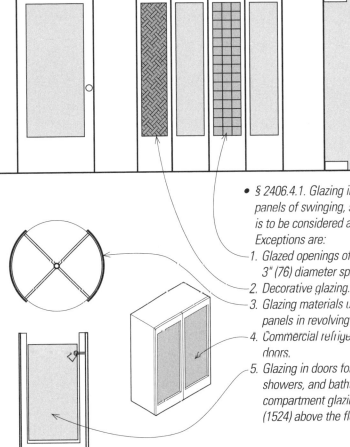

- § 2406.4.1. Glazing in all fixed and operable panels of swinging, sliding, and bifold doors is to be considered a hazardous location. Exceptions are:
1. Glazed openings of a size through which a 3" (76) diameter sphere is unable to pass.
2. Decorative glazing.
3. Glazing materials used as curved glazed panels in revolving doors.
4. Commercial refrigerated cabinet glazed doors.
5. Glazing in doors for hot tubs, saunas, showers, and bathtubs, as well as compartment glazing that is less than 60" (1524) above the floor of the enclosure.

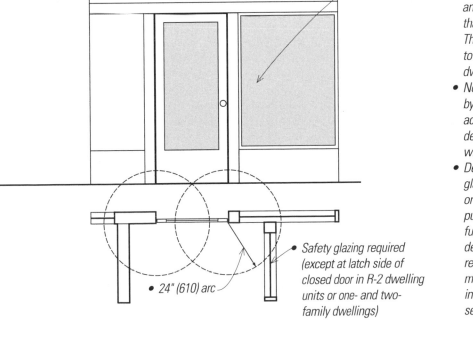

- • 24" (610) arc

Safety glazing required (except at latch side of closed door in R-2 dwelling units or one- and two-family dwellings)

- § 2406.4.2. Glazing in fixed or operable panels where the nearest edge of the glazing is within a 24" (610) arc of either vertical edge of the door in a closed position and the bottom edge of the glazing is less than 60" (1524) above the walking surface. This does not apply to glazing perpendicular to the plane of the closed door in residential dwelling units.
- No safety glazing required when separated by a permanent wall or barrier or when access is to a closet less than 3' (914) in depth if glazing complies with § 2406.4. for windows.
- Decorative glazing is excepted. Decorative glass is defined as being "carved, leaded or Dalle glass or glazing material whose purpose is decorative or artistic, not functional; whose coloring, texture or other design qualities or components cannot be removed without destroying the glazing material and whose surface, or assembly into which it is incorporated, is divided into segments."

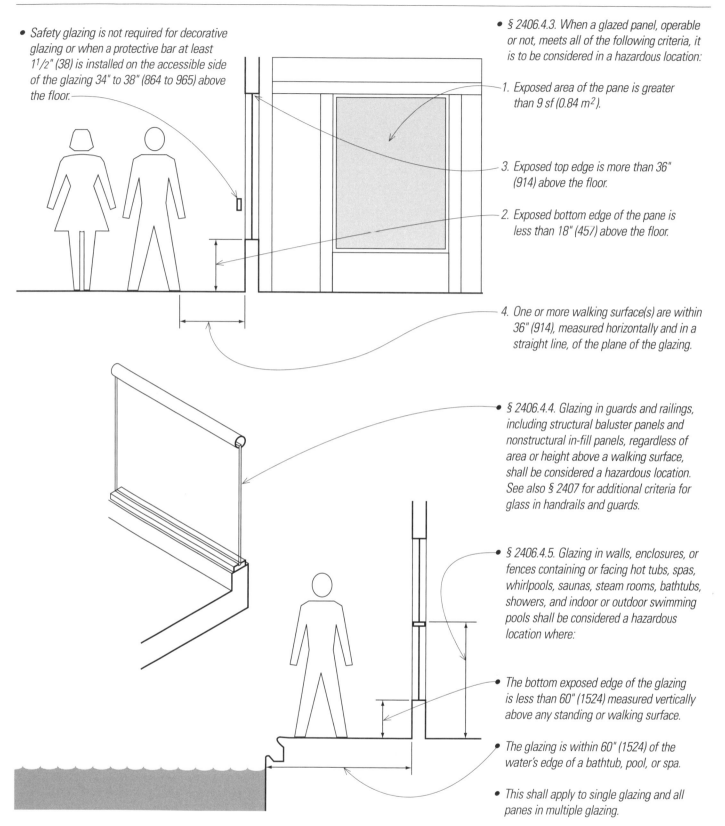

- Safety glazing is not required for decorative glazing or when a protective bar at least 1¹/₂" (38) is installed on the accessible side of the glazing 34" to 38" (864 to 965) above the floor.

- § 2406.4.3. When a glazed panel, operable or not, meets all of the following criteria, it is to be considered in a hazardous location:

1. Exposed area of the pane is greater than 9 sf (0.84 m²).

3. Exposed top edge is more than 36" (914) above the floor.

2. Exposed bottom edge of the pane is less than 18" (457) above the floor.

4. One or more walking surface(s) are within 36" (914), measured horizontally and in a straight line, of the plane of the glazing.

- § 2406.4.4. Glazing in guards and railings, including structural baluster panels and nonstructural in-fill panels, regardless of area or height above a walking surface, shall be considered a hazardous location. See also § 2407 for additional criteria for glass in handrails and guards.

- § 2406.4.5. Glazing in walls, enclosures, or fences containing or facing hot tubs, spas, whirlpools, saunas, steam rooms, bathtubs, showers, and indoor or outdoor swimming pools shall be considered a hazardous location where:

- The bottom exposed edge of the glazing is less than 60" (1524) measured vertically above any standing or walking surface.

- The glazing is within 60" (1524) of the water's edge of a bathtub, pool, or spa.

- This shall apply to single glazing and all panes in multiple glazing.

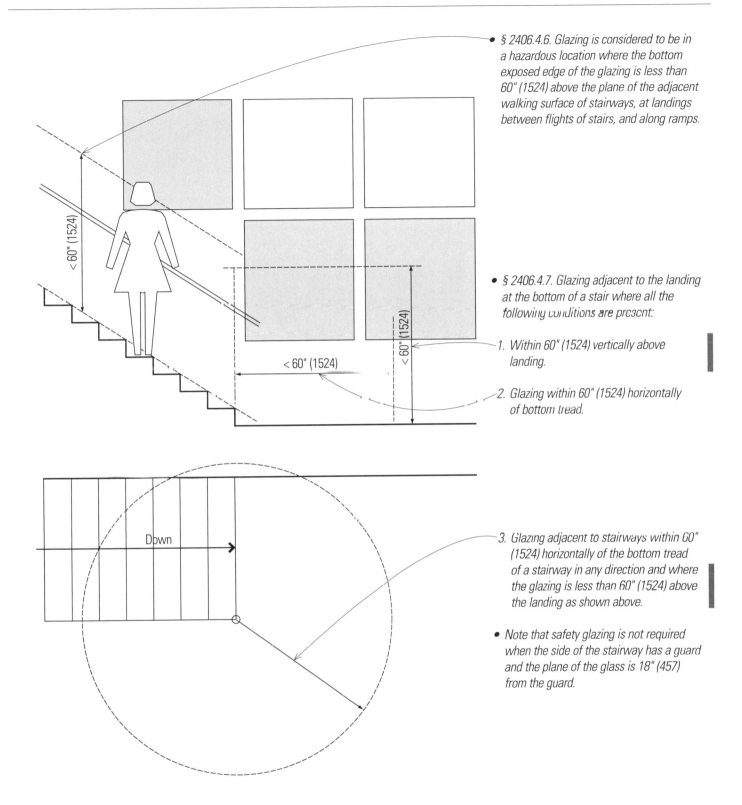

§ 2406.4.6. Glazing is considered to be in a hazardous location where the bottom exposed edge of the glazing is less than 60" (1524) above the plane of the adjacent walking surface of stairways, at landings between flights of stairs, and along ramps.

§ 2406.4.7. Glazing adjacent to the landing at the bottom of a stair where all the following conditions are present:

1. Within 60" (1524) vertically above landing.

2. Glazing within 60" (1524) horizontally of bottom tread.

3. Glazing adjacent to stairways within 60" (1524) horizontally of the bottom tread of a stairway in any direction and where the glazing is less than 60" (1524) above the landing as shown above.

Note that safety glazing is not required when the side of the stairway has a guard and the plane of the glass is 18" (457) from the guard.

Chapter 25: Gypsum Board and Plaster

Code requirements for the use of gypsum wallboard, gypsum panel products, lath, gypsum plaster, cement plaster, and reinforced gypsum concrete focus on durability and weather-resistance of the materials. The standards in Chapter 25 relate to quality of construction, not to quality of appearance. A key measure of where standards for exterior walls are to be applied is determined by the weather exposure of the surface. Weather-exposed surfaces are defined mostly in Chapter 2, as one might expect, with three exceptions that are not to be considered as weather-exposed surfaces. This is another reminder of how important it is to read and understand how the code uses definitions. Weather-exposed surfaces are considered to be:

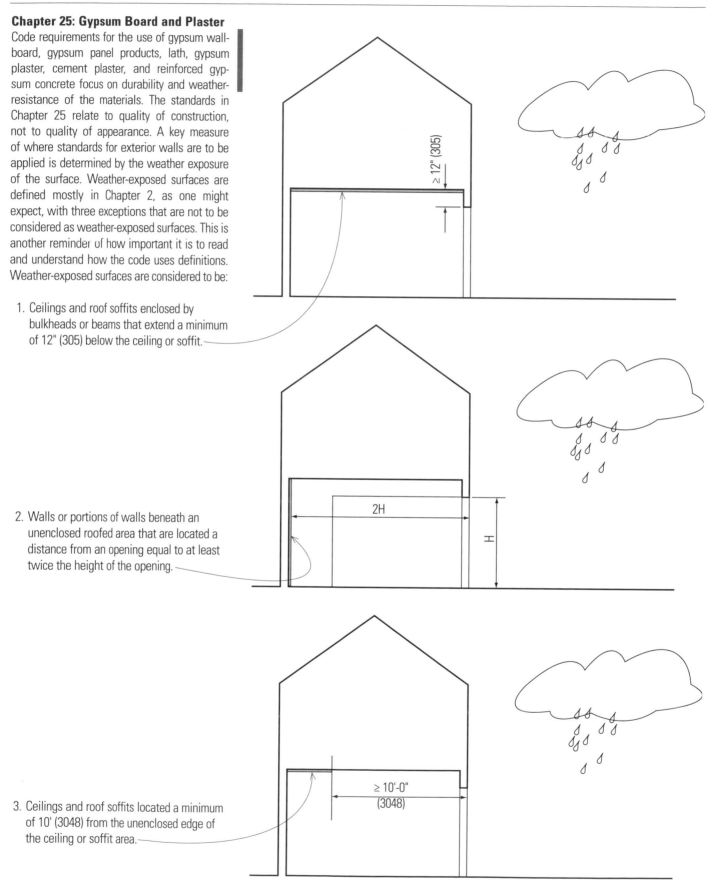

1. Ceilings and roof soffits enclosed by bulkheads or beams that extend a minimum of 12" (305) below the ceiling or soffit.

2. Walls or portions of walls beneath an unenclosed roofed area that are located a distance from an opening equal to at least twice the height of the opening.

3. Ceilings and roof soffits located a minimum of 10' (3048) from the unenclosed edge of the ceiling or soffit area.

Vertical and Horizontal Assemblies

§ 2504 requires wood framing, stripping and furring for lath or gypsum board to be a minimum nominal thickness of 2" (51) in the least dimension. Wood furring strips over solid backing may be 1x2 (25 x 51).

- *Minimum nominal thickness of 2" (51) for wood framing and furring strips*

Shear Wall Construction

§ 2505 permits gypsum board and lath-and-plaster walls to be used for shear walls. The use is dependent on the type of wall-framing materials. Wood-framed walls and steel-framed walls may be used to resist both wind and seismic loads. Walls resisting seismic loads are subject to the limitations of Section 12.2.1 of ASCE 7.

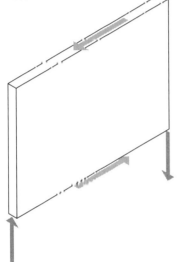

Gypsum Construction

§ 2508 governs both gypsum board and gypsum plaster. They are not to be used where they will be directly exposed to weather. Gypsum board joints are to occur at framing members except where the edges are perpendicular to the framing members.

- *Minimum thickness of 2" (51) for vertically erected studless solid plaster partitions*

- *Fasteners are to be applied so as not to fracture the face paper with the fastener head. Screws are typically used, driven far enough to depress the surface without breaking the paper. This allows covering the fastener with finishing compounds while fastening the material securely.*
- *With few exceptions, most fire-resistance-rated assemblies are to have joints and fasteners treated.*

Gypsum Board in Showers and Water Closets

§ 2509 governs the use of gypsum board as a base for tile or wall panels for tubs, showers, and water closet compartment walls. All gypsum board used in these situations is to be water-resistant. Note that water-resistant gypsum board cannot be used in these applications if a vapor retarder is used in shower or bath compartments.

Materials

§ 2506 and 2507 specify that gypsum board and lath and plaster materials are to meet code-designated AISI and ASTM standards. Materials are to be stored to protect them from the weather.

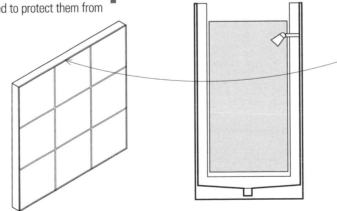

Base for tile in showers and water closets is to conform to the requirements of § 2509.2 and be of glass-mat gypsum backing panels, nonasbestos fiber-cement backer board, or nonasbestos fiber-mat reinforced cementitious backer units per Table 2509.2. Note that this list does not include water-resistant gypsum board. These requirements also apply to the ceilings in shower areas.

Exterior Plaster

§ 2510 covers lathing and furring for cement plaster. Per § 2510.6 water-resistive barriers are to be installed as required in § 1404.2 and, where applied over wood-based sheathing, the barrier is to include a water-resistive, vapor-permeable barrier with a performance at least equivalent to two layers of a water-resistive barrier complying with ASTM E 2556, Type I. The individual layers are to be installed independently such that each layer provides a separate continuous plane and any flashing (installed in accordance with § 1405.4) intended to drain to the water-resistive barrier is directed between the layers.

§ 2512 requires cement plaster, also called stucco, to be applied in three coats over corrosion-resistant metal lath or wire fabric lath, or applied in two coats over masonry or concrete. The three coats have specific names and functions. Table 2512.6 specifies curing times and minimum intervals between each coat for each of the cement plaster coats.

• Flashing, over inner layer of water-resistant barrier, ship-lapped installation, with flashing drainage directed between layers

• Sheathing and wall structure

• Outer layer of water-resistant barrier, ship-lapped installation

• Exterior stucco layer

• The base or scratch coat builds up the thickness and has a roughened surface for increased adhesion of the next layer. Minimum curing time is 48 hours, and the interval before the second coat is 48 hours for exterior plaster.

• The brown coat, so called because it is a darker color than typical finish coats, smooths out the scratch coat but still is to have sufficient roughness to provide a bond for the finish coat. The second coat is to be smooth within $^1/4$" (6.4 mm) in any direction under a 5' (1524 mm) straight edge. Minimum curing time is 48 hours and the interval before the final coat is 7 days for exterior plaster.

• The third or finish coat is applied over the second coat.

• The first and second coats are to be applied under proper weather conditions and kept moist for 48 hours. There is to be a 2-day interval between the first and second coats and a 7-day interval between the second and finish coats. Wetting and the finish intervals are intended to minimize cracking of the finished surface. Deviations from the application intervals are allowed for certain plaster mixes containing admixtures and accelerated curing procedures per referenced standards.

• There is to be a weep screed at the base of the wall to allow moisture that enters the plaster surface to drip down the water-resistant membrane and escape at the bottom.

Chapter 26: Plastics

Chapter 26 covers a wide variety of plastic building materials that can take many diverse forms. Foam plastic boards and shapes, plastic insulation, plastic veneers, plastic finish and trim shapes, light-transmitting plastics for glazing, and plastic composites, including plastic lumber, are all covered by this chapter.

Because plastics are typically flammable, the code places restrictions on their use related to their flame spread and smoke generation. Foam plastics are typically to have a flame spread index of no more than 75 and a smoke-developed index of no more than 450 when tested at their anticipated thickness.

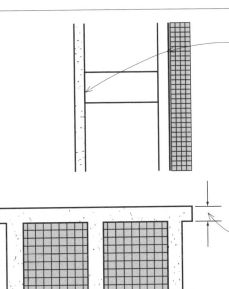

• A thermal barrier of $^1/_2"$ (12.7 mm) gypsum board is to separate foam plastic from the interior of a building. Equivalent materials may be used if they meet the acceptance criteria specified in § 2603.4.

• § 2603.4.1 allows the thermal barrier to be omitted in specific instances as set forth in § 2603.4.1.1 through § 2603.4.1.14.

• The thermal barrier may be omitted if the foam plastic insulation is covered on each face by at least 1" (25.4 mm) of masonry or concrete.

• A thermal barrier is not required when the foam insulation is part of a Class A, B, or C roof-covering assembly and if the assembly passes specified fire tests.

• Or if the roof assembly is separated from the interior of the building by wood structural panel sheathing not less than 0.47" (11.9 mm) thick, is bonded with exterior glue, with edges supported by blocking, tongue-and-groove joints, or other approved type of edge support, or an equivalent material.

• In attics or crawl spaces "where entry is made only for service of utilities," thermal barriers are not required if the foam insulation is covered with any of the specified protective materials.

• A thermal barrier is not required to be installed on the walking surface of a structural floor system that contains foam plastic insulation when the foam plastic is covered by a minimum nominal ½-inch-thick (12.7) wood structural panel or approved equivalent.

• An exception allows for the use of foam plastic as part of an interior floor finish.

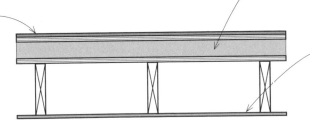

• The thermal barrier specified in § 2603.4 is required on the underside of the structural floor system that contains foam plastic insulation when the system occurs in a floor/ceiling assembly and the underside of the structural floor system is exposed to the interior of the building.

PLASTICS

In buildings not of Type V construction, limitations are placed by § 2603.5 on the use of foam plastic insulation in exterior wall assemblies. It is acceptable to use this material, which often occurs in exterior insulation and finish system assemblies and in manufactured exterior panels, when they meet the code criteria.

Foam plastic insulation may be used in exterior wall assemblies of buildings not of Type V construction in the following instances:

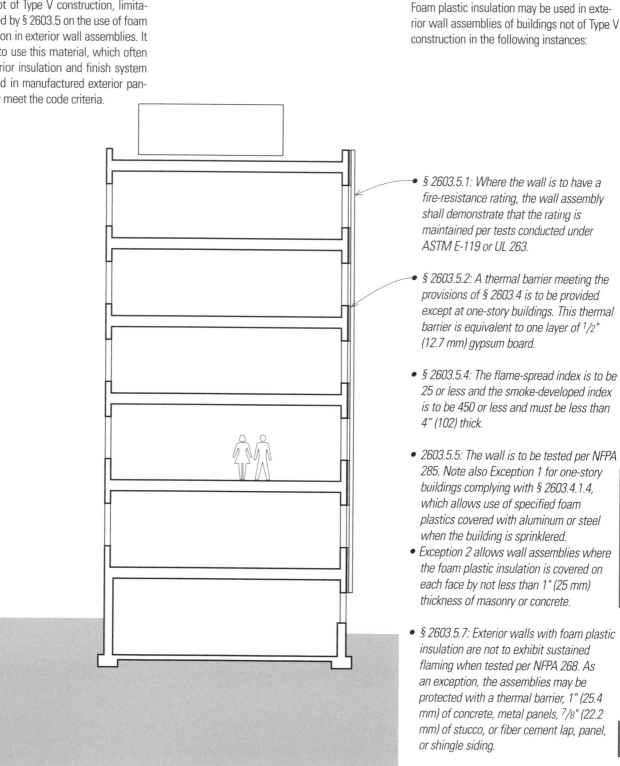

- *§ 2603.5.1: Where the wall is to have a fire-resistance rating, the wall assembly shall demonstrate that the rating is maintained per tests conducted under ASTM E-119 or UL 263.*

- *§ 2603.5.2: A thermal barrier meeting the provisions of § 2603.4 is to be provided except at one-story buildings. This thermal barrier is equivalent to one layer of 1/2" (12.7 mm) gypsum board.*

- *§ 2603.5.4: The flame-spread index is to be 25 or less and the smoke-developed index is to be 450 or less and must be less than 4" (102) thick.*

- *2603.5.5: The wall is to be tested per NFPA 285. Note also Exception 1 for one-story buildings complying with § 2603.4.1.4, which allows use of specified foam plastics covered with aluminum or steel when the building is sprinklered.*
- *Exception 2 allows wall assemblies where the foam plastic insulation is covered on each face by not less than 1" (25 mm) thickness of masonry or concrete.*

- *§ 2603.5.7: Exterior walls with foam plastic insulation are not to exhibit sustained flaming when tested per NFPA 268. As an exception, the assemblies may be protected with a thermal barrier, 1" (25.4 mm) of concrete, metal panels, 7/8" (22.2 mm) of stucco, or fiber cement lap, panel, or shingle siding.*

Light-Transmitting Plastics

§ 2606 governs plastics used for ceiling light diffusers, glazing in skylights, glazing in walls, glazing in showers, and light-transmitting plastics in light fixtures. These materials are divided into two classes based on their burning rate. Class CC1 has a burning extent of 1" (25.4 mm) or less per ASTM D 635. Class CC2 materials have a burning rate of 2 1/2" per minute (1.06 mm/s) or less, per the same test.

§ 2606.7 prohibits the use of light-diffusing plastic systems in interior exit stairways and ramps and exit passageways in large assembly occupancies and I occupancies, unless the building is sprinklered.

Light-Transmitting Plastic Wall Panels

§ 2607 allows plastics to be used as light-transmitting wall panels in buildings other than Group A-1, A-2, H, 1–2, and 1–3 occupancies. There are limitations on area and panel sizes based on the location on the property and the class of the plastic material. Table 2607.4 lists allowable areas, and vertical and horizontal separations between plastic wall panels. The areas and percentages listed in the table may be doubled for buildings that are fully sprinklered. Panels are to be separated by distances as noted in the table unless a flame barrier extends 30" (762) beyond the exterior wall in the plane of the floor.

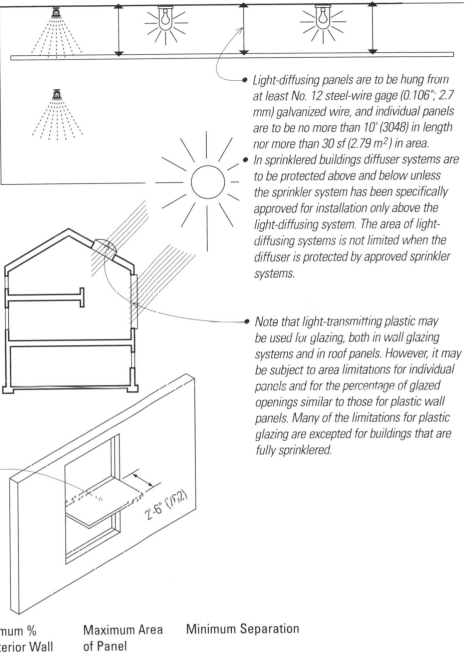

- Light-diffusing panels are to be hung from at least No. 12 steel-wire gage (0.106"; 2.7 mm) galvanized wire, and individual panels are to be no more than 10' (3048) in length nor more than 30 sf (2.79 m²) in area.

- In sprinklered buildings diffuser systems are to be protected above and below unless the sprinkler system has been specifically approved for installation only above the light-diffusing system. The area of light-diffusing systems is not limited when the diffuser is protected by approved sprinkler systems.

- Note that light-transmitting plastic may be used for glazing, both in wall glazing systems and in roof panels. However, it may be subject to area limitations for individual panels and for the percentage of glazed openings similar to those for plastic wall panels. Many of the limitations for plastic glazing are excepted for buildings that are fully sprinklered.

Fire Separation Distance	Class of Plastic	Maximum % of Exterior Wall	Maximum Area of Panel	Minimum Separation
Under 6' (<1829)	Plastic panels are not permitted			
6'–10' (1829–3048)	CC1	10%	50 sf (4.7 m²)	8' (2438) vertical, 4' (1219) horizontal
	CC2	Not permitted	Not permitted	
11'–30' (3353–9144)	CC1	25%	90 sf (8.4 m²)	6' (1829) vertical, 4' (1219) horizontal
	CC2	15%	70 sf (6.5 m²)	8' (2438) vertical, 4' (1219) horizontal
Over 30' (>9144)	CC1	50%	unlimited	3' (914) vertical, none horizontal
	CC2	50%	100 sf (9.3 m²)	6' (1829) vertical, 3' (914) horizontal

Electrical Systems

Chapter 27 specifies that electrical systems are to be designed and constructed in accordance with NFPA 70, the *National Electrical Code* published by the NFPA. Emergency and standby power systems are to be designed in accordance with the IBC, the IFC, NFPA 70, and NFPA 110 and 111.

The *International Building Code* contains scoping requirements for provision of emergency and standby power as defined in the *National Electrical Code.* Among these are:

- Emergency power for voice communications systems in Group A occupancies per § 907.5.2.2.5.
- Standby power for smoke-control systems per § 404.7, 909.11, 909.20.6.2, and 909.21.5.
- Emergency power for exit signs per § 1013.6.3.
- Emergency power for means of egress illumination per § 1008.3.
- Standby power for accessible means of egress elevators per § 1007.4.
- Emergency and standby power for high-rise building systems:
  - Fire command center
  - Fire pumps
  - Emergency voice/alarm communications systems
  - Lighting for mechanical equipment rooms
  - Elevators

- Standby power for elevators per § 1009.4, 1009.5, 3003.1, 3007.8, and 3008.8.

Note that the code requires emergency and standby power systems to be maintained and tested in accordance with the *International Fire Code.*

Mechanical Systems

Chapter 28 requires mechanical appliances, equipment, and systems to be constructed, installed, and maintained in accordance with the *International Mechanical Code* and the *International Fuel Gas Code.* Masonry chimneys are to comply with both the IMC and Chapter 21 of the *International Building Code.*

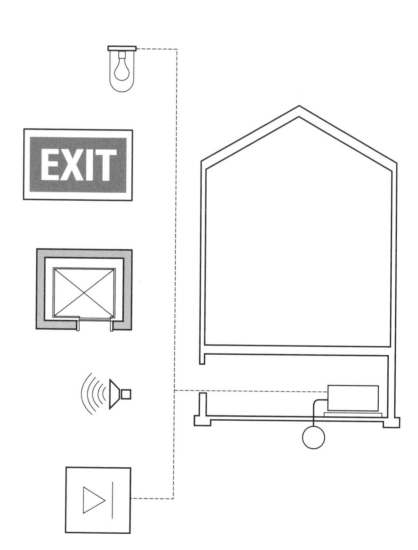

Plumbing Systems

Chapter 29 requires that plumbing systems be constructed, installed, and maintained in accordance with the International Plumbing Code.

Minimum Plumbing Fixtures

§ 2902 and Table 2902.1 specifies the number of plumbing fixtures to be provided in various occupancy groups. This table has cross references to the International Plumbing Code for such items as the number of urinals in relation to the number of water closets. Thus the two codes must be read together when determining the number of fixtures.

Fixture counts are determined by the occupancy type of the building and by the number of occupants as determined under the code. Table 2902.1 sets out requirements for water closets (urinals are per the IPC, as noted above), lavatories, bathtubs/showers, drinking fountains, kitchen sinks, and service sinks. The number of fixtures is based on observations of use patterns for various occupancies.

Occupants are to be presumed to be half-male and half-female unless statistical data demonstrating a different distribution of the sexes is approved by the building official. In certain occupancies, there are to be more women's fixtures than men's. This is based on use patterns where women take longer to use facilities than do men. Also, certain assembly occupancies have fixture counts based on use patterns during concentrated times, such as intermissions during theater performances.

Fixture counts for residential occupancies are expressed in terms of numbers of fixtures per dwelling unit, rather than by occupant load.

Occupancy	Water Closets Male	Female	Lavatories	Tubs Showers	Drinking Fountains	Other
Restaurant	1/75	1/75	1/200	—	1/500	1 service sink
Theater	1/125	1/65	1/200	—	1/500	1 service sink
Arena	1/75 first 1500, 1/120 for # > 1500	1/40 first 1500, 1/60 for # > 1500	1/200 (m) 1/150 (f)	—	1/1,000	1 service sink
Mercantile	1/250*	1/250*	1/750	—	1/1,000	1 service sink
Business	1/25*	1/25*	1/80	—	1/100	1 service sink
Single-Family	1/dwelling		1/dwelling	1/dwelling	—	1 kitchen sink, 1 clothes washer connection /dwelling

*Separate facilities will be required in many cases per § 2902.2. See also § 2902.3 for public toilet requirements.

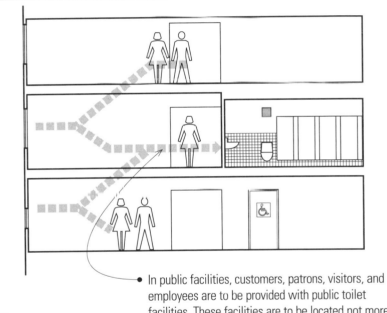

• In public facilities, customers, patrons, visitors, and employees are to be provided with public toilet facilities. These facilities are to be located not more than one story above or below the space needing the facilities. The path of travel to such facilities is not to exceed 500' (15 240). In conjunction with Chapter 11, the path of travel should be accessible, or alternate accessible facilities should be provided.

• Where a building or tenant space requires a separate toilet facility for each sex and each toilet facility is required to have only one water closet, two family/ assisted-use toilet facilities are permitted to serve as the required separate facilities. Such toilet facilities are not be required to be identified for exclusive use by either sex.

• Per § 2902.3.6, toilet rooms are not to open directly into a room used for the preparation of food for service to the public.

ELEVATORS AND CONVEYING SYSTEMS

Chapter 30 governs the design, construction and installation of elevators and other conveying systems, including escalators, moving walks, personnel hoists, and materials. We will discuss requirements with significant design impacts.

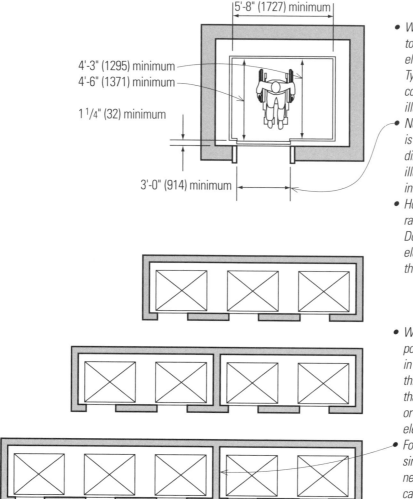

5'-8" (1727) minimum

4'-3" (1295) minimum
4'-6" (1371) minimum

1 1/4" (32) minimum

3'-0" (914) minimum

- Where passenger elevators are required to be accessible per Chapter 11, the elevators are to comply with ICC A117.1. Typical elevator cab dimensions and controls for accessible elevators are illustrated.
- Note that when the elevator door is centered on the elevator car, the dimensions are different than those illustrated. See ICC A117.1 for further information.
- Hoistways are to have fire-resistance ratings as required by Chapters 6 and 7. Doors in elevator shafts, including the elevator car doors, are to comply with the requirements of Chapter 7.

- When four or more cars serve the same portion of a building, they are to be located in two separate hoistways. The purpose of this requirement is to minimize the chance that a fire or other emergency can disable or contaminate with smoke all of the elevators in a bank.
- For example, three elevators can be in a single enclosure, but five elevators would need a shaft division between two sets of cars.

- Elevators are typically not allowed to be used for egress unless part of an accessible means of egress per § 1009.4.
- Standardized signage is to be posted near elevators not used for egress stating:

  IN CASE OF FIRE, ELEVATORS ARE OUT OF SERVICE, USE EXIT STAIRS

Elevators as a Means of Egress

Provisions of the code in § 3008 allow passenger elevators to be used for occupant self-evacuation during fires. The elevators must meet the criteria of § 3008 for fire sprinklers, shaft protection, elevator lobbies, and communication systems. Where elevators compliant with this section are provided, per § 3008.1.1 they may be substituted for the additional egress stair required by § 403.5.2 in buildings with occupied floors higher than 420' (128 m) in building height.

Note that using elevators as a means of egress is a new and evolving concept in egress system design. The use of elevators for egress under § 3008 should be discussed in detail with the AHJ early in the design process.

§ 3008.6.3. Lobby Doorways

Other than the door to the hoistway, each doorway to an occupant evacuation elevator lobby shall be provided with a 3/4-hour fire door assembly complying with § 716.5. The fire door assembly shall also comply with the smoke and draft control assembly requirements of § 710.5.3.1 with the UL 1784 test conducted without the artificial bottom seal.

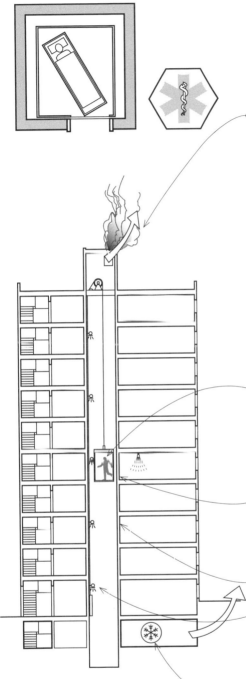

- In buildings four stories or more in height, at least one elevator is to be provided for fire-department emergency access to all floors. This elevator is to be sized to accommodate a 24" x 84" (610 x 1930) ambulance stretcher, in a horizontal and open position (that is, not partially folded up). This elevator is to be identified with the star of life, the international symbol for emergency medical services.

- Hoistways of elevators that penetrate more than three stories are to have a means of venting smoke and hot gases to the outer air in case of fire. Vents are to be located at the top of the hoistway and must be open to the outer air or through noncombustible ducts to the outer air. The vent area is to be not less than 3 1/2% of the area of the hoistway, but not less than 3 sf (0.28 m²) per elevator car.
- This is not required in fully sprinklered buildings, but even in sprinklered buildings, it is still required in R and I occupancies where overnight sleeping occurs.
- Other than independent plumbing for drains or sump pumps for the elevator shaft itself, elevator shafts are not to be used for plumbing or mechanical systems.

- **Special provisions for high-rise buildings > 120' (36 576) tall:** Per § 403.6.1 no fewer than two fire service access elevators, or all elevators, whichever is less, are to be provided. Each fire service access elevator is to have a capacity of not less than 3500 pounds (1500 kg).

- Per § 3007.3 an approved method is to be provided to prevent water from infiltrating into the hoistway enclosure from the operation of the automatic sprinkler system outside the enclosed fire service access elevator lobby.
- The enclosure for this elevator is to be a 2-hour rated shaft complying with § 713.
- The hoistway is to be illuminated with a minimum of 1 foot-candle (11 lux) for its entire height.
- Elevator lobbies per § 3007.6 are required at the fire service elevator.

- Elevator machine rooms for solid-state elevator controls are to have an independent ventilation or air-conditioning system to protect against overheating of the control equipment. Most elevator controls are now solid-state, so this should be assumed to be applicable in almost all installations. The system design criteria for temperature control will be determined by the elevator-equipment manufacturer's requirements.

Escalators

Per § 3004.2.1, escalator floor openings are to be enclosed per § 713 unless the requirements of § 712.1.3 are satisfied. Note also that per § 1003.7, escalators are not to be used as a component of a required means of egress.

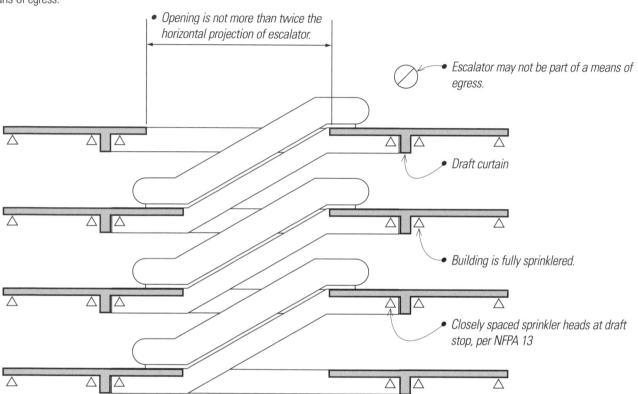

- Opening is not more than twice the horizontal projection of escalator.

- Escalator may not be part of a means of egress.

- Draft curtain

- Building is fully sprinklered.

- Closely spaced sprinkler heads at draft stop, per NFPA 13

20
Existing Structures

The requirements for existing buildings, which previously were located in Chapter 34 of the IBC, have been removed. Existing buildings are now addressed by a separate code, the *International Existing Building Code*. There are no longer any existing building provisions contained in the IBC.

Bibliography

2010 ADA Standards for Accessible Design. U.S. Department of Justice, 2010.

2012 International Building Code. International Code Council, Inc., 2012.

2012 International Building Code, Code and Commentary. International Code Council, Inc., 2012.

2012 International Energy Conservation Code. International Code Council, Inc., 2012.

2015 International Building Code. International Code Council, Inc., 2015.

2015 International Energy Conservation Code. International Code Council, Inc., 2015.

2015 International Fire Code. International Code Council, Inc., 2015.

ACI 318–14 Building Code Requirements for Structural Concrete. American Concrete Institute, 2014.

ACI 530–13 Building Code Requirements for Masonry Structures. American Concrete Institute, 2013.

AISC 341–10 Seismic Provisions for Structural Steel Buildings. American Institute of Steel Construction, 2010.

AISC 360–10 Specification for Structural Steel Buildings. American Institute of Steel Construction, 2010.

ASCE 5–13 Building Code Requirements for Masonry Structures. American Society of Civil Engineers, 2013.

ASCE 7–10 Minimum Design Loads for Buildings and Other Structures with Supplement No. 1. American Society of Civil Engineers, 2010.

ASME A17.1–2013/CSA B44–13 Safety Code for Elevators and Escalators. American Society of Mechanical Engineers, 2013.

ANSI/AWC NDS–2015 National Design Specification (NDS) for Wood Construction with 2012 Supplement. American National Standards Institute/American Wood Council, 2015.

AWC STJR–2015 Span Tables for Joists and Rafters. American Wood Council, 2015.

AWC WFCM–2015 Wood Frame Construction Manual for One- and Two-Family Dwellings. American Wood Council, 2015.

Building Codes Illustrated, Fourth Edition, A Guide to Understanding the 2012 International Building Code. Francis D. K. Ching and Steven Winkel. John Wiley and Sons, Inc., 2012.

Building Construction Illustrated, Fourth Edition. Francis D. K. Ching. John Wiley and Sons, Inc., 2008.

CPSC 16 CFR Part 1201 (2002) Safety Standard for Architectural Glazing Material. Consumer Products Safety Commission, 2002.

DOC PS-1–09 Structural Plywood. Department of Commerce, 2009.

DOC PS-2–10 Performance Standard for Wood-Based Structural-Use Panels. Department of Commerce, 2010.

Fair Housing Act Design Manual. Barrier-Free Environments Inc., for the U.S. Department of Housing and Urban Development, Office of Fair Housing and Equal Opportunity and the Office of Housing, 1998.

GA 600–09 Fire-Resistance Design Manual, 20th Edition. Gypsum Association, 2009.

Guide to the 2010 ADA Standards. Lawrence G. Perry, AIA. Building Owners and Managers Association, 2011.

ICC A117.1–09 Accessible and Usable Buildings and Facilities. International Code Council, Inc., 2009.

NFPA 13–13, Installation of Sprinkler Systems. National Fire Protection Association, 2013.

NFPA 70–14, National Electrical Code. National Fire Protection Association, 2014.

NFPA 72–13, National Fire Alarm and Signaling Code. National Fire Protection Association, 2013.

NFPA 110–13, Standard for Emergency and Standby Power Systems. National Fire Protection Association, 2013.

NFPA 285–12, Standard Fire Test Method for the Evaluation of Fire Propagation Characteristics of Exterior Nonload-Bearing Wall Assemblies Containing Combustible Components. National Fire Protection Association, 2012.

Nondiscrimination On The Basis Of Disability by Public Accommodations and In Commercial Facilities. The Americans with Disabilities Act, 28 CFR, Part 36.

Significant Changes to the International Building Code, 2015 Edition. Douglas W. Thornburg, AIA, John R. Henry P.E., Jay Woodward. International Code Council, Inc., 2015.

TMS 402–13 Building Code for Masonry Structures. The Masonry Society, 2013.

TMS 403–13 Direct Design Handbook for Masonry Structures. The Masonry Society, 2013.

Index